► STUDENTS! ESSENTIAL ACCESS INFORMATION FOR HOUGHTON MIFFLIN VIDEO CASES

EXPLORE TEACHING IN ACTION

Are you interested in what happens in actual classrooms? Do you want to know how in-service teachers handle a variety of situations in the classroom? Watch the Houghton Mifflin Video Cases and explore how new and experienced teachers apply concepts and strategies in real K-12 classrooms. Integrated into your text, these four- to six-minute video clips cover a variety of different topics faced by today's teachers and allow you to experience and reflect on real teaching in action.

To access the Houghton Mifflin Video Cases:

1. Using your browser go to: **college.hmco.com/PIC/ryancooper11e**

2. Select the student website

3. Click on HM Video Cases

4. You will be prompted to enter the passkey below and to choose a username and password

5. Select a video case from the list of options

Passkey: DY6ZJI48NCVNJ

Access is provided for free with the purchase of a new Ryan/Cooper, *Those Who Can, Teach,* Eleventh Edition textbook and will expire six months after first use. If you have a problem accessing the website with this passkey, please contact Houghton Mifflin Technical Support at: **http://college.hmco.com/how/how_techsupp.html.**

ENHANCE YOUR LEARNING EXPERIENCE

Houghton Mifflin Video Cases are integrated with your new copy of Ryan/Cooper, *Those Who Can, Teach,* Eleventh Edition, through boxed features in the margins of the text. The cases include video clips and a host of related materials to provide a comprehensive learning experience.

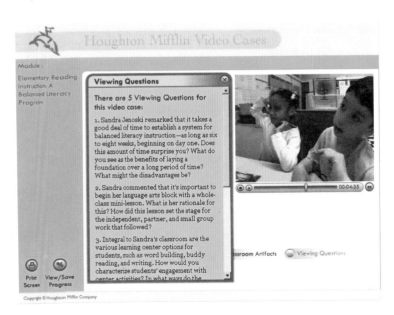

Reflect on the teacher's approach and assess how you might handle the situation by considering the **Viewing Questions.**

Watch textbook concepts come to life through video clips and bonus videos of real teachers applying teaching models and addressing key topics in their own classrooms.

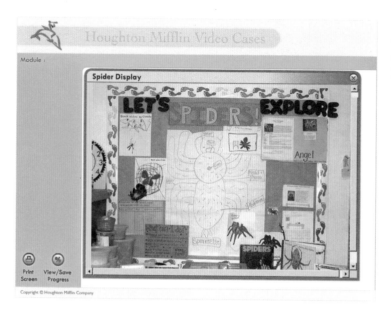

View **handouts and materials used in the class** and gain ideas for your own portfolio.

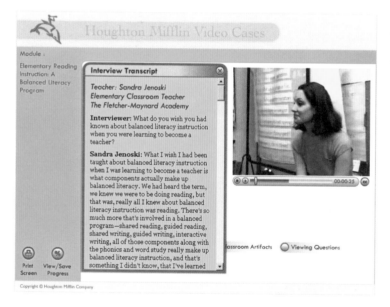

Read detailed **interviews with the teachers** as they explain their approach, how they engage students, and how they resolve issues.

Valuable package opportunities to accompany *Those Who Can, Teach!*

▶ *Kaleidoscope: Readings in Education,* Eleventh Edition, © 2007 by Ryan/Cooper

This popular reader, a perfect companion to *Those Who Can, Teach,* contains 70 selections by some of the most distinguished scholars in education along with writings by practicing teachers. Its comprehensive scope and effective pedagogy invite readers to participate in important discussions about education in a more informed way.

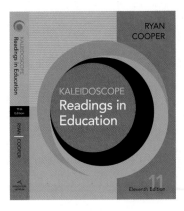

▶ Houghton Mifflin Guide Series

These brief paperbacks examine important topics in education in greater depth and can be packaged for free with *Those Who Can, Teach,* Eleventh Edition.

The current list of titles includes:

- ▶ *New!* An Educator's Guide to Student Motivation
- ▶ *New!* An Educator's Guide to Teacher Reflection
- ▶ *New!* An Educator's Guide to Differentiating Instruction
- ▶ An Educator's Guide to Diversity in the Classroom
- ▶ An Educator's Guide to Classroom Assessment
- ▶ An Educator's Guide to Field-based Observations
- ▶ An Educator's Guide to Inclusion
- ▶ An Educator's Guide to Technology Tools
- ▶ An Educator's Guide to School-based Intervention Programs
- ▶ An Educator's Guide to Classroom Management

Eleventh Edition

Those Who Can,
TEACH

KEVIN RYAN
Boston University

JAMES M. COOPER
University of Virginia

EXPANDED VERSION WITH EDUCATOR'S GUIDES AND VIDEO CASES MANUAL:

James M. Cooper, Series Editor
University of Virginia

AN EDUCATOR'S GUIDE TO TEACHER REFLECTION
Barbara Larrivee
California State University

AN EDUCATOR'S GUIDE TO TECHNOLOGY TOOLS
Cheryl Mason Bolick
The University of North Carolina at Chapel Hill

AN EDUCATOR'S GUIDE TO DIVERSITY IN THE CLASSROOM
Carl A. Grant
University of Wisconsin—Madison

AN EDUCATOR'S GUIDE TO FIELD-BASED CLASSROOM OBSERVATION
Gary D. Borich
The University of Texas at Austin

HOUGHTON MIFFLIN COMPANY
Boston   New York

THOSE WHO CAN, TEACH, ELEVENTH EDITION
by Kevin Ryan and James M. Cooper
Copyright © 2007 by Houghton Mifflin Company. All rights
reserved.

Publisher: Patricia Coryell
Senior Sponsoring Editor: Sue Pulvermacher-Alt
Senior Development Editor: Lisa Mafrici
Senior Project Editor: Jane Lee
Editorial Assistant: Kristen Truncellito
Senior Art and Design Coordinator: Jill Haber
Senior Photo Editor: Jennifer Meyer Dare
Senior Composition Buyer: Chuck Dutton
Manufacturing Manager: Karen Fawcett
Marketing Manager: Laura McGinn
Marketing Associate: Erin Lane

Text Credits: p. 213: From National Education Technology
Standards-Connecting Curriculum and Technology. Copyright
© 2000, ISTE (the International Society for Technology in
Education), (800) 336-6191 (U.S. and Canada) or (541) 302-3777
(International), cust_svc@iste.org, www.iste.org. Reprinted
with permission. p. 255: "Boston University Educator's
Affirmation," By Steven Tigner. Reprinted with the permission
of Steven Tigner. p. 224: From Kenneth R. Howe, "A
Conceptual Basis for Ethics in Teacher Education," *Journal of
Teacher Education*, 37, May-June 1986, pg. 6. Reprinted with per-
mission. p. 383: "Letter from a Homeschooling Mother."
Reprinted with permission. p. 435: From Gary Cornog, "To
Care or Not to Care," in *Don't Smile Until Christmas: Accounts of
the First Year Teaching*, edited by Kevin Ryan, pp. 18-19.
Copyright © 1970. Reprinted with permission of Kevin Ryan.
p. 465: "Great Teachers," by Reg Weaver, President of the
National Education Association. Reprinted with permission. p.
466: "The Role of the Professional Union," by Albert Shanker.
Reprinted by permission of American Federation of Teachers.
p. 481: Copyright © 2000 by Houghton Mifflin Company.
Reproduced by permission from *The American Heritage
Dictionary of the English Language,* Fourth Edition

AN EDUCATOR'S GUIDE TO TEACHER REFLECTION
by Barbara Larrivee and James M. Cooper
Copyright © 2006 Houghton Mifflin Company. All rights
reserved.

Senior Sponsoring Editor: Sue Pulvermacher-Alt
Senior Development Editor: Lisa Mafrici
Editorial Assistant: Dayna Pell
Manufacturing Coordinator: Chuck Dutton
Marketing Manager: Jane Potter

AN EDUCATOR'S GUIDE TO TECHNOLOGY TOOLS
by Cheryl Mason Bolick and James M. Cooper
Copyright © 2003 Houghton Mifflin Company. All rights
reserved.

Senior Sponsoring Editor: Sue Pulvermacher-Alt
Senior Development Editor: Lisa Mafrici
Editorial Associate: Sara Hauschildt
Editorial Assistant: Liliana Ritter
Manufacturing Manager: Florence Cadran
Marketing Manager: Nicola Poser

AN EDUCATOR'S GUIDE TO DIVERSITY IN THE
CLASSROOM
by Carl A. Grant and James M. Cooper
Copyright © 2003 Houghton Mifflin Company. All rights
reserved.

Senior Sponsoring Editor: Sue Pulvermacher-Alt
Senior Development Editor: Lisa Mafrici
Editorial Associate: Sara Hauschildt
Editorial Assistant: Liliana Ritter
Manufacturing Manager: Florence Cadran
Marketing Manager: Nicola Poser

AN EDUCATOR'S GUIDE TO FIELD-BASED CLASSROOM
OBSERVATION
by Gary D. Borich and James M. Cooper
Copyright © 2004 Houghton Mifflin Company. All rights
reserved.

Senior Sponsoring Editor: Sue Pulvermacher-Alt
Senior Development Editor: Lisa Mafrici
Editorial Associate: Sara Hauschildt
Editorial Assistant: Trinity Peacock-Broyles
Senior Manufacturing Manager: Florence Cadran
Marketing Manager: Jane Potter

THOSE WHO CAN TEACH, ELEVENTH EDITION, VIDEO
CASES MANUAL
Copyright © 2006 by Houghton Mifflin Company. All rights
reserved.

Custom Publishing Editor: Dee Renfrow
Custom Publishing Production Manager: Christina Battista
Project Coordinator: Jennifer Feltri

This book contains select works from existing Houghton Mifflin Company resources and was produced by Houghton Mifflin
Custom Publishing for collegiate use. As such, those adopting and/or contributing to this work are responsible for editorial
content, accuracy, continuity and completeness.

Printed in the United States of America.

ISBN-13: 978-0-547-08394-0
ISBN-10: 0-547-08394-7
1043274

1 2 3 4 5 6 7 8 9 – CM – 09 08 07

Houghton Mifflin
        Custom Publishing

222 Berkeley Street • Boston, MA 02116

Address all correspondence and order information to the above address.

Brief Contents

v

Contents

Part Two   *Teachers*   149

Part Three *Foundations and the Future* 263

Part Four   *The Teaching Profession 392*

13   What Are Your Job Options in Education?   392

14   What Can the New Teacher Expect?   417

15   What Does It Mean to Be a Professional?   448

Preface

This book, *Those Who Can, Teach,* is a book of questions. In fact, it was written in the first place to answer the question, "What are the things people beginning their formal study of education should know?" We have organized the chapters of our book around a series of questions that are likely to be of special concern to prospective teachers, and that we believe are key to the central issues and concerns of teaching and learning. We hope that these questions provide direction and focus to readers' study well beyond the time they spend with this book. In addition, for those who are still undecided about teaching, we believe that the search for answers to these questions will help them clarify their career goals.

▶ Purpose and Audience

Those Who Can, Teach is intended as a basic text for courses variously titled "Introduction to Education" or "Foundations of Education." We originally wrote this book because we couldn't find the kind of textbook our own students and the students of many of our colleagues needed and wanted—a book that involves prospective teachers in the real issues of schooling and education and that gives them a clear view of the skills and knowledge they will need to be successful professionals.

▶ Content of the Eleventh Edition

Those Who Can, Teach, Eleventh Edition, presents a frank, contemporary examination of the field and foundations of education and, especially, the teaching profession. Although the text is firmly based in educational research and scholarship, it seeks to convey the important knowledge and issues in the field of education in a way that effectively bridges educational research and classroom practice. For this purpose, we rely heavily throughout the book on a narrative style, using the words of practicing teachers wherever we can in an effort to place the book's content in very human terms.

We have organized the book around four themes, each theme representing one of the four parts. Part One, "School and Students," asks students to reflect on what may be their central question at this point: "Why teach?" Having thought about and probably having imagined themselves teaching, this chapter enables readers systematically to reflect on whether teaching is the work for them. We follow with an examination of what defines a school and a review of its competing purposes. Next, two chapters focus on the diversity of the American students and the new and old social issues surrounding them. We then discuss what it is that schools are trying to teach elementary and secondary students, and we deal with some of the tensions around this critical topic. Part Two, "Teachers," explores three important dimensions of a teacher's work: first, what it takes to be an effective teacher; second, what the growing emphasis on educational technology is all about and what the teacher should be able to do; and third, what the ethical and legal issues are surrounding the work of the teacher. Part Three,

"Foundations and the Future," deals with "something old and something new." The practice of education rests on a body of thought and experience. Therefore, we attempt to lay out the primary lines of thought, or educational philosophies, that speak to teaching and learning. American schools are also part of a unique national experiment to educate all of our nation's people to the fullest extent possible. The chapter entitled "What Is the History of American Education?" paints a "warts-and-all" picture of our attempts to fulfill that high ideal. This part ends with a close look at one of the most talked about and pressing issues facing educators: reform of our schools. We give this special attention because new teachers will undoubtedly be entering schools that are struggling to change and improve. Part Four, "The Teaching Profession," examines teaching from a number of vantage points: what the current job situation is in various parts of the country and in the different levels and subject specialties; what a new teacher can expect from students, fellow teachers, administrators, and others; and what it means to be a member of a profession. This part ends with a final chapter revisiting the all-important question, "Why teach?" Having reflected on the book's questions and issues, readers should now be ready for deeper reflection about whether to join the teaching profession.

▶ Features of the Revision

Teaching, learning, and the condition of our schools have been in the headlines almost continually in the three years since our last edition. Education is big news from Main Street to Pennsylvania Avenue. As the link between education and the well-being of both the individual and the nation becomes more obvious, real change and proposals for change are more in evidence. In this edition, therefore, we have tried to sort out the most significant developments without losing sight of the enduring issues facing students and teachers.

Among the most significant changes in this edition are:

- A **new Chapter 16, "Why Teach? A Final Word,"** and chapter reorganization to return "Why Teach?" to its popular place as Chapter 1. The new Chapter 16 reprises the "Why Teach?" question to encourage a final reflection and to bring the book full circle.
- At the end of each chapter, we have included a **new** "**For Debate**" feature that helps students use the materials available on the web as well as interact online with other readers to discuss important questions raised by the book.
- We have also provided linkages to relevant **Houghton Mifflin Video Cases,** which provide students with real-life teaching examples of problems, methodology, and teaching styles that add another layer of richness to the realistic case studies offered by this book. We are very excited about these new video cases and how they can help prospective teachers understand better the realities of schools and classrooms. Video cases are correlated to chapter content with a **new marginal video case boxed feature.**
- The chapter on social problems and tension points has been divided so that the tension points (gender and sexual orientation, equal opportunity, and school choice) have been moved to different chapters to discuss them in conjunction with related topics throughout the book.
- Two features that appeared in previous editions, "Policy Matters!" and "Open for Debate," have been updated and moved to the Houghton Mifflin website to make room for other material in the book and to make greater use of web

technology to provide new opportunities for students. Some of the "Leaders in Education" features have also been moved to the website.

▶ Continuing Features

As you are probably well aware, education is a dynamic field of study and practice. Americans, young and old, make a huge investment in their schools. We are continually examining them; we are continually criticizing them; and we are continually changing or modifying them. As in previous editions of *Those Who Can, Teach,* we are responding to the changes in schools with changes in this book:

- A huge topic on the educational scene is standards-based education, and we have treated its many implications for teachers in a number of chapters. To help make the connection between standards and content crystal clear, we've included a correlation chart in the front of the book. The ten core principles of INTASC are correlated to the chapters and pages in the eleventh edition.
- We have updated recent federal legislative actions, including coverage of the No Child Left Behind Act and 2004 IDEA reauthorization.
- Our earlier focus on student diversity and multiculturalism has been updated and expanded to reflect the changing demographics of our schools. The growing concern in society and among educators over ethics and character is also mirrored here.
- Our courts, too, have been busy handing down decisions, which are having profound effects on our schools. We keep students updated on the directions of the decisions.
- Our society's ever-changing answer to the question, "What is most worth knowing?" is, of course, mirrored in the school's curriculum, and we have thoroughly updated the new curricular emphasis and school reform movements.
- We continue to believe that it is important for teachers to have a knowledge and appreciation for some of the outstanding teachers, both from the past and the present. **"Leaders in Education"** features profile some of these outstanding teachers in the textbook, and more on the website, where students can link to in-depth biographical information.
- We all live in a world of information overload, if not overkill. Educators in recent years have been pointing out that, unless we stop and reflect on what we read, our chances of holding the information and having it become *meaningful* are greatly reduced. On the other hand, if we stop and consider an idea and evaluate it in the light of our own experience, then we *own* the information. With this in mind, in each chapter we continue to include in the eleventh edition three or four **"Pause and Reflect"** stops, each containing two or three questions for your consideration. We urge you to participate in this crucial aspect of the book because your responses can lead to greater self-understanding.
- One of the frequent complaints made by new teachers is that "no one ever told us what it is really like out here in the trenches." Although these complaints are sometimes unfair (people tried to tell them, but they weren't listening!), we have, nevertheless, from the very first edition of this book tried to reflect, through case studies and reports of teachers, the real world of schooling. In this eleventh edition, we continue to offer the popular **"Voices from the Classroom"** feature. We solicited contributions from a number of our former students and their teacher-friends, and we are enormously pleased with what they

wrote. Each chapter has a reflection or comment on one of the chapter's key topics. Most contributors are new teachers; a few are veterans. All tell it like it is.

- Reflecting technology's omnipresence in education today, we have expanded our coverage of educational technology with resources, such as software programs and URLs, and references to standards that are found in the dedicated technology chapter and throughout the text.

Although much is new in the eleventh edition, key qualities have been retained. Chief among them is the book's informal writing style. We have tried to communicate the seriousness surrounding professional topics and, at the same time, reflect the humor and humanity that is part of the professional life of a teacher. We are helped in this "experiential" aspect of our book by the presence in the text of the actual words of practicing classroom teachers. In addition, many of the events described were experiences that happened directly to us when we were teaching in public schools. We believe (and hope) that this writing style and heavy use of narrative give the text a greater sense of reality.

Both of us have been classroom teachers and are long-time teacher educators. As such, we have, from our very first edition to this eleventh edition, continually tried to keep one question uppermost in our minds as we have labored on this book: What does the new teacher need to know and be able to do in order to succeed in today's school? Answering that question is the challenge and the mission of *Those Who Can, Teach.*

▶ Accompanying Teaching and Learning Resources

The eleventh edition of *Those Who Can, Teach* is accompanied by an extensive package of instructor and student resources.

- ***Kaleidoscope: Readings in Education,*** **Eleventh Edition,** is a companion book of readings that can be used either in conjunction with the text or as a separate volume. This collection of seventy selections, approximately 30 percent of which are new in this edition, contains works by some of the most distinguished scholars in education, along with the writings of practicing teachers. Many of the authors and reports of research cited in *Those Who Can, Teach* are included in this book of readings. We have specially marked several key classic readings in education. Also, an easy-to-use chart in *Kaleidoscope* cross-references topics discussed in *Those Who Can, Teach* with the readings in *Kaleidoscope.* Both books can be packaged together at a special discount price.
- ***Instructor's Resource Manual with Test Bank,*** prepared by Mary Ware of SUNY, Cortland is offered at the Instructor's website and includes a transition guide, sample syllabi, student objectives, chapter overviews, supplementary lecture and discussion topics, class activities, student study guides, practice quizzes, selected references and media resources, school observation activities, and a section of 5–6 case studies with discussion questions. The test bank contains multiple-choice, short answer, and essay questions. The IRM includes a cross reference to *Kaleidoscope,* the companion reader.
- **The Houghton Mifflin Testing Computerized Test Bank** provides instructors with the assessment items from the Instructor's Resource Manual with Test Bank in an electronic format for ease of use. This bank of test questions is compatible with both PC and Macintosh computers.
- **Expanded Companion Website** provides resources for instructors and students, including: ACE Self Quizzes; links to key topics in each chapter; additional

"Voices from the Classroom" and "Leaders in Education" boxes; "Open to Debate" and "Policy Matters!" features for students to review and discuss in the Eduspace course discussion board; and links to updated and expanded information and additional reflection questions, classroom observation guides, and tips for creating a teaching portfolio.

- ***New* Houghton Mifflin Video Cases.** Available online and organized by topic, each "case" is a four- to six-minute module consisting of video files presenting actual classroom scenarios that depict the complex problems and opportunities teachers face every day. The video clips are accompanied by "artifacts" to provide background information and allow preservice teachers to experience true classroom dilemmas in their multiple dimensions.
- ***New* Eduspace.** Houghton Mifflin's new powerful, customizable, and interactive online learning tool, ***Eduspace,*** powered by Blackboard, offers a convenient, user-friendly platform to manage, customize, create and deliver course materials online. In addition to its handy gradebook, discussion board, and other course management tools, Eduspace provides text-specific interactive components such as videos, reflective journal questions, test items, and additional materials to aid students in studying and reflecting on what they have learned.
- **Blackboard and WebCT Cartridges** that include premium text and study guide content made platform-ready for online courses.
- **The Houghton Mifflin Guide Series.** These are brief paperbacks that examine important topics, such as "Diversity in the Classroom," "Classroom Assessment," "Inclusion," "Technology Tools," "Teacher Reflection," "Motivation," and "Differentiated Instruction" in more depth.

▶ Acknowledgments

Whenever any of us put pen to paper or fingers to the keyboard, we stand on the shoulders of others. This is certainly true of this book. We are indebted to many people. In the writing of this book, we are especially appreciative of the help given by the following individuals. Most notably, Lee McCanne, Brooke Graham Doyle, and Elizabeth Langran contributed the chapter on technology and the teacher, entitled "What Should Teachers Know About Technology and Its Impact on Schools?" Additionally, we thank a number of scholars for the invaluable contribution of their research and writing to various chapters, specifically: Cathleen Kinsella Stutz for Chapters 2 and 8; Susan Tauer for Chapters 9 and 12; and Larry Kaufman for Chapter 10. We also wish to thank William Geulcher for writing one of the cases in Chapter 2 and Steven Tigner for his portrait of Socrates and his helpful suggestions on the chapter entitled "What Are the Philosophical Foundations of American Education?" Special thanks go to our colleagues and students for their many good ideas and continuing support, in particular, the teacher contributors to the "Voices from the Classroom" feature. A number of reviewers also made key contributions to the organization and content of this edition, most notably:

Larry Arnson, Gwinnett Technical College

Andrea T. Cortez, Parkland College

Leslie K. Day, Buffalo State College

Cheryl J. Edwards, Southeastern Louisiana University

Diane Hembacher, California State University, Dominguez Hills

Kathleen Hursh, SUNY Geneseo

Carol S. Lorek, Northern Arizona University

William R. Martin, George Mason University

Arturo Monteil, South Texas Community College

Stephen A. Schmitz, Central Washington University

Karen A. Vuurens, South Texas Community College

Mary C. Ware, SUNY Cortland

Brian Yusko, Cleveland State University

A special acknowledgment is due to Marilyn Ryan for the substantial intellectual and psychological contributions she made to the several editions of this book.

Writing and revising a book is a multifaceted process. Many people provide advice—some solicited and some not. We believe, however, that our best source of advice on this book and its companion, *Kaleidoscope,* has been the team we've worked with at Houghton Mifflin. Lisa Mafrici, senior development editor, has been the one who has gracefully orchestrated the coming together of the many pieces of this book and *Kaleidoscope.* Sue Pulvermacher-Alt, senior sponsoring editor, had the responsibility of overseeing the "big picture" surrounding this project and *Kaleidoscope.* We are enormously appreciative of her dynamic and thoughtful leadership. Jane Lee, senior project editor, has deftly handled the copyediting process and all of the final stages of production. The developmental editor for this edition has been Sheralee Connors, who has been a terrific source of good ideas, cartoons, quotes, and practical suggestions. A good revision editor has to have a fine sense of what to keep and what to drop. We are convinced that Sheralee is a gifted poker player because she truly "knows when to hold 'em and knows when to fold 'em," and all of this with the greatest tact. Finally, we acknowledge the thousands of students for whom this book is written. Your new learning as you become teachers is central to our work as authors. We value your feedback on how we are doing and invite you to respond by sending us your comments through the Houghton Mifflin website.

Kevin Ryan
James M. Cooper

1 *Why Teach?*

Chapter Preview   People take education courses for several reasons. Three in particular are common. First, as citizens, people need to know how a major institution like the school system works so that they can make informed choices within their communities and at the voting booth. Second, as parents or potential parents, they need to know a great deal to be intelligent partners with the schools in their children's education. Third, those who are considering a career in teaching need to understand the profession they may enter. This text, by and large, is written with this third group in mind. And this chapter, more than any other in the text, focuses on those exploring the teaching profession. Its purpose is to help you answer a fundamental question: Why should I become a teacher? As you read the cases of representative teachers that follow, we hope you come to understand more fully your own motivations for teaching. This chapter also emphasizes that:

▶ A great variety of motivations lead people to select teaching as their occupation, and often the same person has more than one reason for choosing teaching.

▶ Teaching, like other occupations, often attracts people because of the rewards it offers them. The rewards of teaching can be divided into extrinsic and intrinsic rewards.

▶ In deciding whether to become a teacher, you can draw on a number of sources of useful experiences, including actual encounters with teachers and children, vicarious classroom experiences, guidance from friends and acquaintances in the profession, and—most important—your own personal reflections.

► Examining Your Motives for Teaching

If you teach, it is quite likely that by the end of your second year of teaching you will have had both of the following experiences:

1. Someone at a party or some other social gathering will ask you what you do and how you like teaching. Soon the person will tell you that he or she has always wanted to be a teacher and regrets having become a stockbroker/ bookkeeper/sales representative/flight attendant/disc jockey, and that he or she may still give it all up and become a teacher.

2. You will get to know an experienced teacher who confides in you that he or she deeply regrets having become a teacher. While in college, the person felt definitely cut out for teaching and actually enjoyed it in the beginning. But gradually, he or she became fed up with the whole thing—bratty kids, pushy administrators, the same old faces in the teachers' lounge, the instant-expert parents, the overemphasis on standards and high-stakes testing. Now the person feels trapped in teaching and sees no way to get out.

The purpose of this chapter is to keep you from becoming "the other person" in either of these situations. It is to help you make a well-thought-out decision about what to do with your life, particularly if you are still undecided about becoming a teacher.

Knowing Your Own Motives

Visit the website for a biography of Socrates.

Centuries ago, Francis Bacon told us "knowledge is power." Much earlier, Socrates (one of civilization's great teachers, whom we discuss in the chapter entitled "What Are the Philosophical Foundations of American Education?") recognized the enormous power of self-knowledge when he urged "Know thyself." Understanding one's motives in something as important as a career choice is crucial to good decision making. A superficial motivation to teach can, and frequently does, lead to failure and disappointment. For instance, you may admire and want to emulate a former teacher. And you may, out of respect for this person, decide to teach without ever analyzing whether you have the ability, skills, attitudes, or drive to do so. Or you may think it is admirable to like and help children. But in the process of actually working with, say, sixth-graders, you may discover that you can't stand sixth-graders or that you are not even particularly interested in children. We do not want you—or your students—to be trapped in such a situation.

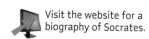
■ understand your real motives

Clarifying your motives helps you to identify your strengths as a person and as a prospective teacher and to cope with your shortcomings. Someone whose desire to teach grows out of a passion for art history has to know how to guard against hostility toward students who don't share that love of art. More than a few frustrated teachers have been heard to mutter, "Those ungrateful little whiners aren't worthy of Shakespeare" (or French infinitives, or the wonders of the protoplasmic process, or the niceties of quadratic equations). In any event, we have written this chapter—and, indeed, the entire book—in the hope that you will use it to gain a greater understanding of how you and a career in education might fit together.

■ make a list

To begin that process, we would like you to take a moment to write down on the blank lines that follow, or on a separate sheet of paper, what you think and feel are your motives for wanting to be a teacher. If you are not completely sure whether you want to be a teacher (this probably applies to many of you), list your motives both for and against becoming a teacher. It is important that you actually write them out, because we are going to return to this question, "Why teach?" and your motives later in the text.

■ multiple motive

We use the plural, *motives,* for a particular reason. Most of us have mixed motives, some altruistic and some personal, regarding what is important to us. Our motives often conflict, and sometimes they are incompatible. In addition, one motive is rarely enough to explain a choice as complex as the career in which we plan to spend a large part of our lives.

Why Become a Teacher?

Motives for **Motives against**

_____ _____

_____ _____

_____ _____

_____ _____

_____ _____

The Habit of Reflection

■ did you answer?

If you did not stop reading to think about your motives for becoming a teacher or to commit yourself in writing, well, you are probably like many other readers. But stop now and think about what kept you from seriously engaging the question. Your answer may tell you a good deal about yourself as a learner and, incidentally, about the educational system of which you are a product. Have you been trained to devour pages and pages without really confronting the issues conveyed by the words? Have you learned to disregard your own views, even about issues quite central to you? If your answers to these questions are *yes,* you are like many, many other students. However, we hope this will be a different kind of book and a different kind of reading-questioning-thinking experience for you.

■ using this book

We want your reading of this book to be unlike others you might read: things you pick up, spend time with, and put down again without having been moved or changed in any way. Because we are teachers, we want this book to have a very special impact on you, and to help you make good decisions about whether you want to be a teacher and about what kind of teacher you want to become. For these reasons, you need to read this book in a different way. Take the book on fully! Encounter it! Fight with it! Improve it by adding yourself to it. That old, tired cliché, "You get out of it what you put into it" truly applies here. So, again, if you didn't think about and write down your motives for teaching, it might be good to go back and have a try at it.

■ the habit of reflection

And, one more thing. As you will see throughout this book (and particularly in the chapter entitled "What Makes a Teacher Effective?"), we believe that effective teachers, indeed effective people in many areas of life, succeed in part because they are mindful of what they are doing. They reflect on their attitudes and performance, always looking for ways to improve. This practice of **reflection** is a habit you can use even now, as part of your career choice process. We think that recording what you think today, revisiting your thoughts throughout the term, and then noting what you think at the end of your class will help solidify any choice you make about teaching. We hope that by the end of the semester (and the end of reading this text), you will develop a greater understanding of what it means to teach, of what teachers do, of how schools operate within their communities and society, and of a number of other issues you will need to consider to make a wise decision about whether teaching is right for you. To that end, we have inserted "Pause and Reflect" sections with questions. Again, to get the full benefit from this text and your course, we urge you to use these opportunities to develop the habit of reflection.

Comparing Your Motives to Others'

■ can you find yourself among these?

Having answered the question "What are my motives for wanting to become a teacher?" (and we surely hope you have), here are a few examples you might check against your own list:

- I really like the idea of having a positive influence on 25 (or 150) kids every day.
- I can't think of anything else to do with my major.
- Teaching seems to be a fairly secure, low-risk occupation with many attractive benefits, including lots of vacation time and time to raise a family.
- I always loved history/mathematics/science/literature, and teaching seems to be a career that will allow me to work with a subject matter that I love.
- I can't imagine anything more important to do with my life than helping children with disabilities learn to cope with, and even overcome, their barriers.
- The instruction I had in school was incredibly bad, and I want to correct that situation.
- My parents would really be pleased and proud if I were a teacher.
- Quite simply, I love children.
- I enjoy being in charge and being able to influence students.
- I really don't know what else I could do. I know about teaching, and I think I could do it.
- I'm concerned that society is falling apart, and I want to look out for the kids.
- One of my students might become a famous painter, or the president of a major foundation, or who knows what. It would be great to have a strong impact on just one significant life.
- I really want to become a principal/coach/guidance counselor/college professor/ educational researcher, and teaching seems to be the way one has to start.
- I have strong religious beliefs and see teaching as a good and useful way to live my life.
- Education seems as if it's going to be the action field of the future, and I want to be part of it.
- Businesses are increasingly interested in training and educating their employees, and I want a career as a private-sector educator working in corporate America.
- I want to have fun in life, and as a teacher, I'll have fun and get paid for it!
- I have always felt I have a calling, a vocation, to be a teacher.

■ changes over time?

You may also be interested in seeing whether or not answers to the question "Why teach?" have changed over time. Why did the teachers you had in school select teaching as a career? Why did your parents' teachers decide to teach? The information in Table 1.1 comes from a study conducted every five years by the

TABLE 1.1 Principal Reasons Selected by All Teachers for Originally Deciding to Become a Teacher, 1971–2001 (%)				
Reason	**1971**	**1981**	**1991**	**2001**
Desire to work with young people	72	70	66	73
Value or significance of education to society	37	40	37	44
Interest in subject-matter field	35	44	34	36
Influence of teacher in elementary or secondary school	18	25	27	32
Influence of family	21	22	21	19

Adapted from Table 49, *Status of the American Public School Teacher* (Washington, DC: National Education Association, 2003), p. 68.

■ categories of rewards

National Education Association. Notice the striking stability of the motives from one generation of teachers to the next. For instance, from 1971 to 2001, the prime motivation, "desire to work with young people," varies by only one percent. Similarly the third most cited reason, "interest in subject-matter field," has also changed by only one percentage point. Amid all the social change of recent decades, men and women are drawn to the work of teaching by the same desires. As we'll see next, the rewards often match the desires of those who teach.

▶ The Rewards of Teaching

As we have seen, an individual's response to "Why teach?" can run the gamut from "What's in it for me?" to "How can I help others?" Moreover, our individual motivations can change and may be quite different at different times and in different moods. As social psychologist Peter Drucker quipped, "We know nothing about motivation. All we can do is write books about it." On the other hand, the motivational *factors*—those qualities that reside within teaching—are clearer and relatively constant. Researchers have identified a set of occupational rewards that can help us sort out both the attractive and unattractive qualities of a career in teaching.[1] The two broad categories of rewards are extrinsic and intrinsic rewards. **Extrinsic rewards** are the public, external attractions of an occupation, such as money, prestige, and power. The **intrinsic rewards** of an occupation are the internal psychic or spiritual satisfactions one receives from one's work, such as a personal sense of accomplishment or an enjoyment of the work itself. It will undoubtedly be no surprise to the reader that teaching is somewhat out of balance, receiving generally high marks on one set of rewards and low marks on the other.

Extrinsic Rewards

■ modest salaries

Teaching has rarely been cited for its abundance of extrinsic rewards. Although it offers more extrinsic rewards than occupations such as law enforcement and coal mining, when compared with other professions, teaching ranks low in extrinsic compensations.

■ **Salaries**   As you will see in the chapter entitled "What Are Your Job Options in Education?" teachers' salaries, as well as benefits such as retirement plans and

At twenty-two, I graduated Phi Beta Kappa. I had choices at my fingertips: law school, grad school . . . corporate America, here I come! Adults swelled their chests in pride. My peers practiced the "on my way to a Lexus" shuffle. Then the question: "And what are your plans after graduation?" Answer: "I'm moving to New York to teach elementary school in the South Bronx." As a twenty-three-year-old teacher with sore feet and twenty-eight incredible kids, my explanation reminds me of a song. I had a choice to sit it out or dance. I chose to dance.

—Thalia Theodore, *Washington Post* (Dec. 2, 2001), p. F1

■ variable status

health care, have improved substantially in recent years, and there are encouraging signs that steady gains can be expected. Nevertheless, compared with salaries in occupational fields with similar educational requirements (for example, a college degree and specialized training), teachers' salaries do not compare well. Whereas salaries in some professions usually begin low and then increase significantly, salaries for teachers may rise only modestly over the course of an entire teaching career. However, the importance of salary, like the whole issue of monetary needs, varies enormously from one individual to the next. And, as you will also see in the chapter entitled "What Are Your Job Options in Education?," teachers' salaries vary significantly from one geographical location to the next.

■ **Status**   Status refers to one's position in a group—that is, where one stands in relation to others. The status of a doctor or a beggar is rather clear, but the status of a teacher is more difficult to discern. To young parents entrusting their child to the schools for the first time, the status of the teacher is quite high. To the same parents twelve or fifteen years later, on hearing that their child wants to become a teacher, the status may be somewhat diminished. Our nation's current commitment to reform our educational system is, however, having a positive effect on the status of teaching. Figure 1.1 shows the results of a public opinion survey that asked which of eight

FIGURE 1.1
Profession That Provides the Most Benefit to Society

Source: From David Haselkorn and Louis Harris, "The Essential Profession: A National Survey of Public Attitudes Toward Teaching, Educational Opportunity, and School Reform." Reprinted with permission of Recruiting New Teachers, Inc., 1998.

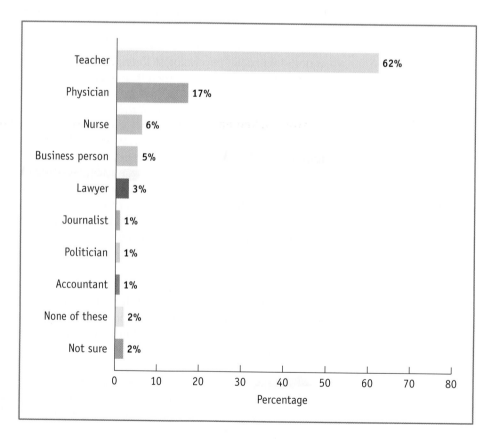

professions (including physician, lawyer, nurse, and journalist, among others) "provides the most important benefit to society." Respondents put teaching first, by close to a four to one margin over physicians (62 percent versus 17 percent). This was a big improvement over a poll taken a decade earlier, in which only 35 percent of respondents put teaching first.[2]

■ power over others' lives

■ **Power** Power is not usually seen as one of the rewards of teaching, but it nevertheless is a quality that "resides in the office." Anyone who claims that teachers do not have power has forgotten what it was like to go to school without having done the assigned homework and to sit in fear of being called on by Mrs. Gotcha. The power of the teacher is not a dollars-and-cents power, like that possessed by a corporate chief executive officer, but any individual who can make another's day or ruin another's year has power. Although, as sociologist Dan Lortie has observed, "Teachers are not supposed to *enjoy* exercising power per se,"[3] the public opinion survey discussed earlier made it quite clear that the public sees the quality of teachers as the greatest influence on student learning.[4]

The sole advantage of power is that you can do more good.

—BALTASAR GRACIAN,
THE ART OF WORLDLY WISDOM, 1647

■ flexibility and personal control over time

■ **Work Schedule** There is an old joke about a student in an education course being stumped on an exam by the question "What are the three best things about a career in teaching?" Finally, in desperation, he writes, "June, July, and August." He probably flunked, but he did have a point. Compared with other workers, teachers spend much less time at their work sites. If we ignore what teachers do at home by way of preparing lessons, correcting papers, and checking homework, we can say they work six or seven hours a day for fewer than half the days of the year. Compared with those in power and status occupations, such as corporate finance or medicine, teachers have less demanding work schedules. Also, teachers have much more flexibility and personal control over how they use their time. For many men and women family life is a top priority, and the time spent close to home and on summer vacations are major plusses for a career in teaching. Teachers' work schedules therefore are one extrinsic reward that carries a great deal of weight.

Intrinsic Rewards

Extrinsic rewards, such as company stock options or yearly bonuses, are quite tangible. Intrinsic rewards are, by their very nature, in the eye of the beholder. What is one person's intrinsic reward, such as taking a busload of students on an overnight fieldtrip to the state capital, is another's living nightmare. However, the most satisfied teachers are usually those attracted to its intrinsic rewards.

■ the joy of helping others

■ **Students**   The attraction of working with students has long been one of the strongest rewards perceived by teachers. The daily contacts, the conversations and exchanges, and even the struggles to motivate a student are a deep source of satisfaction for many teachers. Seeing children learn, grow, and develop—seeing them able to do things that they were unable to do at the beginning of the school year— is a genuinely fulfilling experience. Being important to others satisfies profound human needs for most of us, and teachers know about and appreciate this potential to affect the lives of others. Nearly three out of five (58 percent) teenagers surveyed mentioned teachers when researchers asked them to tell who or what had influenced them to become the kinds of people they are.[5]

> *To hear lessons and control restless children six hours a day through thirty-six weeks in a year is wretched drudgery, but to train and develop human minds and characters is the most inspiring work in the world.*
>
> —ELLEN HYDE, TO THE GRADUATING CLASS OF THE FRAMINGTON NORMAL SCHOOL IN 1886

This reward is particularly meaningful to elementary school teachers, who spend so much time with the same group of fifteen to thirty children. Secondary school teachers, who focus on a particular subject matter and see as many as 150 students in a day, identify working with students as an important attraction but not always to the same degree as their elementary school counterparts do. Jaime Escalante, described in the Leaders in Education feature in this chapter, was a secondary-school teacher who always focused on students as the reason for his teaching career.

■ contribution to society

■ **Performance of a Significant Social Service**   In the award-winning film about early Renaissance England, *A Man for All Seasons,* Sir Thomas More says to Richard Rich, the man who eventually betrayed him, but who at the time was seeking a cushy job at court, "Why not be a teacher, Rich? You'd be a fine teacher. Perhaps a great one." Disappointed, Rich replies, "And if I were, who would know it?" More then says, "You . . . your pupils . . . your friends . . . God—not a bad public, that." To many teachers, the greatest satisfaction derived from teaching is the sense that they are doing important work for the common good. This realization buoys them up and helps them tolerate the less attractive aspects of teaching. As we saw in Figure 1.1, members of the general public seem to agree that teaching provides valuable benefits for society. Whereas workers in government and business are aware, in an abstract sense, that they are contributing to the social good, teachers have daily flesh-and-blood testaments to the importance of their service directly in front of them. Many college professors report that they see more and more college students not only seriously considering teaching as a career but also selecting teaching specifically because they see it as service to the nation and a way to pay back the country. For some students the deeper motive behind the performance of this service for others is a religious one. They see teaching as a way to serve God through being of service to the young.

> *A man of humanity is one who, in seeking to establish himself, finds a foothold for others and who, desiring attainment for himself, helps others to attain.*
>
> —CONFUCIUS

■ collegiality

■ **Stimulation and Support from Fellow Teachers**   When describing the work of teaching, researchers often report on the sense of isolation many teachers experience.[6] Nevertheless, for many teachers their contacts and interactions with colleagues are an important intrinsic reward. Teachers enjoy the shoptalk and ca-

Houghton Mifflin Video Cases let you see real teachers and real students in real classrooms. The cases not only let you watch how teachers handle common classroom situations and employ key teaching strategies, but they also allow you to examine worksheets, notes, and other classroom artifacts.

The video case *Teaching as a Profession: Collaboration with Colleagues* provides a more in-depth look at how teachers can work together. As you watch the clips and study the artifacts in the case, reflect upon the following questions:

1. How does the collaborative process shown in this case demonstrate the habits of reflection discussed earlier in this chapter?
2. Does the planning process in which these teachers are engaged look like something you would enjoy as part of your career?

■ teaching as pleasurable activity

maraderie that is a natural part of school life. Because teachers are not always rewarded for their individual job performance or for their expertise, feelings of competition are less prevalent than among occupational groups such as salespeople or lawyers, who must establish and hold a clientele. Teachers know they are part of a highly cooperative venture.

■ **The Work of Teaching** For many teachers, the process of teaching is a meaningful reward in itself. Whether it is explaining an idea, working with small groups, or designing instructional units, the actual work is highly gratifying. Like a pianist moving through a favorite sonata or a lawyer cross-examining a witness, teachers often draw their deepest satisfactions in and from the act of applying their craft. One teacher describes this feeling in this chapter's Voices from the Classroom. Of course, teachers vary in which activities they find rewarding. Some draw their rewards from establishing a nurturing, cooperative environment, some from unraveling complicated problems for students, and some from seeing students work and learn independently. For these teachers, all else pales before their deep sense of fulfillment in simply doing the work of a teacher.

As you continue reading and doing the work of this course, we urge you to keep alive in your mind the issues of intrinsic and external rewards, of personal satisfactions and of the "fit" between you and the work of the teacher. Begin now with some quiet reflection.

Pause and Reflect

1 ▸ Which of the extrinsic rewards discussed above applies to you most? Which of the intrinsic rewards?

2 ▸ As you have probed your own motives for considering teaching, what have you learned about yourself?

This teacher obviously enjoys her students and the work of teaching.
(© Elizabeth Crews)

VOICES FROM THE CLASSROOM

Elida Laski taught kindergarten for three years in Chula Vista, California, and is now a literacy coach for three early learning centers in the Boston public school system.

Are You Born with It?

In my second year of teaching, a colleague told me, "Good teachers are born, not made, and you were born with it." After four years of teaching, I still wonder about this comment. What is that *it,* that certain something that distinguishes excellent teachers? Do you have to be born with that certain something in order to be a good teacher? If you are born with *it,* do you always know that teaching is the profession for you? Is it true that some people are just not made for teaching, or can anyone learn what it takes? How do you know if you are meant to be a teacher?

I never intended to be a teacher. In fact, it was not until my senior year of college that, as a frustrated pre-med student, I entertained the idea of teaching and took two education courses. Immediately, I knew that teaching was for me! I had done very well in the pre-med track, but I never felt invested in what I was studying. Education courses required just as much, if not more, time and thought, and they were exciting in a way pre-med had never been. Education offered me the academic rigor of the sciences but also appealed to my heart.

Teaching demands systematic thought and reflection in order to deliver the instruction and analyze situations. It requires a solid understanding of content and pedagogy to be critical of new trends and develop curriculum. However, I believe it is instincts that humanize teaching—the gut feeling of what will work or not, the sense of how to connect with each child, the ability to juggle ten things at once and be fired up rather than stressed out, and so much more. Being in the classroom is still an adrenaline rush. I put in twelve-hour days without thinking twice. I cannot go to a store, museum, or park without thinking how I might apply what I see to my classroom. The joy of teaching, itself, drives me. That, I think, is the *it.* Whether you can learn *it* or have to be born with *it,* I still cannot say.

 Visit the website for more Voices from the Classroom.

▶ Sources of Useful Experience

One of the major educational insights applied to schooling in recent years concerns individual differences. There is a new appreciation for the unique learning styles and the unique learning problems of children and youth. As a result, the "one-true-way" approach to education is gradually slipping by the boards. The same insight about individual differences applies to making an intelligent career choice. Because people learn in such diverse ways and differ so much in what they already know and need to learn, we can give only sketchy guidelines here. We recognize four categories of experience that may help you answer the question, "Should I teach?" You should use the four sources in whatever combination best fits your present stage of life and career decision making.

Real Encounters

■ romantic images versus real children

Students who plan to be teachers should test their commitment to teaching by putting themselves in actual school situations. As much as possible, students of teaching should observe in schools and participate in various activities that give them **real encounters** with children and adolescents. Some teaching candidates avoid actual contact with the young until they begin student teaching, only to find

You cannot acquire experience by making experiments. You cannot create experience. You must undergo it.
—ALBERT CAMUS (1913–1960)

■ ways to get your
  educational feet wet

that young people are much different from the romantic images they have manufactured. "Those nasty little fifth-graders are so disgustingly . . . juvenile!" one shocked student teacher said. Frequently, too, teaching candidates limit their encounters to typical elementary and secondary school students. They do not consider teaching children with mental or physical disabilities or even becoming a specialist such as a reading teacher. As a result of their past experiences, they have been exposed to only a narrow segment of the opportunities and challenges of teaching.

Increasingly, school districts are using college students as teacher aides and assistant teachers, both during the regular school year and in summer school. And a large number of teacher education programs have cooperative arrangements with schools that give college students opportunities to play various roles within the school, usually as part of their coursework in teacher education. As we mention in the chapter entitled "What Are Your Job Options in Education?" we particularly urge prospective teachers to take the opportunity resulting from the current teacher shortage and become substitute teachers. Although the work is demanding, there is much that will be learned from it. Besides the valuable experience and the money earned, these substitute teaching stints often lead to regular teaching positions in the future. School districts typically are more interested in hiring someone they have seen in action rather than strangers who they only know from résumés and references.

If your schedule doesn't permit substitute teaching, many schools also gratefully accept part-time volunteer help from education students. Schools, however, do not exhaust the opportunities. There is much to be said for nonschool contact with children, such as camp counseling, playground work, after-school recreation projects, work in orphanages and settlement houses, and youth-related church work. Other possibilities include coaching a team or sponsoring a youth club. The opportunities are many. The important thing is to get your feet wet—to get the feel of working with young people in a helping relationship.

Real-world experience with children can help you make an informed decision about teaching as a career.
(© Bob Daemmrich/ PhotoEdit)

Vicarious Experiences

■ the teacher in fiction and film

Not all learning has to take place in the school of hard knocks. In fact, civilization itself requires that we be able to capitalize on the experiences of others. Artists and other talented people can make others' experiences accessible to us for enjoyment, edification, or both. Great fictional classics such as *Good-bye, Mr. Chips,* by James Hilton, and *The Corn Is Green,* by Emlyn Williams, portray teachers and schools, as do somewhat more contemporary novels such as Bel Kaufman's *Up the Down Staircase* and Evan Hunter's *Blackboard Jungle.* (All four of these books have been made into films.) There have also been some fine nonfiction accounts of teaching; among the best are Tracy Kidder's *Among Schoolchildren,* Samuel G. Freedman's *Small Victories,* and Esmé Raji Codell's *Educating Esmé* (all are cited in the **For Further Information** section at the end of this chapter).

Films, such as *The Emperor's Club, Mr. Holland's Opus, Music of the Heart, Lean on Me, Dangerous Minds, Pay It Forward, Dead Poet's Society,* and *Stand and Deliver,* as well as some television shows such as *Boston Public,* are other sources of **vicarious experiences** that help us both relive our own experience in school and see it in a different light. However, that light is often distorting. Leslie Swetnam has reported on how the media, particularly film and television, twist the public's image of the teacher. Swetnam states, "Problems arise from the misrepresentation of who teaches, where they teach, how they teach, and what demands are placed on teachers, thereby creating an alarming distortion with consequences serious enough to warrant the concern of all educational professionals."[7] Her analysis of the most popular media presentations of teachers and schools shows that they overrepresent male teachers, secondary schools, minority teachers, and urban schools. Other distortions are that classes are small; teaching typically means the adult is talking (often with the skill of a Dennis Miller or Chris Rock!) and, when the class finally gets around to it, learning is fun, fun, fun.[8]

One genre of films that is especially distorting includes those that present teachers as perverts and sadists, film such as *The Breakfast Club, Election,* and *Sugar and Spice,* as well as hoards of others. The less said about those films, the better. There has also been a parade of comedies about school life, such as *The School of Rock, Ferris Bueller's Day Off,* and *Summer School,* which . . . well, don't exactly flatter traditional teachers. However, if approached with a critical eye, all these media images of teaching can prepare us for certain aspects of teaching and school life. We need to remember, however, that books, films, and television tend to portray school life at its extremes, featuring heightened situations well beyond the typical experiences of most teachers. The drama of teaching, on the other hand, is quiet, long term, and terribly real.

Guidance

■ advice from others

Another aid is the advice and counsel gained from those who know you. Besides parents and friends (who sometimes are too close to you to be objective), you can consult former teachers, career placement counselors, and your college professors. Your professors of education can be particularly helpful, because besides knowing you, they usually are familiar with the realities of teaching. You should use caution when seeking guidance from others, however. First, choose people who know you well rather than those who have seen you just at your better moments. Second, do not expect a comprehensive computer printout of hard data with a firm decision at the bottom line. If you get a few glimpses of insight from

Write down the advice of him who loves you, though you like it not at present.

—ENGLISH PROVERB

the person whose advice you are seeking, be satisfied. Third, be wary, since many people are compulsive advice givers. People often generalize on the basis of too little knowledge, and they are sometimes just plain wrong. Receive advice openly, but follow it cautiously.

Reflection

■ taking time out to think

The most important aspect of the real school encounters, guidance, and vicarious experiences you collect is that they provide you with data for reflection. As we mentioned earlier and emphasize throughout this book, the value of these experiences will be lost if you do not think about them. People are often so busy experiencing things, or getting ready to experience them that they fail to truly reflect on what they have done in a manner that will ensure that they get the most from the experience.

We cannot stress this point enough. Reflection goes to the very heart of why we have written this book. Both of us are convinced that many people make sloppy decisions about becoming teachers. Often, they have not asked some of the fundamental questions about themselves and about schools. This is precisely why we have organized this book around a series of questions, such as "Why teach?" and "What is a school and what is it for?"

Pause and Reflect

1 ▸ Are you really and truly using all the resources available to you to help you make a conscious and clear decision about your future career? What can you do to enhance your chances of making a good career decision?

▶ Case Studies in the Motivation to Teach

This section offers two case studies that illustrate common motives for going into teaching. Each case study is followed by a set of questions and a comment. The cases are intended as examples of how particular abstract motives take shape in teachers' lives. You may want to discuss the cases and the accompanying questions with other people. The shared experience of reading the cases and responding to the questions should help you probe and understand your own motivations. Finally, the cases and accompanying comments raise important issues about the nature of teaching.

| **Case Study** | ## The Desire to Teach a Particular Subject |

Julia Tucker had been a star science student since junior high school. She received a partial scholarship to study chemistry in college and earned high marks in everything connected with science. She also derived a good deal of personal satisfaction from quietly showing her mostly male teachers and fellow students that a female could excel at science. When she graduated from college, she was heavily recruited by a chemical engineering firm. She immediately fell in love with her job. It took a little longer (two years), but she fell even more in love with Nicholas, a chemist, who was working on the same project. They got married, and, a year and a day later, Justin was born. Julia was back at work in six weeks. Both Nicholas and she hoped to have four children, but it didn't work out that way. There was no second pregnancy.

■ a midlife career switch

Julia was disappointed, but she took it philosophically. After all, she had a wonderful job, a loving husband, and a son who was the joy of her life. Everything was fine until Justin went off to middle school and began taking science courses. Julia couldn't wait to help him with his science homework. She stayed up late reading his science textbooks. She found all sorts of excuses to talk to his teachers about science education. She found herself daydreaming at work about how to teach various scientific concepts to children. And she was also gradually losing interest in the highly specialized type of chemistry she was doing. So, after a great deal of soul searching and several late-night conversations with Nicholas, she quit her job and went back to school to get a teaching license in chemistry.

That was more than a year ago. Now Julia has a job, but hardly the job she fantasized about in her old lab or the teaching position for which she prepared. To her surprise, the only available position (other than ones that would force her to move the family) was at the elementary level, as a fifth-grade teacher. The school superintendent realized that Julia would be a real asset to his school district, but he did not have an opening in the high school for two more years, when the chemistry teacher was scheduled to retire. So he presented Julia with a proposition: she could take some methods courses over the summer (at district expense), become a fifth-grade teacher for two years, help establish a new elementary science curriculum, and be the coordinator of the annual science fair. At first, Julia was quite wary about this possibility. She thought it would mean throwing away a good deal of her specialized knowledge and risking failure as an elementary-school teacher, even though it would be for only two years. But after talking it over with Nicholas and getting great support from her son, she reluctantly agreed.

A funny thing happened during the summer, as Julia took the methods courses and prepared herself for her fifth-graders. She became more and more enthused about

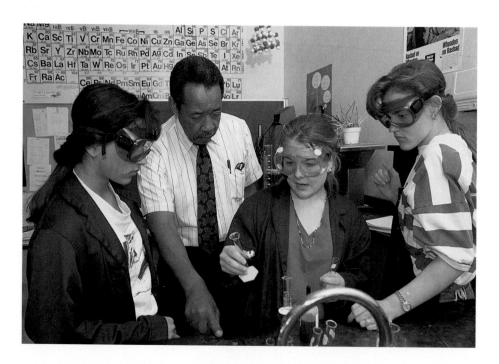

A chemistry teacher helps students with titrations. (© Bob Daemmrich/Stock Boston)

teaching children who she believed were "just becoming interested in the outer world." When she actually started working with her fifth-grade students a couple of months ago, she was hooked. They were so alive, so responsive, and so hungry to know about the world. What a challenge! Thoughts of ever becoming a chemistry teacher took a back seat to the elementary classroom.

■ evaluation and concerns

Now, in November, however, Julia has misgivings. There is a flatness in her class that worries her. Much of the September curiosity has turned into an early case of the midwinter blahs. Moreover, her supervisor has conducted the first formal observation of Julia's teaching, and she is curious about the supervisor's opinion.

"So, Suzanne," Julia says at their post-observation conference. "How did I do? You were writing up such a storm, I thought you would need another notebook!"

"Oh, I hope you didn't find that distracting. I probably should have warned you that I would be scribbling away."

"No, that's fine. I'm just curious to know how I did."

"I'd much rather hear what *you* think, Julia. How do you think the class went?"

"Well, I think pretty much as usual. They were a little quieter, perhaps because you were in there, but in general, that was an average class."

"I did notice it being quiet, Julia. How do you feel about that?"

"As a matter of fact, I'm confused by it. Since September, the decibel level has been steadily falling in all my classes, but particularly when we are doing science. I couldn't get them to shut up in September. They ate up everything I presented, especially science. They just seem to have lost interest."

"From what I just saw, and from what I have observed passing by your door these weeks, I'd agree. Interest looks low."

"Suzanne, I've really worked to find topics that will interest them. I built a whole unit on pollution last month with writing assignments and mathematics worked in. They said they were interested in heredity, so next month, we're going to do family histories with interviews and collections of family facts and artifacts. They were all excited about this in September, but now I'm stumped. What is the matter?"

"Quite honestly, Julia, I had a feeling that this would happen."

"What do you mean?"

"Well, when you came to interview last June, we were thrilled at the possibility of getting someone so knowledgeable and so experienced, and particularly someone who loves science so much. But those same qualities made us hesitant, too."

I love to learn in order that I might teach; and I get no joy from learning anything if I alone am to know about it.

—Seneca

"I'm not getting you, Suzanne. I know we were all concerned that I didn't have traditional preparation for elementary teaching. You're not saying I know too much and I like science too much, are you?"

"Yes and no. No, you don't know too much. And your love of science is a terrific asset. But, at the same time, these qualities are

■ sometimes love for a subject gets in the way

keeping you from being the potentially fine teacher you can become. Julia, let me be honest with you. You are drowning these kids with information—and not just in science. It seems to me that you're doing all the work. What worked so well for you during your student teaching, with high school juniors and seniors, just doesn't work with these elementary school wigglers."

"Honestly, Suzanne, I'm not giving them high school material. This work is within their range. I don't mean to sound defensive, but really. . . ."

"Julia, think 'romance.' "

"Romance? I thought you told me to do health and human sexuality in the spring!"

"No, no. Romance. Like in 'the romance of science' and 'the romance of writing.' Do you remember telling us during your interview how you fell in love—your words, Julia—fell in love with science in the fifth grade when you had to do a project for the science fair? Well, what I think you ought to do is a little time traveling and think about what caused *your* romance with science. Was it a fascinating question? An unsolved problem? The excitement of maybe solving a problem the adults couldn't? Or was it a teacher pumping facts and theories into you?"

"Uh-oh. I think the dawn is breaking. I've been too busy talking at them and trying to teach them some basic information."

"Right. You've been so busy telling them about what you love that you forgot romance. You forgot that romance is a two-way street. It's a classic mistake of rookie teachers, even ancient ones like you. Sometimes you can get away with it in high schools, but not in elementary schools."

"So what do I do now?"

"Well, let me put aside these notes, and let's see if you and I can put a little romance into the rest of the week's lessons."

"A little pedagogical seduction! Suzanne, I think you found the key!" ■

Pause and Reflect

1 ► How would you characterize Julia's motivation to teach?

2 ► What sorts of things do you think her students were thinking and feeling about her classes?

3 ► Julia is clearly an outstanding resource to the school. What, however, are her liabilities?

4 ► What clues should Julia have been picking up?

5 ► What are some things Julia might do to stimulate romance for science in her students?

Comment

We probably all have had teachers whose excitement and enthusiasm for their subject were contagious. Love for a particular subject matter or content is an important and commendable motive for teaching. A major purpose of school is to pass on to the young the best of society's knowledge. Another important purpose is to help young people develop basic skills and attitudes, especially a love for learning. A teacher who has a passion to convey his or her subject matter is often quite effective at both of these goals. Such teachers often push students very hard, but they are frequently the ones who make the greatest impact on us.

■ a balanced approach to subject matter

But carrying love for a particular subject to an extreme can cause trouble. Real learning is usually built on students' interest. Their interest in or love of learning can be blunted when the lover (the teacher) is too overpowering or too insistent. The great teacher, however, like the great lover, knows how to draw out another's interest and help students "fall in love."

■ covering all subjects responsibly

There is another danger for the teacher who is "blinded" by love of a subject. This teacher may be so busy teaching what she or he enjoys that the rest of the curriculum gets shortchanged. For example, the English teacher who loves interpreting literature often finds it easy to avoid slugging it out with grammar, punctuation, and other essential writing skills. The elementary school teacher who loves science, like Julia, may fail to give the other subjects their due. Although this tendency to focus on what we know and love and to avoid what we do not know or like is understandable, it is also irresponsible. It is unfair both to the students and to later teachers, who will expect students to have a command over the avoided or neglected content.

Neither Julia's motive nor her problem is uncommon. Teachers who are strongly motivated by the desire to teach a particular subject matter need to be somewhat cross-eyed. While keeping one eye on what they want to teach, they need to keep the other eye on the students and their day-to-day progress and needs.

Leaders in Education

Jaime Escalante (B. 1930)

It is early in the fall term at Garfield High School in East Los Angeles, once a crime-ridden school filled with low achievers but now famous for outstanding calculus students. It is the morning after the second game of the World Series, and, as he enters the class, the teacher, known as *el professor*, shouts out his first question: "Who won the game?" After a pause, the students begin to chant enthusiastically, "Dodgers! Dodgers!" Having captured their attention, Jaime Escalante moves to the math lesson. Slapping a baseball into his mitt, he says, "As *X* approaches *A*, *F* of *X* is the trajectory. Could be a curve ball." And they are off—teacher and fifty-nine students—on a journey into the mysteries of calculus.

Jaime Escalante, the son of an elementary school teacher, was born in La Paz, Bolivia, and began his own teaching career before age twenty. While he was a high school math and physics teacher, his students began to accumulate prizes, and he soon gained national recognition. Still in his twenties, he organized the first Bolivian national symposium of physics and math teachers. In 1963, amid growing social strife in Bolivia, Escalante, now married with two sons, decided to take his wife and young family to the United States.

The next ten years were years of adjustment and struggle, years when Escalante learned English, went back to college, and worked as a busboy and a cook. When he finally graduated, he took a job in the fast-growing computer industry and studied for the California Teaching Certificate in his free time. When the news came that he had passed the test and would be assigned to a run-down, troubled high school in the *barrio*, Escalante turned his back on a substantially larger paycheck and headed for Garfield High School.

When the school's accreditation was threatened because of its students' low academic performance and high dropout rate, Escalante made his move. Supported by reform-minded administrators, he began setting high standards and making serious demands on students. They were not allowed into his class unless they proved that they had done their homework. He skillfully used the time-honored carrot-and-stick approach. The carrot was college and the world of opportunities higher education opened up for them. The stick was his constant challenging of them: "You *burros* have math in your blood! Our Mayan ancestors were the first to develop the concept of zero!"

Jaime Escalante, the subject of the Academy Award–nominated film *Stand and Deliver*, later taught at Hiram Johnson High School in Sacramento, Calif. He has hosted the PBS series, *FUTURES with Jaime Escalante*, produced by the Foundation for Advancements in Science and Education. Further, he has received numerous awards, including the prestigious United States Presidential Medal of Honor and has been admitted to the Bolivian Hall of Fame. But he is more than the man who has helped hundreds of Mexican-American children discover self-discipline and learning and the enormous self-pride that comes with those accomplishments. Escalante is a tide turner. He has set an idea in motion, the idea that the poor and immigrant children in our country are capable of great intellectual feats. He has shown how remedial, slowed-down education can be replaced by demanding, accelerated education. "My skills are really to motivate these kids, to make them learn, to give them *ganas*—the desire to do something—to make them believe they can learn." He has always been clear about why he taught: his love of young people and his love of his subject. Although he has recently retired from active teaching, Escalante remains a clear and forceful spokesman for quality education, especially for minority chil-

dren. He has taken a strong position against extensive bilingual education, believing it handicaps rather than helps Latino students. Instead he urges a demanding education that will give minority students the knowledge and skills they need to compete in a demanding world. His educational views are captured in his famous motto, "Determination + Discipline + Hard Work = Way to Success."

 Visit the website for more information about Jaime Escalante.

Case Study

The Desire to Aid in the Renewal of Society

Fred Harvey was in his late thirties. His disposition was so pleasant, and a smile came so readily to his face, that one of the other teachers in the large metropolitan high school referred to him as "everybody's Dad." Fred had a remarkable ability to remain relaxed when everyone else was tense, and he often broke up emotionally-charged faculty room situations and staff meetings with an appropriate quip or humorous question.

■ teaching the students nobody else wants

Each year, Fred asked to teach the Curriculum II freshman history class. Of course, his request was always granted because the Curriculum II classes were considered the dumping ground for slow students and students who had given up. Some of the other teachers regarded the Curriculum II classes as "punishment." Yet, year after year, Fred worked happily with students nobody else really wanted.

Fred's freshman history class was one of the most active in the whole school. He often took his students beyond the walls of the school on expeditions to day court, the police station, jail, through industrial plants in the area, and, most years, he also sneaked a baseball game into the fieldtrip lineup. Yet his classes were not characterized by fun and games. The students worked very hard on long and involved homework assignments, intricate discussions of problems, and demanding tests.

One year, Fred invited another teacher to speak to the class about shipbuilding in the eighteenth century. The talk went well, and after the session the other teacher, Todd Vincent, commented to Fred that the discussion following his talk had been very different from what he had anticipated; the questions were thoughtful and displayed observation of detail that the guest speaker had not expected from a "bunch of Curriculum IIs."

Fred laughed. "You know, Todd," he said, "they amaze me, too, sometimes. Most of these kids really have behavior problems, not intellectual ones. If you looked at their case histories, you'd find that the majority of them were 'dropped through the ranks.'"

"What do you mean?" asked Todd.

"I mean that they were in regular classes a good bit of their scholastic lives. But when they became problems in class, their teachers decided that the cause of their poor behavior was that the work was too hard for them. So most of the children in this class really represent the rebels, the nonconformists, the 'antisocials.' These are the kids who some teachers claim 'won't go along with the system.' They're the kids about whom many teachers say, 'I don't care if they learn history as long as they become good citizens.'"

"Yes, but you must admit that very few of them will go to college. Most Curriculum IIs just drop out," said Todd.

■ the danger of low expectations

"Maybe you're missing my point," said Fred. "I guess I'm saying that people can't be 'good citizens' unless they are contributing members of society, and that they should contribute something they think is worth contributing. If they can't get the basic tools that make a person productive, how can they be good citizens? It's a lot more than getting jobs or making decent livings. As a matter of fact, I feel these kids are much more capable than the kids we send to the university."

"In what sense?"

"In the sense that they are the least accepting of society as it exists now," replied Fred. "If you talked to some of them for an hour or so, you'd find that they really feel the school is hypocritical in many ways, and they aren't afraid to point out the hypocrisies. They'll tell you, for instance, that there are two sets of rules in the school, two sets of discipline procedures, two sets of privileges, and all the rest."

"But I hear the same thing from my 'honors' classes," Todd protested. "Those kids know about the double standard, too. They often tell me that an honors student here can get away with anything from cutting class to smoking in the john."

"You've got me wrong again, Todd. What these kids are saying is not that we expect too much of them but that we expect too little. For instance, if a kid dropped from an A to a C in your honors history course, what would happen?"

"The kid would probably get a 'request' to go in and see the counselor," Todd replied.

"That's right," Fred continued. "When a kid everyone believes is bound for college does poorly, bells go off and people get concerned. They try to help the kid take a look at what's wrong. If one of these students goes from a C to an F, though, everyone says, 'Well, what more do you expect? The kid's only a Curriculum II and doesn't have the ability to sustain a C.' And they get all the inexperienced teachers and martinets in the school. Oh, they know that if they become real problems, they'll get counseling and possibly even better teaching. But that isn't their complaint. They know that the system isn't out to punish them. They know the system would rather they just float along and not bother anyone. That's the double standard in this school: those who are cared about and those who aren't. That's what these kids will tell you."

"You know," said Todd, "you're not just talking about the Curriculum II classes. I think the same thing is generally true of Curriculum I classes. It seems that a kid who's really bright gets a lot of attention, and so does the kid who is really slow, but it's that kid in the middle. . . ."

"Right," said Fred. "The kids in this class are the bottom of that middle group in terms of the concern they arouse from the system. And they know it. Yet, as you saw today, they are capable. We owe them a decent set of expectations. I've maintained high expectations for the kids. I would prefer to slightly overmatch them intellectually than undermatch them, because no development is possible when you're being undermatched constantly."

"Don't they complain about being pushed too hard?" asked Todd.

"Oh, sure! There's always a good deal of moaning, particularly in the early weeks, until they realize I don't dance to that tune. Pretty soon they settle in and decide to go along with the program. But then they realize that they are actually learning. At that point, they're hooked. They're mine, and I wouldn't trade teaching them for anything!"

"Well, Fred, this has been most instructive. I came to teach and I ended up learning."

"Me, too. That's what keeps me going. And Todd, please come back next semester."

■ double standards in schools

Those who educate children well are more to be honored than they who produce them; for these only give them life, those the art of living well.

—ARISTOTLE

■ answering students' needs

Pause and Reflect

1 ▶ How is Fred's commitment to social renewal specifically shown in his classroom teaching?

2 ▶ According to Fred, what is the criterion for assignment to Curriculum II classes in his school? Was this true of your high school?

3 ▶ What is the double standard of which Todd Vincent spoke, and how do you explain it? What is the double standard of which Fred spoke, and how do you explain it? Did either of these double standards exist in your school?

4 ▶ How do Fred's expectations for his students differ from those of most teachers you have known? In what other ways is he different from most of the teachers you have known?

5 ▶ What do you think were Todd's major misconceptions as a teacher?

6 ▶ What does Fred see as the role of academic disciplines in education? If you had to, how would you argue against his position?

Comment

In addition to the serious injustice of underchallenging many of our students, Fred was reacting against the perversion of an important idea: teaching good citizenship. In Fred's school, as in many others, the idea of teaching good citizenship has been badly distorted.

During the 1930s, in a reform started by the American educator and philosopher John Dewey, many schools adopted the policy of awarding a grade for citizenship. Dewey and many of his followers envisioned training for citizenship as a process of working out in class actual problems that arise in a democracy. They saw the schools as an appropriate place to teach students about democratic decisions and to give them low-risk but real practice in such decision making in a context where mistakes were not "for keeps."

The role of the teacher remains the highest calling of a free people. To the teacher, America entrusts her most precious resource, her children; and asks that they be prepared, in all their glorious diversity, to face the rigors of individual participation in a democratic society.

—Shirley Hufstedler, former U.S. Secretary of Education

As sometimes happens with reforms, educational and otherwise, the processes introduced to the classroom by reformers degenerated into empty forms. Good citizenship came to mean docility, doing what one is told. Students could earn "good citizenship" grades by "playing the game" and not bothering anyone. Citizenship became a code word among teachers. A teacher who was given a class of "low achievers" or "discipline problems" was sometimes told, "Don't worry about the academics with these children. Just make them good citizens." Parents were told that their child wasn't a very good student but was "an excellent citizen." This meant that even though he or she didn't learn anything, the child did without question everything that students were supposed to do.

■ misuse of citizenship grade

The use of a citizenship grade as a conduct mark is an absolute travesty of the system Dewey and the reformers designed, for, as Fred noted, in reality good citizens are not docile sheep who can be "conned" with impunity. The long-term effect of the misinterpretation of citizenship as conformity and docility has been to discredit it as an appropriate goal for schooling. Yet, in Fred's case, we see a person consciously attempting to develop educated citizens. Fred's visits to courthouses, legislative sessions, and factories, as well as the classroom study of major social problems, are very much in keeping with what Dewey—and, indeed, Thomas Jefferson and James Madison—had in mind when they spoke of educating for freedom.

▶ A Final Word

When we were racking our brains for a title for this book, someone reminded us of the nasty comment George Bernard Shaw, the late-nineteenth-century Irish playwright, made about teachers: "Those who can, do. Those who can't, teach."

While possibly true then (which we doubt), it certainly is false now. In recent decades, the importance of education for the well-being of individuals *and* society has become more and more clear. Much of America's power and prosperity has resulted from our deep commitment to education. And teachers have been the keys to our educational achievements. One thing is crystal clear to thoughtful observers: we need even better schools and better teachers. Shaw was dead wrong. *Those who can, teach.*

Key Terms

extrinsic rewards (5)   real encounters (10)   vicarious experiences (12)
intrinsic rewards (5)   reflection (3)

For Reflection

1 What questions about your own motivation for teaching has this chapter raised?

2 In your experience, did your teachers ever speak to you directly about their reasons for teaching? Did some teachers "tell" you by their actions what their motives for teaching were? Can you give an example?

3 If you are currently planning to teach, what events in your life have helped you discover why you want to teach?

4 Review the list of motives for teaching in the section of this chapter called "Examining Your Motives for Teaching." Put an *E* before those expressing an extrinsic motive, an *I* before those reflecting an intrinsic motive, and a *U* for "uncertain."

5 Have you acquired the *habit of reflection* that is so necessary to make the most of your preparation to be a teacher? If not, what steps can you take to become more reflective?

For Debate

The website for this textbook offers you a link to EduSpace, which lets you take part in electronic discussion with students who are also using this book now. We strongly suggest that you visit EduSpace and share your views on the central question of this chapter: "Why teach?" To help get the discussion started, here are some questions you may want to address:

1 What do you feel are good reasons for becoming a teacher? Are there any unacceptable reasons for teaching? If so, what are they?

2 How certain in a decision does a prospective teacher need to be before committing to further teacher education courses? How sure does the person need to be before going to work as a teacher?

For Further Information

PRINT RESOURCES

Esmé Raji Codell, *Educating Esmé: Diary of a Teacher's First Year* (Chapel Hill, NC: Algonquin Books, 1999).
This book is an inspiring, irreverent, and hilarious diary of a teacher's first year—in short, a wonderful read.

Marva Collins and Civia Tamarkin, *Marva Collins' Way* (Los Angeles: Tarcher, 1982).
This book takes the reader inside the world of one of America's most inspiring and controversial teachers. Marva Collins describes her method of educating the children others forgot.

Pat Conroy, *The Water Is Wide* (New York: Bantam Books, 1994).
This is a thinly veiled account of the author's first years of teaching on a small island off the coast of South Carolina. It is a moving account of how, through his efforts to transform the lives of poor children and their families, the teacher transformed himself. The book has been made into a highly acclaimed film, *Conrac*.

Sam M. Intrator, *Stories of the Courage to Teach* (San Francisco: Jossey-Bass, 2002)
This is an excellent collection of stories by teachers about teachers. It is filled with passion, humor, and, yes, courage. This book was inspired by Parker Palmer's book (below) and he provides its introduction.

Tracy Kidder, *Among Schoolchildren* (Boston: Houghton Mifflin, 1989).
The author spent the entire school year observing a fifth-grade teacher and produced a rich and fascinating account of a teacher's year. The book shows how one teacher shaped and moved the lives of her students.

Jay Mathews, *Escalante: The Best Teacher in America* (New York: Holt, 1990).
This is the biography of Jaime Escalante, who is profiled in this chapter and is the subject of the film *Stand and Deliver.* Escalante wins over his students, largely urban Hispanics, with a combination of challenges to pride, demands of dedicated hard work, and demonstrated love.

Parker Palmer, *The Courage of Teaching: Exploring the Inner Landscape of a Teacher's Life.* (San Francisco: Jossey-Bass, 1997)
The autobiographical account of a dedicated teacher's life will provide the reader with a rare inside view of a skilled teacher's interior life. Palmer tells why and how to connect with students and gets to the core of "Why teach?"

WEB RESOURCES

The Association for Supervision and Curriculum Development. Available at: **www.ascd.org.**
This site in general, and **http://www.ascd.org/cms/index.cfm?TheViewID=1367** (*Supporting New Teachers*) in particular, provide varied and rich support for beginners.

The U.S. Department of Education. Available at: **http://www.ed.gov/teachers/become/about/edpicks.jhtml?src=ln.**
Comprehensive and current, this website is designed to support first-year teachers. It can provide you with many answers to everyday questions.

Learn NC. Available at: **http://www.learnnc.org/newlnc/newteach.nsf/FrontPage?OpenForm.**
This website, which is maintained by the North Carolina Department of Education, is an example of the services that many state departments of education are offering to help beginning teachers.

2 What Is a School and What Is It For?

Chapter Preview   In this chapter, we want to explore with you two related and fundamental questions, "What is a school?" and "What is it for?" We pose them and talk about them to aid you in forming your ideas about the issues that lie behind them. It seems unlikely that you can make a good career choice if you lack a fundamental understanding of the institution you are considering entering. Further, if you hope to survive and be happy within an institution, you will need to know how it is put together and how it works. For example, you need to know what the institution says it is doing and what, in fact, it actually does. You need to know a particular school's expectations of you as a teacher so that you can decide how to respond or if you wish to respond at all. Finally, if you hope to improve the schools—that is, make them better because of your involvement with them—you need to have a realistic view of what is now going on in the schools and develop your vision of what the schools can and should become. This chapter emphasizes that:

▶ Education is a large, all-encompassing endeavor, whereas schooling is simply one aspect of an education.

▶ Schools are cultures and therefore play a critical part in passing on a society's values to the young.

▶ The purpose of school determines much of what happens in school. You can determine the aims of a school by reading formal statements of purpose and by relying on your own experiences in and observations of schools.

▶ Research is giving us more accurate answers to the age-old question "What is a good school?"

What, then, is a school? This may not sound like a profound question; in fact, it probably seems rather tame, but as the late U.S. senator and linguist S. I. Hayakawa once wrote, "If fish were scientists, the last thing they would study would be water." We think it is important to examine schools themselves, something so much a part of our lives that they become almost invisible to us. Again, we ask you to stop reading and seriously to reflect.

Pause and Reflect

1 ► How would you answer the question, "What is a school?"

Your reaction to this question reflects who you are and what your experience with school has been. Perhaps you responded in one of the following ways:

- A school is an agency that weans children from the protective warmth of the family and trains them for what society has decided is useful work.
- A school is a place where they fix your mind so you think like everyone else.
- A school is where children fall in love with learning.
- A school is a tax-supported baby-sitting agency.
- A school is a place where young savages have a chance to become civilized by engaging the world's most precious wisdom.
- A school is a place where we explore who we are and how we can become full, creative human beings.
- A school is a "fun palace."
- A school is an institution where the dead wisdom and worn-out skills of the past are force-fed to the young.
- A school is where education takes place.

Each of these descriptions says a great deal about the school experience of the person who formulated it. Our conviction is that your definition of *school* is a cognitive map that greatly affects how you put together information and impressions of schools.

► Education and Schooling

Before we burrow in on schools, we need to clarify an important distinction, the difference between *education* and *schooling*. In simpler, premodern societies, when a boy could learn to be a man by following his father around and imitating the men of the village and a girl could learn to be a woman by doing the same with her mother and the other women, schools were not necessary. Formal schooling became a social necessity when the home and the community were no longer effective or competent at training the young through informal contacts. Most modern societies have realized that education is too important to be left to chance. Whereas important things are sometimes learned on street corners, and grandparents often are excellent teachers, the formal educative process is simply more reliable. Still, there are nagging doubts that herding youngsters into school buildings for six or seven hours a day, five days a week, is the most effective way to educate our children.

In fact, it has been quipped that today, children interrupt their education to go to school. The distinction between schooling and education implied by this remark is important. Like school, education has myriad definitions. We have sprinkled a few such definitions here and there throughout the book for you to sample. Before we go further, though, we should look at the two concepts in more detail.

Education

■ definition of education

For the moment, let us say that **education** is a process of human growth by which one gains greater understanding and control over oneself and one's world. It involves our minds, our bodies, and our relations with the people and the world around us. Education is also characterized by continuous development and change. The end product of the process of education is learning.

All of us have two educations: one which we receive from others; another, and the most valuable, which we give ourselves.

—JOHN RANDOLPH

Education is much more open-ended and all-inclusive than schooling. Education knows few bounds. It includes both the formal learning that takes place in schools and the entire universe of informal learnings, from hooking a worm on a line to burping a baby. The agents of education can range from a revered grandparent to the guests on a late-night television talk show, from a child with a disability to a distinguished scientist. Whereas schooling has a certain predictability, education quite often takes us by surprise. We go to the movies to relax and come home with a vivid sense of the horrors of warfare. We get into a casual conversation with a stranger and discover how little we know about other religions. Education is a lifelong process; it starts long before we begin school and should be an ongoing part of our entire lives.

■ takes place everywhere

Education and learning are not confined to schools.
(© Michelle D. Bridwell/PhotoEdit)

Schooling

■ definition of schooling

In contrast to education, **schooling** is a specific, formalized process, usually focused on the young, and whose general pattern traditionally has varied little from one setting to the next. Despite minor variations in teaching practices among schools, for example, schooling remains a rather uniform practice throughout the United States. Throughout the country, children arrive at school at approximately the same time, take assigned seats, are taught by an adult, use the same or similar textbooks, do homework, take exams, and so on. The topics they learn—from fractions to the three branches of American government—have usually been mandated in advance.

I have never let my schooling interfere with my education.

—MARK TWAIN

Schools are created for the express purpose of delivering a certain type of educational experience, which we call the *curriculum.* Teachers receive preparation and are employed to fulfill the purposes of schooling as defined by the curriculum. The curriculum (discussed more fully in the chapter entitled "What Is Taught?") represents what a community believes young people need to know to develop into good and productive adults, or it at least includes what the school policymakers in a particular community believe young people need to know. In effect, a school's curriculum represents a **social bet.** It is what the older generation thinks the young will need to live well in the twenty-first century. If the curriculum turns out to be a losing bet, the individual and social consequences are severe.

■ curriculum as a social bet

Keeping the differences between education and schooling clearly in mind is often particularly difficult for the people who should be most sensitive to them— that is, teachers who *do* education *in* schools. People enter teaching because they wish to educate others. They may be committed to a particular educational philosophy. Usually, however, the everyday experiences of working in a school cause their allegiances to shift from abstract educational ideals to the network of personalities and ideas surrounding the particular schools where they teach. They become invested in schooling, in the way things are—that is, the routines of homework, quizzes, and detention—and to varying degrees, they tend to lose focus on the larger issues of education. For this reason alone, it is important for the teacher to keep alive the questions "What is a school for?" and "What is my contribution to this child's and this class's education?" We will have more to say on this topic when we get to examining your ideas in the chapter entitled "What Are the Philosophical Foundations of American Education?"

Pause and Reflect

1 ▶ Which have been the most important learnings in your life—those from your nonschool education or from your schooling?

2 ▶ What do you think has been the most important thing you have learned in school, and what has been the most important thing you have learned outside of school?

▶ Schools as Cultures

■ meaning of culture

A *society* is a grouping of individuals bound together by various connections. Some of the connections might be shared geographic space or similar racial features, but what really connects people is their shared culture. A *culture* is composed of beliefs about what is right and wrong, what is good and bad. It also includes the dominant ideas, stories and myths, artistic works, social habits, and organizations of a group. Another key aspect of culture is language and the ways people use it in relationship to one another. Every group of people who live together in relative harmony can be said to share a culture. Someone once defined culture as simply "just the way we are 'round here." Without a common culture, every time we walked into a room or passed someone on the street, we would grope for a way to respond. Our culture tells us what to do.

All sorts of cultures exist. A family possesses a culture. The U.S. Marine Corps possesses a culture. After a few weeks and months, a college dorm assumes a distinctive culture. A school also possesses a culture. Think about it: each school you have attended has had its own culture—a set of beliefs, values, traditions, and ways of thinking and behaving—that distinguishes it from other social institutions and other schools.

Cultures, including **school cultures,** can be good or bad, leading to good human ends or poor ones. A strong, positive school culture engages the hearts and minds of children, stretching them intellectually, physically, morally, and socially. A school with a weak, negative culture may have the same type of facilities, student-teacher ratio, and curriculum as a neighboring good school, but it may have a weak, negative effect on students. Everyone, students and teachers, goes through the motions, but with few of the positive effects that the strong-culture school provides.

Socialization

Besides food, shelter, and loving care, adults pass their culture on to their young. A major part of any culture is the skills and attitudes necessary to function in that particular society. In our contemporary American society, we expect that most people will try hard to get along with one another, work cooperatively, and look after their families. This task of passing on a society's culture to the young is called **socialization,** defined as the general process of social learning whereby the child learns the many things he or she must know to become an acceptable member of a particular social environment.

Besides the family, the major socializing agencies in the life of a young person are schools, peer groups, religious institutions, youth organizations, political and economic institutions, the mass media, and, in some cases, work environments. Each of these agencies has its own values, norms, and mores that it attempts to teach so that the individual child will know how to act and behave in a manner acceptable to other agency members. Some agencies, such as the school, are formally created and organized, and some, such as the peer group, are informally created and organized.

Schools, as one of the most common institutions in the United States, have a significant role in teaching young people how to be social in the American context. Every school attempts to socialize children by getting them to value those things the school teaches both explicitly and implicitly. The more successful students tend to accept these values, whereas many of the less successful ones reject the ways of thinking and behaving that the school tries to teach.

■ schools value compliance, competitiveness

What are these values, and how are they communicated to students? One researcher suggests that schools value several specific ways of thinking and behaving.[1] One is compliant behavior as opposed to personal initiative. Students soon learn to give the teacher what she or he wants or expects. Reward systems used by schools teach students to "read" both the teacher and the system to determine just what is expected to get the grade, the teacher's attention, or the sticker with

Perhaps the greatest of all pedagogical fallacies is the notion that a person learns only the particular thing he is studying at the time.

—B. Bradford Brown

■ reading school cultures

the smiling face. Similarly, competitiveness is learned through the examples of athletics, grading systems that compare students to one another, and ability grouping to separate students into classes according to their individual achievement levels. The many ways in which students learn what a school values include how the school allocates time to subjects of study, the rules established for the school, and even the architecture of the school.

As a future teacher, you should work to be able to *read cultures*. What rules of behavior, rituals and ceremonies, and accepted patterns of teacher-student interaction are communicated to students at a particular school? Does the "climate" of the classroom and the school suggest warmth, support, and nurturing of individuals, or do you observe a mood of disinterest, regimentation, and antipathy among staff and students? Most importantly, what is the school's deeper message about what stance its students should take toward the current culture?

▶ Schools as Transmitters or Re-creators of Culture

Education is simply the soul of a society as it passes from one generation to another.

—Gilbert K. Chesterton

There are two views or two models of how American schools should socialize our students: (1) the school as the social institution where the young receive from the older generation the very best of their culture and (2) the school as the social institution where the young learn skills and become agents of social change.

Transmitting Culture

■ schools reflect culture

In the model of the school as acculturator, schools exist to advance society by ensuring that the young know and appreciate the dominant ideas and values of their society's culture. The goal of cultural transmission in the American public schools is to teach the American way of looking at the world and the American way of doing things. This desire to ensure that the young share the common culture may explain why, in many U.S. school systems, we teach American history in the third, seventh, and eleventh grades. It can also explain why, for instance, we give little attention to the history of China, even though China is the most populous nation on earth and has one of the world's oldest and richest cultural heritages.

Without even being conscious of it, our teachers instruct our young in our version of reality and our way of handling the real world, and so, too, do the schools of other countries. Schools in northern India, for instance, differ markedly from those in Ghana, and both have sharp differences from their counterparts in the United States. However, the schools of each country are attempting to perform a similar function: to transmit the unique culture of the country to its newest members, the young.

Usually people who view schools as transmitting culture talk about society as an organism, a living thing that can thrive or deteriorate based on how well different elements of society function together. When a society is healthy, its various components (the government, schools, communities, families, and individuals) each do what they ought to be doing and they each work in concert with each other. Conflict, from this point of view, is negative, and society should work toward finding consensus among various groups and toward eliminating any conflict. From this perspective then, it is vitally important that the older generation, including parents and teachers, help the young find value and meaning in their own culture so they too will internalize its values and contribute to its smooth functioning.

■ **Acculturation and Diversity**   Several dangers lurk in this tendency of schools to concentrate on transmitting the dominant culture. If schools offer the young an understanding of only the prevailing culture, the result may be an attitude of smug cultural superiority, which often leads nations and individuals to foolish actions. In cultural terms, what we do not know we often do not respect, and without mutual respect people easily become enemies. In recent decades instantaneous electronic communications, missile-delivered nuclear weapons, and interdependent national economic structures have increasingly made the world a global village, and our students must learn how to function in this new world.

Moreover, in recent decades the United States has experienced an enormous immigration from Southeast Asia, the Middle East, Central America, and elsewhere. These new Americans tend to be young. They and their children are hungry for education. Although they are eager to learn American ways and American culture, teachers and students need to be respectful of the cultures these students bring with them.

Sometimes, schools, as part of acculturating children, tend to pull them away from their individual ethnic backgrounds. For example, one out of five of our students go home at night to families where English is a second language. As they become acculturated, using English becomes more important for these children, and their first languages become something private and rarely used in public. Other school models, more commonly, try to acculturate the child while supporting his or her ethnic heritage. Elementary schools in Calexico, Calif., serve large populations of newly arrived Mexican children. Teachers design the classrooms so that American and Hispanic cultures are honored and children learn to operate effectively in both languages.[2] The presence of new Americans can be a valuable resource in the effort to increase multicultural understanding and appreciation. Therefore, although American schools need to transmit American culture, we must realize that what we call "American culture" has always embraced many cultures. Nevertheless, a primary responsibility of the schools to assist foreign-born students in the acquisition of a high level of English proficiency stands. We will return to this thorny issue when we discuss multiculturalism and bilingual education in the chapter entitled "Who Are Today's Students in a Diverse Society?"

Reconstructing Society

Some of the issues just mentioned, including threats from international terrorists and nuclear weapons; a highly interdependent world economy; large numbers of immigrants; and the hunger, suffering, and social injustices rampant in our modern world, have led some educators to the view that schools must become the tool of social reconstruction. Instead of seeing schools as places where the collective wisdom of the past dribbles down to those who have the capacity and interest to make use of it, these educators assume a much more active, even assertive, role for the school. From this perspective, schools and teachers should work toward activating student interest and commitment to improving society. Unlike those who wish to transmit culture, educators who wish to reconstruct society accept the existence of conflicts between different groups and look at them as important ways to understand these groups' view of social problems.

Margin notes:

■ need to understand other cultures

■ arrival of new cultures

Visit the material at the website to link to more information about acculturation and diversity.

■ acculturating immigrant students

■ school as social leavener

The great aim of education is not knowledge but action.

—HERBERT SPENCER

These **social reconstructionists** see the school forming the young into agents of change and participating in the decision about how society needs to change. They have little reverence for the accumulated wisdom of the past and more concern for the world's problems and the necessity to create a new order. They see the successful student not so much as a cultivated person but as an autonomous citizen ready to join with others to tackle the world's ills and help in the reconstruction of society.

Even among social reconstructionists, however, a wide range of emphases and views are evident. Social reconstructionists fall into two broad categories: *democratic reconstructionists* and *economic reconstructionists*.

■ **Democratic Reconstructionists**   **Democratic reconstructionists** see the solution to certain trends and current issues, such as racism, poverty, and the destruction of the ecosystem, in an aroused and skilled citizenry.[3] The school's mission, then, is to prepare students for vigorous participation in their government. The focus of schooling is on developing knowledge of democratic processes, critical thinking skills, and group process skills so the student can fruitfully work with others for social improvement. In more active programs, students actually select, study, and work on a community environmental problem, such as the polluting of landfills with unrecycled garbage. (We will return to this concept of democratic reconstructionism later in this chapter, in the discussion of Thomas Jefferson, and in the chapter entitled, "What Is the History of American Education?")

■ **Economic Reconstructionists**   **Economic reconstructionists** tend to take a harsher view of the dominant culture and see schools as the pliant servants of those in power. Instead of humanistic institutions attempting to free individuals from their own lives' limitations, schools are institutions operating for the economic powers-that-be. The influence of corporate values is seen in many phases of school life, from the way textbooks are used to our widespread use of testing.[4] Moreover, economic reconstructionists often argue that schools *claim* to serve the needs of all while, in fact, serving the needs of the elites, or those with the most power. Economic reconstructionists usually see schools as disguising that fact, either by their own naivete or by their willing support of the system that already exists. Because of their deep suspicions of, and sometimes outright disgust with, capitalism, economic reconstructionists are often called *neo-Marxists*.

■ Paulo Freire

One noted economic reconstructionist was the Brazilian educator Paulo Freire. Freire's first book, *The Pedagogy of the Oppressed,* describes his work with poverty-stricken, illiterate peasants in his native Brazil.[5] As Freire tried to teach these adults to read, he saw they were trapped in an economic and social web over which they had little control. He saw, too, that the normal mechanisms of education, such as grading and control by the teacher, imposed on the peasants a passivity and subservience to authority. For Freire, the typical methods and routines of schooling are a form of oppression in that they keep people from becoming fully human. To counter this, Freire taught literacy by helping the peasants to (1) name their problem (a polluted water supply); (2) analyze the problem (sewage contamination of the springs); and (3) collectively take action (design and build a new sewage system) to solve the problem. In this manner, education becomes a tool both to develop the human potential of people, such as the ability to read, and to free them from oppressive conditions such as poverty and disease. Currently, two American educators in particular, Henry Giroux and Michael Apple, are voices for this economic reconstructionist view.

■ critics of social reconstructionism

Although both democratic and economic reconstructionists focus on social problems and try to foster in students the attitudes and skills necessary to solve them, the economic reconstructionists question more deeply the fundamental economic and social arrangements in a society. They see education as a necessary means for restructuring the power structures in a society. For them, money, power, and control of education are tightly bound together. Critics of the social reconstructionists' approach to education see it as naive and wrong-headed. Critics emphasize that our current economic and social relations are too fragile and serious to be toyed with by innocent and immature children.

■ **The New Globalization** As we gingerly enter this new century, a relatively new concept of the world as a highly interrelated and interdependent community is emerging. Increasingly, our students need to be educated in terms of this global interconnectivity, clearly drawing on the best ideas of the past, and they also need to be ready to address the fresh demands of a new world. For our educators, that is a big job!

Pause and Reflect

1 ▶ Which of these two broad educational approaches, transmitting the culture or reconstructing the culture, has the most appeal to you? Why?

▶ Four Basic Purposes of School

One thing you may think you know best is school. After all, it's likely that you have spent the better part of your life in schools. Isn't it obvious what schools are and what they do? Perhaps. Yet most of us tend to think of schools in limited ways. Our own experiences within a relatively few schools influence what we think about all schools and what we understand of schools in general. For that reason, it is important to look at schools from different vantage points to gain more perspective on schools as a whole by looking at them from a more distant view. What we just looked at, using the schools for "transmission of the culture" or for "reconstructing society," represent rather broad, general purposes for schools. Now we are going to examine four purposes for schools that are closer to the everyday reality of teachers and students.

"What should our schools be trying to do?" This is a fairly straightforward, almost innocent question. However, it is a question that can stir fierce arguments amongst different groups. If residents have strongly conflicting views about what their community's schools should do, the question can rip apart the fabric of a community. The question taps into serious disagreements about what different people think of contemporary American culture and society and what they want the schools to do for their children. What you should understand, however, is that questions about school, such as what it is and what it should do, are by no means new questions. People have argued, discussed, and written about what schools should do for hundreds of years.

To help illustrate that point, we have included several quotes about schools. Some were written centuries ago; others have been written in the past decade. As you read each quote, think about how each speaker characterizes the functions of schools and education and also think about your own schooling.

Intellectual Purposes

Jacques Barzun is a cultural historian who writes frankly about the current state of schools in America. As you read his quote, try to decide what Barzun sees as the primary purpose of schools.

> What do we really want from our schools? . . . Given the public's muddled feelings about brainwork (which is what "excellence" refers to) and the parental indifference up to now about what their children are being taught, the school has a double fight on its hands: against ignorance inside the walls and against cultural prejudice outside, the prejudice lying so deep that those who harbor it do not even know they do. . . . The difficulties of schooling . . . do not change. . . . Difficulties remain. It will always be difficult to teach well, to learn accurately, to read, write and count readily and competently; to acquire a sense of history and develop a taste for literature and the arts. . . . For this purpose no school . . . is ever just right; it is only by the constant effort of its teachers that it can even be called satisfactory.[6]
>
> —JACQUES BARZUN

■ primacy of intellect

If you said that Barzun is emphasizing the academic or *intellectual* purposes of schools, you would be right. One longstanding purpose of schools has been to foster the intellectual development of the young. Barzun is one among many who contend that promoting academic learning is the single most important purpose of schools.

■ rationality makes us human

Most people who highlight the intellectual purpose of schools believe that the development of reason, through intellectual pursuits, leads to individual enlightenment. Rationality, or the ability to know, to think, to reason, is seen as an attribute distinct to humans, and, more importantly, the capacity that *makes us*

The function of schools that comes first to most people's minds is the intellectual function.
(© Bob Daemmrich/The Image Works)

human. Many of those who rank intellectual purposes as the highest priority see school as the one institution most common to all people. They believe, therefore, that promoting intellectual development in schools is essential so that all children have the opportunity to become rational human beings.

The intellectual purpose of school is included in every school's mission. The way it is manifested, however, can look different from school to school. Some schools exist for the sole purpose of helping students develop their intellects. You may have heard about or even attended a secondary school that requires students to study "the Great Books" or that requires five or six core academic subjects for all students. Other schools simply include the study of academic disciplines along with numerous co-curricular activities.

■ "Great Books" and core academics

Political and Civic Purposes

Now, let's consider another quote. It highlights a different purpose of school. You will be able to tell by the writing style that it was written some time ago; however, the idea the writer expresses is one that has been a constant in American public schools since their beginning.

> [E]ven under the best forms [of government], those entrusted with power have, in time . . . perverted it into tyranny; and it is believed that the most effectual means of preventing this would be to illuminate . . . the minds of the people at large, and more especially to give them knowledge of those facts, which history exhibiteth . . . [that] they may be enabled to know ambition under all its shapes. . . . [7]

—THOMAS JEFFERSON

You will read more about Jefferson's contributions to the American public schools in the chapter entitled "What Is the History of American Education?". For now it is important simply to see that Jefferson hoped that American schooling would help establish and sustain the United States of America, an infant nation. One of the overriding concerns of the early political leaders was, in fact, how people would learn to be American citizens and *not* English subjects.

■ schooling to sustain democracy

With this quote, the *political and civic* purposes of schooling are underscored. Jefferson thought schools could help people learn how to govern themselves wisely and justly. The need for schools to prepare students for their political and civic lives persists to this day. The only sure way for any country to have a well-informed citizenry is through the systematic education that schooling can bring. That need may be more or less prominent during certain times, but the political purposes of schools have always been one of the primary reasons public schools exist.

In your own schools, you may have seen political and civic purposes emphasized through voter registration drives, citizenship education programs, even community service and outreach programs, but schools also promote these purposes by *how* they teach the students to read, to write, and to discuss ideas rationally.

Next in importance to freedom and justice is popular education, without which neither freedom nor justice can be permanently maintained.

—JAMES A. GARFIELD

Economic Purposes

Let's consider one more perspective and see how you would link it to your own school experiences. Jean Anyon, an educational researcher, has investigated the connection between economics and schooling for a number of years.

> When inner city students and their access to the range of services provide a realistic expectation that education will lead to better jobs, life, and future, as is expected in most middle-class and affluent homes, then the students will have a reason to make an educational effort. Realistic expectations that education will make a substantial, positive difference in the lives of their students may also motivate teachers and other school staff to a higher level of performance. At that point teachers, principals, and a quality curriculum can more easily make a difference in the lives of the inner city poor.[8]
>
> —Jean Anyon

What is the question that Anyon raises about the connection between a student's schooling and his or her occupation? What are the criticisms she seems to be leveling against schools in American society? As this quote suggests, many Americans think that schools primarily serve an *economic* purpose—that is, they believe that schools help students obtain the skills and knowledge required to attend college or to get a job.

Think about how you approach your own college education. If you and the student body of your campus were interviewed right now about why you are attending college, many of you would say that you attend college because you expect to earn a more comfortable living with a college degree than without one. Americans generally expect that more schooling leads to greater personal wealth, and, in general, they are right. On the whole, high school graduates do obtain higher-paying jobs than those who didn't complete high school, and college graduates earn more than high school graduates.

■ the job-sorting role of schools

Americans also expect that schools will prepare students for their future, regardless of whether that future includes a college education. High schools support that expectation by including courses of study that are *college preparatory* or *vocational*. Many Americans accept without question that schools guide students into curricular tracks that seem matched to their abilities and inclinations so that the mathematically inclined students will enroll in such courses as calculus and advanced placement (AP) physics and the labor-oriented students will enroll in cosmetology or computer repair courses. The tacit assumption underlying the economic purposes of schools is that well-schooled people and people *appropriately schooled* are vital to a strong national economy, regardless of whether they become business leaders or laborers. We will see later in the chapter that Anyon, among others, has questioned the practices that rest on this assumption, pointing out that curricular tracking and instructional practices are not always related so much to students' individual abilities as to their expected role in the work world.

The economic purposes of schooling have profound effects both on the individual student and society as a whole. You may have heard news accounts of the need for a "well-educated workforce" or the "new demands of working in global industries." Pundits pronounce to one another what the new global economy will demand, and those predictions often trickle down to schools. For instance, many school systems have placed renewed emphasis on teaching foreign languages in order to equip graduates to do business in other countries.

Social Purposes

We have identified intellectual, political, and economic purposes of schools, but one more purpose has yet to be identified. This can be called the *umbrella purpose* for schools because it is so all encompassing. Consider this last quote and think about what it means.

> If . . . education has a collective function above all, if its object is to adapt the child to the social milieu in which he is destined to live, it is impossible that society should be uninterested in such a procedure. . . . It is, then, up to the State to remind the teacher constantly of the ideas, the sentiments that must be impressed upon the child to adjust him to the milieu in which he must live.[9]
>
> —ÉMILE DURKHEIM

This quote draws attention to the *social purpose* of schools. How would you paraphrase this quotation? At some point in your life, you may have heard that schools also teach "social skills." What exactly does that mean to you? You may have heard the old adage, "It's good to be smart, but if you can't get along with people or don't know how to work with others, then it doesn't make much difference how much you know. . . ."

■ adapting the child to society

Émile Durkheim was a French sociologist in the early twentieth century. One of his primary interests was the school's responsibility in promoting a healthy social order. For him, schools existed to help mold or guide students into what their society needed and expected of them. A teacher's job was to help students understand their role in the broader social order.

Durkheim's idea that schools must work to help students adapt to social expectations still holds currency today. Think of how many times elementary school teachers impress on pupils how important it is to *share* with each other. Who decided that we needed to learn to share? Think of how frequently middle and high school teachers remind students to give their best effort on their homework or a project. What does "best effort" mean? Why not encourage students to "kick back and go with the flow?" Think, also, of how schools and teachers emphasize punctuality and the importance of meeting commitments on time. These attributes are emphasized, in part, because they are characteristics prized by most employers. Further, the capacity to share, being sensitive to issues of time, and keeping commitments are habits that have wide value in marriages, family life, and life in the community. Those are three human qualities that illustrate how schooling helps children learn and adapt to social conventions. Because the social nature of schooling is so important, we will return to it later in the chapter.

Pause and Reflect

1 ► Thinking back on your high school experiences, how were these four purposes (intellectual, political, economic, and social) evident in your schooling? Was one more dominant than the others? Which one? Why was this one purpose more dominant in your particular community?

2 ► Which of these four purposes of education do you believe ought to be given the greatest weight in the organization of schools?

▶ What Do Studies Reveal About the Nature of Schools?

What happens in schools, and how does the activity in a school contribute to or detract from its purpose? Researchers often look at the everyday events of human life and see patterns of which the rest of us may be only vaguely aware. In the next several pages, we present a few of these studies and examine the patterns the researchers noticed, focusing first on elementary schools, then on middle schools and junior highs, and finally on high schools.

Life in Elementary Schools

■ Jackson's study

One of the best perspectives on how time is usually spent in the elementary classroom is provided by Philip W. Jackson's classic study *Life in Classrooms*.[10] Anthropologists have taught us that the humdrum aspects of human existence have cultural significance and that we must look at the most routine events in an elementary classroom if we are to understand what happens there. Are certain trivial acts repeated many times? How often do they occur? What is their cumulative effect on the child? What do they teach the child? Jackson's observations of elementary school classrooms show how revealing the answers to these questions can be.

Have you ever figured out how many hours a child spends in school? In most states, the school year is 180 days. The day typically begins at 8:30 AM and ends at 3 PM, a total of six and one-half hours. Thus, if a child doesn't miss a day of school, he or she spends more than 1,000 hours in school each year. Including kindergarten, the average child by the end of sixth grade will spend upwards to 7,000 hours in elementary school. How are those hours typically spent?

You may think first of the curriculum, which is so many hours of reading, language arts, mathematics, science, play, social studies, music, art, and so on, but what do students really *do* when they are studying these subjects? They talk to each other or the teacher. They read silently and aloud. They yawn. They look out the window. They raise their hands. They line up. They stand up. They sit down. In short, they do a number of different things, many of them commonplace and trivial. To understand why some of these things happen, we first need to look at what the teacher does.

■ controlling discussions . . .

■ The Teacher's Role   Jackson has observed that the elementary school teacher engages in as many as a thousand interpersonal interchanges each day.

The teaching-learning process consists, for the most part, of talking, and the teacher controls and directs discussion. The teacher acts as a *gatekeeper*, deciding who shall and who shall not speak. (One may debate whether this *should* be the teacher's role, but clearly most teachers function this way.)

■ . . . supplies, privileges

The teacher also acts as a *dispenser of supplies*. Because both space and resources are limited and the number of students wishing to use them at any one time is likely to be greater than the supply, the teacher must dole them out. A related function is the *granting of special privileges* to deserving students: passing out the milk, sharpening pencils, taking the roll, or free time at the computer. Although little teacher time is involved in awarding these special jobs, they are important because they help to structure the classroom socially as a system of rewards and punishments.

■ . . . time

Timekeeping is another teacher responsibility. It is the teacher who decides when a certain activity ends and another begins, when it is time to stop science and begin spelling, and when to go outside for recess. In some schools, the teacher is assisted in timekeeping by bells and buzzers that signal when a period is over. As Jackson observes, things happen because it is time for them to occur and not because students want them to happen.

■ result of crowded conditions

All these teacher functions can be seen as responses to the crowded conditions in the classroom. If the teacher were dealing with one student at a time in a tutorial situation, gatekeeping, dispensing supplies, granting special privileges, and timekeeping would not be necessary, but since a tutorial setting is not possible, much time and energy are spent keeping order. The resulting atmosphere has unavoidable effects on the students. What are some of the consequences for students in crowded classroom conditions?

■ **What Students Experience** One inevitable outcome for students that results from the teacher's "traffic management" functions is *delay*. Because students' actions are limited by space, material resources, and the amount of teacher attention they can command, there are definite limits on their freedom in class. In addition, because the class ordinarily moves toward a goal as a group rather than as individuals, its slowest members often determine the pace of progress.

■ waiting

Waiting is therefore a familiar activity for elementary school children—that is, waiting in line to get a drink of water, waiting with arm propped at the elbow to be called on to answer a question, waiting to use the scissors, waiting until

Waiting and delayed gratification are common occurrences in elementary school classrooms.
(© Elizabeth Crews)

others have finished their work to go on to the next activity, waiting until four other students have finished reading aloud for a chance to do so, and on and on.

■ denial of desire

Denial of desire is another common experience for the elementary student. A question goes unanswered, a raised hand is ignored, talking out of turn is not permitted, relief of bodily functions is allowed only at specified times. Some denial is necessary and probably beneficial, but one thing is certain: delayed gratification and denied desire are learned in school, and a certain amount of student frustration is bound to develop.

■ interruptions

Students also experience frequent *interruptions* of many sorts, such as interruptions of seatwork by the teacher to give additional instructions or to clarify one student's question, interruptions when messages from the principal's office are read aloud to the class, interruptions for fire drills, interruptions when the teacher is working with one student and another student misbehaves, and so on. Students are expected either to ignore these intrusions or to quickly resume their activities.

The emphasis on an inflexible schedule contributes to the sense of interruption by often making students begin activities before their interest has been aroused and stop at the height of their interest when the schedule dictates that they must begin another task.

■ social distraction

A related phenomenon is *social distraction*. Students are often asked to behave as if they were alone, when in fact they are surrounded by thirty or so other people. During assigned seatwork, for example, communication among students is often discouraged, if not forbidden. To be surrounded by friends, sometimes seated across from one another at a table, and not be allowed to talk is a difficult and tempting situation. As Jackson remarks, "These young people, if they are to become successful students, must learn how to be alone in a crowd."

It is a miracle that curiosity survives formal education.

—Albert Einstein

Delay, denial, interruption, and *social distraction,* then, are characteristic of life in elementary classrooms. Given these classroom conditions, it seems likely that the student who either possesses or quickly develops patience would find school more tolerable than the student who lacks it. The ability to control desires, delay rewards, and stifle impulses seems to be characteristic of successful students, whereas less successful students exhibit less patience and more impulsiveness.

■ patience is a necessity

Life in Middle and Junior High Schools

■ many grade configurations

■ **Types of Schools**   Our knowledge about this next topic is limited somewhat by the variety of grade-clustering patterns evident in our schools. A national survey of middle-grade practices and trends found that schools around the country enrolled seventh-grade students in about thirty different grade spans. For example, some schools were structured to educate all students in grades K–12; others served primarily elementary and middle grades such as K–8; and yet others served middle to high school students such as grades 7–12. Some schools were structured just for students in the middle grades, but even within this group there was great variety. Middle schools mainly contained students in grades 6–8, but also in 5–8, 5–7, and 6–7. Other schools were strictly 7–8 schools, and another grade configuration of junior high schools structured students in grades 7–9, 6–9, or 5–9.[11]

■ varying school sizes

Researchers at Johns Hopkins University found direct relationships between grade configuration and such important educational characteristics as school goals, report card entries, course offerings, instructional practices, relationships between students and staff, and other trends in middle-grade practices.[12] One factor related to the organization of middle grades was size. In the various schools examined, enrollment in grade 7 ranged from five students to more than 2,250. Consider for a moment the very different educational experiences these students will have in their middle school years in regard to familiarity with peers, class size, teacher contact, opportunities to participate in extracurricular activities and so forth.

■ varying school goals

School goals were also examined across different grade configurations. Regardless of the grade span of their schools, most principals identified mastery of subject matter and basic skills as the most important goals at their institutions. However, secondary goals of educational importance varied by the school organization. As might be expected, principals of K–12 schools assigned more importance to higher-level skills such as reasoning, problem solving, and creative thinking. Principals of K–8 schools put less emphasis on personal growth and developmental issues such as self-esteem and self-knowledge than principals of middle schools.[13]

The goals that schools set for students influence middle school education in other ways as well, including the curriculum offered and the instructional methods used. The same study found that schools serving younger students, such as K–8, typically offered fewer elective courses such as home economics or keyboarding for students in the middle grades. Seventh- and eighth-grade teachers used drill practices more often and made less use of higher-order thinking activities such as writing essays, using computers, and discussing controversial issues. These schools, however, also reported greater use of such methods as peer- or cross-grade tutoring.[14]

■ staffing patterns

Another distinction among schools of different grade configurations was seen in staffing patterns. Classroom structure for students in the middle grades varied from completely self-contained classrooms, in which one teacher taught one group of students all major subject areas, to completely departmentalized schools in which each teacher specialized in a single subject area and taught several different classes of students. As you might expect, schools serving younger students (K+) had a larger percentage of self-contained classrooms, whereas middle schools showed a greater percentage of departmentalized staffing.[15]

■ licensure patterns

Teachers also differed by type of licensure held. Teachers with secondary licensure were more likely to be subject matter oriented, and middle-grade students who were taught by subject matter experts showed higher levels of achievement. On the other hand, teachers who were licensed in elementary education were likely to be more student-centered and tended to focus on both the academic and personal development of individual students. The research indicated that relationships between students and teachers in self-contained classrooms tended to be more positive.[16]

Visit the material at the website to link to more information about middle and junior high schools.

■ **Developmental or Academic Purposes Foremost?** So we see a variety of educational experiences occurring along a number of dimensions in the middle grades. Is one means of educating students in the middle grades best? Probably not. No one pattern is superior for all students. The many aspects of diversity we have just examined, from grade configuration to school goals to teacher orientation, appear to present a series of trade-offs in educating students in the middle grades. What is consistently being identified as important for educating students in the middle grades, however, is that the developmental needs of early adolescents must be acknowledged and considered in developing and organizing programs.

■ developmental needs in early adolescence

Increasingly, the middle school years are being seen as a crucial time in the formation of an individual. Early adolescence is characterized by a variety of developmental needs and dramatic variations in the maturation rate. One researcher has identified seven key developmental needs that characterize early adolescence:

- Positive social interaction with adults and peers
- Structure and clear limits
- Physical activity
- Creative expression
- Competence and achievement
- Meaningful participation in families, school, and communities
- Opportunities for self-definition[17]

While both younger and older students have these developmental needs, it is particularly important that they be met by schools serving the middle years. Not meeting these needs often results in a young person's alienation from peers, loss of a sense of self-worth, and the onset of all sorts of destructive behavior from fighting to escapism into drug use and promiscuity. As one specialist observed, "Every child wants to believe in himself or herself as a successful person; every youngster wants to be liked and respected; every youngster wants physical exercises and freedom to move; and youngsters want life to be just."[18]

There is, however, a countertrend in recent thinking about middle schools. Critics see this period as the soft spot in our educational system because of the curriculum's failure to focus on academic learning. They question what is seen as an over-focus on psychological and development issues, such as self-esteem and interpersonal skills. Describing "the lost years of middle schooling in the U.S., grades 6, 7 and 8," as "an intellectual wasteland" and "the 'Bermuda Triangle' of American education," such critics are calling for a return to the K–8 pattern and a more rigorous, discipline-focused curriculum.[19]

Pause and Reflect

1 ► What was the grade-clustering pattern in your junior high or middle school? Do you believe it was the best pattern for you?

2 ► What do you think there is about the middle school years that makes meeting the development goals cited above more crucial than other periods?

3 ► Has your experience led you to agree or disagree with those who believe that academic achievement takes second place to personal growth in many of today's middle schools?

Visit the material at the website to link to more information about research on high schools.

Life in High Schools

No aspect of our public educational system has received more study than our high schools. This is probably because so many people are worried about our teenagers and dissatisfied with the educational experiences we are providing them. Although conducted with reform in mind, the studies, some of them hardly new, provide important insights into how students and teachers live and carry on in our high schools.

high school similarities

For instance, in 1983 the Carnegie Foundation for the Advancement of Teaching released a study, *High School: A Study of Secondary School in America,* intended to guide discussion about needed reforms in American secondary education. In this investigation of fifteen supposedly unique schools, the researchers found striking commonalities among them.[20] Typically, a school day is divided into six or seven fifty-minute periods (although in recent years, high schools around the nation have been experimenting with a wide variety of class-time structures). Hall passes, dress codes, and rules against smoking are often part of life in a high school. From most principals' points of view, absenteeism, class cutting, and parents' disinterest are moderately serious problems; fights, thefts, and vandalism are more serious problems.[21] High school is a place where young people experiment with growing up, find the support that may not be available at home, and attempt to accomplish a variety of goals. These goals range from marking time to finding social acceptance, and from developing job skills to preparing for intellectual challenges. Although some high schools have departed from this picture, this description still fits the great majority of our schools.

■ **Inside Classrooms** What happens in classrooms during those typical six- or seven-period days? In a review of instructional practices in American classrooms, Larry Cuban concluded that the high school of today is *remarkably similar to the high school of the 1890s*.[22] Cuban gathered descriptions of more than 1,200 classrooms. He examined how classroom space was arranged; the ratio of teacher talk to student talk; the manner of grouping the teacher used for instruction (whole-class, small-group, or individual); the presence of learning or interest centers used by students as part of a normal school day; and how much physical movement students were allowed within the classroom. Cuban found that, just as in the 1890s, today's high school classes are characterized by whole-class instruction, teachers talking most of the time while students listen, little student mobility, and a narrow range of activities completed by the entire class at one time.

■ same as the 1890s

The researchers who carried out the Carnegie study found similar characteristics. They noted, for example, a standardized use of classroom space: rooms equipped with rows of desks for thirty or more students, a teacher's desk at the front of the rows, and the traditional black or green chalkboard. The use of time is also routine, consumed by procedural tasks like taking attendance and keeping records, although relentlessly interrupted by announcements on the intercom, pep assemblies, photo sessions, and many other distractions.[23] The study also describes teachers' powerlessness over the factors that influence the quality of instruction they can deliver: the number of students in a class, the lengths of school days and periods, the formats of report cards, the courses that will be taught, and even the textbooks that will be used.

■ pressure on teachers

Pressures of time and heavy student loads invite traditional, teacher-centered instruction, such as lecturing, question-and-answer sessions, and routine homework assignments. Too often, students play passive roles in classrooms dominated by regimentation and conformity.[24]

■ **Multiple Purposes** Tracing the history of the high school, the lead Carnegie researcher concluded, "[H]igh schools have accumulated purposes like barnacles on a weathered ship."[25] Americans seem to want high schools to accomplish everything. The resulting confusion of goals is evident in the variety of goal statements adopted by the states for their schools, in the written goals found in teachers' manuals or school district curriculum guides, and in teacher and student responses when asked about school goals.

■ multiple goals

In an attempt to accomplish these multiple purposes, high schools have developed a comprehensive curriculum with many elective courses. How do students decide what to take and what not to take among dozens or, in some cases, hundreds of courses? Students report that their choices are guided more by parents and peers than by guidance counselors or teachers.[26] The researchers conclude that students' academic programs may be shaped most decisively by the

■ influence of tracking

"tracks" in which they are enrolled. *Academic* tracks stress the traditional subjects of English, history, mathematics, science, and foreign languages as preparation for college. A *general* track usually allows a greater number of elective courses and less rigorous versions of the traditional subjects. *Vocational* tracks may include a combination of academic and job-related courses; students in these tracks are preparing for a job after graduation. Because of the variations in courses required for these different tracks and the differing standards for student achievement among them, a high school education can take on myriad meanings.

■ The Shopping Mall High School

Another group of researchers suggest that the high schools' characteristics resemble those of a shopping mall, with an emphasis on variety and choice for the consumer.[27] Given a diverse student body with many different interests, high schools have offered a diverse curriculum in an attempt to provide something for everybody. Students are expected to make their own course selections; the schools maintain neutrality in regard to students' or parents' choices among the many alternatives offered. The customer has the final word.

■ classroom "treaties"

Staying with the shopping mall metaphor, the study found that some customers (students) are serious about buying, others are just browsing and looking for ideas on what to buy, and still others are at the mall to meet their friends and "cruise." Faced with customers with such different levels of commitment, teachers reach accommodations, or treaties, that promote mutual goals or keep the peace. For example, some teachers make their deals crystal clear when they advise students, "Don't get into my class if you don't want to work." If students don't want to play by these rules, they don't have to take the course.

> *Kids may do poorly in school not simply because they aren't motivated to study or because they lack ability, but because they are intent on maintaining their standing in a crowd that regards academic achievement as uncool.*
>
> —B. Bradford Brown

Most classroom treaties are not this formal or public. Some teachers make unstated, but somehow quite clear, compromises with students uninterested or unwilling to do the work of a course, "Don't hassle me and I won't hassle you. I'll let you slide through if you don't interfere with the students who want to work."[28] These *tacit* arrangements are made to accommodate students and teachers in a manner satisfactory to all. If teachers preach or push too hard, some students resist. To avoid resistance, individual teachers strive to find the appropriate balance in their classrooms between requiring academic rigor and allowing students to opt out of learning entirely. As one teacher commented, "I think I get along fairly well with most of the kids, but to be perfectly truthful, I think I get along because I don't put a lot of pressure on them."[29]

■ specialty shops

■ differences in opportunities

Within the shopping mall high school can be found "specialty shops," the niches for students and families wanting more learning and school engagement. These can include top-track programs, special education programs, vocational and technical education programs, and extracurricular programs like marching band or football. Because the students in these programs have been designated as special, they tend to receive special attention. In contrast, the average or unspecial students are generally ignored by the specialty shops; they do not receive the additional commitment of time, personal relationships, and intensity of learning generally given to specialty-shop students.

> *There must be such a thing as a child with average ability, but you can't find a parent who will admit that it is his child.*
>
> —Thomas Andrew Bailey (Former Florida State Superintendent of Schools)

School personnel were not precise about who the middle students were, using terms such as *average, general, normal,* and *regular,* so the researchers concluded, "Few characteristics of the shopping mall high school are more significant than the existence of unspecial students in the middle who are ignored and poorly served."[30] These students have no important allies or advocates. Their treaties are characterized by avoidance of learning, not engagement. Schools may try to nurture these students' self-esteem, but do not make academic demands on them. As a result, parents of these students occasionally demand a specialty program for their children or transfer them to private schools where purposes are more focused and attention is more personal. Without these opportunities to experience the purpose, push, and personalization of a specialty shop, the unspecial students become the losers in the educational marketplace.

As one reviewer of this study notes,[31] the researchers' evidence supports generalizations made by previous high school observers. For example, although students may have equal access to a high school education, enormous differences may exist in the opportunities available to them within their schools. The "treaties" notion of this study emphasizes the power that teachers and students have to negotiate the quality of education. Effective schooling, however, is marked by a consensus of purpose, high expectations for students, and a supportive climate. What can schools and teachers do to help *all* students be winners? The suggestions are many, but reading the shopping mall high school study may provide a starting point for thinking about the problem.

■ exceptions to the norm

These pictures of life in high school classrooms contrast with glimpses of teachers who challenge their students to think, to express themselves creatively, and to struggle with difficult questions. Students in such classes are pushed to perform as individuals; their teachers share a vision for them that includes high expectations of success. Which picture of high school life is accurate? Undoubtedly both. The issue is, in which direction, in general, are our high schools moving?

Pause and Reflect

1 ▸ Are these findings and descriptions of high school similar to what you saw in your high school experience?

2 ▸ The high school years are often said to be "the best years of your life." Do you agree with this assertion and why? If not, what could and should be done to change the high school experience?

A New Call for High School Reform

In 1996 the Carnegie Foundation for the Advancement of Teaching and the National Association of Secondary School Principals released a joint report entitled *Breaking Ranks: Changing an American Institution.* This national study offered many suggestions for improving the quality of American high schools. Among the factors cited for particular attention were personalization, coherence, time, and technology.[32]

■ personal adult advocate

■ **Personalization**   Finding American high schools too large, impersonal, and rigid, the report recommends that high schools break into units of no more than 600 students so that teachers and students can get to know one another better. Each teacher should be responsible for no more than ninety students each term. Every student should have a *personal adult advocate* who knows him or her well and follows the student's progress throughout high school. No student should be able to remain anonymous, and each student should feel special to some adult in the school. Each student should have a *personal progress plan.* Just as every student with a disability must have an individualized education program (IEP), as described in the chapter entitled "Who Are Today's Students in a Diverse Society?," a student's progress plan would set learning goals that are continually reevaluated. Convinced that personalization in education is crucial, the Gates Foundation (supported by Bill Gates, the founder of Microsoft) has recently donated over 50 million dollars to develop sixty-seven small high schools serving New York City's minority students.[33]

■ connect subjects to real world

■ **Coherence** High schools should identify the essentials that all students must learn to graduate. Instead of organizing the school by disciplinary departments, the report calls for a reorganization that more closely links the various subject matter areas so that learning makes more sense to students in terms of the real world and the application of what they know. Tests must also be aligned with what is taught so that both are consistent with each other. This recommendation for coherence has been reinforced by the recently enacted federal No Child Left Behind legislation discussed throughout this text.

■ identify essential learnings

■ **Time** Flexible, innovative scheduling should replace the fixed fifty-minute periods that dictate the amount of instructional time devoted to each course. The Carnegie unit (the standard type of course credit) should be abandoned or revised so that it no longer equates seat time with learning. Instead, high schools should identify a set of *essential learnings* in literature and language, math, social studies, science, and the arts, the areas where students must demonstrate achievement to graduate. Furthermore, schools should operate twelve months a year.

■ develop technology use

■ **Technology** High schools should develop long-term plans for using computers and other technologies in all aspects of learning and teaching. Each high school should have a technology resource person to consult with and assist the staff.

In the years since the Carnegie report was issued, we have seen moves in some schools around the country toward some of these ideal states outlined in the report, but many observers believe that most U.S. high schools remain far from ideal learning institutions. One thing we can be certain of is that the American high school will continue to be a center of controversy and concern. Worrisome achievement scores and outbursts of violence, such as those in the late 1990s, will keep public attention focused on this segment of our educational system. Reform is in the air, and we'll discuss it in some depth in the chapter entitled "How Should Education Be Reformed?"

▶ What Is a Good School?

■ school as human "product"

First, the obvious: not all schools are good schools. Second, good schools do not just happen. They are *made.* A school is the product of people's intellectual and physical energies, and, at any particular moment, the way a school happens to be reflects the multiplicity of efforts that have gone into creating and maintaining it. Further, like towns and civilizations, schools also rise and fall. They are human creations—dynamic and continually on the move.

No school, at least in the authors' experience, is "right" or "good" for all students, but although we believe this is true, we also believe that some schools are strikingly better than others—that is, some schools provide a significantly better education for a much larger percentage of their students than do others. These schools, referred to in the educational literature as **effective schools,** are the focus of this section.

One major problem associated with this question of effectiveness is what criteria to apply. Effective or good in what dimension? In engaged and happy students? In a teaching staff with high morale? In the percentage of students who get promoted or graduate? Go on to college? What kinds of colleges? How many succeed in business or professional life? In athletics? Socially? Ethically? *Effective,* as currently defined in most of the educational research literature, refers to students' achievement test scores in basic skills such as reading and mathematics. Although such tests measure skills that are hardly the only objectives of education, achievement in these academic areas is an important and widely acclaimed outcome of schooling. Also, achievement in reading and mathematics is easier to measure than good citizenship, artistic development, or passion for ideas.

Characteristics of an Effective School

■ definition of effective schools

Beginning about twenty-five years ago, a number of educational researchers began looking for the characteristics or qualities of effective schools.[34] Among the most significant characteristics they found to be correlated with high achievement in the basic skills were high expectations for student performance, communication among teachers, a task orientation among the staff, the ability to keep students on task, the expenditure of little time on behavior management, the principal's instructional leadership, the participation of parents, and the school environment.

■ high, "can-do" expectations

■ **The Teacher's Expectations**   Through their attitude and regular encouragement, teachers in effective schools communicate to students their belief that the students will achieve the goals of instruction. In effect, the teachers get across to students a "can-do" attitude about learning. We discuss teacher expectations more in the chapter entitled "What Makes a Teacher Effective?"

■ high degree of colleagueship

■ **Communication Among Teachers**   Teachers in effective schools do not operate in a vacuum, each in his or her isolated classroom. Instead, they talk among themselves about their work. They converse about one another's students. They know the curricular materials and activities that go on in one another's classrooms, and they are helpful to one another. In short, effective schools have teachers who are good colleagues.

■ serious attitude

■ **Task Orientation**   The faculties of effective schools are highly task oriented. They begin instruction early in the class period and end instruction late in the period. The staff approaches its teaching responsibilities with a serious air and wastes little time in class. Whether the classes are formal or informal, underneath the surface of events lies a seriousness of purpose that is communicated to students.

■ keep students working

■ **Academic Engaged Time**   *Academic engaged time* (or *academic learning time*) refers to the amount of time students are actually engaged in relevant content-related activities. As we describe in the chapter entitled "What Makes a Teacher Effective?," this characteristic involves the ability of a teacher to get students

VOICES FROM THE CLASSROOM

Denis Gray is a law and justice teacher at Brighton High School in Boston, Massachusetts.

What Is a Good School?

I teach in an urban high school, and it's a good school. For me, there are three criteria for what makes for a good school:

1. The vast majority of its teachers want to have maximum impact on students through instruction.

2. Students have internalized the value of education and want to learn.

3. Most importantly, the educational and ancillary needs of all students are met.

To say the least, making this a reality in the lives of students does not go unchallenged. Students continually test us to determine whether we are "for real." Someone has said, "Students do not care what you know until they know that you care." Difficult students, in particular, test us. They test our patience, our self-control, our professionalism, our integrity, our faith, and our hope. Then, there are the self-doubt questions: "Am I a good teacher?" "Could my actions be interpreted as racist?" "What could/should I be doing that I'm not?"

There are many models and methodologies for instructing and learning. Most of them assume that students *want* to learn. Yet the reality is that for many students, there is a profound disconnect between education and success. They see that multimillion-dollar athletic contracts are signed by high school students. Colleges that should know better are not interested in ensuring that their athletes graduate. Many of our parents shower their children with the latest designer clothes and sneakers. Many of my students have part-time jobs to ensure that they always have pocket money. In their minds is the question, "If I get what I want now, why do I need an education?" Then there are issues of alienation and mistrust. Many students view the education we are trying to give them as the attempt by the "establishment" to "mess with their heads."

Of the three criteria, I believe No. 3 to be the most important. Today's urban school, as a matter of social conscience, must address the psychosocial needs of its students as never before. Today's teacher, as a matter of personal conscience, is required to assume many roles in students' lives, including being parent, protector, counselor, and confidant. It is a tough and complex job, but it's a job I love.

 Visit the website for more Voices from the Classroom.

---

engaged in academic tasks, such as reading or solving math problems, and to keep their attention on these instructional activities. Research has demonstrated a tight link between the amount of time devoted to academic learning tasks and students' achievement.[35]

■ maintain classroom order

■ **Behavior Management**   We have all been in classrooms with teachers who spent huge chunks of time trying to quiet students to get them "on task" or who, in the course of correcting one student, disturbed all the rest, causing a ripple of distraction throughout the room. Teachers in effective schools have learned techniques to minimize the time devoted to managing students. They are efficient both in handling discipline problems and in implementing the learning activities. In addition, these teachers do not routinely resort to corporal punishment, because they use other techniques to deal with student behavior.

Good communication among teacher, student, and parents is key to good teaching.
(© Bob Daemmrich/The Image Works)

principal as instructional leader

The Principal Principals play an important role in effective schools. Instead of being faceless bureaucrats aimlessly shuffling papers, the principals of effective schools are instructional leaders. They have strong views on the purposes of education and are vitally concerned about the quality of teaching and learning in their schools. Still, the principal is perceived as democratic in approach and cooperative in relationships with faculty. The effective principal gains teachers' confidence and clearly communicates to them a vision of what the school should accomplish and how each teacher can contribute toward this end.

parent involvement

Parents An effective school reaches out and draws in parents instead of ignoring them or keeping them at arm's length. Parents are treated as key members of the learning team, as partners with the professional staff in helping their children achieve academic success. In addition to aiding in students' intellectual achievement, the involvement of parents can help improve their children's self-concepts, work habits, and attitudes toward school.

environment conducive to learning

The School Environment Schools that promote learning have climates or environments that support a teacher's efforts to teach and students' efforts to learn. A school that has an environment that is calm, safe, pleasant, and orderly is conducive to learning. On the other hand, a school with an environment that is unsafe, hostile, and generally unruly is rarely a place of learning—at least not academic learning.

another view

Attempts to answer the question "What is a good school?" are still incomplete. Although the characteristics cited are those identified by several extensive

The video case *Parental Involvement in School Culture* lets you view one example of how parents can contribute to an effective school. As you watch the clips and study the artifacts in the case, reflect upon the following questions:

1. Which of the other aspects of an effective school and of effective teaching can you see in the portrayals in this video case?

2. Were parents involved in the schools you have attended? How? How could their involvement have been improved?

3. Do you feel comfortable about involving parents in your classroom as a teacher? If not, what can you do now to address your concerns?

Good schools . . . arise from the crucible of their cultures.

—HOWARD GARDNER

■ a few universal features
■ other qualities of effective schools

research projects, studies continue. Different studies often come up with different characteristics. A ten-year study of 140 schools in the Chicago area, which looked for more holistic measures of effectiveness (rather than just academic achievement), came up with a somewhat different list. Among the characteristics the study found to be associated with successful schools were coherence; good communication within the school community; vital subgroups of teachers (work groups with meaningful responsibilities); a wide range of student incentives (prizes and other forms of recognition); a clear disciplinary policy; and an extracurricular program stressing service to others.[36] Perhaps the reason the research has not clearly delineated for us the characteristics of effective schools is that not enough schools exist where these qualities prevail.

Nevertheless, it appears that whether one is measuring school effectiveness by test scores on math and reading tests or by the more holistic measures, certain features stand out in the schools that most successfully socialize students to behave in ways that the school values. The principal, faculty, and staff in such schools:

- Agree on what they are doing and why something is being done
- Have high expectations for students and clearly communicate them
- Consistently enforce rules
- Provide an environment conducive to the accomplishment of learning tasks and the regular monitoring of students' academic progress

We have a strong suspicion that a number of qualities besides those mentioned here dramatically contribute to the making of a good school. Among these characteristics are a pervasive sense of curiosity, a passion for excellence, a strong belief in students' capacity to grow, and an environment of kindness and support.

▶ The Unfinished Work of the Schools

■ need for balance

As we mentioned at the start of this chapter, our question "What is a school?" has no single satisfactory answer. Schools are human inventions. People bring schools into being for a variety of social purposes. The overall purposes of schools are to advance the common good and help people live happy and successful lives. However, if schools are to serve a society, they must at least keep pace with that society. Many people who are concerned about our schools believe that the schools are moving very slowly while the rest of society experiences dynamic change. They believe, in effect, the schools are out of step with the society, usually being either too far ahead, which is the rarity, or lagging behind (the more common situation) the needs of the people they exist to serve. Schools, like every social institution, need to continually assess what they are *really doing*. They need, too, to see, first, if their purposes and goals are the right purposes and goals, and second, to determine if, indeed, they are achieving those purposes. If you become an educator, you need this commitment to continual examination and renewal of the schools.

Nevertheless, the purposes for which schools are brought into being are still vital. People, particularly parents, have a great desire for good schools for their children, and, as you will see later in this book, many excellent ideas are being generated and movements are under way for the renewal of our schools.

▶ A Final Word

■ today's challenges

Some readers may be uncomfortable with the idea that it is their job to renew the schools. Many may believe that becoming a good classroom teacher is sufficient. Teachers, however, are more than technicians in charge of their classrooms. As professional people, they and their teacher colleagues must have a forceful and clear voice in deciding how they render their services. It follows that the teacher is not simply responsible for his or her own performance but bears responsibility for the total educational enterprise. To live up to this responsibility requires a deep understanding of the schools and much hard work. Still, though, it is the very critical nature of the problems confronting the schools that makes teaching such an exciting occupation today. In the immediate future, education is where the action will be. You have a chance to complete this unfinished work of the schools.

Key Terms

democratic reconstructionists (30)
economic reconstructionists (30)
education (25)
effective schools (45)

school cultures (27)
schooling (26)
social bet (26)

social reconstructionists (30)
socialization (27)

For Reflection

1 Can you think of some pieces of information you picked up on the street that you later "unlearned" in school? Can you think of some things you learned in school that your experience later taught you were untrue? Which has happened more often? What is your reaction?

2 Has reading the accounts and research on the various levels of schools caused you to reconsider the grade level at which you would like to teach?

3 What do you think about the school as transmitter of the culture rather than of "the truth" or "just the facts"? What are some problems with the school being a transmitter of culture? What happens if the national government takes a very strong hand in this? What examples from history can you think of in which a government used schools to promote a particularly dangerous culture?

4 How would you describe the cultures of the schools you have attended?

5 This chapter cites several factors that are associated with good schools. Which five factors are, in your opinion, the most important, and why do you think so?

For Debate

Enter EduSpace from the website to discuss the following questions with other students who are using this book now.

1 How did you answer the question: What is a school? Why? What were your reactions to some of the answers listed on page 24?

2 Read the Policy Matters! summary, "School Dress Codes," at the website. After considering how dress codes might affect or be affected by school culture, post your answers (or respond to other students' answers) to the "What Do You Think?" questions listed in the Policy Matters! feature.

For Further Information

PRINT RESOURCES

Jacques Barzun, *Begin Here: The Forgotten Conditions of Teaching and Learning* (Chicago: University of Chicago Press, 1991).
This book by one of the leading proponents of the academic or intellectual approach lays out a strong case that American schools have badly strayed from their original purposes. In addition, Barzun offers a positive vision of how to recapture this classical tradition.

Ernest Boyer, *Basic School: A Community for Learning* (Princeton, NJ: The Carnegie Foundation for the Advancement of Teaching, 1995).
This was the final book of one of education's great practitioners and spokespersons. Practical wisdom is woven into a clear description of the kind of schools we can and should have.

Terrence Deal and Kent Peterson, *Shaping School Culture* (San Francisco: Jossey: Bass, 1999)
Examining a major theme of this chapter, the authors explore how schools reflect the culture and are themselves culture-shapers. They address the school-culture issue from the perspectives of the past, the present, and the future.

Lisa Delpit and Joanne Kilgour Dowdy [eds.] *The Skin That We Speak: Thoughts on Language and Culture in the Classroom* (New York: New Press, 2002)
This book is a collection of thirteen old and new essays. Although the major focus is on the language of African American students, the books overriding theme is the linkages between classroom language and the school's role as transmitter of culture.

Andy Hargreaves, *Teaching in the Knowledge Society: Education in the Age of Insecurity* (New York: Teachers College Press, 2003).
The author takes a fresh look at what it means to be a teacher in the modern age. In addition, this book sheds light on the work of teachers in different school settings.

Sarah Mondale, ed., *School: The Story of American Public Education* (Boston: Beacon Press, 2001)
This edited book is based on an excellent four-part PBS television series. Among other things, it shows the connection between the will of a people and the purposes of their schools.

Diane Ravitch and Joseph P. Viteritti, eds., *New Schools for a New Century* (New Haven, CT: Yale University Press, 1997).
This collection of essays reflects our nation's struggles with school reform. What emerges is the view that to break away from our current factory-model schooling, radical changes, such as charter schools or choice and new contractual arrangements, are needed.

Allison Zmuda, Robert Kuklis, and Everett Kline, *Transforming Schools: Creating a Culture of Continuous Improvement* (Alexandria, VA: ASCD, 2004)
This book is a highly readable, fictional account of how a group of educators changed the culture in a school to achieve higher student achievement and higher levels of satisfaction for both students and teachers. Behind the story, though, is a blueprint to bring about systematic school change.

WEB RESOURCES

Eisenhower National Clearinghouse, *ENC Online*. Available at: **http://www.enc.org.**
ENC is a rich resource of research-based ideas about school improvement and curricular materials for classroom teachers from kindergarten through twelfth grade, particularly in mathematics and science.

Lee Shiney and Lajean Shiney, *Teacher's Edition Online: Tools for Teachers*. Available at: **http://www.teachnet.com/.**
This website contains many resources for teachers, including links to information on such topics as classroom management, advice to student teachers, attention deficit disorder, drugs and violence in schools, and gangs.

3 Who Are Today's Students in a Diverse Society?

Chapter Preview   In some ways, children never change. The pictures of children in our classic literature are as true today as when they were first written. Look at the conniving, mischievous Tom Sawyer, the overly curious Alice in Wonderland, or the tenacious Mafatu in *Call It Courage*. These characters are endearing to us in part because we have all known children like them. Real children of today are also very much like the children of yesterday or the children of tomorrow. Certain stages of cognitive, social, emotional, and physical development have been identified, and a similar progression through these stages occurs for everyone. We all have basic psychological and physical needs that cut across racial, cultural, age, and gender boundaries. You learn a great deal about these subjects in your courses in child or adolescent development and educational psychology. As a teacher, understanding these stages of development and areas of common needs gives you insight into student behavior and helps you develop appropriate classroom experiences.

However, it is also important to be sensitive to the great differences among students and to factors in our society that are directly affecting their lives. In this chapter, we hope to make you more fully aware of the diversity in our society and classrooms, the range of abilities among the students you will encounter, and the schools' attempts to address all these areas of diversity. We also hope to make you more deeply sensitive to the sorts of issues, potential problems, and benefits related to this diversity. This chapter emphasizes that:

▶ Studies of the demographic makeup of the country indicate shifts in ethnic composition.

▶ All children have basic needs. Being aware of and understanding these commonalities help us accommodate the diverse needs of students.

▶ Students have many strengths and abilities that extend beyond the traditional emphasis in our schools on linguistic and analytic abilities. Approaches that recognize multiple views of intelligence and differing learning styles emphasize the great diversity in student learning and ability.

▶ Gender issues affect the curriculum, classroom interactions, and achievement levels.

▶ Schools address the individual needs of students through multicultural, bilingual, special education, and gifted and talented programs.

▶ To cope in today's classroom, teachers must be aware of many dimensions of student diversity.

▶ Sources of Student Diversity

You will see diversity in your students along a number of dimensions, including who the students are, what they need, and their various kinds of abilities:

■ racial and ethnic diversity

- Students in your classroom are likely to come from a variety of *racial and ethnic backgrounds,* representing many different cultures and ways of looking at the world. Cultural differences between teachers and students can give rise to a variety of misunderstandings unless you make an attempt to learn more about your students' backgrounds and expectations. Multicultural education approaches can help students learn to appreciate the contributions of all people.

■ language diversity

- Some of your students may speak a primary *language other than English.* We will see that parents, educators, and policymakers have become divided, often bitterly so, over the best way to teach these English language learners in U.S. public schools.

■ academic diversity

- Another dimension of diversity will be seen in the academic *abilities, achievements,* and *learning styles* of your students. Some students will enter the school environment and immediately do well. Other students will appear not to respond to your teaching. One of your biggest challenges as a teacher will be to provide a variety of experiences and learning.

■ students with differing needs

- Students in your classroom will develop at different rates and probably will display *diverse needs.* Recognizing diverse needs will help you better understand some student behaviors and perhaps increase your insight into how to respond.

■ avoiding gender stereotypes a challenge

- *Boys and girls* are different, even when they come from the same socioeconomic, racial, or ethnic group. They are raised differently, and often society has different expectations of them. Treating boys and girls equitably as individuals and not as gender stereotypes is a constant challenge for both male and female teachers.

Diversity in the classroom means that your students will come from a wide range of cultural backgrounds, may speak a first language other than English, and may have a variety of learning abilities and learning styles.
(© Mary Kate Denny/PhotoEdit)

◼ gay/lesbian students

- Regardless of your own beliefs on the subject of homosexuality, if you are going to teach in the public schools, you may very well teach *gay and lesbian students*. As a teacher, you will be challenged to establish and maintain a safe and supportive classroom environment for these and all of your students.

◼ socioeconomic diversity

- Your students will come from families with varied *socioeconomic backgrounds*. The benefits of being a child from a family in a higher socioeconomic class show up in school performance; children from such families typically do much better academically than students from families in lower classes. Teachers and schools are challenged to help students from these families. This topic is discussed in more detail in the chapter entitled "What Social Problems Affect Today's Students?"

▶ Racial, Ethnic, and Cultural Diversity

◼ demographic changes

Although American society has always been composed of various races, ethnicities, and cultures, today we are experiencing great cultural diversity. The term *race* refers to people with common ancestry and physical characteristics, whereas the term *ethnicity* applies to people who share a common culture, usually including language, customs, and religion.

 Visit this chapter of the website to link to up-to-date statistics on this topic.

Public school classrooms include an even higher percentage of minorities than the population as a whole. Although about 32 percent of the total population are members of racial or ethnic minority groups, 40 percent of school-age children are minorities, a figure that will continue to increase in the coming years.[1] As shown in Table 3.1, birth rates among minority groups are higher than those of white Americans, and immigration patterns are contributing to the increasing size of the minority population.

◼ increasing minority school population

These national averages disguise the fact that minority groups are unequally distributed across the country. The fastest-growing states also have high percentages of minority youth. For example, the four states of California, Texas, New York, and Florida will have more than one-third of the nation's young people by 2010, and the youth population of each of these states will be more than 52 percent minority. By that same year, about twelve states will have more than 50 percent minority youth populations.[2] In the forty-seven urban school districts that constitute the "great city schools," including those in New York City, Los Angeles, and Chicago, an overwhelming majority of students are from minority groups.

TABLE 3.1 Projections of the U.S. Population Age 0–17, 2000–2020 (millions)

Youth	2000	2010	2020	Change
Total youth*	71.8	73.8	79.3	+10.4%
White, non-Hispanic	45.4	42.7	42.4	−6.6%
Hispanic (of any race)	11.0	13.7	17.2	+56.4%
Black, non-Hispanic	11.3	12.2	13.4	+18.6%
Other races†	4.1	5.2	6.3	+54%
Increase in total minority youth = +10.5 million, or +40%				
Decrease in total white youth = −3 million, or -6.6%				

*May not add exactly because of rounding.

†Includes American Indians; Alaskan Natives; Asian and Pacific Islanders.

Source: U.S. Bureau of the Census. *Table M. Population by Age, Race, and Hispanic Origins: 1990 to 2050.* Available at: **http://www.census.gov/prod/1/pop/p251130/p251130b.pdf.**

As might be expected with increasing cultural diversity, teachers will encounter more students whose native language is not English and whose ethnic and cultural backgrounds reflect a Hispanic or Asian heritage. We discuss these English language learners later in this chapter.

With the development of a richer, more varied society, differences in values and family expectations are also more evident. For example, some families may place a premium on school and higher education, whereas other families may emphasize early entry into the workplace. But even though you will encounter a range of familial expectations for school achievement, all children deserve the best educational experience they can get while in school. Recognition of racial and ethnic differences can provide the understanding and insight needed for more effective instruction.

Cultural Pluralism: Not There Yet

■ "melting pot"

At one time, the United States was considered a "melting pot" of many different kinds of people. Immigrants were expected to give up the language and customs of their homelands and adopt the language and customs of their new country. During the nineteenth and early twentieth centuries, schools contributed to the concept of the melting pot by socializing and acculturating immigrant children to American ways while discouraging them from maintaining the ways of their homelands. Some states even passed laws forbidding instruction in any language but English. The basic idea was to produce a society with one dominant culture. This process of incorporating an immigrant group into the mainstream culture is often referred to as *enculturation* or **assimilation.** Many European immigrant groups were easily assimilated into the dominant American culture, but, as described in the accompanying box, people of color were often prevented from doing so.

■ cultural pluralism

The concept of the melting pot has generally been replaced by the notion of **cultural pluralism,** which calls for an understanding and appreciation of the cultural differences and languages among the nation's citizens. The goal is to create a sense of society's wholeness based on the unique strengths of each of its parts. Cultural pluralism rejects both assimilation and separatism, a philosophy that suggests each cultural group should maintain its own identity without trying to fit into an overall American culture. Instead, it seeks a healthy interaction among the diverse groups in our society—that is, each subculture maintains its own individuality while contributing to our society as a whole. As some commentators put it, cultural pluralism argues for replacing the melting-pot metaphor with that of a "mosaic" or "tapestry" in which the individual parts are still distinct but combine to make a unique whole.

■ cultural pluralism not a reality

Many people have promulgated cultural pluralism as a desirable goal, but it does not currently exist in the United States. Although racial, ethnic, and cultural diversity do exist, equality among the various groups does not. In general, racial and ethnic minorities do not share equal political, economic, and educational opportunities with those of the dominant culture, even though our society espouses such equality. In addition, some people resist the notion of cultural pluralism as a desirable goal. Some opponents argue in favor of assimilation, contending that cultural pluralism will undermine our country's common traditions, historically derived from western European cultures. Others favor separatism. Unfortunately, American schools, too, have often failed to support cultural pluralism. Traditionally, public schools have been run for the benefit of those in the dominant cultural group, excluding minority groups from receiving the full range of benefits.

Acting White

Two researchers, Signithia Fordham and John Ogbu, studied a predominantly African American high school, Capitol High, in Washington, D.C., to see how students' sense of racial identity enters into the process of schooling and affects academic achievement. They conclude that many African American students underachieve academically because they are afraid of being accused of "acting white."

Fordham and Ogbu argue that, because they have been excluded from true assimilation in economic, political, social, and psychological arenas, historically subordinate minorities like African Americans have developed a sense of collective identity, or sense of peoplehood, in opposition to the social identity of white Americans. This opposition includes protecting their identities and maintaining boundaries between themselves and white Americans. Thus, if an African American student behaves in a manner that is typical or representative of the white majority, the student's peers negatively judge that person as "acting white."

Ford and Ogbu discovered that students at Capitol High School, which had a 99 percent African American student body, exerted strong pressure to reassure one another of black loyalty and identity by discouraging students from engaging in certain behaviors that were interpreted as "white." Being an academic high achiever was one such unacceptable behavior. Fordham and Ogbu found that many students succumbed to peer pressure and purposely underachieved academically. Many of these students were afraid of being labeled *brainiacs,* a term meaning that a person was smart but also a jerk. Worse yet for male students was to be known as a *pervert brainiac.* To be known as a brainiac was to question a male student's manhood, but to be known as a pervert brainiac left little doubt and was the kiss of death among peers.

Students who wanted to achieve academically and still be considered an accepted member of the peer group tried various strategies to avoid antagonizing their peers, including engaging in athletic activities, acquiring the protection of "tough guys" in return for assisting the latter in their schoolwork and homework, and clowning around. These students were careful not to brag about their academic achievements or to bring attention to themselves, but even in these instances, the researchers conclude, the students would do much better if they did not have to divert their time and attention into strategies to conceal their academic pursuits.

What are the implications of these findings? Clearly, schools must find ways to reinforce black identity that are compatible with academic achievement. Similarly, the African American community must convince black children that academic pursuit is not synonymous with acculturation into white society. If the community can demonstrate that academic achievement is valued and appreciated, children will get a different message.

Source: Signithia Fordham and John U. Ogbu, "Black Students' School Success: Coping with the Burden of 'Acting White,'" *The Urban Review* 18, no. 3 (1986), pp. 176–206.

Schools that embrace cultural pluralism seek to promote diversity and to avoid the dominance of a single culture. Their curricula are infused with the histories and contributions of diverse groups. These schools attempt to use the cultural patterns of the students to provide instruction and promote learning. They may use the multicultural education approaches described next. The goal is for students to be comfortable operating both within their own cultures and in others as well. Students from all racial, ethnic, and cultural groups are urged to participate in the school's various social, athletic, and governmental activities. These schools seek to eradicate the academic achievement disparities among the various racial, ethnic, and cultural groups. In short, the goal for schools that aim for cultural pluralism is that no particular cultural group either dominates or is excluded from those activities and accomplishments that schools value.

Multicultural Education

■ definition and goals

Multicultural education represents one approach to meeting the educational needs of an increasingly diverse student population. Spurred by the civil rights movement of the 1960s, multicultural education is a response to economic inequality, racism, and sexism in American culture. Originally used in conjunction with improving the lot of "people of color," the term has been broadened to include gender, disability, and other forms of diversity. Its goals include reducing prejudice and fostering tolerance, improving the academic achievement of minority students, building commitment to the American ideals of pluralism and democracy, and incorporating minority groups' perspectives into the curricula of our schools. Like the concept of cultural pluralism on which it is based, multicultural education rejects both the notion of the melting pot and separatist philosophies.

At least five different approaches to multicultural education have been identified, which helps explain why the term often has very different meanings for different people:

 The video case *Culturally Responsive Teaching* shows an example of a multicultural lesson that also helps students develop their writing skills. As you watch the clips and study the artifacts in the case, reflect upon the following questions:

1. Which of the approaches to multicultural education listed in this chapter does the class shown in the video case represent?
2. How might teachers plan meaningful multicultural instruction for other grade levels or subjects?

1. *Teaching the exceptional and culturally different*, which helps students achieve academically and socially within currently existing schools by building bridges between the students' backgrounds and the schools to make the curriculum more "user friendly."

■ different approaches

2. *Human relations*, which attempts to build positive relations among members of different racial/cultural groups and between males and females.
3. *Single-group studies*, which focus on programs that examine particular groups, such as African American studies or women's studies.
4. *Multicultural*, which promotes cultural pluralism by reconstructing the whole educational process around the perspectives of diverse racial, ethnic, cultural, and social classes.
5. *Multicultural and social reconstructionist*, which teaches students to examine inequality and oppression in society and to take action to remediate these inequalities.[3]

■ social justice

Multicultural education is not just for members of minority racial or ethnic groups, but for all students, including those with western European heritage. A major goal of multicultural education is to help students from diverse cultures learn to cross cultural borders and to participate in a diverse, democratic society. True multicultural education does not consist of only black history or women's history months. Instead of simply adding on information about particular groups, leaving the rest of the curriculum untouched, real multicultural education presents multiple perspectives and viewpoints to help students understand how events and facts can be interpreted differently by various groups.

In addition to valuing cultural diversity, multicultural education is based on the concept of *social justice*, which seeks to do away with social and economic inequalities for those who have been denied these benefits of a democratic society. African Americans, Native Americans, Asian Americans, Hispanic Americans, women, individuals with disabilities, people with limited English proficiency, people with low incomes, members of particular religious groups, and individuals with different sexual orientations are among those groups that have at one time or another been denied social justice. Educators who support multicultural education see establishing social justice for all people, but particularly for those who have experienced discrimination, as a moral and ethical responsibility.

■ **An Ongoing Debate** Many school districts are attempting to permeate their curricula with a multicultural emphasis, believing that attention to multicultural education is our society's best way to combat the prejudice and divisiveness among the different subcultures of our nation. By developing mutual respect for and appreciation of different lifestyles, languages, religious beliefs, and family structures students may help shape a better future society for all its members.

Some educators, however, are concerned about what they believe are potential dangers of multicultural education in the schools, including all of the following:

■ concerns and controversy

- It may destroy any sense of common traditions, values, purposes, and obligations.
- It may divert the schools' attention from their basic purpose of educating for civic, economic, and personal effectiveness.
- It attacks the problem of minority students' underachievement by advocating an emphasis on self-esteem rather than hard work.
- It substitutes "relevance" of subjects studied for instruction in solid academics.
- It may undermine a sense of a common morality because no universal moral positions are considered acceptable to all elements of our society.

These critics do not argue against the need to preserve and value the achievements of the diverse ethnic and racial groups of our country, but they reject the position that everything is of equal value, that the schools have a responsibility to teach every possible belief and value, and that behavior is moral if it is believed to be so by any group.[4] These critics assert that there are limits to pluralism and that those limits must be articulated by schools and school leaders. Other critics of multiculturalism include those who completely reject the concept of cultural pluralism, preferring an assimilationist perspective whereby schools are charged with forging one dominant American culture in which English is the only acceptable language.

Thus, the major thrusts of multicultural education are not without controversy. Multicultural education has often been cast as a reform movement, designed to address inequity and discrimination resulting from the race, religion, socioeconomic status, gender, age, exceptionality, or language of students.[5] As with any attempt to solve social problems, excesses and overexuberance can occur. Nevertheless, schools do need to accommodate larger minority populations in a way that removes barriers while preserving the basic purposes of schooling.

■ culturally responsive teaching

One day our descendents will think it incredible that we paid so much attention to things like the amount of melanin in our skin or the shape of our eyes or our gender instead of the unique identities of each of us as complex human beings.

—FRANKLIN THOMAS (FORMER PRESIDENT OF THE FORD FOUNDATION)

■ **Teaching Implications** One method for teachers who want to acknowledge and accommodate cultural diversity in the classroom is through **culturally responsive teaching.** Many educators have documented how cultural identity, communication styles, and social expectations of students from minority cultural groups often conflict with the values, beliefs, and cultural assumptions of teachers.[6]

The school's middle-class culture often places students from other cultures at a disadvantage in understanding the school's cultural codes and communication styles. Teachers who recognize this can implement an *equity pedagogy,* a style of teaching that uses instructional materials and practices that incorporate important aspects of their students' family and community culture.

For example, a teacher whose class contains mostly immigrant children from Central America can place maps of both Latin America and the United States around the room, provide magazines and games in both Spanish and English, and play salsa music as background for certain activities. This teacher might also recognize that for many students from a Latin culture, establishing direct eye contact with an adult authority figure is a sign of disrespect, so she does not establish that expectation of her students. Knowing and understanding your students' cultural backgrounds can help you make your classroom more inviting and can increase their academic achievement.

Pause and Reflect

1 ▸ What are the pros and cons of living in a culturally pluralistic society?

2 ▸ In your opinion, is this preferable to a "melting-pot" or assimilationist approach to diversity? Why or why not?

3 ▸ Does the idea of multicultural education make sense to you? Why or why not? If so, what version of multicultural education appeals to you most?

▶ English Language Learners

■ non-English-speaking students

Almost 4 million **limited English proficient (LEP)** students are enrolled in public elementary and secondary schools (about 8.4 percent of the total enrollment) and the number has increased every year for the last decade.[7] The large majority of LEP students are concentrated in the states of California, Texas, New York, and Florida. Across the country, LEP students speak more than 100 different languages. Spanish is the non-English background of the great majority of LEP students (77 percent), followed by Vietnamese (2.4 percent), Hmong (1.8 percent), Korean (1.2 percent), Arabic (1.2 percent), French (Haitian) Creole (1.1 percent), and Cantonese (1.0 percent).[8] All other language groups represent less than 1 percent of the LEP student population.

Visit this chapter of the website to link to up-to-date statistics on this topic.

You might think that these non-English-speaking youngsters are from recent immigrant families, and some of them are. More than 2 million immigrant youths enrolled in U.S. schools in the past decade, and many of them are non-English speakers. As these children and youth enter schools, most will need to make sense of a new language, a new culture, and possibly a new way of behaving. An important function of teachers and schools is to offer a source of stability for students who are experiencing rapid change in their lives.

A surprisingly large number of students with limited English proficiency, however, were born and raised in the United States but have not learned English at home or in their community. Seventeen percent of all U.S. five-to-twenty-four-year-olds spoke a language other than English at home, and 6 percent spoke English with difficulty.[9] Many of them also lack basic skills in the language spoken at home, which makes it more difficult to teach them English at school.

The Government Response

Students whose native language is not English constitute one of the most conspicuous failure groups in the American educational system. Because of their difficulty in speaking, writing, and understanding English, many of these LEP students fall further and further behind in school, and overwhelming numbers drop out before finishing high school.

■ *Lau v. Nichols*

To cope with this problem, Congress passed the Bilingual Education Act in 1968 and subsequently amended it a number of times to provide federal funds to develop bilingual programs. Much of the expansion of bilingual programs in the 1970s can be attributed to a series of court cases, the most notable of which was the 1974 U.S. Supreme Court case of *Lau* v. *Nichols*. The case involved a class action suit on behalf of Chinese-speaking students in San Francisco, but it had implications for all of the nation's non-English-speaking children. The Court found that "where inability to speak and understand the English language excludes national origin–minority group children from effective participation in the educational program offered by a school district, the district must take affirmative steps to rectify the language deficiency in order to open its instructional program to these students."[10] Basing its ruling on the Civil Rights Act of 1964, the Court held that the San Francisco school system unlawfully discriminated on the basis of national origin when it failed to cope with the children's language problems.

Although the *Lau* case did not mandate bilingual education as the means to solve the problem, subsequent state cases did order bilingual programs. With the advice of an expert panel, the U.S. Office of Civil Rights suggested guidelines for school districts to follow, the so-called Lau Remedies. The guidelines "specified that language minority students should be taught academics in their primary home language until they could effectively benefit from English language instruction."[11]

Bilingual Education Models

■ different models

Students with a native language other than English have two goals in school: learning English and mastering content. Several types or models of **bilingual education** programs have been designed to help them reach these goals. In the *immersion model*, students learn everything in English. Teachers using immersion programs generally strive to deliver lessons in simple and understandable language that allows students to internalize English while learning academic subjects. The extreme case of immersion is called *submersion*, wherein students must "sink or swim" until they learn English. Sometimes students are pulled out for *English as a Second Language (ESL)* programs, which provide them with instruction in English geared toward language acquisition.

> *Our common language is . . . English.
> And our common task is to ensure
> that our non-English-speaking
> children learn this common language.*
> —WILLIAM BENNETT (FORMER U.S.
> SECRETARY OF EDUCATION)

The *transitional model* provides intensive English-language instruction, but students get some portion of their academic instruction in their native language. The goal is to prepare students for regular classes in English without letting them fall behind in subject areas. In theory, students transition out of these programs within a few years.

Maintenance or *developmental* bilingual education aims to preserve and build on students' native-language skills as they continue to acquire English as a second language.

Bilingual Education Controversies

■ bilingual critics support immersion model

Choosing the best method for educating students who need to learn English has become a divisive political battle. In the early 1970s language-minority speakers and their advocates fought for bilingual education as their right, but today many of them are expressing doubts about the effectiveness of bilingual programs. Civil rights and cultural issues are giving way to concerns that non-native English speakers are just not sufficiently mastering the English language, and that, in turn, is keeping them from fully participating in American life. Although some educators believe students who use English as a second language should be educated in their native language as well, critics insist such an approach doesn't work. The critics believe the best path to academic achievement for language-minority students in most cases is to learn English and learn it quickly. Too many bilingual programs, they say, place LEP students into slower learning tracks where they rarely learn sufficient English and from which they may never emerge. These critics basically support an immersion model of bilingual education, opposing the transitional and maintenance models.

■ many still support bilingual education

In response, supporters of transitional and maintenance models argue that students can best keep up academically with their English-speaking peers if they are taught at least partly in their native languages while learning English. They also cite research indicating that instruction in the native language concurrent with English instruction actually enhances the acquisition of English.[12] These advocates say it is not fair to blame bilingual education for the slow progress some

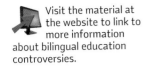

Visit the material at the website to link to more information about bilingual education controversies.

◼ California, Arizona, and Massachusetts abandon bilingual education

students are making. The problem is that becoming proficient in any second language takes longer than just one or two years. They also point out that there is a shortage of well-qualified, fully bilingual teachers, so in many cases the problem with bilingual classes is not the curriculum but the quality of instruction. Some school systems have used teacher aides who speak the child's language to help connect the child and the school. The use of bilingual peer tutors may also help provide a greater sense of stability.

The transitional and maintenance models of bilingual education are in growing jeopardy, however, as first California, Arizona, Massachusetts, and now other states threaten these bilingual programs. In 1998, California voters passed Proposition 227, which called for LEP students to be taught in a special English-immersion program in which nearly all instruction is in English, in most cases for no more than a year, before moving into mainstream English classrooms. Proposition 227 basically ended transitional and maintenance models of bilingual education in California, except when sufficient numbers of parents specifically request that their children continue in them. Many parents, administrators, and teachers are concerned that all children, not just LEP students, will be affected as mainstream teachers grapple with students who may be unprepared to deal with grade-level work in English after one year in immersion. The legality of Proposition 227 was challenged in the courts, but in 2001 a federal appeals court upheld the law. By 2003, English-language learners in California elementary and middle schools had improved their overall scores on state standardized tests for the fifth year in a row. Supporters of Proposition 227 argue that the test scores improved as a result of the law being implemented. Bilingual education supporters, on the other hand, point out that average scores have risen for all students and that the rate of increase in scores for LEP students still lag behind those of English-speaking students.

◼ need for bilingual teachers

Despite this controversy, many school districts are in desperate need of bilingual teachers, particularly those who speak Spanish and Asian languages. If you speak a second language or still have time to include learning a language in your college program, you could help meet a serious educational need and, at the same time, greatly enhance your employment opportunities. Speaking a foreign language, especially Spanish, is also an asset for the regular classroom teacher who may have Spanish-speaking students in class.

Pause and Reflect

1 ▸ How can you help prepare yourself for the diversity you are likely to encounter in the classroom?

2 ▸ What experiences with diversity will you bring to the classroom? How do you think these experiences help you as a teacher?

▸ Diverse Abilities

◼ traditional focus on small range of abilities

In some ways, many of our schools today are not structured to address students' diverse abilities. In the following section, we look at the theory that students may have many abilities and talents not tapped by traditional schooling. We also explore learning styles to see how different students learn and perhaps broaden your views on approaches to teaching. Then we briefly examine characteristics of students along a range of disabilities and talents. We'll see that schools and teachers must make special efforts to educate students effectively who vary from average either because of learning problems or because they are academically gifted.

Multiple Intelligences

Howard Gardner, a leading psychologist, proposes that we should move toward educating **multiple intelligences,** of which linguistic and analytic abilities are only two facets. In Gardner's books, *Frames of Mind* and *Multiple Intelligences: The Theory in Practice,*[13] he explains that we all have strengths, weaknesses, and unique combinations of cognitive abilities. Gardner states that people have at least eight distinct intellectual capacities that they use to approach problems and create products:

Visit the material at the website to link to more information about multiple intelligences theory.

■ eight different abilities

1. *Verbal/linguistic intelligence* draws on the individual's language skills, oral and written, to express what's on the person's mind and to understand other people.
2. *Logical-mathematical intelligence* is a person's ability to understand principles of some kind of causal system, like a scientist does, or to manipulate numbers, quantities, and operations, like a mathematician does.
3. *Spatial intelligence* refers to the ability to represent the spatial world internally in the mind, like a chess player or sculptor does.
4. *Bodily-kinesthetic intelligence* is the capacity to use your whole body or parts of your body to solve a problem, make something, or put on some kind of production, like that of an athlete or a performing artist.
5. *Musical intelligence* is the capacity to "think" in music and to be able to hear patterns and recognize, remember, and manipulate them.
6. *Interpersonal intelligence* is the ability to understand other people, an ability that we all need but is particularly important for teachers, salespeople, and politicians.
7. *Intrapersonal intelligence* refers to having an understanding of yourself and knowing your preferences, capabilities, and deficiencies.
8. *Naturalist intelligence* refers to the ability to discriminate among living things (plants and animals) and to have sensitivity toward features of the natural world, such as rock formations and clouds.[14]

Most of our schools tend to emphasize a curriculum that specifically targets the predominantly linguistic and analytic abilities students need to do well on commonly used standardized tests and deemphasize or exclude other possible intelligences. This constricted focus on a limited range of abilities results in an education system that teaches and reinforces only certain types of achievement. Children who are strong in linguistic and analytic tasks are likely to be successful in school and feel a great sense of achievement. Other children, even though they may be very competent or even gifted in nontraditional school tasks, may experience frustration or failure in school. In Gardner's theory, abilities in diverse areas would be valued as indicators of intelligence and be considered worthy of further nurturance and development in school.

■ fostering diverse abilities

■ **Teaching Implications**   Acknowledging and fostering individual abilities in a variety of areas is one way teachers can help students. To address varied intelligences, Gardner emphasizes learning in context, particularly through apprenticeships. Student development in an area like music should be fostered through hands-on practice and experiences.

TABLE 3.2 Multiple Intelligences Menu

Linguistic Menu	Musical Menu
Using storytelling to explain _____ Conduct a debate on _____ Write a poem, myth, legend, short play, or news article about _____ Create a talk show radio program about _____ Conduct an interview of _____ on _____	Give a presentation with appropriate musical accompaniment on _____ Sing a rap or song that explains _____ Indicate the rhythmical patterns in _____ Explain how the music of a song is similar to _____ Make an instrument and use it to demonstrate _____
Logical-Mathematical Menu	**Interpersonal Menu**
Translate a _____ into a mathematical formula _____ Design and conduct an experiment on _____ Make up syllogisms to demonstrate _____ Make up analogies to explain _____ Describe the patterns of symmetry in _____ Others of your choice _____	Conduct a meeting to address _____ Intentionally use _____ social skills to learn about _____ Participate in a service project to _____ Teach someone about _____ Practice giving and receiving feedback on _____ Use technology to _____
Bodily-Kinesthetic Menu	**Intrapersonal Menu**
Create a movement or sequence of movements to explain _____ Make task or puzzle cards for _____ Build or construct a _____ Plan and attend a field trip that will _____ Bring hands-on materials to demonstrate _____	Describe qualities you possess that will help you to successfully complete _____ Set and pursue a goal to _____ Describe one of your personal values about _____ Write a journal entry on _____ Assess your own work in _____
Visual Menu	**Naturalist Menu**
Chart, map, cluster, or graph _____ Create a slide show, videotape, or photo album of _____ Create a piece of art that demonstrates _____ Invent a board or card game to demonstrate _____ Illustrate, draw, paint, sketch, or sculpt _____	Create observation notebooks of _____ Describe changes in local or global environment _____ Care for pets, wildlife, gardens, or parks _____ Use binoculars, telescopes, microscopes, or magnifiers to _____ Draw or photograph natural objects _____

Source: Reprinted with permission from Linda Campbell, "How Teachers Interpret MI Theory," *Educational Leadership*, 44 (September 1997), p. 18.

Even traditional subjects should be taught in a variety of ways, such as those listed in the Multiple Intelligences Menu in Table 3.2, to address the varied intelligences of both students and teachers. For example, history might be taught through a number of media and methods, ranging from art and architecture to biographies and dramatic reenactments of events. Assessments should also be tailored to different abilities and should take place in a learning context as much as possible.

While the theory of multiple intelligences is very popular with many educators and resonates with their own experiences, it should be noted that a number of psychologists have criticized the lack of scientific measures of Gardner's various intelligences. There is concern on the part of some that schools, in attempting to address a range of abilities, may not stress enough the importance of verbal and mathematical abilities, which they say are critical to success in our society. In particular, critics worry that Gardner's theories are contributing to the end of ability grouping in schools.[15]

Nevertheless, multiple intelligences theory offers teachers some ideas for expanding instructional repertoires and infusing variety into lessons. It provides a framework for enhancing instruction and a language to describe the efforts. Currently a number of schools across the country are applying the theory in the classroom on a day-to-day basis. These efforts should contribute to our knowledge and skills in this area.

Differing Learning Styles

Visit the material at the website to link to more information about learning styles.

Another approach to individual abilities and differences is the theory of learning styles. A **learning styles** approach to teaching and learning is based on the idea that all students have strengths and abilities, but each student may have a preferred way of using these abilities. Whereas Gardner's theory of multiple intelligences centers on the *content* and *products* of learning and has its roots in an effort to rethink the theory of measurable intelligence, learning styles theory addresses differences in the *process* of learning and the different ways people think and feel as they solve problems, create products, and interact.

■ varieties of learning styles

There exist a number of different theories and models of learning styles. One approach looks at four modalities for learning: visual (seeing), auditory (hearing), kinesthetic (moving) or tactile (touching), and is based on the idea that different people prefer different modes of learning. For example, some people learn better by reading (visual), while others prefer learning by doing (kinesthetic or tactile). Other models look at learning styles for processing information. For example, some learners absorb information concretely and in a sequential manner. Other learners focus more on ideas and abstractions, while still others like to learn socially.

If students do not learn the way we teach, then let us teach the way they learn.

—KENNETH DUNN

■ disagreements over implementation

A learning styles approach to teaching is currently receiving a great deal of attention in education. Although few schools adhere strictly to any one "model," the approach is being applied in varying forms and intensities in many schools. Key advocates and researchers of a learning styles approach to education agree that individual strengths and abilities should be emphasized, but they disagree on how to put the theory into practice. Some educators call for a formal assessment of each student's learning style and then a prescription for appropriate teaching methods for that individual. Others believe that students should be assessed and matched with teachers having similar learning styles. Still others warn that current tests are not yet technically adequate, and that using these tests may actually harm students because they may result in improper labeling of individuals and their so-called learning styles.

■ keys for teachers

■ **Teaching Implications**   Rather than label students as having a particular learning style, many educators argue that curriculum and instruction should offer varied lessons that appeal to a range of strengths, abilities, and learning preferences over time. Teachers need to accommodate different learning styles by systematically varying teaching and assessment methods to reach all students. Flexibility and variety are the keys; don't assume that all students learn the way you do, and don't undervalue students just because their learning styles differ from yours.

Differentiated instruction, as described in the "What Is Taught?" chapter, is a powerful way to address academic diversity. Websites on how to differentiate instruction are listed at the end of that chapter in the **For Further Information** section. Technology can also help in varying instruction and assessment methods. As teachers become more familiar with new technology, they are making use of CD-ROMs, video/audio, World Wide Web sites, and other multimedia tools that offer students varied ways to access materials and learning experiences.

Pause and Reflect

1 ▸ In Howard Gardner's list of intelligences, which are your strongest? How do you know?

2 ▸ Should teachers and schools focus on fostering a variety of abilities such as those identified by Gardner, or should they concentrate on developing verbal and mathematical abilities? Explain your position.

3 ▸ What are the general characteristics of your learning style? If you don't know, visit one of the websites on learning styles and take an inventory to discover your preferred ways of learning.

4 ▸ How will you account for various learning styles in your students?

Students with Disabilities

■ types of disabilities

Within the range of diversity your students will display, some will have disabilities. The types of disabilities you may encounter are many. For example, you may have students with mental retardation, emotional disturbance, learning disabilities, attention deficit disorders, speech or language impairments, multiple handicaps, autism, traumatic brain injuries, orthopedic impairments, visual impairments or blindness, and hardness of hearing and deafness. Table 3.3 shows the

Visit this chapter of the website to link to up-to-date statistics on this topic.

TABLE 3.3 Specific Disabilities Among Children Age 6–21: Total and Percentage for Each Category

Disability	Number	Percentage*
Specific learning disabilities	2,887,115	49.2%
Speech or language impairments	1,093,581	18.6%
Mental retardation	605,267	10.3%
Emotional disturbance	477,627	8.1%
Other health impairments	338,658	5.8%
Multiple disabilities	128,552	2.2%
Autism	97,904	1.7%
Orthopedic impairments	73,821	1.3%
Hearing impairments	71,222	1.2%
Developmental delay	45,128	0.8%
Visual impairments	25,845	0.4%
Traumatic brain injury	20,743	0.3%
Deaf-blindness	1,615	0.2%
ALL DISABILITIES	5,867,078	100%

*percentages may not add up to 100 percent due to rounding.

Source: *Twenty-fourth Annual Report to Congress on the Implementation of the Individuals with Disabilities Education Act* (Washington, DC: U.S. Department of Education, 2002), p. II-20.

percentage and number of students in each of the officially recognized categories. During the 2001–02 school year, 5.87 million students, ages six to twenty-one, received federal aid for their disabilities; these students represented almost 12 percent of the total public school population. Over 600,000 additional children, ages three to five, also received federal aid for their disabilities.[16] In the fiscal year 2005, the federal government distributed over $11.6 billion to the states for students with disabilities.[17]

■ Public Law 94–142

■ **Special Education**   The term **special education** is often used as a designation for services designed for students with disabilities. In 1975, the *Education for All Handicapped Children Act (PL 94–142)* established the right of all students with disabilities to a "free appropriate public education" (FAPE). The law specified that each such student must be provided with an **individualized education program (IEP)** outlining both long-range and short-range goals for the child. Since that time, a number of other federal laws have reinforced and extended the commitment to special education.

The video case *Inclusion: Classroom Implications for the General and Special Educator* introduces you to an elementary-school teacher who has several special-needs students in their classes, and shows some of the specialists and adaptations that can help those students succeed in an inclusion setting. As you watch the clips and study the artifacts, reflect upon the following questions:

1. What were some of the strategies that the general teacher and the specialists used to keep the entire class functioning smoothly? Have seen other successful strategies throughout your own education?
2. Do you find the work of the general teacher or that of one or more of the specialists more interesting as a potential teaching position for you?
3. What information from this video case do you believe will be most helpful to you in your career as a teacher?

■ **Preschool Legislation**   *The Education of the Handicapped Act Amendments (PL 99–457),* passed in 1986, provided for early intervention for children from birth to age two who are developmentally delayed. For states that choose to participate, programs must include a multidisciplinary assessment of the child's needs, a written **individualized family services plan (IFSP),** and case management. Services may draw from a variety of areas, such as special education, speech and language pathology, occupational or physical therapy, or family training and counseling, depending on the developmental needs of the child.

PL 99–457 also stated that FAPE must be extended to children with disabilities ages three to five years. Although state and local education agencies administer these programs, they may contract with other programs, agencies, or providers to supply a range of services, such as programs that are home-based for part of the day. Families play a particularly important role in preschool education, and instruction for parents is to be included in the IFSP whenever that is appropriate and the parents desire it. When students reach school age, they are covered by the provisions of the Individuals with Disabilities Education Act (IDEA) discussed in the next section.

■ early intervention

■ **IDEA and ADA**   In 1990, Congress passed two significant federal laws: the *Individuals with Disabilities Education Act (IDEA),* subsequently amended in 1997 and again in 2004, and the *Americans with Disabilities Act (ADA).* IDEA amended the Education for All Handicapped Children Act of 1975. ADA ensures the right of individuals with disabilities to nondiscriminatory treatment in aspects of their lives other than education.

Six principles provide the framework of IDEA, around which education services are designed and provided to students with disabilities:

■ basic provisions of IDEA

- Fair and appropriate education (FAPE)
- Appropriate evaluation

- An individualized education program (IEP)
- Least restrictive environment (LRE)
- Parent and student participation in decision making
- Procedural safeguards

■ IEP's function

Because of the wide variety of disabilities and infinite degrees of severity in which these conditions may be found in individual students, IDEA mandates that a "free appropriate public education" be defined on an individual basis, using the written IEP first mandated in 1975. The IEP states the child's current levels of educational performance, short-term objectives and annual goals, services to be provided, and criteria and schedules for evaluation of progress. Thus, the IEP helps ensure that the educational goals designed for the child are appropriate to individual learning needs and that these plans are actually delivered and monitored. Provisions must be reviewed and revised annually—more often if necessary. Teachers, parents or guardians, special educators, other professionals, and the child (whenever appropriate) are all involved in the development and approval of the IEP. IDEA also requires that all older students with a disability (usually ages fourteen to sixteen) have an individualized plan for making the transition from school to work or additional education beyond high school through age twenty-one.

■ least restrictive environment

■ mainstreaming

■ inclusion

Like the original act of 1975, IDEA further stipulates that services for students with disabilities be provided in an LRE, meaning students with disabilities should be educated with children who are nondisabled to the greatest extent appropriate. Determination of what constitutes the **least restrictive environment** has been subject to great debate. The social and academic benefits of the regular classroom must be weighed against the unique educational needs and individual circumstances for each child. The term **mainstreaming** has long referred to the practice of placing special education students in general education classes for at least part of the school day while also providing additional services, programs, or classes as needed. More recently, the term **inclusion** has been used to mean the commitment to educate each child, to the maximum extent appropriate, in the regular school and classroom. Compared with mainstreaming, inclusion, particularly *full inclusion,* as it is sometimes called, generally indicates an even greater commitment to keeping students with disabilities in regular classrooms. Thus, it usually involves bringing the support services to the child rather than moving the child to services located in separate rooms or buildings. One special education teacher describes the beginning of her school year in this chapter's Voices from the Classroom.

Controversy over Inclusion

■ pros and cons of inclusion

Full inclusion has become a civil-rights issue, compared by some to racial desegregation. Advocates of full inclusion argue that segregated education for students with disabilities is inherently unequal and therefore a violation of the rights of the children who are segregated. They also argue that traditional special education programs have resulted in a costly special education bureaucracy that has not shown the expected benefits in terms of academic, social, or vocational skills. Among the benefits of full inclusion for children with disabilities, they say, are higher expectations and better socialization, as well as greater acceptance of human differences by nondisabled children. The Breaking Out box describes how one student with autism benefits from inclusion.

VOICES FROM THE CLASSROOM

Christine Hamm is currently a special education teacher for students with moderate to severe mental retardation at Anthony T. Lane Elementary School in Alexandria, VA. Previously, she served for three years as a Learning Disabilities teacher.

Co-Teaching and Scheduling

As I started my third year of teaching, I wondered what the new school year would be like. In my position as a sixth-grade LD (Learning Disabilities) teacher, I had adjusted to working with many different students and several general education teachers. I knew how much this position required being flexible and being able to work around other people's schedules to meet my students' needs.

I had a feeling that this year would bring more challenges, however, as I would be working with a group of twelve students and four new teachers. A new school had just opened nearby, and several of the teachers I previously worked with had transferred, so I was going to be dealing with a different sixth-grade team. Based on the IEPs I had piled up in front of me, it looked as though I'd be spending some part of my day working with students in my resource classroom, and the rest of my day co-teaching with two different teachers in two different general edu-

cation classrooms. Faced with this information, the scheduling nightmare began!

As my students enjoyed their first day playing getting-to-know-you games and organizing their binders in their general education classrooms, I sat surrounded by grids and calendars. I ran around to various rooms to catch people while I could, to ask questions about their pending schedules. It would be the end of the first week of school before I had even a draft schedule in place.

Then it was time for revisions—one after the other, based on changes to "specials," such music, PE, art, and library. I also had to factor in speech, occupational, and physical therapy services for some of the students, as well as counseling and social-skills groups. I made sure to schedule myself a few hour-long blocks in which to do testing and work on IEPs. I did so with the realization that, soon, these blocks would be filled with students needing help preparing for tests, making up missed homework assignments, etc. Beyond working with other teachers, parents, and of course the students and their individual needs, scheduling is by far the most difficult task when working in a resource and co-teaching position!

 Visit the website for more Voices from the Classroom.

Visit the material at the website to link to more information about inclusion.

Critics, on the other hand, say that both teachers and students are being hurt in the following ways in the rush to embrace inclusion:

- Parents of nondisabled children often worry that the curriculum standards will be lowered by the inclusion of students with learning disabilities and that those students with attention-deficit hyperactivity disorder (ADHD) or emotional problems can be a disruption to their classmates and teachers.
- Some special educators voice concern that full inclusion may result in diminished or inadequate specialized services for students who have special needs. They point out that the regular classroom may not be the best setting for every child. Violent or emotionally disordered children, for example, may pose a threat to themselves and their classmates. These educators are wary of eliminating the range of service delivery options currently available in favor of a pure inclusion model. Furthermore, they argue, there is little evidence that inclusion

Breaking Out: One School System's Success with Autistic Children

Robert Goodfellow, age six, has Asperger's Syndrome, a mild form of autism that combines uncanny knowledge and awkward social skills. Students with Asperger's may be masters in mathematics, science, or computers, for example, but require daily drilling on such basics as how to make eye contact or maintaining appropriate distance from other children.

Before he joined a special program in the Seattle school system, Robert would sit alone in his yard, peeling bark off of sticks he would find. He seemed fascinated by the process of removing the bark, often singing songs over and over again as he worked on the sticks. He also refused to bathe, clip his nails, or comb his hair.

Robert, however, has benefited greatly from a new program in the Seattle school district. With his teachers' encouragement, Robert has channeled his obsessiveness in more socially accepted ways. He has become an expert on the Seattle Mariners baseball team and has learned how to juggle extremely well. His new knowledge about the batting averages and other minutia of the Mariners, plus his juggling, have enabled Robert to relate better socially with his peers. They now admire his new knowledge and skills.

Students with Asperger's Syndrome tend to excel in subjects that interest them, but other aspects of school may be difficult for them. For example, the hustle and bustle of recess or lunch can be extremely stressful. The Seattle program aims to help children like Robert function in their world without alienating others by their eccentric behavior. Robert and other Asperger's students attend mainstream classes as much as possible, sometimes with a school aide, and only go to small special education classes when they need to work on a particular skill. The special education teachers function as case managers for the children, monitoring their schedules, serving as their advocates, and teaching them lessons on behavior, social skills, and life skills. Students in grades 1–4 are given visual cue cards to remind them of appropriate classroom behavior, such as raising their hands before speaking and sitting still.

There is no cure for autism disorders, but "high-functioning" people with autism can make useful, even outstanding, contributions to society. The Seattle school district began its program in 1997 with a single elementary-school pilot class for such high-functioning autistic children. Two years later the program was expanded districtwide, and twelve classes are now offered in elementary, middle, and high schools. There are plans to add even more classes in upcoming school years.

Because autism is one of the fastest-growing categories of disability in special education, it presents new challenges to school districts. The Seattle program has attracted considerable attention, and educators from around the country and even Japan and Korea have visited to learn more about how to help high-functioning autistic children succeed in school.

Source: Lisa Fine, "Cracking the Shell," *Education Week,* November 21, 2001, pp. 22–29.

---

programs strengthen students' academic achievement. (However, the same criticism could be made of many special education programs.)

- Overworked classroom teachers have complained that they are given inadequate resources and training to deal with students with disabilities. Ideally, when students with disabilities are included in regular classrooms, their teachers receive special training and help from a special education teacher who serves as either a co-teacher or a consultant. Cases are cited, however, in which teachers have been given sole responsibility for a class of thirty students, with as many as ten having disabilities. True collaboration between general education and special education teachers is essential for inclusion to work effectively.

FOR BETTER OR WORSE

FOR BETTER OR FOR WORSE © Lynn Johnston Productions. Distributed by Universal Press Syndicate. Reprinted with permission. All rights reserved.

■ special education costs

In too many instances, critics say, when children with disabilities are moved from resource rooms and self-contained classrooms into regular classrooms, the necessary supports do not follow. One reason is that some school districts use the cover of inclusion as a way to cut costs for special education services. Part B of IDEA originally authorized Congress to contribute up to 40 percent of the average per pupil expenditure (APPE) for each special education student. With over 6 million students served under IDEA, schools are qualified to receive $18 billion in federal funds. Unfortunately, in 2004 the federal government provided just under 20 percent of its commitment rather than the 40 percent specified by law, leaving the states and local school districts with a shortfall of $10.6 billion.[18] With voters reluctant to increase school taxes, and many school districts facing budget cuts as a result, some school boards and administrators see the inclusion movement as a way to save money by reducing funding for special education.

The 2004 re-authorization of IDEA committed the federal government in principle to paying 40 percent of the average per-pupil cost of educating a special education student by 2011. This is especially important since the 2001 "No Child Left Behind" law requires that special education students take the same achievement tests that regular education students take, although sometimes with certain accommodations.[19] Without additional funding, many special education students will not pass these tests, and their schools will fail to meet the provisions of the law. For more on the "No Child Left Behind" law, see the chapter "How Are Schools Governed, Influenced, and Financed?"

■ inclusion becoming widespread

Despite criticisms, one thing is certain: inclusion of children with disabilities is becoming increasingly common in American schools. More and more students with disabilities are taking part in regular classroom and school life with their nondisabled peers. Inclusion seems to thrive in schools that have a shared vision of the school's purposes; strong lines of communication among teachers, administrators, and parents; and cultures of innovation and reform. In many schools with successful inclusion programs, the presence of students with disabilities has sparked other reform initiatives such as cooperative learning, peer teaching, team teaching, authentic assessment, and interdisciplinary instruction.

■ **Assistive Technology**   Just as many students use contact lenses or glasses to help them compensate for poor eyesight, students with disabilities may rely on a variety of technology-based innovations to help them learn better. The term **assistive technology** refers to the array of devices and services that help people with disabilities perform better in their daily lives. Devices such as motorized chairs, remote control units to turn on appliances, voice recognition systems, ramps to enter and exit buildings, and computers can all assist people with severe disabilities. Computers are especially important in allowing many students with a range of disabilities to participate in normal classroom activities that would otherwise be impossible, and we discuss their use more in the chapter entitled "What Should Teachers Know About Technology and Its Impact on Schools?"

■ assistive technology incorporated into IDEA

Congress incorporated definitions of assistive technology in IDEA, declaring that such technology must be provided whenever necessary as an element of free and appropriate public education. Thus, assistive technology must be considered a potential component of the IEP for each student with disabilities.[20] As a new teacher, you should be prepared to encounter situations in which a child uses technology as a medium for interaction and engagement within your classroom.

■ **Teaching Implications**   Students with disabilities will likely be in your classroom for varying amounts of the school day, depending on the types and amount of support services they are receiving. How will you deal with the different needs of these children?

■ avoid stereotypes

It is most important that you do not stereotype these students. Certainly, different disabilities will have different implications for student learning. For example, a student with mental retardation may require repetition and practice to master simple concepts, whereas a student who uses a wheelchair may learn even the most difficult material quickly. Even within the parameters of each type of disability, however, you will probably encounter a wide range of differences. Consider two students identified as having learning disabilities. One may display a low-average intelligence quotient (IQ) and have extreme difficulty in mathematics; the other may have an extremely high IQ and have difficulty in reading. Both of these students have a learning disability, but you would not provide the same instruction for each of them or have the same expectations.

■ expect diversity

The point is to approach instruction for these children as you would for other students in the classroom: expect diversity, anticipate a range of abilities, and look for the particular strengths and learning profiles of each student. A helpful resource for recognizing student abilities and suggesting instructional strategies will be the special education teacher(s) in your school. The more you and a special education teacher can coordinate instruction and services for your students with disabilities, the better the students' educational experiences are likely to be.

Here are a few other suggestions about how you as a regular education teacher can be effective in teaching children with disabilities in your classroom:

■ guidelines for teaching students with disabilities

1. Be open to the idea of including students with disabilities in your classroom.
2. Learn about each child's limitations and potential and about available curriculum methodologies and technologies to help the child learn.
3. Insist that any needed services be provided.
4. Pair students with disabilities with children who can help them.
5. Use a variety of teaching strategies, including hands-on activities, peer tutoring, and cooperative learning strategies.
6. Avail yourself of opportunities for co-teaching with a special education teacher.[21]

Pause and Reflect

1 ▶ Have you had any contact with individuals with disabilities (for example, a relative or neighbor)? What did you learn from this relationship that might be helpful in your teaching?

2 ▸ What is your position on the issue of "full inclusion"? What reservations, if any, do you have?

3 ▸ Do you have any concerns about your ability to work with students who have disabilities? What do you think will be the most rewarding aspects of working with these students?

Gifted and Talented Students

One of the most challenging types of students is the gifted or talented child. The term *talented* most often refers to an ability or skill (for example, musical or artistic talent) that may not be matched by the child's more general abilities, whereas the term *gifted* usually includes intellectual ability. The gifted child is extremely bright, quickly grasping the ideas and concepts you are teaching and making interpretations or extrapolations that you may not even have considered. Gifted children may also have a creativity that shows itself in original thinking or artistic creations.

Students who are gifted and/or talented are sometimes overlooked when educators talk about students with special needs. Although special educational care and services for students with disabilities have long been recognized and accepted, American education has been slow to accept the notion that gifted children require special adaptations in both curricula and teaching methods. Because the idea of giftedness implies an elitism to many Americans, it seems undemocratic to provide special services to children who already enjoy an intellectual advantage. However, as one educator says, "Highly gifted children are as far from the norm in the direction of giftedness as the severely retarded are in the other direction."[22] Therefore, they do have special needs.

■ high dropout rate

As a result of neglected needs, gifted and talented students drop out of school at rates far exceeding the dropout rates for their nongifted peers. Many of those who stay in school feel unchallenged and become bored and apathetic. The result is that many of our brightest and most talented minds are being turned off or underdeveloped. Only recently have school districts begun to make serious efforts to identify gifted children and develop special programs for them.

■ meanings of gifted and talented

■ **Identifying Gifted and Talented Students**   The areas in which states identify gifted and talented students can range from intellectual to psychomotor to artistic, with many variations. Through its evolution, the study of giftedness has moved increasingly toward more *inclusive* definitions and away from more *exclusive* ones. As we described earlier in the chapter, intelligence is now thought by many to be composed of multiple factors, not just one or two as was previously thought. As a result, in many schools, the definition of giftedness is shifting away from an emphasis on general intellectual ability toward the recognition that giftedness occurs in a variety of areas, such as mathematics, language, spatial ability, and kinesthetics.

■ reliance on scores and grades

■ avoid cut-off points

In the past, school districts have tended to rely heavily on general intelligence and achievement tests in their assessment of students' intellectual abilities, as well as on teacher recommendations and grades earned in school. There is a danger, however, of letting the tools used to identify the children become synonymous with the *definition* of gifted and talented. To avoid this danger, teachers and administrators must study and interpret the data the tools provide rather than take the data at face value and use them for hard-and-fast cut-off points. Whether to recommend a child for a special program is a decision that should be made by the responsible teacher and other professional educators on the basis of their objective and subjective appraisals of the student, the nature of the gifted program or activity, and the atmosphere in which the student lives and goes to school. Parents should be a significant part of these discussions. The point is that the complexity of the variables involved requires that individual decisions be made by professionals using their best judgments rather than according to arbitrary, predetermined cut-off points on tests.

■ minorities underrepresented

A major concern in the identification of gifted and talented students centers on the underrepresentation of economically disadvantaged students, learning-disabled students, and certain minority students. Asian American students are well represented in gifted and talented programs, but African American and Hispanic students are underrepresented in terms of their proportion in the total school population. Thus, educators and parents are concerned that the measures being used to identify gifted and talented youngsters may work to the disadvantage of African Americans, Hispanics, and children from low-income families. The problem of identification is especially acute for bilingual children and children adjusting to a new culture.

Visit the material at the website to link to more information about talented and gifted children.

■ **Programs for Gifted and Talented Students** Programs for gifted and talented students exist in every state and in many school districts, but the exact number of students served cannot be determined because not all states and localities collect this information. We do know, however, that by the year 2002, thirty-one states reported serving almost 2.6 million K–12 gifted students and spending at least $624 million on gifted and talented programs.[23]

The two main strategies for serving gifted children are **acceleration** and **enrichment.** With an accelerated curriculum, gifted children can learn at a pace commensurate with their abilities, allowing them to progress to advanced materials faster than their age norms or grade levels. Enrichment activities, on the other hand, provide gifted students with opportunities to go beyond the regular curriculum in greater depth and breadth, to engage in independent or collaborative inquiry that develops their problem-solving abilities, research skills, and creativity.

■ various approaches

Current educational programs for gifted and talented students are quite varied. Some programs establish special schools that are designed only for gifted or talented students and have special admission requirements. In such schools, stimulating courses can be devised and taught without concern for students who might be unable to keep pace, and teachers and students can be recruited on the basis of their talents.

Other programs adapt and enrich the regular school curriculum for gifted and talented children by grouping these students together for all or part of their instruction. This option normally is more flexible and practical than special schools. Classes can be established on a continuing or short-term basis, in any subject area, with the intention of either enriching or accelerating the student.

■ inclusion of gifted students

Most gifted and talented students, however, are likely to receive all, or nearly all, of their education in regular classrooms. In many school districts, in fact, separate programs for gifted students are being curtailed or phased out. The primary reasons for this trend are the spread of a philosophy that favors mixed-ability grouping, the cessation of tracking, and a lack of funds for separate gifted programs. The move to meet gifted students' needs within the regular classroom is parallel to the inclusion movement in special education. Some advocates for gifted education programs are disturbed by this trend, concerned that gifted students will be shortchanged in the regular classroom. They fear that teachers will concentrate their efforts on struggling students or that gifted students will be drafted to serve as tutors for these students rather than working to their own potential. Supporters of the current trend, however, believe that most gifted students' needs can be met in the regular classroom if teachers can differentiate curriculum and instruction for them and increase the level of challenge.

Still others argue that it is important to keep a continuum of programs and services available for gifted students if for no other reason than that they represent a valuable resource to the nation. Along with the regular classroom, these educators argue, the options should include pullout programs, special classes, and separate centers and schools. A range of giftedness exists, and whereas some students will do just fine in a regular classroom, others can benefit from different programs.

■ **Teaching Implications**   If you want to focus on teaching gifted students, your state may be one of the twenty or so that require you to obtain a gifted endorsement to your teaching license. It is more likely, however, that you will discover certain students in your class to be gifted or talented and, lacking any special program, you will be responsible for teaching these students as part of your regular class. Or, if your school or school district has special programs for gifted and talented students, you may be expected to work with resource teachers to help prepare individualized education plans for these students. What do you need to know?

■ guidelines for teaching gifted and talented students

If 2 + 3 is always going to be 5, why do they keep teaching it to us?

—A GIFTED FIRST-GRADE STUDENT

1. Recognize that gifted pupils generally learn the standard curricular skills and content quickly and easily. They need teaching that does not tie them to a limited range, that is not preoccupied with filling them with facts and information, but allows them to use the regular class as a forum for research, inquiry, and projects that are meaningful to them.

2. Realize that these students are persistently curious. They need teachers who encourage them to maintain confidence in their own ideas, even when those ideas differ from the norm.

3. Teach these pupils to be efficient and effective at independent study so that they can develop the skills required for self-directed learning and for analyzing and solving problems independently. Allow students of varying abilities to work together in areas of high interest, such as social action research projects.

4. Help students apply complex cognitive processes such as creative thinking, critiques, and pro and con analyses.

5. Expand your ideas concerning what instructional materials are available. Consider businesses, religious groups, national parks, and resource people as sources of potential instructional materials in addition to the textbooks and reference books available in the school. Be sure to investigate any technological resources that are available, including World Wide Web sites and other electronic links to information and knowledgeable people outside the school.

6. Use differentiated instructional strategies such as flexible grouping, "tiered" assignments (in which all students explore the same topic but the level of questions or products produced varies depending on students' abilities),

learning centers, student contracts, and mentorships. (See the chapter entitled "What Is Taught?" for more on differentiated instruction.)

7. Implement *curriculum compacting,* in which teachers test students on what they already know on upcoming units. Students who demonstrate mastery in advance are allowed to accelerate through the material or pursue enrichment activities while the unit is being taught to the rest of the class.

8. Match students with *mentors* to help develop talent and engage students in relevant and applied problem solving. Mentoring programs encourage independent growth, increased self-confidence, and a willingness to reach out into new, untried areas.

Pause and Reflect

1 ▸ What do you think will be the most challenging aspect of teaching gifted or talented students? How can you prepare for that challenge? What will be most rewarding?

▶ Diverse Needs

In addition to the diversity of racial, ethnic, and cultural backgrounds, as well as ability levels that we have discussed so far, another element of diversity occurs within each individual. We all have basic physical and psychological needs, including needs for belonging, safety, and self-esteem. Our needs, however, may vary in their prominence and expression because of individual circumstances. Your students bring their own individual histories and backgrounds, as well as conditions that have influenced how and whether certain needs have been satisfied. For example, a child from a stable, secure home may have different needs than a child who has not had this kind of security. One way to understand the diverse needs of students is to see how one prominent psychiatrist and educator, William Glasser, has conceptualized the basic needs of all individuals.

Glasser's Choice Theory

■ choice theory

Glasser begins with the premise that each of us is born with fundamental needs for survival, love and belonging, power, freedom, and fun.[24] Throughout our lives, our motivations, actions, and behaviors are attempts to satisfy these needs. Glasser's idea, called **choice theory,** is that if we understand and identify these needs within ourselves, we can make conscious choices about how best to meet them. The recognition of our ability to make choices results in personal empowerment: we have control over how we choose to react to external events and information.

Glasser believes that teachers should empower their students through the use of choice theory. He states that effective teachers combine the needs of students with classroom assignments or activities. The more students are convinced that their schoolwork satisfies their needs, the harder they will try and the better work they will produce. For example, when asked what is the best part of school, many students respond, "My friends." According to Glasser, this expresses the students' built-in need for friendship, love, and belonging. Rather than structure classroom settings to suppress this need, such as by emphasizing independent seatwork or

Schools help students meet social, as well as academic, needs.
(© Charles Gupton/CORBIS)

teacher lectures, teachers should find ways to let students associate with others in class as a planned part of learning. Glasser refers to this kind of cooperative grouping as the use of *learning teams.*

■ learning teams, power needs

Teaching students in cooperative learning teams also meets students' needs for power. Using the term *power* synonymously with *self-esteem* or *sense of importance,* Glasser explains that to fulfill this need students must have the sense that someone they respect listens to them.

The video case *Motivating Adolescent Learners: Curriculum Based on Real Life* shows how one middle-school math teacher helps students meet some of the needs Glasser describes. As you watch the clips and study the artifacts in the case, reflect upon the following questions:

1. Which of the student needs described by Glasser are met by working in the school store?
2. What are some other ways that teachers might help students meet their needs for power and belonging?

Unfulfilled needs for power often result in a number of undesirable attention-getting behaviors. Glasser believes these misguided efforts to achieve power are the source of 95 percent of discipline problems in school. In accordance with choice theory, he suggests that teachers structure opportunities for students to fulfill needs for power appropriately during the school day. In addition to learning teams, in which students interact and listen to one another in the learning process, Glasser suggests that teachers provide opportunities for student input and a forum for students to be heard. Glasser also recommends self-evaluation of homework, classwork, and tests. He believes that students need to be encouraged to set their own standards for quality work and to evaluate whether they are meeting those standards. This helps satisfy the need for power and instills an internal standard for achievement in education and work.

Glasser proposes that students' needs for freedom and fun, although important, are not at the core of problems in schools. Students generally understand the need for some structure in dealing with large groups of people, and they realize that rules and regulations must govern behavior in school, even though they limit individual freedom. Although fun is an essential need, students who have a sense of belonging in school and a forum for personal power are already likely to be experiencing fun.

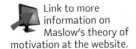

Link to more information on Maslow's theory of motivation at the website.

Glasser's theory of personal empowerment provides one interesting way of viewing and identifying a wide variety of student needs. Other approaches, such as Abraham Maslow's hierarchy of needs theory, may also be useful. The most important point is that teachers must be aware of their students' varying needs and respond accordingly in the classroom.

Adolescent Subcultures

■ how crowds are labeled

Teenagers often satisfy their needs for belonging, power, and fun by forming crowds, or groups that share common characteristics and reflect status among their peers. Most schools have crowds of elites, average students, and outcasts, with various terms used to describe them, including *jocks, preppies, rockers, brains, punks, freaks, kickers, gangstas, nerds/geeks/dweebs,* and *goths.* Elite groups, such as the jocks and preppies, are the "leading crowd," who enthusiastically participate in, and receive the endorsement of, the school. The outcasts, such as the punks or the goths, tend to have an adversarial rather than cooperative relationship with the high school because they believe school doesn't serve their needs well. The outcasts are contemptuous of the elites' interest in student government and athletics, while the elites reject the outcasts' resistance to authority and achievement.

■ symbols of membership

Each crowd has attitudes, behaviors, or dress characteristics that distinguish it from all other crowds. Clothing and adornment are probably the most powerful symbolic indicators of category membership, although each crowd also tends to stake out particular territories of the school as its own. As members of these adolescent subcultures, teenagers can express their own attitudes, explore personal relationships, and test themselves against others. For example, a high school we know recently cancelled its fall dance because the student body could not agree on the genre of music to be played. There were six contenders, each with a solid group of supporters. After weeks on controversy and amid angry talk of boycotts, school authorities gave up in frustration and called off the event.

■ adolescent development and crowds

Membership in teenage subcultures begins to form in the middle and junior high schools as crowds develop around particular interests such as athletics, academics, student government, drugs, and tastes in cars and music. Often, teens don't even select a group as much as they are placed into one because of their image among their peers. These groups strengthen as the teenagers begin to move away from their families, and peer membership becomes a type of new family where youngsters find comfort and support. By senior year, however, the hold of the subcultures on students has weakened. The students develop more self-confidence, and they seek greater personal freedom. At this point, the friendship group becomes a drag on their autonomy. Until that happens, however, the teen subcultures exert a strong influence on the values of their members.

Most high schools have done a reasonably good job of making academically and socially oriented students an integral part of school life. They have been less successful with other subcultures like the various outcast groups. In fact, because groups like the punks or goths reject the schools' values, the schools may be reinforcing their alienation. Finding ways to bring members of alienated subcultures into participation in their schools, bring the loners or outsiders into greater contact with their peers, and channel peer influence as a positive force is a major challenge for high school and middle school educators.

Pause and Reflect

1 ▶ Are you comfortable with the idea of sharing power with students through such techniques as having them evaluate their own homework? Why or why not? What other ways can you think of to empower your students or help them meet their social needs?

2 ▶ What kinds of school activities might be appealing to members of traditionally outcast groups?

▶ Gender

Earlier in this chapter, we made the point that some racial and ethnic groups have been denied equal educational opportunities throughout our country's history. Another group, women, has also suffered discrimination and denial of equal educational opportunities; historically, women in our society have been denied educational and employment opportunities routinely extended to men. In recent years, however, considerable progress has been made to address these inequities. For example, women now constitute the majority of college students and have gained admittance into many professions from which they were previously excluded. Teachers must be alert to avoid unfairness in their treatment of either girls or boys.

■ differences in socialization

Fairness and equality may be difficult to achieve, however, because by the time they get to school, boys and girls are already used to being treated differently. From very young ages through adulthood, society holds different expectations for males and females. These expectations, in turn, generate different patterns of behavior toward boys and girls. Whether it is pink or blue clothes, G.I. Joe or Barbie dolls, video games or drawing kits, or football helmets or ballet slippers, boys and girls get different messages from society about what is expected of them. Society tolerates aggressive behavior more in boys than in girls. Boys are encouraged to be independent, whereas girls often are expected to conform to accepted norms.

The video case *Gender Equity in the Classroom: Girls and Science* shows how one middle-school science teacher meets the needs of all his students: boys *and* girls. As you watch the clips and study the artifacts in the case, reflect upon the following questions:

1. This section of the chapter describes several ways in which boys and girls are treated differently in school. Which of these does this teacher avoid? How?
2. Did your own teachers treat male and female students differently? What do you think was the result?
3. In addition to those listed in this chapter, what are some ways that you, as a teacher, can be fair to boys and girls in your classes?

Classroom Interactions and School Achievement

This situation is not confined to the home. Numerous observational studies have concluded that teachers treat boys differently than girls, often to the girls' detriment, although teachers are generally unaware of their behaviors that favor boys.[25] Research suggests that in subtle and not-so-subtle ways, female students get the message that boys are more important than girls because teachers pay more attention to boys.

At all levels of schooling, for example, male students have more interactions with teachers than do female students. Although boys receive more criticism from teachers than do girls, they also receive more praise. Boys receive more precise feedback from teachers than do girls. Males are more likely to dominate classroom discussions, whereas females tend to sit quietly. Boys are more likely to call out, and when they do, teachers are apt to accept the call-out and continue

■ males dominate interactions

Boys often dominate classroom discussions unless teachers take steps to ensure participation on the part of girls. (© Myrleen Ferguson/PhotoEdit)

with the class. When girls call out, a much less frequent occurrence, the teacher's typical response is to correct the inappropriate behavior. As a result, boys receive more attention simply by demanding it. As Myra and David Sadker, two leading researchers in gender equity research, report, "As victims of benign neglect, girls are penalized for doing what they should and lose ground as they go through school. In contrast, boys get reinforced for breaking the rules; they are rewarded for grabbing more than their fair share of the teacher's time and attention."[26]

■ biased curriculum materials?

Cultural influences are also at work. Several other researchers have charged that gender bias abounds in the schools and is even taught informally in the curriculum. Textbooks, other reading materials, and educational software, despite recent attempts at improvement by publishers and authors, often still portray females as more helpless than males. Although sexism has decreased in many texts, these researchers argue that examples of gender stereotyping, tokenism, and omission often still occur in references to girls and women.

■ AAUW report

■ effects of gender bias

The American Association of University Women (AAUW) issued a controversial report in 1992, *How Schools Shortchange Girls,* describing various ways in which girls are adversely treated in schools and the achievement gaps between boys and girls that result.[27] In 1998, the AAUW updated those findings in *Gender Gaps: Where Schools Still Fail Our Children.* This latter report contends that, although much progress has been made to reduce academic gender gaps, some still remain. Girls have closed the gap in terms of the number of courses taken in mathematics and science, but gender differences remain in the kinds of courses taken, with boys more often taking advanced courses. Girls are also much less likely to enroll in computer science classes in high school than are boys. On the other hand, girls take more advanced-placement (AP) courses in English, biology, and foreign languages. The long-term effects of gender bias taught or reinforced in schools are potentially many: fewer women are in professions and occupations that emphasize mathematics and science, such

If women are expected to do the same work as men, we must teach them the same things.

—PLATO

as engineering and medicine; fewer women are in executive leadership positions in business, government, and education; and women have lower earning power because fewer of them are represented in positions of leadership.

The AAUW report concludes that the goal of school excellence that propels the standards movement is the same goal behind gender equity, yet few states that have adopted standards acknowledge equity issues in their language. Addressing the learning styles of all students, the report argues, is the best way to ensure high educational attainment for boys and girls.[28]

■ not everyone agrees

Some observers challenge the assertion that schools discriminate against girls. One clinical psychologist researcher at Harvard University argues that schools don't accommodate boys' learning styles and classroom needs. Boys perform best, he reports, when they have frequent recess breaks and are able to roam around the classroom. Boys are also more likely to enjoy argument and lively classroom debate, which is often discouraged.[29]

Researchers also cite the fact that the large gaps between the education levels of women and men that were evident in the early 1970s have essentially disappeared for the younger generation. Although females still lag behind males in science and higher-level mathematics achievement, high school females on average outperform males in reading and writing, take more credits in academic subjects, are more likely to be inducted into the National Honor Society, are more likely to attend college after high school, and are as likely to graduate with a postsecondary degree. Furthermore, two-thirds of all students receiving special education services are boys. If schools were really so biased against females, they argue, why are women doing so well academically?

Certainly women have made tremendous progress in educational attainment. What remains to be seen, however, is how these attainments will be rewarded in the marketplace. The average earnings of female high school graduates, aged 25–34 are 85 percent of what their male counterparts receive. Even worse, female college graduates in the same age bracket earn salaries that are only 60 percent of what their male counterparts receive.[30] Women have made important advances recently in gaining equal educational opportunities with men, but our society still seems to favor males when it comes to prestigious jobs and salaries.

■ **Teaching Implications**   What can you do to make sure that you are being fair to both male and female students in your classroom? To ensure sex-equitable learning environments in classrooms, teachers should consider the following steps:

- Have high expectations for all students.
- Examine instructional materials to be certain that sex role stereotyping or bias does not occur.
- Examine the frequency with which students are called on and the kind of responses that they provide the students to ensure that gender biases are not occurring. This can be done by audiotaping teacher/student interactions and listening to unintended patterns of interaction.
- Look at who uses or is encouraged to use computer technology in the classroom. Often, boys tend to monopolize computers and other technology.
- Eliminate the assignment of sex-stereotyped tasks.
- Organize classes so that students don't segregate themselves by sex.
- Model sex-equitable behavior.

▶ Sexual Orientation

You are likely to have gay and lesbian students in your classroom, especially if you teach at the middle or high school level, and you are apt to encounter gay and lesbian parents of students at any level.

■ schools hostile to homosexuals

There is considerable evidence that school is often a hostile environment for young homosexuals. Teenagers tend to ridicule differences in general and homosexuality in particular. Gay and lesbian students have often experienced taunting, harassment, and even violence because of their sexual orientation. Teachers and administrators who condone such name calling as "queer" or "faggot" while prohibiting profanity or racial slurs are also promoters of hostility toward homosexual youth. In fact, there have been recent cases where gay students won lawsuits against school officials for failing to maintain a safe school environment and to discipline students who regularly tormented them.

■ gays, a high-risk population

The hostility that gay and lesbian youth encounter in school is mirrored in the larger society, which bombards them with messages that they are outcasts. This hostility leaves many of them isolated, frightened, and uncertain about their own worth. As a result, gay students are a high-risk population. Many run away from home or are thrown out by parents, abuse drugs and alcohol, suffer from depression, or attempt suicide. One youth risk behavior survey conducted in Massachusetts found that more than one-third of self-identified gay, lesbian, or bisexual teenagers reported having attempted suicide in the previous twelve months.[31]

The National Education Association, the American Federation of Teachers, and the Association for Supervision and Curriculum Development have all passed resolutions calling on their members and school districts to acknowledge the special needs of homosexual students, provide supportive services such as counseling and support groups, and implement anti-harassment measures. In 1993, Massachusetts became the first state to ban anti-gay discrimination in public schools, and establish a statewide "safe schools" program. By 2001, four other states had followed suit. In 1997 the U.S. Department of Education issued guidelines spelling out that "gay or lesbian students" are covered by federal prohibitions against sexual harassment.[32]

However, the issue of homosexuality is extremely controversial, and actions urged by these organizations are certain to provoke opposition by some community members who believe such steps would signal that the schools are condoning homosexuality. Some people believe that while touting tolerance, gay and lesbian organizations are actually seeking to promote homosexuality among students. In spite of such controversy, all students, regardless of sexual orientation, have the right to a safe and supportive learning environment. As educators, we also have the responsibility to promote the emotional well-being of all of our students.

■ **Teaching Implications** There are many things that schools and educators can do to make school safer for all students, as well as those who are gay or lesbian, including the following:

- Establish classroom guidelines about name-calling.
- Address all name-calling immediately.
- Respect different points of view.
- Make no assumptions about students' families or their sexual orientations.
- Be role models for how all students should be treated with respect and dignity.

Pause and Reflect

1 ▶ Do schools treat boys and girls equally? What examples can you cite to support your response?

2 ▶ Do you have any beliefs or attitudes that would inhibit you from treating gay or lesbian students fairly in your classroom? If so, what, if anything, do you intend to do about it?

▶ The Teacher's Response to Diversity

So far in this chapter, we have presented a great deal of information about the diversity of the children you will be teaching. Ultimately, how these children are educated will come down to you and your daily interactions with them in your classroom. How will you deal with diversity?

Teacher-Student Disparity

■ the typical teacher

Consider what we know about the typical teacher today. Women and whites predominate in the teacher force; 75 percent of all public school teachers are women, and almost 91 percent of those teaching in public schools are white.[33] Despite efforts to increase the number of minority teachers (see the chapter entitled "What Are Your Job Options in Education?"), this gap between teachers and students is likely to continue for some time. Profiles of preservice and beginning teachers show similar gender, racial, and ethnic patterns. Most of these teachers, moreover, come from relatively stable family backgrounds. The majority of teachers and future teachers in our classrooms, then, come from very different backgrounds than many of the students they teach.

■ preparing for student diversity

As we mentioned in the chapter "What Is a School and What Is It For?" the more alike students and teachers are in social and cultural characteristics, the more they share tacit expectations about behavior and academic performance. However, as social and cultural characteristics become increasingly disparate, teachers need to rely on solid pedagogical training to overcome these differences. Too often white educators have been reluctant to recognize that their own backgrounds and the culture of the school have an effect on learning. As an incoming teacher, you will need to know about the commonalities and differences among students, and you will need to learn specific methods and techniques for addressing the plurality of culture and learning styles you will encounter.

Diversity: A Complex Phenomenon

The school programs described in this chapter have been designed to address student diversity and create a more equal educational opportunity for children in our school systems. An inherent danger in these approaches to addressing diversity, however, is the tendency to label children and form stereotypic images of who they are. Remember that student performance in school is affected by many factors, including social and cultural trends. The educational groupings we have been discussing are an administrative convenience, not a naturally occurring segmentation of children. Within each of these groups, each child will vary along a number of dimensions and have very different learning profiles of strengths and weaknesses.

■ differences, not deficits

Rather than thinking of minority students as having a culture that is valid, albeit different, from theirs, teachers sometimes think of these students as deficient. We encourage you, as a teacher, to remember that we are talking about *differences* in students, not necessarily deficits. Teachers are challenged to recognize the diversity of cultures represented by their students and to address these cultures in their teaching.

Implications for Teachers

Given this profile of the cultural discrepancy between students and teachers, and the complex diversity of today's student body, how can prospective teachers best prepare? Here are some steps you can take now:

■ steps to take

- Seek out experiences to broaden your understanding of societal and cultural commonalities and differences (for example, travel to foreign countries).
- Spend time in communities whose residents differ from you in terms of ethnicity, culture, or language.
- Volunteer in schools that differ from those you attended.

Once you have your own classroom, what can you do to address diversity there? Here are some guidelines:

- Learn about and appreciate the values and backgrounds of your students.
- Teach to your students' strengths rather than making them feel incapable or deficient.
- Provide a variety of educational experiences, and find ways for all students to achieve recognition from you and their peers for being good at something.
- Coordinate expertise and support with your students' parents or caregivers and other professional staff at the school so that students get a consistent message.
- Recognize that the schools' traditional emphasis on middle-class values such as individual learning and competition may clash with the values represented by their students' cultures. Teachers can provide opportunities for students to learn ways to succeed in today's dominant culture, but they must also respect the value systems in students' home lives and help them, in positive ways, to bridge the gap between the two worlds.

▶ A Final Word

At one time, the only business of schools was to educate students, but now, because of the increasing complexity and diversity of our students' lives, other needs are being addressed and incorporated into the way schools are approaching "education." A major goal of this chapter has been to make you aware of the complexity of issues that directly affect many children's lives and their ability to get an adequate education.

■ help for teachers

You may be getting concerned about whether you can handle the range of diversities you may face in your classroom. Be assured, however, that you are not in this alone. Various assistance systems have been devised to help the teacher respond to the range of student needs. Besides having other teachers and administrators to help you, most schools have specialists, such as nurses, school psychologists, and counselors, who often can give you valuable advice or direct help to your students.

A growing number of parent councils involve parents in giving advice and helping to deal with problems. Teacher aides may be community members who speak the language of substantial minorities in the schools. Interns or students from the local college may help as well, providing another adult in the classroom.

You will need to use all the resources available to you, including parents and other professionals. Some teachers may initially feel threatened by this involvement or have a sense that the classroom is their "turf." As we have seen throughout this chapter, however, our students need the coordinated expertise and support of all school professionals and the crucial link with parents to be given a fair shot at acquiring the good education that is their due.

Key Terms

acceleration (73)
assimilation (54)
assistive technology (70)
bilingual education (60)
choice theory (75)
cultural pluralism (54)
culturally responsive teaching (57)

enrichment (73)
inclusion (67)
individualized education program (IEP) (66)
individualized family services plan (IFSP) (66)
learning styles (64)

least restrictive environment (LRE) (67)
limited English proficient (LEP) (59)
mainstreaming (67)
multicultural education (56)
multiple intelligences (62)
special education (66)

For Reflection

1 How do you compare to the profile of the typical teacher described at the end of this chapter?

2 Would you like to be a teacher of gifted or talented children? Why or why not?

3 What other elements of diversity will you find in your students that have not been discussed in this chapter? How will you be sensitive to these differences?

For Debate

Read the Policy Matters! summary, "The Battle Over Bilingual Education," on the website, and consider the issues it outlines regarding teaching English language learners, and then go to EduSpace to post your answers (or respond to other students' answers) to the "What Do You Think?" questions listed in the Policy Matters! feature.

For Further Information

PRINT RESOURCES

Frank Coffield, David Moseley, Elaine Hall, and Kathryn Ecclestone, *Should We Be Using Learning Styles? What Research Has to Say to Practice* (London: The Learning and Skills Research Centre, 2004).
A thorough examination of thirteen different models of learning styles regarding issues related to reliability, validity, and pedagogical uses.

Lisa Delpit, *Other People's Children: Cultural Conflict in the Classroom* (New York: The New Press, 1995). Asking why schools have such a hard time making school a happy place for poor children and children of color, the author concludes that most classrooms are dominated by a white perspective and too few teachers acknowledge that children of color have perspectives of their own.

Howard Gardner, *Multiple Intelligences: The Theory in Practice* (New York: Basic Books, 1993).
A mixture of previously published articles and lectures and chapters written specifically for this book explain the theory of multiple intelligences and how it can be applied in today's schools.

Geneva Gay, *Culturally Responsive Teaching: Theory, Research and Practice* (New York: Teachers College Press, 2000).

The author makes a convincing case for using culturally responsive teaching to improve the school performance of underachieving students of color.

Manjari Singh, "Gender Issues in Children's Literature," (Bloomington, IN: ERIC Clearinghouse on Reading, English, and Communication, 1998). ED424591 98. Available at: **http://www. kidsource.com/education/gender. issues.L.A.html.**
An ERIC Digest report on how the genders are portrayed in children's books, and how these portrayals contribute to the images children develop of their own role and that of their gender in society.

Judy W. Kugelmass, *The Inclusive School* (New York: Teachers College Press, 2005).
Looking at a public elementary school, the author shows how committed educators can collaborate to maintain a creative, inclusive educational environment and still rise to the demands of state-imposed standards.

Murray Milner, Jr., *Freaks, Geeks, and Cool Kids: American Teenagers, Schools, and the Culture of Consumption* (New York: Routledge, 2004).

WEB RESOURCES

University of Virginia, *Office of Special Education: A Web Resource for Special Education.* Available at: **http://curry.edschool.virginia.edu/go/specialed.**
This website at the Curry School of Education at the University of Virginia contains much information about special education, including the history of the field and types of disabilities. It also offers discussion groups, electronic addresses of special educators, and much more.

Multicultural Pavilion. Available at: **http://curry.edschool.virginia.edu/go/ multicultural.**
This website at the Curry School of Education, University of Virginia, has many resources for incorporating multicultural aspects into a curriculum.

National Clearinghouse for English Language Acquisition. Available at: **http://www.ncela.gwu.edu.**
Funded by the U.S. Department of Education, this site contains hundreds of articles, links, databases, and online assistance in the area of English language acquisition.

Association for Supervision and Curriculum Development (ASCD). Available at: **http://www.ascd.org.**
ASCD has many resources on multiple intelligences and learning styles. Click on Education Topics, *Multiple Intelligences,* for more resources on this topic.

The author looks at adolescent subcultures, concluding that teenagers are obsessed with status because they have so little real economic or political power. He explores the various subcultures found in American secondary schools.

Sonia Nieto, *The Light in Their Eyes: Creating Multicultural Learning Communities* (New York: Teachers College Press, 1999).
This book draws on research in learning styles, multiple intelligences, and cognitive theories to portray the ways in which students learn. It also discusses the social context of learning and the influence of culture on learning.

Guadalupe Valdes, *Learning and Not Learning English* (New York: Teachers College Press, 2001).
This book addresses the difficulties surrounding the teaching and learning of English for second language learners by focusing on the lives and experiences of four Mexican children in an American middle school. Raises important questions about current ESL teaching policies.

Learning Disabilities Resource Community, *Multiple Intelligences Inventory.* Available at: **http://www.ldrc.ca/projects/miinventory/ miinventory.php.**
This site tests which intelligence you favor.

VARK Questionnaire. Available at: **http://www.varklearn.com/english/ page.asp?p=questionnaire.**
This questionnaire assesses whether learners prefer visual, aural, reading-writing, or kinesthetic learning.

Learning Style Inventory. Available at: **http://rrcc-online.com/%7Epsych/ LSInventory.html.**
This is another test of visual, auditory, or tactile preferences.

Paragon Learning Style Inventory. Available at: **http://www.calstatela.edu/faculty/jshindl/plsi/.**
This inventory is somewhat similar to the Myers-Briggs personality tests used in business that give you a four-letter description of your style.

American Association of University Women. Available at: **http://www.aauw.org.**
The AAUW is an organization of 150,000 college graduates dedicated to equity and education for women and girls. It conducts many studies on gender issues.

4

What Social Problems Affect Today's Students?

Chapter Preview Rarely a day goes by when the American public is not assaulted by news of some heartbreaking event or newly revealed problem involving the nation's young. Because formal education is so much a part of their lives, many of the youth-related issues and problems spill over and affect our schools and classrooms. This chapter explores some of the most sensitive and controversial issues in American education. Naturally, in such a short space we can treat each topic only briefly. However, we urge you to pursue additional reading on each issue.

This chapter emphasizes that:

► Many school-age children are affected by critical problems that directly influence their lives and often spill over into the classroom. Among these problems are severe poverty, homelessness, teenage parenting, child abuse, alcohol and drug abuse, and adolescent suicide.

► Violence and vandalism are not confined to urban schools; they are problems in all of our schools and in our society.

► School dropout rates, although improving, reflect disparities among various groups and foreshadow future societal problems.

► Sex education remains as controversial as ever, although concern about acquired immune deficiency syndrome (AIDS) has strengthened the argument for proponents of sex education.

The children who stream into a teacher's classroom each September bring their own personal histories. Although they may wish to start afresh with the beginning of the new school year, much of who they are is wrapped up in their past and their current out-of-school lives. It is likely that some of these students bear deep scars from their past experiences and that some are currently caught up in desperate widespread social problems. We wish to make you more fully aware of and more deeply sensitive to the sorts of problems your students may bring to your classroom. While many of the troubles and pathologies we discuss in this chapter, such as drug use, teenage pregnancies and school violence, appear typically among secondary school students, almost all have their roots in the lives of elementary school students. All teachers, therefore, need to be alert to these problems. We are not suggesting that you should be Mr. or Ms. Fix-It, taking in troubled children and, with a few quick adjustments to their psyches, sending them out into the world cured. We do, however, want you to recognize the healing power of education, which gives structure, purpose, and hope to youngsters whose daily lives often lack these stabilizing and motivating influences.

▶ Recognizing Risk Factors

■ teacher-student gaps

In the chapter entitled "Who Are Today's Students in a Diverse Society?" we talked about changes in our society that are resulting in increased diversity among today's students. These conditions affect many students' lives, but they do not necessarily prevent them from getting an education. However, some changes or trends in society do pose a more direct threat to the performance of students in school. Many teachers may have difficulty recognizing and adapting to differences that contribute to the problems some children bring to the classroom. As we discussed in "Who Are Today's Students in a Diverse Society?" most teachers come from relatively stable backgrounds. Although a teacher's stable background can be a source of strength, it also means that children often inhabit different worlds than their teachers. Often there are gaps between teachers' and students' social class and their personal exposure to major social problems.

■ problems tend to cluster

In our discussion, we deal with several difficult conditions and problems, including poverty, homelessness, child abuse, alcohol and drug use, teenage parenting, sexually transmitted diseases, adolescent suicide, violence, and school dropout rate. As you will see in the following discussion, these pervasive societal problems do not occur in isolation but actually tend to cluster or overlap. In real life, it is difficult to separate out discrete sources of social problems. The compounding of risk factors contributes to the incredible scope of these problems and places a number of students at risk for not completing or succeeding in school. For such **at-risk students,** as they are often called, the chances are great that they will have difficulty getting an adequate education.

What are some of these risk factors? Six key measures include the following:

- The child is not living with two parents.
- The head of the household is a high school dropout.
- Family income is below the poverty line.
- The child is living with a parent or parents who do not have steady, full-time employment.
- The family is receiving welfare benefits.
- The child does not have health insurance.

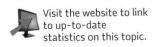
Visit the website to link to up-to-date statistics on this topic.

FIGURE 4.1

Child Poverty and Birth Circumstances

Source: *Kids Count Data Book 2004* (Baltimore: The Annie E. Casey Foundation, 2004), p. 38. Reprinted by permission of the Annie E. Casey Foundation.

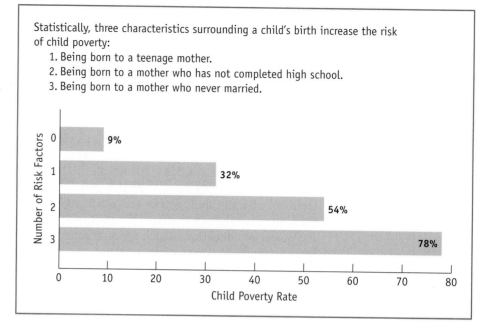

Statistically, three characteristics surrounding a child's birth increase the risk of child poverty:

1. Being born to a teenage mother.
2. Being born to a mother who has not completed high school.
3. Being born to a mother who never married.

■ risks multiply with each added factor

We know that these family variables do not necessarily compromise children. Many children from families with these risks overcome the odds to succeed in school and in life. Research indicates, however, that when several of these risk factors are present, fewer children make it. As one prominent author states, "The research . . . shows that the more risk factors are present, the greater the damaging impact of each. But the impact is not just additive—risk factors multiply each other's destructive effects."[1] Nationally, 9.2 million children are growing up with four or more of these risk factors. Nearly 30 percent of African-American children and almost 25 percent of Hispanic children are in the high-risk category, compared with only 6 percent of white children.[2] Compounding the problem is the fact that multiple-risk families are often concentrated in economically and socially isolated communities that have limited job opportunities, poor schools, low-quality public services, and higher levels of crime and drug use. Figure 4.1 shows the relationship between living in poverty and other risk factors.

Let's examine some of these risk factors in more detail, starting with the changing patterns of the American family.

▶ New American Family Patterns

■ no "typical" family

In recent decades, our society has experienced dramatic changes in how families are structured. The once common image of the "breadwinner" father, a housewife mother, and two children of public school age now accurately describes only a very small percentage of households in the United States. So what is the typical family of our students like today? Actually, there is no longer one "typical" family pattern. Rather, a number of economic and societal trends have resulted in families that come in many forms that, in turn, have a pervasive influence on children in school.

Family Composition

■ single-parent households

An increasing number of children are being raised by single parents. Sixty-eight percent of children under 18 live with two married parents. Twenty-three percent of all children live only with their mothers, 5 percent live only with their fathers, and 4 percent live with neither parent.[3] A breakdown of the figures by racial group reveals that 23 percent of white children, 65 percent of African American children, and 35 percent of Hispanic children live in arrangements other than two-parent families.[4]

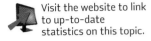 Visit the website to link to up-to-date statistics on this topic.

The rate of divorce has influenced the composition of our families, particularly among couples who have children. More than half of today's new marriages will end in divorce. In addition to divorce, other factors such as births to single parents, separation, and death of a parent contribute to the number of children living in single-parent households or possibly with grandparents or aunts and uncles.

Being a child in a family in which the parents' marriage is conflict ridden and unhappy may be less preferable in some ways than living in a single-parent family, but single-parent families have one major disadvantage: lower incomes. Nearly five times as many children who live with only their mothers live in poverty, compared to children living in married couple households.[5] Single-mother families have been called *the new poor.* It is not just the absence of one parent but the loss of a two-parent income that puts a special burden on these families. More difficult to pin down is the effect of only one parent bearing the daily chores of monitoring, supporting, and guiding the school-age children.

Another result of high divorce rates is the increasing number of children living in blended families with stepparents, stepsiblings, and/or half-siblings. In some cases, divorced parents share physical custody of the children, with the result that the children must split their time between parental households. As we discussed in the chapter entitled "Who Are Today's Students in a Diverse Society?," you may also have students whose parents are of the same gender.

■ teaching implications

Changes in American family patterns will likely influence your interactions with students and their parents in a number of ways. For example, in divorce situations it may be difficult to keep both parents informed of their child's progress, or a single parent may have a very heavy workload and may be unable to attend parent-teacher conferences at the usual times. Varied family patterns will also require more sensitivity in daily interactions, such as avoiding asking students to bring a note from "your mother." It would perhaps be better to say "your parent" or "the person who takes care of you."

Family Relationships

Family composition affects the amount of time children and their parents have to spend with each other and can also affect the quality of that time. For a single parent, the combination of a job with the necessities of maintaining a family, such as cooking, cleaning, and grocery shopping, does not allow for a great deal of leisure time to spend supervising and enjoying the children. Many single parents do a fine job of raising their children, but the hardships are considerable.

■ working parents

Even two-parent families can face challenges. Many mothers now go to work or return to work when their children are very young. In 32 percent of two-parent families, both the mother and father worked all year, full time.[6] Two-career families must balance the needs of childrearing and family life with the demands of

VOICES FROM THE CLASSROOM

Christa Compton taught high school English in Columbia, South Carolina, for nine years. She was South Carolina's Teacher of the Year in 2001 and is currently finishing a doctoral program at Stanford University.

Families and School

My students show up with hearts burdened by terrible losses. Angela's father was murdered when she was very young, and she still grieves for a man she only vaguely remembers. Marcus was put up for adoption at birth by his teenage mother, and his adoptive mother died of cancer two years ago. Peter is angry because his mother recently moved out of the house, and he blames her for breaking up their family. Many other families have been torn apart by divorce, and fathers are increasingly absent in their children's lives.

All of this means I have to work hard to earn students' trust, an especially difficult task with those who have been disappointed by other people they have trusted. If students don't find a sense of belonging at home, it becomes even more important to find it at school, so I try to create a supportive community within the class. I uncover the story of each kid's life and design activities that build relationships among the students. Throughout the year, we write sympathy cards when one of us is grieving, applaud the students who make the honor roll, welcome back the students who return from an absence, and do whatever we can to express concern for each class member.

It helps to observe their behavior and moods from day to day. Sometimes just a quiet comment can reassure them that someone cares. At other times, students reveal their anxieties in a written assignment, so I write notes on their papers to let them know that I am there to support them.

They desperately want someone to pay attention—to praise their successes, to notice when they are sad, to share the daily torments and victories that are the hallmarks of adolescent life. When they feel dismissed, I can provide encouragement. When their lives are chaotic and unpredictable, I can offer safety and consistency. I might be the one person they can count on, and I refuse to let them down.

 Visit the website for more Voices from the Classroom.

---

two work environments. Neither Mom nor Dad is as available as she or he used to be to attend daily to children's social, intellectual, and moral development.

Almost 80 percent of today's students live in families in which either both parents work or the only parent works full time.[7] Now, when many children return home from school, they watch television rather than talk with their parents. Coming home to an empty house or apartment after school is standard for an estimated 4 million "latch-key" children in our country.

America's future will be determined by the home and the school. The child becomes largely what it is taught, hence we must watch what we teach it, how we live before it.

—Jane Addams

For parents of younger children not yet in school, working outside the home raises the issue of adequate childcare. If both parents, or the only parent, go to work full time, who is taking care of the children? Grandparents and extended family used to pitch in and help, but today it is less common for a family to settle in one location near relatives for extended periods. Parents who have to work, especially single parents, can easily be caught in a bind, and they often must settle for whatever child care they can find or afford.

- "latch-key" children
- child care issues

School and Teacher Responses

- schools play a larger role

In addition to limiting the amount of time children spend in close contact with their parents, the trend toward two-career and single-parent families also has a direct impact on the schools. In the past, teachers could count on more support from families; now teachers often find it difficult to even get in contact with many parents. In the past, young people were actively involved outside of school in family and community, but today the school is being urged to play a larger role in expanding and guiding the limited experiences of children.

In this situation, the more dramatic social problems, such as poverty and homelessness, take on even greater urgency for the schools. Schools are being asked to deal with the new problems being brought to them by the facts of modern family life and our changed economy. Many schools have responded to child care needs by offering both before- and after-school programs. For example, many schools provide both breakfast and lunch programs. Schools may offer enrichment and recreational programs or on-site day care before and after school to address student and parental needs. Some schools even stagger their bus schedules to accommodate students who stay for after-school programs. Some schools, such as those following the model developed by James Comer—described in the "Leaders in Education" box—have responded in a very different way, by redesigning the whole school to make effective teamwork with families a priority.

Leaders in Education

James Comer

James Comer is a public health physician and psychiatrist who, through his work with low-income schools in New Haven, Conn., has shown that it is possible for low-income African American children to achieve at high academic and social levels.

After receiving his M.D. from Howard University in 1960, Comer entered the public health service. He became interested in the study of how policies and institutions interact with families and children and began to see the school as the place to improve the life chances for children from difficult home situations. He decided that a career in psychiatry would enable him to address the social problems that plagued the people with whom he worked, and in 1964, he began his psychiatric training at Yale University.

At Yale, Comer worked with the inner-city New Haven schools to find out why they were not helping African American children and how they could be made to do so. He wanted to give these children the same opportunities in life that education had given him. The more he worked with children, the more he came to believe that schools were the only places where children trapped in poverty and failure could receive the support their families could not give them.

With the help of a Ford Foundation grant, Comer became the director of the School Development Program with the New Haven public schools. A team of educational and mental health professionals consisting of Comer, school administrators and teachers, a social worker, a psychologist, a special education teacher, and other support staff worked to involve parents in developing a social skills curriculum that integrated academic disciplines. The curriculum included four major areas: politics and government, business and economics, health and nutrition, and spiritual and leisure time, all areas in which the students would need proficiency to succeed in school and to lead productive lives. Through the curriculum, the students became more aware of their community and of how their involvement in it could make a difference.

By adopting child development and behavioral science research, the team concentrated on problem solving rather than blame fixing and made decisions based on consensus. This consensus process gave each team member a sense of participation and ownership of decisions. The project was a great success: students' standardized test scores rose dramatically, project schools had higher attendance rates than other New Haven schools, and students graduated to become school leaders in their later schooling.

The Comer Model emphasizes the social context of teaching and learning. No academic learning is possible, Comer asserts, unless there is a positive environment at the school where teachers, students, parents, and administrators like one another and work together for the good of all children. Built around three elements—a school governance team, a mental health team, and parental participation—Comer's model seeks to create schools that offer children stable support and positive role models. With the school and parents working successfully together, no conflict arises between home and school. The students learn desirable values, disruptions at school are reduced, and both teachers and students have more time and energy to focus on academic and social skills learning.

Among the many sites that have successfully implemented Comer's approach, now known as the School Development Program, are Washington, D.C.; Dade County, Fla.; Dallas; Chicago; Detroit; San Diego; and New Orleans. Many school districts have chosen this program's structure and processes as a way to implement site-based management.

 Visit the website for more information about James Comer.

■ social services provided through schools

■ **Interagency Cooperation**   In addition to their own responses, many schools work with other agencies to help meet the changing needs of students and their families. These schools offer nontraditional programs that coordinate agencies dealing with health, and social and recreational services. These interagency programs enable the schools to deliver needed social and health services to students and their families to promote success in school. For example, the coordinated school health initiative responds to the risk factors that threaten children and youth by providing student health services. The initiative assesses the health problems in particular school communities, builds consensus on what services should be provided, and puts together a comprehensive approach to improving children's health using agencies that address health, mental health, dental health, social services, recreation, and youth development. The guiding principle of the coordinated school health initiative is that schools and communities can do much more with their current resources if they work together in partnership rather than as separate, isolated agencies. At least 1,500 school-based health centers are operating in the United States.[8]

Pause and Reflect

1 ► Does your own family background reflect traditional or emerging family patterns? How do you think your upbringing will affect your ability to teach students from different family situations?

2 ► How can you prepare to work effectively with a variety of parents and caregivers?

▶ Poverty

■ the widening income gap

The rich are getting richer and the poor are getting poorer. This well-known phrase describes the extremes of different socioeconomic levels in our society today. **Socioeconomic status (SES)** is the term used by the U.S. Bureau of the Census to classify economic conditions of people using a family's occupational status, income, and educational attainment as measures of status. Individuals high in income, occupational prestige, and amount of education are considered to be high in socioeconomic status and are usually seen by others to be upper-class people who are influential in their communities. In contrast, people low in socioeconomic status are seen as being lower-class people who have little prestige or power.

Who Are the Poor?

The poorest 40 percent of American citizens receive 12 percent of the national income, whereas the wealthiest 20 percent receive 50 percent.[9] In 2004, the number of impoverished Americans was 37 million, or 12.7 percent of the population.[10]

 Visit this chapter of the website to link to up-to-date statistics on this topic.

Numerically, the majority of poor Americans are white; however, the *rate* of poverty is higher among minorities. Eight percent of whites, 25 percent of African Americans, 22 percent of Hispanic Americans, 24 percent of Native Americans, and 11 percent of Asian Americans live below the poverty line ($19,484 for a family of four in 2004).[11]

■ one in six children are poor

Although poverty rates declined through the 1990s because of a booming economy, they have risen over the last few years. The problem of poverty is now pervasive, and the prospects for breaking its grip on children are particularly bleak. As Figure 4.2 shows, almost 18 percent (13 million) of American children live in poverty, the highest rate among all age groups and the highest in any

FIGURE 4.2
Percentage of Children Under 18 Living in Poverty, by Race/Ethnicity and Year

Source: Carmen Denavas-Walt, Bernadette D. Proctor, and Cheryl Hill Lee, U.S. Bureau of the Census, *Income, Poverty, and Health Insurance Coverage in the United States: 2004.* Current Population Reports (Washington, DC: U.S. Government Printing Office, 2005). Available at: http://www.census.gov/prod/2005/pubs/p60-229.pdf.

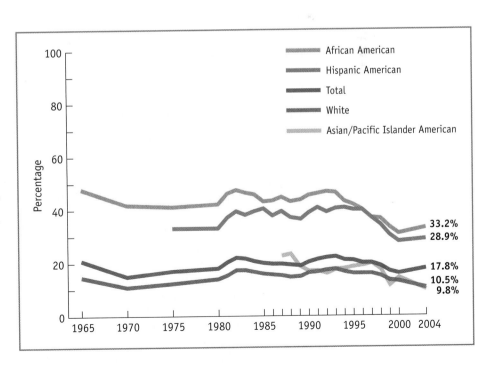

industrialized country. Children make up about one-fourth of the population, but they constitute 35 percent of the poor. More than 53 percent of the children in families headed by females are poor.[12]

■ the working poor

In the past, poverty was assumed to be the result of unemployment, and for many this is still true. Nearly 18 million American children, or 25 percent, are growing up in households in which no parent has a full-time, year-round job.[13] Many people do, however, hold regular jobs but still find themselves in poverty.

America is losing sight of its children. In decisions made every day we are placing them at the bottom of the agenda, with grave consequences for the future of the nation.

—ERNEST BOYER

Thirty-two percent of children living in poverty had at least one parent working full-time all year.[14] After World War II, many high school graduates could get manufacturing jobs that required minimal education yet paid quite well. A high school graduate could support a family of four, buy a house, own two cars, and live comfortably. The American job market has now changed. Many manufacturing jobs can now be done more efficiently and effectively by machines, and many of those that are still done by people have been moved to countries with low-wage workers. The U.S. job market for unskilled workers today is found mostly in fast-food establishments and service jobs that typically pay minimum wage and offer no benefits. Full-time employment at the current minimum wage is not enough to support a family above the poverty line.

Homelessness

For families in or close to poverty, the threat of homelessness is very real. Families in poverty often pay more than one-half of their annual incomes in rent. With such a large percentage of income consumed by rent payments, one incident or emergency in the family can disrupt this tenuous equilibrium and jeopardize the family's ability to maintain a home. Imagine, for example, the domino effect that could occur from mechanical difficulties with the one family car. Even minor repairs costing $50 to $100 may be beyond the family's budget. Without a car, the family breadwinner may be unable to get to work and the children unable to get to day care. It does not take long in such a situation to lose a job or a long-awaited slot in a child care center. If the main earner cannot work, paying rent can soon become impossible. It is easy to see why housing, which consumes so much of annual income, is a particularly vulnerable area for families in poverty.

■ obstacles for homeless schoolchildren

There are about 1 million homeless children and youth in the United States, and more than 750,000 are of school age.[15] Imagine the obstacles for a homeless child trying to get an education. Uprooted from their homes, many live in shelters or other locations in distant parts of town. Attending school may require extensive transportation, which parents are not likely to be able to afford. Enrolling children in a school near a shelter may be a difficult and intimidating process for parents struggling with daily survival. Many parents, believing they will be homeless only for a short time, may not even try to transfer their child's enrollment. As days turn into weeks and months, the child may miss a great deal of school. If the child is fortunate enough to attend school, other difficulties may arise, such as the stigma of wearing dirty and ragged clothes, being unwelcome by other children or school officials, or being unable to stay awake in class.

Some homeless children are on their own, having run away from home or been ejected from their families. Many of these chronically homeless youth have been physically or sexually abused, and many suffer from drug or alcohol abuse, poor nutrition, inadequate sleep, exposure to the elements, and lack of health care. School can be a stabilizing force in the lives of these children, but it can also exacerbate their problems. In 1987, Congress passed what is now known as the Stewart B. McKinney Homeless Assistance Act, to provide protection for the educational needs of homeless children and youth. The legislation provides grants to states to make available money for the educational needs of homeless children. It also requires states to ensure that these children are educated with the rest of the youth in their area and not isolated and stigmatized.[16]

■ homeless children require teacher's support

You may have homeless children in your classroom; if so, they are likely to require support and understanding from you. Some may be malnourished or physically dirty because they lack access to shower or tub facilities. They may show emotional needs. Other children may make fun of them. Your support and caring could provide them with hope and be crucial in improving their chances for success. More than anything else, homeless children need homes. As their teacher, you cannot be expected to provide the homes they need, but hundreds of local and federal programs serve runaway and homeless youth, and these agencies will help you work with these youngsters. Through them, some may find shelter.

School and Teacher Responses

■ two views of schooling

Many people in our society have thought that we could eliminate poverty through education and that, through schooling, it would be relatively easy to free people from the chains of impoverishment. The efforts have been well intentioned but often too little, too late, and in retrospect, sometimes naive. With poverty so prevalent, schools have a challenging problem, partly because they are not designed to serve poor children. The schools in this country were created and continue to be supported by the middle class to perpetuate the middle-class way of life. There is nothing particularly startling about this. Middle-class people want their children to be like themselves or possibly somewhat better. Therefore, they have built and continue to pay for a school system that reflects their values and supports the way of life with which they feel comfortable.

Some critics, however, see the middle-class bias of our schools in a more sinister light, as part of an enslavement system. They claim that schools do not help develop the individual talents and strengths of poor children, and that they also make these children believe they are losers. After eight to eleven years of schooling, many of these young people see themselves as unable to fit into the middle class and as people who, at best, will do society's menial work.

Although some of these critics see this system as a conscious plan of our society, we do not. Such a cynical view suggests that the teachers who are toiling in the urban and rural slums are either people of evil intentions or simply dupes. In our view, many of the most heroic teachers alive are those struggling to aid people oppressed by poverty.

Our past and present inadequacies in educating the children of the poor tempt some to turn away and devote their energies to more solvable problems. Our nation cannot do this. Ours is an evolving society. As a people, we are not finished with our own development. Eradicating the ravages of poverty and its withering effect on children should be at the top of our agenda as citizens of this nation and as educators. Although there are many important and solvable problems to work on, we cannot afford—in justice—to ignore this one.

■ social classes have hidden rules

One educator, Ruby Payne, has written extensively about issues of poverty and how schools can understand better the unique needs of children of poverty.[17] Payne describes *hidden rules,* unspoken clues that individuals in different membership groups use in decision making. Among the middle class, work and achievement are driving forces in decision making, whereas in **generational**

Prosperity is a way of living and thinking, and not just money or things. Poverty is a way of living and thinking, and not just a lack of money or things.

—Eric Butterworth (minister and author)

poverty (being in poverty for two generations or longer) the driving forces are survival, entertainment, and relationships. According to Payne, the hidden rules guiding people who live in poverty mean that relationships and entertainment are more important than achievement. For example, in generational poverty, people are possessions. It is worse to steal someone's girlfriend than a thing. Also, conflict is often resolved by physical fighting, whereas in the middle class fighting is done verbally.

Payne's major point is that unless educators understand these hidden rules that govern the behavior of those from generational poverty, they are unlikely to respond in appropriate ways. Schools tend to reflect middle-class values, which is why children from poverty backgrounds, who don't know middle-class hidden rules, often feel out of place. Payne suggests that, for students from generational poverty to value academic learning, a significant relationship must be present, and academic tasks need to be referenced in terms of relationships. The significant relationship can be with the teacher or with other students and friends. Payne cites an example of how a teacher working with a seventeen-year-old who did not do his homework on positive and negative numbers, suggested that it would be OK if his friends cheated him at cards. The student was furious at the idea. The teacher said that he wouldn't know if they were cheating him or not because he didn't know positive and negative numbers. He grabbed a deck of cards to show the teacher that he did know how to keep score. The teacher said, "Then you do know positive and negative numbers. I expect you to do your homework." From then on the student did his homework regularly.

Pause and Reflect

1 ▸ Why do you think it is so difficult for the schools to overcome the effects of poverty on the academic achievement for poor children?

2 ▸ What are the challenges in teaching poor children?

3 ▸ Are you interested in teaching children from poverty situations? Why or why not?

4 ▸ What decisions of yours have been based on hidden rules related to your social class? How can you prepare to adjust or reveal hidden rules to meet the expectations of students you teach?

▶ Teenage Parenting

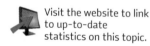
Visit the website to link to up-to-date statistics on this topic.

■ relationship of teen pregnancy and poverty

The bad news is that each year almost 900,000 American teenagers get pregnant and give birth to some 425,000 children, by far the highest teenage birthrate among the world's developed countries. The good news is that between 1990 and 2002, the birthrate among girls ages fifteen to nineteen declined from 60 to 43 births per 1,000.[18] Still, the annual cost in public funds for teenage pregnancies in America is estimated to be more than $7 billion.[19]

The consequences of early parenthood for teen fathers are generally not as severe as those for teen mothers. Almost 80 percent of teenage mothers are not married and so are particularly vulnerable to poverty.[20] When we combine the difficulties of single parenthood with the likelihood that teenagers will have poor work skills and limited employment experience and, if they find work, will receive low wages, we gain some understanding of why more than half the children from households headed by a female live in poverty. In fact, the poverty rate for children born to a teenage mother who has never married and who did not graduate from high school is 78 percent. Also, many young fathers do not provide financial assistance and support for these children. Because about four-fifths of teenage births occur out of wedlock, male parents often feel little responsibility for their children. Only 30 percent of mothers ages fifteen to seventeen receive child support payments, and most of those received only a portion of the payments that were due to them.[21]

■ steps taken by schools

Not only do teenage parents face the enormous task of juggling childrearing and employment or school, but often they must care for a premature baby who is more likely to have health problems and possible learning difficulties. Moreover, poverty often correlates with worse nutrition, less health care, more homelessness, and less education than for more advantaged families. To lessen this problem, many schools are working with local health officials to ensure that pregnant teenagers receive prenatal care and parenting advice. They are also encouraging these young women to stay in school and graduate. In many cases, the schools are permitting young mothers to bring their babies with them to school.

■ teaching implications

If you are planning on teaching in secondary schools, you may work with some of these young parents and should keep in mind the challenges they face. You should also give some thought to what you would do if one of your students informs you that she is pregnant or that he has gotten his girlfriend pregnant. Know both your legal and ethical responsibilities in these cases. If you plan to teach in an elementary school, be prepared to work with very young parents, some who may be your own age.

To prevent teenage pregnancies, many schools have established sex education programs, and some have clinics where birth control devices can be obtained. Both of these steps, while increasingly common, remain controversial.

Sex Education

■ controversies about sex ed

Issues and questions of sexual behavior and sexual attitudes cut deep in the spiritual and social views of most Americans. It is hardly surprising, then, that our

As pregnant teenagers struggle with the decision of whether to drop out of school, educators are finding ways to encourage pregnant teenagers and young mothers to stay in school and graduate.
(© David Young-Wolff/PhotoEdit)

schools' efforts to educate young people frequently stir serious differences and strong passions. Although most people agree that children should be given information about sex, the controversy centers on three issues: (1) is the school the appropriate institution to offer such instruction; (2) if so, should it limit instruction to strictly factual information, or should the psychological, social, health, and moral aspects of sex also be included in the curriculum; and (3) matching the specificity of the sexual information to the maturity level of the students.

Many people argue that because sex is such an intimate topic and is closely related to religious and moral beliefs, sex education is the responsibility of the home and the church. Advocates of sex education in the schools respond that they would agree with that position if parents did in fact provide adequate sex information for their children. They argue that, unfortunately, this is not the case, contending that the majority of parents fail to assume the responsibility to teach their children about sex. According to advocates of sex education, the public school is the only institution that has access to most children over an extended period, and the responsibility must fall to the school because of the demonstrated failure of the home, church, library, and medical profession to provide effective sex education. Further, courts have supported state boards of education and local school boards' right to offer sex education in the curriculum.

■ dropout problem

■ Goals of Sex Education   Preventing teenage pregnancies is a major goal of any sex education program. As we discussed earlier in the chapter, besides endangering babies, early pregnancies are placing the future lives of great numbers of teenage girls in serious jeopardy, interrupting and often terminating their education. In spite of special counseling and accommodations made for teenage mothers to stay in school, the majority drop out, thus drastically reducing their job and career opportunities.

■ risk of sexually transmitted diseases

Another goal of sex education is to reduce the incidence of sexually transmitted diseases (STDs), but this, too, is controversial, particularly regarding the use of condoms. It has been estimated that about 3 million American adolescents are newly infected with an STD each year, with chlamydia and gonorrhea being the most commonly acquired diseases.[22] While not the most common of the STDs, AIDS is a serious killer, and preventive measures have become a matter of life and death. It is estimated that one-fourth of all new human immunodeficiency virus (HIV) cases occur in people ages thirteen to twenty-one, half are among people under age twenty-five, and the majority of these infections are sexually transmitted.[23]

Almost 50 percent of high school students report that before graduating they have engaged in sexual intercourse (49 percent of males and 48 percent of females). However, only 57 percent of the teenagers who were sexually active in the previous three months reported using condoms, which, although clearly not as effective as abstinence, provide some protection against AIDS and other STDs when used correctly.[24] Many teenagers, however, especially if they are using alcohol or drugs, neglect to use condoms or use them incorrectly.

In addition to preventing pregnancies and STDs, sexuality education also seeks to help teenagers become sexually healthy adults. Sexual health encompasses sexual development and reproductive health, and such characteristics as the ability to develop and maintain meaningful personal relationships, appreciation of one's own body, interaction with both genders in respectful and appropriate ways, and responsible decision-making skills.

Students need not only scientific information about human sexuality and prevention of pregnancy and disease, but help to gain the self-control and strength of character needed to avoid risky and irresponsible behavior. Certainly, one important form of prevention, abstinence, depends on developing the necessary self-control to handle sexual feelings. Further, developing true respect of the opposite sex is an important character-related aspect of sex education. (Read further about the character-related aspects of sex education in the chapter "How Should Education Be Reformed?")

■ what kind of program?

■ **Types of Sex Education** Arguments over the kind of sex education the schools should offer are just as heated as the controversy about whether to offer it. Some support comprehensive sex education programs (also called "abstinence plus") that convey sexual activities as a natural and healthy part of life. While advocating abstinence from sex outside of marriage, these programs also provide information on contraception and disease prevention for those teens who elect to become sexually active. Others believe this approach is in sharp contrast to their moral or religious beliefs; they would recommend an abstinence-based curriculum that teaches students to abstain from sex outside of marriage. Advocates of the abstinence approach argue that when sex education programs teach both abstinence and the use of contraceptives, students receive a mixed message. Further, they think that the only appropriate position for the public schools is to teach and to advocate abstinence, leaving the controversial sex education to others, such as parents, medical professionals, and others. They argue that much of the mass media (i.e., films, TV, popular music) has so sexualized the world of young people that schools may be perceived as legitimizing teenage sex through advocating condoms and other devices, which sends the wrong message to students.

Visit this chapter of the website for an author debate on sex education.

Others believe that the large number of STDs, especially AIDS, has strengthened the position of those who argue for comprehensive sex education programs. They stand behind the view that schools should provide children with the sex education that will help them understand the risks they face and how to prevent or minimize those risks. This view is supported by U.S. Surgeon General's 2001 report on sex education programs, based on a two-year review of scientific papers and conferences. He concluded that comprehensive sex education programs, which combine teaching about the importance of abstinence and providing information about condoms and other methods of contraception, have proven to be most effective. The report noted that the evidence on abstinence-only programs is insufficient to draw evidence-based conclusions on their effectiveness. He also questioned the effectiveness of these programs for teenagers who have already become sexually active.[25] The federal government, however, has weighed in on the side of abstinence-only programs. Since 1996, Congress has committed more than a half billion dollars to abstinence-only programs and no dollars to comprehensive sexuality education.[26]

■ be aware of district policy

Like few other issues in education, the "whats and whens and hows" of sex education are matters of deep and serious controversy in our public schools and in our culture. Rational people of good will have come to very different conclusions about what is best for students. In the meantime, it is possible that you will have students in your class or school who are known to have HIV and other STDs. It is important for you and your colleagues to know school district policy regarding these children and the ways in which the disease can be transmitted. Safeguarding other children while also attending to the rights and needs of the child with an STD requires knowledge, care, and understanding.

Pause and Reflect

1 ▶ What kinds of support do pregnant and parenting teenagers need from their teachers?

2 ▶ Do you think that you will be comfortable and well prepared to deal with your students' questions or remarks about sexuality? If not, how can you prepare now?

▶ Abused and Neglected Children

The education of the young brings us into contact with humanity's best impulses. Occasionally, however, we see the wreckage of its darkest and most vicious urges. For many years, the phenomenon of child abuse was known only to a small percentage of social workers and law enforcement people. More recently, we have become aware of the magnitude of this problem and the variety of forms abuse can take, including physical or mental injury, sexual abuse, negligent treatment, and maltreatment.

■ many cases unreported

Because of the hidden nature of much child abuse and neglect, reliable figures on it are somewhat difficult to obtain. Professionals in the field strongly suspect that most cases are unreported. Nevertheless, 3 million incidents of child abuse or neglect were reported to child-service agencies in 2002. Almost 900,000 of these reported cases were substantiated. About three-fifths of the victims of maltreatment suffered from neglect, about one-fifth experienced physical abuse, and about one-tenth were victims of sexual abuse.[27] Parental substance abuse was reported as a major contributing factor in child abuse cases.

■ effects of abuse

The toll that abuse and neglect take on children's physical, emotional, and psychological development is difficult to assess. Children subjected to violent treatment may sustain injuries that cause serious learning problems in school. Abused children may be withdrawn or have trouble concentrating. They suffer enormous stress, and their self-esteem is low. They sometimes have excessive needs for control because they have experienced such helplessness. Ironically, they may be more likely to abuse their own children in the future.

■ the teacher's responsibility

The classroom teacher will not directly encounter the problem of abuse very often. However, in all fifty states, educators are legally responsible for reporting suspected cases of child abuse. Teachers must be aware of potential signs of abuse and know school policy and procedures for reporting suspected abuse. (See the chapter entitled "What Are the Ethical and Legal Issues Facing Teachers?" for a discussion of teachers' legal obligations regarding suspected child abuse.) Potential signs of abuse include the following:

- Repeated injuries such as bruises, welts, and burns
- Neglected appearance
- Sudden fall-off in academic performance
- Disruptive or passive, withdrawn behavior
- "Supercritical" parents who remain isolated from the school and community [28]

Teachers need to realize that even after an abusive situation has been reported and perhaps disclosed, these children's problems in school will not suddenly end. Children who have been abused have a continuing need for emotional safety and stability, including trustworthy praise, concrete rewards, and constructive ways to control their classroom environment. They need capable adult role models who can provide varied but predictable activities and measurable classroom achievement.

Pause and Reflect

1 ▶ What can schools, teachers, and other social agencies do to help parents and children avoid abuse?

▶ Alcohol and Drug Abuse

Many of the trends we have talked about so far in this chapter can severely stress the functioning of families, provoking self-destructive responses in children. Substance abuse is a particularly destructive response. It may involve the use of alcohol or various other drugs. It may be the act of parents or children. Unfortunately, when one family member gets entangled in substance abuse, the entire family is usually a victim.

■ alcohol, a major problem

Alcohol is the most commonly abused substance, and the first use of alcohol may occur at a young age, sometimes in elementary school. Historically, the greatest number of alcoholic teenagers have been male students, especially those with low grades, but the gap between males and females seems to be closing. The problem of alcohol abuse among high school students is widespread. Eleven percent of eighth-graders, 22 percent of tenth-graders, and 29 percent of twelfth-graders consumed five or more drinks in a row at least once in the past two weeks in 2004.[29] Alcohol use and premarital sex are also related. Teenagers who drink are seven times more likely to engage in sex, and twice as likely to have four or more partners, than those who do not drink. Such behavior can lead to unprotected sex, with the increased risk of AIDS or other sexually transmitted diseases.[30]

The video case *Social and Emotional Development: The Influence of Peer Groups* gives you some ideas about how students experience peer pressure. As you watch the clips and study the artifacts in the case, reflect upon the following questions:

1. What kinds of peer pressure have you felt? How did you cope with the pressure?
2. What else can teachers do to help students resist pressure to try alcohol and other substances, become sexually active, or engage in other hazardous behaviors described in this chapter?

In 2004, the percentages of eighth-, tenth-, and twelfth-graders who reported using an illicit drug during the past thirty days were 8, 18, and 23.[31] These are the lowest figures reported since 1993, but, despite recent declines, student drug and alcohol abuse remain serious problems. As indicated in the previous section of this chapter, many child abuse and neglect cases involve parental substance abuse, which has devastating results for children.

■ physical and emotional damage

Every public school in our country is subject to the Safe and Drug Free Schools and Communities Act, which is now part of the No Child Left Behind Act of 2001. The basic purpose of these laws is to provide safe, disciplined, and drug-free environments conducive to learning by eliminating violence in and around schools and preventing illegal drug use on school property.

■ teaching implications

What should you do if you suspect one of your students is using drugs or binge drinking? The most important thing is to talk with the school counselor about the situation. He or she has been trained to deal with these problems and can offer you advice on both the legal aspects of the situation and ways to assist the student. Students want some level of consistency in actions, not just in words. It is quite distressing to students when educators do nothing to address drug or alcohol abuse. Schools need clear-cut policies about how to handle alcohol and other drugs in the classroom and at school.

FIGURE 4.3

Student Drug and Alcohol Use: Percentage of High School Seniors Reporting Use in the Previous 30 Days, by Year and Substance

Source: University of Michigan, Institute for Social Research, *Monitoring the Future: Secondary School Students 2004.* Available at: http://monitoringthefuture.org/pubs/monographs/overview2004.pdf.

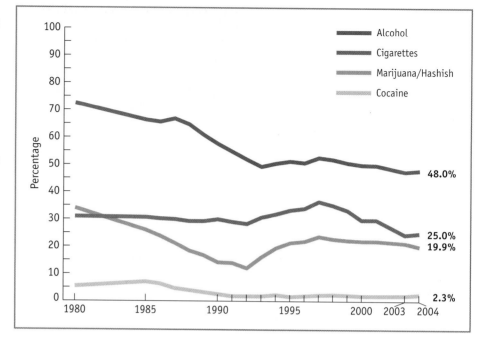

Pause and Reflect

1 ▶ What elements of school culture serve to condone or even encourage student drinking and drug use? What elements could be used to discourage substance abuse?

2 ▶ What can you, as a teacher, do to encourage responsible student substance use behavior?

▶ Adolescent Suicide

Suicide is third only to motor vehicle accidents and homicide as a leading cause of adolescent death in the United States. Each year about 3,900 people ages fifteen through twenty-four take their own lives.

■ suicide patterns

Studies of young people who have attempted suicide and those who have succeeded reveal several patterns. For every teenager who commits suicide, 100 more will try. Every year, one in twelve high school students attempts suicide, and half of all high school students report they have "seriously considered" suicide by the time they graduate. Among those who attempt suicide, the vast majority is female. Girls attempt suicide about three times more often than boys, but boys complete suicide about five times more often than girls.[32] The suicide rate for African Americans ages fifteen to nineteen has increased dramatically since 1980 but is still lower than the rate for whites.

■ risk factors

What puts young people at risk for attempting suicide? Factors include family violence or disruption, mental illness, unemployment, a history of substance abuse, being bullied, and stress in school or social life. Some experts argue that the leading reason why young people are more at risk for suicide now than they were a generation or two ago is the decline of the traditional family unit. To add to the tragedy, young people sometimes engage in copycat suicides. In this "cluster" syndrome, a wave of adolescent suicides plagues an area. In response, hundreds of school districts now offer programs in suicide prevention.

Even though suicide is the third greatest cause of deaths among youth, only one in ten schools has a plan to prevent them. Educators often have the opportunity to recognize children and youths who are suicide risks and to help them get the advice and support they need. Although suicidal behaviors are complex and the warning signs can be ambiguous or misleading, it is important to realize that most young people who commit suicide give warning signs first, to signal their need for help. The American Academy of Child Psychiatry recommends that parents, teachers, and counselors watch for these signs:

■ warning signs

- Changes in eating and sleeping habits
- Withdrawal from friends, family, and regular activities
- Violent or rebellious behavior
- Running away
- Drug or alcohol abuse
- Unusual neglect of personal appearance
- Radical change in personality
- Persistent boredom, difficulty concentrating, or a decline in the quality of schoolwork
- Frequent complaints about physical symptoms that are often related to emotions, such as stomachaches, headaches, or fatigue
- Loss of interest in previously pleasurable activities
- Inability to tolerate praise or rewards[33]

Whom You Will Teach

Proportion of children age three to five who are enrolled in pre-primary education programs: 61

Percentage of high school students who admitted carrying a weapon at school: 17:

Percentage of high school students who reported being in a physical fight in the previous year: 33

Percentage of students who won't graduate from high school: 32

The percentage of children read to by a family member three or more times per week: 84

Percentage of children under age eighteen who are living in poverty: 18

Percentage of high school seniors who report having used an illegal drug in the previous thirty days: 23

Percentage of students age twelve to eighteen who reported gangs at their schools: 20

Percentage of seniors who had five or more drinks in a row at least once during the previous two weeks: 29.

Percentage of high school seniors who have jobs: 65; percentage who work fifteen or more hours per week: 38

Percentage of children under eighteen living in single-parent households: 27

Percentage of children who are overweight: 16

Percentage of thirteen year olds who watch television three to four hours per day: 42; five hours or more: 31

Percentage of sixteen to nineteen year olds who participate in volunteer activities for schools and other organizations: 13

Percentage of students who have disabilities and are served by federal programs: 12

Sources: *Morbidity and Mortality Weekly Report* (Atlanta, GA: Centers for Disease Control and Prevention, July 30, 2004, Vol. 53, No. 29); *NAEP Facts* (Washington, DC: National Center for Education Statistics, October 2001); Carmen Denavas-Walt, Bernadette D. Proctor, and Robert J. Mills, *Income, Poverty, and Health Insurance Coverage in the United States: 2003*, U.S. Bureau of the Census, Current Population Reports (Washington, DC: U.S. Government Printing Office, 2004); *America's Children: Key National Indicators of Well-Being, 2003* (Washington, DC: Federal Interagency Forum on Child and Family Statistics, 2003); *The Condition of Education, 2000-2004* (Washington, DC: National Center for Education Statistics); *Crime and Safety in America's Public Schools* (Washington, DC: National Center for Education Statistics, 2004).

■ teaching implications

If you observe such potential indicators of suicidal tendencies, do not try to handle the burden alone. Seek a support network of the guidance counselor, the school social worker, and/or the school psychologist. Recognizing symptoms and getting professional help for students who behave in this way may prevent their suicides and help them develop coping behaviors to deal with their problems.

▶ School Violence and Vandalism

Massacre at Columbine High School in Littleton, Colorado—15 Die

Gunman Shoots Eighth-Grader in L.A.

Sixth-Graders Plot to Kill Their Teacher

Shooting Rampage by Student Leaves 10 Dead on Reservation

Teen Slashes Five Classmates in Knife Attack

These headlines suggest that America has become a dangerous place for its children. In urban areas, crime and violence from surrounding neighborhoods have spilled over into the schools, affecting children, staff, and teachers alike. In the suburbs, we have seen some horrible examples of students killing other students.

Costs resulting from vandalism or violence include the costs of building repairs, skyrocketing premiums for liability insurance, human costs in terms of injuries to students and teachers, and in extreme cases, even deaths. Many teachers are injured while attempting either to break up student fights or to halt robberies. Student-teacher disagreements also provoke attacks. Still other teachers are injured not by students but by intruders who may be dealing drugs or who see the elementary schools as buildings with little security, populated by women and children.

■ school crime statistics

How extensive is the problem of school violence and crime? Despite the headlines just given, serious violent crime constitutes a small percentage of the total amount of school crime, and homicide is extremely rare. Although the number of multiple homicide events at school has increased and receives national media coverage when it does occur, the chance of suffering a school-associated violent death is less than one in a million. The rate of violent deaths at schools has actually dropped since 1992. The National School Safety Center, a nonprofit group advocating safe schools, tracks the number of school-associated violent deaths. For the 2001–02 school year, the group reports only 5 such deaths, down from 22 the prior year, 44 in 1997–98; and a high of 56 in 1992–93, the first year the organization

Reprinted with special permission of King Features Syndicate.

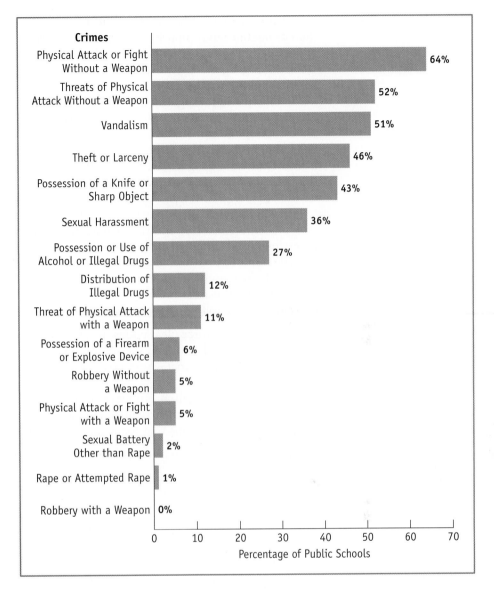

FIGURE 4.4
Percentage of Public Schools with Specific Crimes

Source: *Crime and Safety in America's Public Schools* (U.S. Department of Education, National Center for Education Statistics, 2004). Available at: http://nces.ed.gov/pubs2004/2004370.pdf.

Crimes

Crime	Percentage
Physical Attack or Fight Without a Weapon	64%
Threats of Physical Attack Without a Weapon	52%
Vandalism	51%
Theft or Larceny	46%
Possession of a Knife or Sharp Object	43%
Sexual Harassment	36%
Possession or Use of Alcohol or Illegal Drugs	27%
Distribution of Illegal Drugs	12%
Threat of Physical Attack with a Weapon	11%
Possession of a Firearm or Explosive Device	6%
Robbery Without a Weapon	5%
Physical Attack or Fight with a Weapon	5%
Sexual Battery Other than Rape	2%
Rape or Attempted Rape	1%
Robbery with a Weapon	0%

Percentage of Public Schools

tracked that statistic.[34] Although school-related deaths have declined, many students still fear going to school because of threatened violence. Factors such as weapon carrying, fights, the presence of gangs and bullying create an atmosphere of fear for many students (see Figure 4.4). In 2003, over 5 percent of high school students did not go to school at some point because of safety concerns.[35]

Gangs

Severe violence is often associated with gangs. Once confined to inner-city areas, street gangs are now present in smaller urban areas and suburbs, although in smaller percentages. Urban students are more likely to report street gangs at their schools (31 percent) than are suburban students (18 percent) or rural students (12 percent).[36] The proportion of young people who actually join gangs is quite small, however. The U.S. Justice Department estimates the number of gangs at 24,500 and gang members at about 775,000.[37]

Although gang members are often stereotyped as lower class, some are children of middle-class, suburban families who commit acts of vandalism, robbery, and drug dealing out of boredom or feelings of alienation from family and friends. While most gang members are male, there seems to be a recent rise in the number of females who are gang members, in either all-female or mixed-gender gangs.

Children and teenagers join gangs for a variety of reasons: the excitement of gang activity, peer pressure, physical protection, attention, financial gain, a sense of belonging, and sometimes because they feel ignored by the people they should be close to—usually one or both parents. In many cases, youths are not actively discouraged from gang involvement by their parents. Often parents are unaware that their children are engaged in gang activity. Gangs often display clothing, jewelry, tattoos, or graffiti that distinguish and identify their members.

The character of gang activity has become more violent because gangs are increasingly more involved in drug dealing and other criminal activities. The easy accessibility and spread of guns and the greater tendency to use extreme violence to settle disputes or to avenge even the smallest acts of "disrespect" have also contributed to increased violence.

■ combating gang influence

How can educators minimize the negative influences of gangs? Useful actions include the following:

- Establish and enforce clear codes of school conduct that stress the unacceptability of gang behavior and the prohibition of weapons.
- Establish programs that stress positive youth involvement as alternatives to gang membership.
- Assimilate gang-oriented students into the mainstream—academically, socially, and through extracurricular activities.
- Create school programs that focus on nonviolent conflict resolution and gang prevention.
- Take quick, decisive actions when instances of gang activity occur on school grounds.
- Prohibit gang "colors," insignia, and other signs of gang membership.

Bullying

Everyone who has attended school most likely has memories of themselves or friends of theirs being frightened by a bully. Once dismissed as "kids-will-be-kids" behavior, chronic teasing and bullying are now being viewed by educators as dangerous social acts. One recent study found that schools were more likely to have a serious problem with student bullying (29 percent) than any other discipline problem, with the result that many students stay home for fear of being bullied.[38] In 2003, 7 percent of students ages twelve to eighteen reported having been bullied in the past six months, up from 5 percent in 1999.[39]

Bullying takes a terrible toll on children. Their schoolwork suffers, and their physical and mental health also suffers. Physical and psychological bullying is often reported to be a contributing cause in adolescent suicide attempts. Bullying is also bad for bullies because they rarely learn the consequences of their actions.

■ programs to eliminate bullying

Visit this chapter of the website to link to more information about stopping bullying.

A nationwide program, Bully-Proofing Your School, teaches children to recognize bullying and to develop ways to protect themselves, such as humor and avoidance. Teachers and other school workers also receive training. Civility training is also becoming a popular way to reduce bullying by teaching children how to be kind and compassionate to all people. When the problem persists,

Bullying is common in schools, producing consequences detrimental to both the bullies and victims. Schools are responding with a variety of programs to reduce the incidents of bullying. (© Jonathan Nourok/PhotoEdit)

some schools have developed **zero-tolerance policies** for aggressive behavior and automatically suspend any student who harasses another. By developing a heightened awareness of bullying and its negative consequences, teachers can take actions to make the school environment more hospitable and inviting for all students.

Steps to Reduce School Violence

Concern over school crime and violence has prompted many public schools to take measures to reduce and prevent violence and ensure safety in schools. In particular, concerns about keeping schools secure from outsiders have increased since a 2004 incident in Russia, where terrorists forced their way into an elementary school, killing more than 300 people, 250 of them young students. Measures adopted by schools include enacting zero-tolerance policies regarding weapons—that is, carrying a weapon to school will automatically result in expulsion; creating alternative schools for students with a history of violence; requiring students to wear uniforms; employing various security measures such as requiring visitor sign-in and using metal detectors; having police or other law enforcement officials stationed at the school; and offering students and staff various types of violence prevention programs.

Several aspects of school organization can contribute to student aggression, including high numbers of students occupying a small space, imposition of routines and conformity that may anger some students, and poor building designs that may contribute to the commission of violent acts. Most deadly incidents occur during "transition times"—that is, the start of school, during lunch periods, or the end of the school day. Reducing crowding, increasing supervision, and instituting policies for handling disputes during these intervals can reduce the likelihood of conflicts and their resulting injuries.

The video case *Social and Emotional Development: Understanding Adolescents* shows a group of middle-school boys discussing productive ways to handle stress and anger. As you watch the clips and study the artifacts in the case, reflect upon the following questions:

1. What are your concerns, as a teacher, about violence in the schools?
2. Which of the strategies for teachers and schools listed in this chapter is represented in this case?
3. Can you think of additional techniques that you, as a teacher, could use to defuse potentially dangerous situations in school?

■ school factors in student aggression

■ good relationships reduce violence

Students who enjoy positive interactions with faculty and staff, are academically successful, or participate productively in school activities are less likely to commit acts of violence. One study found that in more than half the cases of school violence, there were warning signs in the form of notes, threats, journal entries, arguments, or physical fights. Teachers who are able to develop close relationships with students may be in a good position to spot these warning signs. Developing mechanisms for reporting threats and other actions that may signal potential violence can also help schools curb these outbreaks.

■ how to reduce violence

What else can schools do to reduce school violence?

- Principals can establish common goals and elicit commitment to the goals from teachers, students, and parents.
- Establish a firm, fair, and consistent system for running the school.
- Establish high expectations for the behavior and performance of students and staff.
- Create a curriculum that supports the values of honesty, integrity, kindness, and respect for others.
- Use a variety of security measures to keep intruders and weapons off school grounds.
- Establish the school as neutral territory for students, control rumors, and squelch loitering and tardiness.
- Create alternative schools for serious offenders.
- Provide students and teachers with training in effective communication.

■ teaching implications

What can teachers themselves do to prevent violence and vandalism?

- Establish a classroom environment centered on respect and kindness, where put-downs, ridicule, and sarcasm are not tolerated.
- Learn how to defuse conflict in ways that save face for both students and teachers.
- Develop intensive skill in classroom management.
- Use peer counseling or peer mediation to train students to handle problems before they become serious.
- Involve students in decision-making processes in areas such as finding methods to handle offenders.

The encouraging news is that although school violence and vandalism are serious problems, they still affect a relatively small percentage of teachers and students in the public schools. The problem probably reflects as much on societal malaise as on the schools. Boredom, frustration, alienation, despair, and low self-concept are characteristics that teenagers may experience in their homes and in society in general, as well as in school. The disintegration of the traditional family and the increasing depiction of violence in the media and in popular music are cited as two major causes of violence in the public schools. As long as violence prevails in society, schools will likely be affected.

Pause and Reflect

1 ► Have you ever been afraid to go to school? Why?

2 ► Were you aware of the problem of school violence and vandalism before you read this chapter? Will it be a major factor in your decision regarding whether or where to teach?

▶ School Dropout Rates

■ different dropout rates

 Visit this chapter of the website to link to up-to-date statistics on this topic.

A disturbing study by the Urban Institute indicates that, nationwide, only 68 percent of high school students receive a diploma and, even more disturbing, only a little more than one-half of students from historically disadvantaged racial and ethnic minorities finish high school. In some high-poverty urban areas, such as New York City and Houston, only 40 percent of all high school students graduate.[40] When we break down these percentages to look at subgroups, (Figure 4.5), we find that only 50 percent of African American youth, 51 percent of Native Americans, and 53 percent of Hispanic youth graduate from high school. Seventy-five percent of White students and 78 percent of Asian American students graduate.[41] Dropout rates are also strongly related to income levels. Youth from

FIGURE 4.5

Graduation Rates for the High School Class of 2001

Source: Data taken from Charles B. Swanson, *The Real Truth about Low Graduation Rates, An Evidence-Based Commentary*, (Washington, DC: The Urban Institute, 2004). Available at: **http://www. urban.org/UploadedPDF/ 411050_realtruth.pdf.**

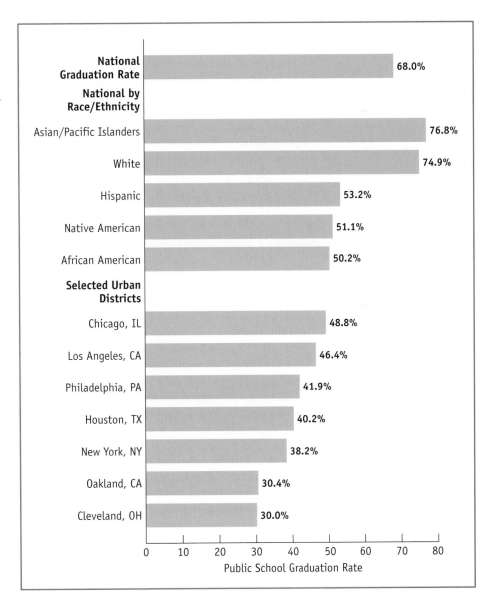

low-income families are six times more likely to drop out than those from high-income families.[42] Dropout rates are highest in schools with a larger proportion of students from low-income families.

■ reasons for dropping out

Besides poverty, what contributes to high dropout rates? Students report poor grades, dislike for school, alienation from peers, marriage or pregnancy, and employment as common causes for leaving school. The most commonly reported factor is poor academic performance. One cause of dropping out is unrealistic expectations about the world of work. Many students with high hopes for the imagined luxury of a regular income fail to realize that wages in the service sector of employment have deteriorated. Other teenagers may envision starting at the bottom of the work hierarchy and, through hard work, eventually climbing the ladder of success. Many of them, however, lack job search skills and end up in jobs with limited potential for advancement. Despite this reality, the strong motivation to work often proves too powerful an incentive and results in a student leaving school. The immediate rewards of the workplace lure some students away from the more remote incentives of staying in school and attaining an education.

I am often asked whether I approve of compulsory education, and I usually reply that I do and that I wish we had it; we only have compulsory attendance.

—JOHN BREMER

■ teaching implications

Students often give warning signs that they are at risk for dropping out. These include increased absences, lethargy in completing work, and preoccupation with things outside of school. Teachers can discourage students from dropping out by showing interest and care in their students and by talking to and encouraging them. Knowing your students well can help you detect changes in their attitudes and work habits.

Pause and Reflect

1 ▶ Can a secondary-level teacher, who may see 150 students a day, get to know them all well?

2 ▶ When you were in high school, did you know any students who dropped out? If so, what were their reasons for doing so?

▶ A Final Word

Given the range of social problems that we have discussed in this chapter and in the preceding chapter, it is not surprising to find that schools bear an ever-growing burden to guide young people's decision making. How well equipped are the schools to handle this task? Creating schools that are safe, healthy, and conducive to learning doesn't happen automatically. The climate in a school is a product of laws, rules, regulations, and, most importantly, attitudes and values held by those who work and study in school. When problems threaten the safety, health, or well being of students, whether within the school or outside its boundaries, educators must intervene in productive ways to ensure a school climate that protects students and promotes learning.

Key Terms

at-risk students (87)
generational poverty (95)

socioeconomic status (93)
zero-tolerance policies (107)

For Reflection

1 What aspects of our culture contribute to the high incidence of child abuse in the United States?

2 Should schools assume responsibility for educating children about alcohol, drugs, sex, and suicide? Why or why not? If so, what aspects of the current curriculum should be dropped to make room for these topics?

3 How can you prepare yourself to address the various social problems that students are likely to bring to your classroom?

For Debate

Read the Author Debate on sex education at the website, and consider the points each author raises about sex education in public schools. Then, go to EduSpace to post your own opinions and concerns about sex education.

For Further Information

PRINT RESOURCES

James P. Comer, Norris M. Haynes, Edward T. Joyner, and Michael Ben-Avie, eds., *Rallying the Whole Village: The Comer Process for Reforming Education* (New York: Teachers College Press, 1996). In this text, James Comer and his colleagues describe the process they have employed to coordinate various resources to create effective school communities in areas of low socioeconomic status.

Children's Defense Fund, *The State of America's Children: A Report from the Children's Defense Fund, Yearbook 2004* (Boston: Beacon Press, 2004). This report makes a compelling case for increasing health and educational programs for children in the United States. Citing numerous shocking statistics, the report makes it clear that the United States, compared with other industrialized nations, is shortchanging its children.

Joan N. Burstyn, Geoff Bender, Ronnie Casella, Howard W. Gordon, Domingo P. Guerra, Kristen V. Luschen, Rebecca Stevens, and Kimberly M. Williams, *Preventing Violence in Schools: A Challenge to American Democracy* (Mahwah, NJ: Lawrence Erlbaum Associates, 2001). This text provides an in-depth ethnographic analysis of violence prevention programs and an assessment of their effectiveness.

Ruby K. Payne, *A Framework for Understanding Poverty* (Highlands, TX: Aha Process, Inc., 2001). This book explains how children from generational poverty possess values and behaviors different from those usually emphasized in schools, and helps educators better understand these differences so they can provide learning supports for these students.

WEB RESOURCES

Children's Defense Fund. Available at: **http://www. childrensdefense.org/.** A private non-profit organization that advocates for children's needs. The website contains key facts about the condition of children in America, relevant legislation, and connections to other organizations advocating for children.

Future of Children. Available at: **http://www. futureofchildren.org/.** *The Future of Children* seeks to promote effective policies and programs for children by providing policymakers, service providers, and the media with timely, objective information based on the best available research. A joint venture of The Woodrow Wilson School of Public and International Affairs at Princeton University and The Brookings Institution.

Education Week on the Web. Available at: **http://www. edweek.org.** Published forty-one times a year, *Education Week* is the nation's newspaper devoted to educational issues, preschool through secondary school. Many of the issues discussed in this chapter are reported on in this periodical, and its website contains an archive section that permits searches for particular topics and issues, particularly the "Hot Topics" section. The site also includes the archives of *Teacher Magazine.*

Virginia Youth Violence Project. Available at: **http:// youthviolence.edschool.virginia.edu.** The Virginia Youth Violence Project identifies effective methods and policies for youth violence prevention, especially in school settings.

Center for the Study and Prevention of Violence. Available at: **http://www.colorado.edu/cspv.**
This site contains many good ideas, references, programs, and links related to violence prevention.

Safe and Drug Free Schools Program. Available at: **http://www.ed.gov/offices/OESE/SDFS/.**
A program of the U.S. Department of Education, the site contains descriptions of model programs, research findings, grant opportunities, and links to related sites.

5 *What Is Taught?*

Chapter Preview   What knowledge is most worth knowing? What should be taught in the schools? The answers to these questions take the form of curricula, and they are often a source of tension among teachers, school boards, education professors, textbook publishers, policymakers, and parents. Currently, these groups are seeking to raise academic standards through common curricular emphases while also accommodating various cultural and ethnic groups' demands for representation in the curriculum.

This chapter emphasizes that:

▶ The school curriculum, which has evolved over time as a result of shifting purposes, consists of all the organized and intended experiences of the student for which the school accepts responsibility.

▶ The present curriculum in most subject areas has been greatly influenced by the recent standards-based reform movement that identifies what students should know and be able to do in each subject area.

▶ Textbooks have such a strong impact on what is taught in the classrooms that some people argue that texts represent a national curriculum.

▶ Major innovative instructional approaches used across the curriculum include interdisciplinary teaching, cooperative learning, critical thinking and problem solving, writing across the curriculum, differentiated instruction, and block scheduling.

▶ The relevance of the schools' curricula to individual and societal problems is a continually debated issue.

Baseball, debating, reading, and biology are all learned in school, along with love and tolerance, independence and frustration, mathematics and dramatics, values and ceramics, woodshop and poise, history and boredom, and computer science and leadership! Some are learned intentionally and others incidentally.

▶ What Is Curriculum?

■ definition of curriculum

We define the **curriculum** as all the organized and intended experiences of the student for which the school accepts responsibility. In other words, the curriculum is not just the intellectual content of the subjects taught but also the methods used to teach them, the interactions that occur among people, and the school-sponsored activities that contribute to the "life experience." Educational theorists have identified several different kinds of curriculum, including the formal, extra, and hidden. Let's briefly examine these different kinds of curriculum.

■ formal curriculum

The planned content and objectives of language arts, mathematics, science, and all the other subject areas available to students constitute the *formal* or explicit curriculum. The states and the local school boards are responsible for determining the subjects that will be taught in this formal curriculum. Later in this chapter, we will examine the formal curriculum of the schools, including trends and controversies in each of the major content areas.

■ "extra" curriculum

At one time, such activities as athletics, band, cheerleading, and debate club were considered to be part of the *"extra"* curriculum, whereas the formal courses of study (history, science, mathematics, and English) were considered curricular. However, this distinction is not particularly useful any more because very important learning also occurs outside the classroom.

■ hidden curriculum

However, what students learn in the environment of the school extends beyond the planned curriculum of courses or subjects they will take, or the extracurricular activities in which they participate. Classroom observers have noted that the schools also teach a *hidden* or informal curriculum through which the classroom and school, as learning environments, socialize children to the values that are acceptable to the institution and society at large. The messages of the hidden curriculum are usually conveyed indirectly and deal with attitudes, values, beliefs, and behavior. The messages of the hidden curriculum can support or undermine the formal curriculum. When the hidden and the formal curriculum conflict, many observers believe the hidden curriculum carries more weight.

What are these attitudes and values, and how are they communicated to students? A major purpose of the hidden curriculum in schools has been to teach students the routines and values for getting along in school and in the larger society. Thus, it tends to have a conservative bent, focusing on preserving the status quo. In the eyes of some critics, the hidden curriculum of the schools works against diversity, equity, and social justice.[1]

■ compliance, competition part of hidden curriculum

One researcher suggests that schools value several specific ways of thinking and behaving.[2] One is compliant behavior as opposed to personal initiative. Students soon learn to give the teacher what she or he wants or expects. Reward systems used by schools teach students to "read" both the teacher and the system to determine just what is expected to get the grade, the teacher's attention, or the sticker with the smiling face. Similarly, competitiveness is learned through the examples of athletics, grading systems that compare students to one another, and ability grouping to separate students into classes according to their achievement. The many ways in which students learn what a school values include how the school allocates time to subjects of study, the rules established for the school, and even the architecture and furnishings of the school.

■ teaching implications

As a future teacher, you should be able to identify what rules of behavior, rituals and ceremonies, and accepted patterns of teacher and student interaction are communicated to students at schools you visit. Does the "climate" of the classroom and the school suggest warmth, support for diversity, and nurturing of individuals, or do observers describe a mood of disinterest, regimentation, and antipathy among staff and students? Most important, what is the school's deeper message about the stance its students should take toward the current society?

Pause and Reflect

1 ▶ How can you determine the hidden curriculum of a school? What clues would you look for?

2 ▶ Thinking back on your own schooling, can you identify some of the messages that you received from the hidden curriculum?

Standards-Based Reform Movement

In this chapter, we examine the formal curriculum, those subjects that are taught in schools and some of the forces and instructional approaches that influence how they are taught. The typical school curriculum is a **subject-matter curriculum,** organized according to subject-matter divisions, and most of the efforts that go into curriculum development are still concentrated around traditional subject matter.

■ curriculum battles

In the chapter entitled "What Is a School and What Is It For?" we discussed how the curriculum is a *social bet* on what knowledge, skills, and attitudes the older generation thinks the young need to know to prosper, personally and economically, in the twenty-first century. There is, by no means, a consensus among the parties involved in placing this social bet. In fact, curriculum decision making can resemble a battlefield in which conservatives and liberals, religious groups and agnostics, whites and people of color, and many other groups grapple to ensure that their beliefs and perspectives are represented in the school's curriculum. These curriculum battles at both the state and local level can be heated, because those engaged believe there is a lot at stake, in essence, the future of the United States.

All that is taught is a commitment to what is thought valuable.

—R. S. PETERS

■ content standards

The strongest influence on a subject-matter curriculum over the last decade has been the *standards-based reform movement,* designed to promote academic excellence and equity. **Content standards** are statements of the subject-specific knowledge and skills that schools are expected to teach and students are expected to learn. Standards-setters often use the shorthand phrase, "what students should know and be able to do," to communicate the purposes of content standards.

■ Goals 2000

In contrast to many other countries, the United States has traditionally had a decentralized system of state and local curricula. The national government has had little influence on what is taught in our nation's schools. During the 1980s and 1990s, however, spurred by concern about the nation's economic competitiveness with other countries, a strong movement emerged toward national curriculum standards, national testing and assessment, and the establishment of national goals. A 1994 law, the Goals 2000: Educate America Act, codified eight national goals to guide future educational initiatives and funded different academic groups to develop national standards in the various subject-matter fields. The National Council of Teachers of Mathematics led the way in 1989 by publishing its mathematics standards, and by a decade later, most subject-specific teacher organizations had followed suit.

By 1996, however, these centralization efforts had lost steam, giving way to a growing consensus that the setting of standards and curriculum should remain the prerogative of the individual states. Interestingly, many states were using the national standards developed by different academic groups in formulating their own state standards. (For examples of current state standards in different subject matter and grade levels, see Table. 5.1.) By the beginning of the twenty-first century,

■ move back toward decentralization

TABLE 5.1 Examples of Content Standards from Several States

Language Arts

Grade Level

K–3	Distinguish different forms of texts such as lists, newsletters, and signs and the functions they serve. (Texas)
2–5	Uses consonant blends, digraphs, and diphthongs to orally decode words. (Georgia)
8	Produce work in at least one literary genre that follows the conventions of the genre. (Pennsylvania)
9–11	Apply knowledge of Greek, Latin, and Anglo-Saxon roots and affixes to determine meaning of unfamiliar vocabulary. (Kansas)
9–12	Identify strategies used by the media to present information for a variety of purposes (e.g., to inform, entertain, or persuade). (California)

Mathematics

Grade Level

2	Use place value concepts to represent whole numbers using physical models, numerals, and words, with ones, tens, and hundreds. (Ohio)
7	The student will solve consumer application problems involving tips, discounts, sales tax, and simple interest, using whole numbers, fractions, decimals, and percents. (Virginia)
K–12	All students will regularly and routinely use calculators, computers, manipulatives, and other mathematical tools to enhance mathematical thinking, understanding, and power. (New Jersey)
Advanced Placement Calculus	The student will use integration to solve problems. This will include areas bounded by polar curves, length of a path (including parametric curves), work (Hooke's law), and improper integrals. (Virginia)

Science

Grade Level

K–5	All students will measure and describe the things around us; explain what the world around us is made of; identify and describe forms of energy; and explain how electricity and magnetism interact with matter. (Michigan)
6–8	Students will know how cells function as "building blocks" of organisms and describe the requirements for cells to live by stating how cells work together to keep the organism alive. (Illinois)

| 9–12 | All students will analyze claims for their scientific merit and explain how scientists decide what constitutes scientific knowledge; how science is related to other ways of knowing; how science and technology affect our society; and how people of diverse cultures have contributed to and influenced developments in science. (Michigan) |
| 9–12 | The student will identify the independent variables, dependent variables, and controls in an experimental setup. (Oklahoma) |

Social Studies

Grade Level

1–3	Construct and interpret maps and other geographic tools, including the use of map elements to organize information about people, place, and environments. (Arizona)
6–8	Describe the social, economic, and political characteristics of Western European society that led to the exploration of the Americas. (Maryland)
9–12	Explain how the design of the U.S. Constitution is intended to balance and check the powers of the branches of government. (Connecticut)

 Visit this chapter of the website to link to more examples of both national and state content standards.

Source: Education World. Available at **http://www.education-world.com/standards/**.

virtually every state had developed its own standards for student learning, and many states backed up their new standards with rigorous accountability measures for both students and educators. The national No Child Left Behind Act of 2001 promoted accountability measures even more strongly, requiring states, by the 2005–06 school year, to administer annual, statewide assessments in reading and mathematics to all students in grades three to eight. For more on this law, see the chapter entitled "How Are Schools Governed, Influenced, and Financed?"

■ controversy over standards movement

The standards movement was immediately surrounded by controversy. Some critics objected to the attention and money lavished on the development and assessment of standards instead of other pressing educational needs, such as habitable school buildings. Other critics were concerned with the testing that usually accompanied the state standards. Many state legislatures linked student passage of standards-based tests with "high-stakes" outcomes, including graduation from high school or school accreditation. Some legislatures made educators accountable for students' learning the standards and passing the assessment tests. Teachers' jobs and students' future education were suddenly at risk if students failed the tests, and educators and students alike felt much more pressure to succeed. In spite of these criticisms, numerous polls show the public overwhelmingly supports the idea of high standards. The chapter entitled "How Should Education Be Reformed?" discusses the current status of national education standards and assessment in more detail.

Pause and Reflect

1 ▶ Study the standards for a discipline area in which you are interested. (You can find standards websites listed at the end of this chapter.) Do you believe they are appropriate for the level of students you would like to teach? Why or why not?

2 ▶ Do you support the use of "high stakes" tests to determine graduation from high school? Why or why not?

▶ What Is the Present Curriculum?

In looking at the courses of study prescribed by the fifty states, we will see that the similarities far outweigh the differences. Parts of this chapter discuss some reasons for this phenomenon, such as the influence of standards-based reform movements in the various states and the uniformity of available textbooks, but for now, let's examine what is presently taught in elementary and secondary schools across the country. At both levels the curriculum is organized into subject-matter areas, which ordinarily are language arts and English, mathematics, science, social studies, foreign languages, fine arts, physical education and recreation, career and technical education, and electives. Most of the national organizations representing teachers of these various subject areas have developed content standards of what elementary and secondary students should know and be able to do in each content area. The websites for these organizations and their respective content standards can be found in the **For Further Information** section at the end of the chapter.

Language Arts and English

Visit this chapter of the website to link to more information about language arts curricula.

The *language arts* program seeks to develop in children the skills of reading, writing, speaking, and listening, as well as a knowledge of culture as represented in literature. The importance of language arts cannot be overemphasized because no subject can be successfully studied without adequate language skills. In elementary schools, most language arts programs focus on helping students develop written and oral communication skills, comprehension and problem-solving strategies, creativity, and appreciation for language and literature. At the secondary level, English courses focus on integration of the language arts using literature as the prime motivator. Among the most commonly read works are *Romeo and Juliet, Julius Caesar, The Scarlet Letter, Macbeth, Huckleberry Finn,* and *The Great Gatsby.*

I have often reflected upon the new vistas that reading opened to me. . . . As I see it today, the ability to read awoke inside me some long dormant craving to be mentally alive.

—MALCOLM X

■ trend toward new media

■ Issues and Trends   Teachers today are selecting literature that is relevant to student interests yet representative of an accepted literary tradition; balancing classic literature selections with works by and about minority groups; instructing students in critical thinking; encouraging writing across the curriculum (discussed later in this chapter); integrating the various language arts by, for example, linking reading and writing together or speaking, listening, and reading; composing and creating in new media forms such as video or World Wide Web presentations; and maintaining a balance between composition and literature in the curriculum. Many English educators are chafing under the pressure to prepare students for state standards-based proficiency examinations that emphasize grammar, spelling, and basic skills, often to the exclusion of explaining classic and modern literature. Adjusting the curriculum and use of standards for children of multiple language and cultural backgrounds constitutes a major challenge for language arts and English teachers.

Education . . . has produced a vast population able to read but unable to distinguish what is worth reading.

—G. M. TREVELYAN

■ phonics versus whole language

Major disagreements exist in the field of reading education. The basic debate is whether reading instruction should emphasize the integration of language arts skills and knowledge in a literature-based approach, commonly known as the **whole language approach,** or focus on **phonics** instruction, an approach to reading that teaches the reader to "decode" words by sounding out letters and

The video case *Elementary Reading Instruction: A Balanced Literacy Program* provides a detailed example of a teacher who balances phonics and whole language approaches for teaching reading. As you watch the clips and study the artifacts in the case, reflect upon the following question:

1. What aspects of the language arts curriculum, as discussed in this chapter, are most likely to apply to the grade levels or subjects you would like to teach?

combinations of letters. The whole language approach to reading stresses that children should use language in ways that relate to their own lives and culture. Whole-language advocates tolerate the use of "invented spelling" by children because it is seen as part of a child's reading development and correcting a child's every spelling error will discourage them from enjoying writing. Whole-language teaching uses such common techniques as daily journal and letter writing, a great deal of silent and oral reading of real literature, and student cooperation.

During the 1970s and 1980s, whole language approaches to reading displaced the phonics approach in many schools. However, discontent with declining reading scores in states that emphasized a whole language approach, notably California, spurred a renewed interest in phonics. In fact, the issue has become politically charged, with conservatives supporting phonics and liberals supporting whole language approaches. Although both the whole language and phonics camps have their strong believers, recent research concludes that it is important to teach explicit, systematic phonics within a context of meaningful literature.[3] *Phonemic* awareness, the understanding that sounds make up language, seems to be crucial in the development of good readers. Thus, a balanced use of both approaches, rather than one over the other, seems to be the key to reading instruction. Many major publishers are now including both approaches in their reading series.

Mathematics

Before the 1950s, schools emphasized student mastery of basic computational skills. In the 1960s, a new type of mathematics curriculum, known as the *new math*, emerged. It saw mathematics as a language that both communicates ideas about numbers and describes the quantitative aspects of ideas and objects. As a result, the new math stressed *structure* rather than drill and computational skills. The new math tended to be abstract, and for the average student, its conceptual theories were of little practical use.

Today the traditional approach featuring drill and practice, computation, and memorization tends to be used in courses for non-college-bound students. College-bound students, after studying algebra and geometry, often take optional fourth-year courses that place strong emphasis on structure, learning by discovery, definitions, properties, sets, rigor, statistics, calculus, trigonometry, and other abstract concepts.

Visit this chapter of the website to link to more information about mathematics curricula.

■ "new math"

■ emphasis on problem solving

■ **Issues and Trends** Mathematics at the elementary level emphasizes the use of hands-on manipulatives to aid students in learning about patterns in mathematics and our base-ten system. Mathematical reasoning and problem solving, rather than the teacher's authority and the textbook, are being urged. Experts in mathematics education are urging teachers to emphasize multiple approaches to solving real problems. These emphases are consistent with the popular constructivist approach to learning, which is based on psychological theories suggesting that people must construct knowledge and meaning for themselves, rather than receiving knowledge passively from teachers or textbooks. (Constructivist approaches to learning are discussed further in the chapters entitled "What Are the Philosophical Foundations of American Education?" and "How Should Education Be Reformed?") Teachers are being urged to focus on conceptual mathematics

Elementary school teachers must build basic understanding in key subjects such as mathematics if students are to succeed in later grades. (© Bill Aron/PhotoEdit)

understanding before focusing on procedural rules. There is a growing body of research that suggests if students learn procedural rules before they learn mathematical concepts, they will score significantly lower than do students who learn concepts first.[4]

use of computers

Calculators and computers are becoming more common, even at the elementary level, as mathematics education focuses less on computational skills and more on developing concepts, relationships, structures, and problem-solving skills. Moreover, the use of computers and computer programming in mathematics classes adds a great deal of practical utility for many students. Not only do computers create interest in the curriculum, but students receive valuable experience that may prove useful as they seek jobs. As described in the chapter entitled "What Should Teachers Know About Technology and Its Impact on Schools?" graphing calculators are seen as important tools to help students understand complex mathematical relationships.

drills can misuse computers

Computers, however, can be misused. One national study examining the use of computers in schools concluded that computers can be an important learning tool when used in simulations and real-life applications of math concepts, but using computers for repetitive math drills actually hurt students' math scores.[5]

integration of skills

In addition to using technology and emphasizing problem solving, mathematics programs have been moving away from the traditional compartmentalization of arithmetic, algebra, geometry, calculus, and so on. As newer topics, such as probability, statistics, and computer science, are emphasized, course designers have begun to integrate a variety of mathematics skills and topics in one course or across several courses. The blending of mathematics with other subject areas, including consumer economics and personal finance, will continue as part of the trend toward broadening students' applications of their mathematical understandings and skills.

Science

Visit this chapter of the website to link to more information about science curricula.

Science in the elementary grades takes advantage of children's natural curiosity about the world around them—plants, seasons, color, light, sound, and animals. In the upper elementary and middle school grades, the curriculum includes weather and climate, the solar system, electricity, and health-related topics. The secondary school science curriculum is still centered around year-long courses: general science, biology, chemistry, and physics.

■ **Issues and Trends**   Two major questions drive science education reform: "Where will the next generation of scientists come from?" and "How can all students be prepared to make informed judgments about such critical and science-based issues as environmental pollution, energy sources, and biotechnology?"

■ Project 2061

For reformers, there has been both good news and bad news concerning science education in the United States. The bad news is that American youth do not know much science. The good news is that the country is reaching consensus on how to remedy the problem. The science curriculum has been undergoing dramatic redirection as a result of Project 2061 (named for the year in which Halley's comet is expected to return), an initiative of the American Association for the Advancement of Science. Inquiry-based learning and a hands-on approach are strong elements in science reform efforts. Addressing both elementary and secondary science, the association's recommendations include the following:

- Reduce the boundaries between academic disciplines.
- Emphasize ideas and thinking skills rather than specialized vocabulary and memorization.
- Help students develop a cogent view of the world by including such key concepts and principles as the structure and evolution of the universe; basic concepts related to matter, energy, force, and motion; the human life cycle; medical techniques; social change and conflict; and the mathematics of symbols.[6]

In the science classroom, wondering should be as highly valued as knowing.

—2061 SCIENCE CURRICULUM

The work of Project 2061 appears to have had a strong effect on both the national standards for science education and many state curriculum frameworks, but as yet, it has been slow to change how science is taught in the schools.

Social Studies

Visit this chapter of the website to link to more information about social studies curricula.

Social studies—the study of people and their ideas, actions, and relationships—is not a discipline in the same sense as mathematics or physics, although it draws on the various social science disciplines (history, geography, political science, economics, psychology, sociology, and anthropology), as well as on religion, literature, and the arts, for its content and methods of inquiry. (A *discipline* has been defined as an area of inquiry containing a distinctive body of concepts and principles, with techniques for exploring the area and for correcting and expanding the body of knowledge.)[7]

■ history dominates

History has traditionally been the leading discipline of social studies at both the elementary and secondary levels and, although other disciplines have made some inroads, it still remains dominant. Recently, efforts have been made to restore geography to the social studies curriculum following assessments that pointed out students' inability to locate countries on maps. Government is also a staple of the social studies curriculum. However, the social studies curriculum at both the elementary and secondary levels is a hodgepodge of approaches.

■ concern for non-European cultures

■ **Issues and Trends**   Currently, a major debate rages over whether the social studies curriculum overemphasizes European history and culture at the expense of Asian, African, and Latin American history and culture. Another concern is the representation of women's roles in the history curriculum. Although many textbook publishers are making efforts to include greater representation of women and people of color in their books, critics argue that the efforts seem feeble and contrived. At all levels, textbooks dominate the social studies curriculum.

■ the "new civics"

Civic learning or **civic education** is another issue gaining the attention of social studies educators. Advocates of this new focus call for courses that will acquaint a racially and culturally diverse student population with the heritage common to the American democratic tradition. These new courses would extend the basic study of American law and government to include trends in history, issues in contemporary society, and questions of character and values. Through critical study of case histories and current news reports, students would learn to apply principles of democracy to everyday concerns they will face as citizens. Practical experiences in civic, cultural, and volunteer activities are also strongly recommended. The "new civics" courses may help unify educators who currently favor many different approaches to the teaching of social studies, including issues-centered, traditional, historical, critical thought, and character education approaches.

Standards have been developed by the various national organizations representing history, geography, economics, civics, and social studies. Unfortunately, these subject standards were developed independently of one another and do not relate to one another. However, the National Council for the Social Studies (NCSS) has articulated a framework to foster academic and civic competence by integrating national standards across various social sciences. Ten themes are highlighted in the framework: culture; people, places, and environments; individuals, groups and institutions; production, distribution, and consumption; global connections; time, continuity, and change; individual development and identity; power, authority, and governance; science, technology, and society; and civic ideals and practices.[8]

Foreign Languages

Visit this chapter of the website to link to more information about foreign language curricula.

Compared with citizens in other nations, Americans are woefully unprepared to speak foreign languages. About 44 percent of students in U.S. public high schools are enrolled in a foreign language course, with Spanish and French being the most popular languages taken.[9] On the bright side, more and more elementary schools are offering foreign language programs in recognition of the ease with which young children learn foreign languages.

■ cultural understanding

■ **Issues and Trends**   Foreign language departments in the public schools are trying to make the study of foreign languages more attractive by expanding their course offerings and integrating language study with concerns for international and multicultural education. Leaders in the field emphasize the cultural foundations of language, asserting that language study increases linguistic competence and cultural sensitivity. CD-ROMs and the Internet assist students and teachers in gaining greater access to current materials from other countries and interacting with key-pals from other countries, thus facilitating teaching and learning. Alternative secondary schools, such as international schools, schools-within-schools, and magnet schools, have also begun to integrate international studies and foreign language study.

■ elementary school emphasis

Early introduction of foreign languages continues to gain support, and concern about U.S. competitiveness in a global economy has led many business leaders and politicians to urge greater emphasis on foreign language instruction. More and more states are responding to these pressures. Techniques used in elementary bilingual education—immersion, partial immersion, or the Foreign Languages in the Elementary Schools Program—have focused instruction on developing fluency in speaking, writing, and comprehension. Proficiency-oriented instruction, which focuses on what the learner can do with language rather than what the learner knows about language, marks modern-day language teaching.

The Arts

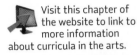
Visit this chapter of the website to link to more information about curricula in the arts.

The arts include visual arts, music, dance, and theater. Art and music in the elementary school are ordinarily taught by regular classroom teachers, although some schools hire specialist teachers in one or both areas. Dance and theater are largely ignored in the elementary school, although children of this age are less inhibited and seem to enjoy these activities more than do secondary students. The small amount of instruction provided in the arts for elementary students contrasts with high school offerings such as drama clubs, orchestras, bands, and dance groups. In most instances, instruction in music or dance during a child's elementary school years takes the form of private instruction outside the public school.

■ aesthetics emphasis

■ **Issues and Trends**   Programs in the arts have tended to emphasize the creation of an art object or the development of a performance, but newer programs center on aesthetic education and art as a way of knowing and perceiving the world. For most students, this trend will be useful.

Art is humanity's most essential, most universal language. It is not a frill, but a necessary part of communication.

—ERNEST L. BOYER

Curriculum specialists have suggested integrating the arts with other subject matter to show the usefulness of the arts and to appeal to a broader range of intelligences. (See the chapter entitled "Who Are Today's Students in a Diverse Society?" for more on the topic of Howard Gardner's theory of multiple intelligences.) There is little doubt that the arts play a crucial role in the development of cultured, educated individuals and that they respond to a deep instinct in humanity. In spite of this recognition, however, the arts remain an "endangered species" whenever budget cuts occur and when high-stakes assessments of standards in language arts, math, science, and social studies dictate what teachers should emphasize in their classrooms.

Physical Education, Health, and Recreation

Visit this chapter of the website to link to more information about the curriculum in this area.

Physical education—education by and through human movement—contributes to physical fitness, skill and knowledge development, and social and psychological development. Currently, physical education curricula are responding to four needs: (1) to develop aerobic capacity to maintain acceptable cardiorespiratory efficiency, (2) to achieve appropriate levels of body fat, (3) to acquire strength to

■ emphasis on fitness

Arts advocates support integrating the arts with the rest of the curriculum. These girls, for example, are studying Macbeth.
(© Bob Daemmrich/Stock Boston)

perform expected tasks of living, and (4) to achieve flexibility and abdominal strength to avoid lower back injuries. To address these needs, sports skills are alternated with fitness development through such activities as swimming, jogging, bicycling, yoga, and cross-country skiing. Students are given information on exercise and nutrition so they can understand how to balance caloric intake and maintain an appropriate body fat level. Physical education teachers are typically licensed for both elementary and secondary school teaching, but teachers usually seek out the age levels in which they are most interested.

health education

The health curriculum addresses such topics as injury prevention and safety, prevention and control of disease (including acquired immune deficiency syndrome [AIDS]), substance abuse, nutrition, family life (sexuality), consumer health, and mental and emotional health. More than most academic subjects, health education strives to change students' attitudes and behaviors to get them to take fewer risks and use preventive measures. Many health educators express frustration that health is not identified as a critical component of the K–12 curriculum and questions about health do not appear on high-stakes tests. Because health is not tested, it isn't stressed in schools as much as health educators would like.

Elective Courses

Most high schools today offer their students a number of options regarding the courses they take. Whereas the average high school student graduates with about twenty units (one year-long course represents one unit), large high schools may offer as many as one hundred courses. The average student, then, will probably choose among optional courses according to individual interests and academic or career ambitions.

■ non-college-bound students

■ **Issues and Trends** Although college preparation has been the major goal of many high schools, efforts have increased recently to provide comprehensive programs for students not planning to attend college. This trend is especially evident in rural areas, where small, local high schools are being replaced by comprehensive regional high schools. Some of the courses involved, such as technology education, distributive education, home economics, business education, and agriculture, are specifically vocational. Others, such as driver education and consumer education, have been added to the curriculum because of an obvious societal need or in response to student interest.

■ more graduation requirements

A trend disturbing those who teach elective courses is the increase in requirements for graduation from high schools, which leaves less time for elective courses. Some argue that a common general education provides the best foundation for future work or academic study; others hope to maintain a large percentage of the curriculum as electives. These issues, when raised by teachers of elective courses, focus attention on the purpose of comprehensive schooling and on what is "basic."

A liberal education is the only practical form of vocational education.

—John Henry Cardinal Newman

Career and Technical Education

Visit this chapter of the website to link to more information about vocational curricula.

The purpose of career and technical education is to provide a foundation of skills that allow high school students to be gainfully employed after graduation. The subject areas most commonly associated with career and technical education are business, trade and industrial, health occupations, agriculture, family and consumer sciences, marketing, and technology.

■ achieving necessary skills

Once known as "vocational education," career and technical education came under fire in recent decades from those who noted its inadequacy in preparing students for careers in high-technology fields or in the country's now dominant service economy. In 1991 the U.S. Department of Labor issued the Secretary's Commission on Achieving Necessary Skills (SCANS) report, which called for all high school students to develop a set of higher competencies and a foundation of skills to be better prepared for the world of work.[10] The report recognizes that both education and businesses will have to change if America is to have a well-prepared work force. The report urges teachers to help students see the relationships between what they study and its applications in real-world contexts and to emphasize real-life problem solving.

■ School-to-Work partnerships

The federal government also supports a School-to-Work program designed to help students develop skills and understandings that will prepare them to adapt to the changing needs of the workplace. Although aimed particularly for students not planning on going to college, many college-bound students also take advantage of these programs to get a "real-world" grounding for future careers. These programs can take many different shapes, from career academies that feature specialized career-oriented curricula in such areas as health professions, business, or law, to paid internships and co-op experiences. Schools work with local businesses to design courses and experiences that will prepare high school students for particular kinds of jobs that meet local business needs. Hundreds of thousands of businesses nationwide now participate in School-to-Work partnerships.

■ more apprenticeship
programs?

■ **Issues and Trends**   The emphasis on high-stakes academic assessments has contributed to a decline in the number of students enrolled in career and technical education. Some educators and labor officials urge that the line between academic and career and technical education should be blurred and that all youngsters should be provided with skills in traditionally "academic" subject areas, including mathematics, science, and English, as well as more applied learning experiences. Some states such as Oregon are moving to require all graduating high school students to have work experience and a career plan. Further, critics argue that the "general education" track in high school, which falls between a college-preparatory track and a strictly career/technical track, should be eliminated because it has no specific purpose. Although just 42 percent of all high school students are enrolled in a general education track, nearly two out of three high school dropouts come from that track. In addition, apprenticeship programs such as those in Germany are being praised. In such a program, students receive on-the-job training with a company for four days a week and participate in classroom instruction on the fifth day. Such programs are designed to help youth move from school to work.

■ "tech-prep" programs

Another promising trend is the development of "tech-prep" programs that link high school and postsecondary study. Tech-prep programs typically involve the last two years of high school and the first two years of college (usually at a community college) and provide an attractive alternative for students who do not plan to attend a four-year college.

Pause and Reflect

1 ▶ What is your view of the issues and trends in your favorite subject field? Are there any other developments that you would like to see?

▶ Assessing Student Academic Performance

Both supporters and critics of contemporary curricula often focus on the results: what do students actually learn from their studies of language arts, math, science, and so forth? The methods of assessing results are themselves highly controversial and will be discussed further in the "How Should Education Be Reformed?" chapter, but in this section, we will look at the results of both national and international studies that attempt to judge the academic performance of American students.

National Assessment of Educational Progress

Visit this chapter of the website to link to the website for the NAEP.

■ "nation's report card"

Since their introduction over thirty years ago, National Assessment of Educational Progress (NAEP) assessments have been conducted periodically in reading, mathematics, science, writing, history, geography, and other fields. Administered to a representative national sample of students, the NAEP assessments are the primary source on educational achievement in the United States, and they have become known as "the nation's report card." Although almost all the states assess their students' progress on content standards, they don't all have the same standards or use the same tests, so comparisons across states are mainly limited to the NAEP data. Assessment occurs at three grade levels: fourth, eighth, and twelfth. Achievement levels are defined as *basic* (denoting partial mastery of knowledge and skills fundamental for proficient work), *proficient* (representing solid academic performance over challenging subject matter for the grade level), and *advanced* (signifying superior performance).

■ how are students doing?

So how are American students doing? See Figure 5.1 for figures on mathematics, science, reading, writing, and U.S. history. In the 2000 science assessments, fourth grade students performed about the same as they had in 1996, whereas eighth-graders did slightly better and twelfth-graders did slightly worse. Twenty-nine percent of fourth-graders, 32 percent of eighth-graders, and 18 percent of twelfth-graders scored at or above the proficient level.

■ math improvements

Unlike in science, students made significant improvements in the 2005 mathematics assessments. In fact, over the past decade, student achievement on the NAEP mathematics tests has improved significantly for all ages and racial and ethnic groups, as much as one year's worth of mathematics knowledge since 1990 for fourth, eighth, and twelfth grades.

■ reading scores steady

Reading scores, on the other hand, remained relatively unchanged from 1992 to 2005, although a modest upward slope has occurred since 1994.[11] The 2005 reading assessment of fourth-graders indicated that 64 percent of the students were at or above the basic level, whereas 31 percent were at or above the proficient level.[12]

■ ignorance of history and geography

Further NAEP assessments reveal that American students are woefully ignorant of history, geography, and civics. In the 2001 history assessment a significant percentage of students—33 percent of fourth-graders, 36 percent of eighth-graders, and 57 percent of twelfth-graders—failed to achieve the expectations for the basic level. The percentages of students who reached the proficient or advanced levels at the fourth, eighth, and twelfth grades were only 18,

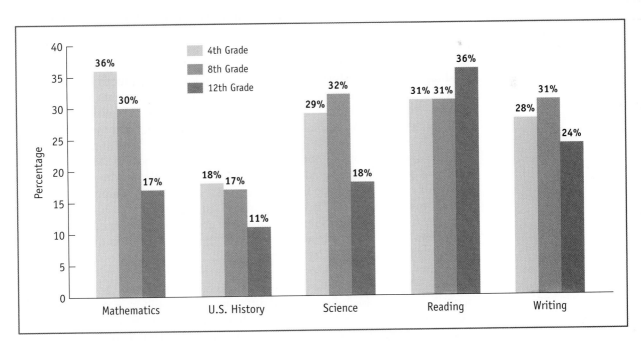

FIGURE 5.1
Percentage of Students Scoring at the Proficient or Advanced Level on NAEP Assessments in Various Subject Fields

Source: The Nation's Report Card. Available at: http://nces.ed.gov/nationsreportcard/site/home.asp.

17, and 11, respectively.[13] In the 2001 geography tests 21 percent of fourth-graders, 30 percent of eighth-graders, and 25 percent of twelfth-graders reached the proficient or advanced levels. In every subject field, therefore, a large majority of American students are failing to achieve the proficient level in the NAEP assessments.

Many of those students are members of minority groups. African American, Hispanic, and Native American students continue to score significantly lower than white and Asian American students, although the gap between African American and white students has been narrowing slightly. Males continue to outperform females slightly on mathematics and science tests, but females significantly outperform males on the reading and writing tests.[14]

International Comparisons

Visit this chapter of the website to link to more information about the TIMSS.

■ poor U.S. *performance*

Compared with the academic performances of students from other developed countries, American students have tended to do poorly, especially middle and high school students. In 1995, the Third International Mathematics and Science Study (TIMSS) tested the mathematics and science knowledge of half a million students at three grade levels—fourth, eighth, and twelfth—in forty-one countries. Eighth-graders from seventeen nations were also tested in 1999. TIMSS was the largest, most comprehensive, and most rigorous international comparison of education ever done.

What were the results? Between 1995 and 1999, there was no change in mathematics or science achievement in the United States for eighth-graders.[15] Of the twenty-one nations that participated in the twelfth-grade tests, the United States outperformed only two, Cyprus and South Africa, in general math and science knowledge. Even our most advanced students, those taking advanced mathematics and physics, scored at the bottom when compared to their counterparts in other countries, and none of the Asian countries, which led the eighth-grade performances, even participated in the twelfth-grade assessments.[16] U.S. students start out performing at high levels in fourth grade, but by the time they graduate, they are performing at unacceptably low levels in both math and science. The two main messages of TIMSS are that (1) U.S. students don't start out behind—they fall behind; and (2) by the time U.S. students finish high school, they are not achieving at the international standards demanded by a global labor market.[17]

The TIMSS is not without its critics. A number of nations in the study did not heed the quality control guidelines in selecting the students who would participate. For example, some countries only tested students in programs concentrating on mathematics and science, making true comparisons across countries difficult. As a result, TIMSS may tell us more about the differing educational systems than about the students.[18] In spite of the criticisms, it is difficult to find much in the U.S. TIMSS data to cheer about.

■ possible explanations

A number of explanations are possible for the differences in mathematics and science achievement test scores between U.S. students and those from high-scoring countries, including cultural differences that result in greater value being placed on education in some countries than in the United States, lower expectations for American students, and more American students holding jobs. Moreover, the TIMSS study revealed that the content of U.S. mathematics and science classes is not as challenging or focused as that of other countries. Many middle school students in the United States are still doing elementary arithmetic and in-

National and international assessments show that by high school, students often fall behind in learning science and mathematics. Unfortunately, most standardized assessments don't measure actual performances, such as these students conducting a science experiment, which can foster a deep understanding of key scientific concepts and methods.
(© Bob Daemmrich/Stock Boston)

troductory science while their international counterparts are studying algebra, geometry, physics, and chemistry. By the senior year of high school, many of our students have stopped taking math and science altogether. Many students never study algebra (about 15 percent), geometry (about 30 percent), advanced algebra (about 40 percent), other advanced mathematics (around 80 percent), chemistry (about 45 percent), or physics (almost 75 percent).[19]

■ breadth instead of depth

Another factor may be the way that mathematics and science are taught. TIMSS researchers have characterized the U.S. mathematics and science curricula as being "a mile wide and an inch deep"—that is, they cover many topics but devote little time to any one topic. The United States is number one in the world in one category—the size of the textbooks—which tend to be encyclopedic rather than focused! U.S. teachers, supported by the textbooks they use, teach more topics but in less detail than teachers from high-scoring countries. Furthermore, when contrasted with Japanese teachers, they focus much more on procedures and skills and much less on concepts, deductive reasoning, and understanding. Surprisingly, however, U.S. teachers assign more homework and spend more class time discussing it than do teachers from Japan and Germany.[20]

■ nonacademic activities

The total amount of time students spend on academic pursuits also likely has an effect on their performance. At the high school level, American students spend much of their school day in such nonacademic activities as counseling, gym, homeroom, driver training, pep rallies, and education about personal safety, AIDS, consumer affairs, and family life. An average of only 41 percent of secondary school time needs to be devoted to core academic work to earn a high school diploma,[21] and that's probably the way most American parents want it. Both parents and students downplay a "nerdish" emphasis on strong academics in favor of preparing "well-rounded" individuals, making it difficult for schools to strengthen their academic requirements beyond a certain point. As long as a majority of Americans feel this way, it seems unlikely that we will see a radical restructuring of schools to emphasize strong academics.

■ lessons learned from TIMSS

We believe there are several lessons to be learned from TIMSS. First, we need to continue setting clear, high standards for what we expect students to know and be able to do in mathematics and science. Second, we need to align everything else we do with those standards: initial preparation of teachers, selection of texts and other curriculum materials, design of assessments, and the continuing professional development of teachers. The difficulty, of course, is that unlike most of the other countries participating in the TIMSS, the United States is highly decentralized in its educational decision making, thus making it extremely difficult to align the various educational components with the standards.

Pause and Reflect

1 ► In your opinion, what best explains the relatively poor performance of U.S. students in international comparisons of student achievement in mathematics and science?

2 ► Do you think the U.S. should have a national curriculum, as do so many other industrialized nations? Why or why not?

► Additional Influences on Curriculum

Although we can examine what is taught in the schools in terms of the subjects offered, the curriculum as students experience it is affected by a number of other factors. The individual teacher, of course, is a major variable in what students actually learn. This whole book is about you as that teacher. The classroom and school context also affect the delivery of the curriculum, as does the academic track to which the student is assigned. We will focus on two other major influences on the curriculum that is actually delivered to students: textbooks and instructional approaches.

Textbooks

■ textbooks as a national curriculum

Education in the United States is constitutionally the domain of the various individual states—that is, the states are empowered to establish curricula and to organize and finance school systems. Unlike in many other countries, there is no national curriculum established by the federal government and implemented throughout the country. Some educational observers assert, however, that we do have a national curriculum of sorts, called *textbooks*. Several recent studies have concluded that most of what teachers and students do in classrooms is textbook related. For example, the objectives and goals for student learning are defined by the textbook (even the text you are now reading), learning activities and materials are provided to teachers as part of the textbook package, and tests geared to the textbook's objectives are usually prepared by the textbook publisher for the teacher's use.

States do have some influence on the content of textbooks. They cast their votes through their decisions on whether or not to use a particular book. Critics, however, have noted the shortcomings of many adoption systems that allow too little time and money to support the selection of excellent texts by qualified personnel.

More than twenty states, mainly in the Sunbelt, have a textbook adoption process in which citizens have the opportunity to examine textbooks being considered for statewide adoption and to express their objections to particular books. Because textbook adoption is a multimillion-dollar business, publishing companies must be careful not to include material that influential groups and factions may find offensive.

With the implementation of content standards in the various states, school boards and faculty responsible for adopting textbooks now examine how well textbooks address their state's standards. However, textbook publishers do not often customize their books for each state. Instead, they adapt the books to the standards of states that have a lot of children and buy a lot of books. Publishers rely on the similarity of standards between states to assure that books geared to the larger states will meet at least some standards in nearly every state. This means that states such as Texas, California, and Florida greatly influence the content of textbooks produced by commercial publishers.

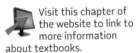

■ call for better textbooks

Visit this chapter of the website to link to more information about textbooks.

A wave of educational reform is directing attention to the quality of the textbooks that determine the curriculum. Some critics claim that texts are "dumbed down" to meet readability requirements; the writing style, designed to meet arbitrary criteria for lengths of words and sentences, can be awkward and stiff. Others believe that textbooks try to include too much material and so lack depth of coverage, a criticism certainly supported by findings from the TIMSS. Critics also complain about typical textbook emphases on skill development instead of the stimulation of students' interest and intellect; these emphases, they say, create texts that are dry, barren of ideas, devoid of concepts, and lacking in the vigorous style that stirs students to comprehend and retain what they read. Whereas some education personnel call for schools to spend more money on textbooks, many others claim that teachers and curriculum developers rely too much on textbooks and not enough on primary sources.

■ multimedia texts

A recent modification of the traditional textbook involves the use of electronic materials. For example, the University of California-Berkeley developed the Full Option Science System (FOSS) for K–8 science, which incorporates CD-ROMs and online interactive activities at both school and at home. Several states have adopted this system as an option for school districts to use in their science curriculum. The discs are available in both Spanish and English. Besides keeping information current, the technology provides access to rich materials and interesting projects such as using interactive and video elements to engage in or observe scientific experiments that would be impractical to conduct in the classroom. The technology also provides alternative assessments by permitting

Universal Press Syndicate

students to answer questions and follow directions on the disc or online. Whether electronic media will make major inroads into textbook adoptions in other subjects remains to be seen. Conventional textbooks, although they lack technological pizzazz, are less expensive and more portable, and do not break down.

One thing appears certain: textbooks, in paper or electronic form, are one of the major determinants of our nation's elementary and secondary school curricula, and that situation does not appear likely to change in the near future.

Innovative Instructional Approaches

Curriculum and instruction are intimately related, and the instructional approaches that teachers use clearly shape how students experience the curriculum. Although these approaches have remained amazingly constant since the 1890s, especially at the secondary level, some alterations to traditional teacher-centered instruction have taken hold.[22] Educators are constantly searching for new ways to deliver the curriculum more effectively. All of the trends discussed here can be used in a variety of subject areas with students of many age and ability levels. We will look at six nontraditional instructional influences on the curriculum: interdisciplinary curriculum, cooperative learning, critical thinking and problem solving, writing across the curriculum, differentiated instruction, and block scheduling.

 The video case *Reading in the Content Areas* shows how two high-school teachers have combined social studies and literature instruction. As you watch the clips and study the artifacts in the case, reflect upon the following questions:

1. How do these teachers achieve the advantages of interdisciplinary instruction described in this chapter, such as making subject matter less fragmented? Do they seem to succeed in making the students feel that learning about 1920s is relevant to their lives?
2. For you as a teacher, what would be the advantages and challenges of planning and implementing an interdisciplinary curriculum or project?
3. What kind of arrangements or support would help with implementing interdisciplinary curricula? Would you, for example, prefer working with another teacher or alone to prepare interdisciplinary projects?

■ **Interdisciplinary Curriculum** Students, particularly secondary students, are often critical of the traditional curriculum, which seems irrelevant to their lives outside of school. They often fail to see how English, history, mathematics, and science relate to them. The curriculum they experience is fragmented and isolated. In one language arts class, the teacher gave the dates of a famous author's birth and death, and asked the students to figure out how old the author was when she died. Silence fell over the room as students pondered the question. Finally, one student said, "It's hard to do math in English class." Students have learned to segment and separate their knowledge into compartments because of the way we teach content.

Many teachers agree. Noting that the real world is not organized by disciplines but contains situations and problems that cut across disciplinary boundaries, these teachers are returning to an old idea of organizing and teaching the curriculum in an integrated and interdisciplinary fashion. Although numerous definitions of **interdisciplinary** or **integrated curriculum** exist, the terms are often used synonymously to mean a curriculum that cuts across subject-matter lines to focus on comprehensive life problems or broad-based areas of study that bring together the various segments of the curriculum in meaningful association.

■ teaming teachers from different disciplines

Visit this chapter of the website to link to more information about interdisciplinary themes.

There are many approaches to developing integrated, interdisciplinary curricula. One of the simplest is for two or more teachers from different disciplinary backgrounds to plan and teach their respective subjects together, seeking different disciplinary perspectives on a particular unit of study. For example, an English and social studies teacher might team together to integrate the study of the nineteenth century through the history and literature of that period.

■ thematic teaching

Another approach is *thematic* in nature. A cross-departmental team chooses themes as overlays to the different subjects. "Inventions," for example, is a theme that could combine science and mathematics in the study of machines and their mechanics, reading and writing about inventors in language arts, and designing and building models in industrial arts. Another example, "health," would permit a number of different subjects to be used to better understand specific health topics (Figure 5.2). Still another thematic approach is to identify concepts that apply in different subjects, such as examining how symmetry, patterns, evidence, and proof apply in mathematics, art, science, social studies, and language arts. For more on integrated thematic approaches, see **"For Further Information"** at the end of the chapter.

■ arguments for interdisciplinary teaching

Proponents of interdisciplinary curricula argue that the merits far outweigh the extra expenditure of time and effort required. Students benefit by experiencing coherence in the curriculum and connections to real-world situations. Critical thinking and problem-solving skills are developed within specific contexts rather than in isolation. Teachers benefit by having students who enjoy learning and by working collaboratively with other teachers. Although interdisciplinary teaching is enjoying a resurgence of popularity, particularly in middle schools, the disciplinary approach to curriculum in the secondary schools is well entrenched and is being reinforced by the development of national standards within each discipline rather than across disciplines. The tension between disciplinary and interdisciplinary approaches to curriculum development will continue for some time.

FIGURE 5.2
Sample Interdisciplinary Approach

Source: Joan Palmer, "Planning Wheels Turn Curriculum Around," *Educational Leadership,* 49, No. 2, October 1991, p. 58. Reprinted by permission. The Association for Supervision and Curriculum Development is a worldwide community of educators advocating sound policies and sharing best practices to achieve the success of each learner. To learn more, visit ASCD at **www.ascd.org.**

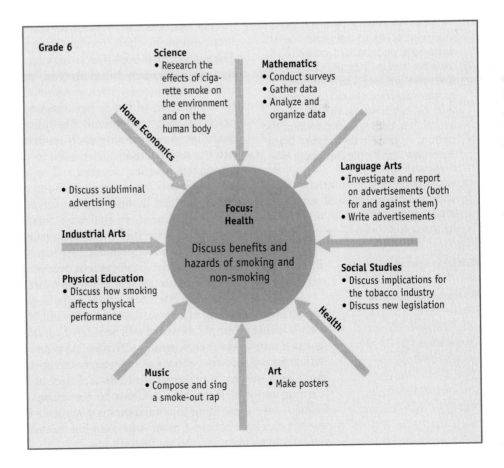

■ **Cooperative Learning** **Cooperative learning** in classrooms is another trend influencing what is taught in the schools. Those who have analyzed the "hidden" curriculum, or the implicit teachings that schools communicate to their students, have observed that American schools tend to reward competitive or individual accomplishment more than cooperative effort.[23] Arguing for cooperative learning techniques, some educators maintain that such techniques can change the ways students learn, their attitudes toward what they are taught, and their perceptions of themselves and others.

Visit this chapter of the website to link to more information about cooperative learning.

■ definitions of cooperative learning

What is cooperative learning? There are many different forms, but all involve students working in small groups or teams to help one another learn academic material. Cooperative learning strategies are organized, highly structured methods that usually involve formal presentation of information, student practice and coaching in learning teams, individual assessment of mastery, and public recognition of team success. Table 5.2 summarizes several such strategies. By their structure and individual assignments, cooperative learning strategies avoid the problem of letting the hard-working students in the group do the work while the other students get a free ride. Cooperative learning strategies have proven successful across grade levels and in different subjects. The effectiveness of cooperative learning, particularly for achievement outcomes, depends on the particular approach used, but overall positive effects have been found on such diverse outcomes as self-esteem, intergroup relations, acceptance of academically handicapped students, attitudes toward school, and ability to work cooperatively.[24]

The video case *Cooperative Learning at the Elementary Level: Jigsaw Model* lets you see one model of cooperative learning in action. As you watch the clips and study the artifacts in the case, reflect upon the following questions:

1. How does the structure of the jigsaw method help avoid the problem of letting some students in a group "coast" while others do the hard work?
2. View the *bonus video* of a student from an expert group teaching his home group. How could the teacher encourage student "experts" to vary their techniques, perhaps using some of the options included in the Ways to Teach list shown among the Classroom Artifacts with the case?
3. Which of the outcomes listed in this chapter (achievement, self-esteem, etc.) seems most likely to be enhanced by this project? Why?

The success of cooperative learning strategies comes from three important characteristics: group goals, individual accountability, and equal opportunity for success. *Group goals* usually take the form of rewards based on team success in academic tasks. To achieve team success, each member of the group must coordinate the completion of his or her assigned task with the other group members; each team member is indispensable. *Individual accountability* involves assessing each student's mastery of the content, with the results usually given back to the group and the individual. Teammates practice together and support and coach one another, but individuals are assessed in the usual ways. The team's success is often judged by how much each team member improves over earlier assessment. In that way, even the least-achieving student can contribute to the team's success by improving over the first assessment. *Equal opportunities for success* are ensured by team scoring systems based on individual improvement over prior performance. This feature reinforces the perception that student effort, not just innate ability, counts.

■ three key characteristics

■ helps at-risk students

Cooperative learning has been found to be a particularly effective instructional tool in teaching at-risk students who benefit from immediate feedback for their learning attempts. It works well because it offers students more involvement in and control over their learning activities. As many schools attempt to do away with tracking and to encourage heterogeneous grouping, cooperative learning provides a means to make all students feel they are essential to the classroom learning process. It enables students to recognize that they all, when given a chance, have something to contribute to everyone's learning. Cooperative learning has quickly become a major instructional method in the United States, particularly in elementary and middle schools.

TABLE 5.2 Selected Cooperative Learning Strategies

Name		Brief Description	Function
1. Student team learning	a. Student Teams Achievement Divisions (STAD)	Four-member mixed learning teams. Teacher presents lesson, students work within teams to make certain all team members have mastered the objectives. Students take individual quizzes. Points awarded based on improvement over previous quizzes.	Appropriate for teaching well-defined objectives with single right answers in most subjects.
	b. Teams-Games-Tournament (TGT)	Uses same teacher presentations and teamwork as in STAD, but replaces quizzes with weekly tournaments.	Same as STAD
2. Jigsaw		Each student on team becomes "expert" on one topic by working with members from other teams assigned same topic. Upon returning to home team, each expert teaches the group, and students are all assessed on all aspects of the topic.	Acquisition and presentation of new material, review, informed debate. Promotes interdependence, status equalization. Used in social studies and other subjects where learning from text is important.
3. Jigsaw 2		Same as Jigsaw, except instead of each student being assigned a particular section of text, all students read a common narrative. Each student receives a topic on which to become expert.	Same as Jigsaw
4. Group investigation		Students work in small groups using cooperative inquiry, group discussion, and projects. Students form two- to six-member groups. Groups choose subtopics from a unit, break subtopics into individual tasks, and prepare group reports.	Developed skills of planning, investigating, and reporting
5. Think-pair-share		Students think to themselves on a topic provided by teacher; then pair with another student to discuss it; then share their thoughts with class.	Generating and revising hypotheses, inductive reasoning, deductive reasoning. Fosters participation and involvement.

■ **Critical Thinking and Problem Solving** A growing interest in helping students become better thinkers and problem solvers is evidenced by the multitude of publications, workshops, curriculum study institutes, journal articles, and course requirements addressing the topics of thinking and problem solving. Although many people favor teaching it, definitions of **critical thinking** vary widely. At the heart of these definitions, however, is the intent to help students evaluate the worth of ideas, opinions, or evidence before making a decision or judgment.

The video case *Cooperative Learning: High School History Lesson* shows a high-school teacher using an informal model of cooperative learning. As you watch the clips and study the artifacts in the case, reflect upon the following questions:

1. Three key characteristics of successful cooperative learning are listed in this chapter. How can teachers, like this one, who use informal groups, achieve those characteristics?
2. One of the students mentions the importance of careful grouping and placing students who can work together in groups with one another. What are some guidelines teachers might use for grouping their students?

■ different approaches

Visit this chapter of the website to link to more information about critical thinking and problem solving.

Many highly intelligent people are poor thinkers. Many people of average intelligence are skilled thinkers. The power of a car is separate from the way the car is driven.

—EDWARD DE BONO

■ problem solving

■ integration with subject areas

■ writing as aid to subject-matter learning

Some educators favor approaches that help students detect bias or identify a wide range of propaganda strategies. The teaching of philosophy is also proposed as a way to provide criteria by which students can judge others' thinking. Still other approaches identify component skills (for example, making inferences, testing hypotheses, identifying assumptions) within the realm of critical thinking and advocate direct instruction in each skill. Socratic questioning (a style of questioning that elicits a clear expression of truth that was implicitly known by the person being questioned) is also suggested as a way to teach the art of thinking.

Problem solving is an element of critical thinking that has received increasing attention and use. **Problem solving** generally refers to the process of either presenting students with a problem or helping them identify a problem and then observing and helping them become aware of the conditions, procedures, or steps needed to solve it. The problem may range from putting puzzles together, to solving simple science or mathematics problems, to solving more complex mental, logical, or social dilemmas. It may be presented as an individual activity, such as when independently predicting outcomes in a reading passage, or may be used with a group, such as when simulating wilderness "survival" activities that require group cooperation. In the many diverse ways of teaching problem solving, the emphasis is on the *process* of reaching a solution. Proponents of problem-solving instruction point out that if students become more aware of their mental processes, they will be able to exercise greater control over their own learning and thinking in future situations. In group problem-solving activities students may also benefit from interacting with one another and being exposed to the variety of approaches used by peers in solving the same problem.

What is the role of critical thought in the curriculum? At one time, educators debated whether students can best learn effective thinking through separate courses or as an integrated part of every course. There is now greater agreement that while students do benefit from stand-alone courses in critical thinking, they must also learn to think within the context of each discipline. The integration of critical thinking into subject areas appears to be the direction of the future, especially since the curricula of the schools are already so crowded. As the "Voices from the Classroom" feature suggests, most students, including those who do not speak English as a first language, can benefit from instruction that emphasizes critical thinking and problem solving.

■ **Writing Across the Curriculum** The **writing across the curriculum** movement has been a center of curricular interest for a growing number of educators since the 1960s. Also called *writing to learn* or *writing to learn in the content areas*, the idea emphasizes writing as a tool for students' learning, not only in English classes but in all subject areas.

How can teachers use the act of writing as the medium through which subject-matter learning takes place? Students in social studies classes may be asked to take a written stand on school issues, moral questions, or political problems. Music students may write their own ballads. Students in science classes may work together to predict the future in story form or to write futuristic headlines and news features. Children in math classes can create their own word problems and

VOICES FROM THE CLASSROOM

Judy Boch graduated from the University of Arizona and obtained a master's degree in Educational Leadership at Northern Arizona University. She has spent a total of nineteen years as a classroom teacher and eight years working as a math and science coach. Judy is currently a third-grade teacher and K–6 Math Coach at Peña Elementary in Phoenix, Arizona.

Triumphs and Setbacks

Up until the time he came to me as a second grader, Raul's content education had been conducted in Spanish. Only in the latter part of first grade did he begin to learn in English. My second-grade classroom was labeled *English as a Second Language (ESL)*, but I spoke no Spanish. The only Spanish that Raul heard in the classroom was from a one-hour Spanish aide and from the other children.

I wondered how I was going to reach this obviously bright and talented boy. This was soon made clear during one of our first math lessons. Having been trained in Cognitively Guided Instruction, I gave the children a story problem and asked them to solve it with their own invented strategies. Although Raul couldn't, at first, read the problem, another child translated for him. Raul came alive! He drew pictures and used numbers to model his strategy to the problem. I knew I was taking a risk that day when I asked Raul to share his strategy with the other students. I wondered if I had made a mistake when he grasped for words to explain. But explain he did! He drew his picture on the board, labeled it with numbers, and wrote a number sentence to match the problem. In short phrases, he shared his thinking sequentially.

Raul blossomed after that day. His English began to improve as he continually volunteered to share his thinking in mathematics. In his math journal, Raul wrote:

"Math is my favrit becuz I get to be the techer. It makes me feel prowd."

Unfortunately, Raul's excitement has not continued. This year, as a Lead Teacher on my campus, I visit Raul's classroom once a week. He is learning math through more conventional methods using the traditional algorithms. It is painful to see him using traditional methods that he really doesn't understand and that take him so much longer than his invented strategies. His teacher says he is becoming unfocused and having discipline problems. Although his English has improved considerably, math is no longer his great equalizer or passion. My only hope is that Raul rediscovers his love and enthusiasm for mathematics. For if he does not, we have failed him.

 Visit the website for more Voices from the Classroom.

keep records of what they have learned, their questions, and their observations. Art classes can write scripts for slide shows and cartoon strips or create illustrated guides and storybooks. Teachers at many grade levels and in many subject areas can ask students to keep informal journals or "learning logs." In these journals students record their responses to what they have read and studied and can then interact with text material and with the teacher's responses to their queries and remarks. These are just a few examples of the many ways teachers use writing as a thinking tool for students to use and apply their knowledge in the content areas.

■ adapt instruction to meet student needs

■ **Differentiated Instruction**   The term **differentiated instruction** is relatively new on the educational scene; however, its practice has been around for a long time. In its simplest form, differentiated instruction tries to respond to student variance rather than adopting a standardized approach to teaching that assumes all learners in a class are essentially alike. The academic diversity of students in

The video case *Academic Diversity: Differentiated Instruction* shows how one teacher adapts a writing workshop to the needs and interests of her students. As you watch the clips and study the artifacts in the case, reflect upon the following questions:

1. As noted in the *video* and *viewing questions,* one of the keys to differentiating instruction effectively is getting to know your students well. How will you, as a teacher, do this?
2. How do posters and handouts, like the *artifacts* included in this case, help provide "access points" to a lesson for students who need extra help?
3. In addition to those listed in this chapter and shown in the video case, what might be some other strategies for differentiating instruction?

Any subject can be taught effectively in some intellectually honest form to any child at any stage of development.

—Jerome Bruner

Visit this chapter of the website to link to more information about differentiated instruction.

Visit this chapter of the website to link to more information about the project approach.

today's classrooms is growing, and one instructional approach won't work for all students. (See the chapter entitled "Who Are Today's Students in a Diverse Society?" for more discussion on various kinds of diversity.) As schools are trying to ensure that all students learn what is expected of them, teachers recognize that they need to diversify their instruction to meet individual student needs. Teachers are trying to tailor their instruction to provide appropriate challenges for gifted students, students who lag behind, and those in between.

Differentiated instruction is a teaching philosophy based on the premise that teachers should adapt instruction to student differences in reading readiness, learning preferences, and interests. According to Carol Tomlinson, a national expert on differentiated instruction, teachers can differentiate three aspects of the curriculum: content, process, and products.[25] *Content* refers to the concepts, principles, and skills that teachers want students to learn. All students should be given access to the same core content, Tomlinson believes. However, teachers can provide different means (for example, texts, lectures, and demonstrations) to give students access to skills and knowledge. *Process* refers to the activities that help students make sense of and own the knowledge being taught. Teachers can vary the activities to provide some students with access to more complexity and others with more support, depending on their readiness levels, student interest, or learning preferences. *Product* refers to culminating projects that students develop to demonstrate and extend what they have learned. These products can vary also, depending on students' interests or learning preferences. For example, some students might prefer to work as a member of a group while producing a play about the topic being studied, whereas others might prefer to work alone to write a term paper. Differentiating content, process, and product for students requires teachers to know their students, their subject, and their materials. (See Table 5.3 for some strategies for differentiating instruction.) There is no formula for differentiation—no one way to address student differences. Rather, it is a commitment to start with students and to make a match between learner and the material to be learned. Its goal is to maximize the capacities of each student.

One popular way of providing differentiation at the early childhood or elementary school level is through the **project approach,** which is an in-depth investigation of a real world topic worthy of children's attention and effort. The project approach uses a set of teaching strategies to guide children through their investigation. The project may involve a whole class or a sub-group of students. Phase one starts with an opening event (story, video, unusual object) designed to capture the students' attention. The teacher then gets the children to map out what they already know about the event. Children then generate questions that they would like to investigate during the project. In phase two, children participate in some type of field trip to investigate the topic and to try to answer their questions. There is a de-briefing of the field trip and sometimes an outside expert is invited to share his or her knowledge about the topic. In phase three, a culminating event takes place, to which parents, other classes, and other interested parties may be invited. Children also have the opportunity to personalize

TABLE 5.3 Strategies for Differentiating Instruction

Many teachers accept the desirability of differentiating instruction, but don't know how to go about doing it. Here are some of the many strategies that teachers can use to avoid lockstep instruction.

Stations	Involves setting up different spots in the classroom where students work on different tasks at the same time. This strategy encourages flexible grouping because not all students have to go to all stations all the time.
Compacting	Involves assessing students before beginning a unit of study so they won't have to waste time learning something they already know.
Complex Instruction	Uses challenging materials, open-ended tasks, and small instructional groups. Teachers circulate among the groups as they work, asking questions and probing student thinking.
Choice Boards	Teacher writes work assignments on cards that are placed in hanging pockets. Teacher asks a student to select a card from a particular row of pockets, which gives the student some choice within circumscribed options. Each row represents work at different levels of complexity.
Problem-based Learning	Places students in an active role of solving problems.
Entry Points	Using some of the multiple intelligences identified by Howard Gardner (see the chapter entitled "Who Are Today's Students in a Diverse Society?" for more on this topic), students explore a given topic through as many as five avenues: narrational (presenting a story), logical-quantitative (using numbers or deduction), foundational (examining philosophy and vocabulary), aesthetic (focusing on sensory features), and experiential (hands-on).
Orbital Studies	Involves independent investigations, generally lasting several weeks, around some aspect of the curriculum. Students select their own topics, and work with the guidance of the teacher.
4MAT	Teachers plan some lessons for each of four learning preferences (mastery, understanding, personal involvement, and synthesis) over the course of several days on a given topic. Each learner can approach the topic through preferred modes of learning. (See the chapter entitled "Who Are Today's Students in a Diverse Society?" for more information about learning preferences.)

Source: Carol Ann Tomlinson, *The Differentiated Classroom: Responding to the Needs of All Learners* (Alexandria, VA: Association for Supervision and Curriculum Development, 1999).

their knowledge through differentiated imaginative activities such as dramatic renditions or story writing.

■ **Block Scheduling**   A report by the National Education Commission on Time and Learning, an independent panel temporarily convened by Congress, stated that time is "the missing element in the school-reform debate." The report urged that the traditional six-hour school day and 180-day year "be relegated to museums as an exhibit of our education past." Advising schools to be less rigid in how they use time, the report also recommended the use of block scheduling and an extended school year.[26] As the accompanying box describes, in another innovative

Looping or Multiyear Teaching

Suppose someone offered you an educational innovation with the following benefits: better teacher/student relationships, improved teacher job satisfaction, extra teaching time, a richer curriculum, increased student attendance, increased student development in social skills and a sense of community, and easy implementation at very little cost. Sound good? Proponents of an old but increasingly common practice called *looping* claim these as among its benefits.

Looping, or multiyear teaching, is a simple concept in which the teacher is promoted with his or her students to the next grade level and stays with the group for several years, typically two but sometimes as many as five. Although not much quantitative research exists on the benefits of looping, qualitative research supports the benefits just mentioned. By keeping the same group of students together with the same teacher, everyone gets to know one another well and feel comfortable in the group. Teachers get to know their students' strengths, weaknesses, and interests. Forging bonds of trust and understanding between teachers and students is at the heart of looping. Teachers who loop have fewer transitions to make at the beginning of the school year and can introduce curriculum topics right away at the start of the second year. They don't have to spend precious instructional time at the beginning of the new year to establish classroom routines and expectations. Instead, teachers can spend the gained time exploring curriculum topics in greater detail.

Administrators argue that looping isn't for everyone, so implementation should be on a voluntary basis. Some administrators urge teaming teachers to implement looping. In that way, students can benefit from different teacher strengths, and if a student has a problem with one particular teacher, another teacher can compensate.

Sources: "Looping—Discovering the Benefits of Multiyear Teaching," *Education Update* 40, no. 2 (March 1998), a publication of the Association for Supervision and Curriculum Development, pp. 1, 3–4; *Looping: Supporting Student Learning Through Long-Term Relationships,* Themes in Education (Brown University: LAB–Northeast and Islands Regional Educational Laboratory, 1997); Cheryl A. Franklin and Mary S. Holm, "Looping," *Encyclopedia of Education,* 2d ed., ed. James W. Guthrie (New York: Macmillan Reference, USA, 2003), pp. 1520–1522.

twist on the traditional school year, some schools are trying out **looping,** a practice that lets teachers stay with the same students for more than a single year.

■ what is block scheduling?

Block scheduling is a "less is more" approach in which students take fewer classes each school day but spend more time in each class. In theory, block scheduling carves out more time for instruction by reducing the amount of time students spend going from class to class and the time teachers spend taking roll and settling down classes. It was relatively rare two decades ago, but grew dramatically during the 1990s. Although block scheduling is not an instructional approach in itself, it does allow and encourage teachers to use cooperative learning, interdisciplinary teaching, critical thinking and problem solving, writing across the curriculum, and other innovative instructional strategies.

■ models of block scheduling

Several models of block scheduling exist. The trimester approach may have classes lasting an hour and twenty minutes; instead of students taking the traditional six classes per semester, they take four each trimester. Courses that used to last a semester now last a trimester, and courses that used to last a year now run for two trimesters. In the 4 × 4 plan, students take four 90-minute classes a day and complete them in a semester rather than a full year. In the A/B plan, students take eight 90-minute classes each semester, but classes meet every other day, four on day A and four on day B. Even more models exist.

The research on block scheduling so far is relatively scarce, and what does exist is often contradictory. Anecdotal evidence indicates that students like the new schedule if teachers are good and keep students' interest through various learning activities, but if teachers rely primarily on lectures, which are longer under block scheduling, students complain. The key seems to be to work with teachers to change their teaching models to make better use of the additional time they have each day the class meets. Teachers seem to like the block schedules because they have fewer students each term (for example, 90 instead of 150), and, as a result, they get to know those students better. In addition, block scheduling allows teachers more in-school preparation time. Teachers of certain disciplines such as music and foreign languages tend to dislike models of block scheduling that don't allow students to work each day on those subjects, arguing that developing skill in their subjects requires daily practice. On the other hand, science teachers tend to like block schedules that allow for longer laboratory periods. Some parents and students are concerned about student absences, which in some forms of block scheduling mean they miss more material and find it difficult to make it up.

Pause and Reflect

1 ▶ Have you had personal experience with any of the instructional approaches described above? If so, were they positive or negative? What made them so?

Current Curriculum Controversies

Given a highly pluralistic society and many different educational philosophies represented in America today, it is little wonder that the questions of how and what schools should teach generate much controversy and debate. In this section we will touch briefly on two of the most highly charged curriculum issues, the question of whether the curriculum should strive to promote American unity or to recognize the diversity of the nation, and the issue of placing students in different "tracks" of study.

■ **Core Versus Multicultural Curriculum** American schools have traditionally played a central role in instilling the ideas and attitudes that maintain our pluralistic society as "one nation." They have helped weave the many ethnic and religious strands together to make a seamless national garment. At least that's the theory. Questions are now being raised about whether schools today provide a shared understanding of our culture, history, and traditions. Does the current curriculum of our schools reflect our national diversity to the exclusion of our national unity? Or is the reverse true?

■ multicultural curriculum

Proponents of a **multicultural curriculum** argue that minority students, whose representation in the public schools is approaching 40 percent and increasing every year, experience a Eurocentric, or Europe-centered, curriculum that gives short shrift to the literary and historical contributions of other parts of the world and to minorities within the United States. As a result, the proponents of multiculturalism argue, youngsters of color see the schools' curricula as being irrelevant to them, not reflective of their cultures or backgrounds. Some multicultural advocates take the position that the current school curriculum needs to be broadened to better reflect the contributions of people of color. Cultural pluralism, a fact of our society, needs to be a fact of our school curriculum, they assert.

Humanity's survival does not depend on reducing differences to a common identity, but on learning to live creatively with differences.

—ANONYMOUS

■ ethnocentric curriculum

A more extreme position is taken by those who demand that the whole curriculum be oriented to a particular ethnicity. For example, some advocates of an Afrocentric curriculum claim that black schoolchildren can learn effectively only in an environment that recognizes and amplifies their African heritage. The theory is that if students learn of the accomplishments of those who share their ethnic identities, their self-esteem will improve, which will promote learning. When schools emphasize the achievements of African cultures, especially ancient Egyptian culture, and of individuals of African descent, students will have a greater sense of pride and be more motivated to learn. Afrocentric curricula are currently being used in a number of large-city school districts.

■ core curriculum

In contrast, proponents of a **core curriculum,** a course of study every student would be required to take, argue that ever since the 1970s, schools have focused on celebrating national diversity and pluralism but have failed to help students develop a shared national identity and common cultural framework. As described in the "What Are the Philosophical Foundations of American Education?" chapter, some advocates of a core curriculum, such as Mortimer Adler (*The Paideia Proposal,* 1983), have promoted the great literary works that have endured over the years as the basic elements of a core curriculum.

■ cultural literacy

E. D. Hirsch, Jr., also endorses the great literary works, but goes beyond them in his push for **cultural literacy** (now called **core knowledge**).[27] Hirsch, sees a culturally literate person as someone who is aware of the central ideas, stories, scientific knowledge, events, and personalities of a culture. Cultural literacy is important, says Hirsch, because authors and speakers make allusions and references in their writing and speaking, assuming that the audience understands these references. If a person doesn't understand the reference, he or she will miss the point and not understand the message. If an author writes, for example, of the "Midas touch," and the reader doesn't know who Midas was, then the point is lost.

Hirsch does not restrict his idea of a core curriculum to the great works of "dead white males," a criticism made of many traditional core curricula; rather, he sees American culture as incorporating the contributions of many ethnicities and subcultures. Hirsch believes that privileged youth gain much of their cultural literacy at home, but since many poor, minority, and immigrant children do not receive cultural literacy at home, it is especially important that they receive it in school. If they do not, Hirsch argues, poor children will not learn those aspects of our common heritage that are necessary to succeed in American society. Hirsch and his colleagues, through the Core Knowledge Foundation, have developed grade-by-grade guidelines for a core knowledge sequence for grades K–8, as well as a series of books entitled *What Every 1st (2nd, etc.) Grader Needs to Know.* Currently, several hundred schools across the country have adopted the core knowledge sequence.

Visit this chapter of the website to link to learn more about Core Knowledge.

In a society as large and pluralistic as the United States, many philosophies and notions of school purpose have committed supporters. How can the schools incorporate in their curricula such diverse ideas of what a school should do? If a certain philosophy is dominant within a given community, the curriculum of the community's schools is likely to reflect that set of beliefs, and those who don't agree will remain dissatisfied. On the other hand, some communities are responding to these diverse philosophical conceptions of the curriculum by providing choice among alternative schools, each with a different curricular emphasis. However, the debate between those who advocate a common curriculum to ensure that all students learn what society has determined is important and those who favor state, local, and individual choice in what is learned will likely continue indefinitely.

Visit this chapter of the website to link to more information about tracking.

■ three common tracks

■ **Tracking**   The curriculum that a student receives is influenced by many factors, including aspirations for further schooling, academic ability, motivation, and vocational interests. Based on these and other factors, students are often placed into academic program *tracks* that determine what courses they take; this process is called **tracking.** The track in which a student is placed can open or close future academic and vocational options. The three most common tracks are academic (stressing the traditional subjects of English, science, mathematics, and foreign languages), general (allowing more electives and less rigorous versions of the traditional subjects), and career and technical (preparing students for the world of work with a combination of academic and job-related courses). Each track has variations in courses required and different standards for student achievement. Within the academic track, further options exist, including advanced-placement (AP) and honors courses.

■ tracking harmful to poor and minorities

During the 1970s and 1980s, tracking came under attack. Several prominent educational researchers produced studies showing that students placed in the lower tracks received an inferior curriculum and less stimulating instruction than students in the academic tracks. Furthermore, these researchers found that poor and minority students were disproportionately placed in the lower tracks, where they had less qualified teachers, less rigorous curricula, and poorer instruction than students in the upper tracks. These researchers also reported that students in the upper tracks did no better than if they had been in mixed-ability classrooms.[28] Tracking became a dirty word, and detracking efforts ensued.

■ strong support for tracking

Other educational studies found conflicting evidence that, while detracking does help the educational performance of low-achieving students, high-achieving students are hurt academically.[29] Parents of these high-achieving students exert considerable pressure to ensure that their children have access to honors and AP classes, resisting efforts to detrack the schools. Furthermore, teachers who teach the high-track students often resist efforts to detrack, enjoying the intellectual challenge and prestige that come from teaching these students. The general sense is that tracking benefits high-ability students but hurts low-ability students, whereas the reverse is true of detracking.

Pause and Reflect

1 ▶ Have the curricula you experienced tended to be more like the multicultural curricula or core curricula described in this chapter? What were the strengths and weaknesses of the curriculum you were taught?

2 ▶ Where do you stand on the tracking issue? Has your own educational background included tracking? How does your background affect where you stand on this issue?

▶ Is the Existing Curriculum Relevant to Today's Society?

In this first decade of the twenty-first century, the world community is confronted with staggering problems. There are 6 billion people on our globe and forecasters project 10 billion by 2050. They need food, shelter, and an education that will lead them to fulfilled lives. The twentieth century saw great advances in manufacturing, agriculture, technology, and the growth of information. However, these advances have not been without costs. Acid rain, for example, polluted our vegetation, wildlife, and the very bodies of millions of people. Together, we and the rest of the world need to stop the systemic despoiling of our planet. Diseases such as AIDS have weakened whole continents. New weaponry, such as nuclear missiles and suitcase bombs, daily threaten the world's peace and progress. A despair brought on by hunger and poverty has bred a desperate terrorism in many corners of the world. It is no overstatement to say that we are in a race for global survival. Schools and teachers play a vital role in this race. In the chapter entitled "What Is a School and What Is It For?" we described the curriculum as a social bet. The stakes of that bet are high. Perhaps the most basic function of all education is to increase the survival chances of the human community.

■ relevance depends on philosophy

Before anyone can determine whether a particular curriculum is relevant to today's urgent needs, some difficult issues must be addressed. In the chapter entitled "What Is a School and What Is It For?" we discuss the purposes of schools and different models of schooling, particularly the school as a transmitter of culture and the school as an agent of social reconstruction. In the chapter entitled "What Are the Philosophical Foundations of American Education?" we discuss four schools of educational philosophy: perennialism, progressivism, essentialism, and romanticism. In judging curriculum relevance, all of these matters come into play, because the relevance of a curriculum depends very much on one's basic beliefs about schooling.

■ two basic oppositions

At the present time, there are conflicting trends in the academic curriculum, each representing a different philosophy. For example, if one considers the school's primary objective to be the intellectual (or mental) training of students, any curriculum that does not emphasize the mastery of certain subject matter and the training of the mind will be judged as irrelevant or wrong-headed. Conversely, if one believes the school should emphasize the development of the "whole child"—the child's emotional and social, as well as intellectual, growth—a curriculum devoted exclusively to English, history, the sciences, mathematics, and foreign languages will be considered inappropriate for many students and thus irrelevant. Those who take the view that education must equip students with necessary work and survival skills may consider a flexible curriculum that includes career and technical courses as most relevant. "The Saber-Tooth Curriculum" (see box) uses a humorous approach as a way to outline the conflicts among different educational approaches.

What one considers to be a relevant curriculum, then, depends on the philosophical position one takes. At the present time, there are conflicting trends in the academic curriculum, each representing a different philosophy.

The Saber-Tooth Curriculum

n his classic satire on curriculum irrelevance, Harold Benjamin (using the pseudonym J. Abner Peddiwell) describes how the first school curriculum was developed in the Stone Age. The earliest theorist, according to Benjamin's book, was a man named New Fist, who hit on the idea of deliberate, systematic education.

Watching children at play, New Fist wondered how he could get them to do the things that would gain them more and better food, shelter, clothing, and security. He analyzed the activities that adults engaged in to maintain life and came up with three subjects for his curriculum: (1) fish-grabbing-with-the-bare-hands, (2) woolly-horse-clubbing, and (3) saber-tooth-tiger-scaring-with-fire. Although the children trained in these subjects enjoyed obvious material benefits as a result, some conservative members of the tribe resisted the introduction of these new subjects on religious grounds. But, in due time, many people began to train their children in New Fist's curriculum and the tribe grew increasingly prosperous and secure.

Then conditions changed. An ice age began, and a glacier crept down over the land. The glacier brought with it dirt and gravel that muddied the creeks, and the waters became so dirty that no one could see the fish well enough to grab them. The melting waters from the approaching ice sheet also made the country wetter, and the little woolly horses migrated to drier land. They were replaced by antelopes, who were so shy and speedy that no one could get close enough to club them. Finally, the new dampness in the air caused the saber-tooth tigers to catch pneumonia and die. And the ferocious glacial

bears that came down with the advancing ice sheet were not afraid of fire.

The thinkers of the tribe, descendants of New Fist, found a way out of the dilemma. One figured out how to catch fish with a net made from vines. Another invented traps for the antelopes, and a third discovered how to dig pits to catch the bears.

Some thoughtful people began to wonder why these new activities couldn't be taught in the schools. But the elders who controlled the schools claimed that the new skills did not qualify as *education*—they were merely a matter of *training*. Besides, the curriculum was too full of the standard cultural subjects, fish-grabbing, horse-clubbing, and tiger-scaring, to admit new ones. When some radicals argued that the traditional subjects were foolish, the elders said that they taught fish-grabbing not to catch fish but to develop agility, horse-clubbing to develop strength, and tiger-scaring to develop courage. "The essence of true education is timelessness," they announced. "It is something that endures through changing conditions like a solid rock standing squarely and firmly in the middle of a raging torrent. You must know that there are some eternal verities and the saber-tooth curriculum is one of them!" (pp. 43–44).

The Saber-Tooth Curriculum was written in 1939, but its continuing applicability seems to be one of the "eternal verities."

Source: J. Abner Peddiwell (Harold Benjamin), *The Saber-Tooth Curriculum.* Copyright © 1959 by the McGraw-Hill Companies. Reprinted by permission of the McGraw-Hill Companies. (NOTE: One chapter of this book is reproduced in *Kaleidoscope: Readings in Education,* the companion volume to this text.)

Pause and Reflect

1 ▶ What goals and knowledge do you believe are most relevant or important for schools to include in their curriculums?

▶ A Final Word

■ which curriculum for survival?

The rather innocuous word, *curriculum,* and the simple question, "What Is Taught?" contain within them nothing less than the keys to our future. Inevitably, schools will have a curriculum and students will learn it, but the actual *stuff* of the curriculum and how they are encouraged to learn it is the key issue. What knowledge from our past should be represented? What from our vast storehouse of scientific and cultural knowledge will they need? What from our moral heritage will they need to

One looks back with appreciation to the brilliant teachers, but with gratitude to those who touched our human feeling. The curriculum is so much necessary raw material, but warmth is the vital element for the growing plant and for the soul of the child.

—CARL JUNG

guide themselves and the nation to make the right choices? What form of classroom and school life will encourage the habits of heart and mind that students will need to take up and meet the challenges they face in the world?

Our collective response will lead to a prosperous and noble future or a future of disappointment and decline. What we select for students to learn in our schools will have a profound effect on their individual futures and on the future of our nation. Indeed, given the power and influence of the United States, the impact of our choices will be global.

What does this have to do with you as a future teacher? Plenty! What should be taught? What do students need to know? These questions are, and will continue to be, debated globally at the highest levels of governments, and here in the United States at national, state, and local school board levels. The person who brings the curriculum into the classroom, who makes thousands of decisions every week about every detail of what and how to teach, is the teacher. Curriculum questions, for this reason, are the special responsibility of teachers, of those who have dedicated their lives to the education of the youth. No small responsibility!

Key Terms

block scheduling (140)
civic learning (civic education) (122)
content standards (115)
cooperative learning (134)
core curriculum (142)
critical thinking (135)
cultural literacy (core
   knowledge) (142)

curriculum (114)
differentiated instruction (137)
interdisciplinary (integrated)
   curriculum (132)
looping (140)
multicultural curriculum (141)
phonics (118)
problem solving (136)

project approach (138)
subject-matter curriculum (115)
tracking (143)
whole language approach (118)
writing across the curriculum (136)

For Reflection

1 In your opinion, should the curriculum emphasize cultural learning common to all Americans, or should it stress the pluralistic nature of our diverse cultural backgrounds? Is it possible to do both?

2 In your opinion, is the prevalent use of textbooks in the schools a positive or negative influence on teaching and learning? Can you see both the benefits and the dangers? If so, what are they?

3 Which of the instructional methods described in this chapter seemed like it would come most naturally to you as a teacher? What can you do to prepare to use other methods about which you don't yet feel comfortable?

4 Specifically, what would you do to improve the curriculum of the public schools?

5 Are there aspects of our current curriculum that you would equate with the *Saber-Tooth Curriculum?* If so, what are they?

For Debate

Read the Policy Matters! summary, "Teaching by Script or Improvisation," at the website, and consider the issues it outlines regarding scripted reading instruction. Then go to EduSpace to post your answers (or respond to other students' answers) to the What Do You Think questions listed in the Policy Matters! feature.

For Further Information

PRINT RESOURCES

Elliot W. Eisner, *The Educational Imagination,* 3d ed. (Upper Saddle River, NJ: Prentice Hall, 2001). The author presents a stimulating, controversial book regarding forces influencing today's curriculum.

E. D. Hirsch, Jr., *Cultural Literacy: What Every American Needs to Know* (Boston: Houghton Mifflin, 1987). This provocative treatise asserts that literacy requires the early and continued transmission of specific information—the common knowledge that enables students to make sense of what they read. (See the Core Knowledge Foundation website at: **http://www.coreknowledge.org.**)

Heidi Hayes Jacobs, *Interdisciplinary Curriculum* (Alexandria, VA: Association for Supervision and Curriculum Development, 1989. An excellent book on how to develop interdisciplinary curricula.

David W. Johnson and Roger T. Johnson, *Learning Together and Alone: Cooperative, Competitive, and Individualistic Learning,* 5th ed. (Boston: Allyn & Bacon/Longman, 1999). This excellent, comprehensive book was written by two of the leading researchers on cooperative learning.

Richard Rothstein, *Class and Schools: Using Social, Economic, and Educational Reform to Close the Black-White Achievement Gap,* (New York: Economic Policy Institute/Teachers College, 2004). This analysis of black-white student academic achievement gap concludes that efforts to close the gap that focus solely on school policies, while ignoring social-class characteristics that influence student learning, will fail.

Carol Ann Tomlinson, "Differentiating Instruction for Academic Diversity," *Classroom Teaching Skills,* 8th ed., ed. James M. Cooper (Boston: Houghton Mifflin, 2006). This chapter guides the reader through the philosophy and strategies for differentiating instruction.

Decker F. Walker and Jonas F. Soltis, *Thinking about Education: Curriculum and Aims,* 4th ed. (New York: Teachers College Press, 2004). This book provides a broad perspective on the basic curriculum questions educators face regarding the purposes, content, design, and structure of educational programs.

Jon W. Wiles and Joseph C. Bondi, *Curriculum Development: A Guide to Practice,* 6th ed. (Columbus, Ohio: Merrill/Prentice Hall, 2002). A comprehensive text offering thorough coverage of K–12 curriculum philosophy, curriculum planning, instruction, and curriculum design. It offers separate chapters on developing curriculum in the elementary, middle, and secondary schools.

WEB RESOURCES

American Council on the Teaching of Foreign Languages. Available at: **http://www.actfl.org.** An executive summary of the national standards for foreign languages can be found at this website.

Mid-continent Regional Educational Laboratory. Available at: **http://mcrel.org.** One of ten regional educational laboratories, this lab has a great set of materials in different subject areas, as well as research reports on effective practice. The website also offers links to other useful sites.

Special Education and Gifted Education. Available at: **http://www.cec.sped.org.** This site contains standards for special educators, not for the children they teach.

The following journals and websites contain many interesting and helpful items for teachers in the respective subject-matter fields. To find both national and state-by-state content standards in the various subject-matter fields, go to *Education World* at **http://www. education-world.com/standards/.**

Art: *Art Education, Arts and Activities, School Arts;* ArtsEdge at the Kennedy Center website, available at: **http://artsedge.kennedy-center.org/.**

Career and technical education: *Industrial Education, Journal of Home Economics; Business Education Forum; Business Education Review;* Clearinghouse on Adult, Career, and Vocational Education website, available at: **http://www.cete.org/acve/.–212+.**

Elementary and early childhood: Clearinghouse on Early Education and Parenting website, available at: http://ceep.crc.uiuc.edu/.

English: *English Journal;* National Council of Teachers of English website, available at: **http://www.ncte.org.** Includes national standards in English and language arts.

Foreign languages: *Modern Language Journal;* Center for Applied Linguistics website, available at: **http://www.cal.org/resources/update.html;**

University of Wisconsin Letters and Sciences website (contains lots of language links), available at: **http://polyglot.lss.wisc.edu/lss/lang/langlink.html.**

Mathematics: *The Mathematics Teacher;* National Council of Teachers of Mathematics website, available at: **http://www. nctm.org.** Includes national standards in mathematics. *School Science and Mathematics;* the official journal of the School Science and Mathematics Association, available at: **http://oregonstate.edu/pubs/ssm/;** Math Forum website, particularly "Ask Dr. Math," available at: **http://forum.swarthmore.edu/dr.math.**

Music: *Music Educators' Journal;* Music Education Resource Links (MERL) website, available at: **http://www1.chapman.edu/soe/faculty/piper/cpiper/MERLmenu.htm.**

Physical education: *Journal of Health, Physical Education and Recreation;* American Alliance for Health, Physical Education, Recreation and Dance website, available at: **http://www.aahperd.org/.** Includes national standards in physical education.

Reading and language arts: *Language Arts, The Reading Teacher;* children's literature web guide, available at: **http://www.acs.ucalgary.ca/~dkbrown/.**

Science: *The Science Teacher, School Science and Mathematics;* Eisenhower National Clearinghouse, available at: **http://www.enc.org;** *Blueprints for Reform: Science, Mathematics, and Technology Education,* available at: **http://project2061.org.** Includes national science standards.

Social studies: *Social Studies, Social Education;* National Council for the Social Studies, available at: **http://ncss.org.** Includes national standards in social studies.

6 *What Makes a Teacher Effective?*

Chapter Preview Effective teaching is much more than an intuitive process. A teacher must continually make decisions and act on those decisions. To do this effectively, the teacher must have *knowledge,* both theoretical knowledge about learning and human behavior and specific knowledge about the subject matter to be taught. A teacher also must demonstrate a repertoire of teaching *skills* that are believed to facilitate student learning and must display *attitudes* that foster learning and genuine human relationships.

This chapter emphasizes that:

▶ Teachers are required to make many decisions as they plan for instruction, implement teaching strategies, and evaluate outcomes of their planning and strategies.

▶ Four major types of attitudes affect teachers' behavior: (1) attitude toward self, (2) attitude toward children, (3) attitude toward peers and parents, and (4) attitude toward the subject matter.

▶ A teacher should have an intimate knowledge of the subject matter being taught, both the instructional content and the discipline from which it derives.

▶ To be able to recognize and interpret classroom events appropriately, a teacher should be familiar with theoretical knowledge and research about learning and human behavior.

▶ Effective teachers demonstrate a repertoire of teaching skills that enable them to meet the different needs of their students. Research has identified a number of these skills in, to name a few areas, classroom management, effective questioning, and planning techniques.

We once knew a teacher who was described as having not twenty years of experience but one year's experience twenty times. The message was that this teacher had stopped growing and developing as a professional after the first year. As someone just starting in your teaching career, this may seem like a remote possibility. After all, there's so much that you know you don't know, and you're eager to learn as much as you can. It is relatively easy, however, to fall into comfortable patterns of teaching, especially after you have gained a few years of experience.

■ developing the habit of reflection

How can you avoid this complacency and stagnation? One way is to maintain your curiosity and develop habits of inquiry and reflection. More and more teacher educators are coming to believe that although it is important to prepare beginning teachers for initial practice, it is even more important to help them develop the attitudes and skills to become lifelong students of teaching. Ideally, rather than relying on authority, impulse, or unexamined previous practice, teachers will continually examine and evaluate their attitudes, practices, effectiveness, and accomplishments. This process of examination and evaluation is often called **reflective teaching.** Reflective teachers ask themselves such questions as, "What am I doing and why?" "How can I better meet my students' needs?" "What are some alternative learning activities to achieve these objectives?" "How could I have encouraged more involvement or learning on the part of the students?" Even when lessons go well, reflective teachers analyze the lesson to determine what went well and why, and how else things might have been done.

Developing the habits of inquiry and reflection should begin now, in your teacher education program. Experiences with schools, teachers, and students will give you many opportunities to reflect on what has occurred. You can use journal writing, observation instruments, simulations, or videotaping to help you examine teaching, learning, and the contexts in which they occur. Comparing your perspectives with those of classmates, professors, and school personnel will broaden your interpretations and give you new insights. As you reflect on your experiences, you will come to distrust simplistic answers and explanations. Nuances and subtleties will start to become clear, and situations that once seemed simple will reveal their complexities.

As you reflect, you are likely to encounter and think about moral and ethical issues. Teachers make moral and ethical decisions every day. When teachers decide how they treat students and others, they make ethical decisions. When they elect to create a classroom climate that fosters trust, safety, and cooperation, they make ethical decisions. When certain examples from history or literature are selected for study, teachers make ethical decisions. In other words, you cannot teach without making ethical decisions. The chapter entitled "What Are the Ethical and Legal Issues Facing Teachers?" discusses this topic in greater detail, but we hope you will study and reflect upon the cases we present throughout this book that reflect moral or ethical issues. By practicing reflective teaching, you will grow and develop as an effective, professional teacher.

▶ Framework for Professional Practice

Visit this chapter of the website to link to more information about the INTASC standards.

In recent years, there have been several attempts to identify what effective teachers should know and be able to do. The Interstate New Teachers Assessment and Support Consortium (INTASC)—which is discussed in more detail in the chapter entitled "What Does It Mean to Be a Professional"—has identified the knowledge, dispositions, and performances that a beginning teacher should possess. As described in the box, novice teachers differ from more experienced experts in several

Differences Between Expert and Novice Teachers

A number of educational researchers have tried to identify expert and experienced teachers and compare them with novice teachers. These studies have identified various ways in which novice and expert teachers differ.

We can think of an expert teacher as similar to an expert chess player. Expert chess players quickly spot trouble areas in any chessboard pattern; likewise, expert teachers quickly recognize trouble spots in a classroom setting. Experts in chess or teaching draw on their hours of experience to build a repertoire of recognizable patterns. In one experiment, expert and novice teachers were asked to look at a photograph of a classroom and identify the class activity. Experts were better able to "read" the classroom, making inferences about what was happening in the picture. When observed in action, expert teachers also show greater ability to gather information in a short time for multiple purposes. For example, an expert teacher may be able to accomplish many tasks in an opening review session: gather attendance information, identify who did or did not do the homework, and locate students needing help with the next lesson.

In comparison, novice teachers described the surface characteristics of the classroom pictures they saw. And when presented with descriptions of student problems, the novices relied again on the literal features of the problems to suggest solutions. Their analyses did not correspond with the higher-order classifications used by expert teachers.

Experts differed from novices in their approaches to planning as well. In a simulated task of planning, experts focused on learning what students already knew about the subject matter to be learned, while novices planned to ask students where they were in their textbooks and then present a review of important concepts. In other words, experts planned to gather information from the students, whereas novices planned to give information to them.

The research suggests that experts in any field demonstrate skill in planning and in classifying problems and formulating solutions. This is no less true for teachers: the expert teacher shows problem-solving skills like those of other experts, whether in chess, bridge, or physics. The studies also indicate that the process of moving from novice to expert teacher takes considerable time because extensive experience is necessary to develop enough episodic knowledge to interpret information about classrooms.

Sources: David C. Berliner, "Expertise: The Wonder of Exemplary Performances." In *Creating Powerful Thinking in Teachers and Students,* ed. J. N. Mangiere and C. C. Block (Fort Worth, TX: Harcourt Brace College Publishers, 1994), pp. 161–186; Greta Morine-Dershimer, "Instructional Planning." In *Classroom Teaching Skills,* 8th ed., ed. J. M. Cooper (Boston: Houghton Mifflin, 2006), pp. 34–40.

ways. Nevertheless, standards for new teachers can help determine the foundations for developing expertise. For that reason, INTASC standards are based on the standards that the National Board for Professional Teaching Standards (also discussed in the "What Does It Mean to Be a Professional?" chapter) has developed for experienced, accomplished teachers. Many states are working in concert with INTASC to implement the standards as part of the states' teacher licensing requirements. The website for the INTASC standards is listed at the end of the chapter, and the ten core standards are listed inside the front cover of this book, along with the appropriate pages in this text where these standards are addressed.

Danielson's Framework for Teaching

■ domains of teaching
responsibilities

Charlotte Danielson has also attempted to define what an accomplished teacher does.[1] Danielson's Framework for Teaching lays out the various areas of competence in which professional teachers need to develop expertise. Danielson organizes the complex activity of teaching into twenty-two components, which are then clustered into four domains of teaching responsibility: (1) planning and preparation, (2) the classroom environment, (3) instruction, and (4) professional

The rapport that effective teachers establish with their students often carries outside the classroom learning environment.
(© Tom Stewart/CORBIS)

responsibilities. A brief review of each of these domains will provide you with a road map of the skills and competencies new teachers need to develop.

■ **Domain 1: Planning and Preparation**   How does a teacher design instruction and organize the content of what students are expected to learn? To be effective in this domain, teachers need to demonstrate that they know their content, pedagogy for teaching that content, their students, how to select instructional goals, what resources they have available to them, how to design coherent instruction, and how to assess student learning.

■ **Domain 2: The Classroom Environment**   Domain 2 consists of the interactions occurring in a classroom that are non-instructional. Effective teachers create an environment of respect and rapport among the students and with the teacher, establish a culture for learning, manage classroom procedures and student behavior, and efficiently organize the physical space.

The mediocre teacher tells. The good teacher explains. The superior teacher demonstrates. The great teacher inspires.

—WILLIAM ARTHUR WARD

■ **Domain 3: Instruction**   This domain constitutes the core of teaching—the engagement of students in learning content. To be effective here, a teacher needs to communicate clearly and accurately, use appropriate questioning and discussion techniques, engage students in learning, provide feedback to students, and demonstrate flexibility and responsiveness.

■ **Domain 4: Professional Responsibilities**   This domain addresses the wide range of teacher responsibilities outside the classroom. They include reflecting on teaching, maintaining accurate records, communicating with families, contributing to the school and district, growing and developing professionally, and showing professionalism. Teachers who demonstrate these competencies are seen as true professionals and are highly valued by their colleagues and administrators.

This framework for professional practice provides several benefits. First, the framework offers the teaching profession a shared vocabulary as a way of talking about excellent teaching. Second, it assists novice teachers by providing a roadmap to excellence in professional practice. Third, the framework provides a structure for discussions among teachers and sharpens the focus for professional development. Lastly, it communicates to the larger community the array of competencies needed to be an effective teacher.

Pause and Reflect

1 ▶ In which of these four domains do you feel most confident about your skills? Which domains do you need to work on?

This chapter will discuss some basic characteristics of effective teachers that are part of Danielson's framework. We particularly emphasize the role of the teacher as a reflective decision maker. We begin with a case study of a new teacher who faces problems that many classroom veterans will find familiar. We will then take a critical look at the many teaching decisions that she had to make.

| **Case Study** | # Carol Landis/A Case of Classroom Decision Making |

Carol Landis/A Case of Classroom Decision Making

As an example of how ordinary teaching situations can lead to useful reflections about effective teaching, consider the case of Carol Landis. Carol is beginning her first year of teaching. She prepared to be a high school social studies teacher, graduated, and accepted a job in her own community, a small city in the Northwest. Most of her students come from solidly blue-collar, working-class backgrounds.

■ the case of Carol Landis

Carol has been assigned three periods of world geography and two periods of American history. We will join her as she prepares the first lesson of a new unit in world geography.

Carol plans to require her ninth-graders to work in groups to prepare panel discussions about a country of their choice. She wants the groups to research the relationships among the geography, political history, and culture of a country and share what they find in panel discussions with the rest of the class. Carol sets these goals for her students: that they work together in groups and that they make effective oral presentations of their research.

■ Carol's questions

When planning how to present the assignment to her classes, Carol has many questions. Do these students know how to use the library? If not, will she need to provide directions for using reference materials? Maybe the librarian has already done this, and they will just need a review. Do these students know what *culture* means or understand general concepts that will help them look for relationships among culture, history, and geography? What background do they need before they start researching a specific country? And do these students know how to work in groups? Have they ever participated in a panel discussion? In planning how to help her students complete this assignment, Carol bases her decisions on what she thinks she knows about them as learners.

Although Carol has already planned this assignment to meet her state's curriculum standards in social studies, she is concerned about whether the books in her room and the library will provide the information her students need. What other resources are available? She knows that other teachers have back issues of *National Geographic,* for example. Maybe she could help students use the World Wide Web to access hypertext links that would tie together geography, political history, and culture for their respective countries.

In addition to the panel discussions, Carol has considered having each student submit a written report. For this first research assignment, however, she decides that an oral presentation by the group is appropriate. Later, she will work with the classes on report writing. In the beginning, she wants her students to enjoy her classes, to feel a part of a group, and to get to know one another, and Carol prefers listening to her students to grading written reports anyway, so this assignment fits her style of teaching.

■ incident with Tom

Despite her planning, when Carol reflects on her second-period class after the first day of library research, she wonders what went wrong. One group argued the whole period and never did select a country. Maybe she should have assigned groups and not let students choose their own partners. She tried to ignore the group, believing they should work out their own differences and come to a group decision. But what if they never work together? She noticed that another group was completely dominated by one of the top students. He decided what country they would research, he assigned the topics, and he told the others where to look for information. When Carol urged the other members to share equally in the group decisions, they asserted, "Tom always gets A's. We don't mind if he tells us what to do." Carol didn't know how to respond to their concern for grades without insulting Tom, so she said nothing.

Later in the period, Tom asked her what religion predominated in Indonesia. Carol wasn't sure but was afraid to admit her lack of information, so she told him, "Just look it up." Tom responded, "So you don't know either?" Carol testily told Tom that she was not his personal encyclopedia. Now she wonders if she overreacted. Maybe she should have admitted she didn't know. Was Tom challenging her authority, or was he just reacting to the sharp tone in her order to look it up? Did she turn Tom and his group against her?

Carol also wonders whether the other groups worked productively. She spent so much time watching the arguing group and Tom's group that she didn't have time to notice whether the chatter from the other groups was work or play. Maybe it didn't hurt to let the other groups have some fun today, anyway. She can direct her attention to them tomorrow.

■ Carol's frustrations

There is so much to watch and monitor when students work in groups, Carol realizes. Many questions arise, such as "Where do I find this?" "Mr. Shaw won't lend me his magazines; what do I do now?" "This library stinks. Why do we have to do this assignment anyway?" and even "Miss Landis, what did you do this weekend?" Carol wonders if she will ever learn to field all her students' questions and comments and distinguish the words on the surface from the real messages. She also worries about what to do about Ron, who started reading a novel about life in Siberian concentration camps. Carol thinks it is the only book she has ever seen him read. But it won't help his group do their project on Kenya.

Maybe this assignment wasn't such a good idea in the first place, Carol thinks, or maybe she just wasn't up to working with her classes in groups. The stares from the librarian and the study hall teacher indicated that they didn't think she could handle her classes, and Carol hasn't even thought about how she will grade her students' panel discussions. Just thinking about it all exhausts her. How will she ever get through another day with that second-period class? ■

▶ The Teacher as a Reflective Decision Maker

■ Carol as decision maker

We present Carol's case to illustrate that the teacher's role can be described as one of a reflective *decision maker*. Indeed, some educational researchers have identified skill in decision making as the most important teaching skill. Some decisions are made as teachers quietly deliberate curricular and instructional goals; many more must be made almost instantaneously as teachers and students inter-

It is in your moments of decision that your life is shaped. Develop your decision-making muscles.

—ANTHONY ROBBINS

act. Let's look at some of the particular decisions that Carol made or will make, dividing them into three basic stages: planning, implementing, and evaluating.

Planning Decisions

Carol wants her students to understand the relationships among geography, history, and culture. But what exactly does she want them to know about these relationships? She must decide the particular kinds of understanding she wants her students to achieve, and this decision affects her choice of teaching techniques.

From a variety of possible techniques, she has chosen independent group work. She has also decided that a panel discussion will provide evidence of her students' learning. These decisions reflect Carol's personal preferences, her goals for her students' learning, and her skills in methods of evaluating their learning. Her decisions are also based on a series of judgments about her students' ability to do research, work in groups, and present panel discussions, as well as on judgments about how long they will need to work together and what resources they will need. Carol may have made some plans for what to do in case her judgments turned out to be wrong, and she needed to adapt her lesson.

Implementing Decisions

Carol, like most teachers, must make many of her decisions almost instantly, as she adapts her teaching to changing classroom conditions. As Carol teaches this lesson or series of lessons, she has to decide when and how to intervene with some of her groups, whether to allow Ron to continue reading a novel, and what responses to make to students' questions.

Evaluating Decisions

After the first day's library work, Carol reflects on her interactions with the students, facing decisions about what adjustments to make in her strategies for the next day. As the groups continue to work, she will also face decisions about how to evaluate the impact of her planning and instruction on her students' learning.

In each of these planning, implementing, and evaluating stages of instructional decision making, Carol chooses among alternative concepts her students could learn, approaches to help them learn the concepts, ways to manage the classroom to encourage their learning, and ways to measure their learning. Could her decisions improve with more adequate knowledge, skills, and attitudes?

▶ Aspects of Reflective Decision Making

In the rest of this chapter, we will explore the areas of competence that help teachers make more effective decisions. We, along with many other educators, believe that to be effective decision makers, elementary and secondary school teachers need to have attitudes, knowledge, and skills essential to the teaching profession. Teachers must ask themselves not only "What am I going to teach?" but also "What should my students be learning?" "How can I help them learn it?" and "Why is it important?" To answer these questions, teachers must be familiar with children and their developmental stages. They must know something about events occurring outside the classroom and about what society requires from the young. They must have enough command of the subject they teach to be able to distinguish what is peripheral from what is central. They must have a philosophy of education that guides them in their role as teacher. They must know something about how human beings learn and about how to create environments that promote learning.

■ areas of teaching competence

What are the specialized skills and attributes of the effective instructional decision maker? The five areas of competence that we consider essential for a teacher are the following:

1. Attitudes that foster learning and genuine human relationships
2. Knowledge of the subject matter to be taught
3. Theoretical knowledge about learning and human behavior
4. Personal practical knowledge
5. Skills of teaching that promote student learning

Teachers draw on their competence in these five areas to inform the many decisions they make as they plan instruction and as they spontaneously interact with the students in their classes. Figure 6.1 indicates the relationship of these areas of competence to the process of instructional decision making. In the remainder of this chapter, we will examine these areas of competence, now and then referring to the instructional decisions that Carol made and the attitudes, knowledge, and skills influencing her decisions.

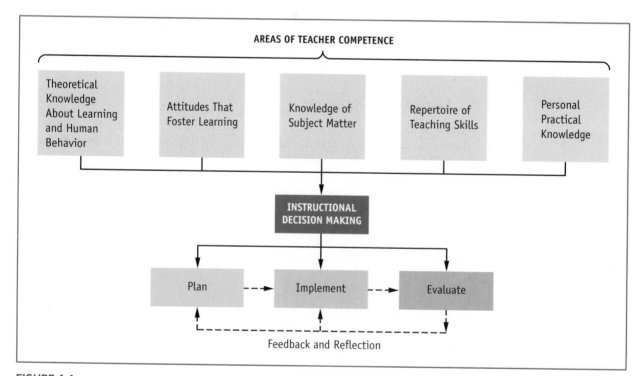

FIGURE 6.1

Relationship of Teacher-Competence Areas to Process of Instructional Decision Making

Source: James M. Cooper, ed., "The Teacher as a Reflective Decision Maker." In *Classroom Teaching Skills,* 8th ed. Copyright © 2006 by Houghton Mifflin Company. Reprinted with permission.

▶ What Attitudes Does the Effective Teacher Possess?

Many people believe that the teacher's personality is the most critical factor in successful teaching. If teachers have warmth, empathy, sensitivity, enthusiasm, and humor, they are much more likely to be successful than if they lack these characteristics. In fact, many people argue that without these attributes, an individual is unlikely to be a good teacher. The Leaders in Education box portrays one teacher known for her positive attitude, Helen Keller's tutor, Anne Mansfield Sullivan.

Leaders in Education

Anne Mansfield Sullivan (1866–1936)

The proof is in the pupil. In this case, Helen Keller, a blind and deaf pupil, was a terror. Wily and mean, Helen was also animal-like. Nevertheless, her teacher, Anne Sullivan, enabled her to become an international celebrity.

Sullivan pioneered the teaching of individuals without sight and without hearing. Today we speak of a *deaf culture,* but this term was not used in the era of Anne Sullivan. "Teacher," as Helen always called her, is credited with making it possible to reach students who were thought to have mental retardation.

The daughter of Irish immigrants, Sullivan was born in Feeding Hills, Mass., on April 14, 1866 and entered the almshouse at eight when her mother died and her father abandoned her and her brother. Half-blind herself, she went to the Perkins School for the Blind in Boston at age fourteen without a toothbrush, hat, or coat; her only possessions were a shirt and stockings tied in a bundle.

At age twenty-one, Sullivan took a job offered by the Keller family in Tuscumbia, Ala., to teach the Kellers' daughter, Helen. Helen Keller was an angry and frustrated child, but she was not stupid. Sullivan saw this and began her assault on Helen's locked mind. Within a month, she made contact with Helen in the now famous pump story, immortalized in the drama *The Miracle Worker.* Sullivan fingerspelled words into Helen's hand, each word suiting an action. Finally, Helen, feeling water over her hand, realized the connection between word and object. She had broken the code and realized that everything had a name.

Sullivan's methods were practical. She taught Helen to play through games and exercises, stimulating her to ask the names of the motions. She kept a menagerie of animals for Helen to help her understand movement. She progressed to abstractions like peace and God as soon as her pupil was ready.

Sullivan wanted to make Helen as normal as possible, giving her every experience she could. She worked at teaching her to sit, stand, and walk properly. As soon as Helen could distinguish between right and wrong, "Teacher" sent her to bed for misdeeds. Laziness, carelessness, untidiness, and procrastination were dealt with by ingenuity, humor, and light sarcasm.

Helen used the manual alphabet for three years before she began to speak. When Helen was nine, Sullivan was rewarded with the words "I am not dumb now." It was one of the most dramatic achievements in the history of teaching.

Sullivan's great discovery was that a child should not be taught each word separately by a separate definition but instead should be given endless repetition of language he or she does not understand all day long. Sullivan continually spelled words into

Helen's hand to mimic the way a hearing child in the cradle absorbs words. This method had never before been put into practice in the education of a deaf child, especially a deaf-blind one.

When Helen attended a school for deaf pupils in New York, Anne Sullivan went along. At Cambridge School and Radcliffe College, Sullivan attended classes, interpreting instruction and looking up words for Helen. She made herself eye and ear to Helen and supplied knowledge to a starving mind as she fired her pupil's drive to study hard. After col-

lege, Sullivan accompanied Helen on worldwide lecture tours as Helen became a famous author and personality.

Extraordinarily close, teacher and pupil spent much of their lives together. The name "Teacher" has been enriched by Anne Sullivan's dedicated life, persistent high standards, and creative instruction.

 Visit the website for more information about Anne Mansfield Sullivan.

Source: Marilyn Ryan

For years, educational researchers sought to isolate the characteristics essential to good teachers. In one comprehensive study, the researcher concluded that effective teachers are fair, democratic, responsive, understanding, kindly, stimulating, original, alert, attractive, responsible, steady, poised, and confident. Ineffective teachers were described as partial, autocratic, aloof, restricted, harsh, dull, stereotyped, apathetic, unimpressive, evasive, erratic, excitable, and uncertain.[2]

Unfortunately, this information is not very useful. After all, what human interaction wouldn't be improved if the participants possessed only positive traits? Two researchers, summarizing fifty years of research on teachers' personalities and characteristics, conclude, "Despite the critical importance of the problem and a half-century of prodigious research effort, very little is known for certain about the nature and measurement of teacher personality, about the relation between teacher personality and teaching effectiveness."[3]

■ definition of attitudes

A person's *attitudes,* or predispositions to act in a positive or negative way toward people, ideas, and events, are a fundamental dimension of his or her personality. Although the relationship between general personality traits and teacher effectiveness has proven elusive, almost all educators are convinced of the importance of teacher attitudes in the teaching process. Attitudes have a direct but often unrecognized effect on our behavior in that they determine the ways we view ourselves and interact with others.

How we think shows through in how we act. Attitudes are mirrors of the mind.

—David Joseph Schwartz

We believe four major categories of attitudes affect teaching behavior: (1) the teacher's attitude toward self, (2) the teacher's attitudes toward children and the relationship between self and children, (3) the teacher's attitudes toward peers and pupils' parents, and (4) the teacher's attitude toward the subject matter.

■ four categories of teacher attitudes

The Teacher's Attitude Toward Self: Self-Understanding

■ recognize own needs as well as students'

If teachers are to help students have meaningful experiences, develop their aptitudes and abilities, face their inner difficulties, and accept themselves as people, they need to know and understand those students. Before teachers can do that, however, they must work at knowing and understanding themselves. Empirical evidence from psychology indicates that people who deny or are unable to cope with their own emotions are unlikely to be capable of respecting and dealing with others' feelings.

For example, unless teachers recognize their own needs and anxieties, they will be unlikely to understand and empathize with their students' needs or expressions of anxiety. They may not recognize that students' inabilities to learn, inattentiveness, impudence, or irritability may be the result of anxiety. Teachers also need to recognize that their own anxieties may make them irritable, causing the students in turn to feel anxious and to show similar symptoms.

■ books about teachers

■ **Ways to Achieve Self-Understanding**   How can one achieve understanding of self and, after achieving it, accept it? A number of potential resources can help promote self-understanding. For example, books by sensitive and compassionate people who have made progress in their own struggles to know themselves can be a valuable aid in self-examination. For prospective teachers, such books might include Sylvia Ashton-Warner's *Teacher,* an account of her teaching experience in a Maori infant school in New Zealand; Tracy Kidder's *Among Schoolchildren;* Herbert Kohl's *36 Children;* and Lisa Delpit's *Other People's Children.*

■ observing in classrooms

Another method is **participant observation,** the process of observing a class and recording what you hear, see, and feel as you observe. You then compare your record with the records of other observers. This experience may show you that what you notice in any given situation is determined largely by habits of thought that you take for granted. It may also show that your "objective" perceptions are often projections of your own subjective state, and so it may tell you more about yourself than about the people you have observed.

■ self-examination

We urge you to regard self-examination as a serious commitment and to undertake it, *as a prospective teacher,* in an effort to make a good decision about whether to teach and to become the best teacher you are capable of becoming. You can start now by examining your responses to the dilemmas presented in the "What Would You Do?" box.

■ Carol's self-concept

Remember Carol's attitude toward Tom when he asked for information she didn't have, and recall her seeming "live and let live" attitude toward the argumentative group and the student reading a novel. What may these attitudes about student behaviors indicate about Carol's self-concept? Is she afraid to admit limitations in her knowledge? Does she hesitate to discipline off-task behavior because she thinks her students will no longer like her? How strong is her need for approval? Maybe Carol overreacts to Tom's request for information because she is insecure with the role of teacher and feels threatened by his authority among his peers. Although Carol's case does not give enough information to answer these questions, we can say with confidence that her self-concept will influence her behavior toward her students. As Carol develops a realistic understanding of herself and her needs and anxieties, she will change her attitudes toward her students and improve her relationship with them.

The Teacher's Attitude Toward Children

Children are sensitive observers of adult behavior, and they often see, and become preoccupied with, aspects of the teacher's attitude toward them of which the teacher may be unaware. Consider how a teacher's effectiveness might be reduced by these feelings or attitudes toward students:

■ negative attitudes

- A strong dislike for particular pupils and obvious fondness for others
- Biases toward or against particular ethnic groups
- A bias toward certain kinds of student behavior such as docility or inquisitiveness
- An uneasiness in working with children who have disabilities

Few teachers are entirely free of negative attitudes at the outset, and self-awareness can be the crucial factor distinguishing a teacher who is able to

What Would You Do?

1. You are a woman, a beginning teacher in a ninth-grade English course. As the first semester proceeds, you realize that one of your students, Fred, has a crush on you. He is always volunteering to help you pass out papers, and he lingers after class each day to talk to you. He finds out your home address and comes to visit you one Saturday morning. His actions are becoming obvious to the other students, who are starting to kid him about his infatuation. *What would you do?*

2. You are generally recognized as one of the most popular teachers in your school. The students look on you as a friend who can be trusted, and you have told them that if they ever have problems, school-related or personal, they should feel free to come to you. One day Maryanne, a junior in one of your classes, seeks you out. Close to hysteria, she tells you she is ten weeks pregnant. You are the first person she has told. She begs you for advice but insists you do not tell her parents. *What would you do?*

3. You are a fourth-grade teacher. Until recently, you have been quite comfortable in your class of twenty-three children. About three weeks ago,

you had to speak to Debbie. Although she is your brightest student, she was continually talking when you were trying to address the class. Since then she has been as cool as ice to you, and you recently discovered a nasty drawing in your desk drawer that was supposed to be you. *What would you do?*

4. You are a white teacher in a somewhat racially tense school. There are seven African American students in one of your classes. Because you fear alienating the African Americans and being accused of prejudice, you make special efforts to treat them fairly. One day, three of your white students come to see you and accuse you of coddling the African Americans and discriminating against whites. *What would you do?*

5. You teach in a school that uses a letter grading system. You have assigned your students a term paper. You know that one student has spent hours and hours on his report, but its quality is quite poor. The student has already expressed his hope that you will take effort into account when grading the reports. *What would you do?*

control and change these attitudes. Thus, it is important that prospective teachers confront their own attitudes early on, perhaps through case studies, group discussions, role playing, or behavioral records of teaching experiences.

■ treat students fairly

When we become aware of our attitudes, we can often control our behavior better, but even then change is neither easy nor automatic. It is difficult to admit to feelings and attitudes that might be considered inappropriate or unprofessional. For example, most teachers would like to believe that they like all their students equally, but this is almost never the case. You will have some students you find charming and others who rub you the wrong way. The important thing is that teachers treat students fairly, which usually means treating them differently. Each child has different needs, and the best way to address these needs equitably is to address them uniquely, including taking into account such factors as race, ethnicity, and gender. As one educator puts it, "If teachers pretend not to see students' racial and ethnic differences, they really do not see the students at all and are limited in their ability to meet their educational needs."[4] The discussion on differentiating instruction in the chapter entitled "What Is Taught?" addresses this issue of treating students differently.

I touch the future. I teach.
—Christa McAuliffe

■ cultivating positive attitudes

■ **Teacher Expectations**   In general, a teacher's expectation that *all* students can succeed seems to make a difference in students' achievement. As a teacher, you need to believe that all your students are capable of high academic achievement and base your beliefs and behavior on the needs, abilities, and aspirations of each individual student.

Teachers do form expectations about a student's performance, and these expectations seem to relate to the student's achievement. The source of a teacher's expectations may vary: a student's social class, race, or gender; information from previous teachers; test scores; or family background information. Research indicates that some teachers expect certain behaviors from students on the basis of stereotypes that they have about particular racial, ethnic, or socioeconomic groups.[5] For example, Asian American students may be encouraged to study mathematics or science because teachers believe they are "good" in those subjects, or teachers may expect more from middle-class students than from lower-class students. Often teachers do not recognize these attitudes and beliefs but communicate them nevertheless in both overt and subtle ways, including the use of praise or criticism to guide a student's performance.[6]

■ self-fulfilling prophecies

If a teacher expects a student or group of students to behave in a certain way, the teacher's attitude may serve as a **self-fulfilling prophecy**—that is, the students may behave in the predicted manner in response to the teacher's attitude and not as a result of the other factors on which the teacher's expectations are based. Thomas Good and Jere Brophy have suggested a process by which teachers' expectations may encourage certain levels of achievement.[7]

First, the teacher forms expectations of specific behavior and achievement for individual students. Then the teacher's behavior toward these students differs according to the expectations. The students perceive the teacher's expectations from how they are treated; this perception affects their self-concept, motivation to achieve, and aspiration to excel. Over time, students of whom much is expected will perform well, and students of whom little is expected will perform poorly. Thus, the result seems to justify the original expectation and fulfill the teacher's unspoken prophecy. The process is not automatic; teachers' expectations are not always fulfilled, but research indicates that teachers can influence which children do or do not achieve in the classroom.

A master can tell you what he expects of you. A teacher, though, awakens your own expectations.

—PATRICIA NEAL (ACTRESS)

PEANUTS: United Feature Syndicate, Inc.

How Do Teachers Treat Low Achievers?

Researchers have not definitely established why some teachers treat students they perceive as high and low achievers differently, but observations of many classroom teachers reveal that they often behave differently toward these two groups of students. Good and Brophy have summarized these differences:

1. Teachers wait less time for lows to answer a question.

2. Teachers give lows answers or call on someone else for the answer instead of giving clues or providing additional opportunities to respond.

3. Teachers reward lows for inappropriate behaviors or incorrect answers.

4. Lows are more often criticized for failure.

5. Lows are praised less frequently for success than highs.

6. Lows may not receive feedback for public responses.

7. Generally, teachers interact less often with lows, paying less attention to them.

8. Teachers call on lows less often for answers to questions.

9. Teachers seat lows farther from the teacher.

10. Less is demanded from lows.

11. Lows receive more private than public interactions; their activities are more closely monitored and structured.

12. When teachers grade tests and assignments, they give highs but not lows the benefit of the doubt in borderline cases.

13. Lows experience fewer friendly interactions, including fewer smiles and other nonverbal signs of support.

14. Lows receive shorter and less informative feedback to their questions.

15. Teachers make less eye contact and respond less attentively to lows.

16. Teachers make less use of effective but time-consuming instructional methods with lows when time is limited.

17. There is less acceptance and use of lows' ideas.

18. Lows are exposed to an impoverished curriculum.

As a teacher, you should make it a point to reflect on your own behavior toward low and high achievers, making sure that you are treating all your students fairly.

Source: From Thomas L. Good and Jere E. Brophy, *Looking in Classrooms,* 9th ed. Published by Allyn & Bacon, Boston, MA. Copyright © 2003 by Pearson Education. Adapted by permission of the publisher.

Pause and Reflect

1 ▶ Can you think of any examples of where a teacher's expectations led to a self-fulfilling prophecy? Describe the circumstances.

2 ▶ What attitudes do you possess that you think will have either positive or potentially negative effects on student learning?

3 ▶ Do you have negative feelings or expectations about any group or type of people? Can you identify the basis of those feelings? Do you want to change them? If so, how might you try?

The Teacher's Attitude Toward Peers and Parents

Much of what we have already said about teachers' attitudes toward themselves and children also applies to their attitudes toward peers and parents. Some attitudes enhance a teacher's effectiveness, and others detract from it.

■ problems with authority

■ **Authority/Collaboration**   One source of conflict may be the teacher's attitude toward those who represent authority (ordinarily administrators but, for prospective teachers, the university supervisor or cooperating teacher). Teachers may find it hard to be themselves while dealing with people who outrank them in position or prestige. Sometimes teachers find they yield too readily to demands from those in authority, and as a result they feel guilty about complying rather than standing on their own convictions. When this occurs, the result is often a continuing undercurrent of resentment toward the person in authority.

If teachers can assume a role of collaboration with those in authority, seeing themselves as part of a valuable partnership in the enterprise of education, they may be able to overcome any predispositions to hostility or any anxiety unwarranted by reality. Resentment of those in authority only prevents communication and understanding.

> Visit this chapter of the website to link to more information about working with students' families.

■ need for recognition

■ **Competition/Cooperation** Some teachers develop a strong drive to compete with other teachers for recognition from both authority figures and students. They try to have the best lesson plans, to be the "most popular teacher," or to maintain the friendliest relationship with the administration. Such teachers are striving to be recognized and rewarded. As a result of this attitude, they sometimes cut themselves off from much-needed help and severely limit their ability to be of help to others. Carol Landis has taken an important first step by enlisting the help of other teachers to get the necessary resources for her students. For the benefit of staff and students, teachers need to cooperate and share ideas.

> *To speak ill of others is a dishonest way of praising ourselves.*
>
> —WILL AND ARIEL DURANT

■ lack of tolerance

■ **Superiority and Prejudice/Acceptance** One attitude that never fails to cause trouble for teachers is a feeling of superiority to other teachers or parents of students. They may feel intellectually superior to colleagues, socially superior to students' parents, or both. Some teachers simply have little tolerance for people who differ from them in values, cultural background, or economic status, and, as a result, they treat others with disdain and contempt rather than patience and respect. Again, effective teachers—those who work well with colleagues and parents to empower children to achieve— show attitudes of acceptance. In their dealings with other teachers and parents, teachers should be real or genuine, value other people as worthy in their own right, and show empathy.

> *Treat people as if they were what they ought to be and you help them to become what they are capable of being.*
>
> —JOHANN W. VON GOETHE

The Teacher's Attitude Toward the Subject Matter

■ must feel enthusiasm

This section is short because our message is simple: it is most important that whatever subject matter you teach, you feel *enthusiasm* for it. Just as students usually can discern the teacher's attitude toward them, they are also very sensitive to the teacher's attitude toward the subject matter. One of the most striking characteristics of the excellent teacher is enthusiasm for what she or he is teaching. The bored teacher conveys boredom to the students—and who can blame them for failing to get excited if the teacher, who knows more about the subject than they do, doesn't find it engaging?

Some teachers find it difficult to feel enthusiasm for a curriculum they haven't constructed themselves, don't identify with, or don't want to teach. The surest way to guarantee that teachers are enthusiastic about what they are teaching is to allow them to teach what they are enthusiastic about. We do not mean this as a mere play on words. We would rather see an enthusiastic teacher teaching

Teacher enthusiasm is usually contagious.
(© Elizabeth Crews)

The video case *Writing Instruction: Process Writing* shows a teacher and a literary specialist who both demonstrate their enthusiasm for writing and their respect for their students. As you watch the clips and study the artifacts in the case, reflect upon the following questions:

1. In this chapter, the authors advise teachers to focus on subjects about which they have the most enthusiasm. How have these teachers applied that advice for themselves? How have they applied it for the students they teach?
2. What expectations do these teachers seem to hold for their students?
3. What are some ways that you, as a teacher, can generate similar enthusiasm and high expectations for your students?

The highest function of the teacher consists not so much in imparting knowledge as in stimulating the pupil in its love and pursuit.

—Henri Frederic Amiel

■ teaching implications

a minor historical topic than an uninspired teacher teaching Shakespeare. As one student put it, "There is nothing worse than sitting in a lesson knowing full well that the teacher is dying to get rid of you and rush back to the staff room to have a cup of coffee." Unfortunately, as more and more states adopt learning standards for students, the latitude that teachers once had to choose content is being greatly curtailed. States expect teachers to teach to the standards, and the high-stakes assessment tests given to students exert considerable pressure on teachers to be certain they "cover the content" contained on the assessments.

If you have to teach something you would rather not, try to develop a positive attitude toward the subject. Enthusiasm: if the teacher has it, life in the classroom can be exciting; if it is missing, there is little hope that students will learn much of significance.

Pause and Reflect

1 ▶ Do you have any concerns about your attitudes toward students' parents, school administrators, or other teachers? If you do, what can you do now to improve your attitudes?

2 ▶ Can you think of any ways that you, as a teacher, might be able to work up more enthusiasm for a topic that does not, at first, seem very interesting?

3 ▶ If you begin to lose your enthusiasm about a certain subject after you have taught it for a few years, what are some ways you might be able to rekindle your interest?

▶ What Subject-Matter Knowledge Does the Effective Teacher Need?

■ structure of the discipline

Very simply, prospective teachers need to understand the content of the subjects they teach, as well as the methods of teaching the specific content. Three important components contribute to a teacher's content knowledge. First, teachers need to understand the subjects they teach well enough to analyze and convey their elements, logic, possible uses, and social biases—that is, teachers need to understand the structure of the subjects they teach. They primarily learn this content in subject-matter courses they take in college. In the case of Carol Landis, she had learned about social studies topics including history and geography in her college courses.

■ curriculum content

Second, the teacher must also understand the content of the school curriculum that pupils are expected to know. Unfortunately, most college courses in the specific disciplines don't prepare prospective teachers to actually teach the knowledge that students are expected to learn. Much of what prospective teachers learn from their study of the academic disciplines is not taught to children and so is not directly applicable to teaching. This is particularly true for elementary school teachers, who are called on to teach content that is rarely taught in universities. For example, a mathematics major preparing to teach elementary school may never have occasion to use differential equations or calculus in the content she or he teaches to elementary-age children. Thus, although studying and understanding specific disciplines is crucial, it is not sufficient for effective teaching. A teacher must also study the actual curriculum taught in his or her school. Carol Landis, for example, worked to make her group project contribute to her students' ability to meet their district's standards in social studies.

■ pedagogical content knowledge

A third type of knowledge shown by effective teachers is **pedagogical content knowledge,** the knowledge that bridges content knowledge and pedagogy. Pedagogical content knowledge represents the "blending of content and pedagogy into an understanding of how particular topics, problems, or issues are organized, represented, and adapted to the diverse interests and abilities of learners, and presented for instruction."[8] The skilled teacher draws on the most powerful analogies, illustrations, examples, explanations, and demonstrations to represent and transform the subject so that students can understand it. For example, a physics teacher who possesses pedagogical content knowledge might use the analogy of water flowing through a pipe to explain how electricity flows through a circuit, but he or she would also know the limitations of such an analogy. Education methods courses in the specific subject areas are where you are most likely to learn pedagogical content knowledge. Carol Landis has learned several methods for teaching social studies content and is now in the process of discovering whether the one she has chosen will be effective with her students.

■ all three types of knowledge essential

These three types of knowledge—of discipline content (including the structure of the discipline), of curriculum content, and of pedagogical content—are, we believe, essential for effective teachers. Did Carol Landis have such knowledge? We suspect not, at least not to the degree that she could communicate information and concepts to her class with the authority and expertise required for effective teaching. In the next section, we will examine more closely another area of the effective teacher's knowledge: theoretical knowledge about learning and human behavior.

Pause and Reflect

1 ▶ What parts of the discipline content you are learning in college do you expect to teach to your own students? What parts are you likely not to teach to them?

2 ▶ Do you recall any teachers of yours who demonstrated especially strong or weak pedagogical content knowledge? How did they demonstrate their level of knowledge?

▶ What Theoretical Knowledge Does the Effective Teacher Need?

Education must bring the practice as nearly as possible to the theory.

—HORACE MANN

Theoretical knowledge about learning and human behavior equips the teacher to draw on concepts from psychology, anthropology, sociology, and related disciplines to interpret the complex reality of the classroom. The teacher who lacks a theoretical background will have to interpret classroom events according to commonly held beliefs or common sense, much of which is, unfortunately, based on outmoded notions of human behavior.

Theories-in-Use

Carol Landis operated on the basis of certain ideas, or what some call *theories-in-use*, which differ from pure theories.[9] A *theory* is an unproved explanation of why something happens the way it does. In its simplest form, a theory is a hypothesis designed to bring generalizable facts, concepts, or scientific laws into systematic connection. On the other hand, a *theory-in-use* is something people have in their heads and apply in their dealings with people and the world. Theories-in-use are often unexamined.

■ typical theories-in-use

We all have these theories-in-use, and they guide us as we make our way through our daily lives. You eat certain foods because you have an idea that they have a healthy effect on the body, or you decide to take a summer job in a public playground, believing that you will get to know children better and that future prospective employers might be pleased or impressed when they hear you have had that kind of experience.

■ Carol's theories-in-use

As you may have observed, Carol Landis has several theories-in-use. For example, Carol has the theory-in-use that groups should operate democratically and not be dominated by one student. She also has a theory-in-use that some children will perform better in school than others; as a result, she expects certain behavior from certain kinds of students. She also has a classroom management theory-in-use that she should give students some leeway before she resorts to firm discipline should they exceed her level of tolerance. Some of Carol's theories-in-use are clearly questionable. A few may have contributed to her problems that day in the library, and some may cause her more problems further down the line. Notice, however, that Carol was not worried about her theories-in-use. She was worried about what she did and what she will do. She didn't question some of her conceptions. Theories-in-use were the last things she had in mind, but they in fact caused some of her problems.

Pause and Reflect

1 ► Has reading about Carol Landis and her theories-in-use helped you identify any of your own theories-in-use or those of teachers you have
known? If so, what are some of those theories-in-use?

Why Study Educational Theory?

The fact that Carol did not reflect on the truth or falsity of her theories-in-use or
try to recall some theories she had learned during her teacher education is not uncommon. Indeed, many teachers question the basic usefulness of theory. Many a
beginning teacher has been told by a senior colleague, "Forget all that theory
they've been giving you in college. Here's what works in the real world." Further,
preservice teachers often complain that courses are too theoretical. They want to
get out to schools, where the action is. This desire (perhaps it is your own desire)
for things that work and ways to cope with real situations is vital, and we do not
want to diminish it. As a teacher, you will need practical techniques and solutions
to real problems, but to need practical tools does not mean that educational theory is less important.

■ why theoretical knowledge
is necessary

The case of Carol Landis illustrates how lack of theoretical knowledge of
classroom management can lead to inappropriate behavior on the teacher's part.
Both theory and empirical research support the notion of being consistent in your
expectations of student behavior, whereas Carol thought it was all right to let students behave as they wished until they crossed her tolerance threshold, at which
point she came down hard on them. Carol probably would not have encountered
such trouble if more of her theories-in-use had been challenged and adjusted.

■ good theories are practical

Like Carol, you may have your own theories-in-use, and these need to be
challenged and tested. The best way to do this is to pit them against other theories and ideas. We believe, moreover, that theoretical information *is* practical. The
problem is not that theory is wrong or unworkable but that many teacher education programs offer students few opportunities to apply theory to practical situations. As the great American philosopher John Dewey said, "Nothing is so
practical as a good theory."* Finally, by giving attention to theoretical knowledge
now, we are looking ahead to the future. In other words, even if it doesn't interest you much at this point, we want you to know that at a later stage of your development, you will encounter theories that will enlighten and enrich your work
with the young.

How Can Theoretical Knowledge Be Used?

A teacher's theoretical knowledge can be used in two ways: to interpret new or
ambiguous situations and to solve problems.[10] (Personal practical knowledge,
on the other hand, is more limited in applicability and is used primarily to respond to familiar situations. We will discuss personal practical knowledge
shortly.) As the box "Teaching: Art or Science?" describes, the "art" of teaching
is knowing how and when to apply research and theory in the quickly paced
classroom.

---

* For the moment we will downplay the fact that John Dewey was primarily an educational theorist.

Teaching: Art or Science?

One of the pioneers of research on teaching, N. L. Gage, professor emeritus at Stanford University, sees teaching as a blend of both art and science. Teaching can be considered an art because teachers must improvise and spontaneously handle a tremendous number of factors that interact in often unpredictable and nonsystematic ways in classroom settings. Teaching cannot be reduced to formulas or recipes for action, in Gage's opinion.

On the other hand, Gage contends that teaching is also a science. Although science can't offer absolute guidance for teachers as they plan and implement instructional strategies, research can provide a scientific basis for the art of teaching. For example, the research on academic engaged time has demon-strated the importance of keeping pupils on task with intellectually challenging, but not too difficult, subject matter.

These two components of teaching, art and science, interact. Empirically derived knowledge of the relationships among teacher behavior, pupil behavior, material to be learned, and desired student learning can guide teachers as they make artistic decisions about their teaching—that is, teachers use their knowledge of the research on these relationships to accomplish the artistry of moving a unique classroom of unique students toward the intended learning.

Is teaching an art or a science? The answer is "yes."

Source: N. L. Gage, *Hard Gains in the Soft Sciences: The Case of Pedagogy* (Bloomington, IN: Phi Delta Kappa, 1985), pp. 4–11.

■ zone of proximal development

■ forming hypotheses and investigating

■ **An Example of Using Theoretical Knowledge**   Let's consider an example of how theoretical knowledge can help a teacher interpret classroom events and solve the problems arising from them. In educational psychology, there is a concept known as the **zone of proximal development,** a range of tasks that a child cannot yet do alone but can accomplish when assisted by a more skilled partner. In other words, the child is on the verge of being able to solve a problem but just needs some structure, clues, help with remembering certain steps or procedures, or encouragement to try. (This assistance, called **scaffolding,** allows students to complete tasks they can't complete independently.) This zone is where instruction can succeed and real learning is possible. The concept of the zone of proximal development derives from the theoretical work of the Russian psychologist Lev Vygotsky, in which he theorized that a child's culture shapes cognitive development by determining what and how the child will learn about the world.

Now suppose that a student, John, is experiencing difficulty doing some percentage problems in math. You, the teacher, understand that the zone of proximal development is influenced by reasoning ability, background knowledge, and motivation. Therefore, you assess John's ability to understand the problems by watching him try to solve one of them. You ask him to explain to you what he is thinking as he attempts the solutions. Is he missing some important understanding, or is he making some procedural error? Are the problems too difficult, or should he be able to solve them with some assistance? If the latter, what kind of assistance does he need? Who should give him the assistance, you or another student?

You decide that John is not lacking any fundamental knowledge and is very close to understanding the correct procedures. You ask Mary, a student who understands percentage problems pretty well, to come over and think aloud as she works on one of the problems. By thinking aloud and having John follow along, Mary provides John with insight into how she goes about solving the problem. You encourage John to ask Mary questions as she goes over her solution. You now ask John to work a similar problem, also thinking aloud as he tries to solve it. This time, he gets the problem correct. You ask him to do a couple more problems and to raise his hand when he finishes so you can check to see if his understanding carried over to the new problems.

■ using theoretical knowledge

How did the theoretical knowledge about the zone of proximal development assist you in helping John? First, you had to determine whether John was close to understanding or missing some fundamental knowledge. Was he in the zone of proximal development where additional coaching or assistance would help him, or would you have to reteach some important knowledge that he didn't have? Second, what sort of scaffolding would benefit John? By having both Mary and John think aloud as they solved the problem, mistakes or errors could be easily determined and, if solved correctly, provide a model for John. An understanding of the zone of proximal development and its related scaffolding strategies represents the kind of theoretical knowledge that can help you interpret and solve classroom problems.

■ taking advantage of opportunities

This example helps show that a teacher needs much more than a common-sense understanding of human behavior. The capable and effective teacher uses theoretical knowledge drawn from various education-related disciplines to formulate and test hypotheses about human behavior in the classroom. In our opinion, the translation of theory into practice cannot be left to chance; you must constantly take advantage of opportunities that allow you to apply theoretical concepts to classroom situations and to receive guidance and feedback from your instructors about the application of these concepts. The field of cognitive psychology, in particular, has recently provided fertile research findings and theoretical concepts for teachers.

▶ Personal Practical Knowledge

■ practical knowledge differs from person to person

Personal practical knowledge is the set of understandings teachers have of the practical circumstances in which they work. Personal practical knowledge includes the beliefs, insights, and habits that allow teachers to do their jobs in schools. This type of knowledge tends to be time bound and situation specific, personally compelling, and oriented toward action. Teachers use their personal practical knowledge to solve dilemmas, resolve tensions, and simplify the complexities of their work. For example, the personal practical knowledge that Carol Landis must develop ranges from learning whether another teacher will loan his collection of *National Geographic* magazines to other classes to clarifying her beliefs about whether assigning students to groups is better than letting them choose their own groups. Because teachers' personal practical knowledge is so intertwined with them as individuals, researchers have not been able to summarize this knowledge into a codified body of teaching knowledge. Case studies of teachers have, however, provided us with rich images of how teachers use their knowledge to make sense of the complex, ill-structured environment that characterizes most classrooms.

■ takes time to develop

Teachers' personal practical knowledge definitely influences the decisions they make. Some researchers argue that a well-informed belief system is the most credible basis for rational teacher decisions. They assert that teachers should become aware of the assumptions that comprise their belief systems. Then, as they develop attitudes and habits of practice, these should be reflected on to ensure conformity to accepted educational principles.[11] Carol Landis, for example, is already reflecting on the educational soundness of her belief that students work well in groups with their friends. As you plan instruction, interact in classrooms, and evaluate instructional outcomes, continually testing your attitudes and habits of practice against sound educational principles can help protect you against poor education decision making.

▶ What Teaching Skills Are Required of an Effective Teacher?

Simply knowing something does not guarantee the ability to act on that knowledge. There is a profound difference between *knowing* and *doing*. Teachers may know, for example, that they should provide prompt feedback to their students on written assignments, but they are not always able to act on that knowledge. Teachers may also know how important it is to hold high expectations for all children, regardless of race, ethnicity, or social class, but then not act on that knowledge. No teacher education program can afford to focus only on theoretical knowledge at the expense of the practice, or "doing," dimension of teaching, just as no individual teacher can rely solely on knowledge of subject matter. All prospective teachers need to develop a repertoire of *teaching skills* to use as they see fit in varying classroom situations.

Among the skills that many educators believe are essential to effective teaching are the following:

■ some essential skills

- The ability to ask different kinds of questions, each requiring different types of thought processes from the student
- The ability to plan instruction and learning activities
- The ability to diagnose student needs and learning difficulties
- The ability to vary the learning situation to keep the students involved
- The ability to recognize when students are paying attention and to use this information to vary behavior and, possibly, the direction of the lesson
- The ability to use technological equipment, such as computers, to enhance student learning
- The ability to assess student learning
- The ability to differentiate instruction based on the students' experiences, interests, and academic abilities

The list of skills just given is far from complete. It does make it clear, however, that teachers need a large repertoire of skills to work effectively with students with varying backgrounds and different educational experiences. (Look at the list of INTASC standards on the inside cover of this book to see how many of these standards require particular teaching skills.) Varied approaches are necessary to meet the many needs of students. As Figure 6.1 illustrated, effective use of teaching skills, along with appropriate attitudes, knowledge of subject matter, and theoretical knowledge, leads to better instructional decision making.

In the rest of this chapter, we will focus on the skills you need in a few very important areas that are often of special concern for preservice teachers: classroom management, effective questioning, and planning techniques. No other dimension of teaching causes more concern for beginning teachers than managing the classroom and maintaining discipline. "Will I be able to manage and control my class(es) so I can teach effectively?" is a question most beginning teachers ask themselves. Because there is such a great concern about this aspect of teaching, we have chosen to spend some time on this skill area first, before turning, somewhat more briefly, to questioning and planning skills.

Classroom Management Skills

Visit the website to link to more advice on classroom management.

■ definition of classroom management

■ no one approach

■ research findings

Classroom management is "that set of activities by which the teacher establishes and maintains those student behaviors that facilitate effective and efficient instruction."[12] Developing teacher-student rapport, establishing productive group norms, and rewarding promptness are examples of managerial behavior. Managerial behavior also includes housekeeping duties like record keeping, and managing time, facilities, and resources in the classroom.

As with most complex teaching skills, classroom management requires a thorough understanding of theoretical knowledge and research findings, as well as practical experience. The knowledge or theory comes primarily from educational, social, and humanistic psychology. As with many other areas of investigation, there is no consensus regarding the one most effective approach to classroom management. Instead there are different philosophies, theories, and research findings, each tending to address particular dimensions or approaches to classroom management. Table 6.1 gives a brief overview of some of these approaches.

The last twenty-five years or so have produced significant new knowledge about effective classroom management practices. The following sections describe some of those findings.

■ **Academic Engaged Time**   Research that focuses on student behaviors, such as academic engaged time, reveals some interesting insights on effective teaching skills.[†] **Academic engaged time,** also known as *academic learning time,* is the time a student spends being successfully engaged with academically relevant activities or materials. Several research studies indicate that academic engaged time in reading or mathematics is strongly related to achievement in those subjects.[13] Simply put, the more time elementary students spend working on reading or mathematics activities that provide them with successful experiences, the more likely they are to achieve in those areas. Although this finding may not seem very startling, observations indicate that tremendous differences exist in the amount of time individual students spend engaged in academic activities, both across classrooms and within the same classroom.

The research on academic engaged time clearly indicates that a primary goal of elementary teachers (and probably secondary teachers, although the research has been limited mostly to elementary schools) should be to keep students on task. We know that classes that are poorly managed usually have little academic learning time. A major task of teachers is to learn how to manage their classes so that students are productively engaged.

■ differences among teachers

Numerous studies indicate that the most efficient teachers are able to engage their students about thirty minutes a day longer than the "average" teacher. If the

† On-task behavior, time on task, and academic engaged time are related concepts. *On-task behavior* is student activity that is appropriate to the teacher's goals. *Time on task* refers to the amount of time students spend engaged in on-task behavior. Academic engaged time adds the dimensions of a high success rate and academically relevant activities or materials to the concept of time on task.

TABLE 6.1 Different Approaches to Classroom Management		
Name	**Major Developers**	**Characteristics**
Behavior modification	B. F. Skinner	Originates from behavioral psychology. Modify student behavior by consistently and systematically rewarding (reinforcing) appropriate student behavior and removing rewards for, or punishing, inappropriate student behavior.
Socioemotional climate	Carl Rogers William Glasser Haim Ginott	Originates in counseling and clinical psychology. Emphasis on building positive interpersonal relationships between students and teachers.
Group process	Richard Schmuck and Patricia Schmuck Lois Johnson and Mary Bany	Originates in social psychology and group dynamics research. Emphasis on teacher establishing and maintaining effective, productive classroom group. Unity and cooperation, as well as group problem solving, are key elements.
Authority	Lee Canter and Marlene Canter	Views classroom management as a process of controlling student behavior, primarily by using discipline. Emphasizes establishing and enforcing rules, using soft reprimands and orders to desist. *Assertive discipline* is a popular manifestation of this approach.

Source: Wilford A. Weber, "Classroom Management." in *Classroom Teaching Skills,* 8th ed., by James M. Cooper (ed.). Copyright © 2006 by Houghton Mifflin Company. Reprinted with permission.

most efficient teachers are compared with the least efficient, daily differences of an hour in academic engaged time appear. If this is spread out over 180 days, students of efficient teachers get 90 hours more of academic engaged time than students of average teachers and 180 hours more than students of inefficient teachers! Differences of this magnitude may help explain why students in some classes learn more than students in others. The box on characteristic behaviors of effective teachers also describes some of the skills these teachers use to keep their students engaged so much of the time.

What Are Some Characteristic Behaviors of Effective Teachers?

In a broad study, educational researcher David Berliner attempted to provide an answer, based on contemporary research on teaching, to the question "What is an effective teacher?" His answer focuses on teacher behaviors that give students the opportunity to spend sufficient time engaged in and succeeding at tasks that help them achieve intended learning. Several behaviors, including the following, seem to distinguish effective teachers from those who are less effective:

- They monitor students' independent work, checking on their progress and providing appropriate feedback, to maintain a high level of student engagement with the task at hand.
- They structure lessons to let students know what is expected of them and what procedures to follow.
- They pace instruction rapidly to deliver a maximum amount of the curriculum to students.
- They ask questions requiring students to analyze, synthesize, or evaluate, demand answers at the same level as the question, and wait at least three seconds for students' answers.

- They communicate high expectations for student success.
- They provide a safe and orderly classroom. Deviant behavior is managed sensibly, and academic achievement is rewarded.
- They foster a convivial atmosphere in their classrooms.
- They capitalize on the instructional and motivational uses of tests and grades.
- They provide feedback to students through praise, the use of student ideas, and corrective forms that allow students to respond appropriately.

This list is not comprehensive; these nine categories of teaching behaviors are only examples of behaviors that distinguish effective teaching, but the relationship of this collection of attitudes, knowledge, and skills to a research base indicates their importance in the repertoire of the professional teacher.

Source: David C. Berliner, "Effective Classroom Teaching: The Necessary but Not Sufficient Condition for Developing Exemplary Schools." In *Research on Exemplary Schools,* ed. Gilbert R. Austin and Herbert Garber (Orlando, FL: Academic Press, 1985), pp. 127–154.

■ **Kounin's Research** Jacob Kounin's research on classroom management in the elementary school grades explains which skills can help teachers improve their classroom management and keep pupils on task.[14] Kounin discovered that effective managers kept students involved in academic tasks, minimized the frequency with which students became disruptive, and resolved minor disruptions before they escalated into major ones. Of the concepts Kounin identified to describe teacher classroom management behavior, three seem particularly useful.

■ "withitness"

The first concept he termed *withitness.* Teachers who are "with it" are those who communicate to pupils and so, by their behavior, appear that they know what is going on. Teachers who are "with it" pick up the first sign of misbehavior, deal with the proper pupil, ignore a minor misbehavior to stop a major infraction, and so forth. Students are often convinced that these teachers have "eyes in the back of their heads."

■ smoothness

The second and third concepts concern the problems of lesson flow and time management. *Smoothness* involves the absence of behaviors initiated by teachers that interfere with the flow of academic events. Examples of teacher behavior that do not reflect smoothness occur when a teacher bursts in on children's activities with an order, statement, or question; when a teacher starts or is engaged in some activity and then leaves it "hanging," only to resume it after an interval;

GRAND AVENUE: © United Feature Syndicate, Inc.

and when a teacher terminates one activity, starts another, and then initiates a return to the terminated activity.

■ momentum

The third concept, *momentum,* concerns the absence of teacher behaviors that slow down the pace of the lesson. Kounin conceptualized two types of slow-down behaviors: *overdwelling* (when a teacher dwells too much on pupil behavior, on a subpoint rather than the main point, on physical props rather than substance, or on instructions or details to the point of boredom) and *fragmentation* (when a teacher deals with individual pupils one at a time rather than with the group or unnecessarily breaks a task into smaller parts when the task could have been accomplished in a single step).

Kounin discovered that teachers who are effective classroom managers emphasize the prevention of disruptions rather than having to deal with them after they occur. Good managers do this by keeping the students engaged in lessons and assignments through effective application of the skills related to withitness, smoothness, and momentum.

■ **Other Research Findings**   Many researchers have replicated and extended Kounin's work on classroom management. Two key principles emerge from this research: (1) good management is preventive rather than reactive, and (2) teachers create well-managed classrooms by teaching their students desired behavior.[15] Here are a few other important recommendations arising from the research:

■ important recommendations

1. *Establish clearly defined rules and routines.* Clear rules and routines decrease the complexity of the classroom, minimize confusion, and prevent loss of instructional time. Having students help make the rules increases their commitment to abide by them.
2. *Ensure students' compliance with rules and demands.* To encourage students to comply willingly with the rules and routines, teachers must gain students' cooperation by establishing positive relationships, sharing responsibilities, and using rewards. This is accomplished more effectively by establishing and maintaining effective learning environments than by relying on authority or the teacher's role as a disciplinarian. Teachers must be willing, however, to administer consequences for repeated misconduct, and able to administer them in a way that is not threatening, punitive, or perceived as unfair.
3. *Involve families.* When families understand what the teacher is trying to achieve, they can provide valuable support and assistance, including helping develop and carry out successful behavior management plans.

■ developing students' responsibility

One school of thought rejects the notion of effective classroom management as a system of rewards and punishments, because these are seen as instruments for controlling people. In this approach, instead of teachers seeing themselves as being in charge and taking steps to maintain that control, they should give up some of the control and help students work together to decide how to be respectful and fair; that is, teachers should help students develop an internal sense of how to work together in a community.[16] The approach may involve times of chaos and uncertainty, but advocates believe that students will learn ethics and democracy in action. One of your responsibilities as a teacher will be to develop a philosophy and ways of operating in the classroom that make sense to you and that accomplish what you value. Your attitude toward the use of rewards and punishments will be part of that development.

Overall, we are learning more about what constitutes effective classroom management behavior. Understanding the related theories and research and practicing the skills that this body of knowledge has identified as effective will help you establish and maintain the conditions that promote student learning. Effective classroom management is a skill that can be taught and learned. (See the box on Kevin and Jim's Suggestions for Classroom Management Problems.)

Pause and Reflect

1 ▶ Do the research findings on academic engaged time surprise you, or do they seem obvious? If you think the findings reflect common sense, why do you suppose teachers vary so much in their ability to keep students engaged?

2 ▶ Are you concerned about your ability to establish and maintain a productive classroom environment? If so, what particularly concerns you?

3 ▶ We have included a number of suggestions for managing a classroom. Which seem most useful to you, and why? Which do you believe you would find most difficult to use, and why?

Questioning Skills

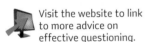

Visit the website to link to more advice on effective questioning.

■ ineffective questioning

The questioning process is a central feature of most classrooms. Studies indicate that teachers may ask hundreds of questions in a day's lessons, but they often fail to ask questions that require students to process and analyze information, and their questions require only a rote response of memorized facts. They also tend to rush students' responses, not giving them adequate time to provide varied and thoughtful answers. Some teachers do not direct as many questions to certain groups of students, such as minority students, girls or boys, or "slower" learners, and thus deprive them of the opportunity to interact actively in classroom learning.[17] Mastery of questioning skills contributes to students' learning and thus is important for effective teaching.

■ **Wait-Time** Good questioning behavior requires that the teacher provide students with sufficient time to think about and respond to questions. What do you think is the average amount of time a teacher waits for a student to respond to a question she or he has asked? Mary Budd Rowe, a science educator, determined in a series of studies that the teachers she observed waited less than one second before calling on a student to respond. Furthermore, after calling on a student, they waited only about a second for the student to answer before calling on someone else, rephrasing the question, giving a clue, or answering it themselves! How

Kevin and Jim's Suggestions for Classroom Management Problems

1. *When students misbehave, check your instruction.* Many behavior problems result from problems with instruction. Students are bored or confused, and their response is to get off task and into trouble.

2. *Take the time to ensure that students fully understand your classroom's rules and procedures.* As the old adage has it, "You have to keep school before you can teach school." At the beginning of the year, and again if and when things begin to break down, teachers need to fix in the minds of their students how the class is to be ordered.

3. *Regularly monitor the entire class.* Successful classroom managers frequently scan the class, noticing what each student is doing. Although the teacher need not react to every sign of off-task behavior or deviation from the established procedure, it is important for students to know that what they are doing is being noted.

4. *Move in on repeated or flagrant breaches of conduct quickly and directly.* Do not let things drift. Students will think you are afraid to confront them, and they may end up confronting you!

5. *Correct in private.* As much as possible, deal with student misconduct in private. Don't disturb the rest of the students and get them off task simply to get one or two students back to work. Also, public reprimanding may backfire and get you involved in a game of escalating remarks with a student.

6. *Don't make empty threats.* Do not say you are going to "do" something to a student or the class unless you have thought it over carefully and are really ready to do it. For instance, do not threaten to call the parents of every child in the room and tell them what rotten children they have unless you have a good deal of time—and alternative plans for next year.

7. *Don't put a hand on a student in anger or even annoyance.* Do not even think of striking a student, no matter how much you are tempted. When a situation is emotionally charged, even your well-intended gesture can be misinterpreted. On the other hand, if students are fighting, you may need to restrain them physically for their own good.

8. *Think through behavior problems.* When your class or an individual student is not behaving up to your expectations, treat the event as a problem-solving activity. Do not flail around or get panicky or discouraged. Coolly identify exactly what the problem is, consider possible causes, and test some possible solutions.

9. *Get help.* If management problems persist and you cannot solve them on your own, get help from a colleague or an administrator. Do not let things fester. Do not be shy about asking for help, particularly about discipline problems, which are so common for many beginning teachers.

10. *Be sure there is a back-up system.* If you need to remove a student from your room, you need to know there is a system in place that will back you up.

11. *Be sure your rules accord with schoolwide expectations.* For example, if the school has decided that chewing gum is tolerable and you crack down on it, you can expect to have more trouble than the issue is probably worth.

can students think carefully or deeply when they have only one second to respond to a teacher's question?

■ results of wait-time training

Rowe followed up these observations with studies designed to train teachers to increase their **wait-time** after questions from one second to three to five seconds. She reported amazing results, including the following: (1) an increase in the average length of student responses, (2) an increase in unsolicited but appropriate student responses, (3) an increase in student-initiated questions, (4) a decrease in failures to respond, (5) an increase in student-to-student interaction,

Through effective questioning techniques, teachers can encourage and promote student participation in discussions. (© Michael Newman/ PhotoEdit)

A prudent question is one-half of wisdom.

—SIR FRANCIS BACON

and (6) an increase in speculative responses. In short, she found that longer wait-times led to more active participation on the part of more students and an increase in the quality of their participation. Subsequent research by others replicated her findings. If questions require students to think about material or generate original responses, they need a longer time to think about their answers than if they are being asked only to recall information from memory.[18]

■ useful techniques

■ Effective Questioning Techniques In addition to wait-time, those who have studied the relationship between questioning strategies and student achievement have identified a number of other techniques as signs of effective teaching. This research suggests that teachers do the following:

1. Phrase questions clearly. Avoid vague questions.
2. Ask questions that are purposeful in achieving the lesson's intent.
3. Ask brief questions, because long ones are often unclear.
4. Ask questions that are thought-provoking and demand original and evaluative thinking.
5. Encourage students to respond in some way to each question asked.
6. Distribute questions to a range of students, and balance responses from volunteering and nonvolunteering students.
7. Avoid asking "yes-no" and "leading" questions.
8. To stimulate thinking, probe students' responses or demand support for their answers.
9. Provide students with feedback about their responses, both to motivate them and to let them know how they are doing.[19]

With knowledge and practice, teachers can learn questioning strategies that engage all students in the verbal interaction that supports learning.

Planning Skills

Visit the website to link to lesson plans and advice on planning.

■ types of planning

Good teaching is one-fourth preparation and three-fourths theater.

—GAIL GODWIN

Another skill related to a teacher's effectiveness is skill in planning. The plans teachers make for lessons influence the opportunity students have to learn, because plans determine the content students will experience in a lesson and the focus of the teaching processes. Effective teachers base their plans on a rich store of perceptions of classroom events and of their students' progress toward educational objectives and content standards. This store of perceptions (ways of looking at students and classroom activities) also helps the teacher make adjustments during instruction when plans must be adapted to the immediate situation.

Teachers do four basic types of planning—yearly, unit, weekly, and daily—and all are important for effective instruction.[20] Research shows that experienced teachers don't plan the way curriculum experts recommend—that is, by beginning with instructional objectives and then selecting instructional activities to meet those objectives. Instead, many elementary school teachers begin by considering the context in which teaching will occur (for example, the materials and time available); then they think about activities that students will find interesting and that will involve them; finally, they ponder the purposes these activities will serve. Secondary school teachers, on the other hand, focus almost entirely on the content and preparation of an interesting presentation.[21] This doesn't mean experienced teachers don't have goals, especially in these days of content standards; rather, it suggests that the interest and involvement of their students are paramount. Because research shows that student achievement is related to academic engaged time, planning should include consideration of how to involve students.

We have looked at three skill areas—classroom management, questioning, and planning—that researchers have identified as competencies demonstrated by effective teachers. (Another important skill relates to the use of technology, to which we devote a whole chapter.) Principals and other school evaluators assess beginning teachers' competence in these and other skills areas as part of their observations of beginning teachers. Standards for new teachers, such as those created by INTASC, discussed earlier in this chapter, also emphasize these skills. Therefore, developing classroom management, questioning, and planning skills should be an important concern for those preparing to teach. Several websites related to these and other skill areas are listed at the end of the chapter.

▶ A Final Word

We think this chapter is an important one because it provides an overview of what a truly effective teacher needs to know and be able to do. It may have been a frustrating chapter if you concluded that there is no way you can achieve the ideal we describe. We share that frustration, since we ourselves have not attained this ideal in our own teaching, and we're not certain that we ever will. Nevertheless, we continue to aspire to be the type of teacher we have detailed in this chapter. If you too can fix your sights on this conceptualization of an effective teacher and continually work toward this ideal, you are certain to observe positive and rewarding results in your own classroom.

Although we can detail the various proficiencies teachers need, noted educational author Jonathan Kozol cuts to the chase in his description of what he would look for in a teacher:

[O]bviously we want people who can teach [their subjects]. . . . But if I had to narrow it down to one characteristic, I would always hire teachers whom I wouldn't mind getting stuck with on a long plane flight to California. I would look for people who are capable of making the world seem joyful, people who are a delight to be with, people who are contagiously amusing human beings. To me, that's more important than almost anything else. I would put the emphasis on the capability to create contagious enthusiasm for life. There are a lot of teachers like that, but not enough.[22]

Key Terms

academic engaged time (171)

classroom management (171)

participant observation (159)

pedagogical content
   knowledge (165)

personal practical knowledge (169)

reflective teaching (150)

scaffolding (168)

self-fulfilling prophecy (161)

wait-time (176)

zone of proximal development (168)

For Reflection

1 Do you agree that having an enthusiastic teacher teach an unimportant subject is preferable to an uninspired teacher teaching a crucial subject? What implications do you see in this remark? On what assumptions about teachers, students, and subject matter is it based?

2 What is the difference between common sense and theoretical knowledge?

3 We have maintained that decision-making skills are important for teachers. What do you think you can do to improve your ability to make good decisions as you plan and deliver instruction?

4 Can you think of any ways that you, as a new teacher, could speed up the process of gaining personal practical knowledge?

5 Which of the classroom skills listed in this chapter seem most important to you? What skills would you add to the list? What skills would you subtract from it?

For Debate

Read the Policy Matters! summary, "Raising Standards for Teachers," at the website, and consider the issues it outlines regarding teacher qualifications. Then, go to EduSpace to post your answers (or respond to other students' answers) to the What Do You Think questions listed in the Policy Matters! feature.

For Further Information

PRINT RESOURCES

James M. Cooper, ed., *Classroom Teaching Skills,* 8th ed. (Boston: Houghton Mifflin, 2006).
This self-instructional book is designed to help teachers acquire basic teaching skills such as writing objectives, evaluation skills, classroom management skills, questioning skills, and differentiating instruction skills.

Charlotte Danielson, *Enhancing Professional Practice: A Framework for Teaching* (Alexandria, VA: Association for Supervision and Curriculum Development, 1996). This useful book, organized around a framework of professional practice, is based on the PRAXIS III criteria, including planning and preparation, classroom environment, instruction, and professional responsibilities.

Thomas L. Good and Jere E. Brophy, *Looking in Classrooms,* 9th ed. (Boston: Allyn & Bacon, 2003).
This excellent book provides teachers with concrete skills that will enable them to observe and interpret the classroom behavior of both teacher and students.

Bruce R. Joyce, Marsha Weil, and Emily Calhoun, *Models of Teaching,* 7th ed. (Boston: Allyn and Bacon, 2004).
This text describes numerous teaching models based on different assumptions about teaching and learning.

Carol Simon Weinstein and Andrew J. Mignano, Jr., *Elementary Classroom Management: Lessons from Research and Practice,* 3d ed. (New York: McGraw-Hill, 2003).
This practical book, based on sound research findings, addresses the major issues in establishing and maintaining effective learning environments. Ms. Weinstein has a secondary version entitled *Secondary Classroom Management* (2003), also published by McGraw-Hill.

WEB RESOURCES

Educators' Reference Desk. Available at: **http://www.eduref.org/.**
Access more than 2000 lesson plans submitted by teachers from all over the United States.

Education World. Available at: **http://www.education-world.com/a_curr/archives/shore.shtml.**
Education World presents a range of information concerning classroom management, including many tips for how to handle certain management problems.

Effective Questioning Techniques. Available at: **http://www.oir.uiuc.edu/Did/docs/questioning.htm.**
This online booklet offers ideas to help teachers ask good questions and create environments in which students are encouraged to ask questions.

Adprima. Available at: **http://www.adprima.com/managing.htm.**
This website provides a number of different topics of interest to teachers, including classroom management.

Funbrain. Available at: **http://www.funbrain.com.**
This site provides games and thousands of assessment quizzes to enable teachers to integrate them into their daily lesson plans.

Kathleen Cotton, "Classroom Questioning," (Portland, OR: School Improvement Research Series, Northwest Regional Educational Laboratory). Available at: **http://www.nwrel.org/scpd/sirs/3/cu5.html.**
A good, brief overview of effective questioning techniques based on research findings.

Interstate New Teacher Assessment and Support Consortium (INTASC). Available at: **http://www.ccsso.org/intasc.html** and **http://www.ncpublicschools.org/pbl/pblintasc.htm.**
A consortium of state education agencies, higher education institutions, and national educational organizations dedicated to the reform of the education, licensing, and on-going professional development of teachers. Their core standards for beginning teachers can be located at **http://www.ccsso.org/intasc.html** or more directly at the North Carolina department of public instruction at **http://www.ncpublicschools.org/pbl/pblintasc.htm.**

The New York Times. Available at: **http://www.nytimes.com/learning/teachers/index.html.**
This newspaper website has daily lesson plans for grades 6–8 and 9–12, as well as daily news "snapshot" activities that can be developed into lesson plans for grades 3–5. This site can be a valuable resource for exemplary lessons and activities, especially by allowing users to access related academic standards for many individual states.

Teachers.Net. Available at: **http://www.teachers.net/.**
This excellent site has an online reference desk, an active chat board, and a lesson plan exchange.

Yahoo!'s Directory of K–12 Lesson Plans. Available at: **http://dir.yahoo.com/Education/Standards_and_Testing.**
This site contains a large variety of resources for testing, assessment, measurement, and benchmarking.

7 What Should Teachers Know About Technology and Its Impact on Schools?

Chapter Preview   The use of technology in the classroom has gained attention as an issue in education. As our society continues to embrace new forms of communication, networking, and computer technologies, our schools are scrambling to keep up. In this chapter, we will explore what teachers should know about technology and its use in the educational setting, what roles technology may take in education, and how those roles may change what students and teachers do in the classroom.

This chapter emphasizes that:

▶ Technology is not new to the field of education.

▶ Schools are being pressured from many sides to incorporate contemporary technologies into instruction.

▶ Students can use computers not just for drill, but also in ways that promote creativity, collaboration, and higher-order thinking.

▶ Technologies can help teachers change their role from dispensers of information to facilitators of students' learning.

▶ Teachers can benefit from the productivity of computers in areas ranging from record keeping to staff development.

▶ The placement of technology within the educational setting affects how it can be used.

▶ Issues involving equity, teacher education, infrastructure, and budgeting will need careful consideration as technological tools become more and more integrated into classroom instruction.

Case Study

■ a technology-enhanced teaching scenario

Patricia Gonzalez/Using Technology to Innovate in Her Classroom

Patricia Gonzalez issues a challenge to her eighth-grade class: "Where should the next landfill be built in our state?" The students are interested in this topic, which they have heard their parents discuss. To find a solution, Patricia's class works with local city officials, who coach them on the mechanics of a geographic information system (GIS). A GIS, in simple terms, is a collection of electronic tools that translate data into a digital map. The power of a GIS comes from its ability to display several layers of maps on the computer screen at a single time. For example, students can look at a map showing population density and then at another that depicts distance from urban areas. They can also view these two maps together as they struggle to choose the site of their landfill. The GIS tools allow students to zoom in and out on an area as they begin to narrow down their choices for the site. Then they can search the GIS database to make sure they will not disturb any known historic or archaeological sites.[1]

After two weeks of investigation, Patricia's class divides into teams to present their choices. Three sites are offered, and a different group presents the case for each location. The culminating activity requires students to role-play a city council meeting, assuming such roles as city councilor, mayor, geologist, and angry citizen.

Two years later, the same students are still using the geographic information system, but now they are in the field collecting water samples near the landfill that was built. Students meticulously record data, which are transferred to a GIS database. They still work with municipal officials, this time to monitor the safety of the landfill. ■

■ teacher as facilitator

Patricia Gonzalez's role in the classroom is far from the traditional view of the teacher as sole dispenser of information. Instead, Patricia functions as a fa-

GIS software allows users to create customized maps such as the one shown here.
(ArcData Online screen capture provided courtesy of ESRI. Copyright © 2000 ESRI, EDT, FEMA. All rights reserved.)

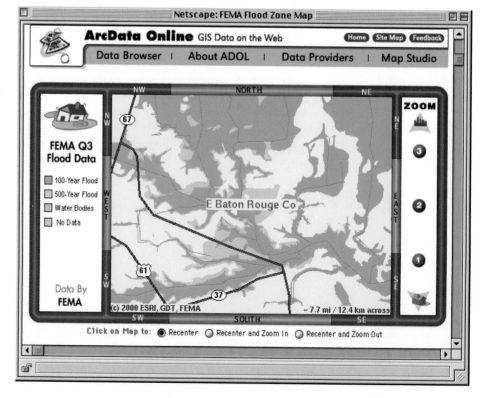

cilitator. She allows her classroom to become an active laboratory where students take charge of their learning and hypothesize about solutions. As she circulates around the room, she challenges her students to consider what evidence they will need to convince an area's citizens that their backyards are the best place for the landfill. Patricia is one reference point that students can consult, along with others, including technology, municipal officials, and other students. For example, she knows the technology skills required by GIS software, but she relies on the expertise of the municipal officials who use it daily to teach her students while she facilitates.

Has Patricia been replaced by the computer? The answer is "no." Teachers, in fact, have an expanded role in this technologically-enriched environment, though this role differs from the traditional one. Later in the chapter, we will explore in more detail how teachers can use computer technologies in instruction and what changes this approach can bring to the roles of both students and teachers. First, though, to put contemporary changes in perspective, let's look at the way technology has affected American schools in the past.

▶ A Brief Look at Education's Technological Past

■ a high-tech wonder of the early 1800s

Today people usually equate educational technology with computers. But technology in a more general sense is by no means new to education. In the early 1800s, a technological innovation was introduced to classrooms that would prove to have a profound impact on teaching. Although advocates called this new tool "invaluable" and it was installed in classrooms throughout the country, many teachers ignored it at first. Schools had to encourage use of this new technology by preparing training manuals with step-by-step instructions to help teachers integrate the device into their lessons. What was this technological wonder? The chalkboard!

Visit the website to link to more information on the history of educational technology.

In the old one-room schoolhouses, where students of different ages worked on various individual lessons, the function of a chalkboard was not immediately apparent. During the nineteenth century, however, classroom structure began to evolve from a one-room orientation to the graded classrooms we know today. When teachers began to teach the same lesson to an entire group of students, the chalkboard came into its own.[2]

■ TV reaches the classroom

The twentieth century brought a variety of technological devices that helped teachers use pictures in the classroom, including the filmstrip projector, the overhead projector, the motion picture, and educational television.[3] Such changes were viewed as so significant that in 1913 technological proponent Thomas Edison stated, "Books will soon be obsolete in the schools. Scholars will soon be instructed through the eye. It is possible to teach every branch of human knowledge with the motion picture. Our school system will be completely changed in ten years."[4]

■ microcomputers become affordable

Similarly, in the 1980s, when microcomputers became affordable, many software products were introduced to drill students on basic skills, and some educational visionaries predicted the end of classroom instruction and the end of the teaching profession as we know it. Of course, the technology never lived up to the hype. Today the most effective and promising technologies are not those that claim to take over the instruction but those that help with it.

I think there is a world market for maybe five computers.
—THOMAS WATSON, CHAIRMAN OF IBM, 1943

As these episodes show, many grandiose claims have been made about the use of technology to revolutionize the instructional process. But the eventual acceptance of any new technology, from the chalkboard to the microcomputer, has been determined more by the needs and demands of the classroom than by the claims of technology advocates.

Once a technology enters the classroom, the uses to which it is put are affected by what we might call the technology's level of maturity. In education, as in other fields, new technologies tend to go through three stages of application:

■ typical stages of technology

1. In the first stage, the technology is applied to things we already do. For instance, when microcomputers were first introduced into education, computer programs were created to simulate flash cards for math drill.

2. As a technology moves into the second stage, it is used to improve on the tasks we do. As an example, a more sophisticated math software application can provide remedial instruction when a student makes the same mistake more than once. It can also expand to cover more math topics and increase motivation by using gamelike activities.

3. In the third stage of maturity, the technology is used to do things that were not possible before. An excellent example is the geographic information system software that Patricia Gonzalez used in our opening case study. Among other things, the GIS software helps students pull together their knowledge and skills from different disciplines in a collaborative manner to solve a problem in their local community. Students use their math skills, for example, to calculate the slope of different areas and see how the results might affect the landfill. This kind of application uses technology in a way that is innovative rather than just allowing us to do old things in new ways.

Following this pattern, the role of any technology in the classroom will tend naturally to change as the technology matures. In addition, teachers follow a similar progression as they become more comfortable with various technologies. Teachers who are just beginning to use technology may start with applications, like drill and practice software, which are similar to something they already do. As they begin to learn about technology's possibilities, they will move on to applications that allow them to innovate. As we examine different technologies, ask yourself at which stage they can be applied and at which stage you would feel comfortable using them.

Pause and Reflect

1 ► How have recent developments in technology affected you and your family?

2 ► When you were in high school, what types of technology were your teachers using? At what stage was the technology applied?

3 ► Do you think the excitement about computers in education will fizzle as it did for educational television, or will computers go the way of the chalkboard, being seamlessly integrated in a meaningful way?

► How Are Schools Being Pressured to Change?

■ do schools prepare students for modern life?

Computer and networking technologies are an integral part of our society. It is hard to imagine a world without ATM machines, email, and pay-at-the-pump gas stations, a world with no microprocessors to run your microwave, TV, DVD player, car, and cellular phone. Now imagine a classroom with no TV, no DVD player (not even a VCR), no phone, and no computer. This classroom scenario is

In the video case *An Expanded Definition of Literacy: Meaningful Ways to Integrate Technology* three teachers talk about the importance of using technology, as well as the benefits and challenges of doing so. As you watch the clips and study the artifacts in the case, reflect upon the following questions:

1. Which of the pressures to use technology described in this chapter are evident in the comments of the teachers in this video case?
2. What roles do the teachers in the video case seem to take when their classes use technology?
3. Which advice from this video case about integrating technology do you believe will be most useful to you as a teacher?

■ sources of pressure

Visit the website to link to more information on technology and content standards.

Once a new technology rolls over you, if you're not part of the steamroller, you're part of the road.

—STEWARD BRAND

easily imagined, for we have all experienced it. Most people agree that schools should prepare students for life in our society. If pervasive use of technology is a fact of life, should the classroom be an exception?

No wonder, then, that schools are feeling pressure to increase their use of technological tools. The pressure is coming from many sources:

1. Parents are placing pressure on schools to use technologies in the classroom. They see a discrepancy between what is taught to their children and the real-world activities they perform every day at work. An example is the debate over the importance of cursive writing as opposed to keyboarding skills: is instruction in handwriting important if most adults will soon be using a keyboard? Parents are concerned not only that their children have access to technology in the classroom, but also that the students learn technology skills to allow them to compete in a job market increasingly powered by technology. Patricia Gonzalez's students, for example, are learning the marketable skills of using technology to collect and analyze data as they solve the landfill problem.

2. Students are placing pressure on schools by knowing more about current technologies than many of the teachers.

3. Teachers are placing pressure on schools because they need both access to technology in their classrooms and training to use the technology effectively. New teachers, in particular, who have used technological tools in college and at home, want to use them in their classrooms.

4. Businesses are placing pressure on schools and governmental agencies to adequately prepare future employees. A report on the "21st Century Skills" needed by today's students identifies digital literacy as a requirement for high school graduates.[5] Computer-based information processing power is doubling every eighteen months,[6] and the pace of change in technology is significantly faster than even the pace in business, let alone that in education. The pressure on schools to keep up, therefore, is intense.

5. Another pressure stems from the perception that America is falling behind the world in educational attainment. Business and governmental agencies march to the drum of global competition: "If America is to compete with the world, America's schools must be the best!" Regardless of their truth, rallying calls like this add to the pressure on schools to use technology.

6. Governmental agencies have moved to support federal, state, and local initiatives to ensure access to technology for K–12 students. Many state departments of education have written "technology skills" into teacher licensure requirements, and national organizations are moving toward specific subject-area technology standards for K–12 students.*

Within each of these groups are voices calling for schools to help close the digital divide—that is, the gap between those who

*For one example, see ISTE's National Educational Technology Standards (NETS) **(http://cnets.iste.org/)**.

are able to benefit from technology and those who are not. These gaps may divide along such lines as socioeconomic status, race, gender, ability, or geographic location. Citizens are concerned that technology is further deepening cleavages between the haves and have-nots of American society.

■ change equals opportunity?

Although we have been speaking of "pressures" for change, they can also be seen as opportunities. Many educators welcome the chance to try new curriculum materials and methods in their classrooms or to help bridge the digital divide. There are also new opportunities for teachers with skills in technology, now an important competitive edge in the job market. Most important, perhaps, there are tremendous opportunities for students, as the next section describes.

Pause and Reflect

1 ▶ What other pressures can you add to this list?

2 ▶ As a teacher, from where do you expect to feel the most pressure to incorporate technology?

3 ▶ What pressures exist on schools to avoid adopting technology?

▶ How Are Technologies Affecting Student Learning?

As our example of GIS software shows, many new technologies have been introduced into the educational setting in the last decade. To facilitate our discussion of these new technological tools, we will group them into content-specific categories, even though some examples will cross disciplines and join subjects, such as social studies and math. Many disciplines use some common technological tools, but how a teacher uses the Internet in science, for example, will differ from how another uses it in English.

■ enhance and engage thinking

Some computer applications can be classified as **cognitive tools** when they are used to engage and enhance thinking.[7] These tools are applications that manage information in ways that allow users to think more clearly, creatively, and critically. They derive their power from their flexibility and their ability to unleash creativity and foster significant cognitive processes. For example, they allow users to organize information in new ways, evaluate it, and construct personally meaningful representations of it. Cognitive tools are not necessarily meant to make learning easier. Instead, they often require students to think harder, more critically, or more creatively than without the tool.[8] Patricia Gonzalez's students were thinking hard and working collaboratively to solve the problem of where to locate the landfill. Much of the working world uses cognitive tools for everyday tasks, and we believe that all teachers and students should have similar opportunities. There are many computer technologies that we might consider cognitive tools. Our discussion will include word processors, databases, spreadsheets, communications tools, tutorials, simulations, multimedia software, drill-and-practice programs, and presentation and publishing tools. Table 7.1 summarizes these tools and their educational benefits.

During my eighty-seven years I have witnessed a whole succession of technological revolutions. But none of them has done away with the need for character in the individual or the ability to think.

—BERNARD MANNES BARUCH

TABLE 7.1 Types of Technology Tools

Technology Tool	Educational Benefits	Example
Word processor	• Easy cut-and-paste procedures and the ability to save and return to a document later encourage editing. • On-screen spell checkers, dictionaries, and thesauruses aid accuracy.	*AlphaSmart,* a portable and user-friendly word processor, is especially popular with teachers who work with younger writers.
Multimedia presentation software	• Combining text, audio, video, and virtual environments helps to communicate complex ideas. • Caters to a variety of learning styles.	*PowerPoint* allows students to easily combine a variety of media or even publish a presentation on the Web.
Drill and practice	• Similar to an interactive worksheet that provides feedback for the user and teacher. • Progress through the program depends on mastery of previous level. • Effective at reinforcing a concept.	*Reader Rabbit* is a popular program to reinforce letter recognition, rhyming words, and word families.
Database	• Organizes and stores complex sets of information. • Users can sort through information and filter unwanted data.	The *Valley of the Shadow* website offers students access to a variety of searchable databases from two communities during the Civil War.
Digital video	• Caters to a variety of learning styles. • Capable of presenting rich and complex information. • Easy editing software empowers students to take a video project from idea to completion. • Drag-and-drop features let students create movies out of still images, and add their own narration or soundtrack.	A digital camera and easy-to-use editing tools in *Windows Movie Maker* or *iMovie* allow students to create visual essays or digital stories.
Graphing calculator	• Quickly generates graphical representations of mathematical functions. • Helps users connect graphical, numerical, and algebraic representations of mathematical functions. • Allows users to input data from real-time experiments.	Students can gather motion data with collection devices connected to the *TI-73* graphing calculator to analyze graphs and look for patterns.

TABLE 7.1 (continued)

Technology Tool	Educational Benefits	Example
Simulation	• Interactive in nature, simulations allow students to reenact an event. • Students assume roles in the event, making decisions to which the software responds appropriately.	*Decisions, Decisions: Local Government* lets students play the role of a mayor facing a dilemma about the city's economic future.
Spreadsheet	• Allows users to form multiple calculations and to see all answers simultaneously. • A powerful tool to manipulate large sets of data. • Includes easy tools to graph.	Students can study a graph of population demographics in a community and use a spreadsheet program, like *Excel*, to predict future changes in that society.
Tutorial	• Provides the initial instruction for a topic in a self-controlled, self-paced environment. • Monitors progress and evaluates the student once instruction is complete. • Students' location within the tutorial can be saved.	*Fundamental Math* allows teachers to individualize their students' instruction in mathematics.
Collaboration over the Web	• Allows for fast, inexpensive worldwide communication and collaboration. • Organizations support these projects, allowing students to participate in legitimate research.	The GLOBE program supports a project that uses data on acid rain and waste disposal collected and submitted by students around the world.

Visit the website to link to all the websites mentioned as examples in this chapter.

■ combining instructional techniques and technologies

Today most educational software applications use a combination of instructional techniques (for example, tutorial, simulation, and interactive multimedia) to achieve the desired outcomes. It would be relatively rare to find an application that neatly fits into only one of these categories. Moreover, teaching approaches that use educational software normally draw from two or more of these categories.

Pause and Reflect

1 ▶ As you read the following sections, consider how teachers are using particular tools. At which of the stages discussed earlier are teachers making use of these technologies? Are teachers applying the tools to things

they already do? Does the technology enhance the teacher's ability? Are teachers innovating with the tools?

English/Language Arts Education

Teachers of many disciplines will find the tools for developing literacy useful. In this section, we will examine word processors, software applications to develop reading skills, multimedia presentation and communication tools, including digital video, and ways to combine technologies across disciplines.

■ ease of editing and rewriting

■ **Writing with Word Processors** Although technology has vastly broadened the avenues of expression available to students, writing ability is still highly valued in our culture, and today many students write using word processing software. The **word processor** provides many benefits over paper and pencil. Editing is less tedious when you don't have to laboriously erase several lines of text or even start over. Using a word processor, students can experiment with different sequences for their paragraphs with little effort. In fact, students who learn to write using word processors are more likely to revise their work and make more substantial revisions than students who learn to write without the tool.[9] Built-in spelling and grammar checks in most word processing software help struggling students to focus on their ideas, and the keyboard itself avoids the handwriting obstacle many students face. These aids are controversial, however; they are not foolproof, and some educators believe they are often a crutch. Nonetheless, the more students edit their writing, the more they learn about the writing process. In this respect, the word processor engages students and enhances thinking, making it a cognitive tool. The addition of an **LCD projector** enables teachers to project a writing example and, either using the "track changes" feature of the word processor or writing directly onto a whiteboard, model the process of editing for students.

SALLY FORTH   **BY STEVE ALANIZ & FRANCESCO MARCIULIANO**

■ expanded definition of
literacy

■ **Communicating in Multimedia** The spread of technology has required an expanded definition of literacy. Students are now becoming literate not just in the written word, but also in video, audio, and multimedia[*] productions. In the chapter entitled "Who Are Today's Students in a Diverse Society?" we discussed Howard Gardner's theory of multiple intelligences and the concept of learning styles, emphasizing that different individuals learn best in different ways. Students who struggle with written expression may enjoy the chance to publish a web page or create a multimedia presentation instead of submitting a traditional five-page essay. Presentation tools, such as *PowerPoint*, can combine text, graphics, audio, and video to communicate complex ideas. Students can use multimedia-authoring programs like *HyperStudio* or *Kid Pix* to create their own interactive presentations or illustrate and present stories.[†] Our current students are the first to have widespread capability of authoring compelling multimedia works using digital tools. Programs such as *Movie Maker* and *iMovie*, now included with the operating systems by Microsoft and Apple, allow students to shift from the role of passive observer to active creator of digital media. Students can use their strengths in expressing themselves while they develop visual literacy, become familiar with valuable tools for the future, and strengthen their ability to analyze and synthesize information.

The video case *Multimedia Literacy: Integrating Technology into the Middle School Curriculum* shows one language-arts class making slide shows to present their research findings. As you watch the clips and study the artifacts in the case, reflect upon the following questions:

1. In what ways are the students using technology in this video case? What is the role of the teacher?
2. This chapter mentions that the use of particular technological tools is not limited to particular disciplines. How could these students use their new ability to create slide shows in another subject area, such as mathematics or science?
3. What are some ways that teachers can balance content instruction with technology-skills instruction, a concern mentioned by the teacher in the video case?

Digital storytelling is a project that can engage even the most reticent students. In digital storytelling, students create images, often by taking digital photos. These images are accompanied by narratives written by the students and recorded with their own voice. For students who are having trouble beginning to write, the pictures they choose can serve as prompts to engage them in the writing step. Because students have chosen and manipulated the images to accompany the narrative, they have greater ownership and connection to their stories.[††] With increasingly affordable digital video cameras and user-friendly software, students can even research, direct, and produce their own digital documentaries. For example, a student could film a Native American elder telling an important story from his or her tribal culture as the culminating project for a unit on storytelling.

Visit the website to link to examples of student multimedia projects.

It is relatively easy to publish student work through the World Wide Web, and knowing their work may end up publicly available motivates students to care more about their creations.[10] Many students enjoy publishing and reading web logs, more commonly known as **blogs.** A blog is basically a journal that is available on the Web. Blogs are typically updated daily using software that allows people with little or no technical background to update and maintain the blog.

■ finding a better match
between instruction and
learning style

■ **Learning to Read** **Drill-and-practice** programs are the earliest form of educational software or educational games. First used as an interactive worksheet,

---

[*] Multimedia productions combine various media such as text, graphics, video, music, and voice narration.

[†] *PowerPoint* is a product of Microsoft (**http://www.microsoft.com/**; telephone: 425-882-8080). For *HyperStudio,* contact Knowledge Adventure (**http://www.hyperstudio.com/**; telephone: 800-321-7511). For *KidPix,* contact The Learning Company (**http://www.kidpix.com/**; telephone 800-825-4420).

[††] For more information on digital storytelling, consult the Center for Digital Storytelling web page at **http://storycenter.org/.**

"Edutainment" Software

A software application that is both entertaining and educational is referred to as "edutainment." Ordinary drill-and-practice software is repetitive by nature, and children can easily lose interest in such mundane tasks. Therefore, software developers added gamelike characteristics to their applications in the hope of motivating users to complete the task. These features also helped to sell the products to students and parents looking for educational activities for the home.

Today, in fact, most edutainment software is designed and marketed for the parents of school-age children, not specifically for classroom use, although some software applications with gamelike features, such as *Math Blaster* and *Oregon Trail,* manage to bridge the gap, proving useful in both the home and the classroom. Since parents often ask teachers to recommend software applications for the home, it is a good idea to know what applications available for home use would complement the school's curriculum.

Not everyone is a fan of such software, however. Some caution, for example, that the many bells and whistles technology offers can reduce learning to a "spectator sport" where students sit back and watch machines do the work. The balance between entertainment and education is a delicate one. Educators must address these problems as technology continues to progress. As you try out educational software, ask yourself whose mind is doing the thinking: the child's or the programmer's?

the software provided feedback to the user, usually by labeling an answer right or wrong, and then presented the next task. Now, many programs monitor the students' progress so they do not move on until they have mastered the current concept. As described in the accompanying box, many of today's drill-and-practice programs also include motivational, gamelike design. Drill-and-practice programs generally increase the fluency of a skill rather than actually teaching it.[11] For example, products such as the *Reader Rabbit** series are popular for reinforcing young children's reading skills, such as letter recognition, rhyming words, and word families. Teachers also use drill-and-practice programs such as *Reader Rabbit* to diagnose students' ability in reading, as well as other subjects, and assign them to the appropriate group.

■ **Making Mind Maps and Webs**   Students and teachers often create graphical representations, known as **mind maps** or **webs,** to demonstrate their understanding of a story or concept. Software such as *Inspiration* or *Kidspiration*[†] use these visual learning techniques to teach students to clarify, organize, and prioritize their thoughts. Mind maps can serve as an alternative assessment tool for teachers who can examine the thinking patterns, interrelationships, and even misconceptions revealed by students' diagrams. *Inspiration* can also be used as a prewriting activity to help students brainstorm, draft, and revise their writing.

■ enhancing what teachers do

■ **Combining Technology and Crossing Disciplines**   Technology can facilitate interdisciplinary connections in a powerful way. Like word processors, multimedia tools are used across the disciplines—from a presentation on the Depression

---

* Reader Rabbit is a product of the Learning Company (**http://www.readerrabbit.com/**; telephone: 800-825-4420).
† Inspiration and Kidspiration are both products of Inspiration Software, Inc. (**http://inspiration.com/**; telephone: 800-877-4292).

that includes music of the era and clips from President Franklin D. Roosevelt's Fireside Chats to a hurricane project with graphs, images, video clips, and links to the National Weather Service website. An example combining several types of technologies and crossing content areas is the *I Lost My Tooth* project.[12] First-grade students around the world use email to share stories and myths about losing their teeth. Using these rich and diverse stories, teachers develop interdisciplinary activities that can make use of a variety of educational tools, both technological and traditional. For example, students study maps, either on computer or on paper, to locate the countries where other children live and ask their "e-pals" about the weather and local heroes of their regions. Students can use drawing software, or old-fashioned crayons, to illustrate their tooth fairy stories. They use their math skills, and perhaps graphing software, to chart the number of teeth lost. In this project, technology is functioning at the second stage we described: facilitating and enhancing what teachers can do.

Science Education

As the case study at the beginning of this chapter showed, technology can allow students to do legitimate scientific investigations on a scale that would otherwise be impossible. Technology enabled Ms. Gonzalez to use a constructivist approach to education that encouraged her students to build their own knowledge on the basis of their experiences. (See the box on constructivism in this section. See also "The Influence of Psychological Theories" in the chapter entitled "What Are the Philosophical Foundations of American Education?" and "What Ought to Be the Elements of Educational Reform?" in the chapter entitled "How Should Education Be Reformed?") Through the Internet, students can find images from a professional observatory in Australia to learn about how supernovae form or monitor the regularity of Old Faithful's eruptions through a live web camera. Putting these technologies in students' hands allows learning to become an active process in which the students do the experiments, draw conclusions, and engage in problem solving, rather than merely reading about an investigation and memorizing the results.

Cognitive Tools and Constructivist Teaching

In the constructivist approach to teaching (discussed in the chapters entitled "What Are the Philosophical Foundations of American Education?" and "How Should Education Be Reformed?"), learning is recognized as an active process. Students engage in constructing their own knowledge on the basis of their previous experiences instead of passively absorbing knowledge as presented by the teacher. This approach to instruction celebrates the differences among students instead of continually trying to build similarities.

Constructivist teachers can find cognitive tools especially helpful. Since cognitive tools do not try to instruct, they do not assume a particular learning style or methodology. Using *Movie Maker* or *iMovie* to create a digital story is a good example of this. The student must bring the goals—and the content to achieve them—to the tool, and then the tool will facilitate the student's discovery of knowledge and construction of meaning.

It is important to note that it is *how* the tool is used that makes it constructivist, not necessarily the tool itself. Although cognitive tools are an excellent match for constructivist methods, many software applications can be used in a similar manner. As with many other aspects of teaching, it is the student's and teacher's ingenuity, creativity, and experience that set the limits of a tool's educational use, not the tool itself.

Although the equipment to conduct many of these experiments is costly, there are ways around these financial obstacles. For example, most city governments own geographic information systems software, and many are interested in partnering with a local school to share their expertise, as government workers did in our case study example of Patricia Gonzalez's class. Many organizations support collaboration between scientists and schools; for a reasonable membership fee, schools receive the technical support they need and an opportunity to work with experts. Such partnerships let students see how people in the "real world" do their jobs, as well as allowing them to participate in interesting projects. This section discusses some of these opportunities, ranging from conducting sophisticated local research that contributes to an organized database to collaborating with NASA scientists via conferencing technology.

■ doing "real" science

■ **Scientific Hardware**   Imagine conducting class beside a stream behind your classroom and having the technology to collect a water sample; instantly and accurately find the pH, temperature, and amount of dissolved oxygen in it; and graph the data on the spot. Revolutionary technology in the form of affordable handheld computing devices, such as the Palm,* and accompanying probes, thermometers, and sensors, allow this to happen. No longer are teachers forced to demonstrate stale experiments in the sterile environment of a lab. Schools are moving toward **ubiquitous computing,** where each student has access to some type of mobile computing device to use inside the classroom, out in the field, and at home. Students can access rich data, do calculations, and test their hypotheses themselves. Science students today do things like measure ozone and sulfur dioxide levels from the air near their schools, or use GPS (global positioning systems) to be "Environmental Detectives"[†] in a simulation to discover the source of groundwater contamination.

■ **Digital Imagery**   Much of science education is based on the skill of observation, and resources that allow students to visualize concepts lead to greater understanding. The use of both still images and video in the science classroom has been greatly enhanced by digital tools. Teachers and students can go online and download images or video clips of processes such as amoeba reproduction or a lunar eclipse. As digital cameras and digital microscopes have come down in price in recent years, students themselves have the ability to capture still or moving images that can be analyzed later, or, with the use of an LCD projector, by the entire class. Processes that are too fast to observe, such as dropping a ball, can be slowed down, and students can use time-lapse capabilities to capture processes that are too slow to see, such as the growth of a plant.[13]

■ **Communication with Other Scientists**   The class doing the stream experiment could take their results a step further and collaborate with students and scientists around the world to examine the effect of acid rain or waste disposal on the earth's water quality. The Global Learning and Observations to Benefit the Environment (GLOBE) program[††] coordinates such a project. GLOBE allows students to collaborate with expert mentor scientists who will answer questions,

---

* Palms are produced by Palm, Inc (**http://www.palm.com/;** telephone: 800-881-7256).
† The MIT "Environmental Detectives" website can be accessed at **http://education.mit.edu/ED/ intro/index.htm.**
†† To learn more, visit the GLOBE website (**http://www.globe.gov**).

engage in the analysis of data, and help students place their measurements in the broader context of global environmental issues. Students and teachers work with other classrooms to collect data at the same time and send it into a computer that aggregates it and returns analyses of all the classrooms' data. The program is a dynamic, legitimate scientific investigation without preprogrammed answers. Students must interpret the results and develop an understanding based on their own experiments.

The important thing in science is not so much to obtain new facts as to discover new ways of thinking about them.

—Sir William Henry Bragg (British physicist 1862–1942)

Collaboration projects are becoming more popular across the disciplines as a variety of communications technologies make it easier to connect with schools, universities, experts, and organizations around the world. Classrooms can connect via email, Web pages, or videoconferencing. Projects such as Global Schoolhouse and NASA Quest* provide opportunities and lesson plans to connect students, teachers, and experts using the Web.

◾ understanding students' cognitive processes

◾ **Enhancing Problem Solving**   Teachers often wonder what their students are thinking, and technology is providing some ways to discover and understand the cognitive processes students use as they solve problems. At Cedar Way High School, students use the *True Roots* program[†] to play the role of forensic scientists trying to determine if a girl is correct in asserting that she was switched at birth in the hospital. Using genetic data, students must try to deduce whether the girl is related to the parents who have raised her. The program tracks students' decisions so that the teacher can later analyze the problem-solving strategy students used. Teachers instruct students not to guess or proceed randomly but to have a systematic plan. To reinforce the idea that problem solving should be a logical exercise, classes often use the program two times over three days. Teachers take the middle day to show students the graphs of their problem-solving strategies. Students try again and are graded on their improvement.[14] Here, technology is functioning at the third stage of progress: offering teachers unique insight into their students' cognitive processes, which they would find difficult or impossible to get otherwise.

The video case *Integrating/Improve Student Learning* shows a high-school science class using a computer simulation to understand and solve questions related to genetic inheritance. As you watch the clips and study the artifacts in the case, reflect upon the following questions:

1. Does the technology that the students are using in this video case fit this chapter's description of a cognitive tool? Why or why not?
2. What is the role of the teacher in this video case? How do you feel about taking this role as a teacher?

Social Studies Education

Digital resources can be used to promote historical thinking and inquiry-based learning in social studies classrooms. Among other tools, social studies teachers across a broad range of topics are making use of technological tools that include online archives, electronic simulations, virtual fieldtrips, and spreadsheets.

◾ doing the work of historians

◾ **Online Archives**   Social scientists are digitizing[††] immense archives and publishing them on the World Wide Web. Without the computer to help organize and

---

* To learn more, visit the Global Schoolhouse website (**http://www.globalschoolhouse.org/**) and the NASA Quest website (**http://quest.arc.nasa.gov/**).

[†] True Roots is produced by IMMEX (Interactive Multimedia Exercises) at UCLA (**http://www.immex.ucla.edu;** telephone: 310-649-6568).

[††] The digitizing process stores documents in an electronic format that allows them to be viewed on the Web and archived in a more permanent form.

manage such large amounts of information, a teacher might be limited to using several photocopied diary entries to expose students to primary sources.* Giving students access to a rich archive that is organized by databases allows them to broaden their understanding of history and do the work of historians.

For example, the *Valley of the Shadow* website[†] contains detailed databases of census results, church records, newspaper articles, military records, and letters about two communities, one southern and one northern, during the Civil War. Users can investigate the answers to questions they pose, such as what was the average number of slaves people held or how did occupations differ in the North and South. Students can incorporate the details they discover into their larger picture of the Civil War, building a richer understanding of the event than facts alone could provide. The role of the teacher changes from dispenser of knowledge to guide through the archives, helping students learn to ask the right questions and examine the sources critically. Students and teachers construct their understanding of history together.

■ **Simulations** A **simulation,** a representation of an activity or environment, is a time-honored and effective teaching technique. Long before software developers began to use the technique, teachers had their classes simulating a newspaper business or a famous court case. A simulation can be a fun way to explore an environment or a concept that would be too expensive, or possibly dangerous, to handle in reality. For this reason, simulations have proven to be a fertile field for educational software developers. A large variety of computerized simulations are available for classroom use in practically every field.

Decisions, Decisions: Local Government[††] is a simulation game in which users assume the role of the mayor of a community facing a dilemma. The town's main employer, a mining company, wants to greatly expand production. The mayor must choose between improved employment opportunities with increased development and keeping the quality of life while risking economic stagnation. The mayor must listen to advisers and weigh the options. The program can be used by the class as a whole, with only one computer, or it can accommodate multiple small groups at individual computers. After students input their decisions, the software reacts and presents them with the results. For example, if the mayor raises taxes, she or he must accept some public dissatisfaction. To come up with every possible scenario and consequence manually would be an overwhelming task for any teacher, but the computerized simulation manages that information easily. The software frees the teacher to be more involved with the students and to mediate instruction.

■ **Virtual Fieldtrips** **Virtual fieldtrips** provide a wealth of opportunities to extend learning. Not limited to social studies, virtual fieldtrips can be used to provide information about a site that students are unable to visit.[15] It is unlikely you will manage a class outing to the Amazon rainforest, for example, but Na-

■ teacher as guide through the archives

■ students assume the role of mayor

■ exploring environments beyond the classroom

Visit this chapter of the website to link to examples of virtual field-trips.

---

* A primary source is a firsthand account. For example, a soldier who fought at the battle of Gettysburg and described it in his diary provides a firsthand account or primary source.
† To learn more, visit the University of Virginia's Valley of the Shadow website (**http://valley.vcdh .virginia.edu/**).
†† The *Decisions, Decisions* series of software titles is available from Tom Snyder Productions (**http://www.tomsnyder.com/**; telephone: 800-342-0236).

The teacher helps a student use a Photoshop program as others watch.
(© David Young-Wolff/PhotoEdit)

tional Geographic's Jason Project* provides a "fieldtrip" through the computer. Hundreds of sites are produced by teachers, agencies, governments, and students themselves.

■ students contribute to local history projects

Student-produced virtual fieldtrips are often used in connection with local history. Students conduct interviews and use digital cameras to take pictures of important sites and people in their community. By using photo-editing software such as *Photoshop,*† the image can be manipulated or enhanced on the computer screen. Students can put their images of local sites into a multimedia presentation program such as *HyperStudio* or *PowerPoint* and add descriptions. These can then be published on the World Wide Web and viewed by others. Students can see themselves as historians who are contributing to the preservation of their community's story.

■ **WebQuests**   A **WebQuest**†† is an inquiry-based learning activity that directs learners in using information from the Web. In a WebQuest, the appropriate tasks and websites are provided so that the students can focus on the analysis of information rather than losing time by searching for it. In the "King Tutankhamen: Was It Murder?" WebQuest§, middle school students take on the roles of medical examiner, reporter, archaeologist, professor, or historian, and explore information about the death of King Tut. Using the provided links, students will visit websites,

* To learn more, visit The Jason Project website (**http://www.jasonproject.org/**).
† *Photoshop* is available from Adobe (**http://www.adobe.com/;** telephone: 800-833-6687).
†† The WebQuest model was developed in 1995 by Bernie Dodge with Tom March. Information about WebQuest can be accessed at the San Diego State University WebQuest site at **http://webquest.sdsu.edu/**.
§ **http:www.pekin.net.pekin108/wash/webquest/**.

then use what they learn to develop a persuasive essay presenting their verdict on whether King Tut was murdered or not.

▮ **Using Spreadsheets and Databases to Connect Disciplines**   Technology helps facilitate interdisciplinary relationships by providing easy access to rich data. The World Wide Web offers easy access to numerous sets of rich, real-world data, while spreadsheets and databases provide powerful tools to manipulate the data. For example, though social studies and math are not two subjects that people naturally connect, students who visit the National Center for Health Statistics website* can find data on the number of live births in the United States, create a spreadsheet to mathematically manipulate and display the information, then analyze the trends based on their knowledge of U.S. history.[16] Social studies problems are analyzed using mathematical and social studies skills, and students are challenged to synthesize data, make predictions, and construct knowledge.

> ▮ forecasting and predicting changes in society

A **spreadsheet** is a software program that allows users to perform multiple calculations. With a simple calculator, students can find only one answer at a time. For complex scenarios, single answers may be too limiting, but a spreadsheet will allow the user to see all the numbers and formulas at once. Any change is immediately reflected in the entire sheet. Using the above example, students are able to calculate whether the number of live births increased or decreased over time. As a tool for forecasting and predicting, a spreadsheet might help students understand the consequences of population changes. For example, during a hypothetical epidemic, students can predict the future population changes and hypothesize the societal effects.

Database tools such as *Fathom*† also allow students to explore statistical data. They can plot functions and create animated simulations from data created by students, gathered from the Web, or from the included data files, which range from the 2000 census data to carbon dioxide levels in the atmosphere. Students could, for example, use Fathom or a similar tool to graph their population projections based on live birth data from the census.

Mathematics Education

From slide rules to calculators, math teachers have relied on technology for years. This section deals with some of the newer uses of technology in math education, including tutorial software, other software, and graphing calculators.

▮ **Tutorial Software**   **Tutorials** are educational software applications designed to provide the initial instruction on a given topic. They are used in most disciplines. Unlike drill and practice, tutorials present the skill or concept, then check for understanding throughout the process, and evaluate the learner's grasp of the topic once the program is completed. More narrative in nature than drill and practice, tutorial software often has the feel of a book placed on computer.

> ▮ self-contained, self-paced software

Tutorial software is somewhat controversial, because many tutorials are intended to replace the teacher as the primary agent of instruction for a particular topic. To achieve this, the software is self-contained and self-paced. Small chunks

---

* To learn more, visit the National Center for Health Statistics website (**http://www.cdc.gov/nchs**).
† Key Curriculum Press produces *Fathom* (**http://www.keypress.com/fathom/**).

of information are delivered to the learner in a careful sequence of instruction designed to adjust to students' needs, allowing them to achieve success. One tutorial program is *CornerStone Mathematics.* * Users move through concepts such as fractions and decimals at their own pace; topics are explained, reinforced, and tested. As with most tutorials, the user's location in the program is saved for a later use if the software must be turned off. Generally more flexible than drill-and-practice applications, these tutorials give teachers a powerful tool for individualizing instruction and monitoring student progress.

■ **Other Math Software**   Certain mathematics-specific software enhances what teachers can do. For example, *The Geometer's Sketchpad*[†] allows students to explore the relationships among points, lines, planes, and angles in an environment conducive to experimentation. Users are offered a palette of tools for drawing and deriving geometric concepts. This cognitive tool enables the user to explore, question, learn, theorize, fail, succeed, and grow.[17]

Visit this chapter of the website to link to the National Council of Teachers of Mathematics.

■ making connections among multiple representations

■ **Graphing Calculators**   Schools are trying to heed the National Council of Teachers of Mathematics' statement that "Electronic technologies—calculators and computers—are essential tools for teaching, learning, and doing mathematics. They furnish visual images of mathematical ideas, they facilitate organizing and analyzing data, and they compute efficiently and accurately."[18] These electronic technologies help teachers and students with some of the same tasks that were conducted without these aids. Many students find it difficult to make connections among the graphical, numerical, and algebraic representations of mathematical functions, for example, but the speed and ease with which graphs can be generated and manipulated using graphing calculators can help students to understand those relationships.

Technology also enhances what teachers and students are able to do. Students can use data collection devices[††] connected to their calculators, such as various sensors or temperature probes, to gather their own data as the basis of their investigations of mathematical phenomena. Learning becomes more active, and students consult with both technology and the teacher.[19] Technology has not replaced the teacher. As students are gathering the data and manipulating the graphical representations, the teacher observes and analyzes how individual students are solving problems and making sense of mathematical concepts.

Foreign Language and ESL Education

The World Wide Web and other communications applications open up vast opportunities in foreign language education. Years ago, it was often a challenge for foreign language teachers to collect materials in the target language. Now students can view authentic materials over the Web, or even use the Internet to communicate to other classrooms in a foreign country. Compare assigning a sterile textbook article about French food to connecting your students with e-pals in French-speaking Africa so they can ask about the cuisine themselves. Furthermore, the World Wide Web offers a wide array of current foreign language publi-

---

* *CornerStone Mathematics* is available from Achievement Technologies. (**http://www.achievementtech.com;** telephone: 888-391-3245).
† Key Curriculum Press produces *Geometer's Sketchpad* (**http://www.keypress.com/sketchpad/**).
†† To find out more about data collection advices, visit the Texas Instruments website (**http://education.ti.com/us/product/tech/datacollection/features/features.html;** telephone: 800-842-2737).

cations that would be far too difficult and expensive to obtain otherwise. Students will find extensive online newspaper collections in languages as different as Arabic and Portuguese, as well as live radio from Guatemala.

A **news group** is a feature of the Web that can be compared with a large wall full of messages in chronological order. When you subscribe to a news group, you join an online discussion that occurs as people post messages and reply to one another. Teachers nationwide log on to these resources to share ideas, find keypals for their students, and converse with other professionals in their field. For example, ESPAN-L* is a news group for teachers of Spanish, and discussion ranges from cultural notes to grammatical points. Students can also log on to news groups and join a discussion in a foreign language. To participate in this real, interactive chat, students are required to put their communication abilities to the test. These engaging ways of learning foreign languages are changing the way we teach and encouraging us to be creative and flexible.

Both ESL and foreign language teachers have numerous websites designed for language learners and teachers. Among the most famous are "Tennessee Bob's Famous French Links"† and "Dave's ESL Café."†† These sites have numerous links to websites with lesson plans, interactive activities, vocabulary and grammar resources, and virtual tourism sites. The Web is rich with resources for learners of almost any language.

Distance Education

School districts vary greatly in location, size, budget, composition of populations, and graduation requirements. Such differences often create educational inequities, particularly when a school district simply cannot afford to provide the quality and variety of courses offered by larger or more affluent districts. **Distance education** is a fast-growing alternative for schools trying to overcome such constraints.

connecting professionals and students

Distance education involves using technology to link students and instructors in separate locations. As we have seen, two-way audio and video allow live interaction between individuals who are hundreds or thousands of miles apart, while the Web allows the rapid exchange of data over distances. Thus, distance education can allow schools to increase educational opportunities by offering courses otherwise prohibited by cost or other constraints.

A congressional report found that distance education can help reverse some of the effects of the nation's long-term population shift from rural to metropolitan areas. This population loss has caused many districts to close or consolidate schools, forcing many rural students to travel long distances.[20] Ironically, the decline of rural populations has often been accompanied by state educational reforms that pressure schools to broaden programs and offer more courses. Many schools find themselves in the awkward situation of having to offer elective subjects for which neither funds nor teachers are available.

an alternative to the traditional high school experience

An explosion in the availability of online courses has alleviated some of this pressure. The Virtual High School (VHS)§ first offered courses in 1997–98 and

---

* To learn more about ESPAN-L and other mailing lists for teachers, visit **http://www.theteachersguide.com/listservs.html.**

† Tennessee Bob's Famous French Links can be found at **http://www.utm.edu/departments/french/french.html.**

†† Dave's ESL Café can be found at **http://www.daveseslcafe.com/.**

§ To learn more, visit the Virtual High School website (**http://www.govhs.org/website.nsf**).

by 2004, it offered 169 courses to more than 4,500 students, including fifteen Advanced Placement courses. Students from around the country use their courses' websites as their starting point. From there they obtain readings and assignments. Students then log on to a daily discussion group in which the teacher conducts a *netseminar*. This flexible arrangement accommodates a variety of school schedules as well as time zone differences. The convenience and additional time for reflection that come from logging on at any point make the netseminar particularly appealing. Students do collaborative projects for the course by exchanging information over the Web. All the makings of a traditional class are present without the face-to-face interaction. Furthermore, schools in more isolated areas or with limited resources can vastly expand the courses they offer to include such diverse classes as Eastern philosophy and the history of aviation. Students below the college level can explore nontraditional academic avenues and connect with peers who have similar intellectual interests. While the VHS intends to enhance the traditional high school experience, other programs are available that offer complete high school curricula for those who are overseas or homebound, or who are nontraditional students.

Technology for Students with Special Needs

Visit the website to link to more information about assistive technology.

Technology tools can be of especially great assistance to students with special needs. For those with disabilities, the tools can help level the playing field by presenting information in a manner best suited to a student's learning style and particular needs. Although using a software program does not replicate the experience of learning from a teacher, the computer is not constrained by the human variables of limited patience and classroom distractions. Using the right software, an alternative, individualized curriculum can be created for students with special needs, paralleling the standard school curriculum.

■ assistive technology

In addition to its direct instructional uses, technology plays a second, very important role for special-needs students. The term **assistive technology** describes the array of devices and services that help people with disabilities perform better in their daily lives. (See the chapter entitled "Who Are Today's Students in a Diverse Society?" for a further discussion of assistive technology and special education.) Students with disabilities may rely on a variety of innovations to help them achieve successful inclusion in regular classrooms.[21]

■ vastly improving the quality of life and education for special-needs students

Computers are especially helpful in allowing students to participate in normal classroom activities that would otherwise be impossible. User-friendly keyboard enhancements simplify typing, and assistive technology can be used to control most basic computer applications. ERICA (Eyegaze Response Interface Computer Aid) is one revolutionary technology that opens up opportunities for special-needs students. Using ERICA's system, which tracks and records the user's eye movements and pupil dilation across a computer display, the mouse can be controlled with eye movement alone, allowing even extremely immobile students to communicate with teachers and classmates.*

The variety of tools to help special-needs students fully participate in school is constantly expanding. The options include a word-predictor feature† that facilitates keyboarding. After the student types a letter or two, the computer pre-

---

* To learn more, contact ERICA (**http://www.ericainc.com/**; telephone: 434-296-3846).
† One such product is *Co-Writer* by Don Johnston Inc. (**http://www.donjohnston.com/**; telephone: 800-999-4660).

Assistive technology such as this helps some students with disabilities participate in regular classrooms with their nondisabled peers.
(© Elizabeth Crews)

sents a list of likely words, and the student simply selects the correct word rather than typing it out completely. Other aids, such as voice recognition software, which translate a student's spoken words into text on the computer screen, or programs that will read text aloud,* can make writing a satisfying experience for students who struggle in this area.[22] Blind students and their teachers can use braille software, which provides easy-to-use, sophisticated print-to-braille and braille-to-print translations.[†]

■ part of IEPs

As discussed in the chapter entitled "Who Are Today's Students in a Diverse Society?," assistive technology must be considered a potential component of the individualized education program (IEP) required under law for each child with a disability. Regular classrooms now often include students with disabilities and other students with special needs, and you should be prepared to work with children who use assistive technology in your classroom.

Pause and Reflect

1 ► To what technologies should students have access?

2 ► Pick the technology that most interests you in this section, and think about how you might use that technology in your classroom. Would it allow you to improve on something you already did? Would you be innovating with the technology?

3 ► Do you have any educational concerns about the use of these technologies in schools?

---

* *DragonDictate* is a popular voice-input program available from Software Maintenance, Inc. (**http://www.ddwin.com/dictate.htm;** telephone: 888-343-3773). *IntelliTalk II* is a talking word processor from IntelliTools (**http://intellitools.com/;** telephone: 800-899-6687).
† Kurzweil Educational Systems offers software for visually impaired students (**http://www .kurzweiledu.com/;** telephone: 800-894-5374).

▶ How Are Technologies Affecting Teaching?

 Visit the website to link to the International society for Technology in Education (ISTE).

■ movement toward standards

As a teacher, you can expect your students to have to meet some standards relating to technology. Some states give technology only a brief mention in their standards, whereas others have separate standards exclusively for technology. In line with the current nationwide move toward standards-based learning (see "What Ought to Be the Elements of Educational Reform" in the chapter entitled "How Should Education Be Reformed?"), the International Society for Technology in Education (ISTE) has produced national technology standards. For example, before completing eighth grade, students should "design, develop, publish, and present products (e.g., web pages, videos) using technology resources that demonstrate and communicate curriculum concepts to audiences inside and outside the classroom."[23] ISTE encourages teachers to teach these skills within the context of their academic curriculum. To this end, ISTE has worked with content specialists to provide resources for incorporating the ISTE technology standards into subject standards for the rest of the curriculum.

This trend is encouraging; however, for technology to be truly integrated as an important part of classroom instruction, several additional shifts must take place in current practices and attitudes. The impact of technology on learning depends more on how teachers use the technology than on the characteristics of the technology itself.

A Different Role for the Teacher

In the video case *Using Technology to Promote Discovery Learning* a mathematics teacher talks about the ways his role has changed with his use of technology in a constructivist fashion, to support students as they build their own knowledge. As you watch the clips and study the artifacts in the case, reflect upon the following questions:

1. In what ways is this teacher's approach similar to the description of constructivist uses of cognitive tools in this chapter? In what ways does his approach differ?

Technology is just a tool. In terms of getting the kids working together and motivating them, the teacher is the most important.

—BILL GATES

■ teacher as leader and co-learner

■ the subject matter drives the technology

Integrating technology into your teaching can change the way you deliver content to your classes. Many schools and teachers have been slow to discover the real potential of new technologies, but some new trends are emerging. Technology can be more effective in a teaching environment where computers help to facilitate instruction and foster a constructivist approach to learning, as discussed in "The Influence of Psychological Theories" in the chapter entitled "What Are the Philosophical Foundations of American Education?" As we have mentioned throughout this chapter, a constructivist approach to infusing technology is related to several other classroom characteristics, including the following:

- *Teacher as a Facilitator.* Think back to the scenario at the beginning of this chapter. Patricia Gonzalez was *facilitating* instruction as needed to bring a deeper understanding and relevance to students. Because of the technology the students employed, she was no longer the sole source of information for her class. By using technology to present basic factual and historical information, the teacher is freed to become much more involved in higher-level evaluation of performance. Teachers can monitor students' projects, guiding their efforts and providing feedback. Instead of being a teller and a tester, the teacher can be a leader and a co-learner. In such environments, teachers must view themselves as "coaches" or "facilitators" who guide students as they use technology to discover facts and concepts.

- *Embedding Technology in the Curriculum.* With the encouragement of groups like ISTE, described above, teaching technology skills in isolation is giving way to a new model of embedding technology skills within the context of the content.[24] A social studies teacher might teach the mechanics of a program, such as *HyperStudio,* as part of a unit on the local community that asks students to create a virtual fieldtrip, as described earlier in the chapter. The subject matter is driving the technology rather than vice versa. In the words of one team of researchers, "we learn best 'with' technology rather than 'from' it."[25]

- *Small Group Instruction.* To better use the available technology, teachers must move from whole-class instruction toward smaller group projects and activities that are conducive to active, engaged learning and student interactions. This is not a shift all teachers warmly embrace. Smaller group work may mean that students learn different things at different times rather than an entire class learning the same material together. In many ways, this resembles the days before chalkboards and full-class instruction. Classrooms that effectively use technology evolve into cooperative rather than competitive social structures, and student assessment shifts from pencil-and-paper testing toward the evaluation of products and progress in meeting established criteria.[26]

The connection between technology and constructivism is not clear, but some researchers are beginning to understand elements of it. We know that teachers who have changed to a more constructivist approach in their classrooms are the same teachers who have used computers consistently and in meaningful ways in their classrooms. These teachers are more willing to discuss subjects in which they are not experts and tend to assign longer, more complex projects. It appears not that the technology makes teachers change but that the technology facilitates changes that teachers already wanted to make.[27]

It is not the strongest of the species that survives, nor the most intelligent; it is the one that is most adaptable to change.

—CHARLES DARWIN

■ technology as facilitator of change

However, change in education is rarely swift. Even highly motivated teachers who regularly used technology took substantial amounts of time (over three to five years) to become comfortable with new technology and able to fit it into their classroom goals.[28] With increasing pressure on schools to incorporate up-to-date technology and with other supporting factors present, such as sufficient funding and on-site technical support, we can expect to see changes in teachers' pedagogy as they become more comfortable with the power of technology.

■ Project CHILD combines traditional and constructivist views of education

Florida's Project CHILD (Computers Helping Instruction and Learning Development)* demonstrates some of the changes in common teaching practices and attitudes toward learning classrooms that help teachers effectively incorporate technology in teaching. Elementary school teachers work together in teams of three, clustered by grade level (K–2 or 3–5). Each teacher focuses on one of three subject areas: reading, writing, or math. After direct instruction from the teacher, students complete independent work while rotating through three stations: a computer station for technology work, a textbook station for paper/pencil work, and activity stations for hands-on work. The teacher also has a teacher station for small group tutorials or individual assistance. The students rotate among the three subject-area classrooms, working with the same three teachers for three years. This systematic approach ensures equitable computer time for all, and teachers can individualize instruction by specifying where students begin working each day. Children often work together to complete group projects and to have maximum computer time, learning from one another and the computer and other materials in each room.

* For more information, visit Project CHILD's website at **http://www.ifsi.org/.**

Project CHILD combines both traditional and constructivist views of instruction. Although teachers offer some traditional direct instruction, one of the aims of the project is to help teachers shift from being the single source of knowledge in their classroom to being a facilitator and coach. While students are using their station time, teachers circulate to facilitate learning.

- how computers are used as a key variable

Students who participated in the program for a full three-year cycle scored better on standardized tests than their peers in conventional classrooms with similar computer-student ratios.[29] These results suggest that an important variable is not simply how many computers students have access to but how those computers are used.

Professional Resources and Communication

In the past decade, we have witnessed a boom in communications. Facsimile machines, cellular phones with web capabilities, satellite broadcasting, and powerful handheld computers have been shrinking our world. With these tools a teacher can communicate with colleagues worldwide, both quickly and cheaply.

- a less expensive technological modification

■ **Email**   Email is an excellent medium for teachers to use in sharing ideas, materials, and resources. Besides being fast and cheap, email can be sent with attachments, so correspondents can share anything from a word processing document to digital video files. It can also be sent to large groups of recipients as easily as to one, making it much more efficient than the telephone or mailings. Teachers can communicate with parents via email, and vice versa, without the disruption of ringing phones and answering machines. Within the school setting itself, email has streamlined the work environment, reduced staff meetings, and decreased the mounds of accumulated paper.

- online teacher resources

■ **The Web**   The Web connects teachers to professional organizations in their field and to vast databases of lesson plans and teaching materials throughout the world. The list of websites at the end of this chapter is just a small sample of an incredibly large and growing resource.

- reducing teachers' isolation through electronic communities

The Web also provides teachers with opportunities to belong to communities of practice to communicate and share ideas. Tapped In* has a free membership for teachers to set up a virtual office and up to two group rooms or classrooms. These spaces allow for synchronous (real-time) chat and asynchronous discussions with other teachers, as well as places to post files, links, and notes. Tapped In has virtual groups on a wide variety of subjects, with events posted each month for online forums.[30]

Classroom Management

Teaching involves many complex tasks. Organizing learning activities, creating or gathering the materials needed, keeping records, managing conduct, and delivering instruction—all of these together add up to a big job. A teacher

---

* Tapped In, a project of SRI International's Center for Technology in Learning, is available at **http://tappedin.org/**.

may have from 25 to 150 or more students every day, with attendance records to be kept and grades recorded for each one. Technology can both complicate and streamline this job. The introduction of technology can affect the dynamics of a classroom, as students are in control of the equipment; this can be a challenge for some teachers who are not used to constructivist learning activities. Technology lessons require careful planning, rearrangement of room configurations, and an alternate plan for when equipment malfunctions. Additionally, teachers have to monitor the appropriateness of language in online communications and the appropriateness of websites viewed. Teachers who are new to technology may find that it can be time consuming at first, but improves over time.[31]

Although integrating technology into the curriculum can take time, teachers can also make use of technology to save them time in other areas of their daily work. As their size and price come down, some teachers are using handheld computers that allow grade input, schedule coordination, file sharing, organization of students' data, and web page downloading in a portable form. Tools such as these allow teachers to spend more time at the art of teaching and less time dealing with paperwork, organization, and materials management. In addition, a variety of software, referred to collectively as teacher productivity tools, can save teachers time by speeding up other management tasks. Popular teacher productivity tools include:

▪ software gradebooks save time

- **A software gradebook,** also referred to as an *electronic gradebook,* is a hybrid application of a spreadsheet and a database. The database functions keep records of student and parent information such as mailing addresses, phone numbers, locker numbers, book numbers, and other details. The spreadsheet functions calculate grades and provide the teacher with statistical information regarding assignments, tests, and performance of students over time. In addition to saving teachers hours of work doing calculations and retrieving student information, gradebook software also gives teachers new ways to identify a student's strengths and weaknesses. Some programs, for example, allow the teacher to print charts of a student's academic performance over time (quarters or semesters) for the student or parent to inspect.

▪ help putting together exams

- **Test generators and question bank software** allow teachers to create a database of questions and then construct tests from them. The teacher can easily create two or three versions of the same test with the questions in a different order or with slightly different questions. This is particularly useful for pre- and post-assessments or for giving a different test to students absent on test day.

▪ more software to help teachers

- **IEP software** helps manage the paperwork involved in the individualized programs required in special education.
- **Time management tools,** such as schedule or calendar software, can help teachers keep track of appointments and schedules.

Pause and Reflect

1 ▸ To what technologies should teachers regularly have access?

2 ▸ Do you envision yourself as a teacher who would be comfortable using technology in a constructivist way, such as Patricia Gonzalez did?

3 ▸ What do you see as the pros and cons of such an approach?

► How Are Computer Technologies Organized for Student Use?

Computer technologies generally operate in several different arrangements within the school setting, and it is useful to think of these arrangements across a continuum from concentrated to infused, as shown in Figure 7.1. When technology is *concentrated*, students are given intense exposure to computers from time to time. Technology that is integrated smoothly into the daily classroom experience is described as *infused*. Several common computer setups exist along this continuum.

Computer Labs

advantages of labs

Computer labs, which usually feature a number of computers in a single room, offer a concentrated arrangement in which all the students use computers at the same time. This setup is ideal for technology education—teaching about the computer or how to employ a particular application. In many labs, a large display station for the teacher facilitates the demonstration of skills for more effective whole-class instruction. Forty-three percent of computers in American schools are found in computer labs and 48 percent are found in classrooms, according to one national survey.[32]

disadvantages of labs

Most computer labs do not lend themselves to interdisciplinary or cooperative group projects because of a lack of open table space, although some teachers foster collaboration by having two chairs around one computer. Access to computer labs is another key factor in their use by teachers. If many classrooms share one computer facility, there may be little lab time for each class, and visits to the lab must always be planned. For these reasons, computer labs tend to foster technology education rather than what we might call education *with* technology, that is, education that uses technology to facilitate learning about other subjects.

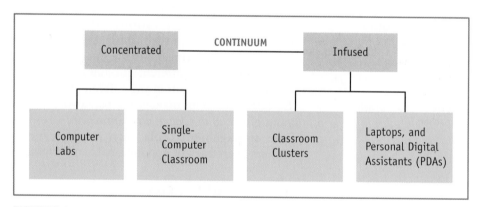

FIGURE 7.1
Arrangements for Computer Technologies
One way to think about the different ways of arranging computer technologies within a school is to consider where each arrangement fits along a continuum, from concentrated to infused. If the arrangement is concentrated, students are exposed to computers in an intense way from time to time, whereas technology that is integrated smoothly into the daily classroom experience is considered infused.

Single-Computer Classrooms

■ productive uses for a single computer

In a slightly more infused arrangement, the single-computer classroom might have the computer on the teacher's desk or rolled into the room on a mobile cart. Until classrooms reach a 1:1 student-computing device ratio, teachers will need to find instructional uses for one or just a handful of computers.

Although a single computer makes it difficult to use the technology for active instructional tasks, with the addition of a projection system teachers can make the rich resources of the Internet available for the entire class. Teachers can demonstrate complex mathematical or scientific concepts by using dynamic visualization programs such as Geometer's Sketchpad or Starry Night, and, used properly, can support student learning and inquiry.[33] Unfortunately, projections systems are increasingly misused by subjecting students to endless and wordy PowerPoint slides in darkened rooms, where students become passive consumers of the technology rather than active learners.

Classroom Clusters

■ clusters are a flexible arrangement

In a more infused situation, a cluster is usually a table or an area of a classroom where three to five computers are available for use at any time by the students in that class. Clusters provide convenient access to computer technologies for a variety of tasks. For example, a teacher might use two of the computers to allow cooperative groups access to cognitive and communication tools and the others as learning stations for specific subjects.

Providing a cluster of computers in each classroom generally requires more of an investment in technology than the other arrangements we have described. Whereas a computer lab of twenty-five computers may afford access for ten classrooms, clusters might require thirty to fifty computers. If a school can afford them, clusters offer a very flexible use of technology in the classroom setting. Teachers can plan to use them in instruction and can set up each computer to fit their needs. This arrangement genuinely fosters education *with* technology. It is not particularly good, however, for technology education, since not every student has access simultaneously.

Laptops and Handheld Computing Devices

■ laptops as the most infused arrangement

By 2003, Henrico County Public Schools in Virginia had teamed with Apple to distribute an iBook laptop to every middle and high school student, as well as all teachers in the district in an effort to provide 1:1 computer access. Their goals in providing more than 25,000 wireless laptops were to improve student achievement, create technology-literate graduates and teachers, and bridge the digital divide in a constructivist learning environment.* While it will be some time (if ever) before all schools adopt laptops for every student, wireless laptop carts (carts of laptops that can connect to the Internet wirelessly and can be rolled into a classroom) provide a good solution to the issue of computer access in the classroom. This arrangement facilitates deep, flexible use of technology by the students and encourages the teacher to assume the role of facilitator.

■ uses of handheld devices

Handheld computing devices, such as Pocket PCs and Palm handhelds, offer the benefit of achieving a 1:1 ratio with a fraction of the cost of laptops, but

* For more information on the Henrico County Public Schools Teaching and Learning Initiative, visit their webpage at **http://www.henrico.k12.va.us/technology/**.

are still primarily a business tool and not created for classroom use. A growing trend in many classrooms is to adapt these business tools for instructional uses, such as word processing or geometry manipulations. In addition, a few affordable educational handhelds, such as AlphaSmart's Dana Wireless, are currently available, and it is likely that in the coming years more will be developed.

Pause and Reflect

1 ▶ Envision yourself teaching with each of these computer arrangements. What would you and your students be able to do in a computer lab? How would that be different if each of your students is able to use a Palm handheld in school? How would your instruction change if you were assigned to a classroom with a single computer?

VOICES FROM THE CLASSROOM

Janet Muller teaches third grade at Duniway Elementary School in Portland, Oregon.

Infusing Technology into the Curriculum

Several years ago, I found myself charged with the daunting task of turning a group of wiggly third graders into sophisticated little techno-wizards. Four new computers were delivered to my classroom and the school district packed me off to a series of amazing classes. Unfortunately I never learned how I could effectively use four computers with twenty-six little children, and I often found myself pondering the value of a computer program based on sign-up sheets.

I began looking for a way to bring some serious technology into my room that would allow simultaneous student access to equipment. Soon, I stumbled onto the Palm Education Pioneer Program (PEP), an experimental online grant program that offered teachers a unique opportunity to design a classroom technology project using Palm handhelds. My proposal was chosen for funding and last fall we received thirty Palm IIIc color screen handhelds . . . and technology in Room 11 changed forever!

Each one of my third graders has his or her own Palm loaded with wonderful websites, and when they arrive each morning, the students "hotsync" to one of the four classroom computers to download updated information. Together, we read the *New York Times* and Reuters News Service each morning. Throughout the day students type their spelling words and check special websites. They zoom through *Encarta* Spanish dictionaries, studying the definitions of unfamiliar Spanish words; take math, geography, and science quizzes; write collaborative stories; draw detailed maps; create animated illustrations; and play interactive critical thinking games.

After a year with the Palms, my students are as well informed about current events as their parents. The average spelling grade is 92 percent and my little kiddos draw maps you have to see to believe! But the most rewarding part of this entire project has been the remarkable technology proficiency these children have developed on their own. Putting a Palm in their hands has provided daily opportunities for problem solving, practicing, and experimentation.

My little third graders WERE transformed into techno-wizards by virtue of opportunity. Rather than waiting for a seat at one of our desktop computers, they've been given an opportunity to take a handheld computer to their seat and use this amazing technology to shine at the important business of third grade.

   Visit the website for more Voices from the Classroom.

▶ What Are the Key Issues in Educational Technology?

You probably realize by now that many features of educational technology have given rise to serious debate among educators, policymakers, and the general public. To achieve the best use of available technology, schools need to reach some consensus on several key issues, including questions about infrastructure and budgeting, education of teachers, parent support, equity for students, and infusing the technology into the curriculum.

Infrastructure and Budgeting

 Visit the website to link to more information about technology and budget issues.

Before technology can be used as an educational tool, schools must have in place the infrastructure to support it—that is, the basic facilities that make the technology usable. At the most fundamental level, the physical plants of American schools are often ill equipped to handle the demands of technology. Of course, a discussion of infrastructure problems immediately raises issues of money, both the initial costs of new technology and the yearly allowances that must be made in school budgets. This section offers a quick survey of infrastructure and budgetary issues and the ways in which they interrelate.

▪ inadequate power supplies

▪ **Electrical Problems** One basic obstacle to technology integration has been inadequate power supplies. For many years, classrooms were designed with only one electrical outlet at the front of the room. A cluster of computers will not run safely from one outlet. Rewiring has cost both time and money as schools join the information age.

▪ expense of wiring

▪ **Network Wiring** Network wiring has been another roadblock on the information superhighway. The Telecommunications Act of 1996 defined equal access to "universal service" to include electronic networking and provided a fund to help reduce the price of wiring each classroom to form a schoolwide network. This fund of $2.25 billion per year is used for local and long-distance phone charges, high-speed data lines, and web access in schools. Depending on how needy a school district is, discounts can be as high as 90 percent.[34] As a result, the majority of U.S. classrooms have Internet connections, though much work still remains to bring the power of the Internet into the hands of students.

▪ student-to-computer ratios improving

▪ **Access** The ratio of students to computers has dramatically improved in K–12 schools in the last fifteen years, dropping from about 125 to 3.8. On average, four students share one computer.[35] This trend is encouraging, but significant gaps remain in terms of the quality of equipment. For example, approximately half of school computers are not capable of running sophisticated applications, processing large amounts of data, displaying graphics, or running several applications at once.[36] The challenge in education is not to simply get technological equipment into schools but to keep it up to date and usable in a daily classroom situation.

▪ continued need for up-to-date equipment

▪ **Technology Budgets** Although costs of personal computers have dropped considerably since they first entered schools, information technology is expensive, especially when it is implemented on the immense scale of public education.

Commercial Influences in Schools: Where Do You Draw the Line?

Schools are faced with competing pressures: Industry demands technologically savvy students. Lawmakers demand tight budgets, which can limit technology purchases. Under these opposing forces, some schools have chosen corporate partnerships as the answer. Many corporations are willing to provide cash or free equipment to schools.

What do these businesses get in return? Businesses see vast potential revenue from the millions of children and teens online, and they want a way to capture those students' attention and money. Some companies, for example, offer schools free software in exchange for the rights to post online advertisements on school computers. These exchanges have proven controversial. Many parents and educators believe public schools should be commercial-free spaces where children grow and develop away from the pressures of advertising. Others feel that advertising is a small concession to make in exchange for the benefits gained.

Issues of student privacy further complicate the dilemma. Some web-filtering software, which businesses have donated to schools, collects data on the demographic characteristics and surfing habits of groups of students, and the information is later sold to other businesses. Recent legislation requires school districts to inform parents if students' personal data is gathered for marketing purposes, and parents can choose for their child not to participate.

Where do you draw the line in protecting students? Is it sufficient to guard their personal information, or should students be shielded from the advertising of corporate interests as well?

Source: Amy Aidman, "Children's Online Privacy," *Educational Leadership* 58 (October 2000), pp. 46–47; *Protecting Children and Communities from Commercialism.* Available at: **http://www .commercialalert.org/n2h2/.**

For example, state and local governments are spending over $5 billion annually to equip schools with computers, networks, hardware, and software.[37] Schools struggling under financial pressure may choose to accept donations of technology equipment in return for access to student information. The accompanying box discusses these questionable practices in more detail.

■ budgets to include repair, maintenance costs

Beyond the basic issue of providing the needed hardware, school administrators must plan for an ongoing technology budget that includes such items as repair costs. Maintaining a network, within a school or among schools, can be a time-consuming task requiring highly trained personnel. Although many such tasks can be contracted out to local businesses, this factor must be accounted for in yearly budgeting.

■ specialists need to support teachers

■ **Support Personnel**   Besides repair personnel to keep the system running, teachers should have access to training and support personnel. Even the most advanced technologies are useless if teachers are not comfortable with their operation. Teachers who encounter technological difficulties may become discouraged and find it easier to avoid using technology altogether. Educational technology specialists who work on-site (in the school itself) are especially important. A technology specialist can act as a safety net for the integration of technology into teaching. Teachers may be more likely to take a risk and try something new if they know help is readily available.[38]

Education of Teachers

Visit the website to link to more information about the INTASC standards.

Because of the excitement and demands generated by new technology, pressures have risen to improve both the preparation of new teachers and the staff development options for in-service teachers.

■ teachers' technology standards

■ Teacher Preparation When you graduate, you can count on having to demonstrate your skills in technology. In addition to National Educational Technology Standards for Teachers (NETS-T),* most states have developed technology components to their certification requirements. Schools of education, much like elementary and secondary schools, are struggling with how to develop competent teachers who will meet these goals. Many instructors indicate that, even with the recent emphasis on computer literacy, instructional technology is not adequately modeled for future teachers.[39] Schools of education are continuing to rethink their programs and are gradually using modern technology to enhance what they offer. To this end, education students often develop electronic portfolios of their work, create computer-based assessments, and use digital video to capture and reflect on their student teaching.

■ in-service and preservice teachers learn from each other

The University of Virginia's Curry School of Education operates the Technology Infusion Project (TIP), which pairs each preservice teacher enrolled in the Applied Teaching with Technology course with a local classroom teacher who has an interest in learning more about using technology in the classroom. During their collaboration, the classroom teacher provides insight about curriculum and classroom practices while the preservice teacher shares the new skills learned in the TIP program, such as multimedia applications or skills in constructivist uses of technology. As both teachers become more familiar with new technologies, they jointly explore instructional possibilities, culminating in a long-term project that they teach together in the classroom. Preservice teachers gain a valuable classroom perspective from a veteran in the field and ground their technology learning in classroom practice, and the classroom teachers gain professional development in technology. Whereas introducing technology into a classroom can be intimidating for some teachers, TIP's collaborative nature makes it a more comfortable experience and provides an extra set of hands to assist with the process.

■ keeping up to date

■ Staff Development Some states are adding more stringent requirements for teachers to renew their licenses. Several states also offer incentives for teachers to develop technology skills; incentives range from paying for classes to buying hardware and software. Teachers report, however, that one of the greatest obstacles to their use of computers is lack of release time to learn how to use technology. Experts do not agree on exactly how training should be offered. Some believe it should be ongoing at teachers' convenience, whereas others advocate an intensive, off-site course with follow-up seminars to allow teachers a chance to learn with undivided attention. With the advent of widespread telecommunications networks, many professional development courses are now offered online.[†] Teachers who cannot be released during the school day can log on at night or during the summer to work through self-paced lessons. Accompanying discussion groups allow time for reflection.

Pause and Reflect

1 ▶ What skills in using media and technology do you think teachers should have?

2 ▶ How can you prepare yourself to use technology in your classroom?

---

* ISTE's NETS-T can be viewed at **http://cents.iste.org/teachers/t_stands.html.**
† One example is CaseNEX (**http://casenex.com**).

3 ► What are your concerns about using technology in the classroom?

4 ► What support systems do the teachers you know have for using technology in instruction? Whom do they ask when they have questions?

Parents

■ parents and children learning together

Technology can be a "hook" to get parents involved or a quick deterrent to send them running. Parents who are not familiar with technology may be intimidated by or fearful of their child's computer use. Technology can become an obstacle between you and your students' parents, but several initiatives are aimed at breaking down these barriers while also educating parents.

Since 1987, Indiana's Buddy Project has worked to increase student achievement using technology in "any time, anywhere" settings to extend the learning beyond the bounds of school.* The Buddy Project supplements existing home and community-based technology to strengthen family involvement in education. For example, participating students in kindergarten through eighth grade take home a Buddy Backpack that is filled with themed activities to do with their families. Parents teach other parents, children teach parents, and children teach one another. The Buddy Project extends the child's learning opportunities beyond the classroom walls while creating a special opportunity for the family to become involved as well. With sensitive training, technology can "hook" parental interest in education. For example, one Indiana farming family was able to use their new technological skills to help turn around their family business.[40]

Equity

■ the digital divide

The U.S. government reports that urban households with incomes of $75,000 and higher are more than nine times as likely to have a computer at home than rural households at the lowest income levels, and more than twenty times as likely to have Web access.[41] Students who use a computer at home have opportunities to develop skills and to explore technology's potential that are not available to students without those luxuries. Initiatives such as the Buddy Project help to equalize the technological playing field that income levels can divide. However, simple access is not the only barrier. One technology expert argues that students from poorer families are more likely to use computers for games, whereas children from middle-class families are more likely to use the computer for online research.[42]

 Visit the website to link to more information about the "digital divide."

Some critics also argue that programs like the Indiana Buddy Project are the exception, and current patterns of technology use in schools contribute to disparities in educational quality. At school, data indicate that poorer students are at a disadvantage. While the presence of computers in schools in wealthier and poorer areas has almost equalized, the digital divide still exists in terms of quality of equipment and type of instruction. For example, underprivileged children are more likely to use computers in a rigid drill-and-practice format rather than in more flexible formats, such as doing online research, that build higher-level cognitive skills. The impoverished city of Camden, New Jersey, spent $8 million on computers and software offered by a software vendor to boost students' scores on math and reading tests to meet the mandatory performance levels set by the 2001 No Child Left Behind law. Elementary and middle school students are in the computer labs up to five times a week, drilling to pass the annual tests. Critics of Camden's approach point to the loss of constructivist activities time and the re-

---

* To learn more, visit the Buddy Project website (**http://www.buddyproject.org/**).

sulting lack of higher-order thinking skills. These critics believe that drilling software can lead to an achievement gap.[43] Besides the basic question of fairness, these inequalities will have implications when these students graduate and look for jobs, without the skills of their more affluent peers.

Technology access and use divides along racial, as well as income, lines. A 2003 report by the North Central Regional Educational Laboratory showed that in the U.S., home computer ownership among Asian and non-Hispanic white households is 12 to 24 percent greater than among other racial and ethnic groups.[44] As computers become more commonplace in schools, teachers need to consider students' access to technology outside of school, particularly in assigning homework.

■ gender inequities

Gender differences also have emerged from the use of technology in education. Researchers argue that certain types of technologies aggravate the differences between boys and girls. For example, many commonly used applications value speed, aggression, and efficiency [45]—qualities that boys tend to display—whereas technology tends to be more interesting for girls when it's used for a relevant problem-solving exercise or collaboration and not as an end in itself.[46] The key to engaging girls in technology appears to be *how* technology is used in the classroom. Tasks that require versatility and collaboration in classrooms (and businesses) that move to a more integrated approach to technology may invite more girls to participate.

■ what teachers can do

Teachers can do a lot to dispel inequities within their own classrooms. Students with little computer experience can be teamed with more experienced users. Classrooms and computer labs can be made available to students before and after school, and teachers can promote gender equity through modeling, attitude, and expectations. Technology need not become a wedge widening the gap between the "haves" and the "have-nots"; but without awareness of the problem, the potential for increased inequity is very real.

Pause and Reflect

1 ▶ Where do you see evidence of the digital divide in the world outside of the K–12 classroom?

2 ▶ How will the digital divide affect you and your classroom?

Integration into the Curriculum

We need to recognize that it is one thing to use technology in isolated classrooms and quite another to make technology a potent force in transforming an entire school or an entire education system.

—Barbara Means

■ essential conditions

For computer technology to become a genuine part of school life, as it has in the business world, the tools of technology must be *integrated* into school behaviors. Integrating technology means bringing the tools of technology into daily learning and teaching activities, just as teachers already do with chalkboards and books. This is not an easy task. Much of this chapter has focused on how computer technologies can be used as tools for student learning, but we have also seen that many support systems must be in place.

What conditions must be present in a school "to create learning environments conducive to powerful uses of technology"?[47] Among other conditions, schools must have the following:

- Student-centered approaches to learning
- Access to contemporary technologies, software, and communications networks

- Educators skilled in the use of the technology for learning
- Technical assistance for maintaining and using technology resources
- Ongoing financial support for sustained technology use
- Content standards and curriculum resources
- Community partners who provide expertise, support, and real-life interactions
- Vision with support and proactive leadership from the education system
- Assessment of the effectiveness of technology for learning

As this list* indicates, real change in education and technology cannot be the job of a lone teacher who is a whiz on the Web or a solo school board member who votes for new software. It must be a systemic change coming from a critical mass of individuals who are committed to the integration of education *with* technology.

▶ A Final Word

One key issue that we have not fully addressed is whether all the "hype" about technology will simply go the way of the filmstrip. Are we spending billions of dollars on fancy hardware, remodeling schools to accommodate wireless networks, and asking veteran teachers to change their ways without reason? What do we lose when we incorporate technology into our teaching? With increased access to vast amounts of up-to-date information and powerful new technologies, are students learning "the basics" as well as they do in more traditional classrooms?

■ align uses with goals

When "techno-reformers" talk about their grand plans, they have one purpose in mind: preparing future employees in a technology-driven work environment.[48] Teachers, on the other hand, have a broader focus: they want to develop healthy bonds with their students that will lead to intellectual growth. Teachers hope to develop responsible, educated citizens who have every opportunity open to them. When teachers see the rapidly changing world of technology in which machines sometimes break, certain applications take a long time to learn, and some programs are not flexible enough to meet their needs, they hesitate to take part in it.[49] While policymakers rush to move schools into the information age, it's important to remember that teachers make up a crucial part of the integration question. In order to reach some consensus, the dialogue should begin not with the goals of technology, but with the goals of schooling. When agreement is found, educators should raise the question of how technology can help reach those goals.[50]

We must adjust to changing times and still hold to unchanging principles.

—Jimmy Carter

■ technology is not the panacea

■ is technology worth it?

Certainly new technologies are no panacea for the classroom, but they offer tools that can help change the classroom from a teacher-centered to a more cooperative and student-centered environment. Students can use technological devices as tools—not toys—in the same ways that they will likely use technology in their future lives. We believe that all teachers should have the opportunity to gain skill in educational technologies, and in particular we believe it would behoove new teachers to develop these skills in the context of their preservice work. Most

---

* International Society for Technology in Education, *National Educational Technology Standards— Connecting Curriculum and Technology* (telephone: 800-336-6191 [United States and Canada] or 541-302-3777 [international]; email: **cust_svc@iste.org; http://www.iste.org.** Copyright 2000. Reprinted with permission.

important, we want you to consider how technology will affect your future classroom. Ask yourself where technology can enhance what you do and where it can allow you to innovate. If it is not accomplishing these goals, ask yourself why you are using it.[51]

Key Terms

assistive technology (200)
blog (190)
cognitive tools (186)
digital storytelling (190)
distance education (199)
drill-and-practice (190)

LCD projector (189)
mind maps (webs) (191)
news group (199)
simulation (195)
spreadsheet (197)
tutorials (197)

ubiquitous computing (193)
virtual fieldtrips (195)
word processor (189)
WebQuest (196)

For Reflection

1 Do you think parents should be concerned about the role, or lack of it, that technological tools play in the education of their children? At what age do you think children should be taught to use computers?

2 Should governments spend billions on technology for schools, or should the money be spent differently?

3 What do you see as the goals of schooling? Are there ways you can use technology to reach those goals?

For Debate

Read the Policy Matters! summary "Web Filtering Software: Censorship or Good Sense" at the website, and consider the issues it outlines regarding protecting students from undesirable Internet content; then go to EduSpace to post your answers (or respond to other students' answers) to the What Do You Think questions listed in the Policy Matters! feature.

For Further Information

PRINT RESOURCES

Larry Cuban, *Oversold and Underused: Computers in Classrooms 1980–2000* (Cambridge, MA: Harvard University Press, 2001).
The author takes a critical and historical look at the use of technology in education.

Richard C. Forcier and Don E. Descy, *The Computer as an Educational Tool: Productivity and Problem Solving,* 4th ed. (Upper Saddle River, NJ: Prentice Hall, 2005).
This is an introductory book in the use of computers as a tool in education.

Jane M. Healy, *Failure to Connect: How Computers Affect Our Children's Minds—for Better and Worse* (New York: Simon and Schuster, 1998).
The author explains how computer use interacts with brain development at different ages.

Robert Heinich, Michael Molenda, James D. Russell, and Sharon E. Smaldino, *Instructional Media and Technologies for Learning,* 7th ed. (Upper Saddle River, NJ: Prentice Hall, 2002).
Now in its seventh edition, this is one of the seminal books on the "how to" of using media in the classroom.

David H. Jonassen, *Computers as Mindtools for Schools: Engaging Critical Thinking,* 2d ed. (Englewood Cliffs, NJ: Prentice Hall, 2000).
Centering on the use of computer applications to foster constructivist, higher-order thinking skills, this is a useful book for learning how to integrate "mindtools" into instruction.

George Lucas *Educational Foundation, Edutopia: Success Stories for Learning in the Digital Age* (San Francisco: Jossey-Bass, 2002).
A collection of stories from innovative leaders in schools who are integrating technology in a meaningful way.

Cleborne D. Maddux, D. L. Johnson, and J. W. Willis, *Educational Computing: Learning with Tomorrow's Technologies,* 3d ed. (Needham Heights, MA: Allyn and Bacon, 2001).
This text combines history, theory, and practice to provide a strong base of knowledge for applying educational technologies in classroom instruction.

Barbara Means, William Penuel, and Christine Padilla, *The Connected School: Technology and Learning in High School* (New York: John Wiley and Sons, 2001). Through case studies of six high schools that have pioneered the use of technology, this book comments on successes and challenges of integrating computers in schools.

WEB RESOURCES

In addition to these printed materials and the websites listed within the chapter, the following list offers some educational websites for you to look through. Remember, however, that these sites are only starting points. For specific information, use a search engine. Also, keep in mind that web addresses can change without warning. If your web browser cannot locate an address, try shortening the address to the next root level. For example, if **http://www.iste.org/Research/Background/Online.html** does not work, try **http://www.iste.org/**. If you still have trouble, try a web search engine and use some descriptive keywords.

Blue Web'n. Available at: **http://www.kn.pacbell.com/wired/bluewebn/**.
A library of award-winning learning sites on the Web, categorized by subject, grade-level, and format.

International Society for Technology in Education (ISTE), *ISTE's Electronic Resources.* Available at: **http://www.iste.org/resources/**.
A superb list of links that covers a wide range of issues including standards, digital divide, professional development, and technology integration.

ISTE, *Learning and Leading with Technology.* Available at: **http://www.iste.org/L&L/index.html**.

Janet Ward Schofield and Ann Locke Davidson, *Bringing the Internet to School: Lessons from an Urban District* (New York: John Wiley and Sons, 2002). This book discusses the findings of a five-year study of Internet use in schools.

A monthly journal available online that offers great suggestions from teachers for teachers on how to use technology effectively in the K–12 classroom.

Kathy Schrock, *Guide for Educators.* Available at: **http://school.discovery.com/schrockguide/**.
A very well-organized list of useful links, with an especially helpful section categorized by subject area.

Edutopia Online. Available at: **http://www.glef.org**.
A rich resource of articles related to the future of public education, with a strong emphasis on technology.

Judi Harris, *Virtual Architecture Web Page.* Available at: **http://virtual-architecture.wm.edu/**.
An excellent resource for teachers who want to explore telecollaborative projects.

Internet Resource for Special Children (IRSC), *disABILITY Links.* Available at: **http://www.irsc.org/disability.htm**.
A helpful site for information and resources about a wide range of disabilities and health conditions.

ERIC Database. Available at: **http://www.eric.ed.gov/**.
A searchable database of journal and nonjournal education literature.

8 | *What Are the Ethical and Legal Issues Facing Teachers?*

Chapter Preview   This chapter aims to sharpen your sense of the ethical dimension of teaching and your understanding of the legal underpinnings of many aspects of school life. We examine several common ethical problems faced by teachers, along with legal issues and recent court rulings that have affected them.

This chapter emphasizes that:

▶ Ethics and the law are closely related, but they also differ.

▶ Ethical teaching has six specific characteristics.

▶ In addition to teaching's everyday ethical dimensions, teachers confront certain other, more complex ethical problems.

▶ Teachers need to understand fully how two basic legal terms, *due process* and *liability,* relate to their work.

▶ Broad areas of the law—from contracts to copyright, from self-defense to religion in the classroom—permeate school life.

▶ Students have rights under the law, such as the rights to due process and privacy, and teachers need to understand and respect these rights.

If each of us were the only person on the face of the earth, we could behave exactly as we chose. We would not have to worry about the rights or feelings of anyone else. We would be free of the constraints and demands imposed by others as we went about doing our own will. Quite obviously, though, this is simply not the case. Everyone who walks the earth is bound by real, if unseen, connections with his or her fellow humans. The English poet John Donne said it most succinctly: "No man is an island."

Our systems of ethics and laws are a major part of these invisible connecting fibers. Together they make civilized society in a neighborhood and coexistence on a planet possible. Ethics, as we say in the chapter entitled "What Are the Philosophical Foundations of American Education?," brings us into the realm of what is the right way to act. **Ethics** refers to a system or a code of morality embraced by a particular person or group. Law is related to, but different from, ethics. A **law** is a written rule that members of a given community must follow. The law is a system of such rules that governs the general conduct of a particular community's citizens.

■ ethics and the law

■ **Laws and Our Ethics**   Whereas ethics may be invisible obligations that we perceive, laws typically are statements that have been hammered out by the legitimate authority of a particular community, state, or nation and are used in court as standards by which to judge, and often penalize, the actual behavior of individuals. As a matter of fact, what someone might refer to as an unstated law is not a law at all but an ethical statement.

■ law as codified ethics

Laws, then, are concrete, made by people and usually written down for the public to see; ethics, on the other hand, consists of ideas that are less tangible and observable. Most of our laws are simply the codification of what we see as our moral or ethical obligations to one another. Sometimes, however, laws are unethical, such as the racial segregation laws that existed in this country only a few decades ago, and sometimes ethical obligations are not written into law, such as the ethical obligation to help the weak, the poor, and the sick.

■ **The Teacher's Responsibility**   What does all this have to do with teachers? First, it is the responsibility of teachers to convey to the young the fundamental moral message that we are all legally and ethically bound to one another. Much of this moral message is embedded in the content of our curricula, from our great stories to our history as a people. Second, a unique set of ethical relationships and legal obligations is embedded in teachers' work, and teachers, therefore, carry a special ethical and legal burden. This second issue is the subject of this chapter.

■ teachers' unique power

At the heart of the teacher's unique ethical and legal relationship with students is power. Like it or not, power resides in the "office" of teacher. Compared with a corporate executive or a military officer, it may not appear that a teacher has a great deal of power, but, in fact, the teacher has a special type of power.

This power arises from the fact that the teacher has an impact on people when they are still at a very malleable stage. The teacher is in command of the classroom insofar as he or she has the responsibility for what goes on. Teachers evaluate their students. They not only "mark" them with tangible symbols that become part of students' official records; they also mark their minds and hearts. Many careers are open to you, but few offer such truly awe-inspiring power, and because of the potential for abuse of this power, there are codes of ethics to guide the teacher and a body of laws governing the work of teaching. Since ignorance of the law (and ethics) is no excuse, we urge you to take the material in this chapter quite seriously.

If you wish to know who a man is, place him in authority.

—Yugoslav Proverb

▶ The Ethics of Teaching

 Visit the website to link to more information about ethics and teaching.

In a sense, individuals lose their "freedom" when they get married, and in a similar sense, people lose their freedom to do as they please when they become teachers. In both situations people make commitments, and ethical constraints come with these commitments. Constrained by ethics, the teacher is not always able to act in a manner that he or she finds most satisfying. For instance, the teacher should not respond with sarcasm to a student's foolish or rude remark. Even though a child—sometimes even a very small child—can provoke a rush of anger, the teacher should not act on that anger. In another, more positive sense, though, ethics are principles that call the teacher to higher modes of professional behavior. It is the ethical principles that teachers follow that mark the teacher's character and the social significance of the profession.

Pause and Reflect

1 ▶ When you think of some of your favorite teachers, can you recall in any ways you would say they exhibited ethical habits or principles?

2 ▶ What would you say is the greatest ethical obligation of a teacher?

Being an ethical teacher means having a rather special relationship with one's students and the other people with whom one works. Consider the following situation, as told to educator Kenneth Howe by a practicing teacher.

Case Study

■ case of Marilyn Henderson

The Characteristics of Ethical Teaching

Marilyn Henderson is a fifth-grade language arts teacher at Willoughby Elementary in South Lake, a medium-size city with a population of roughly 150,000. Marilyn is troubled to learn that Connie Severns, a fifth-grade social studies teacher with whom Marilyn worked previously in another school in the South Lake system, will be transferred to Willoughby. Marilyn believes Connie to be incompetent and is uncomfortable with this knowledge, especially in light of the fact that her students will be moving through Connie's class. As Marilyn recalls, "Connie didn't teach anything; she couldn't teach anything." Others in the district share Marilyn's assessment of Connie as a teacher and apparently with good reason. Connie seems totally to lack control. Children cry and complain about the chaos, some steal things from her purse, and on one occasion, another teacher discovered a child chasing Connie around the room.

Marilyn had previously tried to do something about Connie's incompetence but met with little success. The teachers' union advised her that they would have to stand behind a tenured teacher, and the school administration claimed to have to follow procedures that could take years, according to Marilyn. At this point in time (before Connie's transfer), the principal of Willoughby called the affected teachers together. He, too, was concerned about Connie's transfer and proposed that they discreetly and surreptitiously "write things down" to build a case that they could use to have Connie fired. Marilyn is asked to be a part of this. What should she do?[1] ■

This story provides just a peek at the teacher's ethically complex world. Howe suggests that in dealing with issues involving ethical judgment, we as teachers need to exhibit six characteristics: appreciation for moral deliberation, empathy, knowledge, reasoning, courage, and interpersonal skills.[2]

■ "seeing" competing
   interests

■ Appreciation for Moral Deliberation   We need, first, to see an ethical dilemma such as Marilyn's as a situation characterized by conflicting and competing moral interests (Connie's need for a job, the students' need for a competent teacher, and the other teachers' need to be fair in what they say to and about Connie). We need to see the complex moral dimensions of the problem and appreciate that care must be taken to protect the rights of all parties.

■ feeling what others feel

■ Empathy   *Empathy* is the ability to mentally "get inside the skin of another." We need to feel what the others in an ethically troublesome situation are thinking and feeling. In the case described, we would need to empathize with the principal who is inheriting a questionable teacher, the students and their parents, Connie, and Marilyn and the other teachers.

■ knowing all the facts

■ Knowledge   One of the tools of a teacher who is able to deal effectively with ethical issues is knowledge. We need to remember the facts that will enable us to put an issue in context. What does Connie actually do in the classroom? What formal procedures are in place to deal with ineffective or incompetent teachers? We need to be able to formulate reasonable approaches to the problem and then, from experience, anticipate the consequences of each approach. In Marilyn's case, she needs to be able to think clearly about the alternatives—such as participating in the principal's questionable plan or, perhaps, directly confronting Connie—and she must think through, with some degree of accuracy, what the likely consequences of such action would be. This involves knowledge of the context in which she and Connie are working.

■ thinking systematically

■ Reasoning   To reason is to reflect systematically on an issue. When we reason about an issue, we move through it step by step and draw conclusions, or we may compare a particular event or action with some moral principle and come to some conclusion. For instance, Marilyn may hold as a moral principle that people should not deceive others and, further, that spying is deception. Through reasoning, she may come to the conclusion that what the principal has asked her to do is spying. Of course, this leaves Marilyn with another problem: how to tell her principal that his plan is unethical.

■ confronting, not evading,
   problems

It is easy to be brave from a safe distance.

—Aesop

■ Courage   To feel, to know, and to reason are not enough. To be ethical, we must act, and action sometimes takes courage. To be ethically correct often requires the willpower to act in what we perceive to be the right way rather than in the comfortable way. Frequently, when confronted with a seemingly no-win dilemma like Marilyn's, we tend to ignore it in the hope that it will simply go away. However, as the theologian Harvey Cox sees it, "Not to decide is to decide." Among other things, Marilyn will have to find a way to tell her principal that she simply cannot be a part of his secret reporting network. Besides courage, this will require tact.

■ acting with sensitivity

■ Interpersonal Skills   Acting on ethical principles demands sensitivity and courage. Therefore, teachers need the communications skills to deal sensitively with issues that demand great tact. They need to be able to call up the right words, with the right feeling and tone, and to address the issue at hand openly and honestly.

Ethical Dilemmas in Teaching

Although teachers spend most of their professional lives working with students in an instructional manner, sometimes ethical concerns break in and demand their attention. Recently, as teacher education students interviewed practicing teachers, they asked them to describe an ethical situation they had encountered in the last few years. The two cases that follow are based on those interviews.

As you read each case, take time to reflect carefully on it. As you work through these situations, keep in mind the six characteristics described by Kenneth Howe. Also, discuss these cases with other people. We often see much more in a situation involving ethics and recognize many other possible courses of action once we have talked to others about it.

Case Study

■ drugs in the classroom

A Big Deal or a Little Fudge?

Recently, drugs have plagued your community, and increasingly they are coming into the schools. You are a sixth-grade teacher, and there has been only sporadic evidence of drugs in your building. On the other hand, your principal has been making what seems to you a big deal out of very little in his crusade to stamp out drugs in "his" elementary school. He has threatened the student body, first-graders through sixth-graders, in a special assembly about what will happen to them if they are caught with drugs of any kind. Most of your in-service training time this year has been taken up with the subject of drugs. You are yourself concerned about the misuse of drugs in our society. However, you, like most of the other teachers, find the principal's preoccupation with drugs overzealous and slightly laughable, and you are afraid of what will happen to the first offender he catches.

Coming from lunch, you see Alan, one of your sixth-graders, showing two of his friends a plastic bag containing what appear to be three or four marijuana joints. Startled, but unsure that you have actually seen what he has, Alan shoves the bag into his pants pocket. You act as if nothing has happened and usher the boys into class. To gain time to think, you set the students to work on a composition.

Alan is a kid with a spotty record in the school. His family life is rumored to be rather chaotic, but he has behaved well in your class. You have never seen the slightest evidence that he has been high in school. Knowing Alan, you guess he got the dope from one of his brothers and brought it to school to impress his friends. On the other hand, you could be wrong, and the situation could be much more serious. One thing you are sure of is that if you report what you saw to the principal, as you are expected to, he will move in on Alan like a crazed SWAT team. As you mull all this over, Alan and his friends are nervously watching you and anxiously looking back and forth at one another. Then, suddenly, Alan gets up, comes to your desk, and asks if he can go to the boys' room. What do you do? ■

Case Study

Righting Wrongs?

Donald Mitchell is a veteran history teacher in your high school, and he has "ruled the roost" in the department for the past fifteen years. Many current and former advanced-placement (AP) and honors students adore him. They find him exceedingly challenging, and they claim that his teaching prepares them for the rigors of college.

Apart from his senior AP classes, Mr. Mitchell teaches two sections of American government to tenth-grade students. A number of the students in those two classes have individualized education programs (IEPs). He publicly claims skepticism about many of these students' learning disabilities, doing grudgingly what he has to do to comply with the IEPs. (Learn more about learning disabilities and IEPs in the chapter entitled "Who Are Today's Students in a Diverse Society?")

You have often heard Mr. Mitchell complain about "lowering standards of educational excellence" when he sits with his cronies in the school lunchroom. He does not hesitate to announce to the others about what he sees wrong with the school administration, the student body, and on occasion, even faculty from other departments. His latest pet peeve is the "laxness" with which the English department teaches writing, so he designed a strict procedure for writing his history papers. You have often found Mr. Mitchell to be boorish, but you reasoned that his behavior and opinions are his own prerogative. After all, you think to yourself, his teaching approaches are really a matter of academic freedom.

■ academic freedom or spiteful behavior?

One afternoon, one of your students comes to class visibly upset. Janelle is one of your more challenging students. She has had a few minor run-ins with the vice-principal, and she does not demonstrate much interest in academics. You often have been frustrated by what you see as her lack of motivation and effort. Privately, you ask her what is wrong. She tells you that she has just left Mr. Mitchell's class where she received a paper that was given a D−. You listen to her, reluctant to talk about the grading policies of another teacher. Yet, after calming down, the student tells you that it wasn't the grade itself that made her so upset, but how the teacher returned the papers. She claims that Mr. Mitchell stood at the front of the class stating that some of the students' papers followed the proper format. Others, he sneered, were so riddled with errors and so poorly written that the only use for any of them would be to line a kitty litter bin. He added that he designed his format so that some students would learn to write correctly, but that many of them apparently could not or would not even follow his simple format. With that statement, he scattered those papers on the floor. He passed the satisfactory papers to the rest of the students, and when the rest of the students, all inclusion students, were left without their papers, he glanced at them and said, "Well, go on. They're right there if you want them." And he pointed to the floor.

Janelle tells you that she waited until class was dismissed to pick up her paper from the floor. You excuse Janelle so that she can go to the girls' room, and then you ask to speak to another student who is in that same class. When you ask him, again privately, if anything unusual happened in his history class, the student replies it was a regular class. You're still curious, so you ask him how Mr. Mitchell returned the papers. The student looks at you quizzically and says, "How'd he return the papers? The same way you do. He walked around the room and handed them back to us."

You're very disturbed by the story Janelle told you, and you want to do something to intervene. Yet, the other student's report makes you hesitant. What if nothing unusual did occur? Making an enemy of Mr. Mitchell would not be the politically savvy thing to do, and Janelle, you know, can be difficult at times. Maybe she was just angry at the teacher for some reason and wanted to cause trouble, but what if that story was true? What should you do? ■

Pause and Reflect

1 ▶ Do these situations really involve ethics? Do they involve unfairness or a breach of ethical standards?

2 ▶ Are there complexities that cause ethical conflicts? If so, what are they?

3 ▶ What are the consequences of various courses of action?

4 ▶ Who needs to be considered as you try to decide on courses of action?

5 ▶ What, specifically, would you say or do?

The Everyday Ethics of Teaching

As we hope the preceding case studies make clear, serious ethical issues strongly influence the lives of teachers. Few teachers get very far into their careers without having to deal with situations like these. But these cases do not exhaust the ethical responsibilities of the teacher. There are everyday events that occur in the classroom and school life that have an even greater ethical impact on students.

▪ three ways to influence ethically

Although it is clear that parents have the primary responsibility for the ethical training of their children, schools do have an impact on the character and moral lives of students. (We will discuss character education in the chapter entitled "How Should Education Be Reformed?") Classrooms and schoolyards overflow with issues of right and wrong: a student submits a report that is downloaded from an Internet site; a group of girls start a rumor that another girl is pregnant; a teacher continually and harshly picks on the same student. Events like these send strong ethical messages to students. How the teacher and the rest of the school respond to this ethical dimension of schooling is what we refer to as *the everyday ethics of teaching*. In particular, teachers ethically influence students in three ways: by example, by the classroom climate they create, and by the dialogue they establish.

First, the *personal example* provided by teachers includes the care and manner with which they do their work, how they treat students and others, and their use of examples from history and literature to enrich the ethical understandings of students.

Second, teachers can establish a beneficial *classroom climate* by creating an environment of safety and trust where students are free from fear and ridicule, where a spirit of cooperation and friendly competition prevails, and where students are working hard and feeling the satisfaction of learning.

Living up to basic ethical standards in the classroom—discipline, tolerance, honesty—is one of the important ways children learn how to function in society at large.

—ELOISE SALHOLZ

Third, teachers can establish an *ethical dialogue* in their classrooms by discussing with students the core ethical values such as honesty, respect for others, and responsibility that come into play not only in the study of literature and history, but especially in the real life events of the school.

The everyday ethics of teaching, then, means *doing the job as it ought to be done*. It means realizing the preciousness of the minutes and hours that you spend with students and making sure they do not waste their time with you.

Codes of Professional Ethics

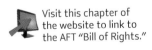

Visit this chapter of the website to link to the AFT "Bill of Rights."

Teachers do not struggle alone when they face ethical issues. Besides their own understanding, reasoning, courage, and other qualities, they have the support of a professional group.* Professional groups, such as those of doctors, architects, and teachers, have special obligations to their clients. Because of their special knowledge and power, they have an ethical responsibility to those they serve.

---

* The extent to which teaching is or is not a profession is an important question and is the subject of the chapter entitled "What Does It Mean to Be a Professional?"

The way teachers do their work is regulated, then, both by their personal ethical standards and by those of the teaching profession. Whereas some professions have formulated their own universal code of ethics (like the Hippocratic Oath taken by all medical doctors), there are several published codes of ethics for teachers. The best known is the code of the National Education Association (NEA). The American Federation of Teachers (AFT) has a "Bill of Rights and Responsibilities for Learning" that deals with the ethical treatment both teachers and students should receive. (You can link to the NEA and AFT statements from the website for this book.) In recent years a number of state departments of education have also developed codes to govern the work of their teachers. Among them is the code in the accompanying box, developed by the Alaska Professional Teaching Practices Commission.

Code of Ethics and Teaching Standards

In fulfilling obligations to students, an educator:

- May not deliberately distort, suppress, or deny access to curricular materials or educational information in order to promote the personal view, interest, or goal of the educator.

- Shall make reasonable effort to protect students from conditions harmful to learning or to health and safety.

- May not engage in physical abuse of a student or sexual conduct with a student and shall report to the commission knowledge of such an act by an educator.

- May not expose a student to unnecessary embarrassment or disparagement.

- May not harass, discriminate against, or grant a discriminatory advantage to a student on the grounds of race, color, creed, sex, national origin, marital status, political or religious beliefs, physical or mental conditions, family, social, or cultural background, or sexual orientation; shall make reasonable effort to assure that a student is protected from harassment or discrimination on these grounds; and may not engage in a course of conduct that would encourage a reasonable student to develop a prejudice on these grounds.

- May not use professional relationships with students for private advantage or gain.

- Shall keep in confidence information that has been obtained in the course of providing professional service, unless disclosure serves a compelling professional purpose or is required by law.

- Shall accord just and equitable treatment to all students as they exercise their educational rights and responsibilities.

In fulfilling obligations to the public, an educator:

- Shall take reasonable precautions to distinguish between the educator's personal views and those of any educational institution or organization with which the educator is affiliated.

- Shall cooperate in the statewide student assessment system by safeguarding and maintaining the confidentiality of test materials and information.

- May not use institutional privileges for private gain, to promote political candidates, or for partisan political activities.

- May not accept a gratuity, gift, or favor that might influence or appear to influence professional judgment, and may not offer a gratuity, gift, or favor to obtain special advantage.

- May not knowingly withhold or misrepresent material information in communicating with the school board regarding a matter before the board for its decision.

- May not use or allow the use of district resources for private purposes not related to the district programs and operation.

In fulfilling obligations to the profession, an educator:

- May not, on the basis of race, color, creed, sex, age, national origin, marital status, political or religious beliefs, physical condition, family, social or cultural background, or sexual orientation, deny to a colleague a professional benefit, advantage, or participation in any professional organization, and may not discriminate in employment practice, assignment, or personnel evaluation.

- Shall accord just and equitable treatment of all members of the profession in the exercise of their professional rights and responsibilities.

- May not use coercive means or promise special treatment in order to influence professional decisions of colleagues.

- May not sexually harass a fellow employee.

- Shall withhold and safeguard information acquired about colleagues in the course of employment, unless disclosure serves a compelling professional purpose.

- Shall provide, upon the request of the affected party, a written statement of specific reasons for recommendations that led to the denial of increments, significant changes in employment, or termination of employment.

- May not deliberately misrepresent the educator's or another's professional qualifications.

- May not falsify a document, or make a misrepresentation on a matter related to licensure, employment evaluation, test results, or professional duties.

- May not intentionally make a false or malicious statement about a colleague's professional performance or conduct.

- May not intentionally file a false or malicious complaint with the commission.

- May not seek reprisal against any individual who has filed a complaint, provided testimony, or given other assistance in support of a complaint filed with the commission.

- Shall cooperate fully and honestly in investigations and hearings of the commission;

- May not unlawfully breach a professional employment contract.

- Shall conduct professional business through appropriate channels.

- May not assign tasks to unqualified personnel.

- May not continue in or seek professional employment while unfit due to (A) use of drugs or alcohol that impairs the educator's competence or the safety of students or colleagues; (B) physical or mental disability that impairs the educator's competence or the safety of students or colleagues.

- May not interfere with a colleague's exercise of political or citizenship rights and responsibilities.*

* The authors slightly modified the form of this code of ethics for purpose of clarity.

A third example is the Boston University Educator's Affirmation, which is taken voluntarily in a special and quite popular ceremony, typically in the junior year, during or after student teaching. Run by the education students, the ritual marks their commitment to the high ideals and standards of the profession. In this, it is similar to the Hippocratic Oath taken by physicians.

Boston University Educator's Affirmation

■ one school's code

I dedicate myself to the life of an educator, to laying the living foundations upon which successor generations must continue to build their lives.

I dedicate myself to the advancement of learning, for I know that without it our successors will lack both the vision and the power to build well.

I dedicate myself to the cultivation of character, for I know that humanity cannot flourish without courage, compassion, honesty, and trust.

I dedicate myself to the advancement of my own learning and to the cultivation of my own character, for I know that I must bear witness in my own life to the ideals that I have dedicated myself to promote in others.

In the presence of this gathering, I bind myself to this affirmation.[3]

▶ The Teacher and the Law

■ rise in litigation

Once upon a time, teachers were like the kings and queens of small kingdoms. Their authority was wide, and their decisions were rarely questioned. Students who would not or could not do the work were "held back" or told not to come back. Students who did not conform to the teacher's standards of behavior were expelled. Students and their parents tended to view education as a special opportunity that put definite responsibilities on their shoulders. In fact, much of the legal authority of teachers was based on the principle of ***in loco parentis,*** or "in the place of parents." In other words, it was generally agreed that teachers acted as parental figures while students were in their care. For that reason, teachers' leeway in treating students was fairly broad and they could make decisions about students, based on what they thought was in the best interest of the student or students.

In the last few decades, however, the attitude toward schooling in our country has changed. The authority of the adults in general and teachers in particular has eroded noticeably, and students are often more fixated on their rights than on their responsibilities. There are many reasons for this change, but suffice it to say that we are a very litigious society. Our country has more lawyers per capita than any other nation in the world. And our increasing tendency to use the courts to settle differences and conflicts has had its impact on the work of the teacher.

The video case *Legal and Ethical Dimensions of Teaching* shows a round-table discussion of real teachers discussing the legal situations they face. As you watch the clips and study the artifacts in the case, reflect upon the following questions:

1. Which of the legal issues listed in this chapter and discussed in the video case are you most concerned that you might face as a teacher?
2. How did this video help you feel more prepared to cope with the legal issues involved in teaching?

The new presence of the law in educational matters is, like many changes, a mixed bag. On the one hand, teachers are often cautioned to remember that students are autonomous, with individual rights that continue to exist even when students pass through schoolhouse doors and are under the supervision of teachers. As a result, teachers are required to be much more deliberate and cautious in their dealings with students to prevent an infringement of students' rights than they were in earlier decades. On the other hand, it can be argued that our new consciousness of the teacher's legal responsibilities and our heightened sense of students' rights have helped rid schools of dictatorial practices by teachers and administrators, the systematic denial of certain rights to students, and the abusive use of corporal punishment.

■ law = collective judgment

Woodrow Wilson once said, "The law that will work is merely the summing up in legislative form of the moral judgment that the community has already reached." Our laws, then, are our collective social judgments and decisions about what is fair. Laws differ from codes of ethics, though, because they apply to all the people, not to a particular group like doctors or teachers. Laws are public, whereas ethics can reflect one's private standards. And laws have judicial teeth, whereas codes of ethics do not. Rarely is a teacher suspended, or expelled, or even sanctioned by the teaching profession for violating general codes of ethics.[4] However, teachers are regularly affected by the law and are occasionally brought to court. The next sections examine some specific areas of law that can affect your work as a teacher.

The Teacher and Due Process

- A young junior high teacher, on a lark, changes his "image." He comes to school one Monday morning sporting a shaved head and a diamond stud earring. He is fired on Tuesday.
- A teacher gives a speech at a meeting of the local gay and lesbian alliance. The newspaper runs a story on the event, and the superintendent asks her to resign quietly.
- A business education teacher who has been teaching for three years has been visited by administrators only twice during that period. He loves teaching and was recently told by his principal that he was a "shoo-in for tenure." Instead of getting the expected letter from the superintendent outlining the upcoming tenure review process, he receives a dismissal notice in May claiming that his teaching is not up to the district's standards.

due process = fairness

All three of these examples represent violations of the teachers' rights to due process. Due process is one of the most important principles embedded in our nation's laws. The essential meaning of **due process** in education is that fairness should be rendered and teachers' rights as individuals should not be violated. Many of the most influential court decisions concerning education, teachers, and the law concern fundamental issues of due process.

Due process protections come directly from two amendments to our Constitution. The Fifth Amendment states that "no person shall . . . be deprived of life, liberty, or property, without due process of law." The Fourteenth Amendment adds, "nor shall any State deprive any person of life, liberty, or property, without due process of law."

The Fourteenth Amendment goes on to stipulate that no person should be denied "the equal protection of the law." Legal rulings related to due process in education often reflect the requirement that individuals be treated equally in their education or by school officials.

substantive due process

■ **Two Types of Due Process**   When judging the fairness of an action, there are two due process concerns. One, *substantive due process,* has to do with the issue itself. The other, *procedural due process,* concerns the fairness of the process followed. For example, if a teacher is fired because he wears a nose ring, this is an issue of substantive due process: Is this matter substantive enough in this particular circumstance to deny a teacher employment? What is a fair decision in this matter? Procedural due process would involve how the case is handled. Suppose the teacher, after hearing several rumors that the nose ring is irking the superintendent, gets a curt letter saying his "services are no longer needed." Is this process fair? Has the teacher had a fair chance to defend himself?

The precise meaning of procedural due process changes from state to state, but the Supreme Court decision in *Goldberg* v. *Kelly* (1970) indicated that "the minimum procedural safeguards . . . demanded by rudimentary due process" would include the following:

procedural safeguards

- The opportunity to be heard at a reasonable time and place
- Timely and adequate notice giving details of the reasons for the proposed suspension or dismissal
- An effective opportunity to defend oneself, including oral presentation of evidence and arguments
- An opportunity to confront and cross-examine witnesses
- The right to retain an attorney
- A decision resting solely on the legal rules and evidence adduced at the hearing

- A statement of the reasons for the determination and the evidence relied on
- An impartial decision maker[5]

Procedural due process exists so that individual teachers and students are protected from arbitrary actions against them. The principle of due process and these guidelines reach into many corners of the teacher's life, as we will see in the upcoming sections.

Contracts, Tenure, and Dismissal

Some of the most fundamental legal issues have to do with the legalities of employment. When, for instance, is a teacher actually hired? How does a teacher know he or she has an actual teaching position? What does having tenure mean for a teacher?

Teachers are not self-employed; they are employees of a school board or, in the case of a private school, of a board of trustees. As employees of a governing body, teachers must be familiar with and abide by the stipulations of the contract issued to them by the school board. If teachers do not fulfill the requirements of the contract, they are at risk of losing their jobs.

■ **Contracts to Teach**   Imagine the following situation. You are a recent college graduate, newly licensed to teach, and you are actively interviewing for teaching positions. Your interview at the Long Meadow school district goes extremely well, and the superintendent tells you she would like you to join the faculty. She tells you that she is going to recommend your hiring to the school board, telling you that for all intents and purposes, you should consider that you have a teaching position, since the board usually votes to approve the superintendent's recommendations. You tell her that you would like to join the faculty, accepting her verbal offer.

Several weeks go by, and you hear nothing from the school district. In the meantime, you are invited to interview at the Centerville school district. When you interview there, you realize it is *the* ideal school district for you. The school administrators seem equally impressed with you, and in several days, the superintendent calls and offers you the position. Although you want to accept immediately, you ask the superintendent for a day to think over the offer. In fact, what you really want to do is find out your status at the Long Meadow school district. Do you really have a job there? If you accept the offer at Centerville, are you violating some legal obligations to the Long Meadow school district?

■ a contract . . . or not?

The simple answer is, it all depends on whether you have a legal contract for employment. A **contract** is a binding agreement between two or more persons or parties. It indicates the rights and responsibilities of each party to the agreement, and all teachers, new or old, sign a contract with their Board of Education or trustees. Contracts differ from district to district and state to state, but generally, contracts include the teacher's salary, course or teaching assignments or instructional areas, the maximum class size, length of school day and school year, and grievance procedures. A **grievance** is the formal expression of a complaint about an unsatisfactory working condition. Grievances typically concern disputes over working conditions; when a person files a grievance, he or she usually argues that the working condition was in violation of the teacher's contract. Additionally, contracts generally indicate if the local teachers' association or union is the official bargaining agent for teachers.

Contracts are for a set period of time. Most new teachers work on a contract that has to be renewed annually if the teacher is to stay on. Even teachers on tenure (to be discussed shortly) sign a yearly contract stipulating the terms of employment. Occasionally teachers work under a **continuing contract,** which states that its terms will remain in force until the teacher is given notice that the contract will be terminated on a particular date.

■ elements of legal contracts

To be considered a legally enforceable document, a contract must do the following:

1. Have a lawful subject matter
2. Represent a meeting of the minds of both parties
3. Include an exchange of something of value (called a *consideration*)
4. Be entered into by parties who are competent to do so
5. Be written in proper form (instead of in vague terms such as "pay the teacher what he or she is worth")

In addition, the school board must act officially to ratify a teacher's contract. Many people assume that contracts must be written. In fact, unless state law requires a written contract, an oral contract that includes all legal requirements can also be legally binding.[6]

So in the above scenario, unless all of the conditions were included in your discussion with the Long Meadow superintendent and the school board acted upon, or *ratified,* the superintendent's recommendation to hire you, you did not have a legally binding offer. Therefore, you could accept the Centerville offer without hesitation.

■ breach of contract

What if that scenario were altered slightly? What if you had signed a contract for the Long Meadow school district and then accepted the Centerville offer? In that instance, you could be held liable for **breach of contract.** A legal contract is binding on both sides—the school district's and the teacher's. If either party violates conditions of the contract, the contract itself is said to have been breached, and the other party can sue for damages.

When an injured party successfully sues the other party for breach of contract, the court may order that the contract be fulfilled, that the injured party receive monetary damages, or both. For instance, the district may have to rehire a fired teacher and pay damages, or a teacher who walks away from a job may have to pay the district's cost of finding a replacement. In addition, anytime a teacher breaches a contract, his or her professional reputation will likely be tarnished. So before you accept a position, you should study the contract carefully and ask about anything unclear to you. That contract will govern many of the important details of your life as a teacher.

Visit the website to link to more information about tenure.

■ **Tenure**   Imagine a few years have passed since you accepted the Centerville position. At what point are you granted **tenure,** or what some states call *continuing contract status?* New teachers are hired on a probationary period, often three years, so that the school district can ensure that the nontenured teacher can teach well enough to be granted permanent faculty status. State law determines when a teacher is eligible for tenure and outlines the requirements for earning tenure or continuing contract status. Some states require that the school board take some positive action to grant the teacher tenure status; in other states, the teacher automatically is granted tenure when he or she successfully completes the probationary period.

■ long-term rights

What does possessing tenure actually mean for a teacher? The word *tenure* comes from the Latin root "to hold," as in "hold that job." So if you become a tenured teacher in the Centerville school district, you are entitled to contract renewal every year. The general purpose of tenure was nicely stated by the Supreme Court of Pennsylvania in 1957: tenure helps to maintain "an adequate and competent teaching staff, free from political or arbitrary interference." In addition, tenure allows "capable and competent teachers" to feel secure and to perform their duties efficiently.[7] Tenure guarantees your position as a teacher in the school district, but does *not* mean that you are guaranteed to have the exact same teaching assignment every year. A teacher can be reassigned to teach second grade after being a fourth-grade teacher for years, or a school district can reassign a tenured teacher to another school in the district.

Tenure is an issue about which both the general public and teachers often have strong views and, just as often, much misinformation. Contrary to the views of many, poorly performing, tenured teachers *can* be fired. There are clear sets of procedures administrators can follow to provide the evidence necessary for dismissal. On the other hand, following the procedures takes a good deal of time and energy if a solid case is to be made. As we discuss next, a school district needs to follow a stricter set of guidelines for disciplining or dismissing a tenured teacher than for teachers who have not yet earned tenure. For this reason, some education critics and school reformers advocate the elimination of tenure, but it is doubtful that will happen in the foreseeable future.

■ **Dismissal**   Occasionally teachers fail; they simply cannot handle the job. Or they make a big mistake, such as striking a child in anger. Occasionally, too, teachers have "philosophical differences" with administrators, sometimes further complicated by mild or severe cases of "personality conflict." These situations and many more may result in an attempt to dismiss a teacher. Dismissal procedures are covered by the laws in each state, and those procedures must follow due process.

■ special conditions

If a school district decides in the middle of a school year (and therefore in the middle of a contract) to dismiss an untenured teacher, the teacher always has a right to a full hearing and due process. On the other hand, if the district decides not to extend a second- or third-year contract to a new teacher, as in the example earlier in this chapter, the situation is less clear. Although in some states an untenured teacher who is not being rehired can demand a hearing, in most states the school district does not have to justify its reasons for not rehiring a teacher on probationary status.

■ tenure as "property"

For tenured teachers, the legal situation is different. Tenure is protected under the Fourteenth Amendment and is considered part of the teacher's "property." Tenured teachers have the expectation that they will have continued employment, so that is considered a "property interest." In a sense, the tenured teacher has "earned" and "owns" the job, and he or she can be separated from it only under very special circumstances. In light of that fact, a teacher can call on the full protection of the law, as she or he would if someone were trying to take away a home or a car. To justify dismissal, the school district must prove that the tenured teacher has violated some provision of the tenure law.

■ dismissal "for cause"

In most states, a tenured teacher can be dismissed only "for cause." States vary concerning what they consider due cause for dismissal, but most require a good reason that will withstand the scrutiny of the courts, such as sexually molesting a student, gross negligence, or gross incompetence. In some states, the law stipulates that a tenured teacher cannot be dismissed without being given opportunity to correct his or her deficiencies. In those instances, the courts usually determine what is "remediable," or faults that could be corrected by the teacher. So, if a teacher demonstrates poor classroom management, that can be seen as something correctable, and most courts would not allow a tenured teacher to be dismissed before he or she was warned about the management problems and given a chance to correct them. Certain actions, however, are so unprofessional that the damage is "irremediable." Being convicted of a crime or engaging in sexual relations with a student are considered irremediable.[8] In those instances, the school district is under no legal requirement to help the teacher correct his or her behavior and dismissal procedures can begin immediately.

■ conduct unbecoming

The most common reasons for dismissal include immorality, insubordination, incompetence, and "conduct unbecoming a teacher." The last reason is a fairly vague term that allows schools some leeway in dismissing a teacher whose behavior is unethical, but may not be classified under the other more specific causes such as insubordination or incompetence. For example, sometimes "conduct unbecoming" means a teacher has used the classroom for purposes other than teaching. One teacher was dismissed because he used class time to advocate that the students, their families, and friends vote for a particular candidate running for superintendent of schools.[9] In another case, a teacher was dismissed for tampering with the school telephone system and eavesdropping on telephone conversations.

It is the responsibility of the courts to weigh the individual situation, to review the law on the subject, and to determine whether the case justifies dismissal.

■ reductions for economic reasons

■ **Reduction in Force**   In most instances, then, a tenured teacher can only be dismissed for wrong behavior or incompetent teaching. The one exception to that is if the school district needs to eliminate some teaching positions for economic reasons. Sometimes the courts allow schools to dismiss teachers as a result of curricular reorganization. For example, a school board might decide to drop its classical language department. Most commonly, however, reductions occur when the school district has a drop in student enrollment and does not need all the teachers that it employs, or experiences a budgetary shortfall that requires teacher dismissals. Under those conditions, a school district can lay off tenured teachers, and the decision about which tenured teachers to dismiss is usually made on the basis of seniority. Called **reduction in force**, or "riffing" in slang, it was common in the 1970s and 1980s, when student enrollments were shrinking, but riffing is rarely used today, except in the case of a district budget crisis.

Case Study

The Teacher and Liability

Lori Spinelli, a middle school Spanish teacher, often employed cooperative learning activities in her lessons so students would have more opportunities to practice speaking and listening to each other. Although the students worked together, Lori often circulated around the room to converse with each small group, using the week's vocabulary words in her brief conversations with them. One afternoon, while she was working with a small group in the front of the classroom, she heard a scream from the back. One of her students, Jared, was writhing in pain on the floor. He had tried to show his group members a certain dance move and had dislocated his shoulder. Later that afternoon, Lori replayed that class in her mind, feeling more and more dread, worrying and wondering about whether she would be held liable for Jared's injury. True, she had been in the classroom, but Lori realized that while she was talking to the group in the front of the room, her back had been turned to most of the students in the room, including Jared. What if Jared's parents held her and the school district liable for their son's injury? ■

Teachers' Liability

Liability means blame, as in "The teacher can be held liable for the student's dislocated shoulder," and other accidents and mistakes—that is, the teacher behaved negligently or intentionally in a way that allowed the injury to happen.

■ areas of liability

Teachers are responsible for ensuring the safety and well-being of their students in their own classrooms and work spaces and in the activities they oversee. This includes fieldtrips and after-school clubs and activities, such as band, sports, and play rehearsals. Teachers are also liable if they do nothing when they observe a student in some potentially dangerous act that eventually turns out to be harmful. Turning one's back on misbehavior in no way lessens this responsibility. Teachers can be held liable for acts of omission.

So Lori has good reason to be concerned. A court trying to determine if her supervision was adequate would focus on whether Lori could have reasonably prevented Jared from getting injured or whether his injury was something that could not have been reasonably anticipated by her.

■ a failure to supervise

Two court cases help shed light on the extent of a teacher's liability. In one case (*Sheehan v. St. Peter's Catholic School,* 1971), an eighth-grader was injured when her teacher took a group of students outside to watch a baseball game, then went back inside the school. In the teacher's absence, a group of students began throwing pebbles at the spectators, and Margaret Sheehan was hit in the eye with a pebble, sustaining a serious eye injury. In that case, the court ruled that the school did not take reasonable precaution to prevent student injury. It is impossible, after all, for a teacher to monitor students if the teacher is inside while the students are outside. The teacher should have anticipated that in leaving the group of students alone, unsupervised, a dangerous situation could develop.[10]

So does that mean, then, that teachers need to be directly observing students at all times? Does it mean that a teacher like Lori would be considered liable for her student's dislocated shoulder? Maybe not.

■ can't supervise everywhere

In another case concerning liability, teachers took a group of junior high and high school students to visit Chicago's Natural History Museum (*Mancha v. Field Museum of Natural History,* 1971). When the group arrived at the museum, the teachers allowed students to visit the exhibition halls on their own. One student, while in an exhibition hall apart from the teachers, was approached and then beaten up by a group of teenagers who did not attend the same school. In this case, the court ruled that the risk of student injury in a museum usually would be "minimal," so it was an unreasonable expectation that teachers should have been able to foresee and prevent the student's beating. Furthermore, the court indicated that expecting teachers to supervise directly every student on the field trip would place such an unreasonable expectation on teachers that few would plan field trips or other educationally valuable activities for their students.[11]

So, even though teachers are required to exercise prudence and foresight in their supervision of students, the courts expect *reasonable* prudence and foresight. Some student injuries are accidents or unforeseen injuries, and in those cases, the teacher is not held responsible.

■ **Liability Precautions**   Indeed, when teachers can demonstrate they have taken reasonable precautions to prevent student injury, courts have not found teachers liable for student injuries. To show that they have been "reasonably prudent," teachers need to be able to demonstrate that:

- They made a reasonable attempt to anticipate dangerous situations.
- They provided proper supervision.
- They took precautions.
- They established rules.
- They gave a warning to minimize the chances of students getting hurt.

■ liability insurance

Because teachers are vulnerable to legal suit, it is important that they be covered by some form of liability insurance. However, in recent years, many teachers have been scared into buying more insurance than they need or, more commonly, into buying insurance when they are already covered by school district insurance policies. Therefore, the new teacher should check on-the-job coverage with the district's personnel director before beginning work.

Certain school activities can be dangerous . . . and an area of potential teacher liability.
(© Sven Martson/The Image Works CMTN2262)

■ automobile liability

One area in which experts claim teachers are particularly at risk is automobile liability. Often teachers volunteer to take students in their own cars to a sports game or on a fieldtrip. Even if teachers have personal insurance, they often do not have enough to cover liability claims if a serious accident happens. Before taking students in a private car, the teacher needs to be sure that the district's insurance policy covers such cases or that his or her own policy is adequate.

To Lori Spinelli's great relief, no charges were brought against her. Lori had established an orderly classroom, and she was in the room when Jared was injured. Other students indicated that Ms. Spinelli had taught them rules of behavior and of courtesy, especially since they would often be working in small groups. Jared was, in general, a well-behaved student, so there would be no reason for Lori to expect that he would decide to jump up and show a dance move to his group members. Finally, her lesson for the class, presenting and practicing written dialogues for their partners, would not be considered a dangerous situation for students. The mere fact that her back was turned to Jared's group wouldn't be grounds to hold her liable. No teacher can face all of the students all of the time. Lori's established good teaching practices and her sound judgment demonstrated her competence. In another situation, in which just a few of those factors were different, a teacher may have been held responsible.

In all these issues of liability, it is important for the teacher to use good judgment. Accidents often "just happen," and there may be no liability. As noted earlier, if a school injury results in a legal suit, the courts will try to determine if the teacher was providing reasonable care and, in general, was acting in a prudent and careful manner.

Reporting Child Abuse

Visit the website to link to more information about reporting child abuse.

In addition to preventing harm to students under their supervision, teachers also have a legal responsibility to safeguard students from abuse and neglect at the hands of their parents and other adults. Teachers in every state are required by law to report suspected child abuse or neglect. The laws vary somewhat from state to state, but they all include two or more of the following elements in their definition of abuse and neglect: physical injury, mental or emotional injury, and sexual molestation or exploitation.[12] If teachers suspect that a student has experienced *any* of those injuries, they *must* report their suspicions of child abuse and neglect to the appropriate authorities. Schools typically have detailed instructions in their faculty handbooks about how to report such suspicions. Additionally, principals or other administrators will often remind teachers of those procedures, so that all teachers understand explicitly the necessary reporting procedures.

A teacher does not have to be *certain* that a child is being abused before he or she makes a report to the principal. Child abuse is clearly one of those areas where it is better to act and be wrong. If a teacher has a reasonable cause to suspect that a child is being abused, that is sufficient grounds for making a report. To protect a teacher from reaction to an incorrect report or from the anger of an offending parent, the reporting is kept confidential. Further, teachers are granted immunity from accusations of slander or any possible libel suit. Without such protection, many teachers would hesitate to report their suspicions. (For a more detailed discussion of child abuse, see the chapter entitled "What Social Problems Affect Today's Students?")

Self-Defense

Schools are very crowded places, and they are crowded, by definition, with immature individuals. Thus, it is not at all surprising that conflicts erupt and teach-

Teachers must be vigilant about possible abuse of their students.
(© Bill Aron/PhotoEdit)

ers find themselves encountering hostile behavior. For instance, a teacher may have to break up a playground fight or stop some students from vandalizing another student's locker, or a student may strike a teacher in anger.

■ "reasonable force"

Self-defense is defined broadly here to take in all these situations. In the first two cases, fighting and vandalism, the teacher is expected to intercede in the interest of safety. In a fight, for instance, the teacher must act to stop the students from hurting one another. Strong words usually are effective, but sometimes the teacher must become physically involved. The operating principle here is "reasonable force." If a teacher uses reasonable force, and if, in the process of stopping the fight and separating the students, a student suffers an injury (say, a strained wrist or dislocated arm), the courts typically will find that the teacher is not liable. If the same injuries resulted from a fight the teacher did not act to stop, he or she may be held liable.

In more obvious cases of self-defense, a student threatens or actually strikes a teacher, and the principle of reasonable force applies here, too. What constitutes reasonable force is generally a matter of common sense, but the heat of the moment can make good judgment difficult. In one case, a male seventh-grader who weighed 110 pounds struck a 220-pound coach. The coach grabbed the boy, lifted him off the ground, and threw him against a wall, breaking the child's back. When brought to court, the teacher-coach claimed self-defense. He lost—big time. Usually in the court's view, it is the teacher's responsibility to keep a level head.

■ assault

■ Assault and Battery A teacher's recourse against an abusive student is governed by assault and battery laws. In legal terms, *assault* has come to mean a threat to do harm. Threats should always be taken seriously and reported to the principal, but their legal status depends very much on the student's ability to carry through on the threat. An angry fourth-grader's threat to "do something terrible to you" does not have the same status as a high school junior's threat to blow up your classroom.

■ battery

Battery means a willful attack on another that results in harm. Being unintentionally knocked to the hall floor by a rushing student is not battery. (It may, however, call for some disciplinary action by the school.) Being intentionally pushed by a student or a parent is an entirely different matter and makes the pusher immediately liable.

Incidents of assault or battery should be promptly reported and disciplinary action demanded or legal charges filed. Often teachers, particularly new teachers, are hesitant about making a fuss or turning offending students in to the proper school authorities. But verbal abuse and physical violence have no place in our elementary and secondary schools.

Freedom of Expression

One of the most treasured rights of American citizens is the freedom of expression. Freedom of expression includes symbolic expression and verbal or written expression. For teachers, freedom of expression also subsumes **academic freedom,** the freedom of a teacher to select course materials and to teach in a way he or she thinks fit. Before we go on, take a moment to consider your ideas about freedom of expression.

Pause and Reflect

1 ▶ Is the freedom of expression limitless? Can a teacher say anything or teach anything, claiming it is his or her right to free expression?

2 ▶ To what degree do you think that you, as a potential teacher, should have the right to select your own course materials or to provide information to students?

3 ▶ Are there any instances in which you think a teacher's freedom of expression should be limited?

◼ Pickering's free speech case

Until about forty years ago, teachers who publicly criticized administrators' decisions or school board policies received little sympathy from judges. The attitude of the courts was that judges had no business interfering in the legitimate affairs of the schools. Things changed, though, as a result of Marvin Pickering.

Pickering, a high school English teacher, wrote a long and sarcastic letter in the local newspaper about his superintendent and school board. He accused them of, among other things, taking the local taxpayers "to the cleaners," making excessive expenditures on athletics, and forcing teachers to live in an atmosphere of totalitarianism. It was later shown that Pickering's information on a number of issues was wrong.

Pickering was fired. He sued for his job, but the original court verdicts upheld the firing.

Pickering's case was appealed before the U.S. Supreme Court in 1968. Because Pickering, an English teacher, made erroneous statements about athletic expenditures and those expenditures were matters of public record, the Court indicated that Pickering did not speak with any greater authority on the matter than any other taxpayer. The Court also found that his comments did not impede his proper performance in the classroom or otherwise interfere with the regular operation of the schools, so the judges reversed the lower courts' ruling and ordered Pickering reinstated and compensated.[13]

◼ *Scoville v. Board of Education*

In effect, the Court said in the *Pickering* decision that society needs to balance the interests of a teacher, as a citizen commenting on issues of public concern, and the interests of the state, as the teacher's employer trying to promote smoothly running schools. So although the Court affirmed the teacher's right to free expression, it pointed out that this First Amendment protection is not an absolute right. A teacher cannot expect to say absolutely anything, then cry out for protection under "freedom of expression." As a U.S. Court of Appeals stated in the 1970s *Scoville* v. *Board of Education* case, "Freedom of speech includes the right to criticize and protest school policies in a nondisruptive manner, but it does not include the use of 'fighting' words or the abuse of superiors with profane and vulgar speech."[14] In many possible situations, such as when teachers become disruptive forces in a school or make irresponsible statements, the courts will not support their expression of their views. For instance, in 1981 the courts ruled against a teacher who had claimed that the racially derogatory comments he made to his principal and assistant principal were constitutionally protected.[15]

The Supreme Court also ruled against teacher John Stroman (*Stroman* v. *Colleton County School District,* 1992) after he circulated a letter harshly critical of school administration. In it, he urged fellow faculty members to stage a "sick out" to show the administrators just how unified the faculty was in their discontent. The Court, however, indicated that urging a "sick out" when individuals were healthy was an appeal for dishonest behavior and conduct unprofessional for teachers.[16]

◼ **Symbolic Expression** Personal expression is not limited to spoken and written words. Dress styles, armbands, and buttons have been used in recent years to "make a statement." Typically the courts support teachers (and students) in these cases of free symbolic expression. A key issue here involves the potential of this type of expression to lead to "substantial disruption" within the school. A school

Reprinted with special permission of King Features Syndicate.

might forbid such symbolic clothing as a teacher's Ku Klux Klan button in a high school with many African American students or students' gang "colors" or jacket insignia if they provoke fighting. These judgments cannot, however, be a matter of a teacher's or an administrator's "taste." Bans on symbolic expression of one's views or preferences must be based on clear indications that the efficiency or safety of the school is endangered.

■ teaching controversial issues

■ **Academic Freedom** A subcategory of freedom of expression, academic freedom, deals largely with issues in the classroom and the teachers' (and students') rights to discuss ideas and read material of their choosing. Academic freedom allows teachers to speak freely about their subject matter, to select reading assignments, and to choose teaching methodologies based on their professional judgment. It is designed to allow experimentation with ideas and to foster an open spirit of inquiry. Academic freedom can meet with opposition when teachers want to discuss controversial or unpopular ideas such as sexual mores, gun control, or abortion. If such issues are a part of the school's curriculum, there is rarely a problem. But when a teacher "adds" them to the curriculum, he or she needs to make a reasonable case that they are relevant to the curriculum. Dismissal for teaching controversial issues may or may not be upheld by the courts. Teaching about volatile issues that may disrupt a particular school, such as homosexuality or the alleged characteristics of different races, is frowned on by the courts. So is teaching controversial material considered unsuitable for the age of the students. In addition, courts have not allowed teachers to use controversial teaching methods that are unsupported by professional opinion or prohibited by reasonable school policy.

Political issues, both local and national, are also points of tension. In the classroom, teachers may discuss current political controversies, but they must deal with them neutrally and in a balanced way. Away from work, advocating a particular cause or political party is fine, but a teacher may not behave as a partisan supporter in the classroom.

■ the *Keefe* case

Particular essays and books that contain sexually explicit material or even words that are offensive to certain members of a community have been a great source of legal controversy in schools. In one important case, *Keefe v. Geanakos* (1969), a Massachusetts English teacher, Robert Keefe, assigned his students an article from the well-respected *Atlantic Monthly* that contained offensive language. Keefe's assignment caused a storm, and he was eventually fired for refusing to agree not to assign the article again. Subsequently, he was reinstated by a circuit court decision because the offending language existed in a number of books already in the school library; because the school board had not notified him that such material was prohibited; and, finally, because that court believed the word in question was not all that shocking to the students. As the decision stated, "With the greatest respect to such parents, their sensibilities are not the full measure of what is proper education."[17]

■ the *Parducci* case

The Court ruled similarly in another often-cited case concerning academic freedom (*Parducci v. Rutland,* 1970). Marilyn Parducci, a high school English teacher, had assigned *Welcome to the Monkey House,* by Kurt Vonnegut, to her eleventh-grade English class. Ms. Parducci was called down to the principal's office the next morning and was told not to teach that story in any of her classes. Parducci disagreed, contending that the short story had merit as a literary work, despite the principal's remark that it was "literary garbage." Parducci indicated to the principal and assistant superintendent that she would continue to teach her eleventh-grade English class using whatever material she wanted and in whatever way she thought best. Parducci was fired from her job, with the explanation that she was "insubordinate" and the course reading had a "disruptive" effect on students. The Court found that the Vonnegut story was not inappropriate reading for eleventh-graders. The finding added that the short story was met with "apathy" by most of the students, so the reading itself could not have created an undue distraction.[18]

■ the not so *Boring* case

Absolute academic freedom at the K–12 level does not exist, however, and some court decisions rule against teachers' perceived academic freedom. A more recent case contrasts the rulings of the Keefe case and the Parducci case (*Boring v. Buncombe County Board of Education,* 1998). Margaret Boring chose *Independence,* a play containing mature subject matter, for her advanced acting class to perform in a statewide competition. After reading the script, however, the school principal informed Boring that the class would not be allowed to perform that play at the state competition. Boring, along with parents of the actors, met with the principal, requesting that he not cancel their performance. He agreed that they could perform the play, but only after certain portions were deleted. The students performed the play, with portions deleted, and won second place at the competition. At the end of that school year, the principal requested the transfer of Boring from that high school, citing "personal conflicts resulting from actions she initiated during the course of the school year."[19] Boring argued that her transfer was in "retaliation" for expression of unpopular views through the production of the play. It was thus a violation of her right to freedom of speech.

The Court ruled in the school board's favor. In the decision, the Court stated that this was nothing more than an ordinary employment dispute, not a matter of public concern. For that reason, the Court found that the dispute did not constitute protected speech. The Court also wrote that school administrators have a "legitimate pedagogical interest in the makeup of the curriculum of the school," and that the "school, not the teacher, has the right to fix the curriculum."[20]

Issues of academic freedom often generate a great deal of heat. When they reach the courts, the following considerations, among others, are brought to bear:

■ relevant considerations

1. The teacher's purpose
2. The educational relevance of the controversial publication
3. The age of the students involved
4. The quality of the disputed teaching material and its effects on the class[21]

Those are critical guidelines to remember when one teaches.[22] Perhaps the most important point to remember is that academic freedom is limited: it cannot be used to protect the incompetent teacher or the indoctrinating zealot.

Copyright Laws

Good teachers are always on the hunt for effective teaching materials: a story that carries a special message, a poem that captures an idea with beauty and economy, an article that contains the latest information about an issue students are studying. Having found the "perfect" piece, it is difficult to resist the temptation simply to copy it and share it with the class, and the wide availability of photocopying equipment makes this practice all too easy.

Printed matter, however, is the product of someone's labor, the same way a painting or a piece of furniture is. In the law, it is considered intellectual property. The creator or author has a legal right to receive a reward for his or her labor. Without such payment, few could afford to write books, plays, or articles. For this reason, first in 1909 and more recently in 1976, the U.S. Congress passed copyright laws to protect writers and publishers from the unauthorized use of their material.

■ justification for copyright laws

For teachers, the heart of the current copyright law is its **fair use** guidelines, which help specify what printed materials teachers may photocopy and under what conditions they may do so. The general principle behind fair use is "not to impair the value of the owner's copyright by diminishing the demand for that work, thereby reducing potential income for the owner."[23] In other words, if people simply copy print materials whenever they want, they will not buy the books, and publishers and authors will suffer. Some copying is allowed, of course, and it is important for teachers to know what they may and may not do.

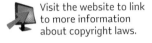 Visit the website to link to more information about copyright laws.

Teachers may:

■ fair use guidelines

- Make a single copy for class preparation of a chapter from a book; a newspaper or magazine article, short story, essay, or poem; or a diagram, chart, picture, or cartoon from a book or magazine
- Make a copy for each of their students of a poem if it is fewer than 250 words and printed on not more than two pages; and one copy for each student of an article or short story if it is fewer than 2,500 words

Teachers may not:

- Make copies of a work for their classes if another teacher in the same building already has copied that same material for his or her class
- Make copies of the same author's work more than once a semester or make copies from the same anthology, text, or periodical issue more than three times a semester
- Create a class anthology by copying material from several sources (a favorite trick of many teachers!)
- Make multiple copies of weekly newspapers or magazines specifically designed for classrooms, or of consumable materials, such as copyrighted games, exercises, and particularly worksheets from workbooks
- Charge more for legally permissible copies than it cost to copy them

These guidelines may seem overly restrictive and technical, but teachers actually have more liberal guidelines for copying than the average citizen does.

■ **Videotapes, Software, and the Internet**   There is a great temptation for teachers to tape material "off the air" and to build tape libraries of material to use in instruction. Although this may be effective pedagogy, it may not be legal. Commercially produced videos are intellectual property and are also covered by our copyright laws. Copyrighted television programs (and most of them are copyrighted) can be kept for only forty-five days, after which they must be erased or taped over. Also, during the first ten days after the taping, the teacher may show the tape only twice: once for initial presentation and once when "instructional reinforcement" is called for. Finally, schools cannot routinely record material for potential later use by a teacher. It can be done only at a teacher's request.

The personal computer has helped to revolutionize American life, in general, and American education, in particular. Since 1976, a huge new source of intellectual property has burst on the scene via the Internet, making it possible to link up to vast worldwide networks of information. It is possible to copy information from government agencies, libraries, legal systems, commercial sites and other schools with the click of a mouse. For example, you may be tempted to copy a research report from an online news information service and make copies for all of the students in your class. However, contrary to what many believe, the Internet is *not* in the public domain. Most Web pages—including the information on them and the code used to create them—are protected by copyright law. Because the Internet is global, it is regulated by an international treaty, the Berne Convention for the Protection of Literary and Artistic Works, to which the United States and most English-speaking nations are signatories. The law in this area is still evolving and until it settles, we suggest you follow the fair use guidelines cited above. Also, many teachers find that their school's media specialist can help them keep up with changes in copyright laws regarding digital, as well as print and video, materials.

Computer software programs are not treated in the same way as text, video clips, or still pictures. Commercially sold software differs from material "taken off" the Internet. Software should not be passed around and copied. In some cases, the software publisher may allow the purchaser to make one backup copy of the software, but making any other copies is a violation of the copyright laws. Although all of this may seem like "overkill," it is important for teachers to follow the rules—not simply because it is the law, but because students will follow their example.

▶ Lifestyle and the Teacher

■ teachers and community values

Teachers bring into their classrooms more than their minds and their lesson plans. They bring their attitudes and values. Elementary and secondary teachers traditionally have been considered extensions of the family in passing on to the young the community's positive values. In past generations, teachers who behaved in ways counter to the community's values were dismissed. Teachers were summarily fired for homosexuality, being pregnant and single, living with someone of the opposite sex, using illegal drugs, being publicly drunk, or committing a crime. However, the late 1960s saw a shift in the balance between the community's right to require certain standards of behavior and the rights of individuals to their own lifestyles and values. Although some areas are still legally quite uncertain, on many questions, judicial opinion (the way judges are tending to rule) is clear.

Pause and Reflect

1 ▶ To what degree do you believe that a teacher's personal life should be truly private? Should what the teacher does on his or her own time always be off-limits for school authorities and be protected by the law? Is the teacher completely free to live his or her life in whatever way he or she decides?

2 ▶ Were there teachers in your elementary or high school experience whose behavior "pushed the envelope" and were in conflict with your community's standards? If so, how did the school district respond? Do you believe justice was served? Was the cause of education served?

Personal Appearance: Hair, Clothes, and Weight

■ less leniency today

Although in the late 1960s and early 1970s the courts tended to rule in favor of teachers' rights to do what they wished with their hair, currently the courts are siding more often with school districts' rights to impose reasonable grooming codes for teachers. Teachers, according to the current view, do not have a *constitutional* right concerning their "style of plumage."[24]

The situation is similar for clothing. Courts are upholding districts' judgments on skirts that are considered too short, as well as the requirement (in some districts) that male teachers wear neckties. Courts are asserting that the First Amendment does not extend to "sartorial choice."

For health reasons, obesity may be its own punishment. However, does a school district have a right to fire a teacher because it decides she or he is too fat? A California school district released a forty-two-year-old female physical education teacher because, at 5 feet 7 inches and 225 pounds, the district felt she was "unfit for service." Her principal argued that she "did not serve as a model of health and vigor" and was restricted in her ability to perform on the trampoline, in gymnastics and modern dance, and in other aspects of the program.[25] Here, though, the court sided with the teacher, claiming that the district had not proved that her girth had impaired her performance.

Private Sexual Behavior

■ the Morrison case

In the past, sexual behavior was considered an area in which a community had a complete right to impose its standards on people selected to teach its children. Currently, however, the courts are increasingly viewing teachers' private sexual habits or preferences as separate from their public, professional lives as teachers. A landmark case involved Marc Morrison, who was fired after his former lover, another male teacher, reported their brief relationship to the superintendent. The school district believed it was on solid ground in dismissing Morrison for several reasons. The district's representatives argued that California's law requiring teachers to be models of good conduct applied to the case, that teachers are required to impress on their charges "principles of morality," and, further, that homosexual behavior is contrary to the moral standards of the people of California.

■ private versus professional life

However, in 1969 the California Supreme Court ruled in Morrison's favor. It acknowledged that homosexuality is, for many people, an uncertain or controversial area of morality. But the court made an important distinction between a teacher's private life and his or her professional performance. Since there was no evidence that Morrison's sexual orientation had ever been part of his relationship with his students, or in any way affected the performance of his teaching duties, or, in fact, affected his relationship with his fellow teachers, he was reinstated.[26]

Similarly, cases involving pregnancy out of wedlock and unmarried couples living together are being settled in favor of the individual teacher. However, the conditions just cited are required. The behavior must not intrude into the classroom or seriously affect the teacher's professional performance.

A teacher would, however, be misguided to think that his or her behavior after school hours is always protected under the law. A tenured California teacher was fired after she was arrested by an undercover policeman for engaging in sexual activity at a swingers' club. California state courts ruled that her behavior at this semi-public party showed "a total lack of concern for . . . decorum or preservation of her dignity and reputation" and that she demonstrated a serious lack of "normal prudence and good common sense."[27] Flaunting one's deviation from the community's standard tends to increase the chances that the courts will uphold dismissal. In all these cases, however, circumstances play a crucial role in the courts' final opinion.

Conduct with Students

■ teacher held accountable

Whereas the courts have become increasingly lenient on issues of private sexual behavior, the line is being held firm with regard to socially unacceptable behavior that spills over into the classroom. One sure way to lose one's teaching position is to make a sexual advance to a student. Usually one incident is enough to sustain a dismissal. The same goes for smoking marijuana, taking other drugs, public drinking to the point of drunkenness, or even using excessively obscene language in the presence of students. In this area, the teacher bears the full weight of the responsibility to be a role model.

Teachers should also realize that they can become "overinvolved" with students, even when no sexual impropriety has occurred. A fourth-grade teacher was dismissed from his job when he became so involved with one of his students that he sued the boy's mother for custody. The child had been allowed to live with the teacher for nine months, but when the mother wanted her son to return home, Drew Kerin, the teacher, sued for custody. The custody battle generated so much publicity that the district fired him. Kerin was found to have "exploited his position as a teacher" and that provided "just cause for termination."[28]

In general, then, except in matters of personal appearance, the courts are allowing teachers a good degree of freedom in their private and personal lifestyles as long as their choices and their behavior do not adversely affect their performance as teachers. Table 8.1 summarizes the court cases and rulings discussed in this and the previous sections.

▶ Law, Religion, and the School

According to the First Amendment to the Constitution, "Congress shall make no law respecting an establishment of religion, or prohibiting the free exercise thereof." During the past two centuries, the American judicial system interpreted this amendment inconsistently with respect to the place of religion in public schools, a topic of high controversy and much public unrest in recent years. The controversy is not new: the role of religion has been a bone of contention since the beginning of public education in the United States.

Among the questions currently being asked are the following:

Visit the website to link to more information about religion and schools.

- What religious observances, if any, are permitted in public school classrooms?
- Is all prayer, public and private, illegal in our schools?
- Are extracurricular religious clubs allowed in public schools?
- May parents insist that schools provide alternative textbooks consistent with their religious beliefs?

TABLE 8.1 Selected Court Cases Dealing with Teachers' Rights and Responsibilities

Issue	Case	Ruling
A teacher's liability for student's injury	*Sheehan* v. *St. Peter's Catholic School* (1971)	A teacher is liable for student injuries (i.e., eye injury) if he or she leaves students unsupervised.
	Mancha v. *Field Museum of Natural History* (1971)	A teacher is not liable for student injuries under unusual circumstances (i.e., fight in a museum) if he or she has taken appropriate precautions.
A teacher's right to free speech (such as criticizing the school authorities)	*Pickering* v. *Board of Education* (1968)	A teacher can criticize the operation of a school as long as this does not interfere with the normal running of the school.
	Scoville v. *Board of Education* (1970)	Freedom of speech does not include the use of "fighting words" or the abuse of superiors with profane and vulgar speech.
A teacher and academic freedom	*Keefe* v. *Geanakos* (1969)	A teacher may not be dismissed only for selecting reading assignments with offensive words.
A teacher and his or her private life	*Morrison* v. *State Board of Education* (California 1969),	A teacher's sexual orientation is not grounds for revocation of licensure, particularly when it in no way affects the performance of professional tasks.

Prayer and Scripture in the School

■ rulings against prayer

Until the mid-twentieth century, religious observances, including Bible reading and prayers, were common in the public schools. In fact, Bible reading and the recitation of the Lord's Prayer were required by constitutions or by statutes in a number of states. In *Abington School District* v. *Schempp* (1963), however, the Supreme Court ruled both to be unconstitutional.

In a 1962 decision (*Engel* v. *Vitale*), the Court had already ruled against the recitation of a nondenominational prayer, holding that Bible reading and prayer violate both clauses of the First Amendment. The Court recognized that the schools involved did not compel a child to join in religious activities if his or her parents objected; nevertheless, the Court held that the social pressures exerted on pupils to participate were excessive. In essence, no distinction was believed to exist between voluntary and compulsory participation in religious activities.

The Court did note that the study of comparative religion, the history of religion, and the relationship of religion to civilization were not prohibited by this

Teaching about religion is not the same as teaching someone to be religious. In our multicultural, multiethnic society, understanding another person's faith will foster tolerance and harmony, a goal common to all religions.

—Margaret Bartley

decision. It would also appear that, although the Bible may not be used to teach religion, it might, if objectively presented, be used in such areas of study as history, civics, and literature. Indeed, most thoughtful people would agree that failure to be conversant with the Old and New Testaments makes understanding of Western history and literature impossible. In the same way, if a student set out to learn about Chinese culture and was not permitted to read Confucius, he or she would be doomed to a very limited understanding.

The Court has also affirmed the right of individual public school pupils who so desire to say prayers and read scriptures of their choice in the morning before school starts or after the regular school day has ended. As discussed in the next section, many students join clubs or groups for these activities. If prayers are said during lunch period, they must be silent. Many students who are religious continue to seek avenues for expressions of beliefs within the public school day, while other students and their families campaign to avoid mixing religious expression with school activities.

The daily recitation of the Pledge of Allegiance has been controversial in some quarters for several decades. Originally challenged on the ground that the compulsory recitation of the Pledge is unconstitutionally coerced allegiance to the country, courts allowed students to opt out of reciting it. This was not enough for a California atheist father who did not want his third-grade daughter to have to listen to the Pledge's phrase "under God." In an extremely controversial ruling in June 2002, the 9th U.S. Circuit Court of Appeals, which has the nine Western states under its jurisdiction, banned the teacher-led pledge for the nearly 10 million public schoolchildren. Two years later, in 2004, the Supreme Court rejected the father's case on a technicality. However, the ban imposed by the 9th Circuit Court has been lifted until the Supreme Court issues a final ruling. We should hear more on the Pledge of Allegiance issue soon.[29]

■ prayer at graduation

The Supreme Court has also determined that the recitation of prayers at a public school function is unconstitutional. In the *Lee* v. *Weisman* case (1992), the principal of a public middle school, Robert Lee, had invited a rabbi to say a benediction and invocation at the middle school graduation exercises, instructing the rabbi to offer nonsectarian prayers. Student Deborah Weisman and her father filed a suit in court seeking a permanent injunction against including prayers in graduation ceremonies. The Court used the following facts to reach its decision: (1) public school officials directed the performance of formal religious exercises at the graduation ceremonies, and (2) although such exercises do not require attendance, they are in a real sense obligatory for all students, even those who object. As a result, the Court upheld the decision of the lower court, ruling that it is unconstitutional to include clergy members who offer prayers as part of school graduation ceremonies.[30]

■ student-led prayer at games

What if the students themselves select the prayer or the person delivering the prayer at after-school events? In 2000, the Court also ruled that student-led, student-initiated prayer at football games violates the First Amendment, in part because attending school football games is mandatory for some students, such as athletes, cheerleaders, and band members and other students who might object to the prayers feel social pressure and/or genuine desire to participate in high school football.[31]

Nevertheless, students who are religious continue to seek avenues for expressions of beliefs within the public school day.

"Meeting at the flag" for morning prayer is a growing movement in our schools. (© Rob Crandall/The Image Works)

Religious Clubs and Prayer Groups

■ religious extracurricular clubs

Are extracurricular religious clubs legal in public schools? Court decisions provide no clear guidelines here. In at least one case, a district judge ruled in favor of such clubs based on students' right to free speech. But a U.S. Circuit Court of Appeals overturned the decision, maintaining that such clubs violated the First Amendment's "establishment of religion" clause. The U.S. Supreme Court did not clear the waters: the five-justice majority upheld the district court opinion on a technical point, but declined to comment on the constitutional issues raised.[32]

■ after-hours student prayer groups

In yet another case, *Board of Education of Westside Community Schools v. Mergens* (1990), the courts ruled that extracurricular religious group meetings held on public school grounds did not necessarily violate the U.S. Constitution. The Court stated that if the school provides a limited public access for other noncurriculum student groups, then, under the Equal Access Act, a student religious group may also use the school building for its meetings. Under these circumstances, then, a student religious group meeting in the cafeteria after school does not violate the constitutional separation of church and state.[33]

Subsequent court rulings have maintained students' rights to use school facilities for religious club meetings, even if the club is directed by adults. The Supreme Court ruled that a school district could not prohibit the Good News Club, a private Christian organization for children six to twelve years old, from meeting in a school building after school hours. The Court stated that the school district had already adopted broad community access to its schools, and in doing so, had created an open forum. Prohibiting the club from meeting violated the club's First Amendment right of free speech (*Good News Club v. Milford Central School District*, 2001). While a key point in the *Good News Club* decision was that teachers do not participate in such meetings, the 8th Circuit Court of Appeals in St. Louis later ruled that a teacher may *on her own time* lead such religious meetings after school.[34]

Religion and Secular Humanism

■ secular humanism issue

The many court cases dealing with prayer in school, extracurricular clubs, and the presence of the Bible in schools, as well as the publicity surrounding them, have had a chilling effect on teachers and administrators. Rather than get involved with what is clearly a controversial set of issues, many public educators have tended to discourage any expression or even mention of religious issues or topics. This, in turn, has caused a reaction from parents and others who think that by ignoring the religious dimension of life, the public schools create a distorted, and ultimately dangerous, view of humankind—a view labeled *secular humanism.* Secular humanism asserts the dignity of human beings, but ignores the idea of God and the spiritual.

Objecting to what they see as the prevailing secular humanism of the schools, some parents contend that such fundamental questions as "What is a person's true nature?" can be treated in schools from every perspective except the religious view. They claim that this is not only intellectually unbalanced, but a danger to their children. Speaking to this issue, one legal scholar has written, "When government imposes the content of school, it becomes the same deadening agent of repression from which the framers of the Constitution sought to free themselves."[35] Many parents are voting not only with their pocketbooks, by turning down school budgets and tax requests for public schooling, but also with their feet, by walking away from the public school system. This trend has fueled a dramatic growth in religious schools and particularly in home schooling in recent years.

Specific objections to secular humanism in the schools have taken a number of forms. Two examples are the controversies over teaching about the origins of the human race and those over the use of certain textbooks.

■ Balanced Treatment Act

■ **The Creationism Versus Evolution Controversy** Major concern over the teaching of evolution dates to the famous 1925 Scopes trial in Tennessee in which a high school biology teacher, John Scopes, was accused of illegally teaching the theory of evolution. Although the trial came to national attention at the time (and again decades later with the award-winning play and film *Inherit the Wind,* based on that trial), no legal precedents were set. The issue returned to the public eye later in the century, when citizens asked for equal time for the biblical account of creation. In 1982, the Louisiana legislature passed the Balanced Treatment for Creation-Science and Evolution-Science Act, which quickly came to be known as the Balanced Treatment Act. The act defined *scientific creationism* as "the belief that the origins of the elements, the galaxy, the solar system, of life, of all the species of plants and animals, the origin of man, and the origin of all things and their processes and relationships were created ex nihilo (from nothing) and fixed by God."[36] In addition to requiring that scientific creationism be taught whenever evolution was taught, the act required the development of curriculum guides and research services for teaching creationism. On the other hand, the act provided none of these resources or protections for those teaching evolution.

After several challenges and lower court rulings, a case, *Edwards v. Aguillard,* reached the U.S. Supreme Court, which in 1987 ruled seven to two against the Balanced Treatment Act. According to the Court, the Balanced Treatment Act was, in fact, not balanced because its provisions favored the teaching of creationism over evolution. Further, the Court asserted, the Balanced Treatment Act was motivated by the legislature's desire to promote a particular religious viewpoint and thereby violated the Constitution's provision against the establishment of a state-sponsored religion. Despite the Court's arguments, few observers think this controversy has been settled. In 1999, the Kansas Board of Education voted to drop the requirement in the state's academic standards that evolution be taught in public schools.[37] Within days, suits were filed challenging the decision.

For several years the creationism-versus-evolution clash has been the battle-ground between those who believe the public schools have become antireligious and are promoting secularism and those opposed to the schools teaching a religious point of view. Recently, however, this controversy has taken a somewhat different turn with the introduction of **intelligent design** theory. This theory suggests that some complex biological structures and other aspects of nature are so complex and so highly interdependent that they could not have developed through Darwinian evolution, or "undirected natural causes." Intelligent design theorists believe there is evidence that "an intelligence" either created or somehow guided their development.

While this theory differs from creationism on several points, it is quite compatible with a belief in God and is frequently explicitly linked with such a belief. Many in the scientific community have criticized intelligent design as mere speculation and a violation of scientific principles because it relies on pre-existing causes to explain natural phenomena. Whatever its merits, intelligent design theory has pumped new life into those who believe the public school curriculum, and science curriculum in particular, have been, de facto, anti-religious.

■ Tennessee case

■ **The Textbook Controversy**   Recent court cases have been launched by fundamentalist Christian parents who argue that texts used in their children's public school classes are anti-Christian and thus a violation of their children's constitutional rights. In a 1986 Tennessee case, a U.S. district judge agreed that students' constitutional rights were violated when they were expelled after they refused to read certain texts. However, the following year a U.S. Court of Appeals reversed the decision of the lower court and ruled that the texts in question did not promote or require a person to accept any religion.[38]

Shortly after, another challenge to the public schools' choice of textbooks was made in Alabama by fundamentalist parents, students, and teachers. Forty-four textbooks used in history, social studies, and home economics courses were cited as advancing secular humanism. In this case (*Smith* v. *Board of School Commissioners of Mobile County*), the courts followed a pattern similar to that of the Tennessee case just described. Initially, the district court ruled that secular humanism is a religion and that some of the textbooks in question did discriminate against theistic religion. On appeal, this decision was reversed, and the court ruled that the textbooks promoted neither secularism nor any other religion.[39]

Guidelines for Religious Neutrality

Table 8.2 summarizes the court rulings on religion and the public schools. Yet with all the cases taken together, teachers may very well remain confused about what they can and cannot do. Thankfully, some attempts have been made to establish guidelines for the teacher and the school.

Thomas McDaniel recommends a *religious neutrality principle* in the classroom and offers the following four guidelines for putting it into practice:

■ suggested guidelines

1. Students may not be required to salute the flag or to stand for the flag salute if this conflicts with their religious beliefs.
2. Bible reading, even without comment, may not be practiced in a public school when the intent is to promote worship

TABLE 8.2 Selected U.S. Court Cases Dealing with Religion and the Schools

Issue	Case	Ruling
Teaching evolution and/or creationism		
Teaching evolution in public schools	*Scopes* v. *State of Tennessee* (1925)	The court upheld the state law permitting the teaching of evolution as an explanation of the origins of the universe.
Balancing the teaching of creationism and evolution in public school curricula	*Edwards* v. *Aguillard* (1987)	Schools teaching the biblical explanation of creation violate the Constitution's provision against teaching a particular religious viewpoint.
Public schooling, prayer, and the Bible		
The inclusion of Bible reading and prayer	*Engel* v. *Vitale* (1962)	Bible reading and teacher-led prayer in schools are in violation of the First Amendment; because of the social pressures involved, there is no difference between voluntary and compulsory prayer in school. However, private prayer and Bible reading are protected.
	Abington School District v. *Schempp* (1963)	Reading the Bible and reciting the Lord's Prayer in public schools are in violation of the First and Fourteenth Amendments; however, the Bible may be studied for historical, cultural, or other general educational purposes.
Reciting nondenominational prayers at public school ceremonies	*Lee* v. *Weisman* (1992)	It is unconstitutional to include adult-led prayers at public school ceremonies because all students are virtually obligated to attend ceremonies like graduations, even those students who object to the practice.
Students reciting nondenominational prayer at extracurricular events	*Santa Fe Independent School District* v. *Doe* (2000)	Schools cannot allow student-led prayer at extracurricular events (e.g., sporting events) because attendance is not completely voluntary.
Public schools and extracurricular religious groups		
Extracurricular religious clubs meeting on public school property	*Board of Education of Westside Community Schools* v. *Mergens* (1990)	If a public school allows a limited public forum for other extracurricular groups, the Equal Access Act indicates that extracurricular religious groups may meet in public school buildings without violating the Constitution.

3. Prayer is an act of worship and as such cannot be a regular part of opening exercises or other aspects of the regular school day.
4. Worship services, such as prayer and Bible reading, are not constitutional even if voluntary rather than compulsory. Consensus, majority vote, or excusing objectors from class or participation does not make these practices legal.[40]

This principle of religious neutrality does not mean, however, that the public school must ignore religion. On the contrary, teachers in public schools are free to study the history and contributions (pro and con) of individual religions with their students, to have them read the Bible as literature, and, in general, to expose students to our culture's religious heritage. When teachers cross the line into advocating a particular religion or involving students in prayer, they become vulnerable to legal action.

A few years ago, as debate over such issues continued, the White House asked the Department of Education to issue a directive on religion in the public schools. The resulting guidelines are an attempt to find a new common ground between religious expression and religious freedom and, further, to correct the perception (or the fact) that schools are hostile to religion. Among the specific points listed in the guidelines are the following:

■ White House guidelines

- Public schools should not interfere with or intrude on a family's religious beliefs.
- Public education should be respectful of religion, should be open to appropriate religious expression, and should teach about religion because it is so very much a part of our nation's history.
- Advocacy of religion by teachers and administrators has no place in public education.
- Students' religious clubs and groups are entitled to hold meetings, to have common prayer, to read scriptures, and to have their meetings publicized through school bulletin boards, newspapers, and public address systems.
- Although school-sponsored prayer should not be permitted, it is appropriate to begin the school day with a moment of silence.[41]

Although this directive from the Department of Education has been well received by many parents and educators, it has not yet been tested in the courts. Nor does it address all of the conflicting issues surrounding religion in public schools.

Pause and Reflect

1 ▶ Do you believe that the textbooks you used as a student, or that you have seen in your fieldwork, promote secular humanism? What can you do, as a teacher, if your assigned curriculum materials seem to you to promote or denigrate a particular religious viewpoint?

2 ▶ Do you believe that controversies about religion in the schools will have a chilling effect on your own willingness as a teacher to have students read religious literature or study the contributions of religions?

▶ Students and the Law

Many of the most important legal issues that affect the lives of teachers relate directly to students and their rights. Students, particularly public school students, have a special status under the law. In this section, we will touch on a few of the more significant and current student-related issues that can affect the teacher.

The Student and Due Process

As described earlier in this chapter, for many years the courts used the legal principle of *in loco parentis* in cases involving students. Teachers following this principle are expected to treat their students in a caring and informal manner instead of in the formal and legalistic manner that governs relationships "out in the world." By the same reasoning, since we do not require due process in the home, for a long time it was not valued in the schools.

■ more explicit rules today

Gradually, though, in court cases such as *Tinker*[42] and others described in upcoming sections, the *in loco parentis* principle has eroded, and the courts have come to appreciate that students often need to be protected from the arbitrary use of authority. As a direct result, many schools have developed clear statements governing procedures for expulsion, suspension, student privacy, freedom of speech and publication, and various breaches of discipline. Informing students of the rules, procedures, and consequences of violations in these areas is a major step toward providing due process rights. Still, the most important aspect of due process is the spirit of fair and evenhanded justice with which teachers respond to the daily events of the classroom.

In terms of disciplinary matters relating to students, schools can operate on a continuum with regard to student due process. For trivial matters or emergencies, schools may act without due process. For matters that may result in a short suspension (one or two days) or some entry on the student's record, schools must use some measure of due process, and for disciplinary matters that may result in a long-term suspension or expulsion, schools must demonstrate careful due process.[43]

Suspension and Expulsion

Ever since schools began, individual students have had difficulty following the rules and staying out of trouble. In recent decades, as schools have tried harder to keep older youth from dropping out, and as drugs and violence have increased in society as a whole, problems have escalated. One of the most dramatic and horrible examples is the massacre that happened at Columbine High School in Colorado in the spring of 1999.

■ rising discipline problems

Educators need to keep in mind that some students, having been compelled to stay in school, find little to capture their imaginations and to motivate them. For these students, school continues to be a place of failure and frustration, and trouble is often close behind. Some of the more common forms of school infractions today are stealing; vandalizing school property or someone's private property; bringing a weapon to school; possessing, using, or selling drugs or alcohol; fighting (or encouraging others to fight); and repeatedly disobeying the reasonable directives of teachers and other school personnel.[44]

■ power of suspension or expulsion

School districts are not powerless in the face of these kinds of disciplinary breaches. For the good of maintaining a safe and effective academic environment, schools have three alternatives: in-school suspension, out-of-school suspension, and expulsion. Typically, in-school suspension is for minor offenses and is brief in duration. Out-of-school suspension and expulsion are, of course, more serious and for a longer period, with expulsion meaning complete separation from the school. This school district power must be wielded in a manner that ensures that students' constitutional rights to due process are protected. And it is here, in the administration of suspension and expulsion, that school administrators in particular have become entangled in the courts.

■ Lopez suspension case

■ **Major Court Cases**   One of the most important cases was *Goss v. Lopez*, a 1975 suspension case involving Dwight Lopez, a high school sophomore from Columbus, Ohio.[45] Lopez was suspended for ten days for allegedly becoming involved in a cafeteria disturbance. This suspension occurred without a hearing and without any prior notification. Although a suspension of this length and without a hearing or prior notice was in accord with the Ohio statutes, a suit was filed stating that Lopez's constitutional rights had been violated because there was no notice or hearing. The case went to the U.S. Supreme Court, which ruled in favor of Lopez on the grounds that students facing suspension from a public school have property and liberty interests and therefore are protected by due process. In addition, the Court stated that "longer suspensions (longer than ten days) or expulsions for the remainder of the school term, or permanently, may require more formal procedures."

■ violation of PL 94–142

In a 1988 case with some similar elements, *Honig v. Doe,* the Court ruled against California school officials.[46] A school district had suspended indefinitely two emotionally disturbed students on the grounds that they were dangerous, and the Court ruled that this suspension was a violation of PL 94–142 (later called the Individuals with Disabilities Education Act (IDEA)), which allows school authorities to suspend dangerous students with disabilities for a maximum of ten days. Longer suspensions require either the permission of parents or the consent of a federal judge.

■ test of zero-tolerance rules

Because of the fear of school violence, exacerbated by the Columbine school tragedy, a number of school districts have adopted a **zero-tolerance policy** toward weapons, drugs or school fights. These zero tolerance policies call for automatic suspension or dismissal for student violators. Court cases involving "zero tolerance" have yet to be heard by the Supreme Court; however, lower courts have already heard cases in which zero-tolerance policies have played a part. A 2000 court case in Illinois, *Fuller v. Decatur Public School Board of Education School District 61,* highlights zero tolerance, as well as the volatile issue of racial profiling.[47] The school district, in accordance with its zero-tolerance policy on fighting, expelled a group of students for two years for starting a fight in the bleachers at a home football game. The fight, from all accounts, including a videotape, was brief but violent; seven spectators were injured. The students argued that the expulsion was because of racial profiling; they were unfairly singled out, they argued, because they were stereotyped as gang members. Further, they argued that because no guns, knives, or drugs were involved, their behavior did not merit an expulsion. The Court ruled that the students failed to present any evidence that their expulsion was in any way based on their race.[48] So, although that court case found no evidence of racial profiling in the school's application of its zero-tolerance policy, it seems likely that future cases will involve both issues in school disciplinary actions.

School dress codes are another area where students' rights and strict (sometimes zero-tolerance) policies are clashing. In response to provocative and immodest student dress, codes are being revised. Among the recent additions: no tank tops or tube tops; no low-riding, hip-hugging pants; no exposed midriffs; no capri pants; no overalls; no pajama tops or bottoms; no sweat pants; no shirts with slogans or offensive illustrations; no athletic jerseys; no hats; no hooded sweatshirts;

VOICES FROM THE CLASSROOM

Rob Famularo, a former sixth grade teacher, has recently been appointed assistant principal of the Eisenhower Middle School in Wyckoff, New Jersey.

Dress Codes

In my very first year as a teacher, I quickly realized the numerous and varied job responsibilities that undoubtedly come with the profession. On any given day a teacher may be asked to be a coach, friend, counselor, helping-hand, disciplinarian, or facilitator, to name just a few. What I did not realize quite so quickly, however, was the number of important decisions I would make on a regular basis. Many of these decisions carry moral, ethical, or legal implications. Consider, for example, the decisions involved in enforcing my public school's dress code.

Although the United States Supreme Court has stated that students relinquish some of their First Amendment rights in school, teachers nonetheless often struggle with the legal and ethical ramifications of controlling student dress and deeming what is "appropriate or inappropriate" attire for school.

There are, of course, lots of theoretical, legal, and ethical questions surrounding dress codes, such as, "Is it the responsibility of a public school to determine what attire is appropriate dress for school?"; "Can a school still make this determination even if a parent objects or disagrees?"; and " How can a teacher make an objective and consistent decision for every student?". These questions, which contain deep moral, legal, and ethical significance, are worthy of thoughtful reflection and consideration by anyone entering the teaching profession.

The situation becomes quite real, however, when the administration sets a specific dress code that I am expected to enforce when students enter my classroom first period in the morning. Can (or should) I tell a female high school student that her skirt is too short or that her shorts are more appropriate for the beach, rather than for school? Or should I simply turn a blind eye to the situation, saving both the girl and me the embarrassment? Am I really doing my job by ignoring the situation? This is when teachers get the chance to truly define their own personal meanings for what seem like abstract legal and ethical questions.

 Visit the website for more Voices from the Classroom.

---

belts are required unless the pants or skirt lack belt loops; shirts and blouses should be tucked in at all times—and should be long enough to stay tucked.[49] While difficult to enforce, as the "Voices from the Classroom" attests, increasingly educators are recognizing that there is a connection between edgy or over-the-line clothes and a school's poor learning environment.

Zero-tolerance policies, while hailed by many as tools to bring greater order and discipline to our schools, are not without their detractors. In recent years there have been a number of highly publicized incidents, such as the suspension of a third grader for bringing a butter knife to school, that have made this policy rather controversial, which only proves that no school policy can substitute for an educator's common sense.

Visit the website to link to more information about zero tolerance policies.

■ rights of pregnant students

■ **Pregnancy, Parenthood, and Marriage** As mentioned earlier, not many years ago, unmarried teachers who became pregnant were routinely dismissed from their teaching positions. Additionally, once a student was discovered to be either married, pregnant, or both, she was dismissed. With regard to students, this policy of dismissal was standard procedure until relatively recently. Pregnant students were considered to be morally corrupting influences on other students, and their presence in school was seen as legitimizing premature sexual activity and early marriage. Although many people still hold these views, the courts have tended in recent years to see such dismissals as discriminatory to young women and a denial of their rights to an education.* The result is that most school districts make arrangements for the education of pregnant students. Nevertheless, vexing issues keep coming up, such as "Should an obviously pregnant cheerleader be allowed to continue cheering?"

■ **Guidelines for Educators**   Overall, in recent years, the pendulum of judicial decisions seems to be moving away from an emphasis on student rights and back in favor of the authority of the schools.[50] Nevertheless, when dealing with matters that might lead to suspension or expulsion, teachers and administrators should follow these guidelines:

■ useful guidelines

- *Documentation.* First, before suspension and expulsion can take place, students must be notified (either in writing or orally) of the nature of their offense and what the intended punishment is.
- *Explanation.* Second, the school must give the students a clear explanation of the evidence on which the disciplinary charges rest.
- *Opportunity to defend oneself.* Third, the school must give the students an opportunity to refute the charges before a fair and impartial individual with decision-making authority.

Corporal Punishment

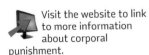

Visit the website to link to more information about corporal punishment.

Although few educational theorists living today advocate it, corporal, or physical, punishment is alive and well in American schools. The Supreme Court has regularly refused to rule on corporal punishment, leaving the issue up to the states. The trend among the states is clearly in favor of banning it. In 1979 only two states had banned corporal punishment in public schools, but currently twenty-eight states prohibit it.[51] A number of other states currently have legislation pending that would abolish corporal punishment. Still, many states leave the decision up to local school districts. In 2000, more than 342,000 students were spanked in U.S. schools.[52]

■ limits on corporal punishment

What does this situation mean for teachers from a legal point of view? First, they must know the rules of their state and school district. Second, they must be aware that the courts have ruled that corporal punishment can be administered only under certain conditions. Thus, teachers must be sure they are using only "moderate" and "reasonable" corporal punishment and using it only to establish discipline. A teacher who severely punishes a child, especially if any permanent disability or disfigurement results, is highly liable to a lawsuit. Also, punishment cannot be administered out of spite, revenge, or anger. In ruling on cases of excessive corporal punishment, the courts scrutinize the teacher's state of mind and motivation. The instruments of corporal punishment and where on the body they can be administered are also matters of concern to the courts. Fists are totally inappropriate; so are switches and canes. Blows must not strike parts of the body

* Title IX of the Education Amendments (1972), which addresses issues of prohibiting sexual discrimination in any education program receiving federal funds, is the basis for most court decisions supporting a pregnant young woman's right to stay in school.

where the risk of injury is high. Also, the punishment must be in scale with the crime—no whipping for whispering, for instance. Apparently the days of the principal's dictum, "The beatings will continue until the morale improves," are over.

Corporal punishment, of course, also entails important ethical considerations. Is it better to paddle a schoolyard bully and keep him in school or have legal hearings and separate him from the possibility of further education? One large problem with corporal punishment is that a ruler on the palm provokes terror in one student, but is all but meaningless for the next student. On the other hand, noncorporal punishment, such as the prolonged separation of an offending student from classmates, may cause true psychic pain for some children. The entire area of dealing with disruptive and offending students needs careful thought and even more careful actions.

Search and Seizure

Many students, even students of junior high and elementary ages, possess and sell illegal drugs. Schools have drug problems because American youth culture is inundated with images of drug use, and drugs are only one problem relating to search and seizure. Despite the risks of suspension or expulsion resulting from many schools' zero-tolerance policies, students also bring alcohol, pornography, and even dangerous weapons to school. As a result, school administrators may be urged to step up their searches of students for possession of drugs, alcohol, weapons, or other illegal items.

■ locker search rules

A student's locker may be searched by an appropriate school official, usually an administrator, *if there are reasonable grounds* to suspect that the locker contains something illegal or dangerous. The New York State courts have gone further in stating that "not only have the school authorities the right to inspect, but the right becomes a duty when suspicion arises that something of an illegal nature may be secreted there."[53] On the other hand, courts have found that it violates students' rights under the Fourth Amendment and is therefore illegal for school personnel to systematically spot-check lockers in hunts for drugs, weapons, or other illicit materials. Students' rights are even more closely protected when it comes to clothing and body searches.

■ probable cause

■ **Reasonableness and Probable Cause**   In the world outside school, authorities must have "probable cause," a substantial reason for believing that the person is in possession of something illegal, for any kind of search of a person or possessions. Yet because schools are specifically designed for the education and supervision of minors, courts have often allowed schools to use greater latitude in their searches. These decisions have been in keeping with the principle of *in loco parentis,* that schools act in place of the parents during the school day. Schools may only need to demonstrate a "reasonable suspicion" that a student was in possession of an illegal substance, rather than demonstrating the "probable cause" that law enforcement officials would need to demonstrate under similar circumstances.[54]

■ criterion of "reasonableness"

The importance of *reasonableness* in cases of search and seizure is shown by the 1985 U.S. Supreme Court case *New Jersey* v. *T.L.O.*[55] A teacher found two high school girls smoking in the bathroom and immediately brought them to the assistant vice principal's office. One girl admitted to smoking, but the second denied not only smoking on this occasion, but even being a smoker. The administrator asked the second student to come to his office, where he opened her purse and discovered a pack of cigarettes, cigarette-rolling papers, marijuana, a pipe, empty plastic bags, a wad of bills, and a list of "people who owe me money." Enter the police. The student was turned over to the juvenile court, where she was judged to be delinquent. She appealed on the basis that the search of her purse had violated her constitutional rights and therefore the evidence against her had been obtained illegally.

The case went to the U.S. Supreme Court, and the student lost. The Court stated, "The legality of a search of a student should depend simply on the reasonableness, under all the circumstances, of the search." Reasonableness appears to be determined, first, by whether or not the search has been initiated by a "reasonable" suspicion. Having seen rolling papers, it was reasonable to look for marijuana, since the two are so often closely related. The second criterion of reasonableness is that its scope and conduct must be "reasonably" related to the circumstances that gave rise to the search. Further, school officials must take into consideration the age and gender of the student and the nature of the offense.

The distinction between "reasonable suspicion" and "probable cause" is a fine line that is not always crystal clear. The prudent guideline for schools in their searches, though, is that any invasive search (body searches, for example) would require "probable cause," whereas less invasive searches (student lockers) would not require as rigorous a standard. In those cases, a "reasonable suspicion" would suffice. Mistakes here, particularly in the case of unwarranted strip searches, can be not only painfully embarrassing to the students, but also very expensive for the school district.

■ custodial responsibility versus rights

Finally, the police do not have the same *custodial relationship*—the same kind of responsibility toward students—that school officials do. Therefore, as a general rule, police need a warrant and the consent of school officials to search individual students or their lockers.

Pause and Reflect

1 ▶ If school authorities hear rumors that there are drugs in students' lockers, do you believe it is correct for them to search students' lockers without their permission?

■ **Drug Tests as Searches**   Most people have heard of potential employees or Olympic athletes taking tests to see if they have any illegal drugs in their systems. Can schools decide to administer such kinds of drug testing for those who go out for sports teams?

In the late 1980s, the Vernonia School District of Oregon noted a surge in students' use of drugs. Athletes, in particular, were leaders in this drug culture. So the school decided to institute random urinalysis to spot check for drug use among the athletes. All students who signed up for a team were required to provide their own and their parents' written consent for testing.

In 1991, a seventh-grader, James Acton, signed up to play football, but was denied participation on the team because he and his parents refused to provide the test consent forms. The family sued, claiming that the drug testing was an invasion of student privacy and an illegal search. The case eventually was decided in the Supreme Court, which ruled in favor of the Vernonia School District. The justices took into consideration several of the district's arguments, including observations that athletes participate in any number of activities, from "suiting up" in the locker room to preseason physical exams, that reasonably decrease their expectations of privacy, and that the drug test was relatively unobtrusive. The Court also considered the severity of the need, based on the widespread student drug use, and ruled that the policy was reasonable and constitutional. In its ruling, however, the Court cautioned against assuming that suspicionless drug testing would be constitutional in all other situations. The Court indicated that in this case, the most salient factor was that the school district was enacting its governmental responsibilities in monitoring and supervising schoolchildren entrusted to its care.[56] In 2002, the Court significantly broadened its ruling to include not just athletes, but all students engaged in "competitive" extracurricular activities, be they football or debating. The ruling reaffirmed and stressed the school's "custodial responsibility." Because search and seizure touches upon such fundamental American rights, schools will probably always need to be vigilant about how school policies and practices align with constitutional rights.

Freedom of Speech

▪ limits of free speech

The right to say what we want, where we want, is the cornerstone of a free society, and as such it is near and dear to Americans. Justice William O. Douglas stated, "Restriction of free thought and free speech is the most dangerous of all subversions. It is the one un-American act that could most easily defeat us."[57] Despite our courts' vigilant protection of this right, however, it is not an absolute right. The great Supreme Court Justice Oliver Wendell Holmes wrote that freedom of speech does not give a person the right to yell "Fire!" in a crowded theater or to knowingly and maliciously say or write lies that damage the reputation of another. In schools, freedom of expression must be balanced with the school's responsibility to maintain a safe and orderly environment and to protect people's feelings and reputations.

▪ *Tinker* case—symbolic protest

▪ **Students' First Amendment Rights** During the 1960s and early 1970s, many social protests and antiwar demonstrations spilled over into the schools, particularly the high schools. In one case, *Tinker v. Des Moines Independent Community School District* (1969), students who had been suspended for wearing antiwar armbands took the issue to court, claiming that the school had interfered with their right to freedom of expression. The Supreme Court ruled in favor of the students, stating that their black armbands were a form of symbolic speech in protest of the Vietnam War and should not be prohibited. A key point in this affirmation of students' First Amendment rights was the passive and nondisruptive nature of the students' protest. According to the Court, there was no evidence that the wearing of armbands would "materially and substantially interfere with the requirements of appropriate discipline in the operation of the schools."[58]

▪ *Fraser* case—lewd speech

▪ **A Shift in Legal Direction: Restricting Student Speech** During the 1970s and 1980s, the *Tinker* case was often cited, but the tide of court opinion in favor of student rights to free speech soon began to recede. In the 1986 case of *Bethel School District No. 403 v. Fraser*,[59] Matthew Fraser, a high school student in Bethel, Wash., nominated another student for vice president of the student government in a formal speech at an assembly before 600 students. Despite the warning of two teachers, Fraser built his speech on an elaborate, graphic, and explicit sexual metaphor comparing the nominee to a sexual organ. The court records of this case fail to tell us the outcome of the election, but Matthew Fraser got the ax. He was suspended for three days and removed from the list of candidates to speak at graduation. Fraser sued and won initially, but when the case went to the Supreme Court, he lost by a seven-to-two decision. The Court affirmed the school's right to "establish standards of civic and mature conduct" and to enforce them.

■ *Hazelwood/Kuhlmeier case—school newspapers*

■ **School Newspapers and Freedom of the Press**   School newspapers have long been the arena for struggles over freedom of speech and freedom of the press. Often the very best efforts to make the paper "vital" and "relevant" draw the newspaper staff into controversies. This is what happened at Hazelwood East High School in the spring of 1983.[60] Attempting to make their paper, *The Spectrum*, speak more directly to the real issues confronting their fellow students, the staff submitted two controversial articles, one dealing with the personal accounts of three Hazelwood students who had become pregnant and the other focusing on divorce and its effect on students.

■ *students' rights lose ground*

In line with standard practice, the advisor and teacher of the journalism class that produced the paper passed the issue on to the principal for his approval. The principal eliminated the two pages containing the offending stories and sent the other four pages to the printer. In response, Kathy Kuhlmeier and the six other journalism students sued, contending that their freedom of speech rights had been violated. Eventually, in 1988, the Supreme Court ruled in favor of the school district. Although dissenting justices complained about the potential for "thought control" and the "denuding of high school students of much of the First Amendment protection that *Tinker* in itself prescribed," the majority supported the principal's actions as legal and responsible. As stated in the majority opinion:

> A school may in its capacity as publisher of a school newspaper or producer of a school newspaper or producer of a school play disassociate itself not only from speech that would substantially interfere with its work or impinge on the rights of other students but also from speech that is, for example, ungrammatical, poorly written, inadequately researched, biased, prejudiced, vulgar or profane, or unsuitable for immature audiences. . . . A school need not tolerate student speech that is inconsistent with its basic educational mission even though the government could not censor similar speech outside the school.[61]

■ **Implications of the Court Cases**   Taken together, the three cases we have just discussed—*Tinker/Des Moines*, *Bethel/Fraser*, and *Hazelwood/Kuhlmeier*—suggest that freedom of speech and expression in schools is hardly absolute. Students may be punished for offensive or disruptive speech or publications. Schools, then, are something like Justice Holmes's crowded theaters, and the students' freedom of speech is somewhat limited. Students can and should express themselves, but in an orderly and nonviolent way. And the school has the right and responsibility to be certain that language is not used to hurt or scandalize the students in their charge.

■ *problems with the Internet*

One cutting-edge freedom of speech issue again involves the Internet. As discussed in the chapter entitled "What Should Teachers Know About Technology and Its Impact on Schools?" the Internet can be a marvelous educational tool, opening up infinite intellectual resources to students. However, it can also expose students to written and visual pornography, obscenity through email, electronic bullying, and chatroom predators. Many school districts have been struggling to respond to these dangers without unduly restricting students' exploration.

Among the responses currently in place are orientation programs on appropriate use of the Internet, more careful supervision of computer stations, and special software designed to block forbidden sites. Many districts have **acceptable use policies** designed to provide rules of the road for students using this technology.

Sexual Harassment

■ Hostile Hallways

Visit this chapter of the website to link to more information about sexual harassment.

A major study by the American Association of University Women (AAUW), entitled *Hostile Hallways,* reported that 81 percent of American students acknowledged that they were the subjects of sexual harassment at some time during their school lives. However, only 11 percent reported the incident to a teacher. One-fourth of the girls and one-tenth of the boys reported being harassed by a school employee. Most harassment, however, was student to student. Teenage girls responded to the survey with stories of pervasive and overt sexual harassment. Girls described sexual jokes and taunts; attempts to snap their bras, lift their skirts, and grope their bodies; and other unwanted physical attention. Boys and girls get the message that girls are not worthy of respect and that it is okay for boys to exert power over girls. Spreading sexual rumors and calling a person gay or lesbian were often reported verbal forms of harassment. Most of the harassment occurred in plain view of others—in hallways, lunchrooms, classrooms, assemblies, and playgrounds, and on school buses.[62]

■ sexual harassment

Since the study first appeared, schools have attempted to address this abuse, focusing in particular on student-to-student harassment. The study's definition of **sexual harassment** is "unwanted and unwelcome sexual behavior which interferes with your life." However, what constitutes sexual harassment in a particular situation can be a thorny issue. For instance, in the fall of 1996, a North Carolina school suspended a *six-year-old* boy who had kissed a female classmate on the cheek for sexual harassment. On the other hand, many readers may know of serious and frightening harassment incidents from their own school experience. One such incident was the subject of a Supreme Court ruling in *Davis* v. *Monroe County Board of Education.*[63]

When LaShonda Davis was in fifth grade in Forsyth, Georgia, her harassment nightmare began. A fellow student began groping her, grinding up against her, and declaring that he was "going to get in bed with her." The girl and her parents made repeated complaints to her teacher and the school principal. After five months, the teacher finally agreed to move the boy's desk to the other side of the room. But the sexual taunting and lewd overtures continued, until finally the family sought legal counsel. Six years after the initial incident, and with much legal work, the suit finally made its way to the Supreme Court. The Court, in a controversial five-to-four decision, ruled for the Davises and against the school district.

What has made this case legally controversial is the perceived danger of our courts being flooded with cases ranging from innocuous flirtations to true, hardcore harassment. Further, judges worry that the budgets of school districts will be drained by the legal expenses involved in fighting frivolous suits. However, in the prevailing opinion, the *Davis* decision stresses that school districts are liable only if they were "deliberately indifferent" to information about "severe, pervasive, and objectively offensive" harassment among students.[64] It appears that while the Court has come to the defense of harassed students, the criteria for what actually constitutes an offense have been set quite high. Nevertheless, the problem of sexual harassment in our schools is out of the closet, and schools, which formerly have taken this issue casually, are now working to respond. Schools can work to avoid the problem by drafting a sexual harassment policy; requiring training programs for administrators, teachers, and students; acting quickly when confronted with sexual harassment; enlisting the support of parents; and instituting disciplinary actions against repeat harassers.

■ prohibited by law

Many schools now have sexual harassment policies that they distribute to students and staff. However, as the AAUW study revealed, neither boys nor girls are likely to report actual incidents to adults for fear of being labeled a "snitch" or suffering repercussions. The challenge for educators is how to change the culture of harassment in schools and to encourage the use of existing resources to address the problem. All our students, boys and girls, have the right to attend schools whose environments are free from such harassment. As a teacher, you cannot ignore such instances when you see them occur. Choose to make such times "teachable moments" by helping students learn to appreciate the dignity of others and ensuring that the classroom is a welcoming environment for all students.

Table 8.3 summarizes the *Davis* case, along with other major students' rights cases discussed in preceding sections.

Records and Students' Right to Privacy

In this information age, most of us probably have a history tucked away on computer disks. For students, the history may consist of school records, various test scores, and ratings by teachers on everything from citizenship to punctuality. Teachers and other staff members judge a student's character and potential, and others use those judgments to decide whether the student should go to this school or get that job. Certainly we need some system of exchanging information about one another; otherwise, we would hire only our friends or attend only those schools where enough people knew us to vouch for us. However, the kind of information in school records may be very imperfect, and the danger that it will be misinterpreted or fall into the wrong hands is great.

■ the Buckley amendment

In the early 1970s, a series of situations came to light in which information was poorly used or parents and students were denied access to records (for example, when a diagnosis was used to justify sending a child to a class for students with mental retardation). In response, the U.S. Congress passed the Family Educational Rights and Privacy Act in 1974. The act, also known as the **Buckley amendment,** outlines who may and who may not see a student's record and under what conditions. Parents, who previously were kept from many of the officially recorded judgments that affected their children's futures, are clearly winners from this legislation. The amendment states that federal funds will be denied to a school if it prevents parents from exercising the right to inspect and review their children's educational records. Parents must receive an explanation or interpretation of the records if they so request.

■ the downside of Buckley

However, the Buckley amendment does not give parents the right to see a teacher's or an administrator's unofficial records. For instance, a teacher's private diary of a class's progress or private notes about a particular child may not be inspected without the teacher's consent.

Although the Buckley amendment has undoubtedly reduced the potential for abuse of information, it has had a somewhat chilling effect on teachers' and others' willingness to be candid in their judgments when writing student recommendations for jobs or colleges. Because students may elect to see a teacher's letter

TABLE 8.3 Selected Court Cases Related to Students' Rights

Issue	Case	Ruling
Students' right to free speech		
Students' right to make a symbolic protest	*Tinker* v. *Des Moines Independent Community School District* (1969)	Students have the right to symbolic protest, if that protest does not interfere with the school's operation.
Students' right to use lewd language for a school speech	*Bethel School District No. 403* v. *Fraser* (1986)	Schools have the right to establish and enforce standards of civic conduct.
Student newspapers and freedom of the press	*Hazelwood School District* v. *Kuhlmeier* (1988)	Because public schools are not public forums, school officials have the right not to publish student articles that may violate the sensibilities of other students.
Students' right to education		
Disabled students with behavior problems	*Honig* v. *Doe* (1988)	Dangerous students with disabilities may not be suspended for more than ten days without parental consent or permission of a federal judge.
Students' school suspension for fighting at a game	*Fuller* v. *Decatur Public School Board of Education School District 61* (2000)	School's policy of zero tolerance for fighting was upheld by courts.
Students' right to freedom from sexual harassment	*Davis* v. Monroe County Board of Education (1999)	School held liable if it ignores excessive sexual harassment of one student by another student.
Students' right to due process		
Students' right to notification and hearing before a suspension	*Goss* v. *Lopez* (1975)	Schools violate students' constitutional right to due process if they suspend students without a hearing.
Students' rights regarding search and seizure		
Students' protection from school searches of personal items	*New Jersey* v. *T.L.O.* (1985)	Schools can search students' lockers and other private items if there is reasonable cause.

of recommendation, some teachers choose to play it safe and write a vague, general letter that lacks discriminating judgments, pro or con, about the student. In effect, some faculty members and other recommenders have adopted the attitude, "Well, if a student doesn't trust me enough to let me write a confidential recommendation, I'll simply write an adequate, safe recommendation."

Nevertheless, the Buckley amendment's impact, in our view, has been positive. In the past, many students lost opportunities for higher education and desirable jobs because of inaccurate statements in recommendations or in their school records. One professor reported to us an incident that occurred in his school in 1975, shortly after the Buckley amendment came into being: "Our counselors at the junior high school where I taught were 'purging' the records of subjective comments with black markers. In one student's permanent record folder, a *Playboy* magazine fell out. It seems a grade school teacher took it from Carl and included it in his permanent record because she wanted future teachers to know what kind of kid Carl really was."

Despite the fact that the Buckley amendment is well over thirty years old, the implications for what constitutes a violation of students' right to privacy concerning his or her educational records are not always apparent. That fact was made all too clear in the fall of 2001, when the Supreme Court agreed to hear a case involving student rights to privacy.

An Oklahoma mother, Kristja Falvo, brought suit against the Owasso Independent School District for violating the Family Educational Rights and Privacy Act. Her son's classroom teacher asked the students to grade each other's quizzes and call out the grades so the teacher could record them. The mother argued that such a practice violated her son's right to privacy because the practice publicly disclosed educational information about him. Ms. Falvo was especially concerned that this practice would have a detrimental effect on his learning. In a 2002 decision, the Supreme Court ruled in favor of the school district, stating that peer grading is not in violation of the Buckley Amendment.[65]

▶ A Final Word

This chapter has been the beginning of what we hope will be your ongoing probe of the important role that two related issues, ethics and law, play in the life of the teacher. Together these issues increasingly permeate the school environment. Whereas ethical issues may raise timeless questions, some laws continually change, and even now the courts may be giving a different complexion to some of the decisions cited in this chapter. Also, the chapter has touched on many issues only lightly and has omitted others because of lack of space. We urge you to move on from this introduction to investigate further the work of the teacher in its larger ethical and legal framework.

Key Terms

academic freedom (235)
acceptable use policy (258)
breach of contract (229)
Buckley amendment (259)
continuing contract (229)
contract (228)

due process (227)
ethics (218)
fair use (239)
grievance (228)
in loco parentis (226)
intelligent design (247)

law (218)
liability (231)
reduction in force (RIF) (231)
sexual harassment (258)
tenure (229)
zero-tolerance policy (251)

For Reflection

1 Can you remember examples of the "everyday ethics" of teaching shown by the teachers you had in elementary and secondary schools? Can you remember examples in which your teachers' ethical behavior was questionable?

2 Do you believe tenure practices are justified and lead to better schools? Why or why not?

3 What do you think about the current controversies over the place of religion in public schools? Of prayer? Of the Bible and other religious works?

4 Teachers are expected to be people of good character and role models to students. What are the limits of this expectation? What are some points at which the rights of the school district end and the rights of the teacher begin?

For Debate

Read the Policy Matters! summary, "School Censorship," at the website, and consider the issues it outlines regarding academic freedom. Then, go to EduSpace to post your answers (or respond to other students' answers) to the What Do You Think questions listed in the Policy Matters! feature.

For Further Information

PRINT RESOURCES

Nel Noddings, *Caring: A Feminine Approach to Ethics and Moral Education,* 2d ed. (Berkeley, Univ. of California Press, 2003).
This is a revision of a distinctive and unique book by a distinguished educational philosopher. The book is a radical challenge to the way we currently approach schooling.

Louis Fischer, David Schimmel, and Leslie Stellman, *Teachers and the Law,* 6th ed. (New York: Longman, 2002).
This book, written by scholars who are lawyers and professors of education, bridges the worlds of the courts and the classroom with great detail and clarity.

Michael W. LaMorte, *School Law: Cases and Concepts,* 8th ed. (Boston: Allyn and Bacon, 2004).
This current text covers both key legal opinions and dissenting opinions, and adds valuable commentary and explanation.

Kenneth Strike and Jonas Soltis, *The Ethics of Teaching,* 4th ed. (New York: Teachers College Press, 2004). This short book is an excellent source for ways to approach the topic of ethics in teaching. It contains a number of practice cases.

2005 Deskbook Encyclopedia of American School Law (Rosemont, MN: Data Research, 2005).
This excellent annual reference book is an easily accessible source on the current law and legal issues surrounding all aspects of public and private education.

Perry Zirkel, "De Jure" column in *Phi Delta Kappan* (Bloomington, IN: Phi Beta Kappa International, Inc). This recurring magazine column reports on important issues of school law and provides an excellent way to follow recent developments.

WEB RESOURCES

Acceptable Use Policies: A Handbook. Available at:
www.pen.k12.va.us/go/VDOE/Technology/AUP/home.shtml.
This handbook, available on the Internet, is produced by the Virginia Department of Education and is a rich source of information on using the Internet in schools and developing acceptable use policies.

The Missouri Department of Elementary and Secondary Education Updates. Available at:
http://www.dese.state.mo.us/schoollaw/freqaskques/index.html.
This excellent website is a gold mine of information on an array of court cases, from school prayer to student-on-student sexual harassment. (Keep in

mind, however, that rulings may, in some cases, apply only to the state of Missouri.)

The Legal Information Institute's Supreme Court Collection. Available at:
http://supct.law.cornell.edu/supct/search/index.html.
This website gives you access to the most important Supreme Court school-related decisions.

ERIC Digests. Available at:
http://www.ericdigests.org/eric-digests.html.
The ERIC Digests are short essays that clearly explain key issues in school law on a wide variety of topics.

9 *What Are the Philosophical Foundations of American Education?*

Chapter Preview   This chapter examines the role of philosophy, a key foundational discipline in the work of the teacher. First, we describe philosophy; then we discuss four different philosophies and analyze their applications to the classroom.

This chapter emphasizes that:

▶ Philosophical knowledge has a fundamental role in clarifying questions of education.

▶ Philosophical thought has distinct characteristics that contribute to the way we know the world. Four branches of philosophy—metaphysics, epistemology, axiology, and logic—relate rather directly to the work of the teacher.

▶ Four philosophies of education—perennialism, essentialism, romanticism, and progressivism—have many practical implications for the classroom teacher.

▶ Psychological theories, particularly constructivism, influence modern educational thought.

▶ Teachers need to have a philosophy to guide their practice. Many develop eclectic personal philosophies that incorporate elements of several major philosophical views.

▶ Discovering your personal philosophy is a lifelong process, but it should begin now.

A medical student who wants intensely to be a surgeon, has marvelous hands, and displays a high level of technical skill, but does not know how the body functions or what constitutes health, can hardly be called a doctor.

An aspirant to the ministry who loves to work with people and possesses a marvelous gift of speaking, but has no opinion about humanity's relationship to God or about the purpose of religion can hardly be suited for religious ministry.

And a person who has a great desire to be with young people, wants to live the life of a teacher, and possesses great technical skill, but lacks purpose and direction is hardly a teacher.

These three individuals are like wind-up toys, moving along blindly without a plan or an intellectual compass. And although this image may be somewhat dramatic, there *are* people who prepare for professions without getting to the core meaning of what those professions are all about. Such directionless behavior can cause problems in any occupation or profession, but particularly in teaching. What kind of a teacher can someone be who lacks a view of what people are and a vision of what they can become? Who cannot clearly define right and wrong in human behavior? Who doesn't recognize what is important and what is unimportant or can't distinguish clear thinking from sloppy thinking? The person who would take on the responsibility for educating the young without having seriously wrestled with these questions is, to say the least, dangerous, for he or she is going against the very grain of what it means to be a teacher. In fact, it is safe to say that such a person is not a teacher, but a technician.

■ philosophy as foundation

This chapter introduces you to philosophy, one of the foundational subjects in education, which, along with history and psychology (and, to some degree, economics, political science, sociology, anthropology, and the law), forms the intellectual underpinning on which the practice of education rests. The study of philosophy helps the teacher systematically to reflect on issues that are central to education, including such basic concepts as *learning, teaching, being educated, knowledge,* and *the good life.*

▶ What Is Philosophy?

Visit this chapter of the website to link to more information about the nature of philosophy.

■ love of wisdom

The word **philosophy** is made up of two root words: "love" (*philo*) and "wisdom" (*sophos*). In its most basic sense, then, philosophy is the *love of wisdom.* Although not all people love wisdom in the same way or to the same degree, all humans are questioning beings—seekers of answers. As children, we are preoccupied with such lofty questions as, "How do I get fewer veggies and more dessert?" Then we progress to such questions as, "How does the teacher always know to call on me when I don't have the answers?" and "What do I need to do to get a decent grade in geometry?" Ultimately, we may move to more fundamental levels of questioning: "Who am I?" "What is the purpose of life, and what am I doing here?" and "What does it mean to be a really good person?"

Fundamental Questions of Existence

Until about one hundred years ago, most people relied on religion and philosophy for answers to such fundamental questions. Whereas religion is said to represent the revealed word of God, philosophy represents a human attempt to sort out by reason the fundamental questions of existence. Many of the great thinkers of Western civilization—Plato, Aristotle, St. Thomas Aquinas, René Descartes,

The real object of education is to have a man in the condition of continually asking questions.

—Bishop Creighton

Jean-Jacques Rousseau, Immanuel Kant, Friedrich Nietzsche, John Locke, John Stuart Mill, William James, Alfred North Whitehead, and John Dewey—have been philosophers. Because education has always been a central human concern, philosophers have thought and written a great deal about education and the questions surrounding it.

The Nature of Philosophy

■ impact of philosophy on our lives

Only a few people in our society are professional philosophers who earn their daily bread (usually a rather meager fare) by pursuing answers to the fundamental questions of life. However, all of us who wrestle with such questions as "Who am I?" and "What am I doing with my life?" are engaged in philosophical activity. Although there is a distinction between the few professional philosophers and the great number of us who are amateurs, the questions we ask and the answers we glean usually have a major impact on the practical affairs of our lives and on how we choose to spend our life force. For instance, the very practical decision of whether to become a teacher, a real estate broker, or a professional bungee jumper almost always has its roots in a person's philosophy of life, whether that person knows it or not.

■ factors that influence our philosophies

In developing a philosophy, we draw on many influences: our experiences in life, our religious views, and our reading of literature, history, and current events. A major difference between professionals and amateurs, however, lies in the precision of their methods. Philosophy is an extremely pure and abstract science. Philosophers work with neither test tubes nor white rats, use neither telescopes nor microscopes, and do not fly off to remote societies to observe the natives. The method or process of philosophers is questioning and reasoning; their product is *thought*.

The Philosopher's Method and Language

■ concern with meanings of words

Basically, philosophers are concerned with the meanings of things and how to interpret those meanings. Therefore, they have an intense interest in the real meanings of words. Although some philosophical discussion and writing involves

" HOW DO YOU EXPECT ME TO LEARN ANYTHING WHEN YOU'RE THE ONE WHO KEEPS ASKING ALL THE QUESTIONS? "

Reprinted by permission from *Phi Delta Kappan*.

technical language, it generally uses "plain language," the ordinary language of people. However, philosophers try to be extremely clear and careful about their use of terms. They do not want their ultimate goal (getting at the meaning of things) to be lost in a thicket of fuzzy language.

Although philosophy appears to deal with simple issues in simple language, behind the philosophers' questions are raging debates about profound issues that can have far-reaching implications. For example, the question, "What is a human?" leads to other questions, such as "When, if ever, can a fetus be aborted?" and "What rights do severely disabled persons have?" Or "Should humans clone humans?"

Pause and Reflect

Before you go much further in this chapter, you should clarify where you stand today. What are your answers to these philosophical questions:

1 ▸ What are the fundamental life questions to which you are seeking answers?

2 ▸ What is or are the ends or goals of an education?

3 ▸ Should a school lay out what is to be learned, or should the students have the larger say in what and how they learn?

▸ The Terrain of Philosophy

■ four branches of philosophy

Philosophy covers a large amount of intellectual turf. The terrain of philosophy is divided into several areas, including four that are particularly important to the teacher: metaphysics, epistemology, axiology, and logic. These four branches of philosophy are central to the educative process and, in fact, speak directly to the work of the teacher.

Metaphysics

■ what is real?

Metaphysics involves the attempt to explain the nature of the real world or the nature of existence. Metaphysics attempts to answer the question "What is real?" without relying on revealed religion, such as the Bible. Further, the metaphysician characteristically believes that it is not possible to address fundamental matters such as the nature of a human being or of the universe, simply by collecting data and formulating statistically significant generalizations. From most metaphysical perspectives, the true nature of a person cannot be captured by measuring or counting alone. A person is more than the sum of his or her height and weight, IQ (intelligence quotient) and SAT scores, and other "vital" statistics.

In probing the nature of reality, the metaphysician asks a whole array of questions: "Does life have meaning?" "Are human beings free or totally determined?" "Is there a purpose to life?" "Is there a set of enduring principles that guide the operation of the universe?" "Can these principles be known?" and "Is there such a thing as stability, or is our world ever-changing?"

■ teachers take metaphysical stands

■ **Metaphysics and the Curriculum**   These abstract questions are ones that the educator cannot dismiss. Ultimately, the purpose of education is to explain reality to the young. The curriculum and how we teach it represent our statement of what that reality is and what part of that reality should we teach. In other words, the curriculum of a school represents what the community believes is *most worth knowing*.

Although teachers may not actually be metaphysicians, they do take a stand on metaphysical questions. If a teacher decides to teach because he or she believes the most important thing in the universe is a human mind, that a career decision is driven by a metaphysical view: the importance of an individual person. The people on school boards also take stands on metaphysical issues. For example, whether a particular school system makes a major investment in educating individuals with severe mental disabilities or emphasizes vocational education depends very much on someone's metaphysical decision about the nature of the person and the place of work in a person's life.

Epistemology

■ what is truth?

Epistemology deals with questions regarding knowledge and knowing. The epistemologist, seeking the true nature of knowing, asks such questions as "What is true knowledge (as opposed to false ideas)?" and "Is truth elusive, always changing and always dependent on the truth seeker's particulars of time, place, and angle of vision?" Some people, whom we call *skeptics,* question our capacity to ever really know the truths of existence. And some, whom we call *agnostics,* are convinced there are no "truths" and that seeking knowledge of ultimate realities is an empty hope.

■ how do we acquire knowledge?

Epistemology deals not only with the nature of truth but also with the ways in which we can know reality. Questions, such as "How do we come to know the truth?" and "What are the sources for gaining knowledge?," are part of the conversation. There are a variety of ways by which we can know, and each of these ways has its advocates and detractors. Among the ways of knowing are by divine revelation, by authority, through personal intuition, from our own five senses, from our own powers of reasoning, and through experimentation.

■ impact on teaching methods

■ **Teaching and Ways of Knowing** Questions concerning knowledge and knowing are, almost by definition, of great concern to the teacher. The epistemological question "How do you know this or that?" goes to the heart of teaching methodology. If a teacher wants her students to have a concept of democracy, how does she proceed? Does she explain the characteristics of different forms of government, such as monarchy and oligarchy, and then the characteristics of democracy? Or does she take a more hands-on approach and have the students do a role-playing exercise during which one student is appointed class dictator and the rest must obey the student-dictator's orders? The student who has only read about democracy "knows" it in an *epistemologically* different way than a student who has been bullied and harassed for several days by a teacher-appointed dictator.

It is becoming increasingly clear, in fact, that individuals differ in their preferred methods of learning. As discussed more fully in the chapter on "Who Are Today's Students in a Diverse Society?," much of the teacher's work is helping the student find the most effective way of coming to know, that is to gain new knowledge.

■ creationist controversy

In some instances, the teacher may find that some people—for example, parents and community members—may have strong opinions regarding these epistemological questions. Many people have strong beliefs about the true origin of humankind and how one knows it. This issue is sometimes called the *creationist controversy,* and it rests on a sharp and fundamental argument over the questions "Who are we?" and "How did we get here?" One faction insists that the public schools should present the evidence of our origin that is given in the Book of Genesis, which we know by divine revelation. Others insist that the way to know the origin of the human race is through the scientific theory of evolution, grounded in the interpretation of artifactual evidence. So behind this ongoing educational controversy is a fundamental question of epistemology.

Axiology

■ what values should we pursue?

Axiology focuses on the nature of what and how we value. As human beings, we quite naturally search for the correct and most effective way to live. In doing so, we engage questions of values. Of course, when different people look at life, they often come up with very different sets of values. For instance, *hedonists* believe in seeking pleasure and living for the moment. On the other hand, *stoics* have an austere way of looking at life and seek to be unaffected by pleasure or pain. Many people regard values from a religious perspective, asserting that unless humanity and the rest of the natural world were originally created by God, existence as we know it is just the meaningless coming together of cosmic dust and debris. In this view, the only genuine values derive from God.

■ teachers and moral values

Most people would agree with Socrates (described in the "Leaders in Education" box) that schools have a dual responsibility: to make people smart and to make them good. To the degree that teachers accept the second function, that is, to assist their students to become good people, they are grappling with an axiological issue. In fact, teachers are intimately involved with questions of moral values. Young people are seeking ways to live lives that are worthwhile, and teachers traditionally have been expected to help students establish moral values both as individuals and as contributing members of society. (See the chapters entitled "How Should Education Be Reformed?" and "What Are the Ethical and Legal Issues Facing Teachers?" for more discussion of this issue.) Moral values such as honesty, respect for other people, and fairness are necessary if we are to live together in harmony. Despite a large core of values on which a majority of people agree, such as respecting others and avoiding violence in settling disputes, other value issues separate people. Certain sexual practices, capital punishment, gun control, and abortion are examples of contemporary social issues that involve a wide range of viewpoints about what is right.

■ issues of right and wrong

■ **Ethics and Aesthetics**   Axiology has two subtopics: ethics and aesthetics. **Ethics** takes us into the realm of values that relate to "good" and "bad" behavior, examining morality and rules of conduct. At one time, teaching children how to deal with issues of good/bad and right/wrong was the primary purpose of schooling. In recent decades the pendulum has swung the other way, and schools have been more concerned with factual and scientifically verifiable knowledge and skills than with ethical knowledge. There are, however, many signs that schools are being called back to help children deal with ethical issues.[1]

The subject of ethics not only teaches us how we can intellectually ascertain the "right" thing to do, but also is often used to help us establish a particular set of standards, such as a code of ethics. In the chapter entitled "What Are the Ethical and Legal Issues Facing Teachers?" we give particular attention to these issues.

■ issues of beauty

The second subtopic of axiology, **aesthetics,** deals with questions of values regarding beauty and art. Many discussions about the value of a particular film,

Leaders in Education

Socrates (469–399 B.C.)

The ancient Greek philosopher Socrates was condemned to death for supposedly corrupting the youth of Athens. Today we know him primarily through the written "dialogues" of his student, Plato. How much Plato's portrayal resembled the actual man is open to debate. Nevertheless, the Socrates of Plato's dialogues has had a deep and lasting influence on both philosophy and education, giving us such common terms as *Socratic teaching, Socratic questioning,* and the *Socratic method.* The following passage explains some of the basic tenets of Socrates' approach.

Socrates expressly denied that he was a teacher in the commonly accepted sense of that term. What he meant by this—at least in part—was that he was not a sophist, a professional pedagogue who, for a fee, would endeavor to transmit some knowledge that he possessed to someone who lacked it. Not only did Socrates charge no fees, he claimed not to have command of any such knowledge.

The learning that Socrates was concerned with simply didn't fit the information-transmission model of education implicit in the Athenian public mind and the teaching profession. Neither did his pioneering focus on virtue and wisdom square well with the popular attachment to honor, fame, and wealth. As he tries to explain at one point to Anytus in Plato's dialogue *Meno,* "[W]e are inquiring whether the good men of today and of the past knew how to pass on to another the virtue they themselves possessed, or whether a man cannot pass it on or receive it from another." Because it was clear that wisdom and virtue could not simply be passed on from one person to another, Socrates sought an alternative way of conceptualizing how such excellences of mind and character were acquired. What was the teacher's role in that acquisition, if not simply being a supplier?

As an alternative to the receiving-knowledge-from-another model, Socrates proposed that learning was "recollection"—that is, a process akin to dredging up knowledge from one's own resources. "Teaching" on this model he later compared to acting as a "midwife"—assisting in the birth of knowledge *in* another person rather than serving as a supplier of it *to* another person. This was to be accomplished in conversation, mostly by skillful questioning and cross-examination ("Socratic teaching," "Socratic questioning," and "Socratic method").

Socrates admitted to behaving like a "gadfly" in this dialectical pursuit of truth, goading people into serious thinking about human living. And he also confessed to acting like a benumbing "sting ray" or "torpedo fish," referring to his ability to render people tongue-tied about matters that they thought they already knew perfectly well—but actually didn't. Not until people felt the sting of not really knowing about life's important matters could they be prompted to inquire into them seriously.

 Visit the website for more information about Socrates.

Source: Reprinted by permission of Steven S. Tigner.

book, or work of art are attempts to come to some aesthetic judgment on the value of the work. Whether a person "has good taste" is an example of a common aesthetic judgment.

Logic

■ the human ability to think

Logic is the branch of philosophy that deals with reasoning. One of the fundamental qualities that distinguishes human beings from animals is that humans can *think.* The pursuit of logic is an attempt to think clearly and avoid vagueness and contradictions. Certain rules of logic have been identified, and they constitute the core of this branch of philosophy. Logic focuses on reasoning and modes of arguing that bring us to valid conclusions. A primary task of the schools is to help children think clearly and communicate logically. Two types of reasoning are commonly taught in schools: deductive and inductive.

■ reasoning from general to particular

■ **Deductive Reasoning**   In **deductive reasoning,** the teacher presents a general proposition and then illustrates it with a series of particulars. The most highly developed form of this approach is the classic method of the syllogism. In a *syllogism,* one makes two statements, and a third statement, a conclusion, is *deduced* or drawn from them. For instance:

All human beings are mortal.

I am a human being.

Therefore, I am mortal.

In deductive reasoning, such as in this example, the general proposition, an abstract concept, is followed by a factual statement, which in turn leads to a new factual statement and the creation of new knowledge, at least for the learner.

As another example, imagine that in October, Mrs. Wells, a fifth-grade teacher, writes on the board:

All trees that shed their leaves at the end of a growing season are deciduous trees.

As a two-week project, Mrs. Wells asks her class to observe and record data about the trees that surround their school. For two weeks, the students observe the three dozen maple trees shedding their leaves during the fall. The teacher then writes her earlier sentence on the board again:

All trees that shed their leaves at the end of a growing season are deciduous trees.

And, using their observational data (and a little intellectual nudging from Mrs. Wells), the students complete the syllogism:

Maple trees shed their leaves at the end of the growing season.
    Therefore, maple trees are deciduous.

Then the students try to identify other types of trees that fit the deciduous classification.

Much of what a teacher does in school is helping children both acquire the intellectual habits of deductive thinking and expand their storehouse of knowledge through this process.

■ reasoning from particular to general

■ **Inductive Reasoning**   **Inductive reasoning** works in the opposite fashion. The teacher sets forth particulars, from which a general proposition is derived or *induced.* For instance, the teacher may wish to lead the students to the discovery that water is essential to plant growth. He gives each child two similar plants (a different type, from weeds to flowers, for each child) and then has each student daily feed one plant with water and leave the other plant without water. After ten days the teacher has the students report the condition of their plants, and from all of these individual reports he leads the students to generalize about the necessity of water to plant life. In fact, they have derived or induced their answer.

■ need for both types of reasoning

While the two forms of reasoning are opposite, both are essential to logical thought and, therefore, need to be developed in learners. Effective teachers design a variety of learning activities, some of which, like the tree example above, help students think deductively, and others, like the plant example, focus on inductive reasoning.

The function of education is to teach one to think intensively and to think critically. Intelligence plus character—that is the goal of true education.

—MARTIN LUTHER KING, JR.

Logic, however, is not confined to inductive and deductive reasoning. To think logically means to think clearly, in many different ways. Teachers need logic in many aspects of their work, from trying to understand the behavior of a child who seems to have an erratic learning pattern to developing tests that accurately measure what has been taught in a course. Most of all, teachers need to model this clear, logical thinking for students.

Overall, the four branches of philosophy—metaphysics, epistemology, axiology, and logic—address some of the major concerns of the teacher. The answers they suggest to the teacher and the implications they have for actual classroom practice are areas to which we now turn.

Pause and Reflect

1 ▶ Which of these four branches of philosophy do you think is of greatest importance to you as a future teacher?

▶ Schools of Educational Philosophy

Visit the website to link to more information about schools of educational philosophy.

Answers to the philosophical questions that pepper the preceding section have almost infinite variety. Over the years, however, certain answers by particular philosophers have received more attention and allegiance than others. These more enduring sets of answers or world views represent schools of philosophy. Some started with the early Greek philosophers and have grown and developed through the centuries. Other schools of thought are more recent and offer fresh, new formulations to ultimate questions.

In this section, we describe four philosophies that have had a major impact on American education and demonstrate the variety of ways in which teaching and learning can be conceived. It is important to keep in mind, however, that many important philosophies relevant to education, such as neo-Thomism and classical Eastern thought, or existentialism, are not included here. In addition, there are major educational ideas that do not quite qualify as "philosophies," but are having a big impact on schools.

■ four philosophies influential in American education

The four philosophies we have selected for this chapter are perennialism, essentialism, romanticism, and progressivism. Behind these rather daunting words are very different ideas of what people are, how we should live our lives, and how we should conduct the education of children. We have selected these philosophies, not because they are our pick of the "Top Four Philosophical Hits," but because of the level of influence each viewpoint has had on American educational thought and practice. We have grouped these philosophies as *subject-centered* or *child-centered*. For each of these philosophies, we present first a brief explanation of its origins and the core ideas it embodies, the implications for teaching and learning, and then a "personal point of view" by a teacher (fictitious) who is committed to that particular philosophy. We have tried to show that these positions are not just windy abstractions or the preoccupations of ivory tower thinkers; rather, they shape what people teach and how they teach it.

Subject-Centered Philosophies

The first two schools of philosophy, perennialism and essentialism, stress the importance of subject matter knowledge in education. Both schools of thought show a strong allegiance to the curriculum and both argue that well-educated students should possess a defined body of knowledge.

■ truth is unchanging

■ **Perennialism**   **Perennialism,** derived primarily from the writings of Plato, views truth and nature, in particular, human nature, as constant, objective, and unchanging. Beneath the superficial differences from one century or decade to the next, the rules that govern the world and the characteristics that make up human nature stay the same. The purpose of life, according to Plato, was the search for these constant and changeless truths, which reside in the nature of things. This search was achieved through the Socratic dialogue or dialectic, a process in which ideas are debated in a back-and-forth discussion until some recognizable clarity (the light) was reached. Essential to undertaking such a pursuit was mental discipline and rational thought processes.

Never mistake knowledge for wisdom. One helps you make a living; the other helps you make a life.

—Sandra Carey

Education is crucial to perennialists because it develops a person's mental discipline and rationality, which are necessary to the search for truths that will help humans avoid being dominated by the instinctual or animal-like side of human nature.

The video case *Middle School Reading Instruction: Integrating Technology* shows how one middle school teacher makes use of an ancient book in a thoroughly modern setting. As you watch the clips and study the artifacts in the case, reflect upon the following questions:

1. Does this teacher's approach represent perennialism, as it is described in this chapter? Why or why not?
2. Which of the other philosophies mentioned in this chapter might be included in this teacher's approach?
3. How well would this teacher's approach fit with your own developing philosophy of teaching?

■ **Perennialism in the School**   For the perennialist, the purpose of education is to find the changeless "truth," which is best revealed in the enduring classics of Western culture. Classical thought, then, should be emphasized as a subject matter in schools. Perennialists believe that schools should teach disciplined knowledge through the traditional subjects of history, language, mathematics, science, and the arts. Perennialists place particular emphasis on literature and the humanities because these subjects provide the greatest insight into the human condition. Although this view of the curriculum is evident in many areas of education, in its most complete form it is known as the *Great Books approach,* developed by Robert Maynard Hutchins, who was president and chancellor at the University of Chicago throughout the 1930s and 1940s and the late Mortimer Adler, a professor at the University of Chicago during the same time period. The Great Books, which constitute a shelf of volumes stretching from Homer's *Iliad* to Albert Einstein's *On the Electrodynamics of Moving Bodies,* are a perennialist's ideal curriculum.

One glance at a book and you hear the voice of another person, perhaps someone dead for 1,000 years. To read is to voyage through time.

—Carl Sagan

For perennialists, the development of the intellect is best achieved through a teacher-directed instructional approach in the early years of schooling. Socratic dialogue is then used to help mature learners question and examine their beliefs in order to move closer to the truth.

■ controversy about
    Eurocentrism

Since the early 1990s, a controversy has arisen over the content of perennialist literature, history, and philosophy courses. Scholars and students have criticized colleges and high schools for promoting a "Eurocentric" view of knowledge and culture, one that ignores the contributions of all but "dead, white, male writers and thinkers." They urge a more inclusive curriculum, one that gives greater attention to women, minorities, and Eastern, African, and Hispanic cultures. And, since 9/11, many are insisting that we need to gain greater understanding of Islamic literature and culture. While some take this movement as a direct attack on the perennialist curriculum, others see it as a natural and useful extension of the perennialists' search for the best of the world's wisdom. One perennialist friend of ours, who welcomes this new approach, suggested, "Sure, students should know about Islamic literature and Eastern philosophy, but they should first get to know their own neighborhood, Western culture."

Education as Preparation for Life

■ disciplined book learning
    prepares for life

*The object of education is to prepare
the young to educate themselves
throughout their lives.*

—ROBERT MAYNARD HUTCHINS

Education, then, is of great importance to perennialists, but it is an education that is rigorous and demanding. Perennialists hold that education is preparation for life, and should therefore not attempt to imitate life or be life-like. Students should engage in a rigorous examination of the classics in order to discover the timeless wisdom embodied therein, rather than focusing on knowledge that might seem personally meaningful.

In summary, the perennialists' view is that one learns through disciplined study of the great works and ideas of the past. It is a view that leans heavily on the authority of the collected wisdom of the past and looks to traditional thought to guide us in the present. As such, the curriculum is structured and clearly defined. Further, perennialists see education as protecting and conserving the best thought from the past. In this sense, the perennialist favors a very traditional or conservative ("conservative" as in *conserving* the best of the past) view of education. The following case study presents the point of view of a more or less typical perennialist teacher.

Case Study

Perennialist Teacher

■ electives as wasted time

I came into education twenty-five years ago for two reasons. First, I was bothered by what I thought was all the nonsense in the curriculum and by all the time my friends and I wasted in school. We were allowed to take whatever courses we wanted, the majority of which were electives which seemed to be little more than the teacher's hobby. There were so many discussions—discussions that seemed to go nowhere and seemed only vaguely to touch on the supposed content of the course. I often felt as if we were simply sharing our ignorance. My second reason for becoming a teacher is a more positive one. I am convinced that our society, our culture, has great ideas, ideas that have been behind our progress in the last 2,500 years. We need to share these ideas, to vigorously teach these ideas to the young. Essentially, I see my job as passing on to the next generation, as effectively and forcefully as I can, the important truths: for instance, about human dignity and the capacity of people to do good and evil.

■ humans not inherently good

That has always been the teacher's role until recent times, when we seem to have lost our way. I am convinced that a society that doesn't make the great ideas and the great thoughts the foundation of education is bound to fail. Nations and societies do falter and fall. The last fifty years have seen several formerly prominent nations slip to the wayside while other younger, more vigorous countries, like Singapore and South Korea, have risen. I am convinced that most of those failed countries fell because of the inadequate education they provided. I am dedicated to the goal of not letting that happen here.

teachers set the rules

I think students are just great. In fact, I've given my life to working with them. But I don't think it is fair to them or to me or to our country to allow them to set the rules, to decide what they want to learn, or to tell me how to teach it. Sure, I listen to them and try to find out where they are, but I make the decisions. My job is to teach; theirs is to learn. And in my classroom, those functions are quite clear. Really, students are too young to know what are the important things to learn. They simply don't know what they need to know. As a teacher, as a representative of the larger culture and of society, that's my responsibility. Turning that responsibility over to students or giving them a huge say in what is taught just strikes me as wrong.

self-discipline needed

I also believe that students should be pushed. School should be very demanding, because life is very demanding. I'm not worried about students' so-called self-esteem. Self-esteem is empty unless it is earned. It will come when they discipline themselves. All of us are lazy when we are young. We would much rather play than work. All of this trying to make school like play is just making it more difficult for students to acquire the self-discipline needed to take control of their lives. What schools are turning out right now—and it pains me to say this—are a lot of self-important, self-indulgent kids. And it's not their fault. It's our fault as teachers and parents.

focus on great ideas of the past

And the answer is so simple! We just need to go back to the great ideas and achievements of the past and make them the focal point of education. When we achieve this goal, the students don't mind working. The students and the other teachers kid me about being a slave driver. I don't really pay attention to that. But I do pay attention to the large number of students, both college-bound and non-college-bound, who come back two or three years out of high school and tell me how much they value having been pushed, how glad they are that I put them in contact with the very best! ■

Pause and Reflect

1 ► Have you seen elements of the perennialist view in your own educational background?

2 ► How much emphasis on classical enduring works do you hope to include in your own teaching?

■ **Essentialism**   **Essentialism** is a uniquely American philosophy of education that began in the 1930s and 1940s as a reaction to what was seen as an overemphasis on a child-centered approach to education and a concern that students were not gaining appropriate and adequate knowledge in schools.

two origins: idealism and realism

■ **The Roots of Essentialism**   Essentialism has its philosophical origins in two older philosophies and draws something from each. From Plato's *idealism*, it takes the view of the mind as the central tool for understanding an objective and unchanging reality, as well as for learning the essential ideas and knowledge that we need to live well. From Aristotle's *realism*, it takes the tenet that the mind learns through contact with the physical world; therefore, to know reality, we must learn to observe and measure the physical world accurately. From our observations, we use our reasoning ability to gain new knowledge. This contrasts with the perennialist view that reasoning alone can lead to truth.

essential skills and knowledge to be learned

The essentialists believe that there exists a critical core of information and skill that an educated person must have. Further, essentialists are convinced that

Essentialists follow Aristotle's idea that students must experience the world around them, as these students are doing on a field trip, to learn from it.
(© Paul Conklin)

■ beyond the classics

the overwhelming number of children can and should learn this core of essential material. The school, then, should be organized to transmit this knowledge and skill as effectively as possible. For the essentialists, then, the methods used to transmit this knowledge and skill are not specifically prescribed. The focus is, instead, on the knowledge that is gained by the students.

Essentialism begins to sound a good deal like perennialism. Although these two views have much in common, some important differences exist between them. For one thing, essentialists do not focus as intently on "truths" as do perennialists. They are less concerned with the classics as being the primary repository of worthwhile knowledge. They search for what will help a person live a productive life today, and if the current realities strongly suggest that students need to graduate from high school with computer literacy, the essentialist will find a place for this training in the curriculum. In this regard, essentialists are very practical. Whereas the perennialist will hold fast to the Great Books, the essentialist will make more room for scientific, technical, and even vocational emphases in the curriculum. Essentialists see themselves as valuing the past but not being captured by it.

■ Core Knowledge program

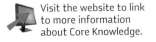
Visit the website to link to more information about Core Knowledge.

The philosophy behind the Core Knowledge program (discussed in the chapter entitled "What Is Taught?"), which speaks in detail about what students from kindergarten to eighth grade should know, is probably best categorized as essentialist. Based on the book, *Cultural Literacy,* by E. D. Hirsch, Jr., this content-rich curriculum stresses academics and learning of specific knowledge.

The ability to think straight, some knowledge of the past, some vision of the future, some skill to do useful service, some urge to fit that service into the well-being of the community—these are the most vital things education must try to produce.

—Virginia Crocheron Gildersleeve

While its emphasis on important ideas and great works of the past makes it attractive to perennialists, the curriculum's focus on current literature and emphasis on science point more to its alignment with the essentialist movement. Currently the Core Knowledge curriculum is being used in nearly 800 American schools.[2]

■ **Essentialist Goals and Practices**   For essentialists, the aim of education is to teach the young the essentials they need to live well in the modern world. To realize this goal, schools should focus on the established disciplines, which are the "containers" of organized knowledge. The elementary years should concentrate on the basics such as the "three Rs." These and other foundational tools are needed to gain access to the disciplined knowledge with which one begins to come in contact in high school.

■ student as learner, teacher as authority

Although there is some debate about what is "essential" in the curriculum, essentialists believe this is not a debate to which children can contribute fruitfully. Therefore, the role of the student is simply that of learner. The individual child's interests, motivations, and psychological states are not given much attention. Nor do essentialists hold fast to what they would call a "romantic" view of children as being naturally good. They see the students not as evil, but as deficient and needing discipline and pressure to keep learning. School is viewed as a place where children come to learn what they need to know. Teachers are not guides, but authorities. The student's job is to listen and learn. Given the imperfect state of the students, the teacher must be ingenious in finding ways to engage their imaginations and minds.

One notable essentialist was James Bryan Conant, a Harvard professor and president for much of the first half of the twentieth century. Concerned about disparities in the knowledge and skills that different high school students brought with them to college, Conant argued for standardization of college requirements for high school students. He was also influential in the establishment of the SAT as a measure of essential knowledge a potential college student needs to possess. While not purely an "essentialist movement," much of the thought and energy behind the drive for state standards, standardized testing and the No Child Left Behind Act [NCLB] has a strong essentialist flavor.

The following case study offers the perspective of a representative essentialist teacher.

| Case Study | ## An Essentialist Teacher |

■ stress on usefulness

■ selecting learning from the past

In my view, the world is filled with real problems, and the young people who leave school have to be ready to take up the challenge of life and solve those problems. So for me, the watchword in education is *usefulness.* I think everything that is taught has to pass the test of whether or not it is useful. My job as a teacher is to find out what is useful and then to make sure the students learn it.

I believe that school should be relevant to the young. However, my view of what is relevant is very different from the views of lots of other people. For me, relevance is not what is personally "meaningful" or a "do-your-own-thing" approach. What is relevant is what helps the individual live well and what benefits humanity. For that we need to look very carefully at the past and sort out the most valuable learning. That is what should be taught and what should be learned. I find the back-to-the-classics approach quite valuable. However, most advocates go too far in concentrating on classics. They also stress the humanities and the arts a little too much and tend to underplay science and technology. If children are going to function in today's world, and if our world is going to solve all the problems it's confronted with, we have to give more attention to science and technology than we have in the past. But clearly the past is the place to begin our search for the relevant curriculum.

It's not the most pleasing or satisfying image, but I think the concept of the student as an empty jug is the most accurate one. Certainly kids come to school with lots of knowledge and lots of interests. However, the job of school is to teach them what they don't know and to teach these things in a systematic and organized way. It's not to fill their minds with isolated fragments of information but to fill them with systematic knowledge. They need tools to learn, and, as they get older, they need human insights and skills that come from the disciplines.

■ task orientation and discipline

Given that there is so much to learn, an emphasis on student "interests" and "projects" and "problem solving" is quite wasteful. There is plenty of time for that outside of school or when school is over. Inside the school, the teachers are the authorities, and the students are there to learn what they don't know. The environment should be task oriented and disciplined. It doesn't have to be oppressive or unjust or any of that. I tell my students that learning is not necessarily going to be fun, but that at the end of the year they will have a great sense of accomplishment. I'd take accomplishment over fun anytime. By and large, most students do too. ■

Learning is not attained by chance; it must be sought for with ardor and attended to with diligence.

—Abigail Adams

Pause and Reflect

1 ▸ What knowledge do you believe will be essential for the students you teach to learn in order to be effective members of their society?

Child-Centered Philosophies

In contrast to perennialism and essentialism, the next two schools of philosophy, romanticism and progressivism, look first to the learner rather than the curriculum. Both consider the development of the learner to be the main purpose of education. A well-educated person does not necessarily have a definite body of knowledge; rather, a well-educated person is able to function well in society and life.

■ condemnation of society

■ **Romanticism** **Romanticism,** or naturalism, is based on the writings of Jean Jacques Rousseau, an eighteenth-century Swiss-French philosopher. In a condemnation of society and the educational system of the time, Rousseau wrote *Emile,* a novel that details Rousseau's ideas about education through the example of a fictional young boy, Emile.

Visit the website to link to more information about Rousseau and *Emile.*

■ **The Education of Emile** Rousseau believed that children are born good and pure, but once exposed to the evils of society, they become corrupted. To keep children good, they need to be isolated from society for as long as possible. Rousseau describes a serene, yet well-controlled bucolic environment for the ideal education of Emile; he is to be educated by a private tutor at the country manor where he lives. Emile's education begins with his exploration of the world of nature surrounding him. From his observations, he may ask questions about the natural world that the tutor answers. There are no formal lessons, no books to read or facts to memorize, no specific curriculum to learn. Emile decides what he learns about and when. As Emile matures, the tutor helps him develop rational thinking skills, but Emile continues to decide the topics of study. When Emile is around fifteen, he is slowly introduced to certain social situations until he is deemed "ready" by his tutor to resist the evils of society and live a productive life in the social world. By the time he is twenty, Emile is ready to take a mate and make a life for himself.

■ purpose is self-fulfillment

■ **Implications for Education**   Unlike the perennialists and essentialists who highlight the importance of educating the individual for society, the romantics consider the individual more important than the needs of society. For the romantics, the purpose of education is individual self-fulfillment, which means that education must help the students develop physically, intellectually, socially, and morally (usually in that order).

■ guided by child's curiosity

Romantics believe that education is a natural process, one that grows out of children's innate curiosity. This curiosity is most obvious during the "why?" phase of young childhood, when nearly every utterance out of the child's mouth is another question: "Why is the dog barking?," "Why is the boy sad?," or "Why is the bird blue?" (Parents often want to ask in return, "Why do you ask so many questions?") Romantics argue that we must let children's interests and curiosity drive their learning. The teacher's job is to respond to the children's questions as they arise and not to impose the learning of subjects that are not of interest to the child. The learner's responsibility is to maintain his or her natural curiosity and desire to learn. Because learning is guided by student interests, there is no set or common curriculum of study for the romantics. Some students may be interested in kayaking, while others want to study photography, and still others may be fascinated by how a DVD player works. As students pursue their own areas of study, the approach to teaching and learning also becomes individualized. Much of the learning is self-directed and self-guided by the students, with teachers serving as sources of information or resources to help the students satisfy their curiosity rather than as taskmasters or authorities on knowledge.

> *A sense of curiosity is nature's original school of education.*
> —SMILEY BLANTON

■ influence on early childhood education

Romanticism has been especially influential in the early childhood and elementary grades. Many early childhood educators, including such pioneers as Maria Montessori, Frederick Froebel, and Johann Pestalozzi, basically agreed with Rousseau's ideas about humans' innate curiosity and using the child's interests to define the curriculum. Although none proposed as radical a school setting as Rousseau's pastoral manor, they did adopt some of Rousseau's other ideas about education, such as providing young children with extensive opportunities to manipulate wooden blocks and clay and other real materials and establishing learning environments which provoke students' curiosity.

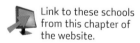

Link to these schools from this chapter of the website.

Today, schools like Summerhill in Suffolk, England, and the Sudbury Valley School in Framingham, Massachusetts, embody many of the beliefs of the romantics. At these schools, there are no set curricula, no formal classes, and no tests. Students decide what they want to study and in some cases are also expected to take responsibility for their learning.

Case Study   A Romantic Teacher

■ wonder turned off by school

Have you ever seen the thrill on a young child's face when he or she figures out how to make something work? What about their wonder as they ask another question about why there are rainbows or thunder and lightning? I see these young children, and then I look at some of the students in school today. Their faces are filled with so much dread or disinterest or boredom that I get disheartened. What happened to that enthusiasm,

Kids' views are often just as valid as the teachers'. The best teachers are the ones that know that.

—Morley Safer, TV journalist

that excitement for learning, I wonder? That schools, which should be places of learning, can turn students off to learning so strongly is the reason I became a teacher. I want my classroom to be a place where students can explore their interests and satisfy their curiosities. I can't make them learn information if it's not something they're interested in.

In my classroom, students decide what they want to study and I help them find the resources. Sometimes we get books from the library, or find websites on the Internet. The Internet has been a wonderful resource for my students. Some of them have been able to have online conversations with professionals in fields like aerospace engineering and bioengineering. Sometimes, I set up face-to-face meetings with professionals in a particular field. Last week, we had a computer programmer in to talk to a couple of students who were interested in learning more about writing code. It's so exciting to see students enthusiastic about what they are learning.

I am aware of the criticism about this approach to learning; students have big holes in their knowledge, they don't learn "the hard stuff," they can't pass standardized tests. My students may not do very well on standardized tests (what do they *really* measure, anyway?), but they do learn the hard stuff! I mean, computer programming, aerospace engineering, and bioengineering? Those are not easy topics to understand. It may be that my students don't know a lot of facts in the standardized subjects, but they know well what they learn because they have selected these topics themselves. They *want* to learn about them, so they do. ■

Pause and Reflect

1 ► How would teachers in public schools, who are held accountable for students' mastery of curriculum standards, be able to follow a romantic philosophy of letting student interest guide the curriculum?

■ nature is always changing

■ Progressivism **Progressivism** is a relatively young philosophy of education. It came to prominence in the 1920s, growing out of the progressive political and social movement of the time. It drew from some of the ideas of Rousseau and from the work of John Dewey, the most influential educational philosopher of the twentieth century (see the "Leaders in Education" box in this section).

Progressivism views nature as being in flux, as ever changing. Therefore, knowledge must continually be redefined and rediscovered to keep up with that change. Whereas other philosophies see the mind as a jug to be filled with truth or as a muscle that needs to be exercised and conditioned, the progressive views the mind as a problem solver. Like the romantic, the progressive believes that people are naturally exploring, inquiring entities. When faced with an obstacle, they will try to find a way to overcome it. When faced with a question, they will try to find an answer. For the progressive, education aims to develop this problem-solving ability.

 The video case *Middle School Science Instruction: Inquiry Learning* shows how one middle school teacher guides students as they develop and test hypotheses. As you watch the clips and study the artifacts in the case, reflect upon the following questions:

1. Does this teacher's approach represent progressivism, as it is described in this chapter? Why or why not?
2. Which of the other philosophies or psychological influences mentioned in this chapter might be included in this teacher's approach?
3. How well would this teacher's approach fit with your own developing philosophy of teaching?

■ **Progressive Education** Progressive educators believe that the place to begin an education is with the student rather than with the subject matter. The teacher identifies what the student's interests and concerns are and tries to shape problems around them. The teacher then helps the student develop strategies to solve the problems posed. The student's motivation to solve the

Leaders in Education

John Dewey (1859–1952)

John Dewey, the founder of instrumentalism, is widely considered the single most influential figure in the history of American educational thought. At the same time, his ideas and beliefs have been frequently misunderstood and misinterpreted, leading to the misapplication of his theories.

Dewey grew up in Vermont, where he attended public schools and the University of Vermont. As a graduate student in philosophy at Johns Hopkins University, he was deeply influenced by the ideas of Charles S. Pierce and William James, founders of pragmatist philosophy. Dewey recognized the implications for education of Pierce's argument that ideas, or propositions, have worth only if they make a difference in future thoughts or actions. Calling his own philosophy *instrumentalism* to emphasize the principle that ideas are instruments, Dewey argued that philosophy and education both involve the practical, experimental attempt to improve the human condition.

Dewey denounced the public school's classical curriculum in the nineteenth century as totally unsuited to the demands of newly industrialized society of the United States. He claimed that the schools were divorced from life and that they failed to teach children how to *use* knowledge. Defining education as a "continuous reconstruction of experience," Dewey said that schools should teach children not what to think but how to think. In his 1916 *Democracy and Education,* Dewey claimed that the schools offered students as future citizens no preparation for the responsibility of citizenship in a democracy. Dewey called for schools to provide a concentrated study of democratic processes and to reflect those processes in the organization of school life, going as far as advocating that students be given the power to make decisions affecting life in the school in a democratic way. He considered participation in life, rather than preparation for it, the watchword of an effective education.

In 1896, Dewey established the University Laboratory School, an elementary school at the University of Chicago. It was experimental in two senses: in its use of experiment and inquiry as the method by which the children learned and in its role as a laboratory for the transformation of the schools. The activities and occupations of adult life served as the core of the curriculum and the model teaching method. Children began by studying and imitating simple domestic and industrial tasks. In later years they studied the historical development of industry, invention, group living, and nature. Dewey wrote that we must "make each one of our schools an embryonic community life, active with types of occupations that reflect the life of the larger society and permeated with the spirit of art, history, and science."

The late 1920s to the early 1940s, the era of progressive education, saw a massive attempt to implement Dewey's ideas, but the rigid (and often inaccurate) manner in which they were interpreted led to remarkable extravagances in some progressive schools. For instance, some educators considered it useless to teach geography because maps changed so rapidly. The role of subject matter was gradually played down in progressive schools, replaced by a stress on method and process. The rationale was that it was more important to produce a "good citizen" than a person who was "educated" in the classical sense. Well into his nineties, Dewey fought vehemently against these corruptions of his views.

The centrality of John Dewey's thought to American education has waxed and waned over the years. Traditionally more popular in universities than in actual classroom practice, Dewey is often invoked by people attempting to make the schools more humanistic and the curriculum more relevant to the current world. Whether in favor or out, John Dewey represents the United States' most distinctive contribution to educational thought.

 Visit the website for more information about John Dewey.

■ student's concerns most important

The teacher's task is not to implant facts but to place the subject to be learned in front of the learner and, through sympathy, emotion, imagination, and patience, to awaken in the learner the restless drive for answers and insights which enlarge the personal life and give it meaning.

—NATHAN M. PUSEY,

FORMER PRESIDENT, HARVARD UNIVERSITY

problem is the key and posing problems based on student interests helps heighten their motivation.

Students should start with simple study projects and gradually learn more systematic ways to investigate until they finally master a variety of problem-solving strategies. Rather than being a presenter of knowledge or a taskmaster, the teacher is an intellectual guide, a *facilitator* in the problem-solving process. Students are encouraged to be imaginative and resourceful in solving problems. They are directed to a variety of methods, from reading books and studying the traditional disciplines to performing experiments and analyzing data.

Method is of great importance to the progressive. On the other hand, knowledge—formal, traditional knowledge—is not given the same honored place. For the progressive, there is really no special, sacrosanct knowledge or subject matter which students must learn. The value of knowledge resides in its ability to solve human problems.

Regarding the school curriculum, progressives believe that a student can learn problem-solving skills from electronics just as easily as from Latin, from agronomy just as well as from geometry. The focus for progressive educators is teaching students *how* to think rather than *what* to think. Progressive teachers often use traditional subject matter, but they use it differently from the way it is used in a traditional classroom. Because the problems students are trying to solve are of paramount importance, the subjects contribute primarily through providing contexts for problems students must solve. Subject matter knowledge may also provide information that leads to solutions. The focus for progressive educators is teaching students *how* to think rather than *what* to think. It is the process, not the product, which is of greater importance. Although both romantic and progressive educators start with the student's interests, progressives have more structure behind their teaching and they have goals for their students, to which we turn now.

■ **The School as Training Ground for Democracy**   Unlike the romantic educator who may see society as a negative influence on the student, the progressive sees society as an integral aspect of the student's life. Progressives view schools as small societies in themselves, places where students are learning as they live life, not simply preparing for life. This gives the progressive school a unique atmosphere, different from a perennialist storehouse of wisdom or a place with the clearly defined roles and authority structures of the essentialists.

■ school as a democracy

Education makes people easy to lead, but difficult to drive; easy to govern, but impossible to enslave.

—HENRY BROOKS ADAMS

Progressive educators believe the school should be democratic in structure so that children can learn to live well in a democracy and become good citizens. They emphasize group activity and group problem solving so that students learn to work with others and help others. This is one reason many teachers who describe themselves as progressive educators are enthusiastic about cooperative learning strategies such as those discussed in the chapter entitled "What Is Taught?"

Implicit in the progressive approach is the belief that children must not only learn to solve their own problems, but also help to solve those of their neighbors. For progressives, one of the main purposes of education is to make society better, which requires people working together to solve problems. It is not uncommon for the problem-solving activities of the progressive school to spill out into the community and involve students in issues like ecology and poverty. In this way, students learn an important principle of progressive education: knowledge should be used to redesign or improve the world.

One notable progressive educator was William Heard Kilpatrick (1871–1965), who was a professor of philosophy of education at Columbia University in New York. He was a follower of many of Dewey's ideas about education, but differed on the importance of subject matter in a child's educational experience. Rejecting formal curriculum study, he developed the **project method** of education in which students work in groups on a topic of interest to them. He believed that students learn only what is of interest to them so that they should be the ones to determine topics of study.

Both progressive and essentialist educators claim their particular approach is the true American philosophy of education. One can make a case that they both are, but each reflects different aspects of the American personality. Progressivism represents our antiauthoritarian, experimental, and visionary side; essentialism speaks to our more practical, structured, and task-oriented side. In recent years, many of the tensions and public debates in American education can be traced to struggles between these two philosophies of education. Clearly, though, essentialist educators gained ground on progressive educators in the 1980s and 1990s. Concerns over the country's global economic competitiveness and the perceived "softness" of our schools have created a receptive climate for essentialist views.

To judge your own sympathy for the progressive approach, see what you think of the following representative statement by a progressive educator.

Case Study	## A Progressive Educator

I'm a progressive educator and proud of it. I'm not ducking that label just because it is unpopular in many quarters these days, usually among people who don't really understand what it is. Quite honestly, for the life of me, I cannot understand how a teacher can be anything *but* a progressive educator.

I'm dedicated to a few simple and, I believe, obvious principles. For one thing, children come into the world with a very plastic nature, capable of being molded one way or another. We should therefore work to surround them with activities and opportunities that bring them in contact with good things. Also, by their nature, children are curious. Instead of rejecting their curiosities, I believe we should build on them. Schools should be exciting, involving places where students are caught up in interesting activities.

■ children molded by environment

I think that I'm a progressive educator because I have looked at my own experiences. I know I learn best when I'm trying to solve a puzzle or a problem that really interests me. And somehow I've always been able to get much more interested in how we're going to solve the problems of our own society than in the affairs of the Athenians and Spartans. I can get much more involved in a research problem about which MP3 player gives the best value for the dollar than about some dry economic problem presented to me by a teacher. And I really don't think I'm different from the overwhelming majority of students.

■ learning through direct experience

I see many of my fellow teachers spending all their energy damming up student curiosity and imposing work on their students. And then the teachers wonder why they themselves are so tired or burned out. I'm sure it's quite tiring to try to convert children into file cabinets and to stuff facts into their heads all day.

One of the things that sets me apart is that I'm not so hung up as others are on what I call the "talky" curriculum. I am convinced that students learn most effectively by *doing,* by experiencing events and then reflecting on and making meaning out of what they have experienced. I think more science is learned on a nature walk than from the same time spent reading a textbook or hearing teacher explanations. I think students learn more abstract principles, such as democracy, from trying to set up and maintain a democratic society in their classroom than from a lot of learned lectures and dusty prose on the subject. I'm trying to get to their hearts and their heads. The traditional approach gets to neither place.

■ focus on current and future problems

To me, life is a matter of solving problems. New times have new problems and demand new knowledge. I don't want my students to be ready for life in the eighteenth century. I want them to be effective, functioning, curious citizens of the twenty-first century. They are going to need to be able to develop solutions to fit new and unique problems. Although much knowledge is important, they need to realize that knowledge is only today's tentative explanation of how things work. Much of what we know now is incorrect and will have to be replaced.

It's not that I think that ideas and content and the traditional subjects are worthless. Far from it. I teach much of the same material as other teachers. However, I get there by a different route. I let the issues and problems emerge and then give the students a chance to get answers and to solve problems. And, as they quickly learn, they have to know a great deal to solve some of the problems. Often they get themselves involved with some very advanced material. The only difference is that now they want to. Now they have the energy. And, boy, once they get going, do they have energy! No, it doesn't always work. I have students who coast, and I've had projects that failed. But I'd put my track record against those of my more traditional colleagues any day. ■

Pause and Reflect

1 ► Did any of your teachers take a progressive approach to teaching? If so, how did you, as a student, respond?

2 ► Do you believe your students would respond well if you chose to implement a progressive approach? What difficulties, if any, do you think you might encounter?

► The Influence of Psychological Theories

Since early in the twentieth century, educational practice has been greatly influenced by the discipline of psychology. Psychology, the scientific study of the mind and human behavior, was a natural influence on the work of teachers, particularly with its focus on how we learn. Over the years, various schools of psychology have emerged, often having roots in particular philosophies. Some of these psychological theories have had a great deal to say to educators. Two in particular have had an impact on our schools: behaviorism and cognitive psychology.

Behaviorism: Conditioning Students or Setting Them Free?

■ learning by rewards and punishments

The psychological theory of behavior modification or **behaviorism** is an educational approach that emerged directly from the pioneering research of B. F. Skinner (1904–1990), who himself was influenced by the social efficiency movement in education of the 1920s and 1930s. Skinner developed the theory called operant conditioning, which viewed learning as the learner's response to various stimuli (for example, sounds, words, or people) present in the environment. Subscribing

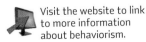
Visit the website to link to more information about behaviorism.

■ measurable objectives,
objective tests

to the view that humans learn to act in specific ways based on the response they receive for their actions (generally reward or punishment), the behaviorist teacher believes that learners need incentives, both positive and negative, as motivators to learn.

In planning for teaching, the behaviorist (1) uses clear objectives, spelled out in terms of the behaviors to be learned; (2) establishes a learning environment, which will positively reinforce desired behaviors and eliminate undesirable behaviors; and (3) closely monitors and gives the learner feedback on progress until the goal is achieved. The curriculum is organized in sequenced, discrete segments. Because the same behaviors and knowledge are desirable for all students, standardization of the curriculum and of measuring progress is important. Behaviorist teachers will often use objective tests made up predominantly of multiple-choice questions to measure how well students have learned the curriculum and to give prompt feedback to students. In some behaviorist classrooms, students are expected to practice a specific skill until they show a certain level of mastery of the skill.

■ behaviorist methods still
in use

In the 1960s and 1970s, many educators made behaviorism their dominant, organizing educational theory. This education movement has been criticized for being teacher dominated and causing teachers to treat students as passive objects to be conditioned. Nevertheless, behaviorism remains a dominant theoretical presence, particularly in the areas of special education and classroom discipline. Many teachers rely on behavior modification practices to get students to be quiet when they see or hear the teacher's signal or to do their best work to get a reward sticker.

Critics argue that a behaviorist teacher exercises too much control over students' learning and focuses on the learning of facts rather than deep conceptual knowledge. In response, behaviorist teachers insist that their goal is to eventually put control of learning in their students' hands once they have learned to respond appropriately to the teacher's prompts.

Cognitive Psychology: Students as Makers of Meaning?

What we want to see is the child in pursuit of knowledge, and not knowledge in pursuit of the child.

—George Bernard Shaw

Over the past twenty-five years, researchers in both medicine and psychology have been investigating the human brain to find out more about its role in human learning and memory. Cognitive psychologists, drawing heavily on the trail-blazing research of Swiss psychologist Jean Piaget (1896–1980), as well as that of the Russian psychologist Lev Vygotsky (1896–1934), and the American psychologist Jerome Bruner (1915–), have discovered a great deal about how people learn to think and solve problems. Their discoveries have led to the development of new theories about learning and cognition that have tremendous implications for how teachers teach. One increasingly popular theory derived from the research findings is that in order for new information to be internalized by the learner, it must be integrated into the learner's pre-existing knowledge base. This process of integration is referred to as **constructivism.**

Visit the website to link
to more information
about constructivism.

■ knowledge constructed

According to this theory, knowledge cannot be *transmitted* directly from the teacher to the learner, but is *constructed by the learner* and, later, *reconstructed* as new information becomes available. Instead of seeing students as partially full vessels waiting to be filled, teachers should view them as actively engaged in *making meaning*. Teachers, therefore, need to create learning situations where students can build their own knowledge rather than having students sit and listen to the teachers' lectures. Constructivism has become so influential in education in recent years that we give it particular attention here.

■ the individual as meaning maker

Constructivists view individuals as having an aversion to disorder. They believe that we are all continually trying to sort things out, to find clues and patterns amid our impressions that will help us to make sense of the world around us. When we encounter something new—say, a strange sound in the night—we immediately attempt to fit it into the patterns or structures we already possess (for example, "That's the midnight whistle of the Ole Ninety-Eight headin' down to New Orleans"). But sometimes we encounter new information that leads (or forces) us to realize that our knowledge base as it is currently "constructed" is incorrect or outdated ("Uh-oh! The railroad retired that train two years ago!"). We may respond in a number of ways: we search for new input from our senses, seeking either to reconstruct the knowledge base or develop different patterns and structures so that the information "fits" ("Maybe that noise was from the hot water boiler and it's about to explode," or "Maybe that creepy guy from the apartment down below is on my fire escape," or "Maybe I shouldn't read Stephen King novels before going to bed!"). In some instances, we may be so convinced of our knowledge base that we refuse to make allowances for the new information. ("No, I'm sure that it was a train whistle. They must have put that train back in service.") Students follow the same patterns as they try to make sense of new information they encounter in school.

VOICES FROM THE CLASSROOM

Susan Dougherty writes about her career as a fourth-grade teacher at Bayberry School in Watchung, New Jersey.

Constructivist Philosophy

As I began my career in education I held firm one belief about students: they must be active participants in the classroom. Twelve years later, I hold that same basic belief but have refined what it means for a learner to be active.

Early in my career *active* meant that my students would not sit in rows and spend the day doing seatwork. My first position as a kindergarten teacher quickly revealed that I might strive for something greater than physical activity. Of course, kindergarten students are active—try and keep them from being anything but active! I came to recognize that while active bodies can be important, what I really wanted was to engage the minds of my students.

As I taught students at many elementary levels, I learned to ask probing questions that required my students to consider their learning carefully. How do you know to add these two numbers? What kind of person do you think the main character of this story is? How would you explain why oil floats on water to someone who didn't understand? While my students were often physically active, acting out scenes from a novel we were reading, experimenting with magnets or prisms, or using pattern blocks to build models of math problems, they also spent time physically inert, but inwardly engaged in active thought.

Soon, however, I was not satisfied with simply engaging the minds of my students. I wanted to reach their hearts. I wanted to awaken a passion for learning within each student. How might a teacher encourage the awakening of such passion? One key, I think, is to allow and encourage the students to ask and seek the answers to their own questions. In this way, students' minds and hearts become active, leading them on a lifelong journey of inquiry and self-motivated learning.

 Visit the website for more Voices from the Classroom.

Cognitive psychologists also suggest that we organize our knowledge in ways that allow us easy access to knowledge we use regularly. These cognitive structures, which are called *schemas* or *schemata,* change constantly and continually as new information is taken in, hypotheses are developed, and theories are tested. These processes of hypothesis development and testing can be done independently or in interaction with others. Thus, real learning for constructivists involves moving from the Trivial Pursuit or Jeopardy type of factual or declarative knowledge to applicable knowledge—in other words, from "knowing what" to "knowing how." To do this, learners must develop cognitive learning strategies for particular kinds of learning tasks; that is, they have to learn how to think through or go about solving problems. One teacher describes how she puts her constructivist philosophy into action in the "Voices from the Classroom" box.

▶ Your Philosophy of Education

At this point, you may well be confused and possibly discouraged. To expect to be able to understand and evaluate critically every aspect of each philosophy is to expect of yourself what few professional philosophers are able to do. What you have just finished reading is a précis of some of the major ideas of Western civilization (see Table 9.1 for a summary). Some of these ideas have been around for centuries, and some are the fruits of twentieth-century thinkers.

TABLE 9.1 Four Philosophies and Their Applications to Education

	Perennialism	Essentialism	Romanticism	Progressivism
Metaphysics: What is real? Does it have meaning?	The meaning of life is the search for unchanging truth found in the collective wisdom of Western culture.	What is relevant is what helps an individual live well and what benefits humanity.	Reality is stable; the meaning of life is derived primarily through self-development away from society.	Reality is in flux and ever-changing, so meaning is in the context of the individual, who is a "problem solver."
Epistemology: Knowledge and knowing—what is truth?	Truth and knowledge are changeless, revealed through guided reflection and in classics of Western culture.	Truth exists in the classics *and* modern science. Students must learn process *and* content. Knowledge is gained through the interaction of experiences and rational thought.	Knowledge is gained through sensory experiences and interaction with one's environment.	Knowledge is gained via individual experience: Truth is individually defined so that emphasis is on learning *how* to learn.
Axiology: Values, ethics, aesthetics	Changeless. Determined by the very nature of reality.	Determined by the natural order of things. Values exist in the best of culture.	Determined by the individual.	Determined by each individual in interaction with his or her culture, based on the shared values of the community or culture.

	Perennialism	Essentialism	Romanticism	Progressivism
Logic: How we think, deductive and inductive	Rationality, especially deductive thought, is developed by studying classics and through the Socratic dialectic.	Rationality is best developed through interplay of deductive and inductive thinking.	Primarily inductive thought, since learning starts with experiences and moves to hypotheses.	Emphasis is on inductive thinking and problem solving.
Purpose, of Education/ Schooling	Educate the intellect; develop in learner rational thought and an understanding of the truths of humankind.	Prepare students to be productive, contributing members of society.	Make learner strong (physically, intellectually, morally) to resist the evils of society.	Helps students become good citizens familiar with the workings of democracy and with good problem-solving skills.
The Teacher	Teacher is expert of content knowledge. Passes on to next generation the accumulated wisdom of the past.	Teacher is expert of content knowledge. Teaches essential knowledge. Maintains task-oriented focus.	Teacher responds to learner's requests for knowledge; does not initiate learning in learner.	Teacher is facilitator of student learning; provides resources for students' problem-solving abilities. Develops students' problem-solving abilities. Helps children do what they want to do.
Teaching Strategies	Cultivates rational powers through contact with the culture's best and through imitation. For older students, Socratic dialogue is key to uncovering truths found in classics.	Avoids methodological frills and soft pedagogy and concentrates on sound, proven instructional methods.	Creates productive learning environment for learner; individualized approach to learning, depending on student interests.	Stimulates students to plan and carry out activities and research projects using group processes and democratic procedures.
The Child	Is there to learn what is taught.	Is there to listen and learn.	Is naturally good and must be protected from the evils of society.	Learns by doing and by discovering.
Curriculum	In younger grades, focus on basic skills to develop mental discipline and rational thought processes. Older learners study materials reflecting universal and recurring themes through which the truths of humanity can be revealed.	Strong emphasis on basic skills in elementary schools and on disciplined knowledge and scholastic achievement in secondary schools.	Dependent on the interests of the learner. No set curriculum, no specific skills to be acquired.	Centered on student's interest in real problems and interdisciplinary solution seeking.

Source: Adapted from a table suggested by James Hotchkiss. Used by permission of James Hotchkiss.

Identifying Your Own Philosophical Leanings

Think of your favorite teacher from elementary or secondary school, or a teacher you have admired during your teacher education. On a separate piece of paper, list some of that teacher's practices that you admire most. Include instructional techniques, classroom management strategies, ways of relating to the students—anything you think helped that person be an effective teacher.

Now, on the same piece of paper, write the philosophical outlook that you think may underlie each practice you admire. This will take some reflection, and you may well find that no single philosophy matches all the teaching characteristics you listed. Use whatever philosophical labels seem most appropriate.

After completing both tasks, what general conclusions can you draw about the philosophy of this teacher you admire? Does your teacher reflect the tenets of a single educational philosophy discussed in this chapter? Or does she or he take an eclectic approach, drawing on different philosophical traditions? Are there ways in which this teacher is too unique to fit any category?

As a final step, reflect on what this tells you about your own philosophical leanings. If you hold this teacher in high regard, presumably you share at least some of his or her philosophical convictions. Is there anything that surprises you about the philosophical beliefs you have deduced? Do they suggest that you are more traditional or more progressive than you supposed? More child-centered or subject matter–centered? More nicely balanced, or just more muddled? What aspects of your own philosophical base do you need to think about further and clarify?

How can you use this summary to help you develop your own philosophy of education? First, recognize that selecting the philosophy by which you will live and by which you will guide your professional activities takes much more investment of time, thought, and energy than reading our short chapter. You can start now, and the suggestion in the box entitled "Identifying Your Own Philosophical Leanings" may help, but developing and refining your philosophy is a lifelong endeavor.

Some teachers, like the teacher-philosophers in this chapter, settle on one philosophical view, and that view structures all of their work. Other teachers lean strongly toward a particular philosophy, even if they may not be fully conscious of their position or be able to give it a proper philosophical label. Typically they have a particular view of the learner, of how the learner should be approached, and of what is most worth knowing.

However, few teachers are philosophical purists. Some teachers, recognizing that they draw ideas from various philosophies, label themselves *eclectics*. But what does it really mean to be an eclectic teacher in contemporary education?

Pause and Reflect

1 ▸ It is perhaps unfair of us to ask you so soon after having read descriptions of different philosophies and theories of education, but, right now, which one holds the great intellectual appeal to you? Which one holds the least appeal? And, "why" to both questions?

Eclecticism: Not an Excuse for Sloppy Thinking

Eclecticism embodies the idea that truth can be found anywhere, and therefore people should select from various doctrines, systems, and sources. The eclectic teacher selects what he or she believes to be the most attractive features of several philosophies. For example, the teacher might take from romanticism the innate curiosity of the learner and from essentialism a curricular viewpoint dominated by the criterion of usefulness.*

■ the lazy kind of eclecticism

Eclecticism is quite popular, but often for the wrong reasons. It sometimes appears as the easy way out of philosophical uncertainty, just taking what you please from the philosophical cafeteria of ideas. ("Let's see now: I think I'll begin with a light vinaigrette salad of romantic individuality and follow that up with a main course of progressive problem-solving projects, but with some hearty perennialist classics as side dishes. And, oh, yes—let's finish with a popular and tasty dessert of essentialist vocational training.") One problem with this approach is the possibility of inconsistency. To take one's view of society from the romantic, who gives primacy to individual freedom, and one's teaching methodology from the progressivist, who stresses group membership and democratic process, is liable to make everyone confused. Selecting eclecticism must not be an excuse for lazy thinking.

■ eclecticism as a real teaching strategy

On the other hand, most teachers feel quite free and justified in borrowing teaching methodologies and strategies that are associated with various philosophies of education. The ardent perennialist teacher may choose to involve his or her sixth-grade students in a "hands-on" project constructing a large topographical map of Odysseus's ten-year journey to his home after the fall of Troy. Conversely, the free-spirited romantic teacher may insist that each student memorize and be able to recite fifty lines of *The Odyssey*. Although this type of eclecticism may, in a narrow sense, seem philosophically inconsistent, at its root is the recognition that no philosophy of education is able to dictate the ideal methodology or learning strategies for all situations or all students trying to learn all subject matter. Related to this is the growing realization (discussed in the chapter entitled "Who Are Today's Students in a Diverse Society?") that different students possess a great range of learning styles and that what works with one student may flop with another. In sum, eclecticism can be a serious philosophical position, and eclecticism in the selection of teaching strategies is quite justified. But, again, the choice to be "eclectic" should not be a substitute for sloppy thought.

Philosophy and Liberal Education

We are not suggesting that you sit yourself down, think through all these issues, and come up with a tight set of philosophical answers that will last the rest of your lifetime. Rather, we hope that we have focused—or refocused—your attention on some of life's most critical questions and on some issues that are at the very core of teaching.

■ opportunities to develop your philosophy

One purpose of the general education component of teacher education programs (that is, the courses in the arts and sciences required of the prospective teacher) is to provide a chance for future teachers to think through these fundamental questions of human nature and existence. A primary purpose of the college curriculum is to present the student with a spectrum of society's best thinkers and their attempts to understand their own existence. On the other hand, the infamous college bull sessions may be where the real philosophical inquiry goes on; they are frequently thinly veiled discussions of what really counts in life and what one should try to do with one's life. In effect, then, both the formal apparatus of college and its curriculum and the informal opportunities to meet, talk, and test your ideas with a variety of people should help you discover where you stand on some of these essential human questions.

* In the process of writing this chapter, we discovered that we are really traditional but progressive essentialists who are searching for a Great Books Club to join.

▶ A Final Word

As we said at the beginning of this chapter, the teacher who will be more than a technician has an obligation to take philosophical issues and questions seriously. Teachers owe it to themselves and to their students to understand where they are going and why they are going there.

As a wise teacher wrote, however, "A philosophy of education cannot be crammed down people's throats. They must feel it to be true in the marrow of their bones and look with trust and approval upon the leaders who attempt to give it expression. It must catch and reflect their temper, not arouse their distemper."[3] Teachers owe it to themselves to make sure that the schools they work in are hospitable—and certainly not hostile—to their own philosophies of education. It is important, therefore, that you be ready both to discuss your own philosophy of education with prospective employers and to inquire about the district's or school's philosophy of education. Do not, however, expect those interviewing you to be able to define their schools precisely according to the particular philosophies described in this chapter. Although educators live out a philosophy of education, we are not always able easily to capture it in words.

Key Terms

aesthetics (268)

axiology (268)

behaviorism (283)

constructivism (284)

deductive reasoning (270)

epistemology (267)

essentialism (274)

ethics (268)

inductive reasoning (270)

logic (269)

metaphysics (266)

perennialism (272)

philosophy (264)

progressivism (279)

project method (282)

romanticism (277)

For Reflection

At the present time, what beliefs do you have about the following: the role of the teacher, the nature of the learner, the nature of the curriculum, how people learn best? Thinking about these topics will help you to begin to formulate your philosophy of education.

1 What role, if any, does religion play in your philosophy of education?

2 Why do you think that superintendents and principals often ask teaching candidates about their philosophy of education?

3 And now, a really hard question: If you are leaning toward eclecticism, in what areas of teaching and learning would you draw on the various philosophies presented?

For Further Information

PRINT RESOURCES

Nel Noddings, *Philosophy of Education* (Boulder, CO: Westview Press, 1995).
This book is an extremely comprehensive and clearly written account of the ideas that have influenced educational practice. The author gives particular attention to modern thought, especially the feminist viewpoint.

Gary D. Fenstermacher and Jonas F. Soltis, *Approaches to Teaching*, 4th ed. (New York: Teachers College Press, 2004).
This slim volume shows how two philosophers can unpack the term *teaching* and explain what is behind several different approaches to instruction.

Jostein Gaarder, *Sophie's World: A Novel About the History of Philosophy* (New York: Farrar, Straus and Giroux, 1994).
This interesting and innovative book is an excellent introduction to philosophy and the history of ideas. The writer is clearly a marvelous teacher, plus a most engaging writer.

WEB RESOURCES

American Philosophical Association (APA). Available at: **http://www.apa.udel.edu/apa/.**
This excellent website provides basic information and reference material on many branches and schools of philosophy.

Larry Shaw, *Five Educational Philosophies.* Available at: **http://edweb.sdsu.edu/LShaw/f95syll/philos/ phintro.html.**
This website, developed by Professor Larry Shaw, is an excellent description of the key ideas competing for dominance in American education.

Gerald Gutek, *Historical and Philosophical Foundations of Education: A Biographical Introduction,* 4th ed. (Upper Saddle River, NJ: Prentice-Hall/Merrill, 2005).
This textbook is a comprehensive and up-to-date account of the competing schools of educational philosophy and their application to schooling. It provides thumbnail sketches of key figures and leads the reader in investigating their thought.

Materials on the Philosophy of Education. Available at: **http://commhum.mccneb.edu/PHILOS/ phileduc.htm.**
This site is a fine collection of further readings, including original sources, on the major philosophies of education. The majority of the material focuses on modern philosophers.

What Is the History of American Education?

Chapter Preview To understand our present educational system, its successes and failures, and the problems it still faces, we must look to our past. There we can identify the forces that have affected and continue to affect the development of American education. This chapter reviews the history of schooling and education in the United States, pointing out seven important themes and examining the contributions that significant men and women have made.

This chapter emphasizes that:

▶ Education in colonial America was originally religious in orientation but differed in form according to geographical area. Schooling in colonial America was not universal; it was primarily for white males.

▶ During the nineteenth century, influenced by the ideas of Thomas Jefferson and Benjamin Franklin and led by such reformers as Horace Mann, free public education became a reality. Common schools at the elementary level were tax supported and open to all children; the purpose was to cultivate a sense of American identity and loyalty.

▶ The nineteenth century also saw the development of public high schools that were designed to prepare young people, within a single institution, for either vocations or college; this goal of providing comprehensive educational opportunities was unique to American education.

▶ Private education has always played an important role in America, particularly in our nation's early days. Even today, about 11 percent of elementary and secondary school-age children attend private schools. Most private schools have a religious affiliation and thus offer alternatives to the public schools' secular emphasis.

▶ Equal educational opportunities for minorities and women have not always existed in America. Ethnic groups such as African Americans, Hispanic Americans, Native Americans, and Asian Americans, as well as women, have had to fight uphill battles to gain educational rights and treatment equal to those given to white males.

Rare is the college student who feels a burning urgency to answer the question, "What is the history of American education?" Unless you are a history buff, you will probably ask yourself, "Why do I need to know this stuff? How will it help me do a better job in the classroom?" In truth, knowing something about the history of American education probably will not directly affect your classroom practices. So why should you study this aspect of education?

■ why study educational history?

First, understanding American educational history will give you a sense of perspective. As educators, we are sometimes accused of being faddist, which implies that we blindly follow each new approach or idea, thinking it is the greatest thing since sliced bread. On the other hand, we are sometimes accused of reinventing the wheel, spending a great deal of energy discovering something that has been in the educational literature for years or was a significant part of the education program of a different culture.

Second, although studying the history of American education will not give you answers to the immediate problems you are likely to face in your classes, it will enable you to better understand the culture and context in which you will work. It will help you obtain the "big picture" of why things operate as they do in today's schools.

Finally, studying the history of education will help you appreciate its truly noble heritage. Schools have been a progressive instrument in the lives of most people who have attended them. They have freed people from superstition and false information and have given them new skills, positive values, and world-expanding visions of what each individual, as well as what we as a people, can become. Some of the greatest people who have walked the earth—Socrates, Jesus, Gandhi, among others—saw themselves essentially as teachers. Teachers, then, are part of an old, progressive, and inspirational human endeavor. Knowing our educational history and gaining a historical perspective will help you live up to and extend this tradition.

The farther backward you can look, the farther forward you are likely to see.

—WINSTON CHURCHILL

▶ Themes in American Education

Reading this book, surrounded by college classmates and friends, may seem a natural step in your educational career. Kindergarten or nursery school led to elementary school, then to middle school or junior high school, then to high school, and now college. You may have taken this progression for granted, assuming that's the way things have always been. Actually, you are enjoying a level of education that was available only to the elite of earlier generations. You are already close to the top of an educational pyramid for which the foundation was laid almost 350 years ago. The growth of the pyramid has been shaped and energized by seven major themes in American educational history:

■ seven major themes

1. *Local control.* Originating in New England during colonial times, the concept of local control of schools spread during the nineteenth century with the common school district system. Because of a fear of a strong federal government, the framers of the U.S. Constitution made no reference to education. As a result, state governments assumed the role of educational authorities and then delegated substantial powers to local school boards. Not until the mid-twentieth century did the federal government really become involved in educational matters.

2. *Universal education.* Education for all children has been a developing theme in American education. In the colonial period, education was reserved for a small minority, mainly white males. During the nineteenth and twentieth centuries, children from various groups previously omitted from educational opportunity (girls, minorities, immigrants, people with disabilities) gained access to elementary and secondary education. Today, a college education is generally available to all who actively seek it.

3. *Public education.* In the colonial period, education was generally private and primarily for the middle and upper classes. Private education still remains a small but important part of the overall educational system, but nationhood brought the spread of publicly supported education. By the early twentieth century, not only was public education widespread but education became compulsory, as well.

4. *Comprehensive education.* The basic abilities to read, write, and do arithmetic were once sufficient to prepare most children for their adult roles in society. However, the growth of urban, industrial life in America during the nineteenth and early twentieth centuries also demanded that people be educated for work. The result was the comprehensive public high school, which includes both training for trades and preparation for college.

5. *Secular education.* In earliest colonial times, the purpose of education was religious training. Beginning in the eighteenth century and progressing through the twentieth, the function of American education became increasingly secular, concerned with producing socially responsible citizens. Religious study has remained mainly in the private sector.

6. *Changing ideas of the basics.* Literacy and classical learning were the main goals of colonial education, whereas practical skills for a pragmatic, democratic society were the aims of the nineteenth-century schools. Technical and scientific literacy were added to the basics in the computer- and space-age late twentieth century.

7. *Expanding definitions of educational access and equality.* In the nineteenth century, the goal for educational access was to build schools in places where children lived and to enroll as many of them as possible. Since that time, the focus on **equality of education opportunity** has expanded. By the beginning of the twentieth century, efforts to equalize education involved offering more curricular choices, including vocational training, to help prepare students for different economic and social roles. Throughout the middle of the twentieth century, the focus was on removing legal, racial, and economic barriers to schooling. From the 1960s through the 1970s, access and educational opportunity became redefined as they became increasingly tied to results. The removal of racial, linguistic, mental, and physical discrimination as the basis for expanded access was augmented by a focus on measuring learning outcomes among different groups as a test of whether improved access led to real educational opportunity. As one noted educational historian noted that, "By the end of [the twentieth] century, . . . expectations had shifted to an emphasis on academic achievement."[1]

Many contemporary educational issues have their roots in these seven themes, which continue to shape the character of American schooling and education. Consider these examples of current issues:

• *Local control.* What should be the role of the federal government regarding education? Should federal legislation, such as the No Child Left Behind law, require states to test students in particular grades and subjects?

- *Universal education.* How can we ensure the quality of education regardless of whether students live in wealthy or poor school districts?
- *Public education.* Should private and religious schools receive public tax support?
- *Comprehensive education.* Should the schools require all students, vocational and college prep, to follow a common curriculum?
- *Secular education.* How should public schools treat the presence of religion in American society and world culture?
- *Changing ideas of the basics.* Is technological literacy a new "basic" of education, and, if so, how will schools finance programs that train students to use new technologies?
- *Expanding definitions of equal access and opportunity.* What should schools do about "achievement gaps" between poor and minority students and students from white or wealthier families?

These are just a few of the issues facing today's policymakers. As you read the rest of this chapter, look for links between historical forces and the key topics and debates in contemporary education. This chapter's tour through history is not a dead-end journey into the past. What happened in earlier generations has had a great impact on the schooling you received and the system you will enter as a teacher.

Pause and Reflect

1 ▶ Why is it important for teachers to know the history of American education? How might you use such knowledge?

▶ Elementary Education

Colonial Origins

Link to more information about colonial schooling at the website.

In the 1600s, some girls received elementary instruction, but formal colonial education was mainly for boys, particularly those of the middle and upper classes. Both girls and boys might have had some preliminary training in the *four Rs*—reading, 'riting, 'rithmetic, and religion—at home. Sometimes, for a small fee, a housewife offered to take in children, to whom she would teach a little reading and writing, basic prayers, and religious beliefs. In these **dame schools,** girls also learned some basic household skills such as cooking and sewing. The dame schools often provided all the formal education some children, especially girls, ever received.

■ apprenticeships

Throughout the colonies, poor children were often apprenticed or indentured to local tradesmen or housewives. Apprenticeships lasted three to ten years, generally ending around age twenty-one for boys and eighteen for girls. During that time, an apprentice would learn the basic skills of a trade and might also be taught basic reading and writing and perhaps arithmetic as part of the contractual agreement.

Although the lines were not drawn hard and fast, the three geographic regions of the colonies—New England, the South, and the Middle Colonies—developed different types of educational systems, which were shaped by each region's particular settlement patterns.

■ town schools

■ New England Town and District Schools   In New England, the Puritans believed it was important that everyone be able to read the Bible and interpret its teachings. As early as 1642, Massachusetts passed a law requiring parents to educate their children. That law was strengthened in 1647 by the famous **Old Deluder Satan Act.** Because Satan assuredly would try to keep people from understanding the Scriptures, it was important that all children be taught how to read. Therefore, every town of fifty or more families was obligated to pay a man to teach reading and writing. With these schools, known as **town schools,** New England set the precedent that if parents would not or could not educate their children, the government was obligated to take on that responsibility.

■ moving schools

When settlers spread out, seeking better farmland, the town schools began to disappear. What emerged in their place was the so-called *moving school,* a schoolmaster who traveled from village to village, holding sessions in each place for several months before moving on. One can imagine how much actual learning occurred under such circumstances!

■ district schools

Discontent with this system of education led to the development of the **district school.** By this scheme, a township was divided into districts, each having its own school and master and funded by the town treasury. The theme of local control of schooling developed in these various kinds of schools. The district school system soon entrenched itself in New England because it was inexpensive to finance and gave some measure of schooling to every child. Laws made attendance compulsory, but they were not very strongly enforced.

Some towns allowed girls to have one or two hours of instruction between 5:00 and 7:00 AM, when boys were not using the school building. For the most part, however, girls had no access to the town elementary schools until after the American Revolution,[2] and if few girls went to school in the towns, even fewer did so in the outlying districts. The theme of universal education, which would include girls, was not to develop until the next century.

The town and district schools were unlike today's schools in many respects. The schools were usually crude, one-room buildings housing twenty or thirty students. The interiors typically were colorless and cold. Heating was such a problem that students usually had to provide firewood.

■ New England Primer

Students entered school around age six or seven and stayed in school for only three or four years. They learned their ABCs, numerals, and the Lord's Prayer from a *hornbook,* which consisted of a page that was laminated with a transparent material made from boiled-down cows' horns and then attached to a flat piece of wood. Having learned the basics, students graduated to the **New England Primer,** an illustrated book composed of religious texts and other readings. Although there were other primers and catechisms, the *New England Primer* was the most famous and remained the basic school text for at least one hundred years after the first edition of 1690.

Foolishness is bound up on the heart of the child; but the rod of correction shall drive it from him.

—NEW ENGLAND PRIMER

■ dreary atmosphere

The learning atmosphere was repressive and grim. Students were under orders to keep quiet and do their work, and learning was characterized by an emphasis on memorization. Group instruction was almost unheard of; each child worked independently, one on ABCs, another on spelling, and another on the catechism. Class recitation was nonexistent. Instead, the master, sitting on a pulpit at the front of the room, called students up to recite to him one at a time.

If students did well, they were praised and given a new task. If they did poorly, they were criticized harshly and often given a rap across the knuckles or on the seat of the pants. It was believed that if children did not pay attention, that was simply a sign of how easily the devil could distract them from the path of righteousness. Such views continued to serve as a justification for severe classroom discipline throughout the first 250 years of American history.

Discipline in colonial schools was often strict and harsh. (© Historical Pictures Service/Stock Montage)

▪ private tutors

▪ **Education in the South** Conditions in the South were quite different from those in New England. Many upperclass Englishmen emigrated to the South, where they established large estates. As opposed to the more centralized conditions in New England, the great distances between southern settlements encouraged plantation owners to educate their children with private tutors, who were often local ministers or itinerant scholars. As in England, education of the poor and orphans was often undertaken by the Anglican Church or by religious groups such as the Society for the Propagation of the Gospel in Foreign Parts.

Most southern settlers were members of the Anglican Church and did not share the Puritan belief that everyone had a religious obligation to learn to read. The lack of concern for general education of the entire community caused public education in the South to lag behind that in other sections of the country for many generations. Town governments established schools, but their administration was usually delegated to a group or corporation, which could collect tuition, own property, hire and fire teachers, and decide curriculum content.

▪ private venture schools

▪ **Education in the Middle Colonies** Unlike Puritan New England and the Anglican Southern Colonies, the Middle Colonies were composed of various religious and ethnic groups. Quakers, Catholics, Mennonites, Huguenots, Baptists, and others each wished to train their children in their respective faiths; Dutch, German, and Swedish settlers also wanted a separate education for their children. As a result, **private venture schools,** which were licensed by the civil government but not protected or financed by it, flourished, and the use of public funds to educate everyone's children did not become customary.

In these private schools, parents paid the teacher directly on a contractual basis. The instructor managed the school and curriculum, accepting or rejecting students as desired. The denominational schools in the Middle Colonies shared the New England concern for proper religious training as a primary goal, but they also began early to offer, in addition to the basics, practical subjects such as bookkeeping or navigation.

Pause and Reflect

1 ► Why did the educational development of colonial America differ among the New England, Middle, and Southern Colonies? In what ways were the educational systems different? Can you see similarities to any of the colonial systems in today's schools?

The Common School

■ emerging idea of common school

Before the American Revolution, the term **common school** referred to schools that provided education for the average person, but it was not necessarily at public expense or available to all. Even in colonial New England, it was the students' parents who had to pay for the schooling. In the first blush of the new republic, however, conditions began to favor **universal education,** the idea that some sort of elementary education should be provided free, at public expense and under public control, for everyone who could not afford or did not want private schooling.

■ Northwest Ordinances

Even though the Constitution had relegated control of education to the states, the impetus for such public schooling came from the federal government, in particular as a result of the enactment of the **Northwest Ordinances** of 1785 and 1787. Concerned with the sale of public lands in the Northwest Territory (from present-day Ohio to Minnesota), Congress passed the Northwest Ordinance of 1785. Every township was divided into thirty-six sections, of which one was set aside for the maintenance of public schools. In the Ordinance of 1787, Congress reaffirmed that "religion, morality, and knowledge, being necessary to good government and the happiness of mankind, schools and the means of education shall forever be encouraged."[3]

■ **Arguments for the Common School**   After the American Revolution, it was recognized that a democratic government would be only as strong as the people's ability to make intelligent choices, which in turn depended on a basic education for all. It was also argued that education was a natural right, just like the very rights for which the Revolution had been fought. During this period, Benjamin Franklin and Thomas Jefferson suggested educational plans, as did other leaders of the Revolution.

If a nation expects to be ignorant and free, in a state of civilization, it expects what never was and will never be.

—Thomas Jefferson

The early period of independence saw an increased concern with citizenship and nationhood. A system of common schooling would strengthen unity. An influx of immigrants in the 1840s and 1850s, following a period of upheaval in Europe, further stimulated demand for an educational system that would serve to "Americanize" the waves of foreigners and keep society stable.

In contrast to European social structure, class membership in America was rather fluid: wealth and social status in this country depended less on the social class into which a person was born. Universal education, one of the key themes of American education, was thus seen by the newly evolving working class as a means of equalizing economic and social opportunities. As a result, another reason given for spreading educational opportunity was that better-educated people would increase productivity and enhance everyone's prosperity while diminishing crime and reducing poverty.

■ McGuffey Readers

In fact, school materials of the time reflected this argument. Whereas the *New England Primer* reflected the religious orientation of much colonial education, the textbooks of the nineteenth century began a trend toward secular education (another of the seven major themes in the history of American education), emphasizing morality and Americanism. No other book was more popular than the six-volume series of ***McGuffey Readers,*** which sold more than 100 million copies between 1836 and 1906. Besides training students in (American) English language and grammar, these texts introduced poetry and the writings of statesmen, politicians, moralists, and religious leaders. "They assumed the Fatherhood of God, the brotherhood of man, the wickedness of war, crime, and inhumanity, and above all, they buttressed the concept of the sacredness of property and bulwarked the position of the middle class in society."[4]

Although at this time universal education was meant only for whites, the same arguments advanced by its advocates were used later to extend equal opportunities for education to include racial and ethnic minorities and children with disabilities, to name just a few groups that have been denied equal educational opportunities. The desegregation efforts of the 1950s and 1960s were based on these very arguments.

■ who pays for universal education?

■ **Arguments Against the Common School** As proper as these thoughts may sound to the modern ear, they often encountered opposition. The arguments against the public common school were based on economics as much as on educational or political principles: why should one family pay for the education of another's children? Many people believed that schooling, especially for the poor, should be the responsibility of religious groups. Still others thought that a free public school would gradually weaken or dilute the particular culture or religion that they had sought to establish in America. If ethnic groups mingled together, what would be the fate of each group's native culture and language? Similar concerns are reflected in the current controversies about multicultural and bilingual education, discussed in the chapter entitled "Who Are Today's Students in a Diverse Society?"

■ what about religious study?

And what was to be done about religious study? The ability of different religious groups to exist together in one school, as in democracy itself, demanded that no one religious group be favored over another. Although there were many competing proposals, the common schools finally settled on the teaching of basic moral values such as honesty and sincerity, as a substitute for direct religious instruction. As described in the chapter entitled "What Are the Ethical and Legal Issues Facing Teachers?" the same issues remain with us today.

■ **Victory of the Common School** Between 1820 and 1920, the establishment of common schools made steady progress around the country. By the middle of the nineteenth century and certainly by the end of the Civil War, thanks in large part to the efforts of Horace Mann (who is profiled in the "Leaders in Education" box) and other common school advocates, the ideal of universal elementary education was generally acknowledged, if not universally practiced. By 1930, eleven states and the District of Columbia had passed compulsory attendance laws in addition to making common schools generally available.

The Common School is the greatest discovery ever made by man.

—Horace Mann

■ public school enrollment burgeons

As a result, between the Civil War and World War I, the number of students in schools grew enormously. In 1870, 57 percent of children between five and eighteen years old were enrolled in some form of schooling. By 1918, more than 75 percent of that age range were enrolled.[5] In 1870, average attendance was forty-five days a year; in 1918, it was more than ninety days. Thus, the hundred years between 1820 and 1920 saw extraordinary growth in the commitment to free, publicly supported, universal education.

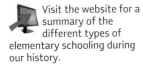 Visit the website for a summary of the different types of elementary schooling during our history.

Leaders in Education

Horace Mann (1796–1859)

Horace Mann was the radical educational reformer of his day. Born in Franklin, Mass., Mann received only the most rudimentary schooling until he was fifteen. Most of his education was self-acquired, a fact that profoundly influenced his philosophy of education. He studied hard to be admitted to Brown University, where he became a brilliant student.

In 1827, Mann was elected to the Massachusetts House of Representatives, and a luminous political career lay ahead of him, but he became committed instead to education and to the use of political methods to bring about educational reform. Asked why he had exchanged the practice of law for education, he answered that "the interests of a client are small compared with the interests of the next generation."

Horace Mann strongly believed in the ideals of the common school and championed its cause throughout his career. He saw education as a tool of liberation by which the poor could raise themselves, African Americans could become emancipated, and children with disabilities could adjust to their handicaps. After all, Mann reasoned, education had brought him fame and position. Thus, more than 150 years ago, the idea of social mobility through education was born in America.

For education to be as powerful a force as Mann envisioned it, he thought the school term must be lengthened and teachers' salaries raised. To make learning more relevant and enjoyable, he helped introduce new textbooks designed to illustrate the relationship between knowledge and the practical problems of society. Mann organized libraries in many schools, making books readily available to students. He believed less in the formal curriculum than in individual learning—undoubtedly because of his own self-education.

Mann was intensely interested in teacher preparation, and he believed teachers should be intellectual, moral, and cultural models for their communities. Mann was responsible for the establishment of the Massachusetts Board of Education and for the founding in 1839 of the first public *normal school* (a two-year school chiefly for the training of elementary teachers) in Lexington, Mass. Although the normal school opened with only three students, the concept spread and was widely imitated throughout the country.

He also made it his aim to abolish the cruel floggings that were then routine in the public schools. Most schoolmasters of the day believed flogging was an aid to learning and that it was their duty to drive the "devil" out of their students. Many of them administered from ten to twenty floggings a day.

Many of Mann's ideas were controversial, but he was most violently denounced for his position on religion in the schools. Although a religious man, he believed religious training belonged outside the schools, which should be run by the state. Because of his views, Mann was attacked from many Boston pulpits.

Mann was regarded as a dreamer and a visionary by many of his colleagues. When he took over the presidency of Antioch College in 1852, it opened its doors to all races and religious sects, and admitted women on an equal basis with men, some educators predicted that these measures would promote the collapse of higher education. Were he alive today, Mann might still be fighting for ideas he espoused more than a century ago, because many people have yet to accept these ideas.

 Visit the website for more information about Horace Mann.

Pause and Reflect

1 ► How are the arguments for and against common schools reflected in to-day's controversies about using vouchers to pay for private or religious schooling?

Other Developments in Elementary Education

■ **European Influences**   From Europe came new ideas about education. One of the most far-reaching experiments was the **kindergarten,** or "children's garden," where pleasant children's activities such as songs and stories were used to lay a foundation before formal education began. Friedrich Froebel of Germany developed the first kindergarten in 1837. The first American experiments were actually made before the Civil War, but in 1873 a public school kindergarten was established in St. Louis, and the idea spread rapidly. Elizabeth Peabody brought Froebel's ideas to the United States and was influential in instituting early childhood education in our country.

■ Pestalozzi

European influence also resulted in greater emphasis on the interests of the child in elementary education (see Table 10.1). Johann Pestalozzi modeled his educational doctrines in a Swiss experimental school at the beginning of the nineteenth century. Pestalozzi attempted to educate the heads, hearts, and hands of his pupils, relying on attitudes of acceptance and love of the individual student to reach large numbers of poor and handicapped children. Among his instructional techniques were *object lessons,* lessons that focused on actual objects and pictures. He also emphasized learning through sense perceptions and sequencing of learning experiences from the known to the unknown. We can still see in American education the influence of many of Pestalozzi's ideas.

■ Herbart

German educator Johann Friedrich Herbart, influenced by Pestalozzi's thinking, stressed that the primary purpose of education was moral development. Herbart also established a highly structured mode of teaching that strongly influenced American teachers during the early part of the twentieth century.

■ Montessori

Many European thinkers, and American educators influenced by them, believed students could learn best by direct experience, by using their senses and relating new learning to their previous knowledge. As a result, some schools incorporated more physical activity and manual training in their curricula. This innovation was designed not to train technical workers but to complement and round out traditional intellectual instruction. Maria Montessori, profiled in the Leaders in Education features at the website, was particularly influential in developing a curriculum that emphasized learning through the senses for young children.

The thoughts of Froebel, Pestalozzi, Herbart, and Montessori, among others, entered American education through their influence on issues of curriculum and instruction. The emphasis on the child's interest and experience, advocated by the progressive educators (described in this chapter and in the chapter entitled "What Are the Philosophical Foundations of American Education?") and still strong in American elementary education, owes much to these European thinkers.

■ less religious training

■ **Curriculum Changes**   The movement toward comprehensive education that occurred during this time period exemplifies one of the key themes of the history of American education. During the colonial period, it was hardly necessary for

TABLE 10.1 Major European Educational Thinkers		
Name	**Dates**	**Major Contributions**
John Comenius (Czech)	1592–1670	Emphasized sensory experience in learning
		Materials and instruction should be based on developmental stages of child growth
		Developed textbooks that were among the first to contain illustrations
		Stressed that schools should be joyful and pleasant places
		Believed we acquire knowledge of world through our senses
John Locke (English)	1632–1704	Believed we acquire knowledge of world through our senses
		Pioneer of the inductive, or scientific, method
		Recommended utilitarian and practical learning in a slow, gradual process
Johann Pestalozzi (Swiss)	1747–1827	Stressed the importance of children learning through their senses and concrete situations
		Advocated love and unconditional acceptance of children; schools should be like warm and loving homes
Johann Herbart (German)	1776–1841	Believed the chief aim of education was moral development
		Developed the concept of curriculum correlation—each subject should be taught so it relates to other subjects
		Believed history, geography, and literature were core subjects
		Developed Herbartian method of instruction: (1) preparation; (2) presentation; (3) association; (4) systematization; and (5) application
Friedrich Froebel (German)	1782–1852	Introduced the kindergarten, or "children's garden," whose goal was the cultivation of the child's self-development, self-activity, and socialization
		Believed the teacher should be a model of human dignity and cultural values
		Songs, stories, and games stimulated the child's imagination and transmitted the culture
Maria Montessori (Italian)	1870–1952	Established preschools run on the principle of allowing children freedom within a carefully designed environment
		Curriculum focused on three types of experiences: practical, sensory, and formal studies
		Created learning materials designed to develop sensory and muscular coordination
		Required considerable training of teachers to implement the structured curriculum

one to know anything beyond the four Rs unless one was wealthy and wanted to go on to college. In the early and mid-nineteenth century, the common school curriculum simply expanded on the colonial curriculum. The primary concern, however, was less with religious training and more with obtaining functional knowledge for life after school. Subjects such as spelling, geography, history, and government were added because they were considered important for good citizenship. Natural science, physical training, and mechanical drawing were also included to provide a complete, well-rounded education.

■ merging of districts

■ **Consolidation** Although the one-room school had served well in the days of the frontier, as areas developed, it became clear that the smaller, poorer districts could not provide the educational opportunities available in larger, wealthier ones. As a result, the early 1900s saw a period of consolidation of smaller school districts into larger, unified systems. In 1910, more than half the states allowed such unification. By the 1920s, the growth of industry and the invention of the automobile (and the school bus) had helped consolidate the large number of one-room schools around the country into centrally located, modern facilities that could serve larger areas better than the old district schools.

■ **The Progressive Education Association** John Dewey (who is discussed more fully in the chapter entitled "What Are the Philosophical Foundations of American Education?") and other educators tried to create new, experimental, child-centered schools in the early 1900s. In 1919, the establishment of the Progressive Education Association was a formalized attempt to reform education according to the following principles:

■ progressive principles

1. The child should have freedom to develop naturally.
2. Natural interest is the best motive for work.
3. The teacher is a guide, not a taskmaster.
4. A student's development must be measured scientifically, not just by grades.
5. Students' general health and physical development require attention.
6. The school and the home must work together to meet children's needs.
7. The progressive school should be a leader in trying new educational ideas.[6]

The progressive school movement eventually went in several different directions. Some educators argued for letting children be free to do whatever they wanted; others tried to make the school into a community center for recreation, adult education, and even social reform. Critics ranged from traditionalist advocates of the subject-centered curriculum to some progressives, like Dewey himself, who argued that the ties between society and the child would be broken if children were granted total freedom to do whatever they wanted.

■ influence of progressives

The 1940s brought a rather conservative reaction to the progressivism of the previous generation. However, it is good to remember that many ideas we take for granted now—such as teaching through student projects, fieldtrips, and nonlecture methods of instruction—were hotly debated innovations that were introduced by progressive educators.

■ special education receives attention

■ **Since World War II** After World War II, the role of the United States in world affairs increased tremendously, thus broadening the scope of educational objectives. The use of the single textbook was supplemented by a great variety of learning resources. Other major developments in elementary education included the rapid increase in kindergartens and an emphasis on providing special educational programs for children with disabilities. Between 1948 and 1953, the number of

■ new curriculum projects

■ education of gifted and disadvantaged

■ back to the basics

schools offering special education services increased by 83 percent, and enrollments in kindergartens in public schools increased from 595,000 in 1939–40 to 1,474,000 in 1953–54.[7]

A number of national curriculum projects were developed and implemented in the elementary schools during the 1950s and 1960s. In response to the Soviet launch of the space satellite *Sputnik,* many of the projects emphasized mathematics, science, and social studies.

Also during this period two types of students received major attention from elementary school educators: the gifted and the disadvantaged. (See the chapter, "Who Are Today's Students in a Diverse Society?" for more on gifted education.) Gifted students received attention because of our nation's concern over the Cold War with the Soviet Union and our perceived need to produce scientific breakthroughs to ensure our military superiority over the Soviets. As the movement for civil and human rights gained momentum, more and more curriculum reform movements also focused on the "culturally disadvantaged" child. In response to judicial decisions and protests by minority groups, the federal government advanced significant financial aid to change schools to better address the needs of these children. Compensatory education programs, such as Head Start and Title I of the Elementary and Secondary Education Act, improved the learning of disadvantaged children. (See the chapter entitled "How Are Schools Governed, Influenced, and Financed?" for more details on compensatory education programs.)

As achievement test and Scholastic Aptitude Test (SAT) scores declined during the 1970s, many parents, politicians, and educators argued that the schools had tried to accomplish too much and had lost sight of their basic purposes. A return to the basics seemed to be the cry of the late 1970s and early 1980s. Today academic rigor continues to be emphasized in the form of content standards, but more programs have been developed to meet the needs of students who are at risk for dropping out.

Although a public elementary school education is now available universally, the issues of what constitutes a proper education—how comprehensive it should be, how secular it should remain, and how basic learning should be defined—are far from resolved. The changing nature of what constitutes the basics of education has been another one of the key themes of the history of American education.

▶ Secondary Education

Link to more information about the history of high school at the website.

Today's *public comprehensive high school* has evolved from earlier forms of secondary education that included colonial *grammar schools* designed to either prepare students for college or for particular careers and private *academies,* popular throughout the nineteenth century.

Early Forms

■ **Latin Grammar Schools**   In the colonial period, all secondary education—that is, all education beyond the elementary level—served the sole purpose of training for entrance to college. The earliest secondary institution was the **Latin grammar school,** whose name gradually came to mean "college preparatory school." The term *prep school* still carries that classical connotation today.

A boy entered a Latin grammar school around age seven or eight and spent the next seven years learning Latin texts written by ancient Romans or medieval scholars. Much work was memorized, and over three or four years the student learned composition and writing of Latin verses. Following this, the student studied Greek, moving in the final year to classical Greek writers and the New Testament. He also might have given some attention to the study of the Hebrew language.

The first Latin grammar school in the colonies is generally considered to have been established in 1635 in Boston. It was public and open to boys of all social classes. The Old Deluder Satan Act of 1647, which required communities of fifty or more families to establish elementary schools, also required communities of one hundred or more families to establish Latin schools. At first, Latin grammar schools were found primarily in New England; a bit later they were instituted in the Middle Colonies.

■ Alternative Forms of College Preparation During the colonial period, many wealthy families in the South either hired tutors or sent their sons back to England for college preparation. Private venture schools were more common in the Middle Colonies. These forms of schooling generally relied on instruction provided by a single schoolmaster, which lacked variety and dependability. Gradually, corporate schools were developed; these institutions were governed by a board of trustees or directors and were able to continue as a corporate endeavor beyond the tenure of any particular teacher.

■ English Grammar Schools The growth of middle-class businesses in the 1700s led to the demand for a secondary education that would provide practical instruction in everything from navigation and engineering to bookkeeping and foreign languages. Thus there arose private **English grammar schools,** which catered to the growing number of students who needed more than elementary instruction but were not interested in preparing for college. Classes were offered at various times and places, sometimes to both girls and boys. Commercial rather than religious subjects were taught. Some subjects, such as music, art, and dancing, were actually not practical but were meant to train students for socializing in polite company.

■ Secondary Education for Females In the 1700s, private venture English grammar schools were more flexible than the Latin grammar schools and, as a result, were the first secondary institutions to accept female students. Depending on the sophistication of the particular school and the preferences of its clientele, girls typically studied the three Rs (reading, 'riting, 'rithmetic), geography, and French, but they also sometimes learned English grammar, history, and Latin. Some practical vocational subjects such as bookkeeping were occasionally taught along with such traditional and socially accepted skills as art and instrumental music.

Because of the somewhat larger number of private venture schools in the Middle Colonies, girls who lived there probably had greater educational opportunity than girls elsewhere. Quaker leaders, including William Penn and French-born Anthony Benezet, were concerned with and supported the education of several deprived groups, such as African Americans and Native Americans—and women.

Margin notes:

■ emphasis on classical education

■ corporate schools

■ commercial subjects

■ greater opportunities for girls

In the South, the daughters of wealthy landowners could receive traditional instruction in the various arts and letters, such as music, dancing, and French, which would give them the social skills appropriate for the lady of a household. By the end of the colonial period, separate class-based education tracks were developed for girls similar to those for boys in the English or Latin grammar schools.

The Academy

A new type of secondary school grew up during the second half of the eighteenth century. The **academy** was an attempt to combine Latin and English grammar schools through separate Latin and English departments within one school. Academies were unlike the Latin grammar schools in that the primary language of the academy was English; they were unlike the English grammar schools in that they included classical subjects in the curriculum. Gradually the academy took the place of both types of school.

■ emphasis on practical studies

■ **Growth of Academies**   The number of private academies grew rapidly after the American Revolution in response to the growing need for practical business training. Around 1850, about 6,000 academies were in operation.[8] Compared with the Latin grammar schools, the academies included instruction for a larger age range, which on the low end overlapped the curriculum of the common schools and on the upper end sometimes provided instruction that was as extensive as that of colleges. Although academies first focused on practical, useful studies rather than on college preparatory courses, over the years the emphasis shifted back to the classical languages and curriculum. Because they were private institutions, the academies were also at greater liberty to accept girls.

■ surge in education for females

■ **Female Academies**   The real surge of development in education for girls and young women came in the first half of the 1800s with the growth of academies and seminaries that were established especially for young women. Female academies were established by Emma Willard in Troy, New York (1821); by Catharine Beecher in Hartford, Connecticut (1828); and by Mary Lyon in South Hadley, Massachusetts (1837). (Learn more about one of these educational leaders, Catharine Beecher, in her "Leaders in Education" profile at the website.) A secondary education acquired at one of these institutions was often the highest level of education women would ever receive. Eventually, some of these academies themselves became colleges.

The female academies had to buck the established tradition against formal education for women, who in many quarters were still considered intellectually inferior to men. The schools compromised somewhat by offering courses related to home economics in addition to more classical subjects.

In practical terms, the leaders of the women's education movement were committed to two goals. One was to produce women who could handle the domestic chores and challenges of wives and mothers intelligently and wisely so as to "become companions rather than satellites of their husbands."[9] The curriculum of female academies therefore was designed to include subjects similar, but not identical, to those at men's institutions. Domestic skills were presented as practical applications of the more abstract traditional subjects. The other goal of women's education was to prepare women as teachers.

The availability of women teachers at low salaries during the late nineteenth century helped keep education costs down but, at the same time, contributed to the low salary problem that is still with us today.
(© The National Archives/CORBIS)

The Public High School

■ practical skills and teacher preparation

Although the private academies reflected the democratic independence of the middle class, their tuition and fees effectively cut out participation by the poorer working class. In the years following the American Revolution, the growing demand for free public elementary education understandably provided a basis on which to argue for free secondary education. Such schooling at public expense was the educational system most appropriate for democracy, it was argued, and the only system that could maintain democracy.

■ early public high schools

Although by no means universally accepted, the argument for free public high schools was a logical one, based on the inequality of providing elementary schools for all and secondary schools only for those who could afford tuition. In 1821, Boston created the first public English high school; a second one, for girls, was established in 1826. Unlike the academies, high schools were governed by the public rather than by private school boards.

The number of public high schools throughout the states increased slowly but steadily as an extension of the common school system. Not everyone, however, favored their spread. Opponents of the idea of public high schools did not dispute the need for common elementary schools. They did argue, though, that secondary school was a luxury and was not within the domain of the taxing authorities. In 1874, however, in the famous **Kalamazoo case** (*Stuart and Others* v. *School District No. 1 of the Village of Kalamazoo and Others*), the Michigan courts ruled that the school district could tax the public to support both high schools and elementary schools. This court case set the precedent for financing public high schools.

The ladder was there, "from the gutter to the university," and for those stalwart enough to ascend it, the schools were a boon and a path out of poverty.

—DIANE RAVITCH

■ multiple purposes

■ **Debate Over the Secondary Curriculum** In the late nineteenth century, debate shifted from whether public secondary schools should be supported to what the content of the curriculum should be. As is still the case today, guidelines for the curriculum were derived largely from the goals expressed for the schools. One goal was to reduce social tensions and strengthen the democratic form of government by bringing together all social classes and ethnic groups.

Another goal was to provide better preparation for Americans to participate, on graduation, in the full range of industrial occupations. In addition, the high schools were to offer specialized vocational and technical training. At the beginning of the 1800s, the appeal of the academies had been to provide training in studies that prepared students for a practical livelihood and not necessarily for college. By the 1840s the same goal was being demanded of public high schools. Seen in retrospect, the academies were really a link between the earlier grammar school and the later high school. High schools were supposed to provide both a terminal educational experience for most students and a bridge to higher education for those who were capable and chose to pursue further studies.

■ a more diverse curriculum

■ The Comprehensive High School   To meet these varied purposes, the secondary curriculum shifted considerably between the Civil War and World War I. The basic mathematics courses in arithmetic, geometry, and algebra tended to be taught in a more commercial and practical context. American literature began to compete with English literature, and commercial English was added to the study of literary English. The classical languages continued to give way to modern foreign languages. In the sciences, physiology, chemistry, physics, botany, and astronomy were joined by meteorology, zoology, forestry, agriculture, and geology. Physical education was added to the curriculum. In social studies, the number of courses in American history grew, although European history continued to be central. Civics and citizenship were added to history. Moral philosophy fell away completely and was replaced by purely commercial courses such as typing, stenography, commercial law, home economics, industrial arts, and manual training.[10] The result was the institution known today as the **public comprehensive high school,** which embodies the notion of comprehensive education, another of the key themes of American education.

During the twentieth century, public comprehensive high schools continued to spread. Between 1890 and 2002, the number of students in public high schools increased as a percentage of all students attending public school, from 1.6 percent to 29 percent.[11] This increase is shown graphically in Figure 10.1.

Growth of Junior High and Middle Schools

Link to more information about middle and junior high schools at the website.

For some time, educators debated the best way to divide grade levels for elementary and secondary training. The main question was when to stop teaching basic skills and start teaching content: Should there be eight elementary grades and four of secondary school, or six elementary and six secondary, or some other arrangement?

■ first junior high schools

In an attempt to resolve these issues, educators began to experiment with various ways to reorganize the grades. Finally, in the school year 1909–10, in both Columbus, Ohio, and Berkeley, Calif., a separate program was established for the intermediate grades seven, eight, and nine. The new grouping was called **junior high school.** By 1926, more than 800 school systems had a six-three-three organization, and that pattern became the dominant one.[12]

■ arguments for middle schools

Since the 1960s, however, the system of five elementary—three intermediate—four secondary grades has become increasingly popular, with a **middle school** for grades six, seven, and eight rather than a junior high school. Advocates argue that

FIGURE 10.1
Enrollment in Public Elementary and Secondary Schools by Level, 1869–70 to 2002, with Projections to 2013 (in Millions)

Sources: Thomas D. Snyder, *120 Years of American Education: A Statistical Portrait* (Washington, DC: U.S. Department of Education, National Center for Education Statistics, 1993), p. 26; William J. Hussar, *Projections of Education Statistics to 2014* (Washington, DC: U.S. Department of Education, National Center for Education Statistics, 2005), Table 1. Available at: **http://nces.ed.gov/pubs2005/2005074.pdf.**

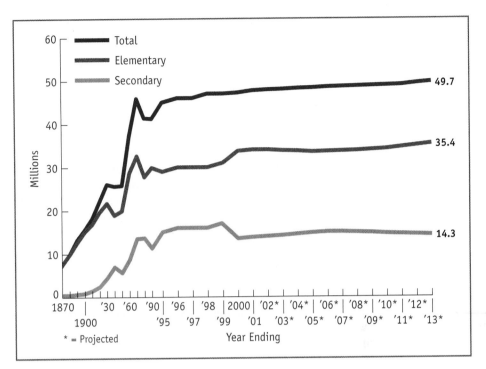

■ emphasis on personal growth

■ criticisms of middle schools

middle schools have significant advantages over junior high schools. For one thing, they offer a unique environment where ten- to thirteen-year-olds are free to grow up at their own rates and where attention is focused on the needs of this age group rather than on mimicking the high school's emphasis on academic and sports competition, as is often the case with junior high schools. Because of the earlier onset of puberty in today's children, sixth-graders may be better served in a school designed for early adolescents in grades six, seven, and eight than in an elementary school. Additionally, giving the ninth grade, which is still considered the first year in the college entrance sequence, to the high school frees middle schools to try new programs and new approaches without having to make them specifically applicable to college preparation.

Since the middle 1980s, there has been a deepening national commitment to the improvement of the education of early adolescents, with a strong emphasis on personal growth and development. To encourage this kind of personal growth, middle schools often use interdisciplinary team teaching, block scheduling, advisory homerooms, and exploratory activities and courses.

However, a recent report questions whether students of this age should be in separate schools.[13] The 2004 report from the RAND Corporation portrays the middle school years as a time when American adolescents feel unsafe, socially isolated, and academically unchallenged, and calls for a reconsideration of stand-alone middle schools. The RAND report relies upon research indicating that young teens do better in K–8 schools than in schools that require a transition to an intermediary school. Additionally, international comparison studies show that the relative performance of U.S. students in mathematics and sciences declines from elementary school to middle school, and national tests of proficiency show that the majority of eighth-graders fail to reach proficiency in mathematics, reading and science. As a result, some critics see the middle schools as having gone "soft," overemphasizing self-esteem building at the expense of academic rigor. These critics see the middle school curriculum as being unfocused, repetitive, and un-challenging. Some critics agree with the RAND study, arguing for doing away with middle schools and going to a K–8 elementary school and a 9–12 high school; while others want to maintain the middle school but increase its academic focus. Advocates for middle schools say that just changing the grade configurations is no magic bullet for improvement. What goes on in the classroom is what really matters, they argue. Programs need to be both academically rigorous and developmentally appropriate.

■ teaching in middle schools

Teachers are the key to what goes on in the classroom. In the past, many states permitted teachers with either elementary or secondary teaching licenses to teach in middle school, but now more of them are upping the academic course-work required of elementary school teachers who want to teach in middle schools in an effort to refocus the middle school curriculum on academic subject matter. A number of states have broadened the licensure eligibility of secondary teachers to allow them to teach as low as the sixth grade. Thirty-three states also offer teacher licenses specifically for middle school that focus on both adolescent development and academic subject-matter preparation. The RAND study suggests that relatively few teachers obtain this type of licensure; only 12 percent to 25 percent of teachers have specialized training in middle-grades education.[14]

Secondary Education Today

Look at the pictures of the two secondary classrooms below, one taken in the late 1800s and one from today. In what ways are they similar? How are they different? The most remarkable observation made about secondary education today is how little it has changed over the last one hundred years. There have been changes, of course, but they have been small relative to the changes that have occurred in American living patterns, values, technologies, and careers. The curriculum revolves around subjects that are taught by specialists and are not very different from the subjects offered in schools during World War I.

■ high school structure resists change

The reason lies in the basic structure of the high school. Its organizing framework, developed in the nineteenth century, persists today across all regions of the country. High schools are complicated organizations, requiring considerable orchestration to work efficiently. A change in one part of the system means that

© Bettmann/CORBIS

© Bob Daemmrich

other parts must also change. As a result, relatively little change occurs. The chapter entitled "How Should Education Be Reformed?" examines recent efforts at structural or system-wide reform.

Pause and Reflect

1 ▶ What made the development of the American secondary school so unique in the history of the world?

2 ▶ How would you group the grade sequence from elementary to secondary school? Why?

▶ Private Education

Private schools have always been part of American education. For more than 150 years, until the growth of the common school movement in the early 1800s, most education in America was private. Historically, private schools have served three major purposes, providing (1) instruction for various religious denominations, (2) an exclusive education for the wealthy, and (3) an alternative for any group that finds the available forms of education unsatisfactory.

■ Catholic school growth

Since the middle of the nineteenth century, by far the largest private school enrollments have been in parochial schools run by the Roman Catholic Church. The earliest Catholic schools existed primarily in the Spanish-speaking Southwest and in French-speaking Louisiana. After 1840, however, Irish and Italian immigration increased the support of Catholic institutions in the North and East. The total number of Catholic schools grew from about 100 in 1840 to about 3,000 in the 1880s, to 8,000 in 1920, and to more than 13,000 in the early 1960s. From that point through the early 1980s, however, many Catholic schools closed. Today, the number of Catholic schools has stabilized at slightly less than 8,000.[15]

Link to more information about private schools at the website.

In terms of enrollment, Catholic schools now have a total student membership of about 2.5 million, compared with an estimated 1.87 million students in other religious schools and an estimated 842,000 in nonsectarian private schools.[16] There are more than 27,000 private schools with a total enrollment of about 5.3 million, or about 11 percent of all students in U.S. schools.[17] The chapter entitled "What Are Your Job Options in Education?" offers more information about teaching opportunities in private schools.

■ discrimination against private schools

The steady reduction in the percentage of private school students in the nineteenth and early twentieth centuries was not only a sign of public school strength; it also reflected outright discrimination and pressure against those who wanted to be "different." An extreme case followed World War I, when Nebraska passed a law prohibiting the teaching of German in either public or private schools. However, in 1922, the U.S. Supreme Court ruled that a state could not interfere with the prerogative of parents to educate their children as they see fit—in this case, at a private school that taught the German language—simply on the grounds of desiring to "foster a more homogeneous people with American ideals."[18] When, in 1925, an Oregon law required all children to attend public school, a Roman Catholic school and another private school successfully challenged the law on the grounds that their Fourteenth Amendment rights were being threatened. In a landmark decision in *Pierce* v. *The Society of Sisters,* the Court overturned the Oregon law, holding that the act "unreasonably interferes with the liberty of parents and guardians to direct the upbringing and education of children under their control."[19]As a consequence of this decision, nonpublic schools survived efforts to eliminate them.

■ still an important alternative

But if public schools have clearly become the principal mode of education in America, it is also significant that private education has remained an important alternative for about 10–12 percent of the population. This fact reflects a paradox. On the one hand, from the early days, private schools have represented the freedom of immigrant groups to pursue life in America and to educate their children as they choose. That privilege was essential to the young democracy and still represents a basic freedom of choice in America. On the other hand, some argue that private education supports a caste system that is, in principle, not democratic. The very existence of private forms of education can be viewed as an implied criticism either of the quality of public education or of its availability on equal terms to all comers, irrespective of class, religion, or race. As discussed in detail in the chapter entitled "How Should Education Be Reformed?" this issue has gained in importance as school voucher plans expand to include private and religious school options.

Pause and Reflect

1 ▸ Do you believe the role of private education is likely to increase, decrease, or stay the same in the upcoming years? Why?

▶ Education of Minorities

The picture of American education that we have drawn up to now has been quite rosy because the educational achievements of this country over the past 350 years are indeed impressive. There is, however, a less pleasant side to the picture. The history of education provides insight into people's values in general, and the educational experience of minorities tends to reflect how a society relates to them. The somewhat idealized image of the melting pot begins to break down when we look at the experience of nonwhite groups.

■ minorities excluded from equal educational opportunities

The United States is a multiracial, multiethnic, and multiclass society. Many people consider it to be one of the most successful mixed societies the world has ever seen. However, it is far from perfect, and many children born into poor or minority-group families face severe disadvantages in their attempts to live decent lives and to climb the ladder of success. Schooling is intended to help individuals in this process. Traditionally, however, ethnic minorities such as African Americans, Hispanic Americans, Native Americans, and Asian Americans have not been given equal educational opportunity in America. Not until the late nineteenth century, for example, did the federal government make any serious effort to provide education for Native Americans. We will see that many groups struggled throughout the nineteenth and twentieth centuries to be a part of the growing access to education that developed for the majority of white students in America. American society is still suffering today from the effects of educational neglect of various minority groups.

As we begin discussing the education of minorities, it is important to note that members of a minority group are often discussed as though they were a homogeneous subgroup of Americans. However, the terms *African Americans, Asian Americans, Hispanic Americans,* and *Native Americans* actually encompass many ethnic, national, and linguistic groups. Although it is convenient to use these broader terms, we should not forget that within each subgroup great diversity exists.

Education of African Americans

Link to more information about the education of African Americans at the website.

For African Americans, the struggle for equal access to schooling and education paralleled the growth of education for the majority, beginning with efforts to simply provide schools. Efforts throughout the twentieth century focused next on offering a broader variety of curriculum options to African American students, and then on removing legal obstacles to equality of education.

■ **Before the Civil War**   As is true of colonial education generally, the earliest motivation to educate African Americans was religious. In New England, as early as 1717, the Reverend Cotton Mather started an evening school for slaves. In the South, the first attempts to educate African Americans were carried out by clergy, particularly English representatives of the Society for the Propagation of the Gospel in Foreign Parts. To dubious slave owners, ministers defended the education of slaves not only as a religious duty to save their souls but also because conversion to Christianity, it was believed, would make them more docile.[20]

■ schools for free African Americans in the North

In the North, schools were established for free African Americans. In 1731, Anthony Benezet, a French-born Quaker, started a school for slave and free African American children in Philadelphia. In 1774, another school was begun by Benjamin Franklin, as president of the Abolitionist Society. In 1787, an African Free School was established in New York City with an enrollment of forty students, which grew to more than 500 by 1820. The city provided funds in 1824 and took over the school in 1834, thus providing education for African Americans before many white children were receiving it.

Prejudices, it is well known, are most difficult to eradicate from the heart whose soil has never been loosened or fertilized by education; they grow there, firm as weeds among stones.

—Charlotte Brontë (from *Jane Eyre*)

Yet conditions were not all bright in the North. In 1833, Prudence Crandall, a white schoolmistress in Canterbury, Conn., began to take in African American girls. The villagers boycotted the school, threw manure into its well, and tried to burn it down. Finally, a mob broke the windows, and the school was closed.[21]

■ education for African Americans prohibited in the South

In the South, following slave rebellions in the early 1800s, states gradually prohibited altogether the teaching of African American children, whether slave or free. Some slaves were taught to read by favorably disposed masters. However, slave owners generally reasoned that reading would lead to thinking, and thinking would lead to the desire for freedom. As the Civil War approached, abolitionist agitation often came from the few liberal colleges, such as Oberlin College in Ohio and Bowdoin in Maine, that allowed the enrollment of African American students.

■ efforts to promote education

■ **The Late Nineteenth Century**   In the period following the Civil War, the seeds for the education of African Americans that had been sown before the war slowly began to sprout. During the period of Reconstruction, from 1865 into the 1870s, the federal government, through the Freedmen's Bureau and, in the former Confederacy, an occupying army, attempted to promote African American voting registration and schooling. Help also came from private and religious philanthropies in the North. Because it was hoped that whites also would benefit from these endeavors, schooling was advocated for the general public as well. Yet the common school movement was weakest in the South and, at first, most whites there refused to participate not only in integrated schools, but also in segregated schools, both of which they believed the northern carpetbaggers were forcing on them.

■ separate schools in South

By the end of Reconstruction, southern whites began to allow the existence of separate schools for African Americans. African American enrollment in the schools, which had been only 2 percent of the school-age children in 1850, was 10 percent by 1870 and 35 percent by 1890, although it dropped somewhat after that during a period of severe repression by the new white state governments.[22] During this period, "Jim Crow" laws were passed separating African Americans from whites in all areas of life.

■ Booker T. Washington

■ Tuskegee Institute—practical education

Into these conditions, a young African American teacher named Booker T. Washington (1856–1915) was called to start an African American normal school in Tuskegee, Ala., in 1881. Originally named the Tuskegee Normal School for Colored Teachers, it was later renamed the Tuskegee Institute. There, Washington found only a few students, no buildings or classrooms, and a hostile white community. Washington, who had been born a slave, realized that the traditional curriculum of the classics would neither prepare his students to help other African Americans learn nor help ameliorate the tensions with the white community. Believing strongly in the idea of learning by doing, Washington instructed his students to build the school themselves. In this process, they learned practical skills, grew produce that could be sold to the white community, and in general showed the whites that African American people could be productive members of society. Booker T. Washington gradually came to be considered the outstanding African American leader of the time by the white establishment.

But a growing number of young African Americans who, unlike Washington, had not been born into slavery believed that Washington's conciliatory policy of training for menial positions in white society would not benefit

The Tuskegee Normal School was established in 1881 by Booker T. Washington.
(© Library of Congress/CORBIS)

Education must not simply teach work—it must teach life.

—W. E. B. Du Bois

African American people in the long run. They believed that practical training is necessary, but there must also be an intellectually sound and academically rich program of study for the "talented tenth" of the student body, who would form the African American intellectual leadership. This was the view of W. E. B. Du Bois (1868–1963), an African American intellectual and scholar who held a doctorate from Harvard.

In 1862, the U.S. Congress passed the **Morrill Act.** This legislation granted each state a minimum of 30,000 acres of federal land with the proviso that the income from the rent or sale of these lands must be used to establish colleges for the study of agriculture and mechanical arts. A total of 6 million acres of federal land were donated to the states. The resulting land-grant institutions, such as the University of Illinois, Texas A & M, and Michigan State University, became the great multipurpose state universities that now enroll hundreds of thousands of students from all segments of society.

■ second Morrill Act

■ 1890 institutions

■ "separate but equal"

In 1890, Congress enacted a second Morrill Act that increased the endowment of land to the original land-grant colleges but forbade the granting of money to a college with an admission policy that discriminated against nonwhites unless a separate facility for African Americans existed nearby. This second Morrill Act thus provided federal support to states to create "separate but equal" colleges for African Americans. As a result of this legislation, a number of so-called **1890 institutions** were created for the higher education of African Americans. Many of these historically African American colleges such as Florida A & M and North Carolina A & T still exist today, but as integrated institutions.

In 1896, in the case of ***Plessy v. Ferguson,*** the Supreme Court upheld the constitutionality of "separate but equal" accommodations for African Americans. Although the ruling originally referred to seating in a railroad car, it was quickly extended to the schools. The practical significance of this ruling was to add federal sanction to the legal separation of African American schoolchildren from white children, most notably in the South, for the next fifty-eight years.

■ southern African American schools impoverished

■ The Twentieth Century   The fact that southern schools for African Americans were not equal to those for whites is woefully clear from looking at financial expenditures alone. In 1912, the southern states, as a group, paid white teachers slightly more than $10 per white child in school but paid African American teachers less than $3 per African American child. In the 1930s, in ten southern states, African American children made up 34 percent of the school population but received only 3 percent of the funds available for school transportation. Discrimination also existed in the distribution of federal funds, particularly in vocational education, the largest and most important educational program subsidized by the federal government.[23]

■ *de jure* segregation

■ *de facto* segregation

Most northern states did not have ***de jure* school segregation,** or *segregation by law,* but the crowding of African Americans into isolated neighborhoods often resulted in ***de facto* segregation**—that is, segregation resulting primarily from residential patterns. Furthermore, large numbers of southern African American children who migrated with their parents to northern cities often had to be demoted because they had not mastered the same amount of material as their northern counterparts. Generally, even in the North, African American teachers taught African American children. One teacher describes her experiences in a segregated school in this chapter's "Voices for the Classroom."

VOICES FROM THE CLASSROOM

Mary Reese is retired and lives in Charlottesville, Virginia. She was an elementary school teacher for eleven years before becoming a principal. She later served as assistant superintendent of schools in Charlottesville, Virginia, and associate director of the American Association of School Administrators.

Teaching in Segregated Schools

College diploma and job contract in hand, I headed to my first teaching job in a small, rural, segregated school. The advice, help, and insights provided by the experienced principal and teachers that first year convinced me that teaching was indeed a good career choice. It mattered not that the "new" books they were excited about receiving turned out to be the "used" books from the white school, and that the children had to walk fairly long distances to get to school because there was no bus transportation provided for them. The belief that a new school year meant a new opportunity to help children created an unbelievable aura of new beginnings.

I later became a teacher in a segregated school in a large urban school district—a school serving students from three public housing units. Again, "new" books, except for newly adopted state textbooks, included used books from other schools. School repairs, if made at all, were taken care of after the needs of the white schools had been attended to.

One of the most powerful insights from both of these experiences was how important the teacher was to the life of the students and the community in which they lived. I taught more than the basic academic skills to students. I assumed the role of family social worker, financial advisor, and any other roles necessary to help students and their parents believe that the school was there for them. I had to convince the student and parent that getting a good education was the key to a better future. I took it as my responsibility to help them learn that segregation was only a barrier if we let it become one.

I became the principal of that urban school after ten years of teaching in it. Shortly thereafter, the school was integrated, and we became a mix of low-income black, and middle-class white students. It was bittersweet to see much of the maintenance work that had been requested and never done, suddenly being taken care of without my having to submit work order requests. It was humiliating to have white parents come and give the woodwork and cafeteria equipment "the white-glove treatment." But it was as equally rewarding to know that their fears would be unfounded because of my belief that the school should be a clean and safe place for any student and staff member assigned there. Because we already had excellent teachers, a strong academic program, and a belief in and requirement of strong parental involvement, integration proceeded more smoothly than in some of the other schools.

 Visit the website for more Voices from the Classroom.

■ however, some gains

Although these conditions continued in varying degrees through the 1940s, some gains were nevertheless achieved. The average daily attendance of African American children increased and approached that of white students. The salaries of African American teachers also increased, reducing the economic gap between African American and white teachers with equal training.

In the late 1940s, the National Association for the Advancement of Colored People (NAACP) began taking cases to the courts. Beginning with universities rather than elementary schools, the NAACP succeeded in having the courts rule that various law school facilities for African Americans were clearly unequal to those for whites.

The stage was then set for the precedent-shattering case of **Brown v. Board of Education of Topeka** (1954), in which the Supreme Court ruled that separate educational facilities are inherently unequal and that laws requiring white and nonwhite students to go to different schools were illegal. This decision held that segregated schools are inherently unequal because the effects of such schools are likely to differ. Thus, a new component was introduced into the theme of educational opportunity: that equality of educational opportunity is defined in terms of the effects, rather than the provision, of schooling. Before *Brown*, the community and educational institutions were expected only to provide equal resources such as teachers, facilities, and materials. Responsibility for the best use of those resources lay with the child and the child's family. In the *Brown* decision, the Court found that even if the facilities and teacher salaries provided were identical, "equality of educational opportunity" would not exist in segregated schools. In the decades since then, many people have come to consider it the responsibility of the educational institution, not the child, to create achievement.

■ **Desegregation Efforts**   In *Brown* v. *The Board of Education*, the Supreme Court concluded that *de jure* school segregation violated the Fourteenth Amendment of the Constitution. Early desegregation efforts therefore were aimed at eliminating *de jure* segregation. Throughout the 1960s and into the 1970s, many school systems, often in response to specific court orders, also attempted to reduce or eliminate *de facto* school segregation. As a result, many school districts underwent desegregation efforts. What have been the results of these efforts? Several researchers have concluded that desegregated schools have accomplished more than mere educational reform—that is, African American students who attended integrated schools experienced desegregation in several aspects of adult life, including attending predominantly white colleges and universities, working in desegregated settings, and living in desegregated neighborhoods.[24]

Busing   Although these long-range findings are quite positive, desegregation efforts have had some negative results. One major problem has concerned busing. Busing students to desegregated schools was one of the most inflammatory issues in education in the 1970s and 1980s. Emotions on the topic often ran very high— so high, in fact, that white parents sometimes slashed bus tires, burned buses, and physically prevented buses from running to avoid having their children bused to other schools.[25]

The federal court system was the prime mover in ordering school districts to employ busing in the desegregation process. For example, the U.S. Supreme Court, in *Swann* v. *Charlotte-Mecklenberg* (1971), concluded that the need to hasten desegregation was great, and busing was deemed an appropriate measure provided the distance of travel was not so great as to risk the health of the children or impinge significantly on the educational process.

Busing to achieve desegregation has had mixed success. One of the most successful busing plans began in Berkeley, Calif., in 1968, and standardized test scores indicated that white, African American, and Asian American students all made better progress after desegregation.[26] On the other hand, in many other communities, attempts to desegregate the schools by busing met with tremendous community resistance.

■ desegregation result

■ court-ordered busing

■ mixed success

■ decline of busing

By the end of the 1980s, court-ordered busing was no longer the preferred method for integrating the schools. Busing, of course, was never an end in itself. It was only one means of integrating society, and polls indicate that even opponents of involuntary busing agree that our society needs to be integrated. As we will see, however, that goal remains elusive.

Big-City Desegregation   A major obstacle to desegregating big-city public schools is that the minority percentage of inner-city populations has increased dramatically during the past several decades. In part, this has been the result of "white flight," an exodus of white students whose parents have chosen to move to the suburbs or place their children in private schools. (This term is somewhat misleading, however, as not only whites are fleeing the city schools; middle-class African Americans are also leaving to give their children a chance to be educated in better schools.) Today, cities such as New York, Los Angeles, Chicago, Detroit, Atlanta, Houston, and Dallas have school minority enrollments approaching 90 percent.[27] How can schools in major cities be desegregated when the percentage of racial minority students is growing and the percentage of white students is decreasing?

■ metropolitan-area strategies

One solution would be to take the emerging residential segregation as given—minority cities and white suburbs—and attempt to overcome its effects on school segregation with metropolitan area–wide school desegregation. In this approach, children would be bused over the entire metropolitan area. However, the Supreme Court has ruled that this approach is justified only if racially discriminating acts of either state or local officials are judged to have occurred in the creation of either predominantly white or African American school districts.

■ Supreme Court reverses direction

In addition, several Supreme Court decisions during the 1990s dramatically reversed school desegregation plans ordered by lower courts, thus eliminating much of the pressure to desegregate schools. In these rulings, the Court has essentially conceded that there are practical limits to what a federal court can do to remedy prior discrimination, and once school districts have corrected initial racial imbalances, they are not required to remedy subsequent imbalances caused by demographic changes. Today the principal cause of segregated schools is not legal action but the choices of individuals whose housing patterns segregate our society and our schools. As long as these patterns persist, desegregation of the schools will continue to be problematic.

■ segregation increasing

Recent Developments   Increasingly segregated residential patterns and the slackening of legal pressures to desegregate during the 1980s and 1990s have led to a phenomenon known as **resegregation;** schools are becoming more segregated again. Evidence suggests that resegregation of African Americans is now fast approaching the levels before 1970. The average white student now attends a school that is 80 percent white, while the average African American student attends a school that is 67 percent African American.[28] In large urban centers, as was discussed earlier, the percentage for African American students is much higher.

■ arguments for resegregation

Although many political and educational leaders remain committed to desegregated schools, others are questioning whether integration is an idea whose time has passed. In many communities, these leaders, typically members of minority groups, call for shifting the emphasis from integrating schools to improving the quality of one-race neighborhood schools. They have lost faith that desegregation is the answer to better schools. These supporters of resegregation argue that it demeans African American children to believe that they can only learn when sitting next to white children in desegregated schools. Some also think that resegregation will protect African-American culture from the gradual eradication that would occur in an integrated setting. Further, they argue, resegregation would relieve African Americans of the disproportionate burden they have carried under most desegregation arrangements.

■ arguments for continued desegregation

Supporters of desegregation counter with the argument that most parents are mainly interested in good schools for their own children, not for the children of others. Accordingly, they say, whites will only support African American students who happen to be in school with their own children. If African American children are to benefit educationally, they need to attend school with white children. Otherwise, resegregation forces poor, largely African American school districts in low-tax-base cities to continue their losing struggle to find educational money that they don't have. As one advocate for desegregation says, ". . . blacks who favor resegregation are doing whites the great favor of relieving both their guilty consciences and their pocketbooks."[29]

Segregation was wrong when it was forced by white people, and I believe it is still wrong when it is requested by black people.

—CORETTA SCOTT KING

■ desegregation does not always lead to integration

Desegregation Versus Integration Another point needs to be made before closing this discussion: desegregation does not necessarily lead to integration. True integration is a very human process that can occur only after desegregation has gone into effect. It happens when people from different racial and ethnic backgrounds learn to be comfortable with one another and to get along together. It means ending racial prejudice and respecting ethnic differences. Anyone who has spent time in racially mixed schools, especially high schools, knows that African American and white students who attend the same school can still be extremely distant from each other. Just bringing together students from different racial groups, social classes, and neighborhood backgrounds will not automatically lead to friendship, understanding, and appreciation of one another. As long as our society remains segregated, efforts to integrate our schools are likely to produce tension, at least in the short run. Integrating individuals with increasingly diverse racial, cultural, and linguistic backgrounds remains one of the great challenges to schools and society.

Pause and Reflect

1 ▶ Where do you stand on the issue of *de facto* resegregation of urban schools? What, if anything, should be done about it?

2 ▶ In what ways did desegregation of American schools work, and in what ways has it not?

Education of Native Americans

Link to more information about the education of Native Americans at the website.

As early as 1622, in an ominous forecast of future policies, one colonist wrote back to England that it was easier to conquer the Indians than to civilize them.[30] The education of Native Americans received less public attention than that of African Americans because Native Americans were considered an impediment to westward expansion, they were far from major population centers, and their dealings were largely with the federal government.

■ education for religious purposes

Initially the education of Native Americans, like that of African Americans, had a religious purpose. Once they had been put on reservations, the Native Americans received schooling from missionaries, who attempted to "civilize"

At the beginning of the twentieth century, special schools for Native Americans, such as the Carlisle Indian School in Carlisle, Pennsylvania, taught basic skills, such as mending clothes, to students. (© CORBIS)

them through the three Rs and, of course, the fourth one—religion. In the 1890s, these missionary schools were gradually replaced by government boarding schools, which tried to forcefully assimilate Native Americans into the mainstream culture, by prohibiting them from speaking their native language and teaching them skills associated with white society, such as farming and mechanical skills for boys and domestic chores for girls. Little emphasis was placed on academics.

The people who had been Native Americans for 20,000 years finally became American citizens in 1924. However, that did not mean they controlled their own education. The federal government, through the Bureau of Indian Affairs (BIA), directed the education of Native Americans until the mid-1970s. During this time Native American participation was virtually ignored, as was acknowledgment of their culture in their educational programs.

By 1965, Native Americans had begun to demand control of their schools, and a few demonstration sites for such tribal schools were funded. These schools were able to include much of the native culture in their curricula, but they were still financially dependent on the federal government, which meant limited instructional materials and lower-paid teachers than in many public schools.

My son, Wind Wolf, is not an empty glass coming into your class to be filled. He is a full basket coming into a different environment and society with something special to share. Please let him share his knowledge, heritage, and culture with you and his peers.

—Robert Lake

- federal legislation

- majority attendance in public schools

Between 1972 and 1975, Congress enacted three bills that affected Native American education and self-determination. These bills encouraged the establishment of community-run schools, offered grants to develop culturally relevant and bilingual curriculum materials, and established an advisory council made up of Native Americans. The Department of the Interior's BIA is still actively involved in educational matters, but now in a supportive rather than directive capacity. The federal government has shifted much responsibility for educating Native Americans from the BIA and tribal schools to public schools. The BIA runs 184 schools, primarily located in Arizona, New Mexico, North Dakota, and

South Dakota. About two-thirds of the schools are operated by Indian tribes or tribal organizations under grants or contracts with the BIA.[31] The schools serve 46,000 students—fewer than 10 percent of all American Indian students enrolled in K–12 schools in the United States. The other 90 percent of Native American students in grades K–12 attend public schools. This trend may have helped reduce the isolation of Native American students. However, because Native American community involvement in public education is slight, the move toward public schooling has resulted in a loss of the limited control Native Americans had begun to exercise over the education their children receive.

■ **remaining problems**

Today the education of the Native American population in the United States, about 500,000 students, is still plagued by poverty, parental alcoholism, underachievement, absenteeism, overage students, and a high dropout rate. Native American students drop out of school more than any other racial group, except for Hispanic Americans.[32] Many Native Americans believe that a culturally appropriate curriculum is needed to overcome these deficiencies and reduce the cultural discontinuities between home and school. Only a small percentage of Native American students have teachers from their same tribe; most of their teachers are white females. One evaluation of Native American schools concluded that they should integrate their programs into a whole-school, standards-based reform effort and increase the participation of the Native American community.

The No Child Left Behind Act of 2001 poses challenges to Native American students who have a long history of struggling on standardized tests, particularly because of their limited English proficiency. States can craft native-language versions of the tests, but that is unrealistic for many states because of the many dialects spoken. Many Native American schools also face a tough time in meeting the law's mandate that all teachers be "highly qualified" by the end of the 2005–2006 school year. In addition, educators worry about the federal law's call for "scientifically based" research in creating school curriculum and instructional practices. Most of the methods of integrating native culture and language into classroom teaching have not undergone the same level of research scrutiny as those used with non-Native American populations, creating concern among Native American educators that these methods will wither away.

Education of Hispanic Americans

■ **discrimination against Hispanics**

The video case *Bilingual Education: An Elementary Two-Way Immersion Program* shows one current approach to teaching children whose first language is Spanish, two-way bilingual education. As you watch the clips and study the artifacts, reflect upon the following questions:

1. How does the scenario depicted in this video case compare with the historical treatment of Hispanic students described in this chapter?
2. How can you begin developing the skills you will need to work effectively with a diverse group of students?

As with Native Americans, the first contact Spanish-speaking people had with the United States was often a result of annexation and warfare. Although they have lived in the continental United States for more than 400 years, Hispanic people came into substantial contact with Anglo-Americans about 200 years ago, and almost from the beginning, there was a cultural clash. Hispanic children first attended religious mission schools, which were gradually replaced by secular public schools. In the process, the Spanish language and Hispanic culture were subjected to a type of discrimination that was perhaps less blatant than that against African Americans but just as pervasive. The common school of the nineteenth and twentieth centuries, although it opened educational and social opportunities in Anglo America for some minority students, often sealed off those opportunities for Hispanic Americans. Hispanic children tended to receive lower scores than Anglo-American children on English-language intelligence quotient (IQ) tests, which not only were written in a language that was not their own, but also reflected white middle-class values. Thus, an image of Hispanic children's intellectual inferiority was reinforced.

■ preparation may be the key

Today, 25 percent of Hispanic students speak mostly Spanish at home. These students are likely to have parents who have less education than those who speak mostly English at home. Only 49 percent of Hispanic students who speak mostly Spanish at home had parents with a high school education or higher, for example, compared with 83 percent who spoke mostly English at home.[33] Children whose parents have not completed high school, and who do not speak English, are less likely to receive at home the background skills and knowledge to begin school successfully. Schools need to develop programs to address the needs of these students, particularly those with limited English proficiency.

■ bilingual education

Since the 1940s, the courts have acknowledged that *de facto* segregation exists between Anglo-American and Hispanic schoolchildren and have required corrective integration plans. The 1965 Elementary and Secondary Education Act provided new support to the education of Hispanics, as it did to the education of Native Americans. Another response has been the establishment of bilingual education programs to provide students with instruction in their native tongue at the same time they learn English. The goal of such bilingual education programs is for students to enter the English-language curriculum at the appropriate age levels for their grades. However, as mentioned in the chapter entitled "Who Are Today's Students in a Diverse Society?" bilingual education programs are being denounced and replaced with English immersion programs in such states as California and Arizona.

■ high dropout rates, low academic achievement

Although significant progress has been made, there is still much concern about the education of Hispanics in the United States. For example, the high school completion rate for Hispanics ages eighteen to twenty-four is only 64 percent, compared with 92 and 84 percent for Anglo-Americans and African Americans, respectively.[34] About 10 percent of Hispanics ages twenty-five to twenty-nine have earned bachelor's degrees, compared with 34 and 18 percent for Anglo-Americans and African Americans, respectively.[35] Furthermore, reading and mathematics proficiencies are significantly lower for the Hispanic population in comparison with the Anglo-American population. The public schools have not served these students well, and the cost in human and economic terms is enormous.

■ fastest growing segment

Hispanic youth represent the fastest-growing segment of the U.S. population. Hispanics now account for more than a quarter of all new entrants into the labor force, and 16 percent of all children under the age of eighteen are Hispanic. As demographers project higher and higher percentages of Hispanic students enrolled in public schools in the twenty-first century, the schools' response to these students' needs will have important consequences for society. Without increased educational attainment, Hispanic Americans will be relegated to low-skill jobs and locked in the lowest socioeconomic brackets, with negative consequences for all Americans.

Education of Asian Americans

■ diverse groups of Asian Americans

The diversity of Asian Americans is evident from the historical beginnings of different groups of Asian Americans in the United States, and it persists in educational issues today. The three largest groups of Asian Americans are the Chinese, Filipinos, and Japanese.

■ discrimination against Asian Americans

Discrimination against early Asian Americans was rampant, especially in the West, where most Asian Americans settled. Although immigrants from China, the Philippines, and Japan often entered the United States to fill the need for hard labor jobs, whites resented the competition for employment. Exclusionary laws limiting immigration of these groups were passed in the late 1800s and early 1900s.

The video case *Diversity: Teaching in a Multiethnic Classroom* shows how the teacher of an elementary school class with a large percentage of Japanese students works with the class today. Watch the clips and study the artifact, and consider the viewing questions that accompany the case. In addition, you may wish to reflect upon the following questions:

1. How does the scenario depicted in this video case stand in contrast to historical treatment of Asian Americans, both in schools and in the larger U.S. society, that is described in this chapter?

2. In one of the *bonus videos*, the two teachers talk about how to best make use of the limited number of students with strong Japanese-language reading skills in the class. If a class had an even smaller percentage of students who shared language other than English, could a teacher conduct a project like this? How? What other ways could a teacher find to incorporate the cultures of English language learners into the curriculum in a way that was useful for all students?

■ recent Asian immigration

■ stereotype misleading

■ language difficulties

■ impediments to parental involvement

Link to more information about the education of Asian Americans at the website.

School segregation of Chinese-American children in California lasted until at least 1946. Japanese-American children in California were forced to attend segregated schools up until World War II. With the outbreak of World War II, the "yellow peril," perceived as emanating from Japanese Americans, resulted in the imprisonment in detention camps of more than 110,000 Japanese Americans, most of whom were American-born citizens. With the end of World War II, discrimination against Asian Americans began to subside. Naturalization rights were extended to resident Asian aliens.

Many Asian Americans benefited from greater job opportunities during the postwar expansion of the American economy. Previous immigration restrictions were lifted in 1965, and the influx of Asian immigrants greatly increased. Since the U.S. withdrawal from Vietnam in 1975, enormous numbers of Indochinese immigrants have come to the United States and entered our school systems.

Asian and Pacific Islanders currently constitute about 4 percent of all students enrolled in public elementary and secondary schools, and this figure is expected to continue to rise for the foreseeable future. Current census estimates indicate that Asian and Pacific Islanders number roughly 11.3 million, or about 4 percent of the U.S. population. It is projected that by the year 2020, this group will reach about 20 million, or 6 percent of the U.S. population.[36]

With the higher educational achievement and income levels of some Asian Americans, this group has often been touted as a "model minority" that has overcome discrimination through hard work, perseverance, and industriousness. However, this rosy stereotype is misleading and at times has contributed to misconceptions and complacency in meeting the educational needs and concerns of Asian American students. The adaptation of more recent Asian immigrants has varied because of a range of educational levels and previous socioeconomic circumstances.

Many recent Asian American immigrants to the United States have little or no knowledge of the English language. This creates formidable language and cultural barriers for students entering the U.S. education system, and may lead to serious family-school discontinuities, alienation from school, and dropout problems. The Supreme Court established in *Lau* v. *Nichols* (1974) that schools must offer students sufficient special instruction to be afforded equal educational opportunity. (See the chapter on "Who Are Today's Students in a Diverse Society?" for more on *Lau* v. *Nichols*.) There is a pressing need for adequate language instruction for this subgroup of Asian Americans, and as immigration continues to increase, this need will likely grow in our school systems.

Parental and community involvement of Asian Americans in the education process also needs to be fostered. However, because of the respect traditionally given educators, parents of Asian American students are hesitant to intervene when they are dissatisfied with their children's educational progress. Another deterrent to parental participation is the fact that a much higher proportion of Asian American families have two parents employed, a situation that makes attendance at traditional teacher conferences or parent-teacher organization (PTO) meetings difficult. Many communities are making efforts to organize and voice the needs of Asian American students.

As the number of Asian American students continues to grow, it will become increasingly important for teachers and administrators to be knowledgeable of and sensitive to the special problems and needs of Asian American students and their families. To serve these students adequately in our schools, it is particularly important to keep in mind that Asian Americans are a changing and complex group whose achievement, aspirations, and learning styles should not be stereotyped.

Access and Equality of Educational Opportunity

From our discussion of the education of minority students, it is clear that, even today, large numbers of minority-group students are leaving school without the academic and occupational skills necessary to function effectively in American society. This is also true of poor students from all ethnic groups. Who, if anyone, is to blame for this situation? The schools? The students? Teachers and administrators? Is the responsibility that of society as a whole, and are the schools merely being made a scapegoat? Talk to five different people, and you will probably hear five different opinions about where blame should be fixed.

■ opinions vary regarding poor achievement

At one extreme are those who think the problem resides in the so-called deficiencies of poor and minority children. Their impoverished home life, their particular cultural milieu, or even their mental capacities are cited as the sources of unequal results in school. At the other extreme are those who claim the problem is in the schools.

Some on this side of the question suggest that the problem is linked to the way schools are governed and financed. Numerous court cases have challenged the school finance systems in various states, charging that when educational spending in rich school districts exceeds that of poor districts by two or three times, students in the poor districts are not getting access to equal educational opportunities. In a number of cases, courts have ordered legislatures to redesign the school finance system. (See the chapter entitled "How Are Schools Governed, Influenced, and Financed?" for more on the topic of equitable school finance.)

Others believe that teaching must be improved, that teachers today neither stimulate nor instruct poor and minority children with the intensity that is needed. Teachers expect these children to do poorly, they claim, and this becomes a self-fulfilling prophecy. As described in the "Who Are Today's Students in a Diverse Society?" chapter, this position assumes that it is the school's obligation to diagnose the learner's needs, concerns, and cognitive and affective styles and to adjust its program accordingly. In fact, the No Child Left Behind Act of 2001, which requires schools to report the academic performance of students in various racial and ethnic groups, is intended to close the academic achievement gaps between white and Asian students on the one hand, and African American, Hispanic American, and Native American students on the other hand. Not everyone accepts this assertion; many argue that the school should do its best to provide equal educational resources for all its students but cannot be held accountable for differences in student learning.

As with most controversies, however, the answer probably lies somewhere in between: many poor and minority students do come to school with certain deficiencies, but the schools need to learn how to overcome them.

Pause and Reflect

1 ► In what ways were the histories of the education of minority groups and women similar and different?

2 ► Limited English proficiency seems to be a major problem in increasing educational attainment for several minority groups. What ideas do you have about how this problem should be addressed?

3 ▶ Do you agree that equality of educational opportunity should be defined by its effects rather than by its provisions? Why or why not?

▶ A Final Word

At the beginning of this chapter, we identified seven major themes that have shaped the history of American education and schooling: local control, universal education, public education, comprehensive education, secular education, changing ideas of the basics, and expanding definitions of access and equal opportunity. If you think back over the issues raised in earlier chapters of this text, you can see the effect of these themes on contemporary education. For example, the universal and public nature of the educational system strikes at the issue of equal educational opportunity and questions of school finance and governance. Current controversies over the content of education—questions about the secular or sacred nature of the curriculum, debate about the need for standards of learning, and efforts to provide excellence in education without sacrificing equality of opportunity—relate to the concepts of secular, universal, and comprehensive education and the definition of what is "basic." Thus, these seven themes continue to play themselves out in our evolving educational system. Table 10.2 lists important dates and events in American education, many of which relate to these seven themes.

TABLE 10.2 Key Events and Curriculum Trends in American Education

Time Period	Key Educational and National Events	Educational Trends/ Emphases and Characteristics of Curriculum	Dominant Educational Philosophies
1620–Revolutionary War	1635—Establishment of the Boston Latin grammar school 1647—Massachusetts Old Deluder Satan Act 1687–90—First edition of the *New England Primer*	Education limited by sex and socioeconomic class. Curriculum emphasized religious training (Bible), moral development, reading, writing, and arithmetic basics.	Perennialism
1770s–1820s	1775–83—Revolutionary War 1783—Noah Webster publishes *American Spelling Book* 1785, 1787—Northwest Ordinances 1788—U.S. Constitution ratified	Education emphasized literacy to make democracy work. Curriculum emphases included moral development, either practical education for career or university education.	Perennialism
1820s–80s	1821—First U.S. public high school 1821—Emma Willard establishes first school for women's higher education 1839—First U.S. public normal school, Lexington, Mass. 1860—First U.S. English-language kindergarten 1861–65—Civil War 1862—First Morrill Act establishes land-grant institutions	Education used to promote "melting pot" assimilation of immigrants and minorities. Curriculum emphases included basic tools of literacy, conservative moral values *(McGuffey Readers)*, cultivation of American identity.	Perennialism

TABLE 10.2 Continued

Time Period	Key Educational and National Events	Educational Trends/ Emphases and Characteristics of Curriculum	Dominant Educational Philosophies
1880s–1950s	1890—Second Morrill Act calls for nondiscrimination in college admissions or "separate but equal" institutions 1914–18—World War 1 1896—U.S. Supreme Court *Plessy* v. *Ferguson* case establishes separate schools for whites and blacks 1930s—Great Depression 1939–45—World War II 1944—GI Bill funds higher education for veterans	Child-centered curriculum became popular, emphasizing activities and experiences rather than verbal and literacy skills, cooperative rather than individual learning activities, citizenship, and self-adjustment.	Progressivism Romanticism
1950s–1970s	1954—U.S. Supreme Court case *Brown* v. *Board of Education* requires desegregation of schools 1957—Soviet Union launches *Sputnik* 1965—Elementary and Secondary Education Act 1971—U.S. Supreme Court case *Swann* v. *Charlotte-Mecklenberg* rules busing may be used for desegregation 1972—Title IX 1975—Education for All Handicapped Children Act (Public Law 94–142) 1979—Department of Education established	Curriculum emphases in the 1950s and 1960s included structure of the discipline and the discovery method of teaching, teaching gifted and talented students. Emphases in the 1970s on mainstreaming, multicultural education, career education, and a flexible curriculum with many electives.	Essentialism
1980s	1983—*A Nation at Risk* published.	Educational reform; reports issued leading to back-to-basics movement, core curriculum, stronger academic requirements. Inclusion and multicultural education grew.	Essentialism Perennialism
1990s	1990—Americans with Disabilities Act 1990—Individuals with Disabilities Education Act	Growing teacher shortage National Education Association (NEA) and American Federation of Teachers (AFT) merger talks fail. Growing standards movement leads to high-stakes testing. Strong technology emphasis. Growing rejection of bilingual education.	Essentialism
2000 and beyond	2001—Leave No Child Behind Act (reauthorization of Elementary and Secondary Education Act) 2004—Reauthorization of IDEA	Federal emphasis on "scientifically based" instructional practices in schools and "highly qualified" teachers.	Essentialism

Key Terms

academy (306)
Brown v. *Board of Education of Topeka* (317)
common school (298)
dame school (295)
de facto [school] segregation (315)
de jure school segregation (315)
district school (296)
1890 institutions (315)
English grammar school (305)

equality of educational opportunity (294)
junior high school (308)
Kalamazoo case (307)
kindergarten (301)
Latin grammar school (304)
McGuffey Readers (299)
middle school (308)
Morrill Act (315)
New England Primer (296)

Northwest Ordinances (298)
Old Deluder Satan Act (296)
Plessy v. *Ferguson* (315)
private venture school (297)
public comprehensive high school (308)
resegregation (318)
town school (296)
universal education (298)

For Reflection

1 Why is it important for teachers to know the history of American education? How might you use such knowledge?

2 How did the moral lessons you were taught in school compare with those taught in earlier American schools?

For Debate

At the website, read the Open for Debate author debate about desegregation. Then, go to EduSpace to post your own opinions and concerns about current trends in desegregation.

For Further Information

PRINT RESOURCES

Larry Cuban, *How Teachers Taught: Constancy and Change in American Classrooms, 1880–1990,* 2d ed. (New York: Teachers College Press, 1993).
This text is a historical examination of instructional practices in American classrooms.

Michelle Fine et al., *Echoes of Brown* (New York: Teachers College Press, 2004).
Integrating a book and DVD, *Echoes of Brown* features a performance by a diverse ensemble of youth from suburban and urban schools who speak back to the victories and continuing struggles for justice and democracy in public schools.

Gary Orfield, Susan Eaton, and the Harvard Project on School Desegregation, *Dismantling Desegregation: The Quiet Reversal of Brown* v. *Board of Education* (New York: New Press, 1996).
This text explores how the desegregation efforts of the 1960s and 1970s are being reversed, particularly by Supreme Court rulings. The authors contend that our nation is making a serious mistake in doing so.

Teresa L. McCarty, *A Place to be Navajo* (Mahwah, NJ: Lawrence Erlbaum Associates, 2001).
An ethnographic account of the Rough Rock, Ariz., People's School, the first American Indian community-controlled school. Rough Rock was the first to teach in the native language and to produce a body of quality children's literature by and about Navajo people.

Diane Ravitch and Joseph P. Viteritti, eds., *Making Good Citizens: Education and Civil Society* (New Haven: CT: Yale University Press, 2001).
This volume brings together leading thinkers from a variety of disciplines to probe the relation between a healthy democracy and education.

Joel Spring, *The American School, 1642–2004,* 6th ed. (New York: McGraw-Hill, 2005).
This book focuses on the social, political, and ideological forces that have shaped the evolution of schooling in America from colonial times to the present.

David B. Tyack and Larry Cuban, *Tinkering Toward Utopia: A Century of Public School Reform* (Cambridge, MA: Harvard University Press, 1995).
This important book on school reforms in the United States argues that utopian policy talk about school reform usually has involved only incremental policy action: "tinkering with the system."

Wayne J. Urban and Jennings L. Wagoner, *American Education: A History,* 3d ed. (New York: McGraw-Hill, 2004).
This book is a relatively brief overview of American education, written by well-known scholars.

WEB RESOURCES

"Lessons of a Century," *Education Week,* January 27, 1999–December 15, 1999. Available at: **http://www.edweek.org.**
Ten monthly installments examining aspects of the educational landscape of twentieth-century America, including the people, trends, historical milestones, enduring controversies, political conflicts, and socioeconomic forces that shaped education.

Library of Congress. Available at: **http://www.loc.gov.** Users of this site will find easy access to THOMAS (legislative information), the Library of Congress catalog, and much more. Particularly relevant for the history of American education is the "Learning Page," which provides information on using materials in the American Memory historical collections, as well as lesson plans and links to related web pages.

11 How Are Schools Governed, Influenced, and Financed?

Chapter Preview   Few beginning teachers are concerned about issues related to school governance and finance. The topic seems remote to them; it is something administrators and representatives of teacher organizations care about, but it does not seem particularly vital for beginning teachers concerned with learning how to survive in the classroom. We feel differently; we believe beginning teachers must have some understanding of the way schools and school systems operate because they will be affected personally by governance and financial decisions. Not understanding how these decisions are made and how they might affect you as a teacher will reduce your effectiveness as a professional.

This chapter emphasizes that:

▶ Legal responsibility for school governance belongs to the state. Traditionally, however, policy decisions and administration have been delegated to local school boards.

▶ In addition to local school boards and state governments, many other groups exercise some measure of influence on educational decisions, either through legal authority or through less formal means. These other groups include professional education organizations, parents, teachers, the business community, the designers of high-stakes standardized tests, the federal government, and the courts.

▶ Court rulings in some states have shifted the responsibility for public school financing from dependence on local property taxes to greater reliance on state support.

How would you explain the fact that:

- A very popular high school teacher was not given tenure?
- The sex education program being planned in your hometown was never implemented?
- A textbook with a fresh approach to the curriculum was removed from circulation after a year, even though the teachers favored its use?
- A coalition of superintendents from poor school districts in your state sued the state government for increased financial support?
- Legislators in New York State banned schools from subscribing to Channel One, a free television news service for school-age children?

It is quite possible that at least one of these questions applies to your local school district or state. They all reflect the struggle for governance, control, and influence over the public schools. This chapter explores how the American educational system is organized, governed, and financed. Although there are legal authorities for the schools and organizations established to exercise this authority, the educational system is strongly influenced by interest groups that do not appear on any organizational chart. We first examine the legal governing authority that exists in most states and then discuss special-interest groups that influence educational policy. Then we look at how the American educational system is financed and how disparities between rich and poor school districts are generating strong challenges to current financing policies.

▶ Who Legally Governs Public Education?

■ education as a state
function

In most countries, the public schools are a branch of the central government, federally financed and administered and highly uniform in curricula and procedures. In the United States, however, responsibility for the public schools has evolved as a state function as a result of the Tenth Amendment to the U.S. Constitution, which reserves all powers to the states that are not specifically designated to the federal government. Each of the fifty states has legal responsibility for the operation and administration of public schools within its own boundaries. In most aspects of public education (we will discuss certain exceptions later), the authority of federal, county, and city education agencies is subject to the will of the state authorities.

■ state versus local control

Although legal responsibility for school governance belongs to the states, policy decisions and administration have usually been delegated to local school boards (see Figure 11.1), which exist because Americans have come to insist on control of schools at the local level. Recently, however, states have been reasserting their policymaking prerogatives.

State Offices and Administrators

At the state level, educational services can be influenced by a variety of actors, from the governor through the many employees of the state's department of education.

■ governors play leadership
role

■ **The Governor and the State Legislature**   Policy analysts agree that the state legislatures are the most influential actors in establishing educational policy. Legislatures wield such power because they make the laws that govern and affect education within their states, and they appropriate the money to fund state

FIGURE 11.1
Organizational Structure of a Typical State School System

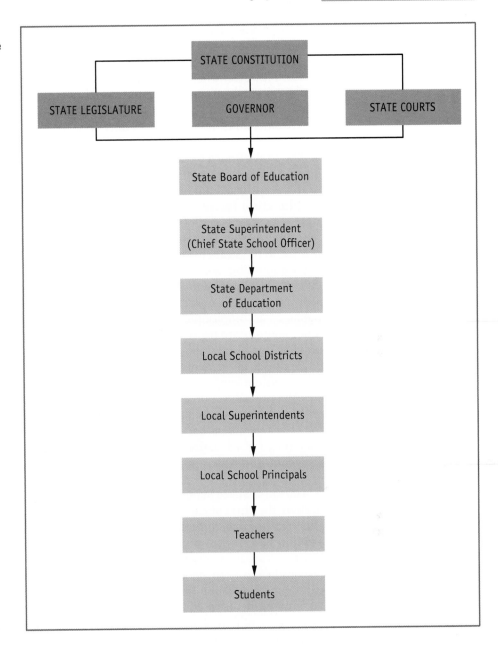

government. In recent years, because of the high profile of educational issues, legislatures' interest in educational policy has increased, particularly in the areas of school finance and establishing standards for student academic achievement.

Like legislatures, the governor's office has the power to affect educational policy but often chooses to do so only on limited issues. Many governors, however, have played more prominent roles, beginning with the educational reforms of the 1980s. Former president Bill Clinton and his education secretary, Richard Riley, for example, became nationally visible as governors through their educational leadership in Arkansas and South Carolina, respectively. President George W. Bush likewise pushed his education agenda as governor of Texas.

On financial issues, the roles of governor and legislature are especially obvious. Governors propose and legislatures act on budgets that contain funding for

■ the "Golden Rule"

school districts. This is, as one wag has stated, the "Golden Rule: Whoever has the gold makes the rules." When state economies are strong, more tax revenues are available to invest in public education, as occurred during the mid- and late 1990s. However, when recessions occur, state governments, facing a loss of tax revenues, cut back on their educational commitments and initiatives, forcing school districts to cut budgets. In either scenario, governors and state legislatures have tremendous influence over educational policy and expenditures.

■ policymaking function

Link to more information about state board of education at the website.

■ The State Board of Education   The state's legal responsibility for public education requires it to establish an organizational framework within which the local school districts can function. The result is the establishment of a **state board of education** to exercise general control and supervision of schools within the state. The state board of education is the state's educational policy-making body for elementary and secondary schools. It typically sets goals and priorities for education in the state; formulates education policy and curricular offerings, including establishing academic standards and their assessment; establishes and enforces rules and regulations for the operation of educational programs; represents the public in matters regarding the governance of education; reports to the public on accomplishments and needs; and makes recommendations to the governor and/or state legislature for the improvement of education. The state board of education also establishes and enforces minimum standards for the operation of all phases of elementary and secondary education from the state to the local school system level.

■ selection of members

The procedure for selecting state board members varies from state to state. In most states, members are appointed by the governor, but in about one-third of the states members are elected by popular vote. The number of members on a state board of education varies from state to state, but a board of nine to fifteen members is typical.

■ duties of chief state school officer

■ The Chief State School Officer   The executive officer of the state board of education, the **chief state school officer,** usually is responsible to the state board of education for the administration of public education. (The actual titles for this position, which vary from state to state, include *superintendent of education, commissioner of education, secretary of the state board of education,* and others.) The responsibilities normally involve serving as the chief administrator of the state department of education (see below) and the state board of education, recommending improvements in educational legislation, arranging studies and creating task forces to identify problems and propose solutions, and reporting on the status of education within the state to the governor, legislature, state board of education, and the public. This officer exercises little direct administrative authority over local educational officials, but his or her indirect influence is widely felt at the local level. The officer is elected by the voters in thirteen states, appointed by the governor in twelve states, and appointed by the state board of education in twenty-four states.

■ The State Department of Education   The **state department of education** (sometimes called the *state department of public instruction*) usually operates under the direction of the state board of education and is administered by the chief state school officer. The state department of education is responsible for carrying out the policies of the state board of education and the laws passed by the state legislature. It consists of a large bureaucracy of officials, often numbering in the hundreds.

■ influence of state departments

Originally organized to provide statistical reports, state departments of education have grown in size, power, and influence. Their primary responsibilities usually include administering and distributing state and federal funds, licensing teachers and other educational personnel, providing schools with technical assistance in improving curriculum and teaching, providing educational data and analyses, providing administration for special programs, accrediting college and university educational licensure programs, evaluating existing programs, and issuing reports. Most schools, school districts, and colleges of education are strongly affected by the policies and actions of these state departments. School and college personnel, including public school teachers, serve on advisory committees and task forces to assist the chief state school officer and the state department of education in their decision-making processes.

The Local School District

To facilitate local control of education, the state creates local school districts for the purpose of carrying out education in conformity with state policy. The school district is thus a unit of the state government and is usually distinct from the local municipal government.

■ board members are state officers

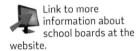
Link to more information about school boards at the website.

In the first place, God made idiots. That was for practice. Then he made school boards.

—MARK TWAIN

■ **The Local School Board** The policymaking body of the school district is the **local school board,** which represents the citizens of the district in setting up a school program, hiring school personnel to operate the schools, determining organizational and administrative policy, and evaluating the results of the program and the performance of personnel. Many school boards are empowered to raise money through taxes. Although school board members are usually elected by the citizens of the local district, they are officially state officers (not simply local representatives), and they must follow the guidelines and policies established by the legislature, the state board of education, and the state department of education. The tension between states' efforts to regulate educational policy and local districts' desire to determine their own policies has increased as states have taken the initiative in the recent educational reform movement.

Methods of selecting school board members are usually prescribed by state law. About 96 percent of the school boards are elected by popular vote, and the remainder are appointed, often by the local mayor or city council.

■ school boards lack diversity

What does the composite profile of school board members look like? As Table 11.1 indicates, the majority of today's school board members are male, white, and between ages forty-one and sixty—demographic characteristics that have changed little in recent years.[1] However, the proportion of women serving on boards has increased from 12 to around 39 percent since 1972. Representation of minorities continues to be small. At least 83 percent of members have annual family incomes over $50,000. Two-thirds of them have at least bachelor's degrees. Most are professionals, managers, or business owners, have children in public school, and consider themselves to be conservative. These figures indicate that in many ways, school board members are not typical of the public they serve. Whether or how this atypical aspect influences their values and decisions is not known. Can you think of any ways in which it might?

TABLE 11.1 Profile of School Board Members

Characteristic	Percentage
Gender	
Male	61
Female	39
Ethnic background	
Black	8
White	85
Hispanic	4
Other	2
Age	
Under 30	0.5
30–39	5.4
40–49	40.1
50–59	33.8
60 or older	20.3
Family income	
Under $50,000	17
$50,000–$74,999	24
$75,000–$99,999	22
$100,000–$149,999	21
More than $150,000	16

Note: Because of rounding, some totals may not add up to 100 percent.

Source: Frederick M. Hess, *School Boards at the Dawn of the 21st* Century (Arlington, VA: National School Boards Association, 2002). Available at: **http://www.nsba.org/site/docs/1200/1143.pdf.**

■ duties of superintendent

■ **The Superintendent of Schools**   The **superintendent of schools** is typically a professional educator selected by the local school board to act as its executive officer and as the educational leader and administrator of the school district. The superintendent is undeniably the most powerful officer in the local school organization. Since the school board consists of laypeople who are usually not education experts, it often delegates many of its responsibilities to the superintendent and staff.

Gathering and providing information to the local school board so it can make informed decisions is one of the superintendent's most important functions. Additionally, the superintendent must recruit, select, place, and promote personnel. Often, too, the superintendent plans the budget and supervises the maintenance, construction, and renovation of buildings.

Decisions about how to improve educational opportunities, including all aspects of curriculum and instruction, may originate with the superintendent. The superintendent generally has responsibility for maintaining harmonious relations with the community by communicating the mission of the schools to the public and marshaling support for district programs.

Theoretically, the superintendent's role is administrative and executive—he or she (only 13 percent of the nation's superintendents are female) keeps the schools functioning, whereas the local school board of education retains policy-making responsibilities. In practice, however, the superintendent has become the major policymaker in the school district.

■ conflict

■ **Superintendents Versus Local School Boards**   The way a school board and superintendent operate together to control a school district depends on their relationship. According to independent observers, this relationship often is one of conflict.

■ high turnover rate often indicative of conflict

One observer, Larry Cuban, asserts that "conflict is—and always has been—the essence of the superintendency."[2] One measure of conflict between superintendents and school boards is the turnover rate: how often superintendents change their jobs. The average tenure for superintendents in urban districts is slightly less than five years, and the national average among all superintendents is just under six years.[3]

Cuban describes the conflict between the superintendent and the school board, or between the superintendent and local private groups, as one of seeming competitors seeking to achieve their goals at the expense of the other participants. Cuban maintains that the issues over which boards and administrators disagree may change as a result of shifting political concerns, changes in school funding or demography, or constantly changing coalitions of teachers or local constituencies. But the relationship remains one of conflict regardless of particular issues. Although school boards hire and fire them, superintendents are expected to lead the board. If they fail to do so, board members are likely to act independently, often with disastrous consequences.

School boards and superintendents search constantly for local constituencies to provide the funding and support for school programs, and with every school board election, new points of view may be brought to the governance of the district. Superintendents must weather these changes in points of view and the emerging coalitions resulting from board member turnover. Sympathies with the schools' mission may be in a constant state of flux, requiring superintendents to exercise coalition-building skills. Their survival as nonelected public officials rests on their ability to mobilize support and manage conflict.

But one thing about today's superintendent is almost a given . . . he must indeed be a political animal.

—Arthur Blumberg

■ **The School Principal**   For the schools within a school district, the superintendent and the local school board of education select professional educators to serve as principals. High schools and middle schools may have a staff of administrators to assist the principal, including assistant or vice principals with specific responsibilities for discipline or curriculum and instruction. At the elementary level, on the other hand, principals may be responsible for more than one school building or may serve part-time as teachers. Whatever the pattern of administrative assignments, those who act as principals are generally considered to be a part of the administrative organization, directly accountable to the superintendent and the local school board of education. (See Table 11.2 for a profile of school administrators.)

■ responsibilities of principal

As administrators, principals usually interview prospective faculty members and make faculty assignments, supervise and evaluate staff members, schedule students and classes, manage school budgets, administer district discipline policies, and procure and dispense supplies. The tasks are many; to list them all would be impossible. Historically, the role of the principal has included management, supervision, and inspection duties. Most importantly, principals are expected to function as instructional leaders for their schools. In a number of states, principals and their teachers are being held accountable for increasing student learning on statewide assessments of achievement.

Effective principals serve as instructional leaders by promoting a productive working and learning environment. They do so by understanding the mission of the school, communicating it to the staff and students, and rewarding excellent performance. They also represent the school to parents and the community. Involving parents and community members in the school's activities and securing their support for these activities are important functions of the principal.

TABLE 11.2 Profile of School Administrators (in Percentages)

	Superintendents	High School Principals	Junior High and Middle School Principals	Elementary School Principals
Sex				
Male	86.8	78.8	66.8	44.8
Female	13.2	21.2	33.2	55.2
Ethnic background				
White	94.9	85.9	83.0	80.8
African American	2.2	8.4	10.5	12.0
Hispanic American	1.4	3.8	5.1	5.8
Asian American	0.2	0.9	0.7	0.7
Native American	0.8	1.1	0.8	0.7
Other	0.5	0.7	—	0.6
Highest degree earned				
Bachelor's	0.3	1.4	1.8	1.8
Master's	32.2	54.8	55.5	53.9
Professional Diploma	22.0	31.6	33.6	34.6
Doctorate	45.3	12.1	9.1	9.7
Salary (12 month)	$125,609	$86,160	$80,060	$75,144

Note: Because of rounding, some totals may not add up to 100 percent.

Sources: "Catherine Gewertz, "School Chiefs Lead the Way in Pay Trends," *Education Week,* June 23, 2004, p. 16; *Schools and Staffing Survey, 1999–2000,* "Public School Principal Survey," "Public Charter School Principal Survey" (Washington, DC: U.S. Department of Education, National Center for Education Statistics. Available at http://www.nces.ed.gov). Parts of this table compiled 7/30/02 by Thuy Dam, National Education Data Resource Center, Request 944315; Thomas E. Glass, Lars Bjork, and C. Cryss Brunner, *The Study of the American Superintendency 2000* (Arlington, VA: American Association of School Administrators, 2000), pp. 17, 128.

■ shortage of principals predicted

Researchers are predicting a shortage of principals during the first decade of the new millennium. The shortage exists in all types of schools—rural, urban, and suburban—and at all levels, elementary through high school. Why the anticipated shortage? Retirements of current principals are a contributing factor. The number one reason, however, is that teachers who might want to become principals believe that principals don't get paid enough for the responsibilities they must shoulder. Many teachers also believe that the job is too stressful and time consuming, and that they would find it difficult to satisfy the demands of statewide assessments, parents, and the community.[4] Also, unlike teachers, in most states, principals do not have tenure as administrators.

Pause and Reflect

1 ▶ From what you have read about the role of the superintendent, what impressions have you formed about the power of the superintendent and the constraints on that power?

2 ▶ The authors of this textbook believe that the hardest job in public education is that of a high school principal. Do you agree or disagree, and what reasons do you have for your position?

3 ▶ In your opinion, should chief state school officers be elected or appointed? What reasons do you have for your position? What arguments can you muster for the opposite opinion?

▶ Who Influences American Public Education?

It is not our intention in this chapter to examine in detail the authority and power that enable various groups to influence certain aspects of public education. However, a brief look at the interplay of influence exercised by professional education organizations, parents, business, standardized testing, the courts, and the federal government yields some fascinating insights into how decisions about public education are actually made.

Professional Education Organizations

Among the most influential forces on the schools are professional education organizations, in particular the National Education Association (NEA) and the American Federation of Teachers (AFT).

■ teacher organizations are powerful

In recent years, the role of teachers' organizations in determining educational policy has greatly increased. At the national level, the NEA and the AFT exert considerable influence on educational policy and legislation. Moreover, the state affiliates of the NEA and AFT are among the most effective lobbying groups in their respective states. (See the chapter entitled "What Does It Mean to Be a Professional?" for more on these two teacher organizations.) State politicians pay attention to these teacher organizations because of their power and influence. The NEA and AFT affiliates have well-articulated positions on selected issues, represent thousands of teachers who can be mobilized to vote for or against particular legislators, and spend considerable amounts of money to make their positions known. At the local level—largely as a result of collective bargaining techniques, including work stoppages or the threat of them—teacher organizations have won more and more power over educational policy.

Just as war is too important to be left to the generals, education is too important to be left to the educators.

—PAUL WOODRING

Today many local teacher organizations, including NEA and AFT affiliates, have won recognition as the official bargaining representatives of their members. Teacher organizations are also demanding that issues previously considered the prerogatives of local school boards and superintendents be subject to collective bargaining. Among these issues are teacher and paraprofessional salaries, clerical and secretarial assistance, curriculum development, fringe benefits, in-service training, class size, textbook selection, and even the appointment of department heads and other school administrators.

■ site-based decision making

Teachers' efforts to negotiate their teaching role and its conditions have not always been welcomed by local school boards and superintendents. However, one recent reform effort to improve schools, **site-based decision making,** has tended to increase teachers' power. The idea behind site-based decision making is that most changes need to occur at the school level, and therefore many administrative and budget decisions should be made at that level, with teachers becoming involved in the decisions that affect them and their students. Site-based decision making transfers much of the budget and decision making from the central school district administration to the individual school level. As a result of such reform efforts, teachers are gaining more authority over important school decisions.

Parents

■ parental influence

Ask educators who has the most influence in determining whether children succeed in school, and they will almost always say *parents*. Parents are their children's

A parent is the most important
teacher a child ever has.

—JOAN BECK

first and primary teachers and the only ones who follow a child's progress from year to year. As the two major forces for educating and socializing children in society, parents and teachers should be natural allies. Too often, however, a wide chasm separates them. Some teachers fear that parents will interfere in their classrooms; others feel pressed for time and don't want to spend the extra effort to communicate with and effectively involve parents. Some parents seem too consumed with the problems of work and raising a family to become involved in schools, whereas others actively participate in various school functions. Research is clear that without effective parental involvement in the schools, most students will not succeed academically. In a national survey of school superintendents, 68 percent identified a lack of parental involvement as the biggest roadblock to student achievement.[5]

The Parent-Teacher Association (PTA) is a loosely knit national organization with almost 6 million members and more than 26,000 local units. The local parent-teacher group, sometimes called the **parent-teacher organization (PTO),** may or may not be affiliated with the national PTA. Local groups devise their own organizations and activities to fit the needs of the local school community. Generally, they serve as a communications link between parents and the formal school organization, with teachers usually acting as representatives of the schools.

Formally, the school system ordinarily operates by means of down-the-line communications, from the superintendent to the principal, to the teacher, and then to the parents. Typically, school systems are less receptive to up-the-line communications from parents or teachers to administrators. But when the formal hierarchy does not respond to up-the-line communications in a satisfactory manner, parents and school officials can resort to an informal communications system in an attempt to get a better response.

An instance of informal communications occurred when the energetic principal of a New Haven, Conn., school in a low-income neighborhood galvanized the PTO in a campaign for a new school to replace the old one. When the city administration raised obstacles, the principal called together the PTO members and other neighborhood leaders to ask their support for the construction of a new school. Within twenty-four hours, they were exerting pressure on the city school board and the administration. Needless to say, the school was built.

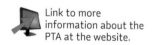
Link to more information about the PTA at the website.

Most PTOs, however, are comparatively impotent in achieving educational aims. Educational reformers are concerned about the ineffectiveness of parent groups, because they know that reforms will last only if parents are actively involved in the work of their schools. Some states have actually passed legislation mandating that schools involve parents in school governance and in the education of the students.

■ parental involvement

Many strategies can be used to increase parental involvement and improve the partnership between parents and teachers. These strategies include frequent parent-teacher conferences; homework hotlines, websites, or emails, through which parents can find out about homework assignments or communicate with teachers; workshops for parents that address a variety of topics; school volunteer programs; and school councils on which parents, teachers, and administrators discuss school policies and practices. Teachers and school administrators must be trained to overcome barriers to effective parental involvement and to create school environments where parents of all races, ethnicities, and social classes feel welcome.

Family support and emphasis on the value of education are extremely important influences on a child's success in school.
(© Joan Clifford/Index Stock)

Business

■ business plays leading role in reform

Throughout American history, concern about the quality of U.S. public education and its ability to produce workers with the knowledge and skills that business needs has prompted partnerships between educators and business executives. In particular, during the 1980s and 1990s, the business community was at the forefront of efforts to restructure public education. Business leaders have been substantially involved in almost every educational reform report. As a result, they have become both the strongest critics and the staunchest advocates for public education. The chief executive officers of such major corporations as Procter & Gamble, Xerox, Apple Computer, Eastman Kodak, Coca-Cola, IBM, RJR Nabisco, and many others have demanded and pushed for educational reforms in state capitols, the halls of Congress, and the White House. More than 100,000 business-school partnerships have been formed since 1983, and business has donated hundreds of millions of dollars to improve elementary and secondary schools. One major effort on the part of business to influence school reform is the

Business Roundtable, an association of chief executive officers of leading U.S. corporations. The Roundtable asks its members to create or join state coalitions of business leaders and others committed to raising academic standards for all students and to ensure that standards reflect the knowledge and skill needed for workplace success.[6] Further information on school restructuring efforts appears in the chapter entitled "How Should Education Be Reformed?"

■ education/economy link

Why should the business community show such interest? The initiatives to improve the quality of American education go beyond altruistic impulses. One source estimates that the education market represents potential revenue of $600 billion for corporate interests. With that kind of money involved, businesses would certainly like to make their presence known.[7] In addition, like the nation's governors, many business leaders are convinced that education reform is essential to the health of the American economy. Competition from Asian and European manufacturers in world markets, a massive U.S. trade deficit, and industry's perception that entry-level workers lack proper job skills have focused attention on educating the American work force. In fact, U.S. companies spend billions of dollars annually on remedial education for their workers.

■ business intrusion?

■ **Purchasing Pressures?**   Not everyone sees business involvement in education as totally positive. Some express concern that financial support from business will lead to business intrusion—that schools may be unduly shaped to meet business needs. Another concern centers on business's provision of free curriculum and instructional materials for teachers. Critics argue that corporate handouts are not just supplementary gifts but sophisticated marketing tools containing subtle and not-so-subtle messages to support the corporation's biases and promote brand identification and product loyalty. For example, Clairol distributes free bags of shampoo to students as they leave school, along with surveys asking whether they had "a good or bad hair day." In another example, a Nike program asks young people to devote a week of classroom time to learning the life cycle of a Nike shoe. Other opponents object to exclusive marketing contracts that schools sign with such companies as Coca-Cola or Pepsi, agreeing to sell only products produced by the particular company in exchange for funding from the corporation. Some people cynically view business's push for the expanded use of technology in schools as an attempt to create a new market for computers and other educational technology.

■ Channel One controversy

Among the most controversial business ventures is Channel One, a commercial service that delivers ten minutes of high-quality news programming directly to public school classrooms free of cost in exchange for two minutes of advertising. A school that subscribes to the twelve-minute newscast receives a satellite dish, two videocassette recorders, a television set for every classroom in the building, and schoolwide cabling to hook it all together. By 2004 about 12,000 middle schools and high schools had signed on, reaching an estimated 8 million students, about 40 percent of the nation's twelve- to eighteen-year-olds.[8] Many educators have attacked the concept as gross commercialism and a dangerous precedent. One state superintendent, an opponent of Channel One, states, "The problem is, they want us to sell access to our kids' minds, and we have no right, morally or ethically, to do that."[9] Supporters argue that the program rouses students' interest in current events, especially since many teenagers don't read newspapers. In addition, supporters argue, the equipment provided by Channel One en-

The classroom is . . . a place in which the claims of various political, social, and economic interests are negotiated. The classroom is both a symbol and a product of deadly serious cultural bargaining.

—NEIL POSTMAN

Many parents and educators express concern that corporate sponsorships allow too much commercial influence into the public schools, while others are thankful for sponsorships that save the schools money.
(© Robin Nelson/PhotoEdit)

ables schools to take advantage of other cable offerings, such as the Discovery Channel, Cable News Network, C-Span, and the Learning Channel. Are the advantages worth the cost? What do you think?

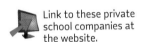

Link to these private school companies at the website.

■ privatization

■ **Privatization Efforts**   Another way business influences education is through the recent movement toward private management of public schools that has occurred in some urban areas. Private corporations such as the Edison Schools, TesseracT Group (formerly known as Educational Alternatives, Inc.), Advantage Schools, and Sylvan Learning, Inc., have contracted with some school districts to provide specific educational services, to operate schools whose students have been performing poorly on academic tests, or to begin new schools with promising designs. One private consulting firm that has tracked the rise of the education industry estimates that about 10 percent of the charter schools operating by the end of the twentieth century were managed by for-profit companies.[10] Advocates of this **privatization** movement argue that private corporations can operate these schools more effectively and less expensively. Opponents, especially teachers' unions, claim that schools operated under a profit motive may shortchange students' welfare in order to make money. They do this, the critics claim, by hiring inexperienced teachers, using unlicensed staff, and eliminating high-cost special education programs. To date, private management of public schools has often led to cleaner buildings, greater access to computers, and more individualized instruction, but the verdict is still out on whether they lead to academic improvement.

■ cooperation or exploitation?

There is no question that the role of the business community in educational affairs has greatly expanded since the mid-1980s, and most people see this trend as positive. Businesses and corporations, with a vested stake in the outcomes of public education, will undoubtedly continue to be major players in the reform of our educational system. The challenge for educators will be to walk the line between partnerships and cooperation on the one hand and exploitation for commercial purposes on the other.

High-Stakes Standardized Testing

■ increase of standardized testing

More and more, policymakers believe that student achievement will not increase markedly until high standards are set and quality work by all students is expected and rewarded. As programs for school improvement proliferated in the 1980s, the trend to assess the quality of schools and teachers by using standardized tests also grew in influence. Currently, forty-nine states have created standards for student achievement linked to some form of high-stakes assessment. Many states also now require high school students to perform well on tests of general academic competence as a prerequisite for graduation, and almost all states require local public school districts to test students at some point(s) between grades one and twelve. The 2001 reauthorization of the Elementary and Secondary Education Act (No Child Left Behind) required states to test students each year between grades three and eight and once in high school if they wish to receive federal funds associated with this federal legislation. (This act is discussed in more detail later in the chapter.) Forty-five states require aspiring teachers to pass a state-prescribed, standardized test before entering a teacher education program and/or before being licensed to teach.[11]

■ overemphasis on testing?

Many educators and parents express grave concerns about what they think is an overemphasis on high-stakes testing. Measuring school excellence by standardized tests poses a danger arising from the limited and simplistic nature of the tests. Evaluation experts warn that tests external to the schools can be limiting if schools pattern their curricula to conform to the content of the tests. Schools may fail to teach what is difficult to test. In some instances, the content and actual form of a test have become the curriculum itself as weeks of classroom drill have centered on previous versions of tests. Some educators and parents see a connection between the rise in student obesity and the emphasis on high-stakes testing as recess and physical education are eliminated or cut back to provide more time for test drilling.

 The video case *Assessment in the Middle Grades: Measurement of Student Learning* shares the views of middle-school mathematics students and their teacher about both standardized and nonstandardized assessments. As you watch the clips and study the artifacts in the case, reflect upon the following questions:

1. In addition to those mentioned by the student and teacher in the video case, what are some other benefits and drawbacks to standardized tests?

2. Look at the exam taken by the students, included in the *artifacts* with the video case. How does the exam allow for authentic assessment, as it is defined in this chapter?

3. What are your biggest concerns about administering standardized tests as a teacher? How can you prepare now to overcome those concerns?

Others worry that standardized tests overemphasize technical information and underemphasize educators' professional judgments about the worthiness of a school's programs. With a national call to stress more problem solving, critical thinking, and writing skills, educators see a contradiction in using standardized tests that don't measure these outcomes. They are calling for more *authentic assessment*—that is, using such things as actual specimens or examples of students' work to determine educational achievement. (See the chapter, "How Should Education Be Reformed?" for more on authentic assessment.)

Pause and Reflect

1 ▶ Did the schools you attended work in partnership with business and industry? Did your education prepare you for further education and entry into the work force? What, in your opinion, is an appropriate relationship between business and schools?

2 ▶ In your opinion, are the schools doing too much, the right amount, or too little testing of students? Why do you say this?

3 ▶ What do you think of Channel One? Do the benefits outweigh the drawbacks? Support your position.

The Federal Government

Although the federal government does not have formal authority over education, all three branches of the government exercise considerable influence over schools in the country through legislation, court rulings and the activities of the U.S. Department of Education.

■ strong court influence

■ **The Federal Courts** The history of education has been shaped by important court decisions on the duties and responsibilities of school officials in such areas as school desegregation, religion in the schools, student rights, and, particularly at the state level, school finance. The U.S. Supreme Court has played a particularly important role in changing educational policy in this country. (See the chapter entitled "What Are the Ethical and Legal Issues Facing Teachers?" for a more detailed discussion of the impact of Supreme Court decisions on American education.) Because its rulings have altered or reduced the power of state and local educational authorities, some of the Court's decisions have generated deep resentment among those who abhor this "federal intrusion" into states' rights. Other people applaud the Court's decisions as steps to make American education more responsive to broad democratic principles. The Court has issued rulings affecting such important educational policies as desegregation, public aid to private schools, rights of people with disabilities, gender equity, and sexual harassment. It recently upheld the constitutionality of the controversial Cleveland voucher plan. (See the chapter entitled "How Should Education Be Reformed?" for a discussion of vouchers and public funding for private and religious schools.)

■ enforcement necessary

However, the courts alone, as powerful as they are, cannot do everything. Often judicial rulings need to be supported by federal administrative and legislative action. In the famous 1954 case of *Brown* v. *Board of Education of Topeka* (discussed

Federal legislation and federal court decisions have significantly affected education, including the education of children with disabilities, many of whom now engage in the same activities as their nondisabled peers as a result of the least restrictive environment requirements of the federal IDEA law.

(© Digital Vision/Getty Images)

in more detail in the chapter on "What Is the History of American Education?"), the U.S. Supreme Court ruled that the doctrine of "separate but equal" had no place in public education. But how was this momentous judgment to be implemented? The Court declared that "all deliberate speed" should be employed to abolish the dual school system for African Americans and whites, but no judicial guidelines were developed to steer the process. As a result, for a decade, almost no changes occurred until the 1960s, when a combination of new congressional laws on civil rights and education and strong enforcement of desegregation by President Lyndon Johnson's administration took place.

Link to the Department of Education from the website.

■ **The U.S. Department of Education**   The Department of Education is a significant part of the federal government, with cabinet-level status and a discretionary budget of almost $67 billion in fiscal year 2005. The department administers a variety of programs passed by Congress, including programs concerned with elementary and secondary education, postsecondary education, educational research and development, vocational and adult education, special education, and civil rights. It also administers funds devoted to the collection of educational statistics. In addition, billions of additional federal dollars for education are administered by other federal agencies, such as the Department of Health and Human Services, the National Science Foundation, and the Department of Defense.

▓ fluctuating federal involvement

The federal government's level of involvement in education often fluctuates depending on whether Republicans or Democrats control the White House and Congress and on the particular ideology professed by the party in power. Republicans generally have sought to decrease the involvement of the federal government in education, even advocating abolition of the U.S. Department of Education, whereas Democrats tend to be more supportive of both the department and federal efforts to improve education. However, under President George W. Bush, the federal government's share of costs for elementary and secondary education has increased from 7 percent to almost 9 percent by 2005. As we'll see in the next section of this chapter, much of this money has been allocated for the raising of standards and for accountability measures.

Pause and Reflect

1 ▸ What other groups, besides those listed, influence education?

▶ How Are Schools Financed?

The total amount of money available to a school district for education is the sum of locally raised revenues, state aid, federal aid, and miscellaneous revenues. During much of the country's history, most of the money used to support public elementary and secondary schools came from local revenue sources, primarily the property tax. But from the late 1970s to the present, for the first time in American history, the states' share of support for public education exceeded the local share (Figure 11.2). Increased state revenues have helped offset the decreases in local funding of the schools. Currently state governments contribute about 49 percent, local governments offer about 43 percent, and the federal government provides about 9 percent toward the financing of public schools.[12]

▓ funding percentages vary

The percentage of revenue received from federal, state, and local sources varies considerably from state to state. Federal contributions for public education range from a high of 16 percent for South Dakota to a low of less than 3 percent

FIGURE 11.2

Percentage of Revenues Received from Federal, State, and Local Sources for Public Elementary and Secondary Schools

Sources: *Rankings and Estimates: Estimates of School Statistics, 2005* (Washington, DC: National Education Association, 2005), p. 94.

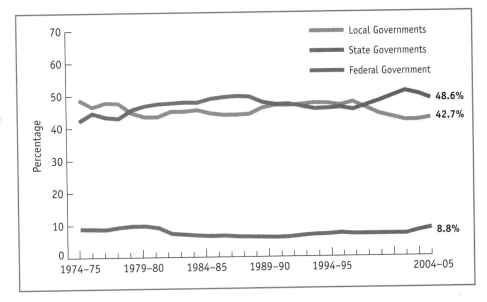

FIGURE 11.3

Expenditures per Pupil

Source: Data in current dollars from *Projections of Education Statistics to 2014* (Washington, DC: U.S. Department of Education, National Center for Education Statistics, 2005), Table 33. Available at: **http://nces.ed.gov/pubs2005/2005074.pdf.**

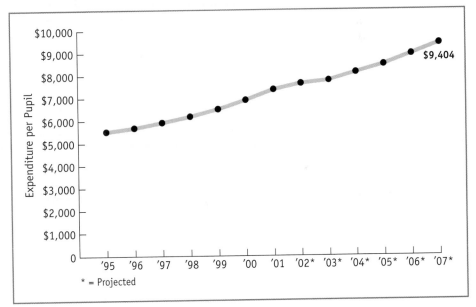

Visit the website to link to up-to-date statistics on this topic.

for New Jersey. Local contributions to revenues range from a high of 61 percent for Nevada to a low of less than 2 percent for Hawaii, which has a statewide school district. Other than Hawaii, which gets 90 percent of its school funding from the state, the state receiving the highest proportion of revenues from state sources is Vermont, at 86 percent, and the lowest is Illinois at 30 percent.[13] Let's look in more detail at state and local spending and funding patterns.

School Spending

■ rising expenditures per pupil

Figure 11.3 shows the upward trend in average expenditure per pupil in daily attendance. The nationwide average stood at $8,554 per pupil for 2004–05. From state to state, however, the per-pupil expenditures vary widely (Figure 11.4), ranging from

FIGURE 11.4

Average Expenditure per Pupil, by State, 2003–2004, Based on Fall Enrollment

Source: Reprinted with permission from *Educational Vital Signs,* 2005. Copyright © 2005 National School Boards Association. All rights reserved.

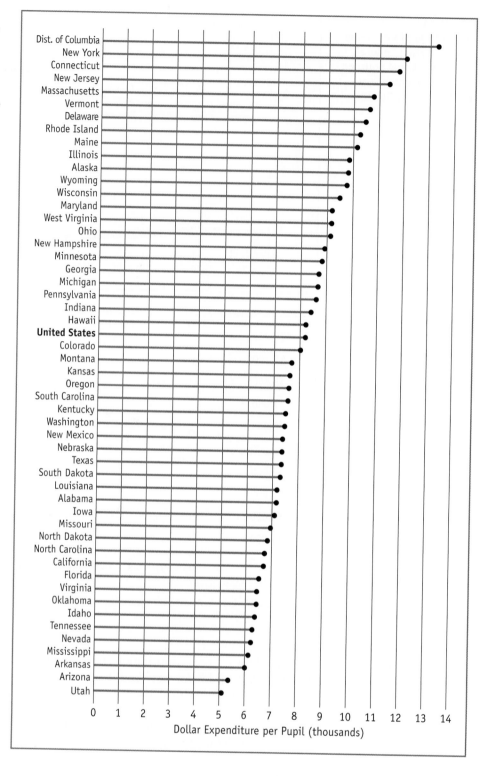

Where Does the United States Stand on Education Funding?

Many politicians, arguing against the need for increased spending on education, assert that the United States already spends more on public education than do most comparable countries but gets worse results. "Money is not the answer," they claim.

We can shed some light on the debate by comparing U.S. educational spending with that of some other countries. To allow for differences in size of the economies, we can consider public spending on education as a percentage of gross domestic product (GDP), the total value of a country's output. The United States spends 3.8 percent of its GDP on public elementary and secondary education, while the average of the thirty-five industrialized countries sampled was 3.5 percent. Countries that spend more than the United States include Norway (4.6), New Zealand (4.3), Denmark (4.2), Sweden (4.3), Portugal (4.2), France (4.0), Poland (4.0), and Belgium (4.0). Countries spending less than the United States include Greece (2.4), Japan (2.7), Germany (2.9), Ireland (2.9), Canada (3.1), and the Netherlands (3.1). Surprisingly, Mexico spends the same percentage of GDP as the United States.

Such figures indicate that the United States devotes only a slightly higher percentage of its resources to elementary and secondary education as the average of other industrialized nations. However, the United States might be expected to spend proportionally more than other countries because of certain characteristics of our school system and society. Our decentralized school system is more expensive than the single, centrally administered system that characterizes many of the other industrialized nations. Our population is more diverse than most countries,' thus presenting unique educational challenges, and the very high number of U.S. children living in poverty creates additional demands for schools. Also, the United States, compared with the other countries, spends a much greater percentage of its public education funds (17 percent) on special education services. Given these factors, our percentage of GDP spent on elementary and secondary education does not seem extravagant.

Sources: Organization of Economic Cooperation and Development, *Education at a Glance, 2004.* Available at: **http://www.oecd.org/dataoecd/62/21/33670978.xls;** Richard Rothstein with Karen Hawley Miles, *Where's the Money Gone?* (Washington, DC: Economic Policy Institute, 1995), p. 8.

more than $15,073 (District of Columbia) per pupil each year to $5,245 (Utah).[14] The reason for these differences is primarily economic. A state's ability to pay for education depends on the income level of its residents and corporations. In general, the southwestern states fund education at lower levels than the northeastern states, but the cost of living in the southwest is generally less than living in the northeast. As a result of lower funding, are students who live in some of the Sunbelt states being deprived of a quality education? The connection between funding and excellence of education is often disputed, but a group of researchers from the University of Chicago, after reanalyzing thirty-two studies on this issue, concluded that higher per-pupil expenditures, better teacher salaries, more educated and experienced teachers, and smaller class and school sizes—all directly a result of higher funding—are strongly related to improved student learning.[15]

State and Local Funding

■ sources of state revenue

State governments use a combination of sales, personal income, corporate income, and excise taxes to generate revenues. Some states fund their schools partly with income from state-run lotteries. State revenue systems are as diverse as school finance plans and reflect the socioeconomic makeup, the political climate, and the educational needs of each state.

■ local governments use
   property tax

Local governments, in contrast, rely primarily on the property tax for income. Most states require the citizens in a school district to vote either on the property tax rate to support education or on the school budget itself.

■ Michigan reform

In an unprecedented move, in 1993 the Michigan legislature voted to eliminate local property taxes as a source of revenue for the public schools. Many observers called the action *bold*, whereas others termed it *reckless*. What made the action so controversial was the fact that the Michigan legislature at that time lacked an alternative funding system to replace the $6.3 billion in local property tax funds for schools. State leaders planned to use the self-inflicted crisis to recast the existing school finance system, which left great gaps in spending power between wealthy and poor school districts. By 1994, the voters of Michigan had voted to increase the state sales tax by 50 percent and raise taxes on cigarettes to replace the greatly reduced property tax, thus permitting the state to reallocate state resources to poorer school districts. Other states have followed the Michigan example of less reliance on local property taxes.

■ unequal funding

Why would districts want to rely less heavily on property taxes? Many knowledgeable educators and politicians argue that one of the greatest causes of unequal educational opportunity is the method used to finance school systems. Because of local districts' heavy reliance on property taxes, districts where property values are high generate much more money to finance their schools than districts where property values are low. Within the same state, for example, the average amount of money spent per child in one district may be more than three times the amount spent in a nearby district. Such spending differentials result in great educational disparities, as measured by pupil-teacher ratios, training and experience of staff, and availability of facilities, equipment, and counseling services.

School Finance Reform and the Courts

■ *Serrano v. Priest*

As a result of numerous court decisions, efforts to equalize the disparities in funding within states have shifted some of the responsibility for funding from local school districts to the state level. In 1971, pupils and their parents filed a class action suit, *Serrano* v. *Priest*, against California state and county officials concerned with financing public schools. The suit charged that the state's school-financing scheme was unconstitutional. The Supreme Court of California supported the parents' claim that the quality of a child's education must not be a function of wealth other than the wealth of the state as a whole. The court also held that the California system of financing schools on the basis of local property taxes violated the Fourteenth Amendment to the U.S. Constitution, which provides equal protection of the law for all citizens.

■ equality as state concern

In 1973, however, the Supreme Court of the United States, by a five-to-four vote, reversed a similar decision (known as the *Rodriguez* case) involving the school finance system of the state of Texas. The Court found that the U.S. Constitution was not violated because the right to an education is not guaranteed explicitly or implicitly by the Constitution. Although *federal* law had not been violated, the Court did indicate that the finding should not be interpreted as a victory for the status quo. In effect, issues of inequity in school finance were returned to the province of the state courts and legislatures. Many state constitutions, unlike the U.S. Constitution, contain equal protection clauses that can be interpreted to include education as a protected right.

Since the *Rodriguez* case, other state courts have ruled that their school financing systems violate their state constitutions. In those states where the finance system has been ruled unconstitutional, the issue has centered on inadequacies in the level of educational opportunities offered to children in the poorer school districts. The courts in those states examined whether the poor children were receiving a sufficient education as required by the state constitution and as measured by contemporary education standards or by comparisons with the best or highest-spending districts. In contrast, in states where the system of school finance was upheld, the courts usually interpreted their state constitutions as guaranteeing only a basic minimum level of funding.[16] As a result of court challenges, more than twenty states have reformed their school finance laws since 1973, and some states are still grappling with the issue.

■ pressures for equality

Educators, parents, and public officials are greatly concerned that the quality of a child's education should not depend on whether the child lives in a school district with high property values. Many of these concerned citizens are urging that state governments become responsible for raising educational revenue and distributing the full costs of local schools to the school districts. The school districts would continue to be in charge of the operation of the local schools but would no longer carry the burden of raising needed money.

Pause and Reflect

1 ▶ Of the methods of school financing discussed in this chapter (local property taxes, state financing through statewide taxes, and state-run lotteries), which do you believe is most equitable? Why?

2 ▶ Do you believe state governments should redistribute money from rich to poor school districts through state taxing power? Why or why not?

Federal Funding

Although the federal government typically provides much less money for public schools than do state or local governments, federal funds are strategically important and have a far greater impact than their proportion of school funding would suggest.

■ categorical aid

■ **Funding in the Past**   Much of federal aid to education traditionally has been in the form of **categorical grants**—that is, the money must be spent for designated purposes (or categories) that are stated generally in the legislation and more precisely by the federal agency administering the funds. As a result, the federal government has been able to influence school districts and institutions that have accepted or sought its aid. For example, to qualify for federal funds to improve its reading program, a school district would have to conform to the guidelines and restrictions accompanying the money. Many financially stricken school districts have been grateful for additional funds, regardless of the regulations they carry.

■ strong funding, 1960–80

During the period from 1960 to 1980, federal education programs thrived. The federal government's share of elementary and secondary school revenues increased from 4.4 to 9.8 percent during this period.[17] Congressional acts provided money to colleges, cities, states, and agencies to finance a wide variety of projects, including construction of buildings and other educational facilities; improvement of instruction or administration; development of educational personnel, including teachers and paraprofessionals, particularly for high-poverty areas; provision of loans for prospective teachers; and funding for educational research.

■ block grants

During President Ronald Reagan's administration (1981–89), categorical grant programs were largely replaced by block grants to state and local education

VOICES FROM THE CLASSROOM

Vidya Bhat graduated from the University of Virginia in 2001, and at the time of this writing was a first-year teacher in the New York City public schools.

Funding Differences Between School Districts

I am a second-grade teacher in New York City, and as a first-year teacher, I find that my expectations of teaching and the realities that I experience are worlds apart.

In September, I imagined a bright cheery classroom filled with beautiful students, as well as a plethora of books, paper, and other necessary educational supplies. Instead, I received an overcrowded classroom, barren of any sort of teaching materials. Much to my chagrin, my situation still remains the same, and it is now April. Although I have some curriculum materials for math, I still do not possess any textbooks for science, social studies, or language arts. More importantly, I have very little quality children's literature to spark my students' interest in reading.

I, like the majority of the teachers in my school, purchase everything from loose-leaf paper to chalk. Because my school does not permit the faculty to use the office's one and only copy machine, I have to pay for all of my own photocopies. While it is a known fact that no one goes into teaching for the money, it is surely disheartening to think that my administration believes it to be okay that teachers have to forgo parts of their salaries toward getting the basics for their classrooms.

The "reason" why I do not have books or supplies, as explained to me by a school staff developer, is simply that there were no school aides hired to unpack and distribute the books and supplies that reside in the supply room. Now, I cannot tell you how many times I have tried to get into that supply room! However, my attempts have been completely unsuccessful. The staff developer further explained that according to our union, teachers and administrators cannot unpack and distribute supplies because it isn't part of our contract, and theoretically, it would be taking away a position from a school aide that would potentially be hired to do that job.

On the bright side, I have a wonderful group of students who are eager to learn. I truly believe in the power of the self-fulfilling prophecy, which is why I do not let my teaching situation depress me. I need to maintain my fresh and positive outlook on the profession so I can make sure that I give my students all the tools they need to succeed. When my older colleagues tell me that I should circulate my résumé in elementary schools outside New York City, I often think about what it would be like to teach in the suburbs. More money, more supplies, more support . . . seems like a teacher's dream. Then I come back to reality and remember my students, who have a classroom with very few books and supplies, and then it finally dawns on me. If all the young teachers leave the urban schools flocking to the comforts of the suburbs, then who will teach New York City's kids?

 Visit the website for more Voices from the Classroom.

agencies. **Block grants** are sums of money that come with only minimal federal restrictions and are transferred from the federal government to the state governments as a block of money rather than by categories. These changes reflected the belief of President Reagan, and of many other Republicans, that the federal government should play a reduced role in educational policymaking. In fact, the federal government's share of support for public education fell from 9.8 percent in 1980 to 6.1 percent in 1990, although by 2005 the percentage had climbed back to 8.8 (see Figure 11.2). Today the federal government employs both categorical and block grant programs.

■ federal role increases with
No Child Left Behind Act

■ **No Child Left Behind Act of 2001**   In 2002, President Bush signed into law the revised **Elementary and Secondary Education Act (ESEA)** (originally passed in 1965), also known as the **No Child Left Behind Act** of 2001 (NCLB). The act is the main federal law on K–12 education, and the revision greatly increases the federal role in education by putting into place requirements that reach into virtually every public school in the country. It called for states to require reading and mathematics tests every year in grades three to eight as well as demonstrable progress toward academic proficiency by all students in every school district of the state. NCLB also requires a **highly qualified teacher** in every classroom. The law also puts pressure on school districts to turn around low-performing schools with a series of consequences for schools that persistently fail to demonstrate **adequate yearly progress** toward having all students meet state standards. The law was accompanied by the largest dollar increase ever in federal education aid, more than 6.7 billion additional dollars for fiscal year 2002, and more money in subsequent years. (See the boxed insert for more details on the provisions of this act.)

No Child Left Behind Act Key Provisions

On January 8, 2002, President George W. Bush signed into law the No Child Left Behind Act of 2001 (NCLB). This law contained the most sweeping changes to the Elementary and Secondary Education Act (ESEA) since it was enacted in 1965. It changed the federal government's role in K–12 education by asking America's schools to describe their success in terms of what each student accomplishes. The act contains the president's four basic education reform principles: stronger accountability for results, increased flexibility and local control, expanded options for parents, and an emphasis on teaching methods that have been proven to work. Major provisions of the law include the following areas.

Annual Testing

By the 2005–06 school year states were required to begin administering annual statewide assessments in reading and mathematics to students in grades 3–8, and to test students at least once during grades 10-12. States may select and design their own assessments, but the tests must be aligned with state academic standards. NCLB also calls for states to administer, by 2007–08, science assessments once during each of the three levels of schooling: elementary, middle, and high school. Test results must include individual student scores and be reported by race, income, special education status, English proficiency, and other categories to measure not just overall trends, but also gaps between, and progress of, various subgroups. Schools may need to report such *disaggregated data* for as many as thirty subgroups of their students.

Academic Improvement

States must set a minimum performance threshold and, within twelve years, all students must attain this level of proficiency. Each state must raise the level of proficiency gradually, but in equal increments over time, leading to 100 percent proficiency. This is known as adequate yearly progress. If a school fails to make adequate progress for two years in a row, the school will receive technical assistance from the district, and the school must provide its students with the option of transferring to another public school. If inadequate progress continues, then more drastic consequences ensue, including possible reconstitution of the school.

Teacher and Paraprofessional Qualifications

By the end of the 2005–06 school year, every public school teacher had to be highly qualified, which means that a teacher has been licensed (including alternative routes) and has demonstrated a high level of competence in the subjects that he or she teaches.

Sources: U.S. Department of Education, "Introduction: No Child Left Behind." Available at: **http://www.ed.gov/nclb/overview/intro/index.html;** An ESEA Primer," Education Week, January 9, 2002, pp. 28–29.

■ mixed reactions to No Child Left Behind Act

Reactions of educators around the country to the No Child Left Behind Act have been mixed. Educators from urban school districts expressed enthusiasm for how federal aid is distributed under the Title I program for disadvantaged students—the largest program in the No Child Left Behind Act (see more on Title I in the following section). The act provides extra funding for school districts with high concentrations of poor children, and urban areas have seen dramatic increases in Title I aid. High-poverty rural areas have also seen significant gains.

■ concerns about NCLB

Although greatly appreciating the increased funding for public education and the concern for students at risk of failure, some of the provisions of the act bothered many educators, particularly the increased emphasis on testing and the lack of attention to increased spending for special education. As one school district superintendent stated: "I have the same concern you're probably going to hear from a lot of educators: this mad rush for testing. . . . It's such a narrow band of information that they're going to use to make crucial judgments."[18]

Others are concerned because the No Child Left Behind Act fails to provide funds for special education services that schools are required by federal law to provide. As one superintendent stated, "Probably the best thing that the federal government could do right now is fund the additional $5 million in special education costs that my district has to pay each year as a result of federal mandates on special education."[19]

In fact, educators and politicians in many states believe that the NCLB, as a whole, has been inadequately funded by the federal government. They cite the costs of increased testing, upgrading the qualifications of teachers, and additional instructional resources required to help struggling learners make adequate yearly progress. Although more federal dollars have been allocated, many state educators believe the amount to be insufficient to meet the needs.

(© John Trever)

Another concern with the law is its provision that if any of the almost thirty subgroups of students fails to achieve passing scores on the state's tests for two consecutive years, then the whole school is rated as failing to make adequate yearly progress. So, even if twenty-nine of the thirty groups passed the tests, the school is seen as failing. For many, this seems unduly punishing. Students attending a school that has failed to make adequate yearly progress can opt to leave that school to attend any other public school. Ironically, in the first few years of the law, it appears that the better students, not the failing ones, are taking advantage of the law's provision to transfer to a new school—certainly not the intent of the law.

■ state standards lack uniformity

It is also important to note that each state sets its own content standards, designs its own assessments of the standards, and sets its passing scores for the assessments. This means that if a state has high standards and requires a high score to pass its assessments, then it is likely to have a higher failure rate among its students. Conversely, if a state has lower standards and does not require high scores, it is more likely to have a higher percentage of its students pass the assessments. A state with high standards may thus be seen in the public's eye as not doing as well as a state with lower standards. This also makes comparing student achievement across states impossible.

Because of these many concerns, various states are putting pressure on Congress and the president to make adjustments in the NCLB law. Several states are threatening to exempt themselves from the provisions of the NCLB law, which would mean forfeiting the federal money that comes with the law. Additionally, the National Education Association and the state of Connecticut have filed suits against the federal government for what they see as inadequate funding of the law. Some leeway seems likely to be given to the states; however, the intent of the law and its main provisions are most likely to continue into the future.

■ **Compensatory Education and Title I**   Although the federal government provides money for a variety of educational programs, its most significant efforts have been to address the needs of children from high-poverty areas who are at risk for educational failure. **Compensatory education** is an approach to creating more equal educational opportunities for disadvantaged children.

■ Title I requirements

Compensatory education was formalized in a section of the original 1965 Elementary and Secondary Education Act (ESEA) known as Title I. Congress continues to strongly support Title I: Improving the Academic Achievement of the Disadvantaged because the money reaches almost every school district and thus provides jobs and services in every congressional district. Few members of Congress will vote against providing these benefits to their districts. Under the 2001 reauthorization of ESEA—the No Child Left Behind Act—Title I is now the largest part of federal spending on public schools.

Title I was designed to do two things: (1) deliver federal funds to local school districts and schools for the education of students from low-income families and (2) supplement the educational services provided to low-achieving students in those districts. Subsequent reauthorizations of ESEA have changed the rules for schools that receive Title I funds. As described in the box on NCLB, to receive money, states and school districts must submit a state improvement plan that includes the adoption of challenging content standards and aligned assessments for Title I students. Schools are now allowed to use their Title I funds on a schoolwide basis rather than only for the poorest students, and they can combine money from multiple federal programs. However, school districts must now rank their schools based on their percentages of poor students and distribute Title I funds accordingly, with the poorest schools receiving the most money per pupil. As mentioned above, NCLB has boosted Title I funding for school districts with high concentrations of poor children by changing the funding formula.

■ Title I funding

Between 1965 and 2005, Title I provided over $185 billion for educational services in almost all of the nation's school districts. Title I now provides more than $14.4 billion each year on behalf of more than 14.9 million children in 47,600 schools. Of the 14.9 million Title I students, about two-thirds are enrolled in grades one through six. Hispanic American students make up 31 percent; African American students, 27 percent; Asian American students, 3 percent; Native American students, 2 percent; and white students, 35 percent of those receiving Title I support. Title I grants serve about 1.8 million preschool and kindergarten children, about 150,000 private school children, some 100,000 students identified as homeless, and about 2.5 million students with limited English proficiency.[20]

■ varieties of compensatory education

Compensatory programs come in many forms. Some are preventive approaches, targeting children who are "at risk" for later school failure during their preschool or infant years. Such programs may help parents learn how to interact more effectively with their babies and young children in the areas of cognitive and psychosocial development. The most famous preschool initiative is **Head Start,** described in the accompanying box.

■ compensatory education beyond preschool

Other compensatory programs target older children and focus on basic skill instruction, tutoring, or remediation in a variety of academic areas. Success for All, described in the accompanying box, is an example of a program implemented in elementary schools. Dropout prevention programs, job training, and adult lit-

Head Start

Head Start is a federal program that aims to improve the learning skills, social skills, and health status of poor children so that they can begin schooling on an equal basis with their more advantaged peers. Since its inception in 1965, Head Start has served over 22 million children.[21]

Although Head Start is over forty years old, the program is not without its critics, and, like other sectors of public education, is undergoing reforms. For the 2005 fiscal year, the federal government budgeted $6.8 billion for Head Start programs. Along with Congress's reauthorization of the Head Start program, however, came a call for a new focus on academics.

Signaling this new emphasis on academics, Head Start was moved in 2005 from the control of the Department of Health and Human Services to the Department of Education. There, Head Start programs, like elementary and secondary schools, are to be held accountable for making progress toward meeting

academic goals. Programs that fail to make satisfactory progress toward meeting these goals face the possibility of having their funding withdrawn after some period of time.

The proposed focus on academics has been strongly opposed by many early-childhood education experts who fear that attention to academic skills will dilute efforts to promote positive social and emotional development and that the health services Head Start currently provides will be abandoned. Others argue that there is no reason why all these goals couldn't be addressed satisfactorily by Head Start programs. Certainly, the students served by Head Start programs need and deserve attention to academic, social, and health concerns in order to prepare them to succeed in school.

 Link to more information about Head Start from the website.

Early intervention programs, such as Head Start, target children who are "at risk" of school failure by intervening in their early years to improve their skills.
(© Syracuse Newspapers/ Gary Walts/The Image Works)

eracy instruction are all attempts to help older individuals improve the quality of their lives through education and to help prevent the cycle of educational disadvantage from being passed down through generations.

■ evaluations mixed

■ early intervention a key

Evaluations of Title I and other compensatory education programs have been mixed. The earliest hopes—that compensatory education would increase student IQ scores and scholastic achievement—have not realized significant results. However, long-range studies that have followed students from preschool to age nineteen, like the study of students in the very successful Perry Preschool Program in Ypsilanti, Michigan, provide other indicators of program success. Effective early childhood programs may result in fewer special education placements, more high school graduations, lower teen pregnancy rates, increased employment and earnings, fewer crimes committed, and greater commitment to marriage.[22] *Early intervention*—beginning the program early in the child's life—may provide the key to success in compensatory education programs.

■ not enough money?

Critics of Title I see little point in strengthening programs that they believe have failed to meet their original goals. Proponents of compensatory education programs argue that, considering the enormity of the problem, expenditures thus far are a mere drop in the bucket. In spite of what seems like an enormous amount of money, only about 50 percent of all eligible children receive services from Title I funds. Because Title I has never been funded at a high enough level to meet the needs of low-income schools and because its resources are widely dispersed, even the recent funding increases have not checked the growing educational crisis in low-income areas.

■ Title I schools show gains

Proponents can also point to recent gains in achievement. A 1999 national assessment of Title I showed that Title I schools were making positive gains in reading and mathematics. The report concluded that Title I schools are benefiting from improved resource targeting, improving alignment of curriculum with standards, and a more cohesive school program through greater use of schoolwide goals and clarification of parent roles. Although the performance of students in high-poverty

Success for All

One compensatory education program that is quite successful is the Success for All program developed by the Center for Research on Effective Schooling for Disadvantaged Students at Johns Hopkins University. The Success for All program restructures the elementary school with one goal in mind: to ensure that all students perform at grade level in reading, writing, and mathematics by the end of third grade.

Success for All schools start early, offering a half-day of preschool and a full day of kindergarten, both focused on providing a developmentally appropriate learning experience for children. The curriculum emphasizes the development and use of language and balances academic readiness with music, art, and movement activities.

The program also implements the center's research findings on one-to-one tutoring, regrouping for reading, family support teams, frequent assessments of learning with immediate help on problems, and the use of an effective reading program. Two social workers and one parent liaison work full time in the schools to provide parenting education and to encourage parents to support their children's efforts. The program also includes tutors for children in grades K–3. Each tutor is a certified, experienced teacher or paraprofessional who works one-on-one with eleven students per day. First-graders get priority for tutoring.

The Success for All program includes ninety minutes of uninterrupted reading instruction each day, during which teachers are asked to follow a fast-paced script written by the Success for All researchers. In spite of its success in teaching students to read, many teachers dislike the reading program, because it tells them exactly what to do throughout their lessons. For some teachers, this process seems contrary to their beliefs about the importance of paying attention to the learning style of each child and varying their instruction accordingly.

Overall, however, evaluation results have been outstanding, much higher than for any other intervention strategy ever tried with at-risk students. Starting with one Baltimore school in 1987, the Success for All program had spread to about 1,500 schools in forty-eight states, serving about 800,000 students, and it has produced dramatic gains in students' reading proficiency. Almost all Success for All programs are in high-poverty, Title I schools. Early programs were more expensive than regular instruction, but that situation seems to have changed. By restructuring elementary schools and reconfiguring the uses of Title I money, special education, and other funds to emphasize prevention and early intervention rather than remediation, the administrators have brought costs in Success for All schools in line with those of other schools that have access to these resources.

The major lesson learned, according to the major developer of Success for All, Robert Slavin, and his colleagues, is that disadvantaged children can routinely achieve substantially greater success in schools that are neither exceptional nor extraordinary. Rather than having to depend on the outstanding principal or charismatic teacher to ensure success, every child, regardless of background, has an excellent opportunity to succeed in school.

Sources: Robert Slavin, "Success for All." In *Encyclopedia of Education,* 2d ed., ed. James W. Guthrie (New York: Macmillan Reference, U.S.A., 2003); Robert E. Slavin and Nancy A. Madden (Eds.), *Success for All: Research and Reform in Elementary Education* (Mahwah, NJ: Lawrence Erlbaum Associates, 2001); Success for All brochure— available at: **http://www.successforall.com/About/sfabrochure. pdf**; Jay Mathews, "As Schools Shop for Success, Teachers Rethink Role," *The Washington Post,* June 21, 1999, pp. A1, A8.

 Link to more information about Title I from the website.

 Link to Success for All from the website.

schools is improving, they remain much further behind their peers in meeting basic standards of performance in both reading and mathematics. The report urges that schools continue to focus on standards for learning, align the curriculum with the standards, reduce instructional reliance on paraprofessionals, and strengthen parent involvement.[23] As the centerpiece of the NCLB law, Title I will likely continue to receive substantial funding increases in the years to come.

Both sides acknowledge that not all programs are equally effective. The best programs achieve desired results, whereas the less effective programs do not seem to have lasting effects on student performance. Both can also agree that, in addition to education efforts, a simultaneous attack should be made on external factors that contribute to low achievement, such as poor housing, family instability, and low income.

▶ A Final Word

■ federal influence is growing

What is the outlook for the future? The federal government, through the NCLB law, has assumed a major role in education in the United States, much more than it played in the past. President George W. Bush has made the NCLB legislation the key to his educational agenda, and has supported increased funding for education to help finance educational reform, even in light of growing federal budget deficits. The strong accountability measures included in NCLB give the federal government influence on education beyond the actual dollars it spends. While states continue to have the major say in educational matters, the federal government is no longer a "silent partner," and this trend is likely to continue in the future.

Key Terms

adequate yearly progress (351)
block grants (350)
categorical grants (349)
chief state school officer (332)
compensatory education (353)
Elementary and Secondary
    Education Act (ESEA) (351)

Head Start (354)
highly qualified teacher (351)
local school board (333)
No Child Left Behind Act
    (NCLB) (351)
parent-teacher organization
    (PTO) (338)

privatization (341)
site-based decision making (337)
state board of education (332)
state department of
    education (332)
superintendent of schools (334)
Title I (353)

For Reflection

1 Do you believe you would like to become a school principal or local superintendent someday? Why or why not?

2 The National Education Association and the National Association of Secondary School Principals make this statement about successful secondary schools: "In good secondary schools, the principal and teachers develop and maintain a variety of cooperative links with the community. Family and community involvement and support complement the efforts of the school." Describe some of the cooperative links you would suggest at either the elementary or secondary level.

3 What role do you think the federal government should play in compensating for educational disadvantages as a result of poverty?

For Debate

Read the Policy Matters! summary "Who Should be Accountable for Getting Results?" at the website, and consider the issues it outlines regarding testing and accountability. Then, go to EduSpace to post your answers (or respond to other students' answers) to the What Do You Think questions listed in the Policy Matters! feature.

For Further Information

PRINT RESOURCES

Vern Brimley, Jr., and Rulon R. Garfield, *Financing Education in a Climate of Change,* 9th ed. (Boston: Allyn and Bacon, 2005).
This comprehensive text examines how schools are financed in this country, the role of the federal government, and significant court cases affecting school finance.

Susan Moore Johnson, *Leading to Change: The Challenge of the New Superintendency* (San Francisco: Jossey-Bass, 1996).
In this text, the author studies twelve superintendents, their models of leadership, and how contexts influence their behavior.

Jonathan Kozol, *Savage Inequalities: Children in America's Schools* (New York: HarperPerennial, 1992).
National Book Award winner Jonathan Kozol presents his shocking account of the American educational system in this best-selling book.

Frederick M. Wirt and Michael W. Kirst, *The Political Dynamics of American Education,* 2d ed. (Berkeley, CA: McCutchan, 2001).
This text presents an analysis of the politics of education by two leaders in the field.

WEB RESOURCES

U.S. Department of Education. Available at: **http://www.ed.gov.**
This home page will keep you abreast of educational initiatives of the federal government. Clicking on the National Center for Education Statistics link (under Programs and Services) will give you access to many government publications and statistics on education. For information on Head Start, use **http://www.acf.hhs.gov/programs/hsb.**

National Education Association. Available at: **http://www.nea.org.**
The NEA website offers many resources, including an annual report on Rankings and Estimates that features many statistics on the states, including average teacher salaries, per pupil expenditures by state, per capita expenditure on education, and many other interesting statistics. To find the report,

go to the Search function and enter "Rankings and Estimates."

Education Commission of the States. Available at: **http://www.ecs.org.**
The Education Commission of the States (ECS) is an interstate compact created in 1965 to improve public education by facilitating the exchange of information, ideas, and experiences among state policymakers and education leaders. ECS produces many policy papers on education issues affecting state policymakers. Go to "Education Issues" and select a particular issue for a review of what's known about the issue. Issues are far ranging, including charter schools, child abuse, brain research, technology, desegregation, and early childhood, among others.

12 How Should Education Be Reformed?

Chapter Preview   This chapter gives you a concentrated look at the educational reform movement. For more than twenty years, politicians and educators have been working vigorously to alter the course of American elementary and secondary education. Though results have been mixed to date, certain patterns and key educational ideas are evident.

This chapter emphasizes that:

▶ Reform has been a part of American education for the past one hundred years.

▶ The current educational reform movement is being fueled by a widespread belief that our schools are not educating many of our students adequately for the demands of our current time, let alone the future.

▶ Although most people agree that schools should educate students to be good citizens, workers, and people, differing educational philosophies and beliefs about purposes of schooling lead to a variety of different approaches to schooling.

▶ Some key educational ideas *ought* to be at the heart of this current reform movement.

▶ Responsibility for school reform resides primarily with state and local educational agencies, with significant contributions from the federal government and national associations.

▶ Teachers are the crucial element in meaningful reform.

It has been said that trying to change or reform our schools is like trying to change a flat tire on a speeding car—something that needs to be done but is nearly impossible to achieve. For nearly one hundred years, attempts have been made to bring about change in American schools, with mixed results. Many of these reform efforts have been fueled by philosophical debates as to what the purpose of schools should be (see the chapter entitled "What Is a School and What Is It For?"). For example, in the early 1900s, with the development of factories, which were seen as a more efficient way of producing goods, some people argued that students could be more efficiently educated if schools looked and functioned more like factories. They also thought that students would become better adult workers if their schools were more like factory assembly lines. Opponents (including John Dewey, who is profiled in the chapter entitled "What Are the Philosophical Foundations of American Education?") thought that schools should educate students to be good thinkers and citizens who, as adults, would work to bring about a better, more equitable society. Thus, our schools became more democratic.

■ debate about need for reform

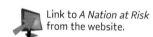
Link to *A Nation at Risk* from the website.

The most recent movement to bring about change in our schools grew out of an influential 1983 report by the National Commission on Excellence in Education entitled, *A Nation At Risk.* In clear and forceful language, the Commission described what it called a "rising tide of mediocrity" in the schools. The report demanded that this tide be stemmed through a greater focus on the academic achievement of students. In the twenty plus years since this report was released, some progress has been made toward reforming schools. How much more can or must be made is open to debate. Some educators and politicians argue that much more still needs to be done to improve our schools, since the reforms implemented to date have not led to many gains in academic achievement. Others disagree, stating that our schools are a great social achievement in that we educate more children to higher levels than any other society in the world. They are encouraged by good news such as significant gains reported among African American and Hispanic students in mathematics during the early 1990s and gains in high school completion rates among African Americans, which now nearly equal those of white, non-Hispanics.[1]

There are also a number of skeptics who believe that the schools, particularly the public schools, are incapable of being reformed. A recent government study stated the problem this way: "The education system in the United States may seem to be, and in some respects is, a chaotic interaction of federal, state and local governments trying to implement sometimes incompatible policies and processes with little central direction."[2]

Some argue that schools, as institutions, are deeply resistant to change and that unlike corporations, whose effectiveness can be judged by bottom-line profits or losses, the effectiveness of schools is all but impossible to measure, in part because their purposes remain multiple. Without a single, clear definition of a well-educated person, schools cannot agree on how to reform themselves.

Still others oppose all these efforts at change, arguing that childhood is childhood and that school should provide continuity and stability in a society in constant flux. Schools fulfill this specific function well and therefore do not need to be reformed. In short, these defenders of the schools ask, "If it ain't broke, why fix it?" Nevertheless, those in favor of serious school reform vastly outnumber these voices of caution and opposition.

Pause and Reflect

1 ▶ Based on your own personal school experiences, do you believe our schools need to be reformed and changed in any major ways? Why?

2 ▶ What do you believe are the most compelling reasons to reform American schools?

■ major motivations for reform

One educator captured the views of many when he wrote that a good school respects and keeps in balance the need "to educate the 'three people' in each individual: the citizen, the worker, and the private person."[3] Using this breakdown, we can categorize the major motivations to reform our educational system as follows:

To Develop a Democratic Citizen:
- There are dramatic differences between the schools serving the children of the rich and those serving the children of the poor.
- Disturbingly high percentages of students know nothing about our democratic traditions and how our government functions.
- There is little understanding of the world and the global role and responsibility of the United States.

To Develop the Good Worker:
- Our way of life and our individual standard of living are closely linked to our nation's ability to maintain its economic leadership, a leadership that is seriously threatened by the comparatively low level of knowledge and skills demonstrated by the graduates of our schools in mathematics, science, and vocational education.
- The world of work is rapidly being transformed, and schools are not keeping pace. As Americans cope with an information age, many of our schools are still trapped in a factory or industrial approach to teaching and learning.

To Develop the Good Person:
- Our children seem to be failing to develop a "moral compass" and the personal habits of responsibility, diligence, kindness, and courage that are associated with mature adulthood.
- Too many students are concerned with personal gain and individual rights rather than the well-being of their community and society.

Keeping in mind these three goals (which are also the three purposes of schooling we discussed in the chapter entitled "What Is a School and What Is It For?") as a basis for reform, we now turn to how our schools ought to be reformed.

▶ What Ought to Be the Elements of Educational Reform?

It is crucial for a builder to have goals and a plan before starting a project. Therefore, before addressing the *what* and *how* issues of school reform, we should take a moment now to consider the question of *ought:* What *ought* to be the nature of this reform? Keep your answers to the following question in mind and compare them to the directions and programs that are part of current reform efforts as you read the rest of this chapter.

Pause and Reflect

1 ▶ Reflect on your own education. Drawing on what you see as the primary purpose of schooling, make a short list of current aspects of schooling that you believe need to be reformed. Your answer should be driven by a view of what we want our schools to achieve, including a set of goals and a realistic plan.

_____

_____

_____

_____

A Call for Excellence

■ the call to excellence

Underlying all the experimental programs, curriculum innovation, and other efforts for school improvement is the commitment to *excellence*. From the *Sputnik* crisis in the late 1950s to the 1983 report by the National Commission on Excellence in Education to the present efforts to implement the No Child Left Behind legislation, excellence has been the rallying cry and the focus of educational reform. Teachers are challenged to ignite in their students a desire to excel in all aspects of school life. A particular concern for educational reformers is that the performance of American students equal or surpass that of students from other countries, particularly those in Asia and Europe. Many educational policymakers insist that American competitiveness will suffer if our students do not excel in all areas of study.

Nearly everyone will agree that we want our students to excel and achieve outstanding results. The more difficult question is how to achieve these results. A number of elements have been advanced as essential for achieving excellence and true and lasting educational reform: high standards, accountability, active learning, a sense of community, a focus on lifelong learning, character education, and teacher development.

High Standards

The reform movement we are witnessing is characterized by the belief that the great majority of students can reach high standards. Students must adopt a serious task orientation toward their studies and show mastery of content that is measured through rigorous tests.

■ earning self-esteem

In the past, teachers were often encouraged to focus first on raising students' self-esteem through positive reinforcement and gentle coaching. In a high-standards environment, self-esteem is seen as the direct by-product of student achievement. Instead of giving self-esteem to students, the teacher sets up learning situations so that students can be successful and earn it. One elementary school captures the twin themes of setting high standards and earning self-esteem by challenging its students with the motto "Your best today. Better tomorrow."

Helping children achieve high standards is a challenge for the teacher, too. It requires that teachers understand individual students by knowing their weaknesses and strengths, interests, and talents. It demands that teachers not only know their subject matter, but also know how to engage students of many different abilities, interest levels, and learning styles. (See the chapter, "What Is Taught?" for more on content standards.)

Accountability

■ teaching to the test?

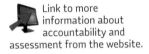

Link to more information about accountability and assessment from the website.

Teachers and schools that set high standards need to find some way of determining if the standards are being met. Some form of accountability is usually required, and it most often comes in the form of standardized tests. During the 1970s and 1980s, a major motivation behind the accountability movement was declining test scores. As is discussed later in this chapter, schools across the country began using standardized achievement tests and so-called *minimum competency tests* to see how they were doing compared with other schools. On the basis of these test scores, the performances of school districts, their teachers, and their students were judged; programs were added or dropped and individuals rewarded or punished. The pressure to boost test scores was intense, and many teachers quite naturally responded by emphasizing in their instruction the knowledge and skills that were being tested. In effect, teachers began **teaching to the test.** What was tested became what was taught.

In the video case *Assessment in the Elementary Grades: Formal and Informal Literacy Assessment,* watch how one second-grade teacher administers several of the forms of assessment discussed in this chapter. Reflect upon videos and other case materials as you consider the following questions:

1. What are the benefits, to teachers, students, parents, and the school, of each of different types of assessment: standardized test, informal assessments, performance assessments, and portfolio assessments?
2. What kinds of useful information can an informal assessment, such as the running record in the *bonus videos,* add to that provided by standardized test scores?
3. What are the benefits and challenges for these same groups of developing a complete assessment program, featuring multiple types of assessments?

These pressures to "teach-to-the-test" have increased even more in recent years as state after state across the country adopted new and more rigorous academic standards. This "high-stakes" testing movement (which we discuss in more detail later in this chapter) has been spurred on by the accountability provisions of the recent federal No Child Left Behind laws. Some critics believe that an unintended consequence of this major reform has been to further focus teachers' instruction and students' learning on the narrow contents of these limited standardized tests.

As instruction narrowed to concentrate more and more on the basics, student scores seemed to improve and state after state reported that their students were scoring above the national average on the standardized tests given. At this point, in state after state and in community after community, what has been called the "Lake Wobegon effect" occurred (named after a fictional town

■ Lake Wobegon effect

portrayed by writer and public radio humorist Garrison Keillor, a place where "all the children were above average"). Each community interpreted its test results to mean that its children were above average.

On closer examination, however, educators and policymakers interpreted the results to mean that the children were becoming overly familiar with the test questions and were able to score well on the tests. Others interpreted the results to mean that the standardized tests being used were inappropriate or invalid. A common complaint was that the multiple-choice tests assessed lower-level thinking skills instead of the higher-order ones for which educators and business leaders were calling.

We must put knowledge directly in the hands of teachers and seek accountability that will focus attention on" "doing the right things" rather than on" "doing things right."

—LINDA DARLING-HAMMOND

■ new type of assessment demanded

Educators and the business community began to call for schools to emphasize critical thinking skills and problem-solving abilities, qualities that are difficult to measure through multiple-choice and other objective tests. Some educators called for a different type of assessment, one that would directly measure real student performance on important tasks. For example, if we want to know how well students can write, we can examine samples of their writing. Or if we want to know how well students understand scientific concepts and can carry out scientific processes, we can ask them to conduct an actual experiment. In other words, the assessment would actually measure what we wanted students to be able to do rather than relying on them to choose the correct response on a multiple-choice test item. This type of assessment is known as **authentic** or **performance assessment.** Advocates claim that authentic assessment involves performance tests that get closer to how students apply knowledge rather than how they store it in their minds.

 The video case _Performance Assessment: Student Presentations in a High School English Class_ shows an extended example of how one teacher goes about assessing her students' creative performances. Reflect upon videos and other case materials as you consider the following questions:

1. The teacher notes that students seem to be more engaged in their learning when they know they will be expected to demonstrate their knowledge via a performance assessment. How might teachers increase students' interest levels for materials that are included on required standardized tests?
2. Do you agree with the teacher that a key goal or benefit of assessment should be to provide students with "ways to feel successful"? In what ways do the various forms of assessment described in this section contribute to or detract from that goal?

One method of authentic assessment involves having students collect their work over time and assemble it to create **portfolios.** These portfolios might showcase students' best work, much like an artist's portfolio. In other instances, the work in the portfolio is representative of work done throughout the semester, showing students' growth over time. In either case, these portfolios can be evaluated by students and teachers to determine learning progress.[4] In many parts of the country, in fact, student teachers assemble portfolios of their own work to show their professional skills when they apply for employment. (See the chapter entitled, "What Are Your Job Options in Education?" for more on teaching portfolios.)

■ portfolios

■ unresolved issues

Authentic assessment is not without its critics and unresolved issues. Whether performance assessments can satisfy the validity requirement (answering the question, "Is this a true measure of what I want to assess?") and the reliability requirement ("Will this test yield a similar result when administered at different times and under different circumstances?") has yet to be determined. Cost is also a major concern. Evaluating writing samples or judging students' success in conducting a scientific experiment is much more time consuming, and therefore more costly, than machine scoring a multiple-choice exam. Standards of judgment present another difficulty. Even if testers use rubrics that specify criteria and standards of assessment, the subjectivity of the human evaluator is an important consideration. In addition, questions remain about how to judge excellence, originality, and creativity in art and writing, let alone math or science. The case of Vermont is a good illustration of the unresolved issues of portfolio as-

Visit the video case *Portfolio Assessment: Elementary Classroom* to see, in detail how this method of assessment can be used. Reflect upon videos and other case materials as you consider the following questions:

1. In one of the *bonus videos,* the teacher mentions the time pressure felt by many teachers. How can teachers pressed for time avoid the temptation described in this book, to "teach to the test"?
2. Can teachers effectively use portfolios to help them meet or cope with demands to teach students the material that will be tested on their standardized assessments? How?
3. What information would standardized test scores add—for a teacher, for parents, and for students—to the information gained from portfolio reflections?

■ humans as active makers of meaning

The video case *Elementary School Language Arts: Inquiry Learning* shows a lesson that takes the constructivist's approach and, as the teacher states it, "put students in charge of their own learning." Reflect upon videos and other case materials as you consider the following questions:

1. How has this teacher prepared the lesson to allow students to take an active role in their learning, as described in this chapter? How might she have prepared differently if she did not take a constructivist view?
2. What are the benefits and challenges for the teacher who takes a constructivist approach? What are the benefits and challenges for students?

■ characteristics of constructivist classrooms

sessment. In the early 1990s, the state of Vermont began a statewide portfolio assessment program for all students at all grade levels. After a few years of implementation, the program had to be suspended because it was proving to be too costly, too time consuming, and with too much variation in the scores.

Whatever form of assessment is used, any educational reform needs to include some way of knowing if students are in fact meeting the standards set and becoming the well-educated individuals that society wants.

Active Learning: The Constructivist's Approach

There is an old saying that all teachers know well: "You can lead a horse to water, but you can't make it drink." Similarly, you can have a child in a classroom, but you can't make him or her learn. Pouring information into students or forcing them to do workbooks or problem sheets won't always do it. Nor will the great majority of students learn if simply allowed to wander through a library or laboratory on their own. Something must happen in learners before they learn. Curiosity? A problem that they want or need to solve? And then, with the direct or indirect help of the teacher, the student "constructs" knowledge from the information available to him or her.

Constructivism is a theory of knowledge acquisition built on the idea that the learner interacts with new information to "construct" meaning from it. (See the chapters entitled "What Should Teachers Know About Technology and Its Impact on Schools?" and "What Are the Philosophical Foundations of American Education?" for more on constructivism.) Constructivism provides a frame of reference for organizing classroom practices so that students learn in all content areas.[5] Contrary to educational practices in which learners passively receive information, the constructivist approach requires that learners actively interact with the information, building on their prior knowledge, attitudes, and values. As learners encounter new information or experiences, they ask themselves, "What makes sense here? What happens when I do this or change that?" In this **active learning** process, learners build and add to their understanding of concepts, rules, and strategies through direct, hands-on experimentation.

How does constructivism embody the call for excellence of educational reform? First, a primary ingredient of the constructivist approach is a learner taking responsibility for his or her own learning. The teacher and the school play important supporting roles, but the initiative of the learner is essential. Students can achieve excellence only if they take responsibility for their learning.

Ideally, constructivist classrooms foster experiential, inquiry-based learning in an atmosphere of intellectual play. Teachers in these classrooms ask challenging, open-ended questions and allow for much wait-time. In short, constructivism incorporates much of what has been written about in this text, including inductive teaching, student-teacher interaction, cooperative learning, multi- and interdisciplinary teaching, and extensive use of new technologies.

Constructivist principles stress the importance of learners being active in creating their own new knowledge. (© Elizabeth Crews)

■ criticisms of constructivism

While constructivism has many virtues, it is but one theory of learning, one way of thinking about how knowledge and understanding are formed, certainly not the only way. Critics are quick to point out that students can "construct" incorrect answers. Further, critics remind us it is a formidable task to translate this theory of learning into a theory of teaching.[6]

Nevertheless, we believe constructivism can be a valuable corrective to much of classroom life. It can bridge the gap between teacher-centered drill or rote learning on the one hand and excessively abstract learning on the other. An ancient Chinese proverb captures well the essence of constructivism: "Tell me and I forget. Show me and I will remember. Make me do it and I learn."

A Sense of Community

■ urban sanctuaries

"Small is beautiful" has been the slogan for many social activists over the last three decades. Social scientists studying adolescents in our cities found what they labeled *urban sanctuaries,* neighborhood organizations that attracted and served inner-city youth, particularly those who were disaffected and drifting toward gangs. These urban sanctuaries had "family-like environments in which individuals are valued and rules of membership are clear. Their activities offer opportunities for active participation and present challenges that result in accomplishments. They are youth driven and sensitive to youth's everyday realities. They assume that youth are a resource to be developed, not a problem to solve."[7] These messages, however, are just beginning to gain a foothold in American education.

■ disengagement of students

Recent years have brought a growing realization that the largest of our schools, although more efficient and cost-effective, can have some destructive side effects. The schools have an aura of impersonality that results in the disengagement of many students. It is common to hear such statements as "I'm lost here," "No one really knows me and no one cares," or "I'm just a name in someone's gradebook." Though these criticisms are directed most often at high schools, they hold for many of our junior high and middle schools and even some elementary schools. Clearly, the larger our schools get and the greater the number of classmates and adults with whom students must interact, the more students disengage, and disengaged students cannot achieve excellence.

Recent studies have found not only a decline in student engagement, and therefore in academic achievement, in large schools but also a decline in faculty morale and an increase in faculty absenteeism.[8] Further, large schools are often equally overwhelming for parents, who tend to remain at a distance and therefore uninvolved in their children's school lives.

■ "houses" of students

■ **Schools-Within-Schools**   School-as-community advocates believe that any school whose principal does not know the names of all the students is too big. Reformers such as James Comer of New Haven's School Development Project and Theodore Sizer, founder and chair emeritus of the Coalition of Essential Schools, argue that a sense of community is essential to the development of an academic environment. In these reform projects, new schools are purposely kept small, and existing large schools are broken up into "houses" of 100 to 400 students. The number of teachers with whom the students interact is similarly reduced, and these houses function as **schools-within-schools.** Because students and teachers stay in the same house for several years, they are able to establish stronger and deeper relationships. Each student is a *known* person rather than a name on a class roster.

One obvious advantage of the house plan is that it allows teachers to plan together and to bring to bear their different perceptions of a child who is having difficulties. In addition, these smaller, more intimate school environments provide a more stable emotional climate for students. Faculty advisors have better knowledge of and more exposure to students and can offer them more help in dealing with students' problems or challenges. In this smaller setting, advocates argue, students are much more likely to achieve the standards of excellence set for them.

Pause and Reflect

1 ▶ Reflecting back on your own recent schooling, did the schools you attended have this sense of community? Your elementary school? Your high school?

2 ▶ Does the college or university you are attending have this sense? What could be done to give it more of a sense of community?

Lifelong Learning

■ need for learning throughout life

In our global, rapidly evolving social and economic environment, people need more than a high school or college education. We must also be capable of continuous learning. The jobs we perform and the tasks we must accomplish today will likely differ ten years from now. Therefore, schools must attend to the habits of mind and the skills that will keep people learning throughout their lives, making them **lifelong learners.** Not only must students become good learners, but in order to be lifelong learners, they also need to be enthusiastic learners. In other words, students must know *how* to learn, and they must *want* to learn.

■ **Tools for Learning**   The human brain is a glorious instrument capable of enormous feats of creativity, from writing symphonies to making scientific breakthroughs. The average brain can store and manipulate more information, by several hundred times, than the largest computers. But the brain has its drawbacks. It loses or "misfiles" information. Numerous and assorted messages enter it through the eyes, ears, and other senses and somehow get lost. When we want to remember an idea, it often is simply "not there," or somehow the information received gets modified so that when we take the exam, we are sure there are two quarts in a gallon and four pints in a quart. Thus, although the brain is humankind's treasure, it is hardly perfect. And to work well, the brain must be trained and well-maintained.

■ training the brain

By *trained,* we mean we have to teach people how to use their brains effectively. Most likely the majority of our readers have been urged a time or two by parents and teachers to "use your brains!" Our meaning is both an extension of that request and a more specialized suggestion. We are urging that we give our brains more power through the use of new tools. In the same manner that reading extends the power of the brain by giving it access to vast amounts of important information, other tools can make the brain more efficient and better able to take in, interpret, process, store, and retrieve information. *Well-maintained* means we continue to make use of these important tools long after we have left the hallowed hallways of schools.

■ tools for learning

A fresh focus on the skills of learning can and ought to be a major part of school reform. Of course, we must attend to the three Rs. We are not suggesting that we give a lower priority to subject matter. Rather, to make knowledge (that is, **intellectual capital**) more useful, students need to learn how to learn. As teachers, we must give our students the necessary **tools for learning:** advanced reading, remembering, recording, researching, test taking, analyzing, and creating. These are the tools that can help students excel, not just in school, but later, in the workplace and in life, in general. (See the box "A Sample of the Tools for Learning.")

Reclaiming Character Education

■ definition of character education

🖥 Link to more information about character education from the website.

The calls for excellence in education are not limited to just academic achievement. Many reformers have also been concerned about excellence of character. Much of the dissatisfaction with schools that has fueled recent educational reform efforts comes from parents and community leaders who believe the schools have not done enough to affect positively the character and ethical values of students. Many reformers are convinced that failure to address these needs of students lies at the heart of the schools' problems. A "good student" has come to mean someone who does well on tests and achieves academically rather than someone who is a good person and who demonstrates characteristics such as responsibility, consideration for others, self-discipline, and the ability to work hard. In order to achieve excellence in student achievement, serious school reform must address the issue of **character education,** which we define as the effort to help the young acquire a *moral compass*—that is, a sense of right and wrong and the enduring habits necessary to live a good life. Character education, then, involves helping the child *to know the good, love the good, and do the good.*[9]

■ objections to character education

■ **Arguments Pro and Con**   Some people argue that the public school has no role in character development and moral education because these are rooted in deeply held religious world views. As such, they are out of bounds to the public school, which should concentrate on cognitive skills exclusively, skills such as reading, writing, and application of the scientific method.[10] These people claim

A Sample of the Tools for Learning

Here is a list of some of the skills, or what we are calling the Tools for Learning, that we believe ought to be taught to all students:

- *Various methods for remembering important information.* This largely involves teaching people how not to forget: how to move information from the fleeting short-term memory to the more enduring long-term memory.

- *Two or three methods of taking notes and saving important information.* Definite skills are associated with capturing what another person is saying, and students should systematically learn these skills.

- *Study reading.* A person practices "study reading" when the material is complex and contains information one wants to remember later. It is quite different from reading a novel or reading a telephone book. It is a set of skills that is at the heart of academic success, as well as success in many jobs.

- *Preparing for different kinds of tests.* Schools should show students how to study for different types of tests, such as objective and essay tests, and how to deal with test anxiety in various situations. Because examinations and tests do not end with graduation, schools should teach students how to cope with and master these challenges.

- *Doing research.* Students need to learn how to get answers to questions by using libraries, the Internet, expert sources, and data-gathering resources of all kinds. In essence, these are the skills of finding and accessing different data sources and using the information to solve a problem.

- *Thinking through a problem in a systematic way.* Instead of jumping to conclusions or relying on how they feel about an issue, students should learn how to think critically.

- *Generating creative ideas.* Much of life in and out of school requires new solutions or imaginative resolutions. Students need to learn techniques for generating novel and creative ideas individually, as well as group-oriented techniques such as brainstorming.

- *Getting the academic job done.* Students need to know how to set goals, develop a work plan, monitor their own behavior, bring a task to successful closure, and gradually become more successful at academic learning. This is important not simply to succeed in school, but because the modern workplace demands these academic skills.

---

that if parents want attention paid to moral values, they should put their children in private schools.

■ whose values?

Others question character education by asking, "*Whose* values should the public schools teach?" In a nation of diverse cultural backgrounds, a nation committed to freedom of thought and expression, is there any one set of values that can be taught without infringing on someone's deeply cherished beliefs? One answer to this objection is that the tax-supported public schools can teach the civic virtues that are necessary for life in a democratic society, such as respect for the rights of others, courage, tolerance, kindness, and concern for the underdog. Another way to approach the answer is to look at a few of the sights we might encounter while walking around some schools, as described in the following paragraph.

Formal education is the playing field on which society vies over values.
—THEODORE SIZER

A counselor is calling a student's home about apparently excused absences, only to find that the parent's letters have been forged. A young boy is in the principal's office for threatening his teacher with a knife. Three students are separated from their class after hurling racial epithets at a fourth. A girl is complaining that her locker has been broken into and all her belongings stolen. A small group of boys are huddling in a corner, shielding an exchange of money for drug packets. Female students complain that they are being rudely groped when their teacher

Character is like a tree and reputation like its shadow. The shadow is what we think of it; the tree is the real thing.

—Abraham Lincoln

■ wide support for certain values

leaves the room. In the playground, two girls grab a third and punch her in the stomach for flirting with the wrong boy.[11]

Schools that tolerate such behavior not only are failing to address the character education needs of their students but also have become places where the intellectual goals of schooling are impaired. In addition, such schools win little support from the general public, the people who pay for public education.

We believe that most educators know it is impossible to educate students in a moral vacuum. The process of schooling necessarily affects the way children think about issues of right and wrong. Further, the overwhelming majority of Americans, regardless of religion, class, or racial background, support certain moral values such as respect, a thirst for justice, honesty, responsibility in our dealings with one another, consideration, compassion, persistence at hard tasks, and courage in the face of adversity.[12] We believe that few people would not wholeheartedly support the schools' vigorous advocacy of these virtues. Teachers and schools can positively influence the development of desirable habits and character formation in numerous ways, but two in particular are worthy of note: using the curriculum and involving students in service activities.

■ moral issues in subject-matter disciplines

■ **Character in the Curriculum**   One major approach is to teach more directly and more vigorously the positive moral values that are embedded in our culture. Our history and literature are permeated with value issues and moral lessons from the past. Instead of simply having students study the facts of a historical period or read a story to build vocabulary or appreciate style, the teacher can confront them with ethical issues and moral lessons that are integral to the subject matter. Instead of merely teaching scientific methodologies and findings, the teacher can have students examine the implications of applied science, such as genetic manipulation. They will see that the use of science and technologies, such as cloning, fossil fuel based energies, and high-speed computers, is not neutral but has ethical implications. As teachers, we must see the content of our curriculum as the carrier of our moral heritage and work to engage our students in that moral heritage.

Character cannot be developed in ease and quiet. Only through experience of trial and suffering can the soul be strengthened, ambition inspired, and success achieved.

—Helen Keller

■ move toward social service

■ **Service Learning**   Knowing about justice, compassion, and courage is one thing; making them a part of one's life and practicing them diligently is another. Students need real opportunities to practice these virtues. As many reformers realize, schools can create opportunities for students, from the early grades on, to help one another and the adults in the school building. As students get older, they can be given more and more responsibility for working with and caring for younger students. In the later stages of high school, groups of students can take on projects in the larger community, such as helping a parent whose child has a disability or assisting with an exercise class at a senior citizens' center. Likewise, individual students can provide companionship to elderly shut-ins or peer counseling to troubled youngsters. The emphasis in such programs is not merely on the study of virtues but also on virtues in action.

Service learning programs are growing rapidly in our schools. By the beginning of this decade, it was estimated that more than 13 million school students were involved in service and service-learning. This represents a dramatic growth.[13] According to a recent survey conducted by the U.S. Department of Education, 64 percent of all public schools and 83 percent of all public high schools

VOICES FROM THE CLASSROOM

Eric Gelfand has taught gymnastics and physical education to preschool through grade 12 students in Washington and Massachusetts for the past thirteen years.

Building Character Education into the P.E. Curriculum

I can remember one of the members of my gymnastics team getting very upset about not winning. Tyler was eleven years old, and anything less than first place resulted in distress, inability to concentrate, and a feeling of failure. His reaction was stronger than others, but many on our team shared the sentiment: self-esteem and success depended on winning. I decided to initiate a discussion of our definitions of winning with the entire team.

In this discussion we discovered that our definition of winning was based on beating others and factors over which we had no control, like the score that the judge would give us. The new definition of winning that we developed focused on giving our best effort in each moment. We also decided to concentrate only on factors that we could control, such as improving our focus and technique, supporting each other, learning from our competitors, and regulating our thoughts and emotions. We decided if we did these things, then we had each won.

Tyler's feelings of self-esteem and success slowly began to change, but not the first time we talked about it, or the tenth time I reminded him to refocus on our new goals, or even on the fiftieth time that he made himself feel good by remembering that he had done his best. Through the efforts of the entire team over a period of three to four years, Tyler arrived at a place where winning meant something very personal and attainable at all times. This evolution meant valuing respect, persistence, temperance, and compassion for ourselves and others above all else. These virtues slowly became habits, which slowly became a part of our character and who we are today. It was incredibly hard to keep ourselves focused on this goal when our society values a very different definition of winning.

In reading this chapter, you will learn that school reform depends on the efforts of individual teachers to help our children become good workers and citizens. What do you think the definition of "winning" is in academics? If the current definition is not attainable by all of your students, how can you change the system or work within it to make every child successful? I believe that the key is to value the building of character as much as achievement within a discipline. It's simple; it just takes a few years of relentless hard work and compassion.

 Visit the website for more Voices from the Classroom.

organize some form of community service for their students. Nearly a third of all schools and half of public high schools provide service-learning programs, where the service that is being provided is linked with the school curriculum.[14] Central Park East, an acclaimed junior-senior high school in New York City's Harlem, requires that each student perform two hours of service every week. The service can be performed in school by, for example, setting up a science laboratory for an experiment, checking out books at the library's circulation desk, or serving food in the school's cafeteria. In the local community, students do a variety of tasks, such as acting as a guide in one of the city's museums or delivering food to shut-ins.[15]

Several states are considering making a certain number of hours of community service a requisite for high school graduation. In 1993, Maryland became the first state to make service an actual requirement. Currently, Maryland high school students are required to perform seventy-five hours of service before they can graduate.[16] We believe schools must succeed in this mission for students' sake and also because a strong program of character education makes teaching a much more satisfying profession.

Professional Development

■ example of U.S. industry

In the 1980s and 1990s, American business and industry dramatically reformed themselves after decades of inefficiency and loss of markets to their global competitors. The result has been a tremendous growth in national prosperity. An important key to this recovery has been a major investment of time and money in the education and advanced training of the American worker. Individuals from the corporate boardroom to the factory floor learned new ways of doing their work. Today, continuing education is a staple in the American workplace.

Along those lines, educational reformers argue that in order to have better-educated students we need to make sure that our teachers are "excellent." To that end, many state departments of education have required teachers to continue their education after their initial teacher preparation. Also, virtually all school districts have salary incentives for advanced training such as college courses, degrees, and workshops.

■ an array of activities

Initially called *in-service education,* the effort to extend the education of teachers is usually referred to as **staff development,** or more recently **professional development.** As such, the term covers an array of activities, including on-site school- or district-sponsored workshops where teachers come together to learn new skills such as searching the Internet, integrating technology into the curriculum, inquiry-based science instruction, writing across the curriculum, or new classroom management strategies; college or university courses and programs, often leading to advanced degrees in specialized areas such as reading, special education, or guidance counseling; and training experiences provided by textbook companies introducing their new curricula to the school. To this list we would add items such as distance learning courses on using technology in the classroom, a teacher-organized book club on women in fiction, an adult education course on yoga and meditation, writing case studies of educational problems or issues that other teachers can use, mentoring new teachers, and a sabbatical year to study the history of Native Americans. The boundaries of what constitutes professional development are often debated, but we believe the essential attribute is that it aids the teacher in becoming a better teacher.

For many practicing teachers, professional development activities often conjure up memories of trudging off to after-school gatherings where they are lectured to by strangers on topics that hold little interest or relevance for many or to state-mandated required courses or workshops that they take in order to renew their licenses. These efforts are at best, minimal, and, at worst, the major stumbling block to true educational reform. Although a school district that hires a teacher and a state that licenses a teacher have the right to require a teacher's continuing education, such a top-down approach is not likely to serve the needs of children in this new century. For educational reform to truly take hold, several changes like the following are needed:

■ four needed changes

1. Schools should be conceived of as **learning communities,** in which everyone—adults and children alike—is always learning.
2. Teachers, specialists, and administrators must see their continuing educational growth as an integral part of their workday.
3. The definition of *professional development* should be broadened to take into account whatever contributes to making an educator more effective.
4. Although teachers must be willing to devote their time and energy to staff development, the cost should be borne by the school district or the state.

Effective professional development does the following for teachers:

■ characteristics of effective professional development

- Focuses on teachers as central to student learning, yet includes all members of the school community
- Focuses on individual, collegial, and organizational improvement
- Respects and nurtures the intellectual and leadership capacity of teachers, principals, and others in the school community
- Reflects the best available research and practice in teaching, learning, and leadership
- Enables teachers to develop further expertise in subject content, teaching strategies, uses of technologies, and other essential elements of teaching to high standards
- Promotes continuous inquiry and improvement of schools
- Is planned collaboratively by those who will participate in and facilitate that development
- Requires substantial time and resources
- Is driven by a coherent long-term plan
- Is evaluated ultimately on the basis of its effects on teacher instruction and student learning, and uses this assessment to guide subsequent professional development efforts

The teacher who has stopped learning is a deadening influence rather than a help to students being initiated into the ways of learning.

—MORTIMER ADLER, AMERICAN EDUCATOR AND PHILOSOPHER

Educational reform expert Michael Fullan suggests that teachers seeking to improve themselves are characterized by four attitudes: they accept that it is possible to improve; they are ready to be self-critical; they recognize better practice than their own; and, most importantly, they are willing to learn what they have to learn to do what needs to be done.[17] In our view, a teacher who is not engaged in learning activities because of lack of opportunity or lack of personal incentive is stunting his or her own career and is a barrier to the educational reform we need.

We now turn to actual reform initiatives, many of which involve one or more of the elements we have described. As in any other type of reform, certain ideas and principles get attention, while others are ignored or lose ground. As you read about the reforms that have been implemented, compare them in your mind both to what you think ought to be done and to what we have been suggesting here.

Pause and Reflect

1 ▶ Which of the reforms above do you most favor? About which do you have doubts? If we made you Czar of American Education, are there any mentioned reforms you would make, and why?

▶ Current Reform Initiatives

■ message of *A Nation at Risk*

Most educators agree that the current reform effort started with the 1983 federal report *A Nation at Risk*. This strongly worded report declared that our nation was in serious danger and that our schools had left the nation vulnerable to our military and economic competitors. The report called for longer school days, more homework and effort on the part of students, tougher grading policies, more testing, and more demanding textbooks. It arrived at a time of particularly widespread dissatisfaction with the public schools. Just two years before the report's release, a *Newsweek* poll revealed that nearly half (47 percent) of the American public believed the schools were doing a "poor" or only a "fair" job.[18] The remainder of the 1980s saw a blizzard of national and state reports, most hitting many of the same themes, and all calling for massive change. The 1990s was a period of intense development of curricular, programmatic, and pedagogic initiatives aimed at bringing about change in schools and better student performance. Several different groups at the national, state, and local levels created proposals for reform. What have been the results?

National-Level Reform Efforts

Since the issuing of *A Nation at Risk* in 1983, education has been at the forefront of the national agenda and has had a prime place in every presidential candidate's platform in the past twenty years. The first President Bush launched an aggressive educational reform effort called **National Education Goals for the Year 2000.** With the support and cooperation of the fifty state governors, this program committed the nation to achieve six educational milestones by the arrival of the new century. Our next president, Bill Clinton, who as governor of Arkansas had been a strong supporter of this reform, added two more goals and recommitted the nation to achieve these goals by 2000.[19]

Learn more about the National Education Goals for the Year 2000 at the website

While well-intentioned, in retrospect National Education Goals for the Year 2000 effort seems somewhat naïve. Goals, such as "By the year 2000, United States students will be first in the world in mathematics and science achievement" are worthy targets, but reaching them would have involved a titanic reformation of our entire educational system. Such an effort was well beyond the currently available educational resources and, apparently, the will of the country.

■ No Child Left Behind

As the year 2000 came and went, the son of the Goals 2000 initiator was elected to occupy the White House. In his first year in office, President George W. Bush, declaring education reform as the "cornerstone" of his administration, proposed a new plan for American education. Called No Child Left Behind, (NCLB) the president's plan, which was the reauthorization of the Elementary and Secondary Education Act, was signed into law in 2002. NCLB is based on four elements of educational reform: accountability, local control and flexibility, expanded parental choice, and doing what works.[20] While more realistic than Goals 2000, the success of NCLB is still uncertain. To qualify for federal funds, states need to be in compliance with several requirements of NCLB, particularly testing elementary students in math and language arts in grades three to eight and once in high school, by the end of the 2005–06 school year. At the start of 2005, however, less than half (23) of the states were in compliance.[21] (See the chapter entitled "How Are Schools Governed, Influenced, and Financed?" for details about the No Child Left Behind Act.)

■ advocates of a national curriculum

■ **National Standards**   Because of the decentralized nature of U.S. education, each state educational agency (SEA) has the authority to decide what students in that state learn. For many years, these SEAs delegated curricular authority to the local educational agencies (LEAs) so that each school district could decide the most appropriate course of study for its students. Critics complained that these practices led to too much variation in what students were learning, raising concerns about both the quality of education received and equality of educational opportunity. These concerns led to a drive for national standards or a national curriculum. E. D. Hirsch Jr., who popularized the concept of "cultural literacy," presents the equality argument, insisting that a national curriculum is needed because so many students move around from state to state and school to school. With a national curriculum, relocated students would be able to integrate easily into their new school environment, with no time lost academically. Hirsch points to facts such as these: one-fifth of all Americans relocate every year; one-sixth of all third-graders attend at least three different schools between first and third grades; and a typical inner-city school has a 50 percent student turnover between September and May.[22] Others make the quality argument by citing the educational excellence attained by France, Germany, and Japan, all countries with national standards and national exams. These proponents insist that a national curriculum will ensure that all students in the United States receive a high-quality education, no matter where they attend school.

■ the critics

Other educators, however, strongly oppose national standards and an accompanying curriculum and testing program, fearing an educational power grab by the federal government. In their view, the idea of Washington bureaucrats, instead of locally accountable individuals, answering the questions "What should our children know?" and "How well should they know it?" seems both educationally flawed and politically dangerous. Opponents also believe that in a large nation with so many racial and ethnic groups and so many regional traditions, a national curriculum would trample cultural diversity and promote a bland sterility. Further, many are convinced that a national curriculum would put disadvantaged students at an even greater disadvantage.

■ the compromise: voluntary standards

So far, Congress has consistently resisted the establishment of a mandatory national curriculum and national subject-matter examinations. Although the No Child Left Behind Act created a national requirement that states test their students' achievement in key subjects every year, each state is responsible for determining the content standards and developing the assessment measures. In sum, the outlook seems to be as follows: national influence, yes; national control, no; obligatory national testing, probably not in the near future.

■ curricular reform projects

Instead of federally mandated standards, **national curricular standards** have been developed by discipline-specific national groups of scholars and educators as part of larger attempts to bring about curricular reform. These curricular reform projects identify not just what students all over the United States should learn at each grade level, but in some cases, how students should be taught.

One such effort, *Project 2061* (sponsored by the American Association for the Advancement of Science), was discussed in some detail in the chapter entitled "What Is Taught?" Others include *Becoming a Nation of Readers* (sponsored by the Commission on Reading) and *Science/Technology/Society (S/T/S)* (sponsored by the National Science Foundation). The National Writing Project, a professional development project for teachers, promotes a process approach to composition and works with 130,000 teachers in forty-nine states to help teach students to become better writers. Likewise, the National Council of Teachers of Mathematics developed new curriculum and evaluation standards that stress students not just *knowing* how to do mathematics but being able to explain what they're *doing* as well. The University of Chicago School Mathematics Project (UCSMP) has created a K–12 curriculum that emphasizes reading, problem-solving, everyday applications, and the use of new technologies. The Algebra Project is a national mathematics project designed to help low-income students and students of color be successful in acquiring the requisite math skills needed in the Information

Age. In addition to these efforts, national projects have already published content and teaching standards in all the major subject-matter areas, including history, geography, and the arts.

These various curriculum reform projects have come about through partnerships among scholars in the discipline, teacher educators, and classroom teachers. Ideas and suggestions flow across lines that were once rigid. University academics observe in elementary and secondary classrooms, and, back on the campus, elementary and secondary school teachers instruct scholars on the realities of teaching their subjects to a wide variety of youthful students.

Some state educational agencies have found these standards to be of great use as they develop statewide curriculum guides and state-mandated tests (we will discuss these under State Educational Reform later in the chapter).

■ schools banding together

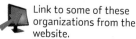 Link to some of these organizations from the website.

■ **National Voluntary Networks**   One of the most interesting recent educational developments is the appearance of networks of schools and school districts. Among these loose, voluntary alliances are two mentioned earlier: the Coalition of Essential Schools begun by Theodore Sizer and the network of schools modeled after James Comer's New Haven School Development Project. Others include John Goodlad's National Network for Educational Reform, Robert Slavin's Success for All Schools, Henry Levin's Accelerated Schools, and a newly established network called Schools of Character, formed by the Character Education Partnership. Schools in these networks commit themselves to a common educational ideal or set of ideals rather than a prescribed course of study or approach to teaching and learning. For instance, the schools in the Coalition of Essential Schools try to put into practice the Ten Common Principles, among which are the following:

- Helping adolescents use their minds well
- Teaching for the mastery of essential skills and acceleration in certain areas of knowledge
- Recognizing the student as worker rather than the teacher as deliverer of information
- Provoking students to learn how to learn
- Reflecting values of trust, decency, tolerance, and generosity in the tone of the school
- Expecting much from students without threatening them[23]

■ summary of current situation

■ **High School Reform**   Most of the reforms of the previous two decades, successful and otherwise, took place in elementary and, to a lesser extent, middle schools. However, in the winter of 2005, a long overdue campaign to reform the country's high schools was launched. The initiators of this transformational project are a coalition of state governors, foundation directors, and business leaders, including Microsoft's Bill Gates, himself a rather successful college dropout.

The group believes that the current American high school is an "obsolete" institution, out of touch with the global world of work and the demands of higher education. They are concerned that our trading partners around the world have more rigorous and productive high schools than those of the United States. In response to these concerns, they are dedicated to several of the changes recommended in this chapter, especially higher academic standards accompanied by a more rigorous curriculum and a better testing and accountability system that measures students' readiness for work and for college.

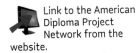

Link to the American Diploma Project Network from the website.

Armed with heavy financial support from businesses and foundations, plus fresh, compelling evidence of the inadequacies of many high school graduates, the coalition is seeking wider support to transform our schools. It has launched the American Diploma Project Network, which in turn is committed to four actions:[24]

1. Raising high school standards to the level needed for success in college or the workforce
2. Requiring all students to take a rigorous college- and work-ready curriculum
3. Developing a test of college and work readiness that all students will take in high school
4. Holding high schools accountable for making sure all students graduate ready for college and work, and holding colleges accountable for the success of the students they admit

Whether this unique partnership of businessmen, foundation directors, and governors has the energy and leverage to change the American high school fundamentally will be one of the most important and closely watched educational questions for the rest of this decade.

■ **Implications of National-Level Reform Efforts**   Overall, two things are clear about education reforms at the national level. First, we are in the middle of a strong push toward national influence on education and, with the No Child Left Behind legislation, the push is getting stronger. Second, there has been a robust response from the states to improve their curricular standards and to hold local school districts accountable for these standards by imposing statewide testing with high-stakes consequences (graduation-dependent testing). The days of strong local control over schools in America may be waning.

State Educational Reform

■ state task forces and commissions

The politics of education is complex and ever changing. At various times and places it can appear to be an asset or a liability. But it is real. Only through understanding and making proper use of politics can education be improved.

—Wendell Pierce

As education became more and more of a national issue, reform also became a hot political topic from the state house to the mayor's office. Statewide task forces were formed by governors, state legislatures, and state boards of education, and a large number were formed by citizens' groups and foundations. Some states had several at the same time. Numerous local school districts established their own blue-ribbon commissions to respond to what was increasingly called *the school crisis.* As the late Ernest Boyer said, "You could draw a 'Keystone Cops' image here of people charging off in different directions and bumping into each other and, in some instances, having a conflict with one another. There is no overall sense of where the problem is and how we should work together to get there."[25] There was, however, one common theme: the **call to excellence.**

Throughout both American industry and education, mediocrity was the dominant criticism, and excellence became the rallying cry of the reformers. Many of these recent state and local task force reports have *excellence* or *quality* in their titles. Because these task forces and reports were sponsored by state governmental agencies or well-connected citizens' groups or educational foundations, their recommendations were quickly turned into legislative proposals for school reform.

■ **Common Elements in State Reforms**   At the state level the "search for excellence" came down to specific proposals for change. The most widely adopted state reforms are described in the following sections.

■ more courses in core
subjects required

An Increase in Graduation Requirements   Instead of one or two years of English and history, states began requiring three and four years in core subjects. For academic high school diplomas, science and advanced mathematics courses were required. The idea of "social promotion," moving students through the grades to stay with their own age groups independently of their performance, came under great pressure and has been eliminated in many places, especially with the advent of mandated tests for graduation (see the section on standards-based education). The U.S. Department of Education reports that the average number of academic credits earned in high school increased significantly. In 2000, high school graduates earned an average of 26.2 course credits, compared to an average of 23.6 in 1990. Even more significant, given the United States' relative poor performance on recent international studies of math and science proficiency, are the gains in academic credits earned in those two content areas. Over the same ten-year period, the average number of course credits in science earned by high school students increased from 2.8 courses to 3.2, and in mathematics the number of courses increased from 3.2 to 3.7.[26] As described earlier, new calls for high school reform urge even more challenging requirements.

■ more time in school

More Academic Learning Time   Research has shown that *quality* instruction time, rather than time merely spent in class, is the key to quality schooling.[27] Nevertheless, in the minds of many educators, the short school day and the long, academically fallow period between June and September are major causes of the poor performance of American students. More time in school overall, they suggest, improves the chances of having more high-quality time. School days, which in many locales were only five-and-a-half to six hours, were lengthened to six-and-a-half to seven hours. The school year, which in many states was between 170 and 175 days or fewer, has been lengthened to an average of 180 days, although states still vary from between 173 days (North Dakota) to 185 days (Illinois) of school per year.[28] Though many of the reform reports recommended that our schools follow the example of Japan (240 days) and Germany (216 to 240 days),[29] no states and relatively few school districts have taken such a major step in lengthening the school year. One reason is that lengthening the amount of schooling is extremely costly.

Even with the lengthening of the school day and year, student academic performance did not improve as much as desired. A second reform initiative focused on the standard 48-minute high school class period as a contributor to students' mediocre performance, and proposed longer periods to allow for a more sustained academic study of a given subject. As discussed in the "What Is Taught?" chapter, *block scheduling*, while having many different iterations, essentially allows for longer periods during the school day so that students can spend more time engaged in learning in a given discipline.

In some states, the idea of **year-round education** has attracted the attention of educators. In most year-round schools, students go to school the same number of days as in traditional schools, but the school days are more evenly distributed throughout the school year. The most popular schedule is referred to as "45–15." Students attend school for forty-five days, then have fifteen days vacation. In the summer, students have six weeks vacation instead of the usual eight to ten weeks. According to the National Association for Year-Round Education, as of 2005 more than 3,200 public schools in forty-six states, as well as many private schools, had adopted some kind of a year-round schedule.[30] Proponents insist that the shorter summer break helps students retain information better. They

Increased graduation requirements and calls for more testing are part of many states' educational reforms.
(© Bob Daemmrich/Stock Boston)

also cite the cost savings for school districts that can house more students without adding new buildings. Critics of year-round education cite the strain such a schedule places on school finances when upgrades such as air conditioning are needed. They are also concerned about disrupting established family life patterns and summer opportunities for teachers' professional development.

Standards-Based Education   Proponents of standards-based education argue that, just as businesses have to meet certain quality standards of production, schools should also be held to certain standards in the education of students. By clearly and precisely identifying what students at each grade level are expected to know, state policymakers can more easily determine the quality and effectiveness of the schools throughout the state. Critics argue that similar reform efforts have already been tried and failed. They also express concern about possible *standardization* of education, which often ignores the individual learning needs of the students.[31]

■ increase in statewide tests

Link to more information about state content standards from the website.

Presently, forty-nine states (all but Iowa) have adopted curriculum or content standards specifying the material that all students in that state are expected to know and at what grade level they should know it. In many cases, these state standards are drawn from the voluntary national standards discussed earlier in this chapter. (See the chapter entitled "What Is Taught?" for examples of state content standards.) In order to make certain that the effort and monies going into their reform efforts are paying off, state legislatures are demanding *accountability*, generally in the form of state-mandated assessments. The result has been a huge growth

Ideas move fast when their time comes.
—Carolyn Heilbrun

GRAND AVENUE   **BY STEVE BREEN**

GRAND AVENUE: © United Feature Syndicate, Inc.

in interest in testing and assessment. In the 1970s, relatively few states had a statewide testing program, a system that assessed whether students met the state's curriculum or content standards. But by 2005, forty-nine states had such programs.[32]

The movement for statewide testing has been a mixed blessing. The statewide tests have been used as educational "report cards" to allow policymakers and the public to see how the schools in different districts are doing.[33] From this information, state educational policymakers can provide financial assistance for the underperforming school districts. But, as was stated in the section on teaching to the test earlier in this chapter, many believe the demand for testing and accountability has increased measure-driven instruction.

■ SES and high-stakes tests

A second concern revolves around the "high-stakes" nature of the tests. In many states (with the urging and backing of federal policymakers), students must pass a state-mandated test to receive their high school diplomas, or to move on to the next grade. Emerging data show that students from lower socioeconomic communities are failing such tests at higher rates than students from higher socioeconomic communities. Some critics suggest high-stakes tests will lead to even greater socioeconomic disparity as failing students will be unable to attend college or get anything but a low-paying job. In response many suggest that, in contrast, the "high-stakes" testing movement is an effort to make American education more rigorous and, thus, graduates who pass the tests will be better equipped to compete in the global market place. Clearly, though, the jury is still out.

Higher Expectations for Teachers   One of the major state-driven reform efforts of the 1980s and 1990s was the move to improve the quality of America's teaching force. Three initiatives in particular were notable: teacher competency testing, stiffening requirements for entering teacher education, and career ladder programs.

■ testing teachers

The first initiative, **teacher competency testing,** was not new, but it underwent massive growth during the last two decades of the twentieth century. Currently forty-four states have some form of teacher testing, typically taking place when candidates are leaving their teacher education programs or before they receive state licensure.[34]

One vexing issue that has plagued the movement for teacher competency testing has been finding an appropriate and valid standard to which all teacher candidates should be held. In some states, the cut-off scores that have often been established are so low as to make them meaningless. In effect, teachers are supposed to demonstrate their proficiency by jumping over a hurdle, but the hurdle has been so low that anyone could jump it. In other states, the standard is considered too arbitrary, dissuading teachers from seeking licensure in those states.

■ changes in teacher education

The second initiative had to do with teacher education. Legislatures across the country have been making changes in the licensure requirements for teaching and in the process of approval for universities and colleges that prepare teachers. In general, the call has been for an increase in liberal education (for instance, the elimination of education as a major in favor of an academic subject such as mathematics or English) and for fewer and better education courses. In recent years, most states have raised admission standards for teacher education programs, reevaluated teacher education programs, or developed unified course requirements for students in such programs.[35] Also, many states have established scholarship or loan-forgiveness programs for college students who wish to prepare for careers in teaching.

■ changes in the career ladder

The third initiative involved **career ladders.** Critics have long complained about the "flatness" of the career structure in teaching. The criticism goes something like this: "Beginners have too much responsibility at the start of their careers and too little opportunity to make the most of their abilities once they really learn to teach. The only way to get promoted in education is to be promoted *away from students,* to become a department chair, curriculum coordinator, or administrator." With the encouragement of state legislatures, a variety of teacher specialty programs, such as master teacher programs, differentiated staffing, and mentoring programs for new teachers, have appeared on the scene. Typically, these programs give experienced teachers new roles, new responsibilities, and usually new rewards. Although these innovations have had somewhat limited adoption, the assumption that "a teacher is a teacher is a teacher" has been dispelled, and new roles, such as mentor teacher and team leader, have been opened to teachers who want new challenges but also want to stay in the classroom, close to students.

■ rising salaries

Higher Salaries for Teachers A key problem revealed by the blizzard of reports published in the 1980s and 1990s was the weak reward system for teachers. Career ladders and other schemes, which expand and enrich the teacher's role, are one way to reward teachers, but more was needed if teaching was to become an attractive professional option for talented students. Salaries were an obvious target. During the 1980s, the average teacher salary increased at a rate twice that of inflation. Since then, average salaries have generally kept pace with inflation.

Visit the website to link to up-to-date statistics on this topic.

Closely linked to this change has been a substantial move to make teaching more attractive by increasing the starting salaries of teachers. In the late 1980s, beginning teachers earned $12,000 to $13,000. By 2004, the national average for beginning teachers was almost $30,500. A more recent phenomenon has been the offering of signing bonuses to teachers, especially in certain hard-to-fill subjects such as math, sciences, and special education. The signing bonuses may be state- or district-funded and typically range from $2,000 to $5,000.

■ performance pay

All across the country the lock-step pay scale by which teachers were rewarded only by years of service and number of courses taken has been altered to allow for **performance pay (pay-for-performance),** a form of recognition and reward for acquiring new knowledge or skills, or for increasing student achievement. Currently, thirty of the fifty states have passed legislation requiring some sort of performance pay.[36]

School Choice

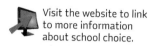

Visit the website to link to more information about school choice.

A reform that has been implemented at both state and local school district levels is to offer families more choices about where their children will attend school. Technically, all parents have a choice as to where they wish to have their children educated. If they do not like the public, state-supported school to which their children are assigned, they can send them to a private or religious school (if there is one in their locale), or they can move to another community where the schools are more to their liking. Another increasingly popular option (as described in the accompanying insert) is for parents to teach their own children at home.

■ constraints on parental choice

The only problem with this view is that not everyone can put it into practice. For the large percentage of parents without the time and ability to conduct home-schooling or the resources to pay tuition at private or religious schools, there really is no choice at all. Therefore, many people are touting **school choice** as an important aspect of access and educational opportunity. They argue that poor parents should have a choice in the schools their children attend, as wealthier parents do. Being able to choose the school your children attend, they argue, is an important way to ensure access to educational opportunity. If the neighborhood public school isn't doing an adequate job, shouldn't parents have alternative choices of schools?

■ public school monopoly?

The advocates of school choice see our current system as monopolistic. The United States, they note, is recognized around the world as a consumer's paradise. Whether it is soft drinks in the supermarket, jeans in a clothing store, or sports cars at the auto dealer, the principle of choice rules—except in K–12 schooling. School choice advocates want to redesign the way we organize education, shifting the decision of where a child must go to school from the school system to the child's parents. They want *market forces* to regulate the schools instead of the educational monopoly that they claim currently operates.

■ **Parents as Educational Consumers**   Advocates for choice say that the current public schools have no real incentive to better serve students, since salaries and benefits are unaffected by either good or poor student results. The teacher who works sixteen hours a day and gives heart and soul to the school is on the same salary scale as the teacher who is the first one out of the parking lot at 2:30 P.M. On the other hand, if the parent can act as a consumer, choice advocates argue, schools will have an incentive to improve. Free-market principles suggest that "more choice equals more competition equals better products at lower prices." Here, the phrase *better products* means better-educated students.

■ arguments for school choice

Supporters of school choice say further that the group getting the worst public education today, our urban minorities, stands to benefit the most. As an example, they point to one of the longest-running choice experiments in the country, District 4 in New York City. Central Park East secondary school and the area's elementary schools are part of a network of schools from which parents can select. Not only has parents' satisfaction increased, but more important, the students' achievement has improved substantially. Poor families that would have had little or no choice now have some options.

Homeschooling

Hilary Tucker is a mother of four children and lives in Auburn, Alabama. She is one of a growing number of parents, dissatisfied with the education their children receive in the local public schools, who have decided to educate their children themselves, most often in their homes. The U.S. Department of Education estimates that there are 1,100,000 children being homeschooled. Reasons for homeschooling vary all the way from concerns about the moral climate in public schools or religious objections to the curriculum to the absence of particular courses of study. In all cases, however, parents strongly believe that they can provide a better education for their children than the public schools can. Regulations for homeschooling vary from state to state. In some states, parents have to submit an educational plan for their homeschooled children; in other states, they merely inform the school and/or the state education agency of their intention to homeschool their children.

Homeschooling these days offers every child an opportunity for a world-class education. It doesn't cost much, and it is adaptable to many circumstances and individuals.

By having personally tailored curricula and individual attention, homeschooled students' time is rarely wasted. My children have their formal lessons during the morning hours, but in some way, the schooling never stops. Besides the basics, my second grader has studied Ancient Greek history this year, along with American history, and is getting a leg up on languages by being introduced to Greek and Latin vocabulary. (On a standardized test, she amused the researcher by identifying the figure of a person behind bars as Socrates in prison.) My preschooler son is working through reading lessons, memorizing poetry, and otherwise engaging in creative activities.

During the afternoons, the kids read and follow their own interests. My seven-year-old has charted the birds that come to our yard. She's learning how to knit and sew (thanks to a family friend, who is better at it than I am). My five-year-old son climbs trees and examines bugs. They work out elaborate fantasies about knights and princesses, pioneer families, and discovered elves. They build forts and press flowers.

For homeschooling parents, offering each child (not just the brightest) the opportunity to become passionate about ideas is worth the sacrifice of having their children under their supervision for most of the day. Students develop the habit of learning, so they don't always have to depend on an instructor. They come to know what it means to master bodies of knowledge and how to reason. They can progress at their own rate. The advanced student is not held back and made to repeat exercises he has already learned. The slower student does not miss building foundational skills because other students are ready to move on. Where the student has weaknesses, he receives extra help. Where there are strengths, he has the opportunity to soar. As a teacher I am able to teach them a time-tested curriculum so the child is spared trendy new subjects that may not be around in ten years.

Perhaps understandably, parents of homeschooled kids are often asked, "What about socialization?" It is true that homeschooled children do not spend their days in a classroom filled with twenty-two peers and are thus deprived of this particular group experience. Yet this freedom from the bustling crowd can be an advantage. The children learn to cooperate with other children of all ages, primarily and significantly their siblings, but friends and peers in sports and other activities, too.

Homeschooling support networks are well developed and very diversified. Most days, tennis, violin, and ballet classes and trips to the library get us out of the house. My son plays in a city t-ball league. They participate in plays with their local homeschool support group. They also have more time with grandparents, neighbors, and other members of the community. And, of course, their friends come over to play. With all this, the children divide their time between other children and the adult world. This is why these students are so strikingly comfortable around people of all ages.

I believe I, and many other parents, can serve my children and society best by educating them in our home. And, besides the impressive progress they are making, I am enjoying it immensely.

 Link to more information about home schooling from the website.

■ benefits for minorities

The choice concept is definitely gaining support across the country. In addition to homeschooling, there are at least three kinds of school choice. The least controversial kind allows parents to choose from among the various public schools that a school district or state operates. Many school districts have created a variety of schools with different goals and purposes, and allow parents to select the one they want their child to attend. The next, more controversial kind of school choice is the charter school concept, and the most controversial kind is school voucher plans. The major political parties have staked out positions on the choice issue, with Democrats favoring choice within the current public school system and Republicans tending to support voucher plans. Although the teachers unions usually give only token support to charter schools, they typically draw support from both Republicans and Democrats.

■ **Public School Choice**   More and more public school systems are offering parents and students options, in addition to the traditional neighborhood school, as to which schools students attend. Some schools have a particular specialty such as mathematics or science. Others are "alternative" schools designed for youth who don't seem to fit well within traditional schools. There are several varieties of public school choice, most of which are fairly noncontroversial. Districtwide or intradistrict choice allows parents to select among the schools within their home district. These school choice options are offered in numerous school districts around the country, including Boston, Seattle, Minneapolis/St. Paul, and District 4 in New York City. Statewide, or interdistrict choice allows students to attend public schools outside their home school district. By 2004, forty-four states, led by Minnesota, had accepted open enrollment programs.[37]

■ variety of public school choice options

■ **Magnet Schools**   These schools represent another form of public school choice. During the 1970s, a number of urban school districts began implementing magnet school programs as a way to reduce "white flight" from the inner cities and as an alternative to forced busing for desegregation purposes. **Magnet schools** are alternative schools designed to provide high-quality instruction in specified areas and in the basic skills. Magnet schools differ from regular schools in three principal ways: (1) magnet schools have a unified curriculum based on a special theme or method of instruction, (2) enrollment is open to students beyond the geographic attendance zone, and (3) students and parents choose the school. In many cases, magnet schools have been established as a method of voluntary desegregation by offering quality education to students who meet admission criteria, regardless of the neighborhoods in which they reside. They are designed to attract (like a magnet) students of all racial and ethnic groups from all areas of the school district, who have a special skill or interest; thus, they offer quality education in integrated classrooms.

■ magnet schools popular

Magnet schools have been established with considerable success in many areas of the country. Once limited to a few large cities, today magnet schools number about 4,000 elementary and secondary schools, serving more than 2 million students.[38] Offering parents a choice of what school their children will attend is a key factor in the popularity of magnet schools. Another factor is that the federal government spent $108 million in fiscal year 2005 to get magnet schools up and running in more than 100 school districts.

■ diversity among magnets

Magnet school programs are diverse. Some emphasize academics: science, social studies, foreign languages, college preparation, and so on. Others stress fine arts or performing arts. Some magnet schools address students with special needs, such as gifted and talented students. Still others take a career or vocation such as engineering or the health professions as their focus. Elementary magnet schools are often identified with a particular teaching style such as emphasis on basic skills, Montessori methods, or open classrooms. Besides diversity, most magnet school programs offer quality.

■ school autonomy

■ **Charter Schools**   Recent years have seen a rapid growth in **charter schools,** and in some ways interest in them has somewhat eclipsed the magnet school movement. Charter schools are public schools that usually belong to a particular school district but have been given a charter that provides them with a large degree of independence. Teachers, administrators, parents, and community representatives who wish to open a charter school in a district negotiate an agreement with the school district or other agency authorized to grant charters. As long as they meet the specifications of their charters, these schools are free to control their own budgets, hire their own consultants, design their own curriculum, and infuse the school with their own educational flavor. These schools are, in effect, independent public schools. Typically, students are chosen randomly from those who apply to attend the particular charter school.

■ site-based decision making

Because they are independent, charter schools usually have a strong element of **site-based decision making** (also known as *site-based management* or *school-based management*), in which participatory decision making is the mode of operation. In theory, the charter school's site-based decision making provides everyone, including teachers, parents, and students, with more say about what goes on in their school and with a great degree of ownership of and commitment to the decisions that are made.

Charter schools are judged on how well they meet the student achievement goals established by their charter, or contract, and how well they manage their fiscal and operational responsibilities. Although charters generally allow schools to be run with substantial autonomy, charter schools must operate lawfully and responsibly with the highest regard for equity and excellence, or their charters will be taken away. By 2004, approximately 9 percent of charter schools had been closed down, primarily because of financial mismanagement or failure to fulfill the conditions of their charter.[39]

■ support by federal government

The first charter schools were authorized in Minnesota in 1991. Although strongly resisted at first, almost all the states have since enacted charter school legislation. By the fall of 2005, more than 3,300 charter schools, mostly elementary, had been established in forty-one states, serving 800,000 students.[40] The federal government committed $319 million in FY 2005 to encourage the growth of charter schools. States vary greatly in the ease with which charter schools may be created and in the number of restrictions and amount of autonomy these schools are granted. Charter schools are most popular in the states of Arizona, California, Texas, and Michigan, where the legislation allowing charter schools is quite permissive.

Many supporters see charter schools as a way to encourage innovation, provide parents with school choice, and still be supportive of the public school system. Opponents wonder why the charter schools should be exempt from regulations while the rest of the public schools must abide by them. They also see charter schools as a form of "voucher light"—that is, a foot in the door toward the creation of school vouchers (discussed following). Evaluations of charter schools' effectiveness are inconclusive at this time. One study, commissioned by the

U.S. Department of Education, concluded that through competition, charter schools are exerting pressure on regular schools within the same district to improve.[41] Often, however, evaluations have been carried out by individuals with vested interests in either proving the effectiveness of charter schools or showing that they are ineffective and lack accountability. More time will be needed to see whether charter schools will revolutionize public education or remain just a boutique innovation.

■ voucher = money

■ **Vouchers**   More controversial than charter schools are school **voucher plans.** In their typical form, vouchers give the parent-consumer the widest array of choices. In effect, this type of plan gives parents a piece of paper, a voucher worth a certain dollar amount, that they can use to help pay the costs for their child to attend the public or private school of their choice. The school collects a voucher from each student who chooses that school and then turns in its vouchers to the state government for real dollars with which to run the school.

■ arguments for vouchers

The voucher idea is based on well-known free-market principles. In a pure choice system, all schools would be public schools, the way all department stores are public stores. Advocates of the voucher system believe it would release an enormous amount of competition-driven creativity in our schools. Teachers and administrators would join together to provide high-quality, unique educational programs that would attract students and parents. Educational institutions would be like most other American enterprises, competing to put out the best possible product—namely, students. Those that succeeded would prosper, attracting many students and therefore voucher dollars. Those schools and teachers that failed to attract or hold "customers" would "go out of business," perhaps to start again with a better idea.

Voucher plans are still relatively novel, and no really thorough test has been conducted to see if they can deliver on their interesting promises. Two districts pioneering voucher plans are Milwaukee and Cleveland. These plans, however, are limited to low-income, mostly minority families. The plans also vary in the

Voucher programs that allow students to use public funding to attend private schools are quite controversial.
(© Tony Freeman/PhotoEdit)

amount of money attached to each voucher (about $5,900 in Milwaukee and $2,700 in Cleveland) and in eligibility regulations. In 1999 the state of Florida passed the first statewide school voucher program for children attending "failing schools."

salvation or disaster?

Some education critics see the voucher concept as the savior of education in America. Others see it as a plot to undermine both the public schools and the democratic spirit of the country. Many politicians who support charter schools oppose voucher plans. They see charter schools as providing choice opportunities to parents and encouraging school reform efforts while staying within the public education system, but view voucher plans as draining money from the public schools to spend on private and religious schools. Vouchers reduce funding indirectly by decreasing public school enrollment, which is one of the factors on which governments base their allocations of money to public schools. (Learn more about school finance in the chapter entitled "How Are Schools Governed, Influenced, and Financed?")

Opponents of voucher plans have voiced several other objections and concerns:

- They argue that voucher plans bring false hopes of school choice because the private schools, not the parents, do the choosing through admissions decisions, and a private school is under no obligation to accept students with vouchers.
- In some proposals, the vouchers are worth only $1,000 to $2,500 per student, seriously limiting the choices of schools for which these amounts would pay the actual costs of tuition.

public funding for religious schools?

- In Cleveland and Milwaukee, religious schools have been the major recipients of the vouchers, which raises concerns about whether spending public dollars for students to attend religious schools violates the principle of church and state separation. In 2002, the U.S. Supreme Court ruled in a 5–4 decision that Cleveland's voucher plan, which empowers parents to redeem tuition vouchers at religious as well as nonreligious private schools, does not violate the constitutional prohibition of "establishment" of religion because government aid goes directly to parents who use it at their discretion. This decision is interpreted as giving a green light to states to implement school voucher plans to assist students attending "failing schools," and we will likely see more school voucher plans being implemented.

teacher unions oppose vouchers

- Many voucher opponents, including the two largest teacher unions, suggest that if voucher plans become widespread, the public schools will lose much-needed revenue and be forced to educate children with great needs, whom the private schools would not accept, while lacking the resources to do a good job.
- Finally, voucher opponents contend that applying market forces to educational institutions doesn't make sense because schools should be driven by the need to serve the public good, not the desire of individuals and corporations to earn profits.

Those who support voucher plans offer counterarguments to many of these objections. For example, although funding private and religious schools with public money is very controversial in the United States, it is less so in many other countries. The United States is one of the few developed nations with such strict limits on parental choice of schools. Most other Western democracies fund private or religious schools with public money, although if these schools accept public money, they usually have to meet certain conditions required by the government.

■ religious schools already get some public money

Voucher supporters also point out that although many people believe U.S. tax dollars fund only public schools, private and religious schools already benefit from public money. The major breakthrough for private and religious schools was the passage of the Elementary and Secondary Education Act of 1965, which funneled millions of dollars into private schools through federal Title I programs to support the education of poor children. In addition, private schools in many states have been receiving assistance ranging from pupil transportation, textbooks, health services, and general auxiliary services to salary supplements for teachers. In general, state assistance in areas other than transportation, milk, school lunch programs, and textbooks has been attacked in the courts.

■ private schools relieve burden on public schools

Another argument in support of voucher plans is that the private schools, which provide education for over 5 million students a year, are lightening the burden of the public schools. If, for example, the Catholic school system collapsed, more than 2.5 million new students would enroll in the public schools, creating a massive shortage of space, teachers, and money. Advocates of private school aid argue that by partially subsidizing private schools to keep them in operation, the public schools can avoid a deluge of students whom they would be unable to assimilate readily. Private elementary and secondary schools spent $33.3 billion during the 2003–2004 school year.[42] If a substantial number of these schools were to shut down, the public schools would incur a substantial portion of these costs.

Like charter schools, the research on the success or failure of various voucher plans is limited and in the eyes of many driven by ideological issues. The issue of school choice is likely to remain a contentious one for some time to come.

Pause and Reflect

1 ▶ Which form of school choice appeals most to you? Why?

2 ▶ Do you support the use of school vouchers for students to attend private or parochial schools? Why or why not?

Local-Level School Reform

Former Speaker of the U.S. House of Representatives, the late Tip O'Neill, was fond of saying, "All politics are local." The same is true of education. Children are educated at their local schools, not at the state capitol or in Washington, D.C. Though some school reform efforts such as the Coalition of Essential Schools Project are national in scope, they are implemented in local schools under the supervision of a school district.

At present, however, the great majority of changes being made in schools are coming at the direction of the various states' departments of education, and educational funds are often linked to how faithfully and quickly a school district implements the desired reform mandates.

■ shortage of local funding for reform

Locally initiated reform efforts, although in no way stopped, have slowed down, partly because of a shortage of local funds. Growing competition for fixed amounts of municipal tax dollars—from police and fire departments to agencies serving the poor and the elderly—and competing thoughts on the primary purpose of public education have made it difficult to secure monies for new, locally supported reform efforts. What we are witnessing is a classic shift in power, with the statehouse dictating to the localities more and more not just what should be taught but how it should be taught.

■ ideas emerge at local level

Though the center of gravity may be elsewhere, the local school district is deeply involved in the current reform movement. Furthermore, the overwhelming percentage of reform ideas that have made their way onto the agendas of national and state reform groups existed first at the local level. They became statewide or national because they succeeded first at the local level. In the future, more innovative ideas such as block scheduling, year-round education, single-sex schools, school uniforms, and site-based decision making, will continue to come up from our local schools.

Pause and Reflect

1 ► Looking back on your own elementary and secondary schoolings, can you recall any locally initiated innovations, unique projects, or experimental programs?

► The Current State of School Reform

■ piecemeal reform

Although we clearly have a new set of educational reform priorities, goals, and expectations, few schools have experienced sweeping changes as a result of educational reform. Some have made fundamental changes in the way they engage children and in what they teach. Most have adopted pieces of reform such as a new districtwide mathematics curriculum, a computer lab, or a career ladder for teachers. Some states have pushed through serious changes that affect the great majority of their schools, but they are the rarities. The school experience of the first-grader or the high school senior is in many ways pretty much the same today as it was in 1983, when the current reform era began.

American education is not like an individual who, after a few life failures, looks in the mirror and says, "That's it; I'm going to get my act together starting today," and from that moment on is a "new" person. American public education is a giant institution, involving almost 15,000 centers of decision making (school boards), well over 55 million people (students, teachers, and administrators), and influences from many quarters of society. And, most importantly, like any institution it has a standard operating procedure. Everyone starting a school year in September (except for the newcomers, the kindergartners) has a clear set of expectations about what school ought to be like. Although chaos would result without them, these expectations make altering the course of schooling quite a demanding task.

Perhaps a better parallel than an individual trying to change the course of his or her life is a large luxury liner plowing through the ocean. Someone convinces the captain that dangerous icebergs lie ahead. The captain first has to be assured that the reports are reasonable, next decide where the safe water is, and then turn the wheel. But because of its size and momentum, the ship may need miles to truly change course. This is where we believe American schools are today. They have heard the message; they have committed to change course and avoid the hazards; they have begun to turn the wheel. Whether the ship actually turns and misses the dangers, we must wait to see.

▶ A Final Word

■ teachers at the center

Clearly, it is the teacher who stands at the center of true school reform. It is the teacher who actually delivers educational services, who creates or fails to create an environment for learning, and who either knows or does not know how to engage students in their own pursuit of excellence. Since 1983, Americans have seen their industries "reengineered" and "restructured," making them much more competitive in the global marketplace. Educational researchers are now suggesting that schools follow the example of outstanding private-sector firms, guiding their reform efforts by the following five principles:

■ principles from private sector

1. Ensure that all front-line workers, the teachers, understand the problem in the same way
2. Design jobs so that all front-line workers have both incentives and opportunities to contribute to solutions
3. Provide all front-line workers with the training needed to pursue solutions effectively
4. Measure progress on a regular basis
5. Persevere and learn from mistakes; remember that there are no magic bullets[43]

The final decisions about educational reform are, by necessity, made by teachers. Although it is discouraging (and even threatening) to know that we have not yet achieved our goal of reforming our schools, we Americans are often at our best when challenged. And clearly school reform is part of the unfinished business of America and the American teacher. A job of critical importance to all of us awaits you.

Key Terms

active learning (365)
authentic (performance) assessment (364)
call to excellence (377)
career ladders (381)
character education (368)
charter schools (385)
constructivism (365)
intellectual capital (368)
learning communities (372)

lifelong learners (367)
magnet school (384)
national curricular standards (375)
National Education Goals for the Year 2000 (374)
performance pay (pay-for-performance) (382)
portfolios (364)
professional development (372)
school choice (382)

schools-within-schools (367)
site-based decision making (385)
staff development (372)
teacher competency testing (380)
teaching to the test (363)
tools for learning (368)
voucher plans (386)
year-round education (378)

For Reflection

1 Are any of the reform initiatives described in this chapter evident in your local schools?

2 Which of the reform efforts described in the chapter most interests you? Why?

3 If monies for schooling continue to be tight, which educational reforms will be most weakened? Which will be least weakened?

4 What do you believe teachers should do to take a more active role in the reform process?

For Debate

1 What aspects of schooling did you list earlier in this chapter as needing reform? Why? Did your opinions change as a result of reading the chapter? Which aspects do you know believe most need reform, and why?

2 Read the Policy Matters! summary, "Class Size, Is Less Always Better?" at the website. After considering the issues it raises about class size, post your answers (or respond to other students' answers) to the What Do You Think questions listed in the Policy Matters! feature.

3 At the website, read the Open for Debate author debate about whether or not public schools are hold a monopoly position in education. Then, go to EduSpace to post your own opinions and concerns about school choice.

For Further Information

PRINT RESOURCES

Gordon Cawelti, *Portraits of Six Benchmark Schools: Diverse Approaches to Improving Student Achievement* (Alexandria, VA: Association for Supervision and Curriculum Development, 1999).
This well-written report offers portraits of excellent public schools with high standards, multiple changes, strong leadership, collaborative teams, and committed teachers—in other words, reform success stories.

Kevin Ryan and Karen Bohlin, *Building Character in Schools: Practical Ways to Bring Moral Instruction to Life* (San Francisco: Jossey-Bass, 1999).
This book offers teachers both a theory and a set of practical steps to infuse their teaching with our core moral values. In addition, the book has many practical lists and materials to promote character in classrooms and schools.

Frederick M. Hess, *Common Sense School Reform* (New York: Palgrave Macmillan, 2004).
Written by a market-oriented educator, this book offers a radically different set of reform suggestions. In the process, Hess engages in a no-holds-barred attack on most of the currently held views on education and on school reform.

David Tyack and Larry Cuban, *Tinkering Toward Utopia: A Century of Public School Reform* (Cambridge, MA: Harvard University Press, 1996).
Two long-time observers of efforts to bring about changes in our schools put our current efforts at school reform in historical context. Further, they lay about a plan, one in which teachers are front and center, for the renewal of our schools.

WEB RESOURCES

Teacher-to-Teacher e-Learning. Available in the "teachers" area at: **http://www.ed.gov.**
This new initiative, developed by the U.S. Department of Education, offers elementary and secondary school teachers online, on-demand professional development training for improving student achievement.

American Diploma Project Network. Available at: **http://www.achieve.org/achieve.nsf/ AmericanDiplomaProject?openform.**
Sponsored by Achieve, Inc., this nonprofit organization created by the nation's governors and business leaders is "working to help states raise academic standards, improve assessments and strengthen accountability in our high schools."

ASCD SmartBriefs. Available at: **http://www. ASCD.org.**
SmartBriefs is a free educational news service that can be received through email. It contains news, commentary, and educational resources.

The Educational Gadfly. Available at: **http://www. edexcellence.net.**
For a conservative slant on educational news and policy developments, you can sign up for *The Gadfly,* a weekly bulletin of policy news, book reviews, and lively commentary by Chester E. Finn.

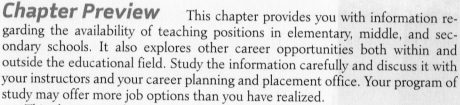

13 *What Are Your Job Options in Education?*

Chapter Preview   This chapter provides you with information regarding the availability of teaching positions in elementary, middle, and secondary schools. It also explores other career opportunities both within and outside the educational field. Study the information carefully and discuss it with your instructors and your career planning and placement office. Your program of study may offer more job options than you have realized.

This chapter emphasizes that:

▶ Many factors influence the availability of teaching jobs. At the present time, some teaching fields face a severe shortage, while in other fields the supply and demand seem balanced.

▶ Teacher salaries have made some gains in recent years, with the average salary of classroom teachers in 2004–2005 estimated at $47,750 and the average salary of *beginning* teachers for 2003–2004 being just over $31,700. Salaries vary tremendously, however, from state to state and from school district to school district.

▶ Certain job-hunting strategies will increase your chances of locating the right job for you. You may have to spend considerable time and energy preparing materials for your job search.

▶ Licensure requirements differ from state to state for both general and specialized areas of teaching.

▶ A wide variety of careers are available to people trained as teachers. Should you be unable to secure a teaching position or wish to change careers after you have taught, the skills you have acquired in teacher education can be transferred to related occupational areas.

▶ No matter what the job market may be at a particular moment, there has never been a surplus of good teachers. Better-prepared teachers will find it easier to gain employment and will improve the teaching profession and its public image.

WANTED: Men and women with the wisdom of Solomon, the patience of Job, and the nerves of David before Goliath. Needed to prepare the next generation for productive citizenship in the twenty-first century, often under adverse conditions. Applicants must be willing to fill in gaps left by unfit, absent, or working parents; satisfy demands of local bureaucrats and state politicians; impart healthy self-esteem; and, oh, by the way, teach content!

Hours: 50 to 60 hours per week

Pay: Growing respectable

Reward: The luxury of always knowing that you are doing something significant with your life

This fictitious ad contains many messages about the roles that teachers play. It also highlights the fact that there is a serious need for skilled new teachers in our nation's schools. As you have thought about teaching as a career, you have probably wondered whether you will be able to obtain a teaching position when you graduate. Although we would like to answer this question for you personally, we obviously cannot. We can, however, provide you with information that may help you increase your chances of obtaining the kind of teaching position you are seeking.

▶ Will There Be Job Openings in Education?

Teaching is a large occupation, representing 4 percent of the entire civilian work force in the United States. There are more than twice as many K–12 teachers as registered nurses and five times as many teachers as either lawyers or professors.[1] With a teaching work force of this size, many jobs exist. Figure 13.1 shows past, current, and projected numbers of classroom teachers in the United States.

FIGURE 13.1
K–12 Classroom Teachers in Public and Private Schools (in thousands)

Source: William J. Hussar, *Projections of Education Statistics to 2014* (Washington, DC: National Center for Education Statistics, 2005), p. 80.

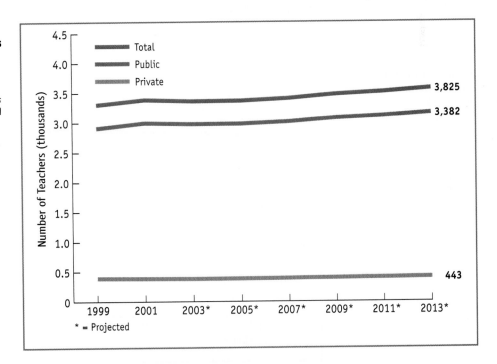

Factors Influencing Teacher Supply and Demand

Many people believe there will be a shortage of teachers in the near future. However, estimates of shortages are based on rapidly changing situations influenced by unpredictable factors. The following sections discuss a number of these factors.

■ **Student Enrollment in Schools** Obviously, when more students are enrolled in schools, more teachers are needed. The good news is that enrollments in public and private schools reached 54.8 million students in 2005 and are projected to increase to 56.4 million in 2013. In the United States, enrollments in secondary schools will increase until 2007, at which point they will decline to 2004 levels by 2013. Enrollments in elementary schools will rise gradually over this period. (See Figure 13.2.) The number of classroom teachers is expected to increase over 300,000 from 3.5 million in 2004 to 3.8 million by 2013, with the number of secondary school teachers increasing at a faster rate than the number of elementary school teachers.[2]

■ **Class Sizes** During the 1980s and 1990s, the demand for new teachers was boosted by declining class sizes, especially in California. In 1996, for example, California provided more than $750 million to cut class sizes in grades K–3 from as many as thirty students to twenty, requiring an estimated 26,000 additional primary school teachers.[3]

Nationally, current class sizes now hover around twenty-one students per teacher in the public elementary schools and slightly more than twenty-three students per teacher in public secondary schools. Class sizes in private schools are slightly smaller than in public schools, averaging a bit more than twenty students per class for both elementary and secondary schools.[4] However, the changes in class sizes during the next few years are expected to be small, and they will not likely affect the demand for new teachers in any significant fashion.

■ **Enrollment in Teacher Education Programs** Across the nation, about 200,000 teachers are prepared each year; however, only about 60 percent of those

Margin notes:

■ rising student enrollments

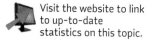 Visit the website to link to up-to-date statistics on this topic.

■ stable class sizes

■ many teachers elect not to teach

FIGURE 13.2
Enrollment in Public and Private Schools (in millions)

Source: William J. Hussar, *Projections of Education Statistics to 2014* (Washington, DC: National Center for Education Statistics, 2005), p. 45. Available at: **http://nces.ed.gov/pubs2005/2005074.pdf.**

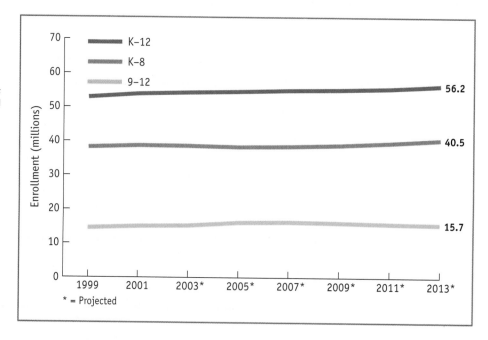

prepared to teach actually enter the classroom. And of these, 30 to 50 percent leave teaching within the first five years.[5] Thus, an adequate number of teachers are prepared to meet the demand, but because so many choose not to teach or to stop teaching after a few years, the supply doesn't match the demand for new teachers.

Link to more information about geographical teacher needs from the website.

■ **Geographical Location**   Location significantly influences the teaching job market. Some communities have far more applicants than available teaching positions. University towns, for example, usually have a great surplus of teachers. Although large urban areas historically have had more teachers available than they needed, they are now experiencing significant teacher shortages. One study examined the nation's largest urban school districts and found that almost all of them had an urgent need for teachers in at least one high-need area, such as special education.[6] Rural America traditionally has had difficulty attracting and holding onto teachers because of lower salaries and a more sedate lifestyle than that sought by many young teachers. There are not enough qualified teachers who are willing to teach in urban and rural schools, particularly those serving low-income students or students of color.

■ jobs available in Sunbelt and Midwest states

Student enrollments in different geographical regions of the country are following different patterns, as well, which influences teaching opportunities. Enrollments, and teaching opportunities, are increasing in the western and southern parts of the United States and declining in the northeastern states. Generally speaking, teacher vacancies are greatest in the West (California, Arizona, Nevada, Hawaii, and Utah); the Great Plains/Midwest (the Dakotas, Minnesota, Iowa, Nebraska, and Missouri); and the South and South Central states. There are fewer vacancies and/or more competition in the Great Lakes states (Wisconsin, Michigan, Illinois, Indiana, and Ohio) and the Middle Atlantic states (Delaware, District of Columbia, Maryland, New Jersey, New York, and Pennsylvania).[7] Supply and demand in the Northeast appears to be fairly balanced.

Teachers tend to be more "place bound" than many other professionals, however. That is, because of family commitments or the importance of geographical location, many teachers seeking jobs are reluctant to stray far from home. Even though teaching jobs may be available in Las Vegas (which they are!), teachers from the Northeast, for example, may not want to relocate to Nevada.

■ job availability depends on teaching field

■ fields with teacher shortages

■ **Subject Matter and Grade Levels Taught**   Teachers are not interchangeable units. They are prepared for different specialties (for example, special education, elementary education, art, or secondary social studies), and the job market in each of these subfields is different. Moreover, the job market for specific subfields may change often. It is unwise, therefore, to decide whether to become an English teacher because you have heard that today there is generally either a surplus or a shortage of such teachers. There have been and continue to be chronic national teacher shortages in certain subjects, including speech pathology; special education (all areas); bilingual education; audiology; mathematics; science (physics, chemistry, earth and physical science, biology); English as a second language; technology education; and Spanish. There is some surplus of teachers in elementary education, health and physical education, and social studies. However, as of 2004, no teaching fields were considered to have a considerable surplus of teachers.[8]

■ shortage of minority and male teachers

In addition to looking for teachers in the subjects just listed, schools are seeking increased numbers of minorities and males. Because 79 percent of all teachers are female, schools want to increase the number of males in the teaching

There is a demand for male teachers at the elementary school level, where they compose less than 10 percent of the teaching force.
(© Frank Siteman / PhotoEdit)

force, especially at the elementary school level, where only 9 percent of the nation's 1.3 million public school teachers are men.[9]

■ aging teacher work force

■ **Retiring Teachers, Teacher Turnover, and Returning Teachers**   An estimated 2 million new teachers will be needed during the next ten years. One factor that bodes well for the long-term job outlook is that teachers, like much of the rest of the American work force, are getting older. More than one-quarter of teachers are at least fifty years old, and nearly half will retire over the next decade.[10]

Another factor influencing job availability concerns the percentage of eligible teachers who elect not to teach or those who leave teaching after a few years.

Teaching was the hardest work I had ever done, and it remains the hardest work I have done to date.

—ANN RICHARDS (FORMER GOVERNOR OF TEXAS)

As mentioned earlier, 40 percent of those prepared to teach elect not to enter teaching, and of the 60 percent who do teach, 30 to 50 percent leave teaching within the first five years. Sadly, the brightest novice teachers, as measured by their college-entrance exams, were the most likely to leave. Factors influencing the high turnover included poor working conditions, dissatisfaction with student discipline, lack of mentoring, and unhappiness with the school environment.[11]

What is difficult to estimate is the number of licensed teachers, currently not teaching, who might re-enter the teaching force if jobs are readily available. When teacher shortages have been predicted in the past, these returning teachers have filled the anticipated shortages. Whether this pattern will continue remains to be seen. Teachers licensed through alternative routes (like those discussed later in this chapter) have thus far made up only a small percentage of the available pool of teachers, but that situation could change if states promote these programs more vigorously.

■ job availability affected by economy

■ **Economic Conditions** In spite of the positive long-term outlook for teaching positions, in times of economic hardship school districts may find it necessary to reduce the size of their teaching forces to balance budgets. During the 1990–91 recession and, to a lesser extent, the 2001 recession, school districts in a number of states found it necessary to issue reduction-in-force notices (RIFs) to teachers, informing them that they were in danger of not being rehired for the following fall. Although painful in the short run, such layoffs in response to future economic downturns will probably be only temporary and will have little overall effect on the long-term demand for new teachers. RIF notices do show, however, that the demand for teachers is greatly influenced by school district budgets, which in turn are affected by the health of the state and local economies.

■ demand for teachers promising

■ federal legislation requiring "qualified" teachers

■ **Summary** What, then, are the job prospects for the future? The situation is promising because the number of classroom teachers in elementary and secondary schools is projected to stay at a high level at least until 2013, primarily because of teacher retirements and teachers who leave the field. Recruitment of teachers recently has become so competitive that many districts are offering incentives to qualified teachers, including paying bonuses ranging from $1,500 to $20,000, closing costs or reduced mortgage rates on home purchases, and relocation expenses. Some states are even considering offering state income tax breaks for teachers.

In the past, if the supply of qualified teachers did not keep up with the demand, states and local school districts have resorted to such practices as increasing class sizes, hiring less-than-qualified personnel, and assigning teachers trained in one field to teach in an understaffed field. These options may be less available now, however, because the federal No Child Left Behind law requires all states to ensure that every public school teacher must be "highly qualified," which means that the teacher has been licensed by the state and has demonstrated a high level of competence in the subjects that he or she teaches. (See the chapter entitled "How Are Schools Governed, Influenced, and Financed?" for more on this legislation.) The requirements of the No Child Left Behind law for highly qualified teachers suggest that the demand for teachers will continue to remain high in years to come.

Keep in mind, too, that demographic projections and supply-and-demand forecasting are not only hard to apply but also very inexact and short-lived. With difficulty, forecasters try to take into account the various factors we have discussed, such as retirement rates, supplies of former teachers re-entering the field, and programs that may attract individuals from nonteaching fields into the profession. What seems to be true for a particular geographic area, a particular teaching field, or a particular year may soon be "out of date."

■ obtain recent information

Therefore, you ought to make every effort to get the most up-to-the-minute information possible about teacher supply and demand. You should consider such information carefully before making a choice about a career in education and, in particular, about a specific subfield within education. This is especially true for people who are unable to wait for openings in their areas of teaching interest or unable to relocate. Sources of data with which to begin your search are your school's career counseling office, the department chairperson's or dean's office, and your state department of education. Also, see the listing of useful references at the end of this chapter.

The bottom line is that demand for teachers is high and is expected to continue to be high in the coming years. Remember, too, that there has never been a surplus of good teachers in any field.

The Severe Shortage of Minority Teachers

One of the greatest teacher supply-and-demand problems concerns minority teachers. At a time when the minority school-age population is increasing rapidly, the number of minority teachers is decreasing. The shortage is severe now and appears likely to become worse.

■ fewer minority teachers

As you saw in the chapter entitled "Who Are Today's Students in a Diverse Society?" enrollments of students from minority groups are increasing and currently are estimated to be about 40 percent of students in public schools (17 percent African American, 17 percent Hispanic, 4 percent Asian/Pacific Islander, 1 percent Native American). Teaching staffs, on the other hand, are becoming more and more white. Ninety percent of public school teachers are white, 6 percent are African American, and only 4 percent come from other minority groups, including Hispanic American, Asian American or Pacific Islander, and Native American or Native Alaskan.[12] Most minority teachers are located in central cities rather than in suburban or rural areas. During most of the 1990s, the graduation rates of minority students from teacher education programs were lower than their percentage distribution in the teaching force. Although minority enrollment in teacher education has been increasing in recent years, the need is still acute.

[Emma Belle Sweet] taught me many things. . . . But nothing could be so important to me and of such enduring quality as her simple, human act of figuratively leading me gently by the hand to a sense of self-respect, dignity, and worth.

—Ralph Bunche (an African American and 1950 Nobel Peace Prize winner)

This shortage of minority teachers is problematic for several reasons. First, the growing number of minority children deserves to have positive minority role models who can help guide them in a world still plagued by racism. Second, white children also need to have minority teachers as positive role models to help them overcome the effects of stereotyping and racism. Third, it is important for our country's well-being to have a teaching staff that reflects the diversity of racial and ethnic backgrounds in our country's population. Fourth, minority teachers are needed to serve as "cultural brokers" to help students navigate their school environment and culture.

■ factors affecting shortage of minority teachers

The shortage of minority teachers exists for a number of reasons. Before desegregation efforts, nearly one-half of African American professional workers were teachers. When schools desegregated in the 1960s and 1970s, resulting in the consolidation of formerly all-black and all-white schools, thousands of African American teachers were dismissed. Today, other professions that pay more and have higher status are actively recruiting minority college students. Another causal factor has been the increasing use of competency tests at either the beginning or the end of teacher education programs. Many minority teaching candidates are either having difficulties with these tests or are being discouraged from even considering teaching as a career.

What can be done to address this problem? Teaching salaries must continue to improve if teaching is to compete with other professions for well-qualified candidates. Assistance programs to help minority candidates perform well on competency tests have been effective in a number of universities and need to be

The shortage of minority teachers deprives both white and minority students of positive role models.
(© Chip Henderson/Stone/Getty Images)

expanded to more colleges. Active recruitment programs for minority candidates must be developed and implemented, and they must reach down into the middle and high schools to encourage minority students to consider teaching as a career. Scholarship and loan-forgiveness programs are needed for students who want to teach but cannot afford college. And the American public must communicate, in a variety of ways, that it values teachers and the work they do.

Employers Besides the Public Schools

Although much of the data presented in this chapter refer to public elementary and secondary schools, teachers can also work in a variety of other school settings. Federal government schools and private schools are two major alternatives to teaching in a local public school.

■ Department of Defense schools

■ **U.S. Government**   A large employer of teachers is the U.S. government. The Department of Defense has 222 elementary and secondary schools in seven states, Puerto Rico, Guam, and fourteen countries around the world, making it the twenty-second largest school district in the United States. These schools enroll approximately 102,600 students and employ about 8,800 educational personnel.* Salaries are comparable to those in the United States, but preference is

* For more information on applying for a job with the Department of Defense overseas schools, write the U.S. Department of Defense, Office of Dependent Schools, Personnel Center, 4040 North Fairfax Drive, Arlington, VA 22203-1635 or call the office at (703) 696-3068.

given to applicants who have at least one year of successful full-time employment as a professional educator.[13]

■ private schools a significant employer

■ **Private Schools** Private education is a highly significant part of the American educational system. There are more than 29,000 private schools in the United States, with an enrollment of more than 5.34 million elementary, and secondary school students and a staff of 425,000 teachers. About 10 percent of the children in elementary or secondary schools attend a private school, with the overwhelming majority attending religion-affiliated schools. (See Figure 13.3 for the percentage of students attending private schools affiliated with various religious denominations.) In addition, there are more than 6,600 private preschools and kindergartens, enrolling 98,000 students, and employing almost 15,400 teachers.

Private schools employ about 12 percent of all elementary and secondary teachers, and projections are that over 500,000 new teachers will be needed in private schools over the next decade.[14] Thus, private schools obviously offer a growing employment opportunity for new teachers. Helpful references for finding teaching jobs in nonpublic schools are provided at the end of this chapter.

■ salaries less in private schools

If you are considering a position at a private school, you should reflect on the relative importance to you of the various rewards of the job. Many teachers who work in religion-affiliated schools do so because of religious motives. These teachers are often willing to work for less money than their public school counterparts, and as a result, the average teacher salary in private schools is about 25 percent lower than that in public schools. In many cases, lower salaries tend to be offset by favorable working conditions. Compared with public schools, private schools have fewer disciplinary problems, stricter discipline, smaller classes, fewer students using drugs, students who are absent less often, parents who are more supportive, more assigned homework, and more time spent in instruction in the central academic subjects. Although private school teachers tend to work about

FIGURE 13.3
Percentage of Students Attending Various Kinds of Private Schools

Source: Stephen P. Broughman and Kathleen W. Pugh, *Characteristics of Private Schools in the United States: Results from the 2001–2002 Private School Universe Survey* (Washington, DC: National Center for Education Statistics, 2004), Table 7, p. 15.

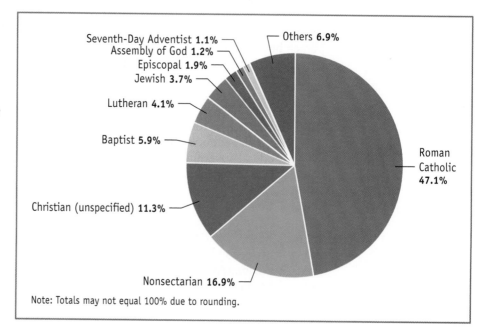

Seventh-Day Adventist **1.1%**
Assembly of God **1.2%**
Episcopal **1.9%**
Jewish **3.7%**
Lutheran **4.1%**
Baptist **5.9%**
Christian (unspecified) **11.3%**
Nonsectarian **16.9%**
Others **6.9%**
Roman Catholic **47.1%**

Note: Totals may not equal 100% due to rounding.

two more hours per week than their public school counterparts, they believe they have more influence over important school policies.[15] Thus, for many individuals, teaching in a private school is an attractive alternative to teaching in the public schools. The "Voices from the Classroom" feature presents one teacher's comparison of the experience of working public and private schools. Recently, however, private schools are finding that they are losing instructors to the public schools. Pay raises and benefits, signing bonuses, and smaller classes have combined to make teaching in the public schools more attractive, particularly as various states relax their licensure requirements, making it easier for private school teachers to move to public schools. Many private schools are responding by raising tuitions to pay for increased teacher salaries.

VOICES FROM THE CLASSROOM

Karen Irving has taught chemistry and other science disciplines at the secondary and college levels for nineteen years, including six years of public high school teaching and six years of private high school teaching.

Teaching in Public Versus Private Schools

I loved the pulse of my urban high school with its creative and energetic faculty. With three other chemistry teachers in our school of just under 2,000 students, we never lacked ideas or opinions about how to best help our students succeed. Sometimes we struggled to match our equipment availability to our classroom plans, but we always benefited from the sharing of experiences and expertise.

In addition to a large and diverse faculty, my urban high school boasted a large and diverse student population. However, with just three to four hours of planning time per week and 130 to 150 students in five sections, as well as science fair projects, science teams, and other extracurricular responsibilities, little time remained in my schedule to offer extra help to my students.

After six years of public high school teaching, I accepted a science teaching position at an independent, college preparatory, girls' school. Because my teaching assignment at the private school included 60 to 65 students in four sections, the amount of time during the school day to plan lessons and work with students (eight hours per week) doubled from what I was used to in the public setting. In addition, because the weekly school schedule included time for faculty meetings and student clubs during the school day, teachers and students shared free time before and after school for help sessions, make-up work, and additional student enrichment. Other conditions were different, too. More parents returned teacher telephone calls, provided necessary home support for learning, made arrangements for students to attend help sessions, attended school functions, and generally worked together with school personnel to ensure that their children received a quality education.

If I had the chance to create an ideal high school environment, I would blend elements of both public and private schools. Ideal High would boast a diverse, creative, and energetic faculty and student population with small classes and sufficient time for teachers to plan and deliver quality lessons. Each student would have the opportunity to reach his or her full potential. Parents, administrators, teachers, and students at Ideal High would share a common vision of an educational community of disciplined effort and academic achievement.

 Visit the website for more Voices from the Classroom.

Pause and Reflect

1 ▶ What are the present and projected teacher supplies in the field that currently interests you? In the geographic area you desire?

2 ▶ Are you willing to leave your current location to find a teaching position? Are you willing to teach in an urban school? A rural school? A private school?

What Are Teachers Paid?

We might answer this question by saying, "Not nearly enough." No one ever went into teaching because of the lure of big money. As we note in the "Why Teach?" chapter, most of the rewards for teaching are personal rather than monetary. Most of teachers' satisfactions come from being of service to others and helping students learn. That does not mean, however, that you have to be a pauper to enjoy the satisfactions that come from teaching. Salaries are a legitimate concern for a prospective teacher; after all, everyone must have sufficient income to meet the costs of living. You will have to decide whether the salary you are likely to make as a classroom teacher will allow you to establish the lifestyle you want. This section will give you some objective facts with which to make your decision.

▪ average teacher salaries

The 2004–2005 average salary of classroom teachers in the United States is estimated to be about $47,750.[16] Figure 13.4 shows the rise in average salaries since the 1990s, and Table 13.1 shows how salaries vary by state and region. The Average Salary column in the table represents the average for *all* public elementary and secondary school teachers, and the Beginning Salary column indicates the average for *first-year* teachers. For teachers in their first year, the average pay across the nation as a whole was just over $31,700, in 2003–04, ranging from a low of $24,032 (Montana) to a high of $40,027 (Alaska).[17]

▪ salary schedules

See an example of a salary schedule at the website.

Most public school salary schedules are usually determined by two factors: years of teaching experience and amount of education, usually expressed in terms of college credit-hours or advanced degrees. Thus, the longer you teach and the

FIGURE 13.4
Average Public School Teacher Salaries

Source: *Rankings and Estimates* (Washington, DC: National Education Association, 2005), p. 78.

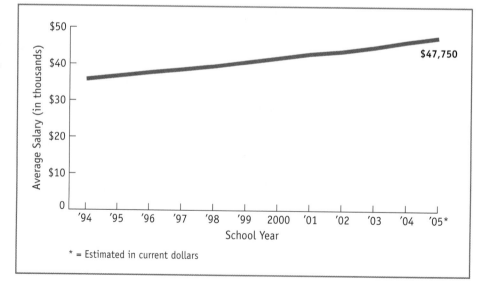

* = Estimated in current dollars

TABLE 13.1 Average and Beginning Teacher Salaries, by State and Region

State	Average Salary ($) (2004–2005)	Beginning Salary ($) (2003–2004)	State	Average Salary ($) (2004–2005)	Beginning Salary ($) 2003–2004
New England			Southeast		
Connecticut	58,688	34,462	Georgia	46,526	35,116
Rhode Island	53,473*	32,902	North Carolina	43,313	27,572
Massachusetts	54,596*	34,041	Virginia	44,763*	32,437
New Hampshire	43,941	27,367	Alabama	38,863*	30,973
Vermont	44,535	25,819	South Carolina	42,207*	27,883
Maine	40,940	25,901	Florida	41,081	30,969
Mideast			Tennessee	41,527	30,449
New Jersey	56,600*	37,061	Kentucky	41,002	28,416
New York	56,200	36,400	West Virginia	38,360	26,692
Pennsylvania	52,700	34,140	Louisiana	38,880*	29,655
Delaware	50,869	34,566	Arkansas	40,495*	26,129
Washington, D.C.	58,456*	36,388	Mississippi	36,590*	28,106
Maryland	52,331	33,760	Rocky Mountains		
Great Lakes			Colorado	44,161	31,296
Michigan	55,693*	34,377	Wyoming	40,392	28,900
Illinois	55,629	35,114	Idaho	42,122*	25,908
Ohio	48,692*	28,692	Utah	39,965*	26,130
Indiana	46,851*	29,784	Montana	38,485*	24,032
Wisconsin	43,466*	28,150	Far West		
Great Plains			California	57,876*	35,135
Minnesota	46,906	30,772	Alaska	52,424	40,027
Iowa	40,347	26,967	Oregon	50,790*	33,396
Missouri	38,971*	28,938	Washington	45,712	30,159
Kansas	39,190	28,530	Hawaii	44,273	37,615
Nebraska	39,456	28,527	Nevada	43,394	27,942
North Dakota	36,449	24,108	U.S. Average	47,750	31,704
South Dakota	34,040	25,504			
Southwest					
Texas	41,009	32,741			
Arizona	42,905*	28,236			
New Mexico	39,328	31,920			
Oklahoma	37,141	29,473			

*estimated

Sources: Average salaries from *Rankings and Estimates: Rankings of the States 2004 and Estimates of School Statistics 2005* (Washington, DC: National Education Association, 2005), available at: **http:www.nea.org/edstats/images/05rankings.pdf.** Beginning salaries from *2004 Survey and Analysis of Teacher Salary Trends,* Table III-2: Trends in Beginning Salary of Teachers 2003–04. Available at: **http://www.aft.org/salary/index.htm**.

more college education you receive, the more money you will make (see Table 13.2 on the website for an example of a school district salary schedule). In addition, some states and school districts have used various forms of merit or **performance pay (pay-for-performance) plans** to reward teachers for exceptional teaching, acquiring new skills needed by the school, achieving national board certification, raising student test scores, or assuming more professional responsibilities. (See the chapter entitled "What Does It Mean to Be a Professional?" for more on national board certification.)

■ fringe benefits

As you can see from Table 13.1, salaries vary considerably from state to state. Each school district determines what it will pay its teachers, with many states setting a minimum base salary below which the school district cannot go. Generally, the large and middle-size school districts pay better than the small ones, and urban and suburban school districts pay better than rural ones. Many school districts offer extra pay for special duties such as directing the band or coaching athletic teams. Some offer summer teaching or curriculum development jobs. Most states and school districts provide public school teachers with a number of fringe benefits, including sick leave, health and life insurance programs, and retirement benefits. When applying for a teaching position, be sure to ask about these benefits.

Pause and Reflect

1 ▶ Are the average teacher salaries reported in this chapter about what you expected? How do the salaries in your geographic area compare with the national average? What might account for any differences that you note?

2 ▶ Judging from the salary information here, what do you estimate your salary as teacher would be? Are you confident that this salary would meet your expenses?

▶ How Do You Obtain a Teaching Position?

The job market is very encouraging for beginning teachers, but regardless of how great the demand for teachers is or how effective you may be as a teacher, school district personnel are not likely to walk up to you and offer you a job unless you have taken a number of the steps that we will outline in this section. We will suggest several courses of action that will greatly increase your chances of finding the best teaching job for you.

Campaign Actively

■ develop a plan

First, you must be determined to campaign actively for a teaching position. Draw up a plan, in writing, of how you will proceed. Don't wait for happenstance. You might get lucky and land a job on your first try, but why take a passive attitude when you can do much to increase your chances of obtaining satisfying employment? For example, try attending job fairs sponsored by various colleges, universities, or school districts.

I'm a great believer in luck, and I find the harder I work the more I have of it.

—Thomas Jefferson

Job seekers often make two common mistakes.[18] One is to try one strategy, wait for results (positive or negative), then try something else. What you should do is pursue many avenues or strategies simultaneously. The second common error is to block oneself out at the wrong stage in the process. Some teachers only halfheartedly write for information or never complete the application form. Others withdraw their applications prematurely. Remember, you can always say "no" to a job offered to you, but you can never say "yes" to one that has not been offered. Keep your options open.

Prepare Materials

■ prepare a good résumé

Next, you need to get certain materials ready. These include your résumé, cover letter, credentials, and transcripts. Your résumé allows you to present yourself the way you want to be presented to prospective employers. Its purpose is to help you get an interview with school district officials. You should make several copies of your résumé.

Many sources are available to help you write your résumé. The office of career planning and placement at your college or university is a good place to start. These offices often run workshops on résumé writing and frequently have samples of well-written résumés for you to examine. The American Association for Employment in Education (AAEE)'s annual *Job Search Handbook for Educators* listed in the **For Further Information** section at the end of the chapter is an excellent source on how to write résumés and on other job search strategies.

■ teaching portfolios

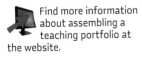 Find more information about assembling a teaching portfolio at the website.

Another set of materials that more and more teachers are using to help them obtain jobs is called a **teaching portfolio.** Just as artists, actors, architects, and journalists use portfolios to display the products of their work, so can teachers. A teaching portfolio can include an organized collection of such items as research papers, letters of commendation or recommendation, pupil evaluations, teaching units, and video recordings of lessons you have taught. There is no set format; you are limited only by your common sense and your own imagination. Remember, the purpose of the portfolio is to market yourself effectively, so don't be modest. A properly constructed portfolio will say much more about you than your résumé ever can. Many beginning teachers are constructing electronic portfolios and making them available to potential employers either as websites or on DVDs. The advantage of an electronic portfolio is that it is easily accessible by potential employers and can be changed or added to as needed. Electronic teaching portfolios are also being used to demonstrate that prospective teachers have achieved standards—such as the INTASC (Interstate New Teacher Assessment and Support Consortium) standards—required for state licensure. The National Board for Professional Teaching Standards (discussed in the chapter entitled "What Does It Mean to Be a Professional?") has advocated teaching portfolios as a means of assessing a teacher's work for national certification. (See the AAEE *Job Search Handbook for Educators* and the website for this book for specific recommendations on portfolio construction.)

■ establish your credential file

■ Buckley amendment

Almost all school districts require credentials, or the whole package from your college recommending you for licensure. Be sure to check with the career planning and placement office about how to establish your **credential file** and what should go into it. Typically this file will include letters of recommendation, a copy of your transcript, and a résumé. Career planning and placement office personnel will help you assemble this file, and they will send copies of your file to school districts on your request. You should start on the file early in your program so you will have time to accumulate the required materials. Letters of recommendation should be recent, and they should come from those who are familiar with your teaching, academic knowledge, and character. Be certain to include letters from your university supervisor and your cooperating teacher in whose classroom you did your student or internship teaching. Be familiar with the Family Educational Rights and Privacy Act, also known as the Buckley amendment, which affords you certain kinds of legal protection regarding what goes into your file.[†]

■ save money on transcript copies

Reproduce unofficial copies of your official transcript. Many applications require that transcripts accompany them. Because colleges charge several dollars per transcript, you can save money by reproducing the transcript yourself. Most

---

[†] A copy of this law appears in the Federal Register 53, no. 69 (April 11, 1998), pp. 11942–11949. It can also be obtained by writing the U.S. Government Printing Office, Washington, D.C. 20402.

school districts will accept unofficial transcripts (those sent from you rather than directly from the college) for the initial screening process. If you receive a job offer, you will then have to provide the school district with an official copy.

■ cover letters

When you send your resumé, transcripts, and other materials to prospective school districts, the package should include a cover letter. The cover letters you write should be addressed individually. The letters may all have the same or similar content, but the recipients should not feel they are receiving a standard letter. And, incidentally, be sure to ask for an interview. That's why you are writing the letter.

Develop Interview Skills

■ prepare for interviews

The success of your personal interview with the school district representative is one of the most important determinants of whether you get hired, so be prepared. Try to anticipate the kinds of questions that might be asked (see the accompanying box for some sample questions). Try role playing with a friend who plays the role of the interviewer while you play the candidate. Audiotape your "interview" so the two of you can criticize it.

Typical Questions Asked During Job Interviews

Most interviews follow a simple question-and-answer routine. Your ability to communicate effectively with a stranger in a stressful situation is critical. Being prepared is the best way to avoid a disorganized answer. Sometimes the interviewer plays "devil's advocate," disagreeing with a position you articulate to see if you will back down from it in deference to an authority figure. You should be aware of this possibility, be prepared to assess your position straightforwardly, and then stand behind it. Avoid "waffling." Your success in interviewing depends on how convincingly you can convey your ability to teach.

Interviews are often subjective, so your enthusiasm, self-confidence, eagerness, and believability will affect the outcome of your interview. Be sincere and mean what you say. Remember to look the interviewer in the eye. First impressions are important, so dress conservatively. Remove visible body piercings! At the conclusion of the interview, restate any important points you want to emphasize. Ask the interviewer for a business card and ask when the selection decision will be made. Send the interviewer a thank-you note; courtesy can make a difference.

Questions you may be asked include the following:

Motivation/Experience/Education

- Tell us about yourself.
- Why do you want to teach?
- Why do you want to work in our school district?

- What grade levels or subjects are you most interested in teaching?
- What do you consider to be your strongest attributes as a teacher? Weaknesses?
- What was your biggest problem in student teaching? How did you resolve it?
- How would you work with students who perform below grade level, especially those from poverty backgrounds?

Teaching Skills

- What is your philosophy of education?
- What are the most important learning outcomes you want your students to achieve?
- What skills and experience do you have in employing cooperative learning strategies or computers for instructional purposes?
- How can you motivate unmotivated learners?
- How would you involve parents to help students learn?
- How do you individualize your teaching?
- What is your grading philosophy?

Classroom Management

- What ideas do you have regarding maintaining classroom control?

- What rules for students would you establish in your classroom?
- How would you enforce these rules?
- Describe the most difficult student discipline situation you have faced and how you handled it.

Professional Responsibilities

- How do you plan to keep growing as a professional?
- What professional journals do you read?
- What added school responsibilities are you willing to accept?

Hypothetical Questions

- What would you do if you caught a student cheating?
- If money were unlimited, how would you improve education?
- How would you handle a student who refused to do the work you assigned?

During a job interview, you will answer many questions. But to gain the information that will help you choose among the jobs offered to you, you will also need to *ask* questions. Remember, you are interviewing the prospective employer, too. Before you accept a position, you will need to know about the following:

Instructional Assignment

- Characteristics of the school district and student population
- Curriculum and resources available
- Typical class size
- Salary and benefits (medical and dental coverage and retirement)
- District's expectations and reimbursement policies for professional development
- Orientation or support services available for beginning teachers

These are just a few suggestions. For additional information on interview questions, see "Interview Questions to Answer and Ask," *2005 Job Search Handbook for Educators* (Columbus, OH: American Association for Employment in Education, 2005), p. 32.

■ empathy for children important

One survey indicated that the major factor school officials look for is whether the candidate has empathy for children. Be prepared to show your empathy, not by saying you have it but through the examples you give from your own experience. You should also ask those who write letters of recommendation for you to emphasize this aspect.

Remember, *you* are also interviewing the school district or specific school. You should look for a good fit between you and your style of teaching and what the school or district expects from you. Don't be so eager to get any position that you ignore the issue of fit. As charter schools continue to develop (see the chapter entitled "How Should Education Be Reformed?") new teachers will have more options to choose from in terms of work climate, educational philosophy, and learning goals. Also consider whether you will have access to an induction program and a mentor teacher. Research shows that having a good mentor teacher increases the likelihood of your success as a teacher. Secondary teachers should also ask whether the number of class preparations is reduced for beginning teachers. Having only one or two types of classes to prepare for makes the first year of teaching much easier than having to make three or four preparations for different courses.

Determine Job Availability

■ use your college placement center

Your next major task is to find out what jobs are available and where. Several strategies are possible. Your college's career planning and placement office receives hundreds of notifications of position vacancies. Contact that office often to see if there are any vacancies that might interest you. Be on the lookout for job fairs, where school districts and potential teachers come together at one site to explore job opportunities. Your college or university may sponsor such a job fair. Another source may be the teacher employment office operated by the state department of education. About one-third of the states run such offices, and you can register with them for free or for a slight charge. These offices send registered candidates a listing of openings in their specialty area for both state and out-of-state vacancies.

■ personal contacts important

Link to Teachers-Teachers.com from the website.

There are also private organizations that keep current nationwide teacher vacancy lists and will try to match your qualifications with those vacancies either for little or no cost. One such organization is Teachers-Teachers.com (available at: **http://www.teachers-teachers.com**). This free service to prospective teachers allows them to post their résumé online, which can be accessed by thousands of schools seeking teachers. (See the **For Further Information** section at the end of the chapter for more information on this website.) Personal contacts too are often very effective in securing a position. Don't hesitate to call friends and acquaintances who might be able to help you obtain interviews. They probably can't get you a job, but they may be aware of vacancies and know whom you should contact. Contacting specific school districts directly is another way to determine what positions are available. Call, write, or visit the personnel office of the school districts in which you are interested. This will ensure that you get current information directly from the school district. Alternatively, use the World Wide Web to see if the school districts that interest you have home pages. If they do, they may very well list their job openings on their pages. Again, the AAEE *Job Search Handbook for Educators* lists and discusses a number of Internet sources with teaching and other educational job opportunities. We have cited a few of these sources at the end of the chapter.

Gain Experience Through Substitute Teaching

■ advantages of substitute teaching

Many education students develop valuable experience, earn some money, and establish an entrance into a school district by serving as substitute teachers. Some universities even offer coursework in becoming an effective substitute. Besides giving you the opportunity to refine your teaching skills, substitute teaching can provide a competitive advantage in the job market. Some school districts are apt to hire full-time teachers from their substitute ranks if the substitutes have done a good job. After all, school officials would rather hire a known teacher in whom they have confidence than take a chance on a new teacher whom they don't know. If you're interested in being a substitute teacher, visit the district personnel office to find out the requirements and attend substitute-teacher training sessions if they are offered.

Pause and Reflect

1 ▶ What ways can you think of to increase your chances of being hired when you are ready to teach?

2 ▶ Which of the interview questions above do you believe you would find most difficult to answer? Which would you find easiest?

▶ How Do You Become Licensed?

- state license required to teach

All fifty states and the District of Columbia require public elementary and secondary school teachers to be licensed to teach by the department of education in the state in which they work. The terms *licensure* and *certification* are often confused or misused. **Licensure** is the official recognition by a state governmental agency that an individual meets state requirements, whereas **certification** is the process by which the profession grants special recognition to an individual who has met certain qualifications specified by the profession. Often, however, the term *certification*, as in, "I'm going to get my certification to teach," is used when *licensure* is meant. This usage is a carryover from earlier times. Today some states continue to use *certification* as a synonym for *licensure*, but in this book, we have tried to distinguish the terms.

Traditional Licensure Programs

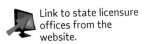 Link to state licensure offices from the website.

Traditionally, to qualify for licensure, a teacher has had to complete an approved teacher education program. Besides conferring a bachelor's or master's degree, which provides the necessary liberal arts background, teacher education programs fulfill the state requirement that prospective teachers take certain education courses or demonstrate certain competencies.

- state exams for teachers

Since the mid-1980s, the overwhelming majority of states have increased the requirements for licensure, adding test requirements such as the PRAXIS examinations (teacher competency exams developed by the Educational Testing Service) or, in some cases, state-developed competency tests of basic skills. Since the No Child Left Behind law requires that "highly qualified" teachers meet standards in the content areas they teach, prospective teachers are examined on their content-area knowledge, as well as pedagogical knowledge. However, the difficulty levels and the required scores to pass these tests vary from state to state. In some states, further requirements for licensure can include U.S. citizenship, criminal background checks, an oath of allegiance, and, in several states, a health certificate.

- differences among states . . .

Because the requirements for licensure differ from state to state, you should become aware of the requirements for the state in which you will seek employment. Someone in your placement office or your school of education most likely will be able to acquaint you with licensure requirements. Your education library probably contains books that list the licensure requirements for all the states. Should you not be successful there, you can call or write directly to the teacher licensure office in the states in which you are interested. A directory of state teacher licensure offices in the United States, along with their website addresses, appears as an appendix at the end of this book. A number of states have reciprocal agreements to accept one another's licenses as valid. If you move from one state to another, you may want to check whether your teaching license is accepted by the state to which you are moving.

- . . . and specialization areas

Besides the basic licenses for teaching at the elementary and secondary levels, many states require different licenses, or *endorsements*, for such specialization areas as special education, bilingual education, and kindergarten. If, as you gain experience, you want to move out of teaching into a supervisory, administrative, or counseling position, you will need a special license.

■ pursue more than one
licensure area

*To those bright young people who
want to enter the profession that has
been so good to many of us—
education—I say, "Good choice!" My
advice to them is not "You're too
smart to be a teacher," but rather,
"You're too smart not to be one."*

—James R. Delisle

If at all possible, you would be wise to become licensed or endorsed in more
than one teaching area. Adding a second field of licensure will make you more attractive to prospective employers, particularly in smaller school
districts, which have less flexibility to hire specialists who teach
in only one area. If you are going to be an elementary school
teacher, having an additional license or endorsement in reading,
special education, early childhood education, or bilingual education would be very worthwhile. Another way to increase your appeal to prospective employers would be to take a major or minor
in mathematics, one of the sciences, or instructional technology.
Elementary school teachers with expertise in these areas are in
short supply. If you are going to teach at the secondary level, you
can broaden your appeal by being licensed to teach in two or
more subject fields. For example, if you are a Spanish major, minor in French; if you are a chemistry major, minor in physics or mathematics. Any
doubling up of teaching fields will work to your advantage.

In summary, individual states use licensure requirements to assure the public that the teachers teaching the youth of our society have been adequately prepared. Licensure requirements should present you with little difficulty as long as
the teacher education institution you attend meets the general regulations of the
state department of education and as long as you maintain contact with the college official responsible for coordinating the education program with the state licensure requirements. But in many states, the traditional route to licensure—
graduation from an approved teacher education program—is no longer the sole
route to gaining a teaching license.

Alternative Licensure

Most states offer alternative routes to licensure, and there is tremendous variation among these options. For example, some states permit **alternative licensure** routes only when there is a shortage of traditionally licensed teachers. Other
states permit alternative routes only at the secondary level. Still other states allow
institutions of higher education to design alternatives to their college-approved
teacher education programs.

■ alternative licensure
requirements

Alternative programs are a response to (1) teacher shortages and (2) the perception on the part of some lawmakers that courses in education contribute little to a teacher's effectiveness. Generally, those licensed through alternative
means hold a bachelor's degree in the subject area they will teach but have taken
fewer credit-hours in professional education courses than are normally required.
Often these candidates are required to have at least a B college grade average and
to have passed a basic skills test and a test in a subject or specialty area.

■ plusses and minuses of
Teach for America

One alternative program that has gained considerable attention is *Teach for
America*. The program recruits motivated undergraduate students with arts and
science majors from select colleges and universities to teach for two years in rural
or urban areas that have had difficulty recruiting teachers. Although the program
has been successful in attracting significant numbers of minority teachers, its
dropout rate is high. Also, the number of teachers produced through the *Teach for
America* program is very small compared with the number graduated through approved teacher education programs.

■ alternative programs—how
successful?

■ alternative routes attract
men and minorities

How successful are these alternative licensure programs? Forty-seven states
have some form of alternative licensure option, but only about 250,000 teachers
in the entire nation were licensed through alternative routes between 1985 and

2005.[19] Formal evaluation studies of alternative licensure programs have been few and have sometimes been conducted by persons with vested interests in the outcomes. However, one analysis of a national sample of teachers who entered teaching through alternative licensure routes concluded that they tended to have lower academic qualifications than those who entered through other routes, were less likely to stay in teaching, and were more likely to be teaching in inner-city schools that serve more economically disadvantaged students.[20] Compared with graduates of traditional teacher education programs, those entering teaching through alternative licensure programs tend to be older, have more work experience in occupations other than education, are more likely to be males, and are more likely to be people of color.[21] Supporters of alternative licensure programs argue that the ability to attract men and minorities into teaching speaks to the need for these types of programs. The federal government allotted $45 million in fiscal year 2005 to help mid-career professionals become licensed as teachers.

Nevertheless, tensions exist between those who want to break college-based teacher education's monopoly and professional educators who believe that completion of an approved teacher education program is the public's best guarantee that a teacher is "safe to practice." The variety of alternative licensure programs across the various states is testimony to the differing views on how teachers should be prepared. The real issue is not whether traditional programs are better than alternative licensure programs. Instead, the important question is what are the most important elements constituting effective teacher preparation, whether through a traditional or alternative program. One thing seems certain: alternative licensure programs will continue to grow to meet the projected need for teachers.

Pause and Reflect

1 ▶ Do you have any opinions about the alternative licensure programs currently offered in most states? What do you see as their strengths? Their drawbacks?

2 ▶ Are you clear about the difference between "certification" and "licensure?"

▶ If You Don't Teach, What Then?

For many different reasons, a substantial number of teachers each year find themselves looking for jobs outside education. Suppose that, despite all your job-seeking efforts, you are unsuccessful in finding the position you want or that after teaching a few years, you decide that teaching is not for you. What will you be prepared to do after your teacher education? Has your preparation equipped you with skills that are in demand in fields outside education?

Transferable Skills

Many non-educational employers are eager to employ teachers and people who have gone through teacher preparation programs because they have skills that many college graduates lack. What generic or transferable skills—that is, skills that are needed in most businesses and professions—are you likely to have developed in your preparation as a teacher? Among the skills and abilities that teachers acquire are the following:

■ teaching skills transferable to other jobs

- Planning and decision making
- Working under pressure

- Conducting performance evaluation
- Keeping records and organizing materials
- Using technology
- Establishing and maintaining good interpersonal relations
- Communicating effectively in oral and written form
- Managing groups of people

In short, many of the skills required of teachers are also required for other types of work. Naturally, additional training may be necessary, depending on the exact type of work. Now let's examine some alternative careers.

Other Jobs

■ jobs requiring teaching experience

In addition to teaching, schools and school districts offer a number of other educational occupations, including librarian, counselor, supervisor, administrator, and school psychologist. Although these roles don't involve full-time teaching of children, they often require some minimum teaching experience and additional licensure. All these roles are important in the educational enterprise. If you decide that you are interested in education but not necessarily in long-term elementary or secondary school teaching, one of these other occupations may be right for you.

You might also investigate employment in early childhood education and day care centers. Because early childhood education is a growing field, numerous new occupations are developing within it, such as reading specialists to help diagnose learning abilities and curriculum specialists to help plan the studies. State, local, and federal government agencies need researchers, planners, evaluators, and others to administer the growing number of early childhood projects they fund. Another growing area is in the field of adult education, which attempts to provide basic education and literacy skills for many adults who lack such competencies and thereby have difficulty finding work in a technology society. Adult education occurs in many venues, including public schools, community colleges, and public service organizations.

■ training and development in corporations

Large businesses also conduct extensive training programs for their employees, and they require the services of people who can design and implement such programs. Many people who have been trained as teachers find their way into such jobs. Several hundreds of thousands of people are employed (full- and part-time) in training and development in the United States.[‡]

■ recreation and leisure jobs

The field of recreation and leisure activities attracts many people trained as teachers. Workers in this field plan, organize, and direct individual and group activities that help people enjoy their leisure hours. They work with people of various ages and socioeconomic groups, the sick and the well, and those with emotional and physical disabilities. Employment settings range from wilderness to rural to suburban and urban, including the inner city. Examples of recreation program jobs include playground leaders; program specialists in dance, drama, karate, tennis, the arts, and other physical activities; recreation center directors; therapeutic recreation specialists; camp counselors and wilderness leaders; senior citizen program leaders; civilian special services directors in the armed forces; and industrial recreation directors. Recreation workers held about 485,000 jobs in

[‡] The American Society of Training and Development, 1640 King Street, Box 1443, Alexandria, VA 22313, can provide more information about corporate career opportunities for teachers. Available at: **http://www.astd.org.**

There are many alternative careers for people trained as teachers but who elect not to teach in schools.
(© Dennis MacDonald/ PhotoEdit)

2002, not including summer workers, and the number is expected to grow between 21 and 35 percent by 2012.[22] The majority worked in local, public tax-supported agencies such as municipal and county park and recreation departments.

jobs in publishing

The publishing industry affords numerous job opportunities for education-oriented writers, technology experts, editors, and salespeople. If you have good writing and analytic skills, you might be interested in helping develop or edit textbooks for use in elementary and secondary schools and in colleges. If you enjoy meeting people and traveling, being a textbook sales representative might appeal to you. Another growing area is the development of computer software related to education. Individuals who combine computer skills, including web design, with an understanding of classroom instruction will have a distinct advantage in the job market.

working for professional organizations

Preparation as a teacher is also important for work related to professional organizations such as the National Education Association (NEA), American Federation of Teachers, Phi Delta Kappa, Kappa Delta Pi, National Council of Teachers of Mathematics, and National Council for the Social Studies. These organizations and others like them hire people for fieldwork, writing, research, and other staff positions.

▶ A Final Word

Many indicators point to a strong demand for teachers in the coming years. Impending retirements in the current teaching force and increased school enrollments are encouraging signs for prospective teachers. However, we don't know how many former teachers will re-enter the job market to compete with recently graduated teachers for the job openings. Successful job searches may require special steps such as relocating to another area or state to secure a teaching position in your field.

As we stated earlier, there has never been a surplus of good teachers. If you and your credentials are good and you are willing to go where the jobs are, you can find a teaching job. Preparing yourself well for school districts' needs, especially gaining expertise in more than one teaching field, can expand your job options and make you more attractive to prospective employers.

America has become an education-oriented society. We are realizing that reaching our individual and national goals depends on achieving high levels of education. This means we are committed to more and better education, to lifelong learning in and out of schools. More than seventy years ago, President Calvin Coolidge said, "The business of America is business." Today and into the future, the business of America is education. Teaching is where the action is and will continue to be!

Key Terms

alternative licensure (410)
certification (409)
credential file (405)

licensure (409)
performance pay (pay-for-performance) plans (403)

teaching portfolio (405)

For Reflection

1 Are there any education-related occupations other than teaching that might interest you?

2 What can you do to increase your employability as a teacher?

For Debate

Read the Policy Matters! summary, "Preparing Teachers: High Standards, Large Numbers, or Both?" at the website, and consider the issues it outlines regarding trends in teacher preparation and licensing. Then go to EduSpace to post your answers (or respond to other students' answers) to the What Do You Think questions listed in the Policy Matters! feature.

For Further Information

PRINT RESOURCES

Richard Nelson Bolles, *What Color Is Your Parachute? 2005: A Practical Manual for Job Hunters and Career Changers* (Berkeley, CA: Ten Speed Press, 2005). This best-selling practical manual for job hunters and career changers is updated yearly.

Roy A. Edelfelt, *Careers in Education,* 3d ed. (Lincolnwood, IL: NTC Contemporary Publishing, 1998). This book explores various educational careers in teaching, administration, higher education, and business and industry.

American Association for Employment in Education, *Job Search Handbook for Educators* (Columbus, OH: The Association).

This annual publication is designed to assist both new and experienced educators in their job searches and is the single most important reference on this topic. The *Handbook* is usually distributed through career planning and placement offices in colleges and universities, but it may also be obtained from the AAEE office at 3040 Riverside Drive, Suite 125, Columbus, OH 43221–2550 or by calling (614) 485–1111. AAEE's website also provides links to public school systems and educational organizations and is available at: **http://www.aaee.org.**

WEB RESOURCES

Council of Chief State School Officers. Available at: **http://www.ccsso.org.**
This organization of the chief state school officers has a useful and informative home page, including links to each state education agency. Click on *Links to State Education Agencies* and choose the state in which you are interested. Some states list telephone numbers and websites of different school districts in the state.

Preparing a Teaching Portfolio: A Guidebook. Produced by the Center for Teaching Effectiveness at the University of Texas-Austin. Available at: **http://www.utexas.edu/academic/cte/ teachfolio.html.**
This online resource provides detailed instructions on how to prepare a teaching portfolio.

Teacher-Teacher.com. Available at: **http://www. teachers-teachers.com.**
Sponsored by several educational organizations, this website allows schools to contact prospective teachers who have posted their résumés on the site. There is no fee for teachers.

References For Locating Sources of Job Vacancies

GENERAL INFORMATION

Directory of Public School Systems in the U.S. Published annually. American Association for Employment in Education, 3040 Riverside Drive, Suite 125, Columbus, OH 43221–2550, (614) 485–1111. Orders may be placed online at: **http://www.aaee.org.**

Education Week. Available at: **http://www.edweek.org.**
Education Week is an independent newspaper published forty times per year. For a subscription, write to Education Week, 4301 Connecticut Avenue, NW, Suite 250, Washington, DC 20008.

Project Connect. Available at: **http://www.aaee.org.**
A national cooperative venture among school districts and university schools of education, Project Connect provides lists of teaching vacancies, either through college placement offices or directly via the website. You can register online for a password; no fees are involved. For your first time, enter the special username (teacher) and password (aswan) to get access.

PRIVATE SCHOOLS

Independent School Management, Inc. Available at: **http://www.isminc.com/pubs/mart/mm.html.**
This organization carries job vacancy listings for teaching in independent schools on its website. Ads are changed every three weeks.

National Association of Independent Schools (NAIS). Available at: **http://nais-schools.org/.**
This organization represents more than 1,200 independent schools nationwide and abroad. Contact the Associate Director of Academic Services, NAIS, 1620 L Street, Suite 1100, NW, Washington, DC 20036–5695, (202) 973–9700. Also visit the website for information on how to secure a teaching job at one of its schools.

TEACHING OPPORTUNITIES ABROAD

U.S. Department of Defense Dependents Schools. Available at: **http://www.dodea.edu/pers/ employment/.**
Teachers in these American schools are U.S. government employees. Contact Department of Defense Education Activity, 4040 North Fairfax Dr., Arlington, VA 22203-1634, (703) 588-3983.

European Council of International Schools (ECIS). Available at: **http://www.ecis.org.**
This organization can provide information about schools in Europe. Contact ECIS, 21B Lavant Street, Petersfield, Hampshire GU32 3EL, UK. Call 44–1730–268244.

International Schools Services (ISS). Available at: **http://www.iss.edu.**
This resource contains names, addresses, and other information on nearly 500 international elementary and secondary schools. Ask for the *ISS Directory of Overseas Schools.* Contact ISS, 15 Roszel Road, P.O. Box 5910, Princeton, NJ 08543 U.S.A. Phone: (609) 452-0990.

The Peace Corps. Available at:
http://www.peacecorps.gov.
Several months of training are provided before living in the host country. Following a stint in the Corps, members have access to a range of programs intended to help them become teachers in the United States. Applications can be made online.

Association of American Schools in South America. Available at: **http://www.aassa.com.**
An association serving forty-one American International schools in South America. Contact the Association at 14750 NW 77th Court, Suite 210, Miami Lakes, FL 33016, (305) 821–0345.

The International Educator (TIE). Available at:
http://www.tieonline.com.
This organization publishes a newspaper five times a year with international job vacancies in teaching and administration. Also, teachers can sign up and have their materials reviewed online by international schools. Contact the Overseas Schools Assistance Corp., P.O. Box 513, Cummaquid, MA 02637, (508) 362–1414

14 *What Can the New Teacher Expect?*

Chapter Preview Starting their career is for most people one of the most exciting and energizing periods of their lives. For most young people it represents their unofficial entrance into the adult world. They are often in a new environment with new people and challenges. They have real responsibilities. This is especially true for new teachers. For many, the transition into full-time teaching is relatively easy and satisfying.

For others, however, the first year is a struggle. Some new teachers are shocked and disappointed by the actual experience of being a teacher. In this chapter, we try to help prospective teachers anticipate some of the problems that lie ahead. All of the material comes directly from the experiences of beginning teachers.

This chapter emphasizes that:

▶ Although prospective teachers may feel that schools will hold few surprises, being on the other side of the desk is a very different experience and can cause a sense of culture shock.

▶ Administrators play an important but often confusing role in the life of the beginning teacher.

▶ Although fellow teachers are an enormous source of learning and support, they can sometimes be a source of difficulty.

▶ New teachers learn much about the job in which they are supposed to be experts: instruction.

▶ Some of the most intense satisfaction and disappointment confronting new teachers come from those they came to help: students.

▶ Working with parents can be surprisingly complex and is rarely what the new teacher has anticipated.

▶ Beginning teachers can follow specific strategies to mitigate problems and heighten their chances for a successful career start.

▶ Teaching invariably has hidden sweetness and secret joys.

■ encouraging job reports

We have good news and bad news for you. First, the good news: forecasters predict that as a result of teacher retirement and population growth, our schools will need 2 million new teachers in the next decade.[1] Not since World War II has there been such a promising job market for teachers. As we describe in the chapter entitled "What Are Your Job Options in Education?," people entering the teaching profession in the first decade of the twenty-first century typically will have a rich variety of options and opportunities from which to choose. So much for the good news.

The bad news is that the first year of teaching can be a rough one—too rough for many beginners. Each year, many new teachers walk into their classrooms with energy, high hopes, and rose-colored glasses, only to face unexpected problems that cause them to give up on teaching or radically lower their sights about their capabilities as teachers. The tips in the "Voices from the Classroom" box gives you an idea of what you might expect the first year.

Rather than ignoring or, worse, sugarcoating these problems, we focus on them, even at the risk of frightening some readers. We do this because we believe that to

VOICES FROM THE CLASSROOM

Lauren Manganiello teaches grades nine, ten, and twelve at Wilmington High School in Wilmington, Mass.

Tips for Your First Year

The most valuable tip I can give to a prospective first-year teacher is that you should expect to work *very hard,* and sometimes *very late,* every night. The summer before I started teaching I worked diligently at preparing units and lessons; still, I had no idea how much work I had coming to me. Granted, the amount of work you'll need to do will depend on your school and your curriculum; I have total control over what I teach, which translates to a lot of work for me. I spend between one and two hours correcting on weeknights and even more on weekends; I spend most afternoons securing the next day's lessons.

Next, expect to do a lot of learning in your first year. Most new teachers are fresh out of college or graduate school and know their specific subject matter very well; however, knowing material and knowing how to teach material are two completely different concepts! Making the switch from higher education back to high school or even elementary school education is a challenge.

Finally, expect to:

- *Struggle*—practice makes perfect, and if you push yourself too hard at the beginning of your career, you might burn out before your time (think of teaching as a marathon).
- Be overwhelmed with paperwork; there's a letter or form for *everything.*
- Meet amazing students who will keep you coming back to your job.
- Have responsibilities outside of your classroom, like corridor duty, study halls or, my favorite, bathroom duty.
- Be shocked by the sometimes cynical conversation in the lunchroom.
- Find some amazing teachers in your department and school who can be your best resources, and best allies.
- *Be surprised*—what you worry about now will seem ridiculous once you're finally in the classroom, and what you've never even given a thought to will suddenly become your everyday amusement, pleasure, or headache!

 Visit the website for more Voices from the Classroom.

be forewarned is to be forearmed, and many of the problems discussed in this chapter can be either prevented or radically reduced in intensity. New teachers can find satisfaction in solving their problems and in succeeding as a professional.

Surprise is a big part of the first year, too. New teachers often report their astonishment at this or that experience or event. The first year is intense because the unexpected demands and the surprises that lurk in what was thought to be a familiar world: the classroom. These surprises often come wrapped in everyday boxes; some contain sweet treasures, and others hold booby traps. We have categorized these surprises in the following way:

■ surprises of the first year

- The school milieu: the shock of the familiar
- Administrators: mixed bag, as well as many hats and pressures
- Peers: a mixed blessing
- Instruction: so much to learn
- Students: friends or fiends?
- Parents: natural allies with different agendas

In this chapter, we will look at each of these categories and try to take some of the surprises out of the first year of teaching. Our larger intention, however, is to help you mobilize yourself by preparing for the problems, developing your strengths, and shoring up your weaknesses.

▶ The School Milieu: The Shock of the Familiar

■ the strange and the familiar

One of the oddest occurrences related to becoming a teacher is the new teacher's sense of strangeness in what is, after all, a very familiar setting. People who become securities analysts, astronauts, or psychiatric social workers know they are moving into a strange environment, and they expect these new work worlds to present them with very different experiences from those they had as students. New teachers, however, are re-entering a familiar setting, even if their schools are not the same ones in which they were taught. Nevertheless, beginning teachers are often overwhelmed by their initial exposure to school.

■ false sense of security

It appears that the new teacher's very familiarity with life in schools is a problem in that it lulls many into a false sense of understanding what is happening around them and thus a false sense of security. "School" is a very complicated network of structures, people, and interactions, and having "studied" school from the perspective of a student is hardly the same as understanding it as a teacher. Being one of twenty-five students sitting and listening to a teacher is quite different from being in front of twenty-five young people and having responsibility for their learning. Also, new teachers have to learn not only a new set of school routines for their particular school but also how to administer those routines. They have to learn their way around a new building and find out how to requisition the supplies they need. They have to get acquainted with their administration, their fellow teachers, and especially their students. And on top of all this, first-year teachers often have to develop lesson plans from scratch. They must build complete units, design bulletin boards, devise an evaluation system, and make up and grade short- and long-term tests. The sheer volume of "newness" puts pressure and strain on the beginners.

A teacher's day is half bureaucracy, half crisis, half monotony, and one-eightieth epiphany. Never mind the arithmetic.

—Susan Ohanian

Culture Shock

■ signs of stress

Beginning teachers' disorientation with what they thought would be the familiar turf of school often shows up in visible signs of mental and physical stress. In the early months of the school year, it is not uncommon for the new teacher to experience depression and self-doubt, outbursts of crying, physical exhaustion, insomnia, crankiness, inability to control temper, and even fits of vomiting before going to school in the morning. One anthropologist claims that the stresses and strains many new teachers experience are similar to the phenomenon known as *culture shock.*[2]

■ school: a foreign culture?

Culture shock is the feeling of dislocation that people experience when they initially live in a foreign country. Peace Corps volunteers, aid workers, exchange students, tourists, and newly arrived immigrants often report that when first thrust into the strange life patterns of a foreign culture, they feel numbingly disoriented, forced to assimilate too much too soon, and afraid they have made a drastic mistake by going to this strange country. It is easy to explain culture shock among Peace Corps volunteers and immigrants, but why teachers? Haven't we just said that teachers, as ex-students, are accustomed to the culture of school?

Rather than saying, "I have a job," I say with delight, "I am a teacher!" It's so much more than a job, it's an awakening.

—STUART D. CHANDLER, FIFTH GRADE
TEACHER, AURORA, CO

Pause and Reflect

1 ▶ Think of a time when you experienced culture shock, and try to remember, in as much detail as possible, how it made you feel. Did you experience it during a foreign visit?

2 ▶ Did you experience any sense of disorientation or depression during your initial months at college? What strategies did you find helpful in getting oriented?

The following account by a new second-grade teacher speaks to the kinds of culture shock problems related to large amounts of "newness" that are experienced by teachers in many situations.*

Case Study

Julia Tucker/Second Grade

The next time I hear someone say, "Teaching is an easy job," I think I'm going to slap their face . . . or cry! I can't believe how tired I am. I've been teaching for five weeks, and it seems as if it has been five months. I never realized that life on the teacher's side of the desk could be so different, so tiring. I remember seeing the old movie *Up the Down Staircase* and thinking it was exaggerated. My kids are younger and don't have the kinds of problems those high school kids in the movie had, but they still have problems, and they are so demanding! They all want my attention, and they all seem to want it at the same time. "Miss Tucker, someone took my pencil! Did you do it?" "Miss Tucker, Ralph and Maxine put gum in my hair." "Miss Tucker, my father doesn't think we're doing enough arithmetic in this class and says I can tell the kids to shut up if you won't." "Miss Tucker, I need to go to the nurse. I have a terrible nosebleed coming on!" And on and on.

---

* All cases in this chapter that are not accompanied by specific citations are slightly altered or fictionalized accounts of situations and problems experienced by the authors or by beginning teachers with whom the authors have worked. The names have been changed to save us all from embarrassment.

And the forms! They never end. Forms for shots. For lockers. For parent volunteers. For books. And we have an attendance procedure here that must have been designed by a sadist! It consumes hours of time. The principal's office continually wants information. I keep filling out forms and sending them in, only to be greeted with more forms. I can't imagine what they do with all the information.

On top of all this, I'm supposed to teach! I leave school in the afternoon—always the last one out of the building—and I'm numb from the hairline down. On some nights, I can hardly unwrap a TV dinner. And I spend what little free time I do have staring at the TV set and having imaginary arguments with Sandra's know-it-all father (whom I have yet to meet) about why we actually are doing just the right amount of arithmetic. What is most discouraging is that Sandra's father wins the arguments.

■ swimming in molasses

Clearly, this has been the most frustrating five weeks of my life. I feel as if I've been swimming in molasses. Student teaching was a breeze compared with this! ■

■ pleasant surprises

But many of the surprises of school life are very pleasant ones. There is much love and human warmth in the classroom. Some of the aspects of school life that you may have dreaded never materialize. The content about which you feel uncertain could turn out to be your strength. Also, within the four walls of the classroom, some people find a new self they didn't know existed.

| Case Study | ## Joan Kinney/High School Mathematics |

All through elementary and high school, I was bashful. In my high school graduating class, I won the Most Shy award. I dreaded being called on, even when I knew I had the right answer! Part of it is that I blush so easily. So my approach was to be like the furniture or the wallpaper and hope that the teacher wouldn't see me. Still, I liked school and always liked my teachers, even the ones that had fun with my blushing. When I decided to become a math teacher, I knew my shyness was going to be a problem, but I figured that I could pass my blushing off as a permanent sunburn.

■ personality transformation

Something happened, though, when I became a teacher. I began to notice a change when I was student teaching, and once I had my own class, it was quite clear: I'm a different person in my class. I feel very outgoing, almost to the point of being aggressive. Also, I've discovered that I'm a ham actor. And what a stage my classroom is! I love it. My students seem to love it, too. It seems so odd that after all these years of trying to be invisible, now I'm discovering a whole new side of myself. ■

▶ Administrators: Mixed Bag and Many Hats

As elementary and secondary school students, most of us had pretty simplistic notions of administrators. The superintendent, if we ever saw one at all, was a vague presence we occasionally glimpsed in the hall talking to one of the staff or in front of a microphone on ceremonial occasions. The principal was much more a part of our school lives as someone beloved or feared, and occasionally both. Even though the principal was near at hand, our student's-eye view was rather one-dimensional. The principal represented AUTHORITY. In all but the rarest instances, the principal stood directly beyond the teacher, supporting the teacher and the system. When, as students, we went to the principal's office, it almost always meant we were in trouble. Now it could mean so many things!

The Multiple Roles of the Principal

■ principals as colleagues

Link to more information about the roles of the principal from the website.

New teachers' relationships with their principals are not so one-dimensional, however. School principals loom quite large in the lives of beginning teachers, and the teacher-principal relationship (as well as relationships with vice principals, department heads, and master teachers) is many-faceted. The principal is, first, a *colleague,* a fellow educator joined with you in the common task of bringing civilization to the young. You are both professionals. You are both part of a common tradition. You probably share common goals (such as improving the educational opportunities of children) and attitudes (for example, that people engaged in the important work of educating the young need more support from the public than they receive). But there is more to this relationship.

■ as leaders

Principals are the *official leaders.* They make decisions or act as the funnel for the decisions of higher authorities. Decisions made by teachers or students are normally checked with principals. Principals speak for the school community to the superintendent, the press, and the local citizens. Nothing is ever quite "official" unless the principal has been involved.

■ as helpers

Principals are *helpers.* They can dispense information and materials, and, as experienced teachers, they are sources of tips, shortcuts, and helpful suggestions. Principals also visit classrooms and hold conferences with teachers, especially new teachers. They are there to aid beginning teachers who are encountering difficulties and confusion.

■ as policymakers

Principals are *policymakers.* A school system is a bureaucracy whose long arm extends from the state commissioner of education to the local district superintendent of schools to the individual school principal. The long arm is, in fact, educational policy, the ideas that are supposed to direct what happens in a school and, more specifically, in your classroom. Principals, in effect, act on behalf of the bureaucracy by introducing teachers to the policies and monitoring the policies' implementation. In addition, principals often set their own policies unique to their school building, such as discipline and dress codes, assembly activities, and a character education program.

■ as crisis managers

Principals are *crisis managers.* When something happens that a teacher cannot handle, the principal's office is where he or she naturally turns for help. A principal needs to know about crises in the school to try to deal with them effectively.

■ as facilitators

Principals are *facilitators.* Schools run on things: pencils, books, paper, heat, hot lunches, sanitary toilets, lights, construction paper, petty cash, and keys. It is the principal's job to keep teachers supplied so that they, in turn, can carry out the aims of the school.

■ as dispensers of rewards

Principals are *reward dispensers.* Principals assign classes to teachers, deciding what kind of children they will teach and whether the children will be at the level or in the subject for which particular teachers are prepared. Principals also assign teachers to extracurricular activities. They can also give or withhold compliments on teacher performance and give or withhold extracurricular duty assignments.

■ as judges

Principals are *judges.* Principals make the decision about a new teacher's qualifications to teach in their school and later decide whether the teacher's performance merits rehiring him or her. After all, first-year teachers are neither permanent members of the faculty nor permanently licensed members of the teaching profession. Principals can write recommendations for or against teachers. They can enhance or destroy people's reputations as teachers. This role of judge is one that new teachers often don't appreciate until it is too late.

as buffers

Principals act as *buffers* between teachers and angry parents (or, occasionally, angry students). Teachers can be quite vulnerable to public attack. Parents hear tales from their children or from other parents and, if they have a question or a complaint to make against a teacher, often go directly to the principal and not to the teacher. The principal is the official "complaint department." This is a delicate position, requiring the principal to be open and responsive to complaints and at the same time support the position of the teacher involved. Such situations call for the skills of high diplomacy.

as sacrificial lambs

Finally, principals are the *sacrificial lambs.* If the community, the teachers, or the school board become dissatisfied with what is going on in a particular school, the school's principal is vulnerable. No one suggests replacing the students or the parents! The tenured staff cannot be dismissed (except under very special circumstances). Thus, the principal, who may or may not be responsible for the reported problem, is likely to be chosen to pay the penalty. The ease with which the principal can be dismissed is, incidentally, a characteristic shared with beginning teachers.

multiple roles

The need to wear all these hats makes for a complicated existence. Today's school principal has a most difficult job, and to do the job well requires the strengths of a field general, a philosopher, a psychiatrist, and a saint. In light of the general shortage of these strengths, it is not surprising that new teachers sometimes find themselves in conflict with their principals. Principals have to make many quick and difficult decisions, often with insufficient information or time, and they are sometimes wrong. When principals observe in teachers' classrooms, they may appear to be there as *helpers,* but they cannot put aside their role as *judges.* At some time in the future, they must make recommendations about teachers to their superiors, and they obviously are influenced by what they have seen during their "helping" observations.

different priorities

Therefore, confusion and potential conflict between the administrator and the new teacher may be expected. In addition, beginning teachers often do not

You Know You're in Trouble When . . .

- You have threatened that if there is one more sound in the classroom, you will personally call every parent to complain—and you hear a sound.

- The principal asks you what you plan to be doing next year.

- You have your students correct their own tests and the lowest mark in the class is 96 percent. And they are smirking.

- It is 10:15 A.M., and the class has ripped through three-quarters of the work you have prepared for the day.

- You return after being sick for three days, and the students chant, "We want the substitute!"

- It feels like February, and it's only late September.

- The teacher across the hall comes in and offers to show your kids how to behave.

- The parents of eleven of your students ask to see the principal, and you are not invited.

- Unsolicited, your principal offers to write a recommendation for your placement file.

- You are convinced you have finally come up with challenging and interesting work for your class, and when you present it, they chorus, "We did that last year."

- After sitting in your class for five minutes, your supervisor starts to look at the clock.

- You walk into your usually noisy classroom, and immediately all the students get in their seats and smile at you.

know how to work in a bureaucracy (that is, make it work for their ends), and sometimes are antibureaucratic, or overly critical and complaining. This can lead them into direct conflict with their administrators, whose job it is to train beginners in bureaucratic procedures and whose *primary responsibility* it is to make sure that the school, as a totality, runs smoothly. Amid these many roles the administrator plays, slippage and breakdown can occur. The following account illustrates such a case.

Case Study	**Steve Mellonwood/Junior High Science**

During the special orientation meeting for new teachers, the principal told us all that whenever we have a problem we should come and see him. He didn't expect us to be perfect, and he felt his major job was to help new teachers. Later that week, he stopped me in the hall and warmly repeated his offer of help. I really took him at his word. So in early October, when I started having trouble planning and finding materials, I just went to see the principal. He was very cordial and, although he talked a lot about himself, he did give me some fairly helpful advice. I went to see him for three short visits. Just talking the problems out seemed to help. I started finding good materials, and my classes really improved. I felt I was really doing well, and I couldn't wait to get to school in the morning.

■ error of first impressions

Then, in early December, I started getting treated in an odd way by some of the senior teachers. They were always asking me whether they could help (sort of like I had some incurable disease), and could they get me a glass of water. It was weird. Finally, I asked two of them in the lunchroom, "Why all the concern?" Well, it came out that the principal had told them that I was having "big trouble," and he had told a number of the senior teachers to do what they could for me. He had not been in to observe me once.

Later in the year he came in for two brief observations (to conform to minimum standards in our district), and he never had time for a conference. He did, however, write up supervisor conference reports. They were lukewarmish and had no specifics. He did mention in both reports that I was improving and overcoming early problems. What improvement? What problems? All he had to go by was what I told him. I got so mad that I wrote him a note to the effect that my self-reported problems had cleared up some time ago and that I felt my teaching was better than his report had indicated. I could see the writing on the wall, though. I started looking for another position and got one without too much trouble. I liked the kids in my first school and many of the teachers. Somehow, though, early on, I had put myself in a box for the principal, and he wasn't going to let me out. ■

An error of first impressions can also work the other way: the administrator who seems severe and distant can turn out to be warm and supportive, as described in the following case.

Case Study	**Victoria Klarfeld/Fourth Grade**

Quite honestly, I was afraid of Mrs. Kelly when I first went for interviews. She seemed so businesslike and talked so much about high standards that I was sure that even if I got the job, I'd end up disappointing her. And after a few weeks with my fourth-grade wigglers, I was afraid I'd never get them to settle down and work on tasks. I was wrong on both counts. The kids settled down—some too much—so that now my biggest problem is getting them excited and alive. And, boy, was I really way off on Mrs. Kelly! She is a jewel! She has so many ideas and gives them to me in the nicest way. I never feel I have to use her suggestions, but in fact I think I've used every one.

■ solid professional support

But what has meant the most is that she has treated me like an adult, a professional. Here I am, right out of college, and she is asking my advice about assembly programs and what to do about the cliques in our school. She has also made sure that the other teachers don't leave me out of things. I'm the only new teacher in the building this year, and they sometimes forget me. Mrs. Kelly has a great way of weaving me into things.

I got very overtired and generally strung out after the Christmas vacation. I was depressed about my teaching and how little time or energy I had for any kind of social life. One day Mrs. Kelly intercepted me on my way to the lunchroom and took me around the corner to a sandwich shop. She knew exactly what was wrong with me and got right to the point, giving me super tips on how to organize my time and plan more efficiently. She even started me on a vitamin program that seems to give me much more energy. She has been terrific to me. She's made the year for me. ■

As the case above indicates, principals (and others who have supervisory responsibility over the beginning teachers, such as lead teachers and department- and grade-level chairpersons) can be a crucial source of professional expertise and moral support. In addition, research shows that supportive administrators actually help teachers to become reflective and solve their own problems.[3] But new teachers need to be proactive and not wait for the help to come to them. Among the potential kinds of help that administrators or supervisors can provide are the following:

■ types of help from administrators

- They may have valuable advice on dealing with specialized problems, such as an extremely reticent student.
- They can put you in contact with specialists in your building or elsewhere in the school district to help you on a range of issues, from curricular matters to dealing with disruptive students.
- They may be able to do demonstration lessons or special presentations in your class.
- They may be able to come to your classroom, observe you in action, and provide focused feedback on your early efforts to carry out a strategy such as cooperative learning.

While we suggest you seek help from administrators and supervisors, we also urge prudence. Do it honestly, directly, and somewhat sparingly.

▶ Peers: A Mixed Blessing

New teachers are vulnerable to many outside forces and also to their own insecurities. If a supportive administrator can turn a potentially disastrous year into a year of growth, a beginning teacher's professional peers can be even more influential in the process of learning how to teach and how to survive in the classroom. The following example is a case in point.

Case Study

Catherine Foley/Sixth Grade

I had a hard time finding a teaching job. I had hoped to teach in my hometown, but there were just no jobs at the level I wanted to teach. The best job was on the other side of the state, and when it became clear that there were no jobs on the local horizon, I took it. I was very excited about teaching; I really felt that I was starting out on an adventure. I was, however, also moving away from my parents. Being so far away from home meant that there were lots of things that were going to be new to me. I had to get a car, an apartment, establish a bank account, and take care of lots of other things—all at once. It was literally like a crash course in being an adult. And that's what I felt like right from the beginning: an adult. It was so different from college and even student teaching. At my school, people treated me like an adult, and they expected me to act like one. For the first months I felt as if I was play-acting at being a grown-up. Well, now I guess the role is comfortable, or maybe I just have my act down pat.

Although I made friends with a few people in my apartment building, I was really very lonely at first. I don't think I would have made it without Joan Silver. Joan teaches in the classroom next to mine. She's been, as she says, "in the trenches" for eighteen years, but she's got more ideas and energy and dedication than any of us fresh troops. Joan was a lifesaver for me. She took me under her wing even before school started. She has been a source of ideas, great materials, and inspiration, and she has never made me feel like a taker or a leech. *I* actually taught *her* some things! That's one of the reasons I admired her so much. She really wanted to know about the new ideas I had learned in my education courses, and she put a lot of them to work in her class.

■ emotional support

I guess we talked every day after school. A lot of the time, we just spent the hour after school laughing. A couple of times the janitor came in thinking there was something wrong, but what he found was the two of us broken up with laughter. And about once a month she would drag me home for dinner. Joan always seemed to know when I was a little low, and that's when she'd insist that I come home with her for dinner.

There's so much to learn in the first year, and not just about subject matter. Important things, like how to get information from the school secretary and how to stay on the right side of the janitor, that you can never learn in education courses. Joan was my guide on everything from how to fill out my planbook to which memos from the front office I had to pay attention to and which I could put in what she called the "circular file."

It seems funny to say this, given the fact that Joan is twenty years older than I am, but I really think she's my best friend. She certainly has made this year a terrific one for me. I hope that during my career, I can mentor other new teachers in the same way. ■

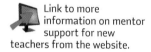 Link to more information on mentor support for new teachers from the website.

Although there is increasing cooperation among teachers and greater access to specialists and aides, for the most part, teachers work independently in their own classrooms and with their own students. When they are engaged in their professional work, they typically are isolated from one another. Although administrators are the official source of support and help for beginners, fellow teachers are a much more accessible and less threatening source of support. As the preceding case illustrates, a teacher's colleagues can be a powerful influence, especially in the beginning. They can be an ever-ready source of ideas and teaching tips and can initiate the newcomer into the customs of the school. Like Joan Silver, a peer can be an inspiration and show by example what the phrase *teacher as professional* means.

■ colleagues more accessible than principals

■ possible negative influence

On the other hand, other teachers can have a negative influence, undermining a beginning teacher's idealism, lowering his or her standards, and offering no help at all. The teachers' lounge is sometimes the venue for serious disillusionment. Many teachers use the lounge to "unwind." Unwinding often involves harsh criticism of students, mockery of administrators, and negative comments about teaching. Although not especially different from similar "off-camera" remarks in hospitals and businesses, such comments in the teachers' lounge can blunt the new teacher's idealism and enthusiasm. The lounge is a source of much learning for beginners, but in some cases the private side of colleagues can be a rude awakening for them.

Although we strongly believe that the teaching profession has a larger percentage of dedicated, selfless people than any other profession (except, perhaps, the ministry), it also has its share of rogues and fools. Beginners should pick their way carefully among this field of new colleagues.

► Instruction: So Much to Learn

■ children's success most important

Ultimately, a teacher's only real problem is his or her students' failure to learn and to develop. All other conflicts, triumphs, and defeats pale in significance if the children are learning and developing their human potential. The degree of the children's success as learners is the best measure of a teacher's success or failure. Although the closeness of the relationship between a teacher's instruction and a student's learning is often overstated, this relationship is crucial. Teacher effectiveness is an area in which there are few naturals. New teachers generally have much to learn in this area of instruction.

One major difficulty is the sheer newness of the role of teacher. After a little student teaching, you suddenly find yourself totally immersed. You are in charge of your own class and responsible for taking it from the first day of school to the last. One particularly vexing problem for the beginning teacher is the search for effective curricular materials, as the following example illustrates.

Grace Joyce/Third Grade

Case Study

Link to lesson plan ideas from the website.

The overriding question of this year has been "What works?" I'm in a constant search for materials. It is never-ending. My kids aren't especially brilliant, but they devour material and look at me as if to say, "Well, what's next?" Our school's curriculum guide is only five years old, but it is terribly dated. The students know a lot of the stuff already. They learned it in lower grades or just picked it up. They are bored by a good bit of the rest, too. I'm constantly squeezing ideas and tips from the other third-grade teachers. They are helpful, but they are in the same boat I am. Sometimes I get a big buildup on a particular workbook or special unit by a teacher who had fabulous success with it. I try it, and I fall on my face with it. Then there are the kids. They are so fickle! A couple of times, I took their suggestions on things they wanted to study and work on. After much work and many late hours, I'd get these classes prepared and the very same kids who were so anxious to make the suggestions couldn't have cared less.

■ "owning" your own materials

My school district has curriculum specialists. Some of them are very good, too. Particularly the math specialist. He would give me *too* much material. I'd spend hours deciding about which approach to use to teach ten minutes' worth of material. The language arts specialist was a sweet lady but very rarely available, and most of her ideas were really out to lunch. I was on my own there. When you get right down to it, you have to make the curriculum and the materials *yours* before they are any good to you. Someone else's great materials are nothing until you have made them your own. This is hard to do the first year. ■

Though the curricular and instructional aspect of teaching can be a thicket of difficulty for many beginners, for others it is very exciting and inspiring.

Nicholas Briggs/Middle School Social Studies

Case Study

School has always been hard for me. But then again, if the truth be known, I've always worked hard. In high school I really got turned on to history, and I think it was then that I decided to become a teacher. In college I took every history course I could. I was way

In this class, a new teacher's creative lesson on DNA is paying off in student interest. (© Bob Daemmrich)

over the required number of history courses for certification. And I was lucky to teach at a very academic high school as a student teacher. I think I did well, too. At least that's what everyone said.

I was really disappointed when I couldn't find any openings as a history teacher. I was getting very discouraged until I was finally offered a middle school job in the same school district where I had done my student teaching. My first thought was to let it go and wait for a "real" history job. What they wanted me to teach was social studies. There was some history involved, but there was also a lot of other social science material to teach. What I really wanted to teach were modern European history and the rise and fall of totalitarianism, and what they wanted was what seemed to me pretty low-level stuff. I was ready to hang it up. I could possibly work for the company my dad works for, or I could go back to school. Well, anyway, I decided I'd give middle school teaching a chance.

■ relearning one's subject

The great surprise of teaching for me was not the kids or anything like that. It was, on the one hand, how little I knew about my strength—history—and, on the other hand, how intellectually exciting teaching in general can be. I had taken tons of history courses and considered myself a super buff, but I had missed the essential meaning of history. That's what I have been learning these first two years, and it has been as stimulating as anything in my life. Now I feel I'm just beginning to understand the purpose of history and what should be taught. I came to teach and probably ended up learning more than my students.

But how do I feel at the end of each day? I feel proud of my students. I feel more knowledgeable about living, teaching, and learning. I feel lucky to be a teacher. I feel . . . full of sparks.

—IRASEMA ORTEGA-CRAWFORD

Incidentally, I was offered the position I thought I really wanted, a position on the high school history faculty. I turned it down. I couldn't be happier than I am here. ■

▶ Students: Friends or Fiends?

Becoming comfortable and sensing that one is effective with children is a major concern for a new teacher, as it well should be—students are the main event! They make the good days good and the bad days bad. The relationship between teacher and students is multifaceted. An important aspect of the relationship is based on how well the students are achieving.

Eileen Black/Fifth Grade

Case Study

■ a moment of panic

I have enjoyed my students this year, probably more than I should have. The only real down moment I had came right toward the end of the year. Something one of the sixth-grade teachers said really shook my confidence. She made some comment at lunch about how much fun-and-games was going on in my class. All of a sudden I began thinking that, although I was having a great time, maybe the kids were having a great time and not really learning anything. I tried to think of what I had taught them that was really important, and my mind was blank. I tried to think of particular students who I thought had really shown a lot of progress, and I couldn't think of anyone specific. I went around that way for a couple of days, and I got sort of panicky.

■ realization of student progress

Finally, almost by accident, I came across one of the student's notebooks, which had all of his work from September, even his diagnostic tests. It was really enlightening. I could almost see the change from week to week in what he knew. The problems became more difficult, but he could master them. His compositions became more interesting, and the mechanics became sounder. His handwriting looked so much more mature. I figured, though, that maybe that was just one student. I asked to look at a few other students' notebooks, and there it was. They had changed. They were different. Not just different but *better*. And I was an important part of that change. ■

It's not what the teacher does that's important. It's what the teacher gets the children to do.

—PHIL SCHLECTY

There can be little doubt, however, that although students are the primary source of a teacher's success, they can also be a source of failure. Three areas in particular cause problems: discipline, social distance, and sex. Behind each of these areas of difficulty is an inaccurate set of expectations the teacher holds about students.

■ changing views of children

One indication of these out-of-line expectations is the sharp change in attitudes people experience as they go through teacher education and into their first years of classroom teaching. Studies have shown that the longer college students stay in teacher education programs, the more positive and warm their attitudes toward students become. But among beginning teachers, positive attitudes toward students drop sharply. In fact, beginning teachers score significantly lower on attitude inventories than students just entering teacher education. Before going on, take a moment to consider these results.

Pause and Reflect

1 ► What are some of your hypotheses about why beginning teachers' attitudes change in this way?

2 ► Can you recall experiencing a new teacher's swing in attitude toward your class? What accounted for it?

Sources of a Distorted View

■ idealism

Our experience in working with college students (for more years than we care to report) convinces us that most students who are preparing to become teachers have high ideals in general and become particularly idealistic about children and education during their preparation. They believe that as teachers they should have warm relations with students, and they want to make the classroom more relaxed and more responsive to the needs of students than it is normally. As college students take more education courses and observe in classrooms, their views of children become more idealistic and, as a result, more positive. By graduation, the rose-colored glasses are firmly affixed.

The class clowns who were so amusing to you in high school are often a very different story when they reappear in your classroom.
(© Elizabeth Crews)

■ skewed view of students

Also, college students have managed to shut out memories of many realities of their own childhood and adolescence. They forget things like the time they joined with the other seventh-graders to put four tacks on Miss Derriere's chair. They blot out all the juicy stories other students have told about the young physical education teacher, even though they knew most were untrue. They forget about how they enjoyed reading (or writing) obscenities about their math teacher on the lavatory wall. They forget how cruel kids can be to kids. Somehow the dark side of human nature recedes from view during teacher education. But fear not; it reappears. Beginning teachers rediscover human fallibility, in their students and in themselves, and all too often, the sad result is that their positive attitudes toward children plummet.

Normally, positive attitudes make a comeback, although they rarely regain the heights they reached during the latter stages of teacher preparation. Nevertheless, the beginner's unrealistic expectations are a great source of his or her problems. And although problems of this kind abound, we will look at just the three areas mentioned earlier: discipline, social distance, and sex.

Classroom Management

Classroom management, classroom control, or discipline (pick your euphemism) is one of those problems that shouldn't exist. After all, school is an opportunity for children. The teacher works hard to help them. It's simple: the teacher is there to teach, and students are there to learn. Unfortunately, though, things do not work out that way.

The great majority of schools, whether kindergartens or high schools, are organized with the expectation that the teacher will be "in charge" of the class. You may not like this, but there are things you can do about it. (For example, zero-tolerance policies in many schools regarding weapons or illegal substances take some of the burden of enforcement off teachers.) But it is still what is generally expected of a teacher by the children, your teacher-peers, and the administration. (We will return to this mat-

The video case *Managing Elementary Classrooms: Basic Techniques* shows how two teachers at different levels keep things flowing smoothly in their classes. As you watch the clips and study the artifacts in the case, reflect upon the following questions:

1. This teacher mentions the importance of starting the day off well, which she accomplishes with morning meeting. In this chapter of the book, the authors also offer seven tips for starting off the school year well. Based on your own educational experiences, what, if any, "don'ts" would you suggest for the beginning of the day or school year?

2. Which of the administrator's roles, described earlier in this chapter, seems to best describe the principal shown in this case? How can the tone set by administrators make it easier or more difficult for a new teacher to maintain classroom discipline?

■ students expect discipline

ter of expectations in the section on social distance in this chapter.) Few (and lucky) are the teachers who do not have to come to grips with their role as disciplinarian.

■ lack of leadership background

■ **Unaccustomed to Being in Charge**   A discipline problem occurs when the expected orderly pattern of classroom behavior is violated. Normally, a breach of discipline is an overt act by one or more students that distracts attention from or interrupts the performance of the task at hand. Few teacher-education students of traditional college age have had much opportunity to be "in charge," give orders, coordinate the activities of a group of people, or say such things as "Quiet down!" or "Stay in your seat!" Students, on the other hand, are accustomed to being taught by experienced teachers who know how to control them, usually rather effortlessly.

Teaching is leaving a vestige of yourself in the development of another. And surely the student is a bank where you can deposit your most precious treasures.

—EUGENE P. BERTIN

Students can sense uncertainty and hesitancy in a new teacher. Moreover, school is not fun-and-games for children. They can get restless and bored. (Remember how long the school day was when you were in elementary and secondary school, how long you had to sit still at a stretch, and how much you had to do that didn't interest you.) These conditions, plus the potential for friction in any group of so many people, make it almost inevitable that first-year teachers will have some trouble establishing the kind of productive relationship with students that they seek.

As we have implied, many new teachers start out with a rather idealized picture of children as victims. They assume that misbehavior is a result of some condition external to the child, such as a disruptive home life or poverty. Often there is the suggestion that something in the teacher's class provokes or brings forth the problem. If only the teacher would "establish the right environment" or "reach out to the child in just the right way" the problem would be solved. This view is a subset of a larger view that people are not capable of evil, only social arrangements are capable of evil—an idea that had many adherents in education at one time and still has some advocates today. This idea that all children are innately good, combined with the first-year teacher's insecurities and search for approval, makes it difficult for many to deal confidently with their role as disciplinarian. (See Kevin and Jim's Suggestions for Classroom Management Problems and Table 6.1, "Different Approaches to Classroom Management," both in the chapter entitled "What Makes a Teacher Effective?")

Case Study

■ faulty assumptions

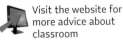
Visit the website for more advice about classroom management.

Carole Foster/Fourth Grade

I was convinced that a good class was a happy class and that I wasn't going to be like those grouchy teachers I remember from my own elementary school. So, in the first part of the year, I let a lot of small infractions go unnoticed: talking during silent reading period, lateness on assignments, yelling out the window to students on the playground, and the like. It was a little hard on my nerves, but I thought I was establishing an open and creative environment. It soon became clear that it was open but not particularly creative. In fact, I first discovered reality when a friendly parent suggested that the room was too noisy and disorderly for the children to get their work done. I tried to "tighten up," but the students were already used to my "open and creative" environment. I just couldn't get them to settle down.

Finally, the straw that broke the camel's back—and almost broke mine—was when the principal came in to observe. The kids behaved horribly. I felt as if they were trying to make me look bad. Whatever their intentions, the situation was not lost on the principal.

"HECKUVA DAY, WASN'T IT, MS. CARPENTER?
NO HARD FEELIN'S ?"

© James Estes

During the follow-up conference, he was very frank with me, telling me that if I couldn't maintain better discipline, he might have to "relieve" me. One thing I particularly remember him saying was, "Carole, if you can't *keep* school, you can't *teach* school." Then he gave me some specific suggestions. Even with those good suggestions, though, I had a very difficult time working my way back in charge and establishing a more civil and orderly classroom. Next year things will be different! ■

In the video case *Managing Secondary Classrooms: Basic Techniques* a teacher discusses the classroom management challenges he faces, and we see his class in action, showing how he overcomes these challenges. As you watch the clips and study the artifacts in the case, reflect upon the following questions:

1. This teacher echoes the point made in this chapter that teachers should maintain a consistent social distance, either relaxed or strict. How does his teaching demonstrate this?

2. How does this teacher demonstrate that he is "in charge," as described in this chapter?

3. What is the most important piece of advice this video case offered for you, as a preservice teacher?

Social Distance

Establishing an appropriate **social distance** from students occupies a good deal of a beginning teacher's attention and energy. Like disciplinary techniques, a correct social distance does not come with a teaching license or one's first job. In the accompanying box, we give you some advice on how beginning teachers can begin developing the appropriate distance on the very first day of school.

Beginning teachers often take refuge in the two extremes of behavior. Many hide their insecurities by acting harshly strict and extremely businesslike, sometimes bordering on hostile. Others attempt to be completely "natural." They reject the stiff, "teacher" image and seek to break down all barriers between themselves and their students. The first extreme, the overly strict teacher, can give rise to long-term difficulties, whereas the "natural" teacher usually has short-term problems.

The problem with playing the role of the overly strict, aloof teacher is that it may become a permanent habit. Acting like a Prussian officer may appeal to a hidden need to make others submissive. Also, one may begin to believe that "a quiet class is a good class."

Kevin and Jim's Guide to the First Day of School

In many areas of life, from job interviews to dating, first impressions are powerful. So too is this the case at the beginning of the school year. With that in mind, we offer a few tips we have picked up along the way.

1. *Teach your very best lesson.* Often teachers use the first day for filling out forms, assigning lockers, and essential but boring "administrivia." Such a day can set a tone for the students that this is going to be just like all the other years, like all the other classes. On the other hand, students will be fresh from the summer, carrying renewed expectations that this year may be different. Capitalizing on this attitude with a really interesting lesson will create important momentum for your class. You can catch up on the forms and other items later in the week.

2. *Establish class rules and procedures.* Although a good lesson is most important, getting classroom management under control cannot be stressed too much. On the first day, at least, let your students know you plan to have an orderly classroom with rules that foster respect and a healthy work environment. We do not imply that you lay down the law but that you let your students know that any group needs to have clear rules and you are open to their suggestions or even codetermination of the rules.

3. *Start learning and using students' names.* As soon as you receive your class lists or rosters, start familiarizing yourself with the students' names. Once you meet your students, start matching names with faces and, whenever possible, use their names. Nothing signals your interest in them and being on top of the situation like using their names on day one.

4. *Be friendly but businesslike.* Often the insecurities of new teachers get the best of them. They vacillate between being Mr. or Ms. Nice Guy and Attila the Disciplinarian. The beginning teacher's early commitment to a friendly but task-oriented atmosphere is the key to its realization.

5. *Share with students your vision for the year ahead.* Students want to succeed. Even the ones with a history of difficulty with other teachers want the new school year to be better. Don't tell them how hard they are going to work. Tell them how much they are going to know at the end of the year and what they can do with this new knowledge.

6. *Establish procedures for communicating with parents.* You need parental support, and students want to know whether you'll contact parents about both good and bad events. Tell them you see their parents as your partners, as your coteachers.

■ overly strict behavior

■ overly "natural" behavior

The problem confronting overly "natural" teachers is that their view of natural behavior often clashes with the children's. The students expect their teacher to interact with them in certain recognizable ways; that is, they expect a certain degree of social distance. They are confused or put off when the teacher acts like "one of the gang." The crux of the problem, then, is that the beginning teacher often wants to be a friend or a pal, whereas the students expect and want the teacher to be an adult. Because they are uncertain and striving to be adults themselves, students seek strength and maturity in their teachers. Often they interpret the beginning teacher's efforts at naturalness and informality as weakness.

Case Study

Jane Candis/Middle School Math

Most of my year was spent alternating between being Wanda the Witch and sweet little Miss Muffet. I started out determined to be different from all those cold teachers I had growing up. I was going to be everyone's sweet Big Sister. I really was surprised when this didn't work. The children didn't respond. If anything, they seemed to be confused. Some of them started treating me like their big sister, and I found myself getting annoyed. They became very familiar and started asking me all sorts of embarrassing questions such as "Are you going on a date this weekend?" or "Did you ever do drugs in college?" both in and out of class. The final straw came when one of my boys—one of my favorites, too—came up to me in the hall while I was talking to a senior teacher. Smiling, he patted me on the back and said, "How's it going, Miss Candis?" I was mortified.

■ first-year insecurities

After that little incident, I became tough. I was all business. If anyone got close to being familiar, I cut them off at the knees. I really said some nasty things. I was just so uptight that I overreacted. I guess I was hurt that my Big Sister routine didn't work. Later I realized that one reason behind my wanting to be Big Sister was simply that I wanted to be liked, at any cost. I guess my insecurities led me to seek approval from my students. Anyway, I spent most of the year going back and forth on this issue—one week being Wanda and the next being Miss Muffet. It was really a strain for both me and the kids. Finally, toward the end of the year, things began to straighten out and I stopped playing a role. It was much more fun that way. I think everyone was relieved. ■

Pause and Reflect

1 ▶ Have you considered the issue of social distance between teacher and students? How much social distance do you believe is appropriate for you?

2 ▶ What are your ideas about how to establish effective discipline in a classroom?

3 ▶ Do you anticipate that classroom control will be a strength or weakness for you?

Sex

■ teacher-student attraction

Sexual attraction and romance between students, and even between teachers, is alive and well in the American school. And most people recognize this. But the idea of sexual attraction or romance between students and teachers generally remains a serious taboo subject. (Except, of course, on TV and the movies!) In fact, there is no surer way to quickly and unhappily end your career than becoming, or even appearing to become, romantically involved with a student.

Beginning teachers are more likely than experienced ones to confront this problem. For one thing, many of them are nearer in age to the students. For another, they are often single, new to the community, and lonely. The strain of the new job may increase their need for affection, and this need may find expression in their relationships with students.

In the same way, students often become attracted to their teachers. They sometimes get what is best described as a "crush" on their teachers, becoming emotionally attached to them, greeting them eagerly in the morning, sending them personal emails and walking them to their cars after school. This too can be a very awkward situation in that the student wants to be treated as special and to feel that the affection is reciprocated. If the teacher rejects or embarrasses the student, the student can be hurt deeply.

Besides the platonic attachments teachers can form to young children, a twenty-two-year-old teacher quite conceivably can find a sixteen-year-old student sexually attractive. Thus, as the following account indicates, high school teachers are particularly vulnerable to sexual attraction or manipulation. Our only advice in this area is an emphatic *don't*.

Case Study

Gary Cornog/High School English

In one class, there dwelt a fair young creature who found me to be an easily flustered appreciator of her many charms. She was a coquette and, to my way of thinking, a dangerous one. She had me at a great disadvantage. While she could liltingly ask special favors of me (such as my continued toleration of her misbehavior in class), I could not cope with her in anything like a spontaneous way. Unless I was in a phenomenally commanding mood, I could expect to hear such daily entreaties as "Oh, Mr. Cornog! Mr. Cornog! Could you come here and help me?" or "Mr. Cornog, I just don't understand!" (All this spoken in a voice of tender urgency.) She would have her left arm raised, her right arm aiding it, and would be leaning forward and upward from her desk so that (I thought) I would not fail to notice her finer endowments (I didn't).

"What is it, Julie?" I would reply, hoping the fear in my heart would not be evident in my voice. It nearly always was.

"Mr. Cornog, there's something here I don't understand. Could you come here and look at it?"

"Don't," I tell myself. *Don't.*

"Read it to me and I'll explain it." (*From here,* I almost added, but that would be too obvious.) No. She's getting up.

"I'll bring it up there."

■ flirtation

She approaches. She arrives at my left side. I note a scent of lemony perfume; an attempt at makeup about the eyes. She leans over to place the book in front of me, and some of her long dark hair grazes my shoulder. By this time I feel thoroughly unwilling to answer any question regarding syntax. *What about private tutoring?* I hear my lecherous innards suggesting. Heaven forbid! My frustration causes me to blurt a response to her query, hoping that she'll return to her seat. The class, by this time, has observed me melting into a limpid pool behind the desk. She must be smiling triumphantly above me, her glory reflected in my devastation.

If only she had been as innocent of malice in her manipulations as I had been tender in my innocence, then all would have been well. Alas, she was not. She thought it great sport to exercise her arts for the benefit of her friends, and I could think of no way to break the spell. I could not ignore her, because then the class would notice my attempt and think that she had really gotten to me. I could not allow her to continue to dominate me, for then the respect I sought would never appear. Who could respect a hen-pecked English teacher? The befuddled teacher doing battle with the temptress every day—what a tableau! What a cliché. It pained me to see myself in such a humiliating posture. It was so absurd.[4] ■

■ experience as authority figure helps

Some first-year teachers become terribly discouraged by their relationships with students. Most of us teach because we like young people and want to work with them. When we are rejected or make fools of ourselves, it is painful. Developing satisfying relationships with students usually involves some initial uncertainty. Most problems with students are a result of inexperience, and the majority of second-year teachers find that most of their previous problems disappear and they feel very much at ease with their students. Experience with children before beginning teaching—as a parent, camp counselor, settlement house worker, or tutor—can also help you learn about how you relate best to children and ease the transition.

▶ Parents: Natural Allies with Different Agendas

■ shared goals

The parent and the teacher are natural partners. Both are working to help the child become a more fully developed person, and both want the child to be happy, sensitive, intelligent, and well balanced. Sometimes, though, the relationship between teacher and parent runs amok and the natural allies become antagonists. Instead of devoting their energies toward understanding and aiding the child, they waste them on conflict with each other.

■ Link to advice for working with parents from the website.

The great majority of parent-teacher conferences are cordial, constructive, and characterized by mutual respect. Although there may be initial problems of perception or communication, the parents' and teacher's shared interest in the child is enough to overcome these minor blocks. However, problems do develop, and they are not always the fault of the parents.

Case Study	## Walter Connor/High School History

In the late winter, we had our annual parents' night. All the teachers were to work with students on displays and projects. And, of course, we had to get lots of students' work up on the board. The drab old school building looked like the Rose Bowl Parade by the big night.

We met the parents in our rooms and gave them an overview of what we were doing for the year. I thought I would be nervous, but somehow I wasn't. I was so distracted and fascinated by their faces. I never suspected that they would look so much like their kids! Or rather, vice versa.

When I finished my talk, I handed out folders of the children's work and told the parents I would be happy to talk with them individually. Most of my students had been doing fairly well, so most of the evening went well. The parents of my two prize ding-a-lings didn't show, an event I greeted with mixed emotions.

One set of parents hung back. I hadn't met them yet, but I knew immediately who they were. They were Bill Russell's parents. Bill is a great big happy kid. He is not bright, and he is quite lazy. All he likes to do is play his guitar, which he is pretty good with. The only time I have gotten any work from him was during a unit on the Civil War. I persuaded him to look up the folk songs and marching chants of the Civil War. He gave a "singing and strumming" report to the class. But after that—nothing! (Bill was carrying something between a D and an F at that time.) Well, the Russells asked a lot of questions, and I stayed with the straight-facts-no-sugar-coating approach, which I was convinced was the right approach. Then Mr. Russell glanced anxiously at his wife, looked over his shoulder to see that none of the other parents was within earshot, and said, "Tell me, Mr. Connor. We're both college men. My son, Bill. . . . I–Is he . . . you know . . . college material?"

I didn't know what to say, so I said, "What do you mean?"

"We just want to know if we should be saving to send him to college. Is he . . . you know . . . college material?"

■ honesty to a fault

All I thought of was that here was a guy who really wanted a straight answer, so I said, "Well, no. I don't think so." Then I looked at Mrs. Russell. I should have looked at her before answering. After the tears came the hostility. "How dare you prejudge my boy! Bill was right! Admit it, you don't like Bill. You are trying to ruin his chances. We work hard to raise our only son, and then some young know-it-all teacher ruins everything!"

Underneath the hysteria, which subsided in about five long minutes, she was right. I was way off base. I had no right to make that judgment. I had known their son for a half year in one course that clearly didn't interest him much. I didn't have enough data.

Well, I made another appointment with them. During that meeting, I saw the frightening intensity of their desire to get my class's number-one guitar player into college. Some good things came out of this conference. Bill's work picked up. He actually ended the year with a C. I was the one who learned a good lesson, though. Wanting to be honest doesn't mean arrogantly abandoning good judgment. ■

The sources of teacher-parent problems are the same as those involved in any human relationship, but encounters are more highly charged than in most relationships. This is to be expected because a child and his or her future are at issue. The following account of Brenda's mother and a new teacher illustrates some of the dynamics that are usually hidden from view.

Case Study	# Ruth Billsbury/Sixth Grade

It happened in late March. Ten days earlier, Brenda's mother called me. She said she wanted to talk to me and asked if there was any day that I stayed late at school. She didn't get off work until 4:30 P.M. and couldn't make it to school until 5:15. I often worked late at school, and so I made an appointment for two days later.

I was curious about why she wanted to see me, and I began to worry. Brenda had something of a reputation in the school. In September, during the teachers' workshop before the opening day, two teachers "sympathized" with me when they heard I had Brenda Carson. They didn't go into great detail why, and I didn't want to ask. However, I was watching Brenda out of the corner of my eye during those first months, and I guess I paid particular attention to her. In recent months, there had been no problems, and I hadn't thought much about her—that is, until her mother called.

■ effects of divorce

Brenda's mother showed up right on time, and after a few pleasantries she said, "Well, I know you're busy, so I'll come right to the point. Three weeks after Brenda started kindergarten, Brenda's father and I separated. After a terrible on-again, off-again year, we decided to get a divorce. It was hard on both of us, but it was crushing for Brenda. She's an only child. Maybe she blamed herself for the breakup. I don't know. In any event, she went into a kind of tailspin. She was trouble at home, and she's been in trouble in school almost from the moment of the breakup. She's no genius, but she's bright enough to do better than she's done. She just dug in her little heels and wouldn't try. She wouldn't bring books home. She wouldn't do assignments. Every time I asked her about school, her standard answer was, 'I hate school.' Once I got working and my life started to settle down, we were able to make a life together. But the school situation was still rotten. None of the other girls played with her. She was never invited to any parties. I even suggested that she invite one of her classmates to stay overnight one Friday night, and the kid refused. We were both heartbroken.

"Then you came along. I don't know what you did to her, but you certainly have turned her around. I sensed it the first day of school. She came home with a funny look in her eye and said. 'This year is going to be different. I can just tell.' She wouldn't say why, but after a few days I guessed. She was continually talking about you—from what you said to her to what kind of car you drive. Honestly, one weekend when we were out grocery shopping, she made me drive by your apartment, she was so curious to find out what it looked like.

"And I guess you know how she's doing in school. I don't think she's missed her homework once. I'm sure she's not your best student, but I know she's doing pretty well, particularly considering the hole she was digging for herself. You look surprised at all this. I figured you might be. Brenda can really keep her feelings to herself when she wants to. But honestly, you have touched that girl in a special place. The difference in her is like night and day. You can't imagine what all this has meant to me. Her pain was my pain, and now it's gone away. Brenda even has friends now.

"Anyway, I just wanted you to know. I just wanted to see you and to thank you personally."

■ unexpected praise

Brenda's mother was out the door before I could respond. It was so unexpected; I don't know what I could have said anyway. That one event has given me a great, great deal to think about. ■

Reasons for Parent-Teacher Problems

The two case studies you have just read illustrate a number of reasons that parents and teachers may have a difficult relationship with each other or even fall into direct conflict.

■ differences in perception

1. *Varied perceptions.* Teachers and parents are quite likely to perceive the same phenomenon in very different ways. The nerve-frazzled teacher perceives a child as a wild, undisciplined, raucous menace. The parents perceive their child as energetic, spontaneous, and sociable. An apparently quiet, shy child may turn out to be a chatterbox in the security of home.

■ evaluation: a sensitive area

2. *Judgments on students.* Evaluation is another area of difficulty. It is part of the teacher's job to make judgments about a child's performance, a process that can touch on some deep insecurities. It can wound the parents' hopes and aspirations, particularly in this age of anxiety when parents see education as their children's royal road to success. In our competitive society, being average is taken by some as failure. For these reasons, the teacher needs to be especially sensitive when dealing with issues of evaluation and would do well to stay away from judgments such as students being "above average" or "below average" or comparing certain children with other students. (Remember Walter Connor above.)

■ social class and communication

3. *Differences of social class and experiences.* Issues of social distance have been at the hub of much parent-teacher antagonism in recent years. Because most teachers are middle class or aspiring to the middle class, they normally have relatively little trouble communicating with middle-class people. But when they deal with parents from a lower or higher socioeconomic class or a different ethnic group, or both, the potential for communication difficulties heightens. Upper-class parents can look down on public schools and treat teachers condescendingly. Poor parents may have had unfortunate and unpleasant experiences with schools and, as a result, regard them with fear or suspicion. Often, these parents speak a different language or dialect than the teacher. What the teacher sees as a humble classroom is to some parents, part of a huge, impersonal bureaucracy. In many urban areas, this impression of the school as a cold, unfriendly, and impersonal institution is supported by the evidence: the school doors are locked, and parents have to pass by police officers and assorted hall guards before receiving a pass to see the head secretary in order to see the teacher. The fact that many lower-class parents, as children, encountered prejudice in schools and found attendance at school more discouraging than helpful makes communication even more difficult.

■ mothers in workforce

4. *Overburdened parents.* Another factor, as we note in the chapter entitled "What Social Problems Affect Today's Students?," is the changing American family. Increasingly, mothers—who, in an earlier era, stayed home, kept house, and guided their children through school—have joined the workforce. Usually, it is very difficult for working parents to get off work to meet with their children's teachers or attend parent-teacher organization (PTO) meet-

ings and after-school functions that would put them in closer contact with teachers. Often these events are unwelcome chores in an already stressful life.

■ students' independence causes pain

5. *The pain of change.* Finally, going to school changes children. School, in fact, exists to help children change in specified ways: to read, to speak a foreign language, to solve problems. And students do change. They master things. They acquire confidence. Or they lose confidence. They become increasingly independent of their parents. Some parents rejoice at their child's growing freedom from them. For others, this process of independence is painful. Hearing her little girl talk about how much she loves her teacher may arouse jealousy in a mother and cause her to act hostile when she meets the teacher. When a high school student comes home from school with political, social, or religious views that conflict with those of his parents, resentment and confusion can result. Thus, it is not uncommon for a parent to approach a conference with the teacher with a sincere mixture of appreciation and hostility.

6. *Privilege and responsibility.* Finally, it is often the parents who give new teachers the sense of what a privilege *and* responsibility it is to be a teacher, as reported by a new teacher in Alaska.

Case Study

■ *in loco parentis*

Scott D. Niemann/Third and Fourth Grades

When the bell rang at 8:15 A.M. on August 28, a new reality entered my mind. Parents stopped by the classroom to familiarize themselves with the new third- and fourth-grade teacher in the village. Some of the concerned looks I spied on the parents' faces as they left their children were heartfelt. Breaking out in a cold sweat, I realized the amount of trust the parents were handing over to me. There was one term that entered my mind: *in loco parentis,* a legal term meaning "in place of the parents." I was taking on the responsibility of a parent! Following the first day, I expressed my concern to a fellow teacher and he replied, *"Encargada!"* He explained how this is a Spanish term often said in Mexico by parents when they are putting their child's life in a teacher's hands. It means we are handing our child over to you and now you are in charge. Wow! What a responsibility. ■

Pause and Reflect

1 ▸ How did your own parents feel about your schools and your teachers? Were their attitudes different when you were in the earlier grades than the later ones? If so, why was that?

2 ▸ Which of these six potential problem areas do you believe represents the greatest threat to you? What are you going to do about it . . . now?

▸ Surviving the First Year of Teaching

■ commit for two years

Link to more advice for your first year from website.

When one of the authors was about to begin his first year of teaching, his battle-scarred department chairman cryptically commented to him, "Promise yourself today that you will teach a second year." At the time, the meaning behind the remark was unclear. However, after the emotional yo-yo of that initial year had taken a few swoops and plunges, the meaning came into sharp focus. A person's first year of teaching is too unusual, too filled with extremes and emotional highs and lows to provide a sound basis for deciding whether teaching is the work on

Being happy in your work will make you a more effective teacher.
(© Will Hart/PhotoEdit)

which one wants to spend one's life. Nevertheless, a whopping 30 to 50 percent of teachers leave the profession within the first five years,[5] presumably many of them first-year teachers. But statistics do not determine personal fate. It is our strongest belief that many of the problems and issues that are behind teachers leaving the field are preventable through planning and a few resolutions. Nevertheless, a single and nontypical year is rarely the basis for a sound career decision.

Begin Now

■ start to work on yourself

First, start now to prepare for the predictable events and problems of the initial year. Make a systematic study of your strengths and weaknesses, with an eye toward using your strengths in the classroom and gradually eliminating your trouble areas. For instance, if you have an especially good reading voice, plan to capitalize on it as a teacher. Students from preschool through college love to be read to. On the other hand, if you are painfully self-conscious and shy, develop a plan to overcome this shortcoming. Don't try to defeat your shyness with big, dramatic gestures, such as trying out for the lead in the college play. Take an incremental approach, using small steps. Plan to speak to someone standing in line next to you whom you don't know; volunteer answers in class. With problematic areas like this, but also with your strengths, seek the advice and help of trusted friends, family, and teachers. Realize that your shyness may never completely go away, but you will gradually feel more and more comfortable speaking and working with people if you push yourself to make small advances regularly. You may surprise yourself—remember Joan Kinney above.

Keep a Teaching Journal

A **teaching journal** can be any notebook that is large enough to hold your teaching thoughts and suggestions. Or, if you prefer working at a keyboard, a computer file can serve the same purpose. Although some teachers started such books in grade school when they first decided to teach, the beginning of one's formal preparation as a teacher is a very good time to begin a journal.

■ benefits of a journal

A teaching journal can be used to record all the useful ideas and strategies you discover, saving them for the time when you are actually teaching. It can include teaching skills learned in lectures or observed in the field, such as how to grade papers effectively or how to give students evaluative feedback on in-class presentations. In addition, it could include methods of disciplining in different situations, easy and efficient ways to take attendance, ways to present particularly difficult concepts, things to do when students get restless or overexcited, and sources of good curricular materials.

Having such a journal serves two functions. First, the teaching journal is a constant reminder that you are preparing to actually be in charge of your own classroom (a fact that often is not in sharp focus for preservice teachers). Second, the journal can be a lifesaver when you are struggling during the first year. A typical journal entry might look like this:

Tuesday, October 7

Ninth-Grade English

Began the introductory lesson on Shakespeare and the Globe Theater today. The biographical info went over only minimally well. Brian and Mark loudly wanted to know why they needed to know when he was born and died and what difference it made. Some of the other kids looked bored as I went into my spiel, and I realized I was probably lecturing too much.

Next time I should review the information that I present, and figure out what's important for them to know and what's extraneous. Just because I'm fascinated with it doesn't mean that it's all appropriate or necessary for a ninth-grader's introduction to Shakespeare. Also, maybe some sort of question-answer sheet about Shakespeare would work better and get more involvement from the kids.

On the bright side, they all seemed to love the Globe Theater model. They really liked the way it opened, showing the cross-section with all the various stage areas. Brian and Mark were among the most interested in the model. The kids also seemed to be able to follow along on their photocopied drawing of the Globe. Jon and Elizabeth (who usually aren't impressed with anything) told me that it was "pretty cool." The next time, maybe I'll start with the theater and allow more time for them to explore it.

Besides offering professional advantages, the teaching journal can be a valuable personal record. One twenty-year teaching veteran in Massachusetts has kept a journal about his teaching experiences throughout his career. He finds that it has "captured the moment," recording what he was thinking and experiencing as he taught throughout the years.

An alternative form of this idea is to develop a card file of "teaching tips," either with index cards or in a similar computerized format. This file of tips can provide quick, easy reference for planning or problem solving.

Keeping a journal is one of the chief characteristics of the *reflective practitioner*, a goal and ideal we have stressed throughout this book.

The Proper Frame of Mind

■ cultivating humility

It is important to have the right frame of mind during your first year of teaching—that is, someone who is untested and who has a great deal to learn. Humility is a virtue that has been all but drowned out in our modern, "We're Number One" culture. Zen masters and teachers of the spiritual life urge the beginner to assume an attitude of submissiveness before what is to be learned. Not weakness, but humility. Many new teachers strive hard to *avoid* humiliation, not realizing that a humble person cannot be humiliated. Instead of assuming a false confidence, one can acknowledge that there is much to learn and open oneself up to that learning.

Making use of this suggestion is somewhat tricky. The humble frame of mind we are urging is one of alertness and quiet observation of your new context, expecting difficulties of some sort but being quietly confident that solutions will come. By all means, it does *not* mean becoming a doormat. In a way, the new teacher should be like a good apprentice: working hard, eyes open, asking questions, and being eager to learn everything possible about the craft.

The love of nurturing and observing growth in others is essential to sustaining a life of teaching. This implies that no matter what you teach or how you present yourself to your students, you have to be on the learner's side and to believe that they can and will grow during the time that you are together.

—HERBERT KOHL

An aspect of having a proper frame of mind is understanding the social and economic context within which your new school exists. Schools vary immensely depending on their social, ethical, religious, and economic make-up. (You will find background information in the chapters entitled "What Is a School and What Is It For?" and "How Are Schools Governed, Influenced, and Financed?") Study your new community and ask questions, so you are not blindsided by attitudes and behaviors that you may be encountering for the first time.

Find a Mentor

■ values of mentor

A first-year teacher can have no greater gift than a good **mentor,** an experienced teacher who is willing to act as a guide and confidant through the first year. Besides all of the information and tips that a mentor can give you, a good mentor is an interpreter-guide on what is essentially foreign turf. A mentor can tell you which pieces of paper from the principal's office need to be responded to immediately, who has the formal power and who has the real power, what the administrators emphasize most in teacher evaluations, and which teachers are most willing to share ideas and which ones are not. Perhaps even more important, a mentor is a friend. (Remember Catherine Foley and Joan Silver above.)

In a completely rational society, the best of us would be teachers and the rest of us would have to settle for something less, because passing civilization along from one generation to the next ought to be the highest honor and the highest responsibility anyone could have.

—LEE IACOCCA

Sixty-seven percent of teachers who have been mentored claim that the experience significantly improved their teaching. On the other hand, only 47 percent of public school teachers report having received such guidance.[6] However, in recent years many school districts have developed special arrangements to help beginning teachers. Some have special induction programs, some have mentor programs, and some have both. In situations where there is no induction program or a mentor is not assigned, we nevertheless urge you to make finding a mentor a high priority.

Make Your Students' Parents Your Allies

We suggest that all teachers, but particularly new teachers, take a very proactive, positive approach to parents. Instead of having them get to know you indirectly through the often distorting eyes and mouths of their children ("My new teacher, Miss Sniddly, hates me. And besides, she can't teach. How come I got stuck with a new teacher?"), help them get to know you and what you will be doing with their children this school year.

■ establish communication with parents

One way to do this is to prepare a short statement to be carried home and signed, introducing yourself to parents and outlining your major goals for the year. Stress that you and they are in a partnership to help their child have a productive year. Let them know how to get in touch with you. Tell them the date for Back-to-School Night and that you are looking forward to meeting them. One new first-grade teacher we heard about sent a letter with a snapshot of herself to her first-graders and their parents once she received her class list in the summer. She wrote a little about herself, told them some of the things they would do during the coming school year, and (for the parents) explained her approach to teaching. Besides being exciting for the students, this technique helped the new teacher start the year (and, more importantly, finish the year) with her students' parents as strong allies.

A second suggestion is that once you have established disciplinary and homework policies, a copy should be sent home for parental sign-off and return.

Third, on the first day, get the home, work, and cell telephone numbers of each student's parents or guardians. The fact that you possess these valuable bits of information will not go unnoticed by your students, particularly those who might be inclined to push the disciplinary envelope.

Fourth, it is a good idea to call all parents early in the fall. In particular, call the parent(s) as soon as a student appears to be falling behind, tuning out, or misbehaving: "Mrs. Tate, this is Philip's teacher. Philip's performance has begun to slip. What can we do to get him back on track?" "Mr. Dee, this is Joan's teacher. Joan just won't stop talking in class. It is interfering with other students and keeping her from doing the work she is capable of. What can we do to make this the good year we all want for Joan?" The key word in dealing with parents is *we,* as in "What can *we* do?" Phone calls should be made and brief notes sent home for positive reasons as well. Such a "good news" call can make a parent's month!

Finally, if problems persist, insist on a parent visit. (Conversations such as "We need to work together to get little Adolph involved in his schoolwork" are helpful for everyone involved.) There is no surer way to get children's attention than to have them realize they are the reason their parents had to leave work early to come to school. And although this is an upsetting bother for many parents, it is usually worth it because of the positive effect it can have on their child's school experience.

Take Evaluation Seriously

The news that they are to be evaluated by their principal or some other administrator is often a surprise to novice teachers. Even more shocking is the revelation that the related evaluation reports are sometimes the cause of not being rehired.

Typically, it is a major job responsibility of principals and other district administrative personnel to visit systematically and evaluate the performance of new teachers. Depending on the district and the conscientiousness of the administrator, this can take place anywhere from once to a dozen times during the first year. Usually, though, there are three or four evaluative visits, followed up closely by feedback conferences during which the administrator goes over his or her observations. Together these evaluative visits play an important part in the school district's decision to rehire the teacher or terminate his or her employment.

■ preparing for and responding to feedback

It is important, then, for new teachers to understand thoroughly how their work will be evaluated. Before you accept a teaching position, be clear about how and when your work will be evaluated. Most school districts have an official evaluation and feedback form, and you should know this well. Check out the department of education's website in your state to see how new teachers are evaluated. If the school or district's evaluator gives you advance notification of a visit, prepare for the occasion. Find out from your mentor teacher what the administrator really stresses in teaching. And do your best. If the evaluator raises issues or makes suggestions for improvement, take them seriously. You do not necessarily have to agree, but you should not casually ignore the issues. In most cases the comments are legitimate, and the new teacher should strive to repair or strengthen the area that was criticized.

Take Care of Yourself

■ physical health

One of the greatest surprises of full-time, fully responsible teaching, as opposed to student teaching, is how tiring it is. Teaching is physically, mentally, and emotionally draining, particularly until one gets conditioned to it—that is, until one gets into "teaching shape." This is true for many jobs. The stress and strain of new employment wear newcomers down and set them up for colds, flu, and other mild ailments. The problem is compounded in teaching because it is such an "in your face" occupation (referring to all those coughing, sniffling, and wheezing faces you encounter every day). A classroom is a magnificent germ factory, with viruses claiming new victims regularly. The teacher who is exhausted, run down, and staying up late reworking lesson plans and correcting papers is a prime target for whatever is circulating in the environment.

■ mental health

The stress and strain of a new teaching position also can cause mild depression. In their first year, few teachers live up to their own expectations. Often new teachers are away from their regular support system of family and friends. Having not yet established realistic standards, they really don't know if they are succeeding or failing. A bad class or even one resistant or disrespectful student can emotionally unseat them. To counter this vulnerability to sickness of body and spirit, new teachers need to give special attention to their health. When you feel yourself becoming overstressed or burnt out, take deliberate steps. Reduce stress directly by trying to solve key problems that are bothering you and look for ways to relieve stress indirectly as well. Plan a weekend away, take vitamins, or join an aerobics class. Instead of getting overtired and run down, beginners need to take special pains to get enough rest, eat well, and get adequate exercise.

Kevin and Jim's Seven Additional Rules for Surviving the First Year of Teaching (Or Seven Compelling Reasons Why Future Teachers Should Not Try to Resell This Book)*

1. *When in doubt, think.* Instead of simply fretting about problems or panicking, use your best tool: your mind. Reflect. Problem solve. Try to identify the problem, possible solutions, and what seems best, and then act and judge whether that option helped the situation.

2. *Don't look for love in the classroom.* Maybe respect, but not love. Don't even expect to be appreciated—that may not come from your students for ten or twenty years.

3. *Deal with your authority problems before entering the classroom.* Come to terms with the fact that you will be responsible for maintaining an orderly and civil environment and think about how you will accomplish this feat.

4. *If you are not organized, get organized.* Coping with the planbooks, student papers, office memos, attendance records, grades, report cards, and so on, requires much more organization than many beginners have practiced.

5. *Love thy school secretary and custodians.* Many beginners fail to realize how important the school secretary and custodians are in enabling teachers to do an effective job and in the "informal communication network" of the school.

6. *Focus on learning.* Many beginners fail to concentrate on making sure their students really learn something and thus have feelings of accomplishment. Students will put up with a great deal of "beginning teacheritis" if they sense they are learning. Remember, however, they usually need to be reminded that they have learned something!

7. *Don't—we repeat, don't—get married two weeks before the start of your first teaching job.* For reasons unknown to the authors, each year, thousands of new college graduates decide to jump at the same time into two of life's most difficult undertakings: beginning a career and starting what they hope will be a lifelong relationship.

* The authors promise that if you follow these seven rules faithfully, you will survive the first year of teaching. You may even like it! On the other hand, if you do not survive the year, return the unused portion of the book to your instructor for a refund.

▶ A Final Word

Much of this chapter has dealt with the trials of being a new teacher. Nevertheless, most new teachers have a great sense of accomplishment and are proud of themselves at the end of their first year. They have learned an enormous amount in nine or ten months. Along with the trials, teaching has its pleasures and bright moments, making it a rewarding and fulfilling occupation for most. English novelist Joyce Cary has written that human joy comes not from the great events but from the little, everyday things, like a good cup of tea. The joys and satisfactions of teaching can lie in mundane happenings and small surprises. As a teacher, you may find joy in the following:

- Experiencing those electric moments when you can *feel* the students thinking and *see* them making new connections
- Watching two lonely kids, whom you brought together, walk down the hall side by side, now friends
- Getting your planbook back from the supervisor with the comment, "These are *excellent* lessons"
- Finding in your box, on a rainy Friday afternoon, a note written in a childish scrawl, "You are my most favorite teacher. Guess who?"
- Shopping at the mall and meeting one of your students, who proudly introduces you to her mother as "my teacher," and being able to tell by the mother's response that you are respected in their household
- Having a former student call to tell you that he has a problem and needs your advice
- Chaperoning a dance and having what you thought was your most hostile student happily introduce his girlfriend to you
- Hearing in the teachers' lunchroom that your supervisor called you "a real professional"
- Being observed by the principal and having your students make you look terrific
- Surviving until June, being bone-tired but proud of what you and your kids have been able to do
- Cleaning out your desk on the last day of school after the kids have been dismissed and finding a box of candy with a card signed by the whole class
- Realizing—be it daily, weekly, or monthly—that what you are doing with your life *really does make a difference*

Key Terms

culture shock (420)   social distance (432)   teaching journal (441)
mentor (443)

For Reflection

1 Can you remember any beginning teachers you have had who fit the scenarios described in this chapter or got into similar situations?

2 How do you explain the different attitudes toward students of teachers in training and first-year teachers? And experienced teachers?

3 If you were to begin teaching tomorrow and were free to evaluate your students in any way you chose (or not to evaluate at all), what would you do?

4 What do you expect to be the major problems you will encounter as a beginning teacher?

5 What can you do now to begin solving those problems?

For Debate

Read the Policy Matters! summary, "Zero Tolerance: The Solution or a False Start?" at the website, and consider the issues it outlines regarding policies designed to reduce violence in schools. Then, go to EduSpace to post your answers (or respond to other students' answers) to the What Do You Think questions listed in the Policy Matters! feature.

For Further Information

PRINT RESOURCES

Esme Raji Codell, *Educating Esme: Diary of a Teacher's First Year* (Chapel Hill, NC: Algonquin Books, 1999). This book is the account of a new fifth-grade teacher in a Chicago inner-city school. Hip, imaginative, and irreverent, the book takes the reader through the teacher's triumphs and travails with students and a particularly dense administrator.

Richard D. Kellough, *Surviving the First Year of Teaching: Guidelines for Success* (Columbus, OH: Merrill/Prentice Hall, 1999). Designed specifically as a survival guide for beginners, this manual is filled with practical tips from first lessons to conducting conferences with parents.

Yvvonne Bender, *The New Teacher's Handbook: Practical Strategies & Techniques for Success in the Classroom from Kindergarten Through High School* (Chicago: Nomad Press, 2003). This short (160 plus pages) book cuts right to the core of the issues and problems confronted by new teachers. The advice is clear, concise and right on target.

Harry K. Wong and Rosemary T. Wong, *The First Days of School: How to Be an Effective Teacher* (Sunview, CA: Harry Wong Publishing, 1998). This highly acclaimed handbook abounds with tips and strategies to help the new teacher get a strong start through motivation and minimizing discipline and the other problems that plague new teachers.

Erma S. Hershman and Dyan M. McDonald, *The Survival Kit for New Teachers: A User-Friendly Handbook*, 2d ed. (Garland, TX: ITPA, 2001). The title says it all. Although this book focuses largely on elementary classrooms, the authors have another 2001 book with a similar title except this is for "new secondary teachers."

Pearl Rock Kane, ed., *My First Year as a Teacher* (New York: Signet/Penguin/Putnam, 1996). This paperback book contains twenty-five narratives of the experiences of new teachers. The accounts are colorful and eye-opening.

WEB RESOURCES

Teachers First. Available at: **http://www.teachersfirst.com.** This website is a treasure trove of information, good ideas, lesson plans and even humor. It is well organized and easy to search for the topic or need of choice.

Web Wonders for Supporting New Teachers. Available at: **http://www.ascd.org/portal/site/ascd/menuitem. 5ef449ab9c0f829abae0e510d3108a0c/ template.article?articleMgmtId= cf8aebb413520010VgnVCM1000003d01a8c0 RCRD.** The Association for Supervision and Curriculum Development site (www.ascd.org) in general, and the one above (Supporting New Teachers) in particular, provide varied and rich support for beginners.

About Teaching and the First Year. Available at: **http://www.ed.gov/teachers/become/about/ edpicks.jhtml?src=ln.** The U.S. Department of Education has a special website to support first year teachers. Comprehensive and current, it can provide you with many answers to everyday questions.

Learn NC. Available at: **http://www.learnnc.org/newlnc/newteach.nsf/ FrontPage?OpenForm.** This website, which is maintained by the North Carolina Department of Education, is an example of the services that many state departments of education are offering to help beginning teachers.

EZ School. Available at: **http://www.EZSchool.com.** This website, associated with Amazon.com, is a treasure of resources for the new teacher. It is filled with good ideas, teaching plans for a range of subject matter, and worksheets.

What to Expect Your First Year of Teaching. Available at: **http://www.ed.gov/pubs/FirstYear/index.html.** This website is an excellent resource for beginning teachers. It combines many of the practical tips and much of the advice in this chapter with several resources helpful to beginning teachers.

15 What Does It Mean to Be a Professional?

Chapter Preview   In this chapter, we focus on the teacher as a professional—that is, as a member of an occupational group. We will see how this rather abstract concept of *professionalism* affects the daily life of the classroom teacher. In effect, we put the role of the individual teacher in the larger context of being a member of a profession.

This chapter emphasizes that:

▶ Teachers can become involved in different types of situations and conflicts in which they will need counsel or support.

▶ Teachers have become more powerful in recent years, but they don't have the same kinds of power that members of some other professions have.

▶ The question of whether teaching is a profession can be judged by reference to specific criteria. Furthermore, cases can be made both for and against teaching being a profession.

▶ There are levels of professionalism, and the National Board for Professional Teaching Standards and its standards for certification are having a substantial effect on teachers.

▶ The National Education Association and the American Federation of Teachers, the most influential teacher organizations, have quite different origins and are competing for the support of classroom teachers.

▶ The teaching profession is still evolving, and much depends on its capacity to maintain the public's trust.

▶ Current educational demands require the teacher to be a continuous learner. Teachers can continue their professional growth in various ways.

■ teaching within a system

The only way to keep our kids foolproof is to keep them away from fools.

—WILL ROGERS

The essence of a career in teaching is close, hands-on work with the young. When people think about becoming teachers, their thoughts and musings usually revolve around working with students. Rarely do they bother with hypothetical issues beyond the scope of the classroom. This is both natural and appropriate because the teacher's success or failure depends on his or her effectiveness with students. Nevertheless, there is much more to being a teacher than this. Teachers work within a system that exposes them to pressures from many quarters. Prospective teachers are often somewhat naive about these pressures and forces, and naiveté can be dangerous, both in making a career decision and in making a successful career.

To help you see this point, we would like you to indulge in a set of daydreams for a few moments. We will offer you a few brief scenarios, and after reading each one, you should reflect on how you might react. As you read each scenario, imagine yourself as a first-year teacher in that ideal classroom you carry around in your head. Assume that you appear to be doing a fine job. You are really enjoying it. Your students are making nice progress. They seem to be interested in their work. A few parents have indicated that although they were initially worried that their precious child was to have a new (in other words, *untested*) teacher, they are pleased with the child's progress in your class. So, things are going very well, until . . .

■ target of pressure groups

1. You get a special-delivery letter from a group called Patriotic American Parents (PAP). You have heard they are very active in your area and are especially interested in schools. Their letter informs you that their lawyer is preparing a case against you for using books that are on their disapproved list. (You didn't know there was such a list, but sure enough, there is, and you have been using books from it!) They claim they have evidence that you are "waging a subtle but nevertheless vicious war against the cause of justice and liberty and have succeeded in temporarily deflecting the minds of some of your students from the truth." Furthermore, they want to know why you display the United Nations flag and why there are no pictures of past presidents on your classroom walls. Finally, you are said to recite the Pledge of Allegiance in a much too hasty fashion, which is clearly a sign of your disrespect for your country. This is the first you have heard of these charges or even of the Patriots' interest in you. You think of yourself as patriotic and are shocked by the letter. They have requested that you respond in writing by next week or they will begin legal proceedings.

■ the invisible contract

2. In late January, the superintendent, who holds a conference with each new teacher, told you she thought you were doing a fine job and that she wanted you to return next year. In passing, she remarked that she would be getting a contract to you in the spring. Toward the end of April, you got a little nervous and called her office. You spoke to her executive secretary, who said not to worry, that you were on the list, and that a contract would be coming before long. You stopped worrying. Today is the last day of school, and you find a very nice personal note from the principal in your school mailbox. He thanks you for your fine work during the year and says he is sorry you will not be back next year. You call the superintendent's office. She is "in conference," and her executive secretary says they are not renewing your

contract. She cannot remember speaking to you in April. She knows nothing about the case. She does know, however, that the Board of Education has put on a lot of pressure for cuts in next year's personnel budget. She ends by telling you, "You must be very disappointed, dear. I know how you feel." No, she doesn't!

conflict with colleagues

3. You noticed something peculiar when you sat down at the faculty dining table one lunch hour. Conversations stopped, and you had the distinct impression your colleagues had been talking about you. A few days later, an older teacher stopped you in the hall after school and said, "I don't want to butt in, but you really are upsetting Mrs. Hilary and Mr. Alexander." Mrs. H. and Mr. A. have the classrooms on either side of yours. Apparently they claim your class makes so much noise that they can't get anything done. Both are very traditional in their approach to education, whereas you believe in a more activity-oriented approach. Although your class is rather noisy occasionally, it is never chaotic, and its noise is usually a by-product of the students' involvement in the task. Twice Mr. Alexander has sent messengers with notes asking that your class be quieter. You have always complied. You hardly know either teacher. You have never really talked to Mr. Alexander except to say hello. Mrs. Hilary, with whom you've chatted, prides herself on being a strict disciplinarian. What she means, you have inferred, is that she is able to keep the children quiet. You know Mr. Alexander is chummy with Mrs. Hilary. You go to the vice-principal, who seems to know all about the case, but only from the Hilary-Alexander angle. Inexplicably, the vice-principal gets quite angry and claims that until you came along, the faculty got along beautifully. Furthermore, you are being very unprofessional in making complaints against experienced teachers. You feel as if you are trapped in a bad dream.

These horror stories, of course, are not everyday occurrences. Also, keep in mind that entrance into any profession has its trials. These accounts are intended to help you realize that you can be an effective teacher and still have trouble keeping your job. What is the common theme running through each of these anecdotes? You, the teacher, were succeeding in your work with children, but forces outside your classroom began to impinge on you. PAP wanted to make a target case of you. The school system bureaucracy was ready to put you on the unemployed rolls. Two of your colleagues damaged your reputation with the faculty and administration. Other than that, it was a super year.

organizational support

Although you may feel confident that you could handle some of these situations, it is doubtful that you could cope with all such cases that might arise. In some instances you would be powerless to respond effectively to your adversaries, and you might end up a helpless victim of circumstance. Fortunately, a teacher is not alone. Like people in many other occupational groups, teachers have organizations whose job it is to protect them from such indignities and injustices. These organizations function on several levels, from the local to the national, and usually their very existence keeps situations like those described from occurring. When they do occur, these organizations are there to support the teacher. At least, that is the way they should work.

It is important to realize that in becoming a teacher, you are not just committing yourself to work with children. You are joining an occupational group composed of other individuals with similar responsibilities, concerns, and pressures whose help you may need and who, in turn, will need your help.

▶ The Status of Teaching: A Profession or Not?

■ professionalism a key question

The question "Is teaching a profession?" probably arouses little interest in many of our readers. Most people thinking about a career in teaching are more interested in whether it will be a personally rewarding way to spend their time than in whether it is a "true profession." Will teaching bring me personal satisfactions? Will it provide an outlet for my talents and energies? Will I be effective with kids? These questions are, we suspect, closer to your skin. Nevertheless, the question of professionalism and the related issues are important to teachers and influence the quality of education teachers provide for children. They will also affect the quality of your life as a teacher. So what actually is a profession?

■ does teaching qualify?

A **profession** is more than a group of individuals all engaged in the same line of work. Professions have a more or less recognizable set of characteristics that distinguish them from nonprofessions.[1] As you read the following list of characteristics, check whether you think teaching qualifies on each premise:

■ ☐ yes ☐ no

1. A profession renders a unique, definite, and essential service to society. Only the people in the particular profession render the service; for instance, only lawyers practice law. The service rendered must be considered so important that it is available to all the people in a society.

■ ☐ yes ☐ no

2. A profession relies on intellectual skills in the performance of its service. This does not mean that physical actions and skills are not needed; rather, the emphasis in carrying on the work is on intellectual skills and techniques.

■ ☐ yes ☐ no

3. A profession entails a long period of specialized training. Because professional work requires special intellectual skills, it requires specialized intellectual training. General education such as that represented by a bachelor's degree is valued but is not considered adequate. The specialized training must cover a substantial period and not be obtained in cram courses or correspondence schools.

■ ☐ yes ☐ no

4. Both individual members of the profession and the professional group enjoy a considerable degree of autonomy and decision-making authority. Professional groups regulate their own activities rather than having outsiders set policies and enforce adherence to standards. Whereas factory workers have very limited decision-making power and are closely supervised in the performance of their work, professionals are expected to make most of their own decisions and be free of close supervision by supervisors.

■ ☐ yes ☐ no

5. A profession requires its members to accept personal responsibility for their actions and decisions and, in general, for their performance. Because the professional's service is usually related to the client's human welfare, this responsibility is an especially serious one.

■ ☐ yes ☐ no

6. A profession emphasizes the services rendered by its practitioners more than their financial rewards. Although the personal motives of any individual professional are not necessarily any higher than any other worker's, the professional group's public emphasis is on service. The Leaders in Education box provides one example of this emphasis on service.

■ ☐ yes ☐ no

7. A profession is self-governing and responsible for policing its own ranks. This means there are professional groups that perform a number of activities aimed at keeping the quality of their services high and looking out for the social and economic well-being of the professional members. Also, these self-governing organizations set standards of admission and exclusion for the profession.

■ ☐ yes ☐ no

8. A profession has a code of ethics that sets out the acceptable standards of conduct for its members.

Leaders in Education

Kay Toliver

"I'm a teacher. What else would I do?" Kay Toliver asks.

Kay Toliver has been instilling a love of knowledge in middle school students in Spanish Harlem for more than twenty-five years. Toliver teaches on the cutting edge of mathematics, stressing thinking and application over computation, and weaving history and art through class discussions into the study of mathematics. Because many of her students come from poor, unstable backgrounds and have poor language skills, she emphasizes writing, reading, and research. Her students must always be prepared to explain their solutions orally, in complete and clear sentences. They are required to keep daily journals, in which they write about what they have learned in class, ideas about how to apply the concepts they study, or simply observations about the class or the teacher. "We don't need different methods to teach so-called disadvantaged children," says Ms. Toliver. She believes that the students' ability to express themselves in well-written English must be acquired hand-in-hand with mathematical discovery. In addition to enhancing writing skills, the journals allow the teacher to gain a glimpse of her students' confusions in mathematics. "A teacher can stand in front of the class and think she's giving a great lesson. But that's not always the truth," she explains.

Kay Toliver's influence is spreading beyond her classroom to videos. In 1995, she was featured in a Peabody award-winning public television special, "Good Morning Miss Toliver." Also, with Jaime Escalante, Toliver contributed to "Interactions: Real Math—Real Careers," a multimedia tool that connects prealgebra math principles to real life in scenarios featuring career professionals. Along with Escalante, Toliver sees the way to future jobs through mathematics, especially for students from the inner city. In addition to the mathematical tools, P.S. 72 children use computers. Toliver feels her students must be technologically competitive. With money she received from one of her many awards, the Presidential Award for Excellence in Science and Mathematics Teaching, she purchased software and computers for her school's computer lab. Recently Kay retired from full-time teaching. However, she's still involved in education, and is in demand as a keynote speaker and teacher trainer. She is the host of a Peabody Award-winning classroom series for elementary math students, "The Eddie Files," and has passed along her classroom strategies in two staff development series, "The Kay Toliver Files," and "Teacher Talk." These materials are influencing a new generation of teachers through their use in professional development workshops and teacher training programs at universities.

Toliver has seen many students who have been exposed to drugs or crime, or both. Frequently, one parent is gone, or a child may be in foster care. Too often a sibling is in jail, and the students' peers are dealing with everyday street life in East Harlem. But having grown up in the South Bronx and East Harlem, she is well acquainted with the world of her students. As a result, discipline is not a problem in Toliver's class. Students understand she is serious and works hard to make math interesting.

"Becoming a teacher was the fulfillment of a childhood dream," says Ms. Toliver. "My parents always stressed that education was the key to a better life. By becoming a teacher, I hoped to inspire African American and Hispanic youths to realize their own dreams. I wanted to give something back to the communities I grew up in."

Learn more about Kay Toliver's approach at: **http://www.nationalmathtrail.org/ ktmathtrail.html.**

 Visit the website for more information about Kay Toliver.

Source: "Inspiring Young Minds: Kay Toliver," by Arwen Larson, *TECHNOS Quarterly,* Winter 1993, Vol. 2, No. 4. Used by permission.

These characteristics, then, are the major requirements of a profession. Few professions satisfy all of them fully. However, the list does serve as a benchmark by which occupational groups can measure themselves and direct their development if they wish to enjoy professional status. With this in mind, let's look at the arguments for and against teaching as a profession.

The Case *AGAINST* Teaching as a Profession

The roots of teaching as an occupation go back to ancient Greece, where slaves called *paidagogos*, or pedagogues, taught children to read and write and helped them memorize passages of poetic history. Despite this long history, however, a careful look at current practices reveals that teaching does not qualify as a profession.

■ teaching not a unique service

■ **A Child's Many Teachers** If education is a teacher's unique function, the teacher certainly has a great deal of competition. Children today learn a tremendous amount from media offerings, including *Sesame Street,* public affairs specials, MTV, and *Sports Illustrated.* The *non*-teacher-educators include parents, ministers, older friends, neighbors, employers, best friends, coaches, scout leaders, camp counselors, and grandparents. The world is bursting with teachers, and those who hold forth in school buildings have only a small piece of the action.

■ training not rigorous

■ **Limited Training** Although teaching has intellectual and theoretical foundations, it requires a rather short period of specialized training (considerably less than some of the skilled trades), and entrance into the occupation is not especially competitive, particularly on intellectual grounds. If it is a profession, it is one composed of college graduates with a sweeping span of academic abilities, varying levels of commitment, and a wide range of motivations for becoming teachers.

Children learn from many adults, both in and out of the classroom.
(© JLP/Jose L. Pelaez/ CORBIS)

■ **Constraints on Autonomy**   Although there is a good deal of talk about teachers' autonomy and decision-making power (and teachers have come a long way since the early days of the country, as described in the box on Rules and Duties for Teachers), in today's classrooms teachers still have a very low level of autonomy and decision-making power. Teachers are at the second rung from the bottom (superior only to students) of the school hierarchy commanded by the local board of education. Unlike lawyers and doctors, who can reject clients, teachers have students assigned to them. They also have supervisors: their principal, lead teacher, department head, and others farther up the chain of command. They teach a curriculum and are responsible for their students' meeting content standards that have been chosen or developed largely by others.

■ little decision-making power

If their supervisors do not like the results, teachers are only rarely protected by their professional group from being fired (or, more gently, "not rehired") by the local school board. Unlike other professions, teachers do not formally evaluate other teachers; administrators do that. Moreover, most of the important decisions that affect teachers' daily lives, even those that bear directly on the standards of their own profession, are made by nonteachers (administrators and citizen school board members). Although teachers are beginning to get more involved in teacher preparation programs and are acquiring some say in the licensing and certification of teachers, laypeople and bureaucrats still wield a great deal of the decision-making power. Some teachers, like factory workers, even have to punch a time clock (or, more genteelly, they "sign in" and "sign out"). In sum, they have very little to say about what goes on in their "shop."

■ little accountability

■ **Responsibility for Their Profession**   Teachers rarely lose their jobs because Johnnie can't read or Samantha failed calculus. After a teacher achieves tenure, it takes some form of gross negligence, clear incompetence, or serious sexual offense for him or her to be fired. As professionals, teachers do very little policing of their own ranks. Their professional organizations are just like other self-serving organizations, whether composed of teamsters or autoworkers—that is, the primary energies of teacher associations and unions go to their own survival and

Rules and Duties for Teachers in the Nineteenth Century

- Teachers will fill the lamps and clean the chimney each day.
- Each teacher will bring a bucket of water and a scuttle of coal for the day's session.
- Make your pens carefully. You may whittle nibs to the individual tastes of the pupils.
- Men teachers may take one evening each week for courting purposes, or two evenings a week if they go to church regularly.
- Women teachers who marry or engage in improper conduct will be dismissed.
- Every teacher should lay aside from each day's pay a goodly sum of his earnings. He should use his

savings during his retirement years so that he will not be a burden to society.

- Any teacher who smokes, uses liquor in any form, visits pool halls or public halls, or gets shaved at a barber shop will give good reasons for people to suspect his worth, intentions, and honesty.
- The teacher who performs his labor faithfully and without fault for five years will be given an increase of twenty-five cents per week in his pay.

From the rules and duties for teachers teaching in an 1872 Missouri school district.

growth. Secondarily, they attempt to protect their members, increase their salaries, and expand their benefits.

■ little involvement

Most teachers, in fact, are minimally involved in professional organizations and their activities. Except when the organization calls a strike—a somewhat contradictory activity for a "profession" supposedly dedicated to serving children—teachers generally just pay their dues. Most teachers claim they are too busy to take an active role in professional affairs. This lack of real involvement in professional activities may stem from the fact that so many teachers have second jobs, either as homemakers or in the after-school labor market. They are unenthusiastic about working for higher standards because one of the first sacrifices to professionalism would be their second job.

■ **Job Security and Salary**   In reality, teachers work in circumstances very different from those of other professionals. Like other public servants, they are hired rather than operating as independent agents. They are on a fixed salary schedule and are protected by tenure laws rather than independently having to find a market for their services. In effect, teaching is a low-paying, relatively high-security job rather than a high-paying, low-security profession. Seniority as a teacher appears to be more important than competence. Talk about professionalism may be personally satisfying to teachers, but it does not conform to the reality of the teacher's occupational life.

The Case *FOR* Teaching as a Profession

The very nobility of the teacher's work is evidence in favor of its status as a profession. Society has entrusted teachers with its most important responsibility: the education of its young. Throughout history, many great thinkers have acknowledged how crucial the work of the teacher is to the fulfillment of personal and national goals. And, as this realization has spread in recent decades, opportunities and rewards for the teacher have continued to improve.

■ service above and beyond the call of duty

■ **Teachers' Commitment to Service**   Service to others is at the very heart of what it means to be a professional. Teachers make large material sacrifices to serve children. The overwhelming percentages of people who teach could find work that in material terms is much more rewarding. Many could command large salaries in business or more lucrative professions. According to a recent survey, teachers even spend an average of $458 of their own money on school supplies and instructional materials each year to make up for the limited budgets in their own schools.[2] This is truly service above and beyond the call of duty!

You have not done enough, you have never done enough, as long as it is still possible that you have something of value to contribute.

—DAG HAMMARSKJÖLD

■ teach difficult skills

■ **The Teacher's Unique Skills**   Although children learn from many people—from parents to television personalities—teachers are the specialists who pass on to the young the key skills they need to participate effectively in the culture. They aid the young in acquiring the most difficult, if not the most important, skills—those that involve thinking and manipulating ideas. Neither reading nor geometry is often learned on the street. They are the indispensable midwives of the "knowledge society." Although teachers do not undergo a particularly lengthy period of specialized training, they are in a sense continually educating themselves.

What office is there which involves more responsibility, which requires more qualifications, and which ought, therefore, to be more honorable than that of teaching?

—HARRIET MARTINEAU

Teachers are expected (and, in most states, required by law) to upgrade their teaching skills and content knowledge periodically.

■ have a domain of control

■ **The Teacher's Autonomy** Teachers have an immense area of personal control. They normally determine the method of instruction. They decide which aspects of the curriculum they will highlight and which they will cover quickly. The limits on their creativity in the classroom are few, if any. After the initial few years of teaching, they are seldom observed and evaluated. Teachers' classrooms are their castles.

If teachers believe they do not have enough autonomy or do not agree with their administrators, they are free to move to another school. However, a teacher's autonomy is accompanied by a responsibility to teach effectively. Like other professionals, teachers must be able to justify the manner in which they render their social services, whether it is grading or disciplinary actions. Teachers take responsibility for their actions and, like other professionals, are open to criticisms of their performance.

Pause and Reflect

1 ▶ Where do you stand on the question, "Is teaching a profession?" To you, what are the best arguments for and against the professional status of teaching?

A Third Possibility: An Evolving Profession

Like most other complex questions, our query about whether teaching is a profession cannot be answered satisfactorily with simple pro-and-con arguments such as those just offered. Also, teachers differ so much in the conditions under which they work, and they possess such varying degrees of knowledge, commitment, and expertise that it is difficult to come up with a definitive answer. In most schools, teachers fulfill many of the criteria of professionals. In other schools, they seem to function as clerks and technicians.

A professional is someone who can do his best when he doesn't feel like it.
—ALISTAIR COOKE

In certain ways teaching clearly is eligible for professional status, and in certain other ways, it deviates sharply from accepted canons of professionalism. On the one hand, teachers provide an intellectual service to the community. They undergo specialized training to master the theoretical basis of their work. Ethical standards guide their work with students. On the other hand, they too often function like many other lower-level white-collar workers and civil servants. Too often seniority and job security are the rules rather than excellence and independence. Like many other occupational groups that are considered professional, at this moment in history, teachers only partially qualify.

■ teaching as an evolving profession

Another way to look at the issue (and one we favor) is to think of teaching as an *evolving profession*—that is, it is in the process of becoming a full profession. What will determine whether teaching becomes a full-fledged profession during your lifetime? Among the factors are the trends toward greater self-determination, better preparation, and recognizing excellence in teaching.

■ **Greater Self-Determination** It may be true that a teacher lacks the autonomy of, say, a small-town lawyer. Yet every profession has limits on its autonomy. For example, today, more and more doctors and dentists are employed by health maintenance organizations (HMOs) and are forming unions to protect their rights against their HMO managers. The crucial point, though, is the direction in which teaching is moving.

To make teaching a full profession, teachers must take on a larger role in the governing of their career affairs. Whereas the direction of the schools and the curriculum should be in the hands of many groups (parents, community leaders, students, and teachers), control over the teaching profession per se should be largely in the hands of teachers. Up to now, the great majority of teachers have taken the attitude "Let George do it," allowing others to make the major decisions about who should teach, how teachers should be trained, and under what conditions they should render their services. This situation will not substantially change until teachers take a major role in making it change.

■ **Better Preparation** To make teaching a full profession, teachers must also demand better preparation requirements. As long as the public believes that any college graduate with a smattering of education courses can walk in off the street and do a teacher's job, people will not treat teachers as professionals. As described in the chapter entitled "What Are Your Job Options in Education?," this dangerous perception may even worsen if, due to teacher shortages, states then issue alternative licenses to individuals without any professional training at all! We are definitely not suggesting that teachers should adopt artificial trappings, like a doctor's smock or a general's uniform, to appear more distinctive and impressive. Rather, teachers must appear better because they *are* better. Like architects and surgeons, teachers must know their work, and it must be imbued with a sense of high purpose. When that happens, the public will decide affirmatively that teachers should be treated as professionals.

■ **Recognizing Excellence in Teaching** We need to realize that not all of the 3 million plus people working in the American schools are interested in and, in some cases, capable of measuring up to the standards of professionalism discussed earlier. At present, what we are calling (and, incidentally, will continue to call) the *teaching profession* is a mixed bag, with a great many transients "just passing through," a great many rather uncommitted teachers, and a great many truly excellent, dedicated career teachers.

More than thirty years ago, an educator captured what we believe to be the essence of the professional teacher in the following statement:

> Let us define a career teacher as one who plans to, and actually does, make a life occupation of teaching; one who is philosophically, emotionally, and spiritually committed, who is never satisfied with what he does and how well he's doing it, and who fully intends to keep on growing for the rest of his life.[3]

This educator went on to estimate that only about one out of four practicing teachers fits his definition. And herein lays the difficulty: until the great majority of teachers qualify by this educator's definition or until there is a qualitative regrouping of those presently identified as "teachers," teaching will not truly be called a profession.

■ need more self-determination

To erect fine buildings and to seek to meet the needs and abilities of all individuals who desire to avail themselves of the opportunities so generously offered without providing teachers with qualifications commensurate with the ideal is a sham.

—I. L. KANDELL

■ recognizing the best

Levels of Professionalism

■ three levels of professional behavior

What people (yourself included) think of the professional status of teaching is clearly important. However, it is dwarfed in importance compared with how you will live out your professional life and how you *will be* as a teacher. One way to think about this is to conceive of teaching as having three levels, or three ways that teachers go about their work.[4] Level One is the *imitative-maintenance* teacher, Level Two is the *meditative* teacher, and Level Three is the *generative-creative* teacher.

■ going through the motions

■ The Level One Teacher   Individuals functioning at Level One are essentially going through the motions prescribed by someone else in a rather mechanical fashion. They tend to be preoccupied by classroom discipline and keeping students busy. They may be successful at getting students *through* their lessons and examinations, but they are somewhat robotic in their narrowly following preset patterns, patterns set out in curriculum guides or textbooks. Level One teachers find security in *teaching to the test* and in what are pejoratively called *teacher-proof materials,* rigid instructional materials that step-by-step guide the teachers' actions. Although not in itself a problem, this *imitative-maintenance* approach doesn't allow the teacher to respond to the unique needs of students or to the special circumstances that continually arise in a classroom. They don't know how to respond to the interesting, off-the-wall question, or when something unexpected happens and they let the "teachable moment" float by. This kind of unimaginative teaching makes teaching more of a technical occupation than a profession.

■ limited reflection

■ The Level Two Teacher   As the label, *meditative,* implies, teachers at Level Two mentally reflect on what they are doing in a classroom, but their reflection lies within a narrow range. They have an awareness of the uniqueness of their classroom and their students, and they go beyond their curricular guides and materials, but their adaptations are few and seem more like tinkering around the instructional edge. They may, for example, deviate from the prescribed teaching guide but not very far. Level Two teachers may vary their instructional patterns to fit certain classroom events—that is, the obvious boredom of students—or they may bring in supplemental materials. However, they are hardly innovative.

■ The Level Three Teacher   There is a large jump to the *generative-creative* level. These teachers focus on their individual students, and they take a wide view of knowledge. They attend to their curricular guides and the prescribed materials, but those materials are launching pads rather than targets of their instruction. Their classrooms are characterized by a great variety of instructional approaches and problem-centered materials. They play off the interests and talents of their students but not in a casual or pandering way. Their expectations for students are high and transcend required tests and examinations. They approach instruction as diagnosticians, seeking the best ways to engage students in their own mental growth. They do not simply transmit knowledge, but they create. They create in students a desire to learn and they create classroom environments where individual students become self-directed learners.

■ creative and effective teachers

Few new teachers burst on the educational scene as Level Three *generative-creative* teachers. Many start at Level Two or attain it quickly. It is important, though, to have an understanding of your current behavior and to work toward this highest level. The very embracing of the goal will put you on the road to full professionalism.

The Level Three teacher finds creative ways to meet the individual needs of students.
(© Bob Daemmrich/ PhotoEdit)

National Board for Professional Teaching Standards

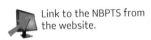
Link to the NBPTS from the website.

Since it began in 1987, an organization called the **National Board for Professional Teaching Standards (NBPTS)** has been working to recognize and provide greater support to superior (or Level Three) teachers. In addition, the NBPTS attempts, in the process, to strengthen the claim of professionalism for the career of teaching and to play a leading role in this effort.

■ standards stimulate achievement

Over the years, the lack of recognizable high standards has discouraged some potentially outstanding people from entering teaching and has lowered the level of aspiration of others. High standards tend to focus people's attention and harness their energies. For example, in long-distance running, the four-minute mile was long considered the unbreakable barrier. For years and years, sports commentators pontificated that it was beyond the capacities of humans to run a mile in four minutes or less. Then, in 1957, Roger Bannister, a relatively obscure British medical student, broke the magic barrier. A new standard was set, and runners reset their sights. The following year, *thirty-seven* runners broke that "unbreakable barrier." Today, breaking the four-minute barrier is commonplace. The reason is that a new standard has been set and people have risen to it in great numbers. The National Board for Professional Teaching Standards is trying to perform a similar function for the teaching profession.

The NBPTS has established standards for teaching practice and has developed a series of board certification assessments based on these standards. As of 2004, just over 32,000 teachers, from all fifty states and the District of Columbia, had achieved board certification.[5] Board advocates believe that these standards allow teachers to gain a highly regarded, professional credential like that available to physicians, accountants, architects, and other professionals.

■ **Core Propositions and Characteristics**   The NBPTS is dedicated to and directed by five core propositions:

■ five core propositions

1. Teachers know the subjects they teach and how to teach these subjects to students.
2. Teachers are committed to their students and their learning.

3. Teachers are responsible for managing and monitoring student learning.
4. Teachers think systematically about their practice and learn from experience.
5. Teachers are members of a learning community.[6]

In addition, the organization has five distinguishing characteristics:

■ five distinguishing
characteristics

1. The NBPTS is for experienced teachers, teachers with a baccalaureate or an advanced degree who have graduated from an accredited college or university and have at least three years of teaching experience.
2. "Taking the boards" is completely voluntary. It is not intended to be a condition of work, like state licensure, but an achievement testifying to an individual teacher's attainment of a high level of professionalism.
3. "Taking the boards" involves submitting oneself to a set of examinations and assessments in particular areas or subject matters such as early childhood, English language arts, and physical education and health. Currently, board certification is offered in twenty-seven different teaching fields, and there are plans for adding more.
4. These assessments are not typical paper-and-pencil tests. Teaching, by its very nature, is a mixture of thought and action and is not measured well by traditional "sit-down" testing. Among the means of assessment are videotapes of one's teaching and an evaluation of one's professional portfolio. Such a portfolio might include examples of students' work, sample lesson plans, and other items that the teacher believes will support his or her candidacy. Candidates do, however, take examinations to assure depth of knowledge in their field. They are also asked to respond to and justify their responses to classroom circumstances that are presented them on CDs.
5. The primary control of the NBPTS is in the hands of a sixty-three-person board of directors. Although administrators, teacher educators, and the general public are represented on the NBPTS, two-thirds of the board members are teachers—a further step toward achieving professionalism in teaching.

■ advantages of the NBPTS

■ **Advantages to Board Certification**   NBPTS certification means a salary bonus for those teachers so designated. The amount varies by state, but can be as much as $5,000 a year for the length of the ten-year certification. Board certification also means that school boards have a recognizable basis on which to award merit pay other than arbitrary and impressionistic criteria, such as "Her children do well on tests" or "He seems to work long hours and is popular with the brightest students." Besides raising salaries, board certification offers a number of other advantages. Teachers who have achieved NBPTS certification are professionally more portable or able to move more freely across state lines. Also, this effort should stimulate research on what constitutes superior teaching. And it should trigger more attention to this research-based knowledge within teacher education and throughout the teaching force. Most of all, it should contribute to the essential but difficult mission of creating a system of recognition for highly skilled and dedicated professionals.

■ arguments against the
NBPTS

■ **Criticisms of the NBPTS**   The NBPTS, however, is not without critics. Some educators claim that there is no solid knowledge base in teaching (as opposed to medicine or architecture) on which to ground the board's assessments. Others see the NBPTS as a public relations move to enhance the status and salaries of teachers with artificial trappings ("Fillmore got himself board certified, but we all know he couldn't teach a duck!"). Still others, suspicious that the NBPTS is controlled by its majority of teacher members, see it becoming a vehicle primarily to serve the economic interests of teachers and to insulate them further from their "clients" (the students and their parents). Finally, some dismiss the NBPTS as just another organization promoting a failed "progressive ideology" (i.e., self-esteem, multiculturalism, and cultural relativity) rather than focusing on content knowledge and whether or not students are *actually* learning. These critics caution at best a wait-and-see attitude, acknowledging the strengths in the idea of a board, but are waiting to see if board-certified teachers really do bring about more student learning than noncertified teachers.[7] Meanwhile NBPTS has commissioned a number of independent research studies, including trying to see if board certified teachers are more successful in producing student learning than non-board-certified teachers. Stay tuned.

As we will see in the next section, the two largest professional organizations, the **National Education Association (NEA)** and the **American Federation of Teachers (AFT),** have been involved in promoting NBPTS certification, as well as performing other professional functions.

What Every New Teacher Should Possess: The Interstate New Teacher Assessment and Support Consortium Standards

■ first tier of skills

In the same year that the NBPTS began its work, the Council of Chief State School Officers (CCSSO) began a parallel work, one that focuses on what prospective teachers ought to know and be able to do in order to attain initial teaching licenses in their states. This effort, which is gathering great support as of late, is to lay out standards for a common core of teaching skills and knowledge for all beginning teachers and standards for teachers in specific subject matter areas and levels of schooling. The CCSSO formed the Interstate New Teacher Assessment and Support Consortium (INTASC) and has been working with the NBPTS to create model standards for "board-compatible" teacher licensing. Although all this talk of NBPTS, CCSSO, and INTASC may seem like alphabet soup, the educators behind these letters are working hard to develop clear and practical standards. The purpose behind these standards is not only to have new teachers across the country possess a common core of professional abilities, but also to lay the foundation for a seamless transition to acquiring the board certification later on. The INTASC standards are, in effect, the "first tier" of skills and knowledge, which all new teachers should possess.

 Link more information about the INTASC standards from the website.

Currently, thirty-seven states have developed and implemented teacher licensing standards that are based on ten core principles developed by INTASC. These ten INTASC standards for all beginning teachers are listed on the inside covers of your book. Find more information on INTASC and the standards at the website that accompanies this book.

Pause and Reflect

1 ▶ What are you doing now to ensure that you meet the INTASC standards as a beginning teacher?

2 ▶ Does the idea of working toward board certification appeal to you? Why or why not?

▶ Professional Associations

■ the need for an advocate

Like other occupational groups such as doctors and teamsters, teachers have associations whose function is to protect their interests and attempt to improve their lot. For example, teacher salaries (which are the major cost of schooling) and other educational expenses come out of the taxpayers' pockets. Tax revenues are used for many purposes, and there is heavy competition among groups that rely on tax money to support their efforts to fight crime and delinquency, increase aid to the elderly and to the poor, and so on. In the rough-and-tumble of a democracy, teachers need someone or something to look out for their interests and the interests of the recipients of their services: children. This is the avowed function of many teachers associations. Protection of teachers' rights and improvement in their rewards and working conditions will not just happen. There is an old saying: "Nobody gives you nothin' for nothin.'" The advances teachers make will occur largely as a result of their hard work and readiness to stand up for what they believe.

■ two competing alternatives

Our primary focus in this section is on the large umbrella organizations of teachers, the NEA and the AFT, because these have the most immediate and sustaining effects on the lives of teachers. In 2002, more than 70 percent of all public school teachers reported belonging to the NEA. The AFT represents slightly fewer than 25 percent. These two large associations claim to represent teachers to the federal, state, and local governments; to educational authorities at the state and local levels; and, finally, to the general public. Both of these organizations also come to the aid of teachers, like those in the vignettes that began this chapter, whose legal rights are being violated or who are being treated shoddily or unethically. It is important to know something about them, because if you become a teacher, they will claim to be speaking for *you*. In fact, many new teachers report being asked to join a professional association their first day on the job.

As you read the following pages, be aware that the NEA and the AFT are and have been in a struggle for the hearts, minds, and membership dues of teachers for decades. Further, each is concerned about advancing its cause and gaining the support of future teachers. Reg Weaver, president of the NEA, and Edward McElroy, president of the AFT, each agreed to write a special letter to the readers of this book, and we urge you to read these inserts. In addition, there is a short insert about one of the newer, smaller professional associations, the American Association of Educators, which is taking a very different approach than the major professional organizations of teachers.

The National Education Association

Link to the NEA from the website.

Founded in 1857, the NEA today is a complex institution that operates on the national, state, and local school district levels and serves a diverse clientele of rural, suburban, and urban teachers. The bulk of its 2.7 million or more members are classroom teachers, but also included are teacher aides, administrators, professors, retired educators, and college students preparing to become teachers. The NEA has some 13,520 local affiliate chapters in approximately 80 percent of the nation's school districts.[8]

■ a range of support services

■ **Services to Members**   The NEA offers its members a wide range of services, from an extensive array of publications to research on issues such as comparative salary scales and the attitudes of teachers on various topics. In addition, its UniServ program has some 1,500 professionals in the field working with teachers, ready

Reformers in the Ranks: The Association of American Educators

Formed in 1994, the Association of American Educators (AAE) represents a fresh approach for teachers who are dissatisfied with the two major professional groups. In its first ten years, it gained 45,000 teacher members in all fifty states. Although not anti-union, the AAE is opposed to many of the stands of the NEA and AFT, such as teacher strikes, opposition to voucher plans, and affirmative action for racial balance. The AAE's key goals are:

1. To encourage and support teachers who embrace certain views on education in America, such as the view that our schools should aim to improve a young person's character as well as his or her intellect.

2. To keep the governance of the organization in the hands of practicing teachers. Currently, more than half the AAE's board of directors is composed of classroom teachers who have won national teacher-of-the-year awards.

3. To keep the focus on educational issues and to stay out of politics. In contrast to the $500 to $700 combined annual local, state, and national dues charged by the major organizations, the AAE dues are a mere $150, and much of that goes for liability insurance.

This lean organization does not try to offer its members all of the supportive services of its larger rivals. It is, however, turning out to be an alternative for those who are tired of paying hefty dues and who disagree particularly with the political stands and social views of the larger organizations.

 Link to more information about the AAE from the website.

---

to give local teachers help in such specialized areas as collective bargaining. A number of special services are also available to members, such as travel programs, insurance policies, mutual fund programs, and book club programs.

◼ NEA as a political force

◼ The NEA and Political Issues   Since the NEA's inception, its goal has been "to elevate the character and advance the interests of the profession of teaching and to promote the cause of education in the United States." In advancing this goal, it regularly comes out against issues such as competency testing of teachers. On the other hand, since 1987, the NEA has supported the NBPTS and has long been a champion of small class sizes and special programs for linguistic and ethnic groups within schools.[9] Further, it has taken forceful positions on other issues. It has, for example, been a vigorous opponent of various voucher plans that call for using public tax monies for religious and other private schools.

If one is going to change things, one has to make a fuss and catch the eye of the world.

—Elizabeth Janeway

When it was started a century and a half ago, the NEA tried to speak for all public educators, teachers and administrators alike. That all changed three decades ago, when two things happened: first, the work of the organization became more concentrated on improving the lot of public school teachers; and, second, it started to flex its muscles in the political arena. In 1976, the NEA for the first time formally backed a presidential candidate (Jimmy Carter), and since then, it has consistently backed Democratic candidates for national and most state offices.

◼ a power on the national scene

The NEA has become a strong political player for various reasons. One political commentator referred to teachers as "bright, articulate, and reasonably well informed, making them naturals for political activism."[10] Also, teachers have the best record of any occupational group in registering to vote—well over 70 percent.[11] Further, the NEA is big and rich. Its sheer size and presence in many congressional districts is a huge asset to any candidate or party it would care to

I ask for philosophy from my union and it gives me politics, partisanship, and public relations. Teachers learn to be pragmatists or they don't survive. Underneath their veneer of practicality, they are dreamers. Truck drivers and longshoremen might not need a philosophical guiding light from their union leaders, but teachers do. Teachers yearn for commitment, for caring, and for conscience.

—Susan Ohanian

 Link to the AFT from the website.

■ the feisty alternative

■ the AFT's recent agenda

■ rumors of merger

support, and a substantial part of the $400 million annually collected from teachers goes to its political war chest.

The Democratic Party has been the recipient of the majority of the NEA's political help. Even though the voting preferences of America's teachers tend to reflect the even split between the two major parties, in recent elections the NEA leadership has doled out between 95 and 99 percent of its political contributions to Democrat candidates.[12] Many, however, question the wisdom of putting all these human and financial "eggs" into one political basket.

The American Federation of Teachers

The AFT's membership is approximately one-third the size of the NEA's, but it represents teachers in key urban areas across the country. Currently it bargains for teachers in New York City, Chicago, Philadelphia, Cleveland, Pittsburgh, Kansas City, St. Louis, Detroit, Boston, Houston, Dallas, Atlanta, and Washington, D.C.[13]

The AFT's leadership is very clear about placing the organization squarely within the American labor movement. The AFT itself is affiliated with the American Federation of Labor and Congress of Industrial Organizations (AFL-CIO), which has a membership of more than 14 million. Further, the AFT is much prized in that it is the fastest-growing union in the entire AFL-CIO.[14] Much of the AFT's growth in the past three to four decades has been due to success in introducing the collective bargaining process in the annual salary negotiations of teachers. The AFT's aggressive techniques, including strikes and the threat of strikes, are credited with substantial salary increases for teachers and with forcing the NEA into more militant tactics. On the down side, however, the shrinking student enrollments in some of our major cities, which are the AFT's real power base, have preoccupied the organization and sapped its energies.

■ **The AFT's Stance on Issues**   Although the AFT is noted for its hard bargaining on bread-and-butter issues such as salaries and benefits, it has also been a defender of academic freedom and greater participation in decision making by teachers. In spite of the fact that the AFT opposes many of the same issues as the NEA, such as vouchers, and shares with it only qualified support for charter schools, the AFT has a more progressive reputation, owing largely to the efforts of its long-time leader Albert Shanker, who died in 1997. Once seen by many as the champion of raw "teacher power" and as concerned only with the good of teachers, Shanker became a strong advocate of educational reform in his later years. He lobbied both his organization and the public in support of many reform efforts such as the NBPTS, certain kinds of merit pay, higher minimum standards for teachers, and longer and more intense teacher education. In contrast, the NEA has only recently come to support many of these reform efforts.

■ **A Possible Merger?**   For thirty years or more, the leaders of both the NEA and the AFT (along with many members of the press) have been discussing merging the two groups into one organization-union that would represent the entire teaching force. The advantages of one giant organization have attracted many people. It has been suggested that political strength in national elections and the ability to call a nationwide school shutdown would give teachers enormous power.

Great Teachers

Reg Weaver, President, National Education Association

A great teacher, Christa McAuliffe, said: "To teach is to touch a life forever."

And, touching lives is what teaching is all about. The process of a pottery maker reminds me of the characteristics of a great teacher. The potter takes a piece of clay, carefully examining it before he or she begins creating and sees the potential of what the piece of clay can become. In the same way, great teachers look at the children in their classrooms.

They see the anxious and excited, who are ready to learn and ready to let you know what they have already learned. They see the shy, who have a lot of hidden knowledge; they are just as anxious to learn, but have problems expressing themselves. Then there are the busy; the ones who may already be disrupting the classroom. The great teacher sees the potential in each of these children and determines how best to motivate and encourage every one of them to achieve academic excellence.

Great teachers know that reaching and inspiring these children is more than a day-long or year-long job. They must spend long hours, many days, weekends, and even time during their vacations to improve their skills and increase their knowledge. "He who dares to teach must never cease to learn."

Great teachers hear a different drummer and travel a different road. They know that parents are the children's first teachers and the community is their first classroom. So, they develop ways to make the curriculum relevant to what the child has learned at home and in the community. Great teachers help their students to realize that their appreciation and dedication to learning impacts their future.

My own life is an example of the value of committed educators. It was the encouragement of caring teachers who helped me to become who I am today. They saw that I had ability, believed in me, and opened my eyes to the opportunities education would unlock. Their example and support were part of why I chose teaching as a career. I am very proud to be a member of one of the most rewarding professions in the world.

Those who choose teaching as a career transform potential into reality. I remember when I was a young child in school, the teacher asked us what we wanted to be when we grew up. Many wanted to be teachers. We loved the way our teacher took time to encourage us, to tell us we could dream the impossible dream and become whatever we wanted to be. The confidence the teacher had in our ability and devotion to learning increased our self-esteem and made us work harder to achieve. Carl Jung wrote, "An understanding heart is everything in a teacher, and cannot be esteemed highly enough. One looks back with appreciation to the brilliant teachers, but with gratitude to those who touched our human feeling."

Great teachers work with parents and community leaders to better understand how to meet the needs of their students, which includes helping to provide a safe and healthy community environment. They face numerous challenges each day, and endure criticisms from individuals who think teaching is a snap. But teaching requires dedication and steadfastness; courage and patience; a sense of humor and strong principles.

It takes very special individuals to become great teachers. They are the creators of renowned scientists, shrewd legal minds, innovative corporate leaders, and effective leaders of this nation and the world. For years I heard George Bernard Shaw's saying, "Those who can, do. Those who can't, teach." The 2.7 million members of the NEA know the truth: Those who CAN, TEACH! Those who care about children. Those who can endure hardships. Those who are not afraid of challenges. Those who recognize that an educated citizenry ensures the survival of this nation. These are the individuals that make up the teaching profession—men and women, sensitive and caring, brave and strong, dedicated to excellence.

Our "help wanted" signs are in every community. The squeamish need not apply. We are looking for highly motivated, highly qualified, and committed individuals to join the teaching profession and the NEA. Together, we can make every community and every school in this nation great for all our children.

The Role of a Professional Union

Edward J. McElroy, President, American Federation of Teachers

Teachers want what children need. Reasonable class sizes, safe and well-equipped schools, high standards for conduct and achievement, and well-prepared and adequately supported teachers would appear on most teachers'—and students'—lists of educational priorities. These goals are reasonable, but not always easy to achieve, especially as an individual. That's where teacher unions come in.

Attaining what teachers want and children need is a guiding principle for the American Federation of Teachers (AFT). An example of this conviction is the way the AFT responded to *A Nation at Risk,* the 1983 report that sounded an alarm about the state of American education. While the report was criticized by many education groups, the AFT acknowledged the challenges it identified and launched headlong into addressing them.

AFT members have numerous options offered by their union for developing their professional abilities, including union-sponsored professional development based on the best and most current education research. The AFT program is designed to help local unions deliver high-quality professional development services, either on their own or in collaboration with their school districts and/or local universities. It meets the criteria for "highly qualified professional development" as defined in the No Child Left Behind Act of 2001.

The AFT also offers members a highly acclaimed biennial conference devoted to professional development. The conference provides classroom educators information about the latest research on school improvement, presentations from leading voices in the field, and scores of workshops tailored to teachers' needs and interests.

The AFT is a founding member of the National Board for Professional Teaching Standards (NBPTS), which certifies teachers according to rigorous standards for what accomplished teachers should know

and be able to do. Many AFT affiliates have negotiated contracts that provide financial support to candidates for certification, as well as salary supplements for board-certified teachers. Some unions have been able to negotiate release time to help candidates complete the certification process.

The AFT is committed not only to improving members' professional knowledge and skills, but also to improving the institutions in which they work. Many AFT local unions are working with school district management to enact school improvement measures with the help of the AFT, which provides technical assistance in applying approaches that have been proven effective. This partnership has helped turn around low-performing schools in districts across the country.

Beginning teachers have all the same reasons veteran teachers have for wanting and needing a professional union, plus another significant factor: new teacher attrition. Close to half of all beginning teachers leave the profession within five years. One-quarter of them will leave after only two years. A number of AFT unions have initiated and participated in induction and mentoring programs for beginning teachers. There is evidence that such programs not only help new teachers stay longer in the profession, but also help them greatly improve their skills early in their careers.

Despite the tremendous changes in American education in recent decades, it is still in many ways a factory system dominated by large employers in which teachers too often do not have an adequate say. Teachers' voices on behalf of their students and their profession are magnified when combined with those of others through their union. The AFT will continue to pursue professional wages and working conditions for teachers, because that is central to attracting, retaining, and rewarding the teachers American students need. At the same time, we will advance our work to strengthen our profession from within. I hope you will consider joining us in this work.

Also, the two organizations historically have spent much of their resources competing with each other to represent teachers in contract talks with local school systems, resources that could be used to improve education and the professionalism of teachers. Although unification would do much to solidify the power of teachers to affect change, internal organizational issues and jealousies have kept the NEA and AFT apart. In 2001, the two organizations stopped fighting and signed the "NEAFT Partnership" agreement, launching "an ongoing effort by the two groups to collaborate in projects ranging from education conferences to political and legal campaigns." In effect, they remain separate and independent, but come together to lobby for common causes.[15] Although hardly a marriage, this agreement appears to be somewhere between "going steady" and deciding to get engaged.

Pause and Reflect

1 ▸ Once you are established as a teacher, does the idea of becoming active in one of these two professional organizations or unions appeal to you personally? If so, what is the attraction?

2 ▸ What questions or concerns, if any, do you have about joining one of the two major teacher organizations?

Other Professional Associations

In addition to the NEA and AFT, there are many other educational organizations. Each supports certain constituents and serves their special interests. Table 15.1 offers a sample of these groups. The ones listed under the heading Specialized Associations of Teachers are primarily for teachers of a particular subject matter or area within the life of the school. Under the second heading, Nationwide Special-Interest Groups in Education, are more broad-based organizations that typically include members of the public, administrators, people from higher education,

TABLE 15.1 Nationwide Organizations of Interest to Teachers
Specialized Associations of Teachers
Council for Exceptional Children **(http://www.cec.sped.org)** National Science Teachers Association **(http://www.nsta.org)** National Council of Teachers of English **(http://www.ncte.org)** National Council for the Social Studies **(http://www.ncss.org)** National Association for Music Education **(http://www.menc.org)** National Association for the Education of Young Children **(http://www.naeyc.org)** Association of Career and Technical Education **(http://www.acteonline.org)** International Reading Association **(http://www.reading.org)** National Council of Teachers of Mathematics **(http://www.nctm.org)** American Council on the Teaching of Foreign Language **(http://www.actfl.org)** National Art Education Association **(http://www.naea-reston.org)** American Alliance for Health, Physical Education, Recreation and Dance **(http://www.aahperd.org)** Association for Education Communications and Technology **(http://www.aect.org)**
Nationwide Special-Interest Groups in Education
National School Boards Association **(http://www.nsba.org)** American Association of School Administrators **(http://www.aasa.org)** Association for Supervision and Curriculum Development **(http://www. ascd.org)** American Educational Research Association **(http://www.aera.net)** Council of Chief State School Officers **(http://www.ccsso.org)** Association of Teacher Educators **(http://www.ate1.org)** American Association of Colleges for Teacher Education **(http://www.aacte.org)**

and teachers. Through journals, in-service training, or professional development institutes, as well as conferences and conventions, these organizations play an important part in keeping teachers informed about research and developments in their fields. It is here where much of the teacher's professional activity goes on. We urge you to consider joining the association closest to your interests.

■ Student NEA

There are also professional associations dedicated specifically to future teachers. The largest of these is the Student National Education Association (SNEA), formerly called Future Teachers of America, which has some 60,000 members in over 900 colleges and universities.[16] As a branch of the NEA, the SNEA offers many of the benefits of NEA membership, such as liability insurance when members student teach, access to the NEA's research files, and subscriptions to its regular publications, *The NEA Handbook* and *Today's Education*.

■ education's honorary societies

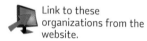
Link to these organizations from the website.

Three other professional groups that are open to prospective teachers include the honor societies of Pi Lambda Theta, Phi Delta Kappa, and Kappa Delta Pi. These associations are international in scope but typically organize around chapters on university or college campuses. They have regular meetings on recent developments in the field, such as constructivist approaches to learning, brain research, and character education. These organizations provide an excellent opportunity for students to meet other education students in a nonclassroom setting and particularly to meet practicing teachers and administrators in a professional but informal setting. If membership in such honorary associations interests you, we suggest first that you check out their websites; second, speak to one of your education professors about which, if any, of the organizations are on your campus and how you can learn about them; and third, call, write, or email the headquarters of these organizations to obtain general information and to learn whether there are chapters on your campus. It is not unheard of for beginning education students to initiate new chapters.

Wanted: A New Professionalism

The term *professionalism* has begun to acquire some negative connotations. Although teachers have had professional organizations for a century, only in the last forty-five years have they employed aggressive trade union tactics. Since then the term professionalism frequently has been equated with "teacher power" and with teachers' capacity to close down schools through strikes and work stoppages. While infrequently used in recent years, the possibility of striking gives teachers real clout. The power of teachers to shut down schools affects not only children's education, but also an entire community's economic health, from the immediate effects on working parents and caregivers to longer-term effects on the community's desirability as a place to live and raise children.

Other negative aspects of professionalism include:

- The growing alliances between the two major teachers' organizations, the NEA and the AFT, and the Democratic Party have tinged teacher professionalism with a troubling political gloss.
- Occasionally teachers will use their "professional status" as a barrier against criticism by children and parents ("How dare you question what I have done? I am a professional!"), making professionalism a cover for self-serving ends.
- In the interest of protecting and expanding the rights of its members, a professional group can be quite insensitive to the needs and rights of the client

group. For instance, insisting on tenure rights for all teachers who have taught for three years or more makes it difficult to get rid of those teachers who turn out to be genuinely incompetent. In the big cities, basing eligibility for transfer to more congenial schools on seniority may be robbing the most difficult schools of exactly the experienced teacher talent they need.

Behind the jargon of professionalism, then, one often finds naked self-interest that can do harm to the teachers' clients—children.

■ behind the jargon

The era of aggressive trade unionism in American industry and frequent labor-management stand-offs seems to have receded in recent years, however. In its place a new, cooperative spirit has brought about a revival of many of our industries. Following slogans of "excellence" and "re-engineering," workers and management have changed the economic landscape. Many see a similar pattern between the practicing teaching profession and their "management" (that is, their school board and administrators). Serious teacher strikes are becoming a rarity. Also, we are witnessing the beginnings of a revival similar to U.S. industry in the "educational excellence" movement and the "restructuring" efforts currently sweeping through our schools. In our view, the issue of teacher professionalism is very much wrapped up in these broader school renewal efforts. Whether teachers are treated as professionals will depend on the bottom line: the performance of our schools. To promote that performance, teachers need to begin with a personal commitment to excellence.

So to all of you who teach, hats off. Yours is an invaluable profession, a calling sure and high and noble, a model we cannot live without if we expect to remain strong and free. Don't quit. Don't even slack off. If ever we needed you, we need you today.

—CHARLES SWINDOLL

▶ Your Own Professional Development

At one time, it was considered adequate for a teacher to obtain an undergraduate education and a teaching license and then have no further training. However, forces both inside and outside the teaching profession have promoted the concept that the teacher must be a continuous learner. Most states have legislated continuing education for teachers. In fact, in more than one-half of the states, it is no longer possible to gain permanent licensure. More and more states are requiring teachers to keep up with developments in their fields or specific areas of education. In "Voices from the Classroom" one teacher describes the moment she first realized how deeply the commitment to lifelong learning can run among teachers.

Link more information about professional development from the website.

Education must not any longer be confined to the young. The young must not look forward to its completion; the old must not look back on it as an accompaniment of immaturity. For all people, education must be made to seem a requirement of human life as long as that endures.

—ISAAC ASIMOV

Central to this drive for the continuing education of teachers, or **professional development,** as it is often called, is the growth of new knowledge and the demand for new skills. A dramatic example is the rising interest in technological literacy. As American society has become increasingly dependent on electronic information services, the needs and advantages of being comfortable and competent with computers, the Internet, CDs, videodiscs, and networking have become more evident. Therefore, elementary and secondary schools and colleges are rushing to provide students with this new competence. And to keep up with the rapidly developing information technologies, teachers, like their students, need to become continuous learners.

VOICES FROM THE CLASSROOM

Theresa Madison teaches grade ten Language Arts at Brighton High School in Brighton, Massachusetts.

Professionalism

Before I began teaching I had a certain vision of what the world of teachers would be like. I prepared myself for hearing a lot of "when you've been around as long as I have" and "when you get to be my age, you'll understand." I felt a sort of pre-embarrassment for all the mistakes I would probably make before I "got it." To me, the profession presented itself as a kind of hierarchy where the big cheese of the school would offer condescending advice and rolled eyes at my rookie mishaps.

Now, only six months into the experience, I am happy to say that my fears were quite wrong. Not too long ago, I went to visit a colleague of mine, Jane, in her classroom during one of her planning periods. She's been a teacher for about six or seven years and at our school for only three. About a minute or two into our conversation, I noticed that the door that adjoined her room with Mrs. Conner's room was open and students were moving between the two. Soon Mrs. Conner herself came bustling in and out of Jane's room, looking for glue sticks and getting a clarification about some graphic organizer.

After asking what was going on, I made a concerted effort to hide my surprise. Jane was asked to take on a smaller class load this year and to spend the remaining time as a literacy coach. She told me that the job included sitting in on classes for a week or so and then working one-on-one with that particular teacher to experiment with different instructional practices and techniques. But Mrs. Conner? She had been teaching for thirty years. This was a woman who had a way with students, parents, and other teachers that I wished I could bottle and sell. It was one thing to smile and nod at staff meetings when younger teachers spoke but to invite a teacher with far fewer years on the job into your classroom was quite a different scenario.

I could only describe the feeling as humbling. Nobody, it seemed, was out to get me, or laugh at my naiveté. The more I began to look around, the more I noticed that many of my colleagues were "age blind." The task at hand was to educate students, and if someone had a better way of doing things or if some workshop came along that could benefit a teacher's practice, then many of these educators were up for another learning experience. I had always heard that teachers were learners for life, but I wasn't sure how many of them bought that old cliché. As it turns out, seeking more for our students and our own practice is not considered a sign of weakness or a stigma by all of those scary veterans; it's simply part of being a professional.

 Visit the website for more Voices from the Classroom.

Types of Continuous Learning Opportunities

■ **Independent Study**   One aim of education is to develop the ability to engage in independent study. *Independent study* is jargon for being able to "go it alone." Although this approach is much discussed among educators, students seem to get little actual practice in choosing and systematically investigating their own areas of interest. Independent study, though, is one of the most important means for continual self-renewal available to you as a teacher. Teachers are confronted daily with things they do not understand about children and knowledge and human learning:

■ self-renewal through study

- Is there anything in this discussion about learning styles and how I can apply it in my classroom?
- What does the new brain research suggest about teaching X and Y?

The video case *Parent-Teacher Conference* shows two teachers role-playing how the conversation between parent and teacher might go at conference time. As you watch the clips and study the artifacts in the case, reflect upon the following questions:

1. Several types of continuous learning opportunities are described in this chapter. Which are represented in this case?

2. Earlier in the chapter, the authors described several aspects of teaching that either contributed to the case FOR teaching as a profession or contributed to the case AGAINST teaching as a profession. Do you believe that conducting parent conferences is a responsibility that can be used as evidence either for or against teaching as a profession? Explain your opinion.

■ forming study groups

■ graduate courses

- What are the fundamental skills of composition that children should know?
- How can I help my students use history for their own benefit?

Such questions are daily grist for the teacher's independent study mill. Of course, your study should not be confined to professional problems. Your own personal interests may lead into such areas as organic gardening, physical fitness, classic movies, the politics of colonial America, the humanizing of the corporate state, or harnessing the media. Not by professional problems alone doth the teacher live!

■ **Group Study**   Group study is another common form of continuous learning for the teacher. It often takes the form of committee work. When a problem arises in the school for which there is no apparent solution, a group of people takes upon itself the task of exploring the problem with a view toward recommending an enlightened course of action. In recent years, to obtain opinions from outside the school, teachers and administrators have begun inviting community residents to these study groups. Typical issues these groups might take on are curricular alternatives, avoiding bullying on the playground, an analysis of the unused education resources in the community, a writing across the curriculum program, and the potential benefits and costs of using paraprofessionals in a high school.

■ **Graduate Study**   A third way for you to continue to learn is to take courses or to work toward an advanced degree. Most colleges and universities offer

Good colleagues make professional growth a pleasure. (© Robin Sachs/PhotoEdit)

The improvement of understanding is for two ends: first, our own increase of knowledge; secondly, to enable us to deliver that knowledge to others.

—JOHN LOCKE

courses suitable for and interesting to teachers. Special and regular courses are offered in the evening, on weekends, and during the summer vacation. Many universities are now offering computer-based distance-learning courses, which enable teachers (and others) to do advanced study without leaving their homes. These courses and degree programs not only allow teachers to gain a deeper understanding of their work but also make it possible for some teachers to train for other jobs in education, such as guidance counseling, administration, or college teaching.

■ programs sponsored by district

■ **Professional Development Programs** A fourth opportunity you will have to grow and learn is to attend a professional development program (sometimes called "in-service") sponsored by the school or school district. Professional development programs are often targeted at school- or district-wide problems or issues. For instance, if students in a particular school are getting unsatisfactory grades on standardized achievement tests, the district may choose to provide special training for the faculty, or the district may decide to switch to a new, supposedly better mathematics program, a change that will also require special training for the faculty. Training often takes place weekly or monthly, before or after school. Also, special days are sometimes set aside on which school is canceled or students are dismissed early so teachers can participate in training.

■ observation and feedback

The more we know, the more we want to know; when we know enough, we know how much we don't know.

—CAROL ORLOCK

■ **Supervision** A fifth form of continuous learning comes through supervision. During a teacher's early years in the profession, school districts provide professional advice that amounts to one-on-one help. For instance, if you are a new high school teacher, your department head may observe your classes regularly and discuss the observations with you, or if you are an elementary school teacher, your building principal or lead teacher may make regular visits and follow them with feedback sessions. Although supervision can sometimes be quite threatening, particularly to nontenured teachers, it offers an opportunity to obtain valuable insight and information about your teaching techniques and skills.

■ mentoring

■ **Mentoring** In recent years, many school districts around the country have instituted mentoring programs whereby more experienced teachers are assigned to assist beginners. (Mentoring is discussed in more detail in the chapter entitled "What Can the New Teacher Expect?") Along with special training, the mentors may receive a reduction in teaching responsibilities, a salary increase, or both. **Mentoring** programs formalize and make more systematic a time-honored process in which an experienced teacher takes a rookie under his or her wing, helping the beginner make the theory-into-practice transition and serving as a nonjudgmental colleague.

■ **Systematic Reflection on Practice** Teaching can become a matter of routine, sometimes a mindless routine. This condition is enormously dangerous to a teacher's development. Even more important than engaging in the activities we have discussed is developing the habit of reflecting on one's practice. If teachers, new or old, are to improve, they need to make systematic reflection on what is happening in their classrooms a regular part of their professional lives. In the "spaces" in their lives—the time between classes, driving home, or working out at the gym—they need to be asking themselves questions like the following:

- What went right in class today?
- What didn't work?
- Which students am I *not* reaching and what should I do about it?
- What can I do to get my uninvolved students more engaged?
- Are there other ways of presenting this material that will connect with students who have different learning styles?

■ reflection is essential

This may explain why we have sprinkled opportunities for you to "Pause and Reflect" throughout each chapter. We are convinced that the true key to sustained development as a professional is the probing habit of reflection and commitment to growth as a teacher.

▶ A Final Word

■ the teacher as both object and artist

A child, unlike any other, yet identical to all who have preceded and all who will follow, sits in a classroom today— hopeful, enthusiastic, curious. In that child sleeps the vision and the wisdom of the ages. The touch of a teacher will make the difference.

—Sharon M. Draper, Teacher of the Year 1997, board-certified teacher

Becoming a teacher may be compared with sculpting a work of art from a piece of stone. The difference is that the teacher is both the sculptor and the stone. The teacher begins with a vision of what he or she wants to be and then sets to work transforming the vision into a reality. The process requires an understanding of the material with which one is working—the self—and of the tools one can use. It also requires a vision of the teacher one desires to become. Finally, it takes long hours of chipping away and then smoothing the surfaces. To be a teacher, particularly a teacher who is continuously moving forward, is a lifelong commitment to be an artist.

Key Terms

American Federation of Teachers
   (AFT) (461)
mentoring (473)
National Board for Professional
   Teaching Standards (NBPTS) (459)

National Education Association
   (NEA) (461)
profession (451)
professional development (469)

For Reflection

1 Do you think it is important for teachers to devote themselves to becoming professionals? If so, what must they do? Are you willing to do it?

2 What do you think about the description of the "career teacher" in the "Recognizing Excellence in Teaching" section of this chapter?

3 Do teachers need a professional organization? What essential functions does such a group perform?

4 At this moment, what seems to you to be the most important issues with which teachers should concern themselves? Increased power? Higher salaries? Better training? Something else?

5 Do you believe it is right for teachers to strike? Why or why not?

6 Which of the ideas for lifelong professional development described in this chapter appeal to you most? Why?

For Debate

Read the Policy Matters! summary, "A Two-Tiered Profession?" at the website, and consider the issues it outlines about the National Board for Professional Teaching Standards (NBPTS). Then, go to EduSpace to post your answers (or respond to other students' answers) to the What Do You Think questions listed in the Policy Matters! feature.

For Further Information

PRINT RESOURCES

National Commission on Teaching and America's Future, *No Dream Denied: A Pledge to America's Children* (Washington, DC: 2003). Available at: **http://www.nctaf.org.**
This report is a follow-up to the bi-partisan commission's initial report, *What Matters Most: Teaching for America's Future.* It examines issues related to teacher retention; strengthening teacher preparation, accreditation, and licensure; and how to build a professionally rewarding career in teaching.

Gerald Grant and Christine Murray, *Teaching in America: The Slow Revolution* (Cambridge, MA: Harvard University Press, 1999).
This book traces the progress of two groups, college professors and precollegiate teachers, pointing out the similarities and differences in the evolution of professions. Drawing lessons from the development of the professorate, the authors point out the steps teachers need to take to continue their progress.

Dan C. Lortie, *Schoolteacher: A Sociological Study* (Chicago: University of Chicago Press, 1975).
This classic book presents a sociological view of the ethos of the teaching profession, that pattern of orientations and sentiments that are peculiar to teachers.

National Education Association, *Status of the American Public School Teacher: 2000–01* (Washington, DC: National Education Association, 2001).
This report is one in a series of studies conducted every five years by the National Education Association. It contains a massive amount of information on who teachers are, what is on their minds, and the conditions of their work.

Eugene F. Provenzo and Gary McCloskey, *Schoolteachers and Schooling: Ethoses in Conflict* (Norwood, NJ: Ablex, 1996).
This short book gives a thoughtful and detailed picture of how teaching has changed in the last third of the twentieth century and the forces at play in a teacher's life.

The Public Agenda, *A Sense of Calling: Who Teaches and Why* (New York: Public Agenda, 2000).
An encouraging report on new teachers' attitudes about their chosen profession, their satisfactions, and their concerns. In addition, the report also deals with the perceptions of administrators of new teachers and their performance.

WEB RESOURCES

American Federation of Teachers. Available at: **http://www.aft.org.**
The AFT's website provides information on the organization and its programs, commentary on current issues, and links to other interesting web pages. Contact the American Federation of Teachers, 555 New Jersey Avenue, NW, Washington, DC 20001.

National Education Association. Available at: **http://www.nea.org.**
This website offers a great deal of information about the NEA and its programs. Contact the

Peter Brimelow, *Worm in the Apple: How the Teachers Unions Are Destroying American Education* (New York: HarperCollins, 2003).
This strongly written book by a noted journalist lays out a case against the major teachers unions and suggests how the profession ought to be reformed.

National Education Association, 1201 16th Street, NW, Washington, DC 20036, (202) 822-7200, FAX: (202) 822-7292.

The National Board of Professional Teacher Standards. Available at **http://www.nbpts.org.**
This website not only has extensive information on the organization and the standards, but also extensive resources of interest to teachers.

16

Why Teach? A Final Word

Chapter Preview   In this short, final chapter we revisit the fundamental question, "Should you choose teaching as your career?" We, of course,
cannot answer such a profoundly personal question for you. However, the chapter presents a few perspectives for your consideration.

This chapter emphasizes that:

▶ The views of those hiring and working with our new teachers are supportive
and positive.

▶ Members of the general public hold strongly positive views of teachers.

▶ The attitudes of new teachers in public and private schools about their career
choice suggest strong career satisfaction.

▶ The "Why teach?" question is critical to a successful career choice *and* success
as a teacher.

We start this chapter with a Pause and Reflect exercise. We ask you to return to the very first question we posed in the initial chapter: "Why teach?"

If you are still considering teaching as a life's work, what are your personal reasons? Write down in the space below what for you are the personal "pros" and "cons" of a teaching career. Since much of the rest of this chapter reports surveys of how others have answered this question, be as detailed as you can.

Reasons for　　　　　　　　　　　**Reasons against**

_____

_____

_____

_____

_____

_____

Compare what you have written here with what you wrote in response to the question "Why become a teacher?" in the chapter entitled "Why Teach?" Have you seen any shifts? If there are changes, how do you account for them? Based on this reflection, how would you characterize your current plans to teach?

▶ Opinions About Teachers and Teaching

Although the decision about whether teaching is the right career for you is intensely personal, as John Donne said in the seventeenth century, "No man is an island," meaning that we are all connected to the "continent" of other people. So, it might be helpful to know what other people think about teachers and teaching. We'll consider the views of the general public, those of administrators, and finally, what teachers who are new to the field have to say about their work.

What Does the Public Say About Teachers and Teaching?

The education of America's children regularly tops the list of the public's social concerns. Particularly now, in the first decade of the twenty-first century, our educational system is receiving major attention from social critics and politicians. Because of this high priority, our teaching force—present and near future—is receiving a good deal of scrutiny. Americans are relying on our teachers to instruct, guide, inspire, motivate, and occasionally prod our children to learn and to learn more than ever before.

■ strong support from public

The public—again, the people whose taxes pay our public school teachers—overwhelmingly acknowledges and supports the nation's teachers. As we reported earlier, when asked to select which group provided "the most benefit to society," 62 percent selected teachers, while only 17 percent selected physicians, the second choice. Only 5 percent chose people in business, 3 percent chose lawyers, and journalists and politicians each received only 1 percent.[1]

Members of the public are also aware of the direct importance of teachers to their students' learning. When asked to rate which factors have the greatest impact on student learning, 44 percent selected the qualifications of the teacher

Surveys reveal that most people consider an effective teacher to be a vitally important factor in a good education.
(© Elizabeth Crews)

over other factors such as class size, socioeconomic status of the family, or the family's involvement and support.[2]

■ teachers are trusted

Finally, the public has a great deal of trust in teachers. According to the *National Credibility Index,* when asked which of the following people is "the most believable when speaking out on public issues," teachers were rated the highest, above members of the armed forces, national experts, and community activists.[3]

What Do Administrators Say About New Teachers?

Nevertheless, amid worries about the academic achievement of students and the cries for increased standards and high-stakes testing, some suggest that teaching now appeals to too many young people with few skills and little drive. Others opine that future teachers are lured to teaching only by the security of regular pay raises and summers off. Is there any truth to these opinions? What do the administrators who supervise them on a daily basis say about the new teachers entering the field?

■ administrators praise new teachers

The opinions of principals and superintendents support those of the general public. A stunning 98 percent of superintendents and principals surveyed agreed with the descriptions of their new teachers as "motivated" and "energetic."[4] As Figure 16.1 shows, rumors that the quality of new teachers has deteriorated are hardly borne out by those who do the hiring. Only 9 percent of these educators believe the quality of the teaching force is declining.[5] We suspect that there are few professions or occupations where supervisors have such high regard for newcomers.

What Do New Teachers Think About Teaching?

■ new teachers happy in their work

An in-depth study, conducted in 2000 with 664 public school teachers and 250 private teachers, all having taught for five or fewer years, paints a picture of how

FIGURE 16.1
What Superintendents and Principals Say About Our New Teachers

Source: Public Agenda, *A Sense of Calling: Who Teaches and Why* (New York: The Public Agenda, 2000), p. 13.

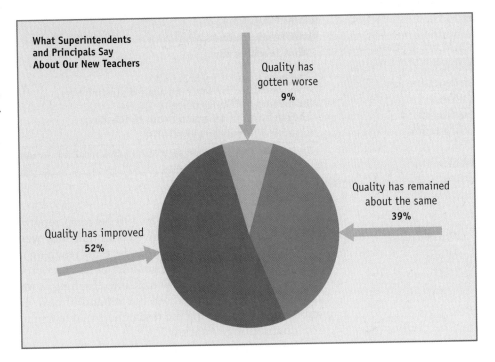

What Superintendents and Principals Say About Our New Teachers

Quality has gotten worse 9%

Quality has remained about the same 39%

Quality has improved 52%

today's newest teachers feel about their work. The researchers aptly titled their report *A Sense of Calling: Who Teaches and Why*, and concluded "most new teachers are highly motivated professionals who bring a strong sense of commitment and high morale to their work."[6] New teachers see themselves as talented and dedicated professionals.

■ teachers need enthusiasm

Reflecting the title of the report, 86 percent of new teachers affirmed that only those "with a true sense of calling" should teach.[7] Nine out of ten claim that the teaching profession demands a high level of energy and effort, requiring more talent and hard work than many other professions. The teachers in this study continually commented on the need for enthusiasm to do the job well. An overwhelming 98 percent described other new teachers with whom they work as sharing in their sense of commitment and enthusiasm.[8] This is hardly the picture of a disappointed and disgruntled group of newcomers.

The best prize life offers is the chance to work hard at work worth doing.

—THEODORE ROOSEVELT

Pause and Reflect

1 ► Do the opinions of one of these groups—the public, administrators, other new teachers—matter more to you than those of the others? Why?

2 ► How important is it to you to know what other people will think about you as a teacher?

► Why Teachers Teach

■ why teachers teach

Let's get back to the question, "Why teach?" by considering those already in the field. Why do teachers teach? *A Sense of Calling*, the study of new teachers described above, reveals some surprisingly consistent answers. As shown in Table 16.1,

TABLE 16.1 Why Teachers Teach	
What Teachers Say	**Percentage Who Say It**
Teaching is work they love to do	96
They would choose teaching again if starting over	80
Teaching is a lifelong choice	75
They get a lot of satisfaction out of teaching	68
They fell into teaching by chance	12

Source: Public Agenda, *Attitudes About Teaching* (New York: Public Agenda, 2003), p. 12.

nearly all of these new teachers (96 percent) reported that teaching is the work they love to do. Four out of five claim that they would choose teaching again if starting over. Three out of four insist that "teaching is a lifelong choice," and two out of three report that they get a lot of satisfaction out of teaching. Contrary to the rumor that many simply drift into teaching, a mere 12 percent say they "fell into teaching by chance." All but a handful have extremely altruistic attitudes about their work, telling the researchers that teaching offers them an opportunity for "contributing to society."

For some teachers, teaching is clearly a short-term career. One in five respondents in the *Sense of Calling* survey indicated that they would probably change careers at some point. Although this figure contrasts sharply with the 50 percent of young college graduates in other fields who say that they expect to change careers at least once,[9] the reference to teaching as a short-term career brings up an important point. The desire to teach for a few years and then to move on to another career or to raise a family is both common and to be respected. Also, our schools are filled with individuals who "dropped in" on teaching and stayed to make it their professional home.

Judging from this study, however, it seems that new teachers show a remarkable certainty that they made the right choice in pursuing a teaching career. It also appears that the majority of today's new teachers have taken the time to reflect on whether teaching is the right career choice for them.

Pause and Reflect

1 ► Does this information on administrators' satisfaction with new teachers and new teachers' satisfaction with their career choice surprise you? What are your personal reactions to this endorsement of teaching?

■ extremely high job satisfaction

Pleasure in the job puts perfection in the work.

—ARISTOTLE

In *A Sense of Calling* the researchers asked these new teachers, "Is teaching satisfying?" and specifically how important it was to them that the work have certain characteristics. Table 16.2 summarizes their responses. An impressive 96 percent report that they are involved in work that they love, and 97 percent are convinced that they are doing important work for the good of society. Eighty-four percent have the peace of mind that comes with knowing one's job is secure.[10]

While not surprising, only 31 percent claim that teaching pays well. Clearly, then, today's new teachers, while not painting a perfect picture, are personally "happy in their work."

TABLE 16.2 Is Teaching Satisfying?

How important is it to you that a job has each of the following characteristics?

	Percentage of New Teachers Responding	
	"Absolutely Essential"	"My Current Teaching Position Has It"
Involves work you love to do	83	96
Allows enough time to be with family	81	79
Contributes to society and helps others	72	97
Provides the supervision and support you need	64	78
Has job security	60	84
Gives the sense that you are respected and appreciated	59	66
Has good opportunities for advancement	33	59
Pays well	30	31

Source: Public Agenda, *Attitudes About Teaching* (New York: Public Agenda, 2003), p. 10.

■ teaching as pleasurable activity

Teachers' widespread satisfaction and love for their work is largely unknown, even among teachers. The "good news" has been lost in the headlines about test scores and other educational problems. The facts are that, by and large, teachers love the job of teaching. Consider the following:

- Seventy-nine percent of teachers agree "strongly" with the statement "I am passionate about teaching."
- Seventy-four percent of teachers say that teaching is a lifelong career choice.
- Ninety-one percent of new teachers believe that teaching matches their skills and interests very well.[11]

A Special Intrinsic Reward

While there is encouraging news that others apparently are happy and satisfied as teachers, nevertheless, it is your life and your choice. Clearly, selecting a career is a personal decision and involves answering many questions, such as "Will I be happy?" "Will this career provide me with a satisfying lifestyle?" "Will I be up to the challenge, and will I find the work satisfying?" and "Will I grow in the experience?" People who are considering teaching as a life's work should grapple with these questions, which surround the motives for choice. But they also need to scrutinize other, deeper motives.

■ teaching, a vocation

Teaching, like nursing, the ministry, and social work, is a service occupation. More correctly, teaching is a **vocation.** Built into teaching is the idea of contributing to the lives of others. For many people, the root of their decision to teach is deeper than a love of subject matter or an attraction to the life of a teacher. Many men and women select teaching for reasons that are, at heart, religious or humanitarian. These people are called to the work.

vo·ca·tion n. 2. An inclination, as if in response to a summons, to undertake a certain kind of work.

—*American Heritage Dictionary*

There are people who come to teaching for a variety of reasons, such as the availability of jobs or summer vacations, but then discover their true calling to teach once they are actually working with

FOR BETTER OR FOR WORSE © 2002 Lynn Johnston Productions. Dist. By Universal Press Syndicate. Reprinted with permission. All rights reserved.

students. We suspect that all teachers who are truly satisfied are people whose choice has been grounded in deeper motivation, whether they felt it before or after they began their teaching careers. It is this deeper motivation that sustains teachers through difficult times and with difficult students. And, although such religious or humanistic reasons for teaching are a private matter, it is a matter that each of us needs to explore very carefully. Of all the questions in this book "Why teach?" is ultimately the most important one. How you answer this question will determine not only whether or not you will teach but what you will actually *accomplish* as a teacher.

▶ A Final Word

■ huge, psychic benefit

In the earlier chapter dealing with the question, "Why teach?" we explored both the extrinsic and intrinsic rewards that come with teaching. One of the intrinsic rewards mentioned was the knowledge that as a teacher you are involved in very important work. This particular **psychic reward** is captured by the story of an American television reporter filming a documentary on the work of the late Mother Teresa and her community of nuns in the slums of Calcutta, India. The reporter came upon a young American nun cleaning the running sores, filth, and infections covering the body of a dying beggar. After filming the young woman carefully cleansing the ruined body of this close-to-death man, the reporter looked down at the nun and declared, "Sister, I wouldn't do that for a million dollars!" Without taking her eyes off her dying patient, the young nun replied, "Neither would I." One of the great intrinsic benefits of a career in teaching—and one not shared by the vast number of other occupations—is the inner certainty that you are doing important work and that you are spending your life well. Those who can, teach.

Key Terms

psychic reward (482)   vocation (481)

For Reflection

1 What issues and questions about your own consideration of a teaching career has this chapter raised?
2 Were you surprise by the survey research on teacher satisfaction?
3 What is your reaction to the positive reports of administrators about the new teachers in the field?
4 Did reviewing the list of motives for teaching in the earlier chapter give you any new thoughts or insights?

For Debate

Now that you have reached the end of this book, we strongly suggest that you visit EduSpace and, once more, share your views on the central question of this chapter: Why teach? If you are comfortable with doing so, share some of the reasons you listed earlier in this chapter both for and against becoming a teacher. How have your answers changed since you made a similar list at the beginning of the book?

For Further Information

PRINT RESOURCES

The Public Agenda, *A Sense of Calling: Who Teaches and Why* (New York: Public Agenda, 2000).
This report, from which much of this chapter is drawn, provides a rich and varied account of the current teaching force and deals with a wide range of issues in addition to the world of new teachers.

National Education Association, *Status of the American Public School Teacher* (Washington, DC: National Education Association, 2003). Available at: **http://www.nea.org/edstats/images/status.pdf.**
This report is a goldmine of information on everything from teacher's attitudes toward their work to salary information. Compiled every five years, the report gives us a snapshot of the profession today in a historical perspective.

Susan Moore Johnson, *Finders and Keepers: Helping New Teachers Survive and Thrive in Our Schools* (San Francisco: Jossey-Bass, 2004).
This book is based on a recent study of new teachers struggling to succeed in a range of different schools. The stories of these teachers are full of insights and useful advice.

WEB RESOURCES

U.S. Department of Labor. Available at: **http://stats.bls.gov/oco/ocos069.htm.**
This government agency maintains an active website on many aspects of employment and careers. It is particularly thorough in its treatment of elementary and secondary school teaching. There is extensive information on the nature of teaching, the employment picture, working conditions, and the job outlook.

About.com. Available at: **http://careerplanning.about.com/library/weekly/aa030901d.htm.**
This all-purpose information website, in addition to a section (curiously) called "Those Who Can Do, Teach," also has an array of sites ranging from the nature of teaching to something called "workplace survival."

Endnotes

Chapter 1

1. Sharon Feiman-Nemser and Robert E. Floden, "The Culture of Teaching." In *The Handbook of Research on Teaching*, 3d ed., ed. Merlin C. Witrock (New York: Macmillan, 1986), pp. 510–511.
2. David Haselkorn and Louis Harris, *The Essential Profession: A National Survey of Public Attitudes Toward Teaching, Educational Opportunity and School Reform* (Belmont, MA: Recruiting New Teachers, Inc., 1998), p. 2.
3. Dan Lortie, *Schoolteacher* (Chicago: University of Chicago Press, 1975), p. 102.
4. David Haselkorn and Louis Harris, *The Essential Profession: A National Survey of Public Attitudes Toward Teaching, Educational Opportunity and School Reform* (Belmont, MA: Recruiting New Teachers, Inc., 1998), p. 2.
5. Mihaly Csikszentmihalyi and Jane McCormack, "The Influence of Teachers," *Phi Delta Kappan* 67, no. 6 (February 1986), pp. 415–419.
6. John Goodlad, *A Place Called School* (New York: McGraw-Hill, 1984); Judith W. Little, "The Persistence of Privacy," *Teachers College Record* (Summer 1990), pp. 509–536.
7. Leslie A. Swetnam, "Media Distortion of the Teacher Image," *The ClearingHouse* (September/October 1992), p. 30.
8. Ibid., pp. 30–32.
9. Ibid., p. 13
10. Dan Lortie, *Schoolteacher* (Chicago: University of Chicago Press, 1975), p. 102.
11. David Haselkorn and Louis Harris, The Essential Profession: A National Survey of Public Attitudes Toward Teaching, Educational Opportunity and School Reform (Belmont, MA: Recruiting New Teachers, Inc., 1998), p. 2.
12. Mihaly Csikszentmihalyi and Jane McCormack, "The Influence of Teachers," *Phi Delta Kappan* 67, no. 6 (February 1986), pp. 415–419. The article is reprinted in this text's companion volume of readings: *Kaleidoscope: Readings in Education*, 10th ed., ed. Kevin Ryan and James M. Cooper (Boston: Houghton Mifflin, 2004).
13. Mihaly Csikszentmihalyi and Jane McCormack, "The Influence of Teachers," *Phi Delta Kappan* 67, no. 6 (February 1986), pp. 415–419. The article is reprinted in this text's companion volume of readings: *Kaleidoscope: Readings in Education*, 11th ed., ed. Kevin Ryan and James M. Cooper (Boston: Houghton Mifflin, 2007).
14. John Goodlad, *A Place Called School* (New York: McGraw-Hill, 1984); Judith W. Little, "The Persistence of Privacy," *Teachers College Record* (Summer 1990), pp. 509–536
15. Leslie A. Swetnam, "Media Distortion of the Teacher Image," *The ClearingHouse* (September/October 1992), p. 30.
16. Ibid., pp. 30–32.

Chapter 2

1. Elliot Eisner, *The Educational Imagination: On the Design and Evaluation of School Programs*, 3d ed. (Belmont, CA: Wadsworth, 1976).
2. Mike Rose, *Possible Lives* (New York: Penguin, 1995).
3. James Shaver and William Strong, *Facing Value Decisions: Rationale Building for Teachers* (Belmont, CA: Wadsworth, 1976).
4. Among the leading spokesmen for this position are Michael Apple and Henry Giroux. See Michael Apple, *Education and Power*, 2d ed. (New York: Routledge, 1995); Henry Giroux, "Critical Pedagogy: Cultural Politics and the Discourse of Experience," *Journal of Education* 67, no. 2 (1987), pp. 23–41.
5. Paulo Freire, *The Pedagogy of the Oppressed* (New York: Herder and Herder, 1970).
6. Jacques Barzun, *Begin Here: The Forgotten Conditions of Teaching and Learning* (Chicago: University of Chicago Press, 1991), pp. 4, 14.
7. Thomas Jefferson, "A Bill for the More General Diffusion of Knowledge." In *Public and Private Papers*, ed. Tom Wicker (New York: Vintage Books/Library of America, 1990), p. 39.
8. Jean Anyon, "Ghetto Schooling: A Political Economy of Urban Reform." In *Exploring Education: An Introduction to the Foundations of Education*, 2d ed., ed. A. Sadovnik, P. Cookson, and S. Semel (Boston: Allyn & Bacon, 2001), p. 53.
9. Emile Durkheim, "Education; Its Nature and Role." In *Exploring Sociocultural Themes in Education*, 2d ed., ed. J. Strouse (Columbus, OH: Merrill Prentice Hall, 2001), p. 57.
10. Philip W. Jackson, *Life in Classrooms* (New York: Teachers College Press, 1990).
11. Ibid., p. 16.
12. Joyce Epstein, "What Matters in the Middle Grades—Grade Span or Practices?" *Phi Delta Kappan* 71 (February 1990), pp. 438–444.
13. Ibid., p. 438.
14. Ernest L. Boyer, *High School: A Report on Secondary Education in America* (New York: Harper and Row, 1983).
15. Henry J. Becker, "Curriculum and Instruction in Middle-Grade Schools," *Phi Delta Kappan* 71 (February 1990), pp. 450–457.
16. James McPartland, "Staffing Decisions in the Middle School Grades: Balancing Quality Instruction and Teacher/Student Relations," *Phi Delta Kappan* 71 (February 1990), p. 466.
17. Ibid., p. 468.
18. NMSA Research Summary #5 Young Adolescents' Developmental Needs (1996). Available from the National Middle School Association at **http://www.nmsa.org/research/ressum5.htm.**

19. Ibid.

20. Jaana Juvonen, Vi-Nhuan Le, Tessa Kaganoff, Catherine Augustine and Louay Constant, *Focus on the Wonder Years: Challenges Facing the American Middle School* (Santa Monica, CA: RAND, 2004). Available at **http://www.rand.org/publications/MG/MG139/**.

21. Ernest L. Boyer, *High School: A Report on Secondary Education in America* (New York: Harper and Row, 1983).

22. Ibid., pp. 21–22.

23. Larry Cuban, *How Teachers Taught: Constancy and Change in American Classrooms 1890–1980* (New York: Longman, 1984).

24. Boyer, *High School*, pp. 141–143.

25. Op. cit.

26. Ibid., p. 57.

27. Ibid., p. 79.

28. Arthur G. Powell, Eleanor Farrar, and David K. Cohen, *The Shopping Mall High School: Winners and Losers in the Educational Marketplace* (Boston: Houghton Mifflin, 1985).

29. Theodore Sizer, *Horace's Compromise: The Dilemma of the American High School* (Boston: Houghton Mifflin, 1984).

30. Powell, op cit. p. 36.

31. Ibid., p. 173.

32. Laurence D. Brown, "A New Metaphor for U.S. High Schools Provides Fresh and Powerful Insights," *Phi Delta Kappan* 67 (May 1986), p. 685.

33. "Seeking Change in High Schools," *Education Week* 28 (February 28, 1996), pp. 1, 9.

34. National Public Radio, "Bill Gates: Creating Small High Schools," September 18, 2003. Available at: **http://www.npr.org/templates/story/story.php?storyId=1434487**.

35. In preparing this section, we have drawn on the following studies: W. B. Brookover, *Effective Secondary Schools* (Philadelphia: Research for Better Schools, 1981); R. Edmonds, "Effective Schools for the Urban Poor," *Educational Leadership* 32 (1979), pp. 15–17; M. Rutter et al., *Fifteen Thousand Hours* (Cambridge: Harvard University Press, 1979); J. Stallings and G. Mohlman, *School Policy, Leadership Style, Teacher Change and Student Behavior in Eight Secondary Schools* (Mountain View, CA: Stalling Teaching and Learning Institute for the National Institute of Education, 1981); R. Blum, *Effective Schooling Practices: A Research Synthesis* (Portland, OR: Northwest Regional Education Laboratory, April 1984); H. J. Walberg, "Productive Teaching and Instruction: Assessing the Knowledge Base," *Phi Delta Kappan* 71 (February 1990), pp. 470–478; T. Toch, *In the Name of Excellence* (New York: Oxford University Press, 1991); and Richard J. Murname and Frank Levy, "What General Motors Can Teach U.S. Schools About the Proper Role of Markets in Education Reform," *Phi Delta Kappan* 78 (October 1996), pp. 113–116.

36. David C. Berliner, "Effective Classroom Teaching: The Necessary but Not Sufficient Condition for Developing Exemplary Schools." In *Research on Exemplary Schools*, ed. Gilbert R. Austin and Herbert Garber (Orlando, FL: Academic Press, 1985), pp. 127–154. Copyright 1985.

37. Edward A. Wynne, "Looking at Good Schools," *Phi Delta Kappan* 62 (January 1981), pp. 377–381.

Chapter 3

1. U.S. Bureau of the Census, *Selected Age Groups for the Population and Hispanic Origin for the United States, July 1, 2003*. Available at: **http://www.census.gov/Press-Release/www/releases/img/cb04-98-table2.pdf**.

2. Harold Hodgkinson, "American Education: The Good, the Bad, and the Task," *Phi Delta Kappan* 74 (April 1993), p. 620.

3. Christine E. Sleeter, "Curriculum Controversies in Multicultural Education." In *Issues in Curriculum: A Selection of Chapters from Past NSSE Yearbooks, Ninety-eighth Yearbook of the National Society for the Study of Education*, ed. Margaret J. Early and Kenneth J. Rehage (Chicago: University of Chicago Press, 1999), p. 261.

4. M. Donald Thomas, "The Limits of Pluralism," *Phi Delta Kappan* 62 (April 1981), pp. 589, 591–592.

5. James A. Banks, "Multicultural Education: Characteristics and Goals." In *Multicultural Education: Issues and Perspectives*, 3d ed., ed. James A. Banks and Cherry A. McGee Banks (Boston: Allyn and Bacon, 1997), p. 7.

6. Geneva Gay, *Culturally Responsive Teaching: Theory, Research, and Practice* (New York: Teachers College Press, 2000); Gloria Ladson-Billings, *Crossing Over to Canaan: The Journey of New Teachers in Diverse Classrooms* (San Francisco: Jossey-Bass, 2001).

7. National Clearinghouse for English Language Acquisition, *Descriptive Study of Services to LEP Students and LEP Students with Disabilities, 2003*. Available at: **http://www.ncela.gwu.edu/resabout/research/descriptivestudyfiles/policy_report.pdf**.

8. Ibid.

9. *The Condition of Education, 2003* (Washington, DC: National Center for Education Statistics. 2003), p. 21.

10. [414 U.S. 563, 571]. Available at: **http://caselaw.lp.findlaw.com/scripts/getcase.pl?court=US&vol=414&invol=563**.

11. Russell Gersten and John Woodward, "A Case for Structured Immersion," *Educational Leadership* 43 (September 1985), p. 75.

12. Raul Yzaguirre, "What's Wrong with Bilingual Education?" *Education Week* (August 5, 1998), pp. 46, 72.

13. Howard Gardner, *Frames of Mind* (New York: Basic Books, 1985); Howard Gardner, *Multiple Intelligences: The Theory in Practice* (New York: Basic Books, 1993).

14. Kathy Checkley, "The First Seven . . . and the Eighth," *Educational Leadership* 55 (September 1997), p. 12.

15. Jay Mathews, "21 Years Later, 'Multiple Intelligences' Still Debated," *The Washington Post* (September 7, 2004), p. A9.

16. 25th Annual Report to Congress on the Implementation of the Individuals with Disabilities Education Act, (Washington, DC: U.S. Department of Education, 2005), p. I-13. Available at: **http://www.ed.gov/about/reports/annual/osep/2003/25th-vol-1-sec-1.pdf**.

17. Information found at **http://www.ed.gov/about/overview/budget/budget05/05action.xls**.

18. "IDEA Funding Coalition Offers Proposal." Available at the National Education Association's website: **http://www.nea.org/specialed/coalitionfunding2002.html**.

19. Joetta L. Sack, "Pressure Building for 'Full' Federal Funding of IDEA," *Education Week* (March 14, 2001), p. 32.

20. Ronald M. Hager and Diane Smith, *The Public School's Special Education System as an Assistive Technology Funding Source: The Cutting Edge* (Buffalo, NY: National Assistive Technology Advocacy Project, Neighborhood Legal Services, Inc., 2003). Available at: **http://www.nls.org/ specedat.htm#_Toc42076243.**

21. The Appalachia Educational Laboratory, *The Link* 14, no. 1 (Spring/Summer 1995), p. 21.

22. Sarah Wernick, "Hard Times for Educating the Highly Gifted Child," *New York Times,* May 30, 1990, p. B8.

23. *The 2001–2002 State of the States Gifted and Talented Education Report* (Washington, DC: National Association for Gifted Children, 2003), pp. 69–70; 150–152.

24. William Glasser, *The Quality School* (New York: Harper and Row, 1990).

25. Myra Sadker, David Sadker, and Susan Klein, "The Issue of Gender in Elementary and Secondary Education," in *Review of Research in Education* 17, ed. Gerald Grant (Washington, DC: American Educational Research Association, 1991), pp. 269–334.

26. Myra Sadker and David Sadker, *Failing at Fairness: How America's Schools Cheat Girls* (New York: Charles Scribner's Sons, 1994), p. 44.

27. *How Schools Shortchange Girls* (Washington, DC: American Association of University Women, 1992).

28. *Gender Gaps: Where Schools Still Fail Our Children: Executive Summary* (Washington, DC: American Association of University Women, 1998). Available at: **http://www.aauw.org/2000/GGES.pdf.**

29. Michelle Galley, "Boys to Men," *Education Week* (January 23, 2002), pp. 26–29.

30. "Annual Earnings of Young Adults," findings from *The Condition of Education, 2002* (Washington, DC: U.S. Department of Education, National Center for Education Statistics, 2002), Table 16-4, p. 157.

31. Lena Sun, "Gay Students Get Little Help with Harassment," *The Washington Post,* July 20, 1998, p. A8.

32. *When Teens Have Sex: Issues and Trends: KIDS COUNT Special Report* (Baltimore: Annie E. Casey Foundation, 1998), p. 14.

33. Thomas D. Snyder and Charlene M. Hoffman, *The Digest of Education Statistics 2002* (Washington, DC: National Center for Education Statistics, 2003), p. 82.

Chapter 4

1. Lisbeth Bamberger Schorr, "Effective Programs for Children Growing Up in Concentrated Poverty." In *Children in Poverty,* ed. A.C. Huston (Cambridge, UK: University of Cambridge Press, 1991), pp. 261–262.

2. *Kids Count Data Book 1999* (Baltimore: Annie E. Casey Foundation, 1999), pp. 6, 10.

3. Federal Interagency Forum on Child and Family Statistics, *America's Children: Key National Indicators of Well-Being, 2005.* Available at: **http://www.childstats.gov/ americaschildren/pop6.asp.**

4. Ibid.

5. Federal Interagency Forum on Child and Family Statistics, *America's Children: Key National Indicators of Well-Being, 2004.* Available at: **http://www.childstats.gov/ ac2003/indicators.asp?IID=112&id=3.**

6. Ibid.

7. Ibid.

8. "School-Based Health Centers—Background," (Washington, DC: The Center for Health and Health Care in Schools, 2003). Available at: **http://www.healthinschools.org/sbhcs/sbhc.asp.**

9. U.S. Bureau of the Census, *Historical Income Tables— Income Equality. Table IE-3. Household Shares of Aggregate Income by Fifths of the Income Distribution: 1967 to 2001.* Available at: **http://www.census.gov/hhes/income/ histinc/ie3.html.**

10. Carmen Denavas-Walt, Bernadette D. Proctor, and Robert J. Mills, U.S. Bureau of the Census, *Income, Poverty, and Health Insurance Coverage in the United States: 2003. Current Population Reports* (Washington, DC: U.S. Government Printing Office, 2004). Available at: **http://www.census.gov/prod/2004/pubs/p60-226.pdf.**

11. Ibid., pp. 41–45.

12. Ibid., p. 11, 46.

13. *Kids Count Data Book 2004* (Baltimore: Annie E. Casey Foundation, 2004), p. 41.

14. Ibid.

15. The Urban Institute, *A New Look at Homelessness in America* (Washington, DC, 2000). Available at: **http://www.urban.org/url.cfm?ID=900302.**

16. *Education for Homeless Children and Youth Program, Title VII-B of the McKinney-Vento Homeless Assistance Act (As Amended by the No Child Left Behind Act of 2001), Nonregulatory Guidance,* (Washington, DC: U.S. Department of Education, 2004). Available at: **http://www.ed.gov/ programs/homeless/guidance.pdf.**

17. Ruby Payne, "Understanding and Working with Students and Adults from Poverty," *Instructional Leader* (Vol. IX, No. 2, March 1996). Available at: **http://www.enc.org/ features/focus/archive/urban/document.shtm?input= FOC-002943-index.**

18. Infoplease, "Teen Birthrates Continue to Decline," September 21, 2004. Available at: **http://www. infoplease.com/ipa/A0193727.html.**

19. *When Teens Have Sex: Issues and Trends* (Baltimore: Annie E. Casey Foundation, 1999), p. 8.

20. Infoplease, op. cit.

21. *Kids Count Data Book 2004* (Baltimore: Annie E. Casey Foundation, 2004), p. 38.

22. *When Teens Have Sex: Issues and Trends: KIDS COUNT Special Report* (Baltimore: Annie E. Casey Foundation, 1998), p. 14.

23. Ibid., p. 14.

24. Ibid., p. 9.

25. *The Surgeon General's Call to Action to Promote Sexual Health And Responsible Sexual Behavior,* July 9, 2001, (Washington, DC: Department of Health and Human Services). Available at: **http://www.surgeongeneral.gov/ library/sexualhealth/call.htm.**

26. *A Portrait of Sexuality Education and Abstinence-Only-Until-Marriage Programs in the States,* (Washington, DC: Sexuality Information and Education Council of the United States, 2004). Available at: **http://www.siecus.org/ policy/states/FundingChart.pdf.**

27. *National Clearinghouse on Child Abuse and Neglect Information.* Available at: **http://nccanch.acf.hhs.gov/.**

28. Cynthia Crosson Tower, *The Role of Educators in the Prevention and Treatment of Child Abuse and Neglect* (Washington, DC: National Center on Child Abuse and Neglect, 1992), pp. 22–27. Available at: **http://www.calib.com/nccanch/pubs/educator/index.htm.**

29. Federal Interagency Forum on Child and Family Statistics, *America's Children: Key National Indicators of Well-Being 2005* (Washington, DC: Federal Interagency Forum on Child and Family Statistics, 2005). Available at: **http://www.childstats.gov/americaschildren/beh2.asp.**

30. Family First, "Teen Drinking." Available at: **http://www.familyfirst.net/parenting/teendrinking.asp.**

31. University of Michigan, Institute for Social Research, *Monitoring the Future: Secondary School Students 2004.* Available at: **http://monitoringthefuture.org/pubs/monographs/overview2004.pdf.**

32. "Youth Suicide Fact Sheet" (Washington, DC: American Association of Suicidology, 2004). Available at: **http://www.suicidology.org/associations/1045/files/YouthSuicide.pdf.**

33. Deborah Burnett Strother, "Suicide Among the Young," *Phi Delta Kappan* 67 (June 1986), p. 759.

34. "Violence and Safety," *Education Week*, Education Issues A-Z. Updated September 15, 2004. Available at: **http://www.edweek.com/context/topics/issuespage.cfm?id=39.**

35. Centers for Disease Control and Prevention, *Morbidity and Mortality Weekly Report,* July 30, 2004, Vol. 53, No. 29. Available at: **http://www.cdc.gov/mmwr/preview/mmwrhtml/mm5329a1.htm.**

36. *Indicators of School Crime and Safety 2004* (Washington, DC: National Center for Education Statistics, 2004), p. vi.

37. Arlen Egley, Jr. and Mehala Arjunan, *Highlights of the 2000 National Youth Gang Survey.* OJJDP Fact Sheet (Washington, DC: U.S. Department of Justice, Office of Justice Programs, Office of Juvenile Justice and Delinquency Prevention, 2002). Available at: **http://www.ncjrs.org/pdffiles1/ojjdp/fs200204.pdf.**

38. *Crime and Safety in America's Public Schools* (Washington, DC: U.S. Department of Education, National Center for Education Statistics, 2004), p. 4.

39. *Indicators of School Crime and Safety 2004*, p. iv.

40. Christopher B. Swanson, *The Real Truth about Low Graduation Rates, An Evidence-based Commentary* (Washington, DC: The Urban Institute, 2004). Available at: **http://www.urban.org/UploadedPDF/411050_realtruth.pdf.**

41. Ibid.

42. Phillip Kaufman, Martha Naomi Alt, and Christopher Chapman, *Dropout Rates in the United States: 2000* (Washington, DC: National Center for Education Statistics, 2001). Available at: **http://nces.ed.gov/pubs2002/droppub_2001/.**

Chapter 5

1. Catherine Cornbleth, "Hidden Curriculum." In *Encyclopedia of Education*, 2d ed., ed. James W. Guthrie (New York: Macmillan Reference USA, 2003).

2. Elliot W. Eisner, *The Educational Imagination,* 3d ed. (Upper Saddle River, NJ: Prentice Hall, 2001), pp. 87–97.

3. Karin Chenoweth, "Reading Wars, Take 2," *The Washington Post Magazine* (May 16, 1999), p. 17.

4. Steve Leinwand and Steve Fleischman, "Teaching Mathematics Right the First Time," *Educational Leadership*, 62, no. 1, (September 2004), p. 86.

5. Jay Mathews, "Study Faults Computers' Use in Math Education," *The Washington Post,* September 30, 1998, p. A3.

6. *Science for All Americans* (Washington, DC: American Association for the Advancement of Science, 1989).

7. Arthur W. Foshay, "Knowledge and the Structure of the Disciplines." In *The Nature of Knowledge: Implications for the Education of Teachers,* ed. William A. Jenkins (Milwaukee: University of Wisconsin Press, 1961).

8. National Council for the Social Studies, *Expectations of Excellence: Curriculum Standards for Social Studies* (Washington, DC: The Council, 1994).

9. *Digest of Education Statistics, 2002* (Washington, DC: National Center for Education Statistics, 2003), p. 70.

10. Secretary's Commission on Achieving Necessary Skills, *What Work Requires of Schools* (Washington, DC: U.S. Department of Labor, 1991).

11. NAEP 2003 Reading Assessment, *The Nation's Report Card.* Available at: **http://nces.ed.gov/nationsreportcard/reading/results/achieve.asp.**

12. Ibid.

13. NAEP 2001 U.S. History Major Results, *The Nation's Report Card.* Available at: **http://nces.ed.gov/nationsreportcard/ushistory/results/.**

14. NAEP 2003 Reading Assessment, *The Nation's Report Card.* Available at: **http://nces.ed.gov/nationsreportcard/reading/results/achieve.asp.**

15. Trends in International Mathematics and Science Study. Available at: **http://nces.ed.gov/timss/results.asp#comparison1995to1999.**

16. Robert B. Schwartz, "Lesson from TIMSS," *Hands On* (Cambridge, MA: TERC, Spring 1998).

17. The National Institute on Educational Governance, Finance, Policymaking, and Management and Consortium for Policy Research in Education, *Policy Brief: What the Third International Mathematics and Science Study (TIMSS) Means for Systematic School Improvement* (Washington, DC: U.S. Government Printing Office, 1998), p. 3.

18. William Schmidt, "Are There Surprises in the TIMSS Twelfth Grade Results?" *TIMSS United States, Report No. 8* (East Lansing, MI: United States National Research Center [TIMSS], April 1998), p. 4.

19. *Splintered Vision: An Investigation of U.S. Mathematics and Science Education, Executive Summary* (East Lansing, MI: U.S. National Research Center for the Third International Mathematics and Science Study, 1996), pp. 5–9.

20. National Education Commission, *Prisoners of Time: A Report of the National Education Commission on Time and Learning* (Washington, DC: U.S. Government Printing Office, 1994), p. 23.

21. Gerald W. Bracey, "Tinkering with TIMSS," *Phi Delta Kappan* 80, no. 1 (September 1998), pp. 32–36.

22. Larry Cuban, *How Teachers Taught: Constancy and Change in American Classrooms, 1890–1980* (New York: Longman, 1984).

23. Robert E. Slavin, *Cooperative Learning*, 2d ed. (Boston: Allyn and Bacon, 1995), pp. 3–4.
24. Ibid., pp. 14–70.
25. Scott Willis and Larry Mann, "Differentiating Instruction," *Curriculum Update*, Association for Supervision and Curriculum Development, Winter 2000, p. 2.
26. *Prisoners of Time*, pp. 10, 31, 34.
27. E. D. Hirsch, Jr., *Cultural Literacy* (Boston: Houghton Mifflin, 1987). Also see the Core Knowledge Foundation's website at: **http://www.coreknowledge.org.**
28. Debra Viadero, "On the Wrong Track," *Teacher Magazine* (January 1999), pp. 22–23.
29. Dominic Brewer, Daniel Rees, and Laura Argys, "Detracking America's Schools: The Reform Without Cost?" *Phi Delta Kappan* 77 (November 1995), pp. 210–212+.

Chapter 6

1. Charlotte Danielson, *Enhancing Professional Practice: A Framework for Teaching* (Alexandria, VA: Association for Supervision and Curriculum Development, 1996).
2. David Ryans, *Characteristics of Teachers* (Washington, DC: American Council on Education, 1960).
3. J. W. Getzels and P. W. Jackson, "The Teacher's Personality and Characteristics." In *Handbook of Research on Teaching*, ed. N. L. Gage (Chicago: Rand McNally, 1963), p. 574.
4. Gloria Ladson-Billings, *The Dreamkeepers: Successful Teachers of African-American Children* (San Francisco: Jossey-Bass, 1994), p. 34.
5. Thomas L. Good and Jere E. Brophy, *Looking in Classrooms*, 9th ed. (Boston: Allyn & Bacon, 2003), p. 75; Gloria Ladson-Billings, "What We Can Learn from Multicultural Education Research," *Educational Leadership* (May 1994), pp. 22–26.
6. Good and Brophy, *Looking in Classrooms*, pp. 77–80.
7. Ibid., p. 71.
8. Lee S. Shulman, "Knowledge and Teaching: Foundations of the New Reform," *Harvard Educational Review* 57 (February 1987), p. 8.
9. Chris Argyris and Donald A. Schon, *Theory in Practice: Increasing Professional Effectiveness* (San Francisco: Jossey-Bass, 1974), pp. 3–19.
10. B. O. Smith et al., *Teachers for the Real World* (Washington, DC: American Association of Colleges for Teacher Education, 1969), p. 44.
11. Richard Kindsvatter, William Wilen, and Margaret Ishler, *Dynamics of Effective Teaching* (White Plains, NY: Longman, 1996), pp. 2–3.
12. Wilford A. Weber, "Classroom Management." In *Classroom Teaching Skills*, 8th ed., ed. J. M. Cooper (Boston: Houghton Mifflin, 2006), p. 236.
13. David C. Berliner, "Effective Classroom Teaching: The Necessary but Not Sufficient Condition for Developing Exemplary Schools." In *Research on Exemplary Schools*, ed. Gilbert R. Austin and Herbert Garber (Orlando, FL: Academic Press, 1985), pp. 136–138.
14. Jacob S. Kounin, *Discipline and Group Management in Classrooms* (New York: Holt, 1970).
15. *Looking in Classrooms*, p. 110.
16. Alfie Kohn, "Beyond Discipline," *Education Week* (November 20, 1996), pp. 37, 48.
17. Good and Brophy, *Looking in Classrooms*, pp. 394–395.
18. Ibid., pp. 393–395.
19. Ibid., pp. 389–395; William W. Wilen and Ambrose A. Clegg, Jr., "Effective Questions and Questioning: A Research Review," *Theory and Research in Social Education* (Spring 1986), pp. 153–161.
20. Greta Morine-Dershimer, "Instructional Planning." In *Classroom Teaching Skills*, 8th ed., ed. J. M. Cooper (Boston: Houghton Mifflin, 2006), p. 27.
21. Ibid., pp. 27–28.
22. Mardell Raney, "*Technos* Interview with Jonathan Kozol," *Technos* 7, no. 3 (Fall 1998), p. 10.

Chapter 7

1. This example is loosely based on a class at Ligon Middle School in Raleigh, NC. Available at: **http://www.ncsu.edu/midlink/gis/hazardous_waste.htm.**
2. David A. Dockterman, "A Teacher's Tools," *Instructor* 100, no. 5 (January 1991), pp. 58–61.
3. Gene White, "From Magic Lanterns to Microcomputers: The Evolution of the Visual Aid in the English Classroom," *English Journal* 73, no. 3 (March 1984), p. 59.
4. Paul Saettler, *The Evolution of American Educational Technology* (Englewood, CO: Libraries Unlimited, Inc., 1990), p. 98.
5. North Central Regional Educational Laboratory & the Metiri Group, *enGauge 21st Century Skills: Literacy in the Digital Age* (Naperville, IA and Los Angeles, 2003). Available at: **http://www.ncrel.org/engauge/skills/skills.htm.**
6. Ray Kurzweil, *The Age of Spiritual Machines: When Computers Exceed Human Intelligence* (New York: Viking, 1999).
7. David H. Jonassen, *Computers in the Classroom: Mindtools for Critical Thinking*, 2nd ed. (Englewood Cliffs, NJ: Prentice Hall, 2000), p. 3. The concept of a computer application as a cognitive tool follows from the idea that "learning is a consequence of thinking"; see David Perkins, *Smart Schools: Better Thinking and Learning for Every Child* (New York: Free Press, 1992), p. 8.
8. David H. Jonassen, Chad Carr, and Hsiu-Ping Yueh, "Computers as Mindtools for Engaging Learners in Critical Thinking," *TechTrends* 43 (March 1998), pp. 24–32.
9. Cleborne D. Maddux, D. LaMont Johnson, and Jerry W. Willis, *Educational Computing: Learning with Tomorrow's Technologies* (Boston: Allyn and Bacon, 1992), pp. 204–205.
10. Matthew Maurer, "Supporting Language and Literacy Development with Technology." In *Leadership in Instructional Technology*, ed. Matthew Maurer and George Steven Davidson (Upper Saddle River, NJ: Merrill, 1998), p. 79.
11. Andrew Trotter, "Teaching the Basics: Beyond Drill and Practice," *Technology Counts '98 in Education Week* (October 1, 1998), pp. 25–27.
12. Diann Boehm, "I Lost My Tooth!" *Learning and Leading with Technology* 24 (April 1997), pp. 17–19.
13. Randy L. Bell, John C. Park, and Doug Toti, "Digital Images in the Science Classroom," *Learning and Leading with Technology* 31 (May 2004), pp. 26–28.
14. Jennifer Underdah, Joycelyn Palacio-Cayetano, and Ron Stevens, "Practice Makes Perfect: Assessing and Enhancing Knowledge and Problem-Solving Skills with

IMMEX Software," *Learning and Leading with Technology* 28 (April 2001), pp. 26–31.

15. Candy Beal and Cheryl Mason, "Virtual Fieldtripping: No Permission Notes Needed. Creating a Middle School Classroom Without Walls," *Meridian* 2, no. 1 (January 1999). Available at: **http://www.ncsu.edu/meridian/jan99/vfieldtrip/index.html.**

16. Hollylynne Stohl Drier, Kara M. Dawson, and Joe Garafalo, "Not Your Typical Math Class," *Educational Leadership* 56 (February 1999), p. 21.

17. David Perkins, Gavriel Salomon, and Tamar Globerson, "Partners in Cognition: Extending Human Intelligence with Intelligent Technologies," *Educational Researcher* 20, no. 3 (1991), pp. 2–9.

18. National Council of Teachers of Mathematics, *Principles and Standards for School Mathematics* (Reston, VA: The National Council of Teachers of Mathematics, 2000), p. 24. Available at: **http://standards.nctm.org/document/chapter2/techn.htm.**

19. Ann M. Farrell, "Teaching and Learning Behaviors in Technology-Oriented Precalculus Classrooms," Ph.D. dissertation, Ohio State University, *Dissertation Abstracts International* 51 (1990), p. 100A.

20. Peter West, "Support Pilot Distance-Learning Projects, Congress Urged," *Education Week* (March 17, 1993), p. 16.

21. U.S. Congress, Office of Technology Assessment, *Teachers and Technology: Making the Connection*, OTA-EHR-616 (Washington, DC: U.S. Government Printing Office, April 1995), p. 1103.

22. Mary Seegers, "Special Technological Possibilities for Students with Special Needs," *Learning and Leading with Technology* 29 (November 2001), pp. 32–39.

23. National Educational Technology Standards for Students (**http://cnets.iste.org/**).

24. Mary Ann Zehr, "Preparing Students for a Digital World," *Technology Counts '98, in Education Week* (October 1, 1998), pp. 33–35.

25. Thomas C. Reeves, "Technology in Teacher Education: From Electronic Tutor to Cognitive Tool," *Action in Teacher Education* 17, no. 4 (1996), p. 74.

26. Carole Bagley and Barbara Hunter, "Restructuring, Constructivism, and Technology: Forging a New Relationship," *Educational Technology* 32 (July 1992), pp. 22–27.

27. Henry Jay Becker and Jason Ravitz, "The Influence of Computer and Internet Use on Teachers' Pedagogical Practices and Perceptions," *Journal of Research on Computing in Education* 31, no. 4 (Summer 1999), pp. 356–384.

28. U.S. Congress, Office of Technology Assessment, *Teachers and Technology: Making the Connection*, p. 41.

29. Sarah M. Butzin, "Using Instructional Technology in Transformed Learning Environments: An Evaluation of Project CHILD (Computers Helping Instruction and Learning Development)," *Journal of Research on Technology in Education* 33 (Summer 2001).

30. Glen Bull, Gina Bull, and Sara Kajder, "Mining the Internet: Tapped In," *Learning and Leading with Technology* 31 (February 2004), pp. 34–37.

31. Cheryl Mason Bolick and James M. Cooper, "Classroom Management and Technology," in Carolyn M. Evertson and Carol S. Weinstein (Eds.), *Handbook of Classroom Management: Research, Practice, and Contemporary Issues*, (Mahwah, NJ: Lawrence Erlbaum, Inc., in press).

32. Ronald E. Anderson and Amy Ronnkvist, "The Presence of Computers in American Schools," *Teaching, Learning and Computing: A National Survey* (1998). Available at: **http://www.crito.uci.edu/tlc/findings/computers_in_american_schools/.**

33. Joe Garafalo, Glen Bull, Randy Bell, and Stephanie van Hover, "Interactive Whole-Class Display Systems," *Learning and Leading with Technology* 32 (October, 2004), pp. 28–31.

34. Andrew Trotter, "E-Rate: The Road Ahead," *Technology Counts 2005, in Education Week* (May 5, 2005), pp. 30–31.

35. Rhea R. Borja, "State Support Varies Widely," *Technology Counts 2005, in Education Week* (May 5, 2005), p. 18.

36. Lori Meyer, "New Challenges: Overview of the State Data Tables," *Technology Counts 2001, in Education Week* (May 10, 2001).

37. Kevin Bushweller, "Technology Spending," *Education Week* (November 3, 2004), p. 17.

38. Lin Foa, Richard Schwab, and Michael Johnson, "Upgrading School Technology: 'Support the Zealots' and Other Pointers for Entering a Strange New Land," *Education Week* (May 1, 1996), p. 52.

39. Sara Armstrong, "The Right Stuff: Curry Graduates Leave College Prepared to Teach" (September 1, 2001). Available at: **http://www.glef.org.**

40. Rockman et al., "Beyond Buddy: The Sustained Influence of the Buddy System Project" (San Francisco: 1998). Available at: **http://rockman.com/projects/buddy/Bey.Buddy98.pdf.**

41. U.S. Department of Commerce, *Falling through the Net: Executive Summary* (Washington, DC: 1999). Available at: **http://www.ntia.doc.gov/ntiahome/fttn99/execsummary.html.**

42. Robert C. Johnston, "Money Matters," *Technology Counts 2001, in Education Week* (May 10, 2001).

43. Alec MacGillis, "Law, Software Fuel New 'Digital Divide,'" *The Baltimore Sun* (September 21, 2004). Available at: **http://www.baltimoresun.com/news/education/bal-te.software21sep21,1,2732113.story?coll=bal=education-storyutil.**

44. North Central Regional Educational Laboratory & the Metiri Group, *enGauge 21st Century Skills: Literacy in the Digital Age* (Naperville, IL and Los Angeles, 2003). Available at: **http://www.ncrel.org/engauge/skills/skills.htm.**

45. Cornelia Brunner, Dorothy Bennett, and Margaret Honey, "Technology, Gender, and Education: Defining the Problem," paper prepared for the AAUW Commission on Gender, Technology, and Teacher Education, October 1998.

46. Cornelia Brunner, "Opening Technology to Girls," *Electronic Learning* 16, No. 4 (February 1997), p. 55.

47. International Society for Technology in Education, *National Educational Technology Standards: Connecting Curriculum and Technology* (2000). Available at: **www.iste.org.** Reprinted with permission.

48. Larry Cuban, "High-Tech Schools and Low-Tech Teaching," *Education Week* 16 (May 21, 1997).

49. Larry Cuban, "Techno-Reformers and Classroom Teachers," *Education Week* 16 (October 9, 1996).

50. Judy Salpeter, "What Does Research Say about Technology's Impact on Education: Interview with Larry Cuban," *Technology and Learning* (June 2000). Available at: **http://www.techlearning.com/db_area/archives/ TL/062000/archives/cuban.html.**

51. Judi Harris, *Virtual Architecture: Designing and Directing Curriculum-Based Telecomputing* (Eugene, OR: International Society for Technology in Education, 1998).

Chapter 8

1. From Kenneth R. Howe, "A Conceptual Basis for Ethics in Teacher Education," *Journal of Teacher Education* 37 (May/June 1996), p. 6. Reprinted with permission.

2. Ibid, p. 6.

3. Steven Tigner, *Educator's Affirmation* (Boston and Toledo, OH: Boston University and University of Toledo, 1989). Reprinted by permission of Steven Tigner.

4. John Martin Rich, "The Role of Professional Ethics in Teacher Education," *Journal of the Association of Teacher Educators* 7 (Fall 1985), p. 22.

5. *U.S.L. Week 4223,* March 24, 1970, quoted in Louis Fischer and David Schimmel, *The Rights of Students and Teachers* (New York: Harper and Row, 1982), p. 323. Much of this chapter is drawn from the material presented in this excellent and highly readable book and also from Louis Fischer, David Schimmel, and Cynthia Kelly, *Teachers and the Law,* 4th ed. (1995), 5th ed. (1998), and 6th ed. (2002). (New York: Addison-Wesley Longman).

6. Louis Fischer, David Schimmel, and Cynthia Kelly, *Teachers and the Law,* 5th ed. (New York: Addison-Wesley Longman, 1998), p. 20.

7. *Smith v. School District of the Township of Darby,* quoted in Fischer, Schimmel, and Kelly, *Teachers and the Law,* 5th ed., p. 31

8. Ibid., p. 38.

9. Ibid., p. 47.

10. Ibid., pp. 76–77.

11. Ibid., p. 101.

12. *Pickering v. Board of Education,* 225 N.E. 2d 1 (1967); 391 U.S. 563 (1968).

13. *Scoville v. Board of Education,* 425 F. 2d 10 (7th Cir. 1970).

14. *Anderson v. Evans,* 660 F. 2d 153 (6th Cir. 1981).

15. *Stroman v.. Colleton County School District,* 981 F. 2d 152 (4th Cir. 1992).

16. Fischer, Schimmel, Kelly, *Teachers and the Law,* 5th ed., p. 166.

17. Mark G. Yudof, David L. Kirp, Betsy Levin and Rachel F. Moran, *Educational Policy and the Law,* 4th ed. (Belmont, CA: West/Thomson Learning), pp. 255–256.

18. Ibid., p. 256.

19. Ibid., p. 257.

20. Fischer, Schimmel, Kelly, *Teachers and the Law,* 5th ed., p. 169.

21. Ibid., p. 169.

22. Thomas R. McDaniel, "The Teacher's Ten Commandments: School Law in the Classroom," *Phi Delta Kappan* 60 no. 10 (June 1979), p. 707.

23. Fischer, Schimmel, Kelly, *Teachers and the Law,* 5th ed., p. 451.

24. Ibid., p. 324.

25. Ibid., pp. 297–298.

26. Ibid., p. 307.

27. Ibid., p. 306.

28. Bill Mears, "Court Dismisses Pledge Case," CNN.Com. Available at: **http://www.cnn.com/2004/ LAW/06/14/scotus.pledge/.**

29. Perry A. Zirkel, "A Bedeviling Message from Providence," *Phi Delta Kappan* 74, no. 2 (October 1992), pp. 183–184.

30. *Santa Fe Independent School District v. Department of Education* (99-62) 168 F. 3d 806.

31. Benjamin Senor, "Even After the Supreme Court Ruling, We're Still in the Dark about Religion Clubs at School," *American School Board Journal* 173 (August 1986), p. 17.

32. Cheryl D. Mills, "Important Education-Related U.S. Supreme Court Decisions." In *Challenges and Achievements of American Education,* ed. Cordon Cawalti (Alexandria, VA: Association for Supervision and Curriculum Development, 1993), p. 192.

33. Caroline Hendrie, "Teacher May Lead Bible Lessons at Her Own School, Court Rules," *Education Week,* September 9, 2002.

34. Stephen Arons, "Separation of School and State," *Education Week,* November 17, 1984, p. 24.

35. Thomas J. Flygare, "Supreme Court Strikes Down Louisiana Creationism Act," *Phi Delta Kappan* 69, no. 1 (September 1987), pp. 77–79.

36. Associated Press, "Science Standard Debates in Kansas," August 11, 1999.

37. *Mozert v. Hawkins County Board of Education,* U.S. Dist. Ct. (E.D. Tenn.) 647 F Supp. 1194 (1987).

38. *Smith v. Board of School Commissioners of Mobile County* no. 87–7216 (11th Cir., 26 September 1987).

39. Thomas R. McDaniel, "The Teacher's Ten Commandments: School Law in the Classroom," *Phi Delta Kappan* 60, no. 10 (June 1979), p. 703. Reprinted with permission.

40. Richard Riley, Secretary of Education, and Walter Dellinger, Assistant Attorney General, *White House press release,* July 12, 1995, pp. 2–4.

41. *Tinker v. Des Moines Independent Community School District,* 393 U.S. 503 (1969).

42. Fischer, Schimmel, Kelly, *Teachers and the Law,* 5th ed., p. 271.

43. Nelda Cambron-McCabe, Martha McCarthy, and Stephen Thomas, *Public School Law: Teacher's and Student's Right,* 5th ed. (Boston: Allyn & Bacon, 2004).

44. *Goss v. Lopez,* 95 S.Ct. 729 (1975).

45. *Honig v. Doe,* 108 S.Ct. 592, 605 (1988).

46. *Fuller v. Decatur Public School Board of Education School District* 61, 78 F. Supp. 2d 812 (C.D. Ill. 2000).

47. Yudof, Kirp, Levin and Moran, *Educational Policy and the Law,* p. 525.

48. Darcia Harris Bowman, "District Dress Code Attracts Nationwide Attention," *Education Week* (October 15, 2003), p. 10.

49. See, for instance, *Newsome v. Batavia Local School District,* 842 F. 2d 920 (6th Cir. 1988).

50. Sureshrani Paintal, "Banning Corporal Punishment of Students." Available at: **http://www.stophitting.com/**

disathome/sureshrani.php; Michael Dobbs, "U.S. Students Still Getting the Paddle—Corporal Punishment Laws Often Reflect Regional Chasms," *The Washington Post* (February 21, 2004). Available at: **http://www. nospank.net/n-l51r.htm.**

51. "Discipline at School (NCACPS): U.S.: Statistics on Corporal Punishment by State and Race." Available at: **http://www.stophitting.com/disatschool/ statesBanning.php.**

52. Fischer, Schimmel, and Kelly, *Teachers and the Law,* 5th ed., p. 268.

53. Ibid., p. 279.

54. *New Jersey v. T.L.O.,* 105 S. Ct. 733 (1985).

55. *Vernonia School District 47J v. Acton,* 115 S.Ct. 2386 (1995) as reported in Yudof, Kirp, Levin and Moran, *Educational Policy and the Law,* pp. 317–320.

56. American Library Association's Censorship and Challenges website. Available at: **http://www.ala.org/ alaorg/oif/censors.html#links.**

57. *Tinker v. Des Moines Independent Community School District.*

58. *Bethel School District no. 403. v. Fraser,* 106 S. Ct. 3159 (1986).

59. *Hazlewood School District v. Kuhlmeier,* 56 U.S.L.W. 4079, 4082 (12 January 1988).

60. Ibid.

61. American Association of University Women, *Hostile Hallways: The AAUW Survey on Sexual Harassment in America's Schools* (New York: Louis Harris Associations, 1993), p. 6.

62. *Davis v. Monroe County Board of Education,* 119 S. Ct. 1661 (1999).

63. Ibid.

64. *Owasso Independent School District v. Falvo,* 534 S. Ct. 00–1073.

Chapter 9

1. In a recent national survey of deans and department chairpersons of education schools and departments, 91.4 percent "agreed" or "strongly agreed" with the statement, "There exists a set of core values/virtues upon which most Americans agree, regardless of race, creed, class or culture, which can and should be taught in schools." See Emily Nelsen Jones, Kevin Ryan, and Karen E. Bohlin, *Teachers as Educators of Character: Are the Nation's Schools of Education Coming Up Short?* (Washington, DC: Character Education Partnership, 1999), p. 7; Association of Supervision and Curriculum Development, *Moral Education in the Life of the School* (Alexandria, VA: ASCD, 1989). Both President Clinton and President Bush have called for greater emphasis on character education in our schools.

2. Personal communication with Mary Kathryn Hassett, Public Relations Specialist, Core Knowledge Foundation, 801 E. High St. Charlottesville, VA 22902.

3. Joseph Justman, "Wanted: A Philosophy of American Education," *School and Society* (May 12, 1956).

Chapter 10

1. Marvin Lazerson, "Access, Outcomes, and Educational Opportunity," *Education Week* (January 27, 1999), p. 46.

2. Willystine Goodsell, *Pioneers of Women's Education in the United States* (New York: AMS Press, 1970/1931), p. 5.

3. R. Freeman Butts and Lawrence A. Cremin, *A History of Education in American Culture* (New York: Holt, 1953), p. 245.

4. Charles W. Coulter and Richard S. Rimanoczy, *A Layman's Guide to Educational Theory* (New York: Van Nostrand, 1955), p. 130.

5. Butts and Cremin, *A History of Education in American Culture,* p. 408.

6. John D. Pulliam, *History of Education in America,* 3d ed. (Columbus, OH: Merrill, 1982), pp. 157–159.

7. Gene D. Shepherd and William B. Ragan, *Modern Elementary Curriculum,* 6th ed. (New York: Holt, 1982), p. 440.

8. Butts and Cremin, *A History of Education in American Culture,* p. 260.

9. Merle Curti, *The Social Ideas of American Educators,* 2d ed. (Totowa, NJ: Littlefield, Adams, 1959), p. 183.

10. Butts and Cremin, *A History of Education in American Culture,* p. 443.

11. Thomas D. Snyder, *120 Years of American Education: A Statistical Portrait* (Washington, DC: U.S. Department of Education, National Center for Education Statistics, 1993), pp. 36–37; William J. Hussar, *Projections of Education Statistics to 2014* (Washington, DC: National Center for Education Statistics, 2005), p. 46.

12. William T. Gruhn and Harl R. Douglass, *The Modern Junior High School,* 3d ed. (New York: Ronald Press, 1971), pp. 46–53.

13. Jaana Juvonen et al., *Focus on the Wonder Years: Challenges Facing the American Middle School* (Santa Monica, CA: RAND Corporation, 2004). Available at: **http://www.rand.org/pubs/monographs/2004/ RAND_MG139.pdf.**

14. Ibid.

15. Mary Ann Zehr, "Private Schools: Catholic Closings," *Education Week* (March 31, 2004), p. 6; Thomas D. Snyder and Charlene M. Hoffman, *Digest of Education Statistics 2001* (Washington, DC: U.S. Department of Education, National Center for Education Statistics, 2002), p. 73.

16. *School and Staffing Survey, 1999–2000* (Washington, DC: National Center for Education Statistics, 2002), p. 47. Available at: **http://nces.ed.gov/pubs2002/2002313.pdf.**

17. Ibid.

18. Herbert M. Kliebard, *Religion and Education in America: A Documentary History* (Scranton, PA: International Textbook, 1969), p. 119.

19. *The Religious Freedom Page.* Available at: **http:// religiousfreedom.lib.virginia.edu/court/pier_v_soci.html.**

20. Earle H. West, *The Black American and Education* (Columbus, OH: Merrill, 1972), pp. 7–8.

21. Eric Lincoln and Milton Meltzer, *A Pictorial History of the Negro in America,* 3d ed. (New York: Crown, 1968), pp. 108–109.

22. *Historical Statistics of the United States, Colonial Times to 1970,* Vol. I, Table Series H 433–441 (Washington, DC: U.S. Government Printing Office, 1975), p. 370.

23. Franklin Frazier, *The Negro in the United States,* rev. ed. (New York: Macmillan, 1957), pp. 427, 432–436, 438.

24. Gary Orfield, Susan E. Eaton, and the Harvard Project on School Desegregation, *Dismantling Desegregation* (New

York: The New Press, 1996), pp. 105–106; Jomills Henry Braddock II, Robert L. Crain, and James M. McPartland, "A Long-Term View of School Desegregation: Some Recent Studies of Graduates as Adults," *Phi Delta Kappan* 66 (December 1984), pp. 259–264.

25. Anthony Lukas, *Common Ground* (New York: Knopf, 1985), a Pulitzer Prize-winning description of desegregation efforts in Boston, Massachusetts.

26. Howard Ozmon and Sam Craver, *Busing: A Moral Issue* (Bloomington, IN: Phi Delta Kappa Educational Foundation, 1972), pp. 33–34.

27. Snyder and Hoffman, *Digest of Education Statistics 2001,* pp. 102–108.

28. Jacqueline Jordan Irvine, "Still Standing in the Schoolhouse Door," *Education Week* (May 19, 2004), p. 38.

29. Richard M. Merelman, "Dis-Integrating American Public Schools," *Education Week* (February 6, 2002), p. 37.

30. R. Freeman Butts, *The Education of the West: A Formative Chapter in the History of Civilization* (New York: McGraw-Hill, 1973), p. 279.

31. Mary Ann Zehr, "GAO: Student Achievement Lagging At Bureau of Indian Affairs Schools," *Education Week* (November 7, 2001), p. 12; Sean Cavanagh, " 'No Child' Law Poses Challenges To Indians," *Education Week* (May 5, 2004), pp. 32–34.

32. Catherine Freeman and Mary Ann Fox, *Status and Trends in the Education of American Indians and Native Alaskans,* (Washington, DC: U.S. Department of Education, National Center for Education Statistics, 2005), p. 120.

33. Charmaine Llagas and Thomas D. Snyder, *Status and Trends in the Education of Hispanics* (Washington, DC: U.S. Department of Education, National Center for Education Statistics, 2003), p. 42. Available at: **http://nces.gov/pubs2003/2003008.pdf.**

34. Ibid., p. 102.

35. Ibid., pp. 8, 72.

36. Snyder and Hoffman, *Digest of Education Statistics, 2001,* p. 58; U.S. Census Bureau, *National Population Projections.* Available at: **http://www.census.gov/population/ www/projections/natsum-T5.html.**

Chapter 11

1. Frederick M. Hess, "School Boards at the Dawn of the 21st Century," a report prepared for the National School Boards Association (Charlottesville, VA: University of Virginia, 2002).

2. Larry Cuban, "Conflict and Leadership in the Superintendency," *Phi Delta Kappan* 67 (September 1985), p. 8. See also Arthur Blumberg with Phyllis Blumberg, *The School Superintendent: Living with Conflict* (New York: Teachers College Press, 1985), p. 32, and Susan Moore Johnson, *Leading to Change: The Challenge of the New Superintendency* (San Francisco: Jossey-Bass, 1996), pp. 77–78.

3. Rhea R. Borja, "Study: Urban School Chiefs' Tenure is 4.6 Years," *Education Week* (February 6, 2002), p. 5.

4. "Education Vital Signs," *American School Board Journal* 190, no. 2 (February 2003). Available at: **http://www.asbj.com/evs/03/2003pdf/ EVS03leadership.pdf.**

5. "Education Vital Signs," *American School Board Journal* 185, no. 12 (December 1998), p. A13.

6. Business Roundtable. Available at: **http://www.businessroundtable.org/.**

7. Henry A. Giroux, "Education Incorporated?" *Educational Leadership* 56, no. 2 (October 1998), p. 13.

8. Channel One website at: **http://www.channelone.com/ common/about/.**

9. Thomas Moore with Nancy Linon, "The Selling of Our Schools," *U.S. News & World Report* (November 6, 1989), p. 40.

10. *Education Week.* Available at: **http://www.edweek.org/ rc/issues/privatization-of-public-education/ index.html?querystring=for-profit%20schools.**

11. Eric Hirsch, Julia E. Koppich, and Michael S. Knapp, "Revisiting What States are Doing to Improve the Quality of Teaching: An Update on Patterns and Trends" (Seattle: Center for the Study of Teaching and Policy, University of Washington, February 2001), p. 16.

12. *Rankings and Estimates: Estimates of School Statistics 2005* (Washington, DC: National Education Association, 2005), p. 94.

13. Ibid.

14. "Education Vital Signs," *American School Board Journal* (February 2005). Available at: **http://www.asbj.com/evs.**

15. Rob Greenwald, Larry V. Hedges, and Richard D. Laine, "The Effect of School Resources on Student Achievement," *Review of Educational Research* (Fall 1996), pp. 361–396.

16. Deborah A. Verstegen, "Financing the New Adequacy: Towards New Models of State Education Finance Systems That Support Standards Based Reform," *Journal of Education Finance* 27 (Winter 2002), pp. 749–782.

17. Thomas D. Snyder, Charlene M. Hoffman, and Claire M. Geddes, *Digest of Education Statistics 1998* (Washington, DC: U.S. Department of Education, National Center for Education Statistics, 1998), p. 169.

18. Erik W. Robelen, "ESEA to Boost Federal Role in Education," *Education Week* (January 9, 2002), p. 28.

19. Ibid., p. 29.

20. U.S. Department of Education, Fact Sheet on Title 1, Part A. Available at: **http://www.ed.gov/rschstat/eval/ disadv/title1-factsheet.pdf.**

21. U.S. Department of Health and Human Services, Administration for Children & Families, Head Start Bureau. Available at: **http://www.acf.hhs.gov/programs/ hsb/research/2004.htm.**

22. Michael Holzman, "Preschool's Effects at 40," *Education Week* (January 19, 2005), p. 33.

23. The Longitudinal Evaluation of School Change and Performance (LESCP) in Title I Schools. Available at: **http://www.ed.gov/offices/OUS/PES/esed/lescp_vol1.doc.**

Chapter 12

1. John Gehring, "College and Minorities," *Education Week* (October 3, 2001). Available at: **http://www.edweek.org/ ew/newstory.cfm?slug=05colleg.h21.**

2. *Industrial College of the Armed Forces (ICAF) 2003 Education Report.* Available at: **http://www.ndu.edu/ icaf/industry/IS2003/papers/ 2003%20Education.htm.**

3. Conway Dorsett, "Multicultural Education: Why We Need It and Why We Worry About It," *Network News and Views* 121, no. 3 (March 1993), p. 31.

4. Quoted in Theodore Sizer and Nancy Fauste Sizer, *The Students Are Watching* (Boston: Beacon Press, 1999), p. 6.

5. For further information on portfolios and authentic assessment see Susan Black, "Portfolio Assessment," *The Executive Educator* (February 1993), pp. 28–31.

6. A. MacKinnon and C. Scarff-Seatter (1997). Constructivism: Contradictions and confusion in teacher education. In V. Richardson (Ed.), *Constructivist Teacher Education: Building New Understandings* (Washington, DC: Falmer Press, 1997).

7. Milbrey W. McLaughlin, Merita A. Irby, and Juliet Langman, *Urban Sanctuaries: Neighborhood Organizations in the Lives and Futures of Inner-City Youth* (San Francisco: Jossey-Bass, 1994), p. 216.

8. Anthony Bryk and Yeow Meng Thum, "The Effects of High School Organization on Dropping Out," unpublished paper, University of Chicago, 1988, pp. 54–68. See also Anthony Bryk and Mary Erina Driscoll, "An Empirical Investigation of the School as a Community," unpublished paper, University of Chicago, 1988, pp. 54–63.

9. Kevin Ryan and Thomas Lickona, eds., *Character Development in Schools and Beyond* (Washington, DC: Council for Research on Values and Philosophy, 1987), pp. 21–26.

10. Barry Chazan, "Against Moral Education." In *Contemporary Approaches to Moral Education* (New York: Teacher College Press, 1985).

11. William Damon, quoted by Amitai Etzioni, *The Spirit of Community* (New York: Crown, 1993), pp. 100–101.

12. "Values Education: Time for Greater Emphasis!" *Phi Delta Kappan* 75, no. 2 (October 1993), p. 145.

13. *Service Learning Is . . .* (Scotts Valley, CA: National Service Learning Clearinghouse). Available at: **http://www.servicelearning.org/article/archive/35/**.

14. Learning In Deed. Available at **http://www.learningindeed.org/research/slresearch/slrsrchsy.html**.

15. Julie Blair, "Kellogg Begins Program to Boost Service Learning," *Education Week* (May 26, 1999).

16. Maryland Student Service Alliance. Available at **http://www.mssa.sailorsite.net/require.html**.

17. Quoted by Mark Edwards in "Turbo-Charging Professional Development," *The School Administrator* (December 1998), p. 36.

18. Thomas Toch, *In the Name of Excellence* (New York: Oxford University Press, 1991), p. 9.

19. Goals 2000: Educate America Act (March 31, 1994); *The National Education Goals* (Washington, DC: U.S. Department of Education, 1994.

20. The No Child Left Behind Act of 2001 Reauthorization of the Elementary and Secondary Education Act Policies and Legislation. Available at: **http://www.whitehouse.gov/news/reports/no-child-left-behind.html**.

21. Lynn Olson, "NCLB: Taking Root," *Education Week* (December 12, 2004).

22. E. D. Hirsch, as quoted by Sara Mosle, *The New York Times Book Review*, September 29, 1996, p. 15.

23. Theodore Sizer, *Horace School: Redesigning the American High School* (Boston: Houghton Mifflin, 1992), pp. 207–208.

24. Lynn Olson, "State Leaders Pledge to Reform Nations High Schools," *Education Week* (February 28, 2005), web version.

25. Quoted by the editors of *Education Week*, "From Risk to Renewal" (February 10, 1993), p. 187.

26. The NAEP High School Transcript Study: Trends in Course Taking: Major Findings. Available at: **http://www.nces.ed.gov/nationsreportcard/hsts/results/trends/findings.asp**.

27. Julie Aronson, Joy Zimmerman and Lisa Carlos, "Improving Student Achievement by Extending School: Is It Just a Matter of Time?" WestEd, 1998. Available at: **http://www.wested.org/online_pubs/timeandlearning/5_conclusions.html**.

28. Chapter Two, Elementary and Secondary Education, *Digest of Educational Statistics*, 2003, National Center for Educational Statistics. Available at: **http://nces.ed.gov/programs/digest/d03/tables/dt126.asp**.

29. Editors of *Education Week*, "From Risk to Renewal," p. 102.

30. National Association for Year-Round Education. Available at: **http://www.nayre.org**.

31. Robert Marzano and John Kendall, "The Fall and Rise of Standards-Based Education," National Association of State Boards of Education Issues in Brief (1998).

32. National and State Standards, Educational World. Available at: **http://www.education-world.com/standards/**.

33. Toch, *In the Name of Excellence*, p. 158.

34. Bess Keller " 'Qualified' Teachers: A Victory on Paper?" *Education Week* (December 8, 2004).

35. Lynn Olson, "Education Schools Use Performance Standards to Improve Graduates," *Education Week* (May 11, 2005).

36. Education World. Available at: **http://www.education-world.com/a_issues/issues374a.shtml**.

37. Education Week on the Web, "Choice." Available at: **http://www.edweek.org/rc/issues/choice/**.

39. U.S. Charter Schools. Available at: **http://www.uscharterschools.org/cs/dia/view/dai/95**.

40. Center for Education Reform. Available at: **http://www.edreform.com/_upload/ncsw-numbers.pdf**.

42. Center for Educational Reform. Available at: **http://www.edreform.com/index.cfm?fuseAction=section&pSectionID=15&cSectionID=97#SCHOOLS**.

43. Richard J. Murname and Frank Levy, "What General Motors Can Teach U.S. Schools About the Proper Role of Markets in Education Reform," *Phi Delta Kappan* 78, no. 2 (October 1996), p. 14.

Chapter 13

1. Richard M. Ingersoll, "Teacher Turnover, Teacher Shortages, and the Organization of Schools" (Seattle: Center for the Study of Teaching and Policy, University of Washington, 2001), p. 14.

2. Debra E. Gerald and William J. Hussar, *Projections of Education Statistics to 2013* (Washington, DC: National Center for Education Statistics, 2003), pp. 46, 80; William J. Hussar, *Projections of Education Statistics to*

2014 (Washington, DC: National Center for Education Statistics, 2005), p. 80.

3. Ann Bradley, "Class-Size Cuts Set Off Hiring Spree in Calif.," *Education Week* (September 4, 1996), pp. 1, 29.

4. Kerry J. Gruber et al., *School and Staffing Survey 1999–2000* (Washington, DC: U.S. Department of Education, National Center for Education Statistics, 2002), p. 3.

5. Eric Hirsch, Julia E. Koppich, and Michael S. Knapp, "Revisiting What States are Doing to Improve the Quality of Teaching: An Update on Patterns and Trends" (Seattle: Center for the Study of Teaching and Policy, University of Washington, 2001), p. 19.

6. *Recruiting New Teachers.* Available at: **http://www.rnt.org/facts/index/html.**

7. *The 2005 Job Search Handbook for Educators* (Columbus, OH: American Association for Employment in Education, 2004), pp. 13–15.

8. Ibid., p. 15.

9. *Status of the American Public School Teacher 2000–2001* (Washington, DC: National Education Association, 2003), p. 90.

10. Hirsch et al., p. 19.

11. *Quality Counts 2000: Who Should Teach?* Fourth annual edition of *Education Week*'s 50-state report card on public education, January 13, 2000. Available at: **http://www.edweek._org/sreports/qc00/.**

12. *Assessment of Diversity in America's Teaching Force: A Call to Action* (Washington, DC: National Collaborative on Diversity in the Teaching Force, 2004), p. 5.

13. *Department of Defense Education Activity.* Available at: **http://www.odedodea.edu/.**

14. Stephen P. Broughman and Kathleen W. Pugh, *Characteristics of Private Schools in the United States: Results from the 2001–2002 Private School Universe Survey* (Washington, DC: National Center for Education Statistics, 2004), pp. 1–3; Catherine Gewertz, "Teacher Need Hits Private Schools Hard," *Education Week* (May 23, 2001), pp. 1, 18.

15. Thomas M. Smith et al., *The Condition of Education 1996* (Washington, DC: U.S. Department of Education, National Center for Education Statistics, 1996), p. 34; James Coleman, T. Hoffer, and S. Kilgore, *Public and Private Schools*, Report to the National Center for Education Statistics, 1981.

16. *Rankings and Estimates* (Washington, DC: National Education Association, 2005), p. 78.

17. Ed Muir, F. Howard Nelson, and Aaron Baldaro, *Survey and Analysis of Teacher Salary Trends 2004* (Washington, DC: American Federation of Teachers, 2005), Table III-2. Available at: **http://www.aft.org/salary/2004/download/2004AFTSalarySurvey.pdf.**

18. Most of the ideas in this section are taken from John William Zehring, "How to Get Another Teaching Job and What to Do If You Can't," *Learning* 6 (February 1978), pp. 44, 46–51.

19. C. Emily Feistritzer, *Profile of Alternate Route Teachers* (Washington, DC: National Center for Education Information, 2005), p. 2.

20. J. Shen, "Has the Alternative Certification Policy Materialized Its Promise? A Comparison of Traditionally and Alternatively Certified Teachers in Public Schools," *Educational Evaluation and Policy Analyses* 19 (1997), pp. 276–283.

21. Feistritzer, pp. 8, 9, and 15.

22. *Occupational Outlook Handbook, 2004–2005 Edition* (Washington, DC: U.S. Department of Labor, 2004). Available at: **http://www.bls.gov/oco/.**

Chapter 14

1. Eric Hirsch, Julia E. Koppich, and Michael S. Knapp, "Revisiting What States are Doing to Improve the Quality of Teaching: An Update on Patterns and Trends" (Seattle: Center for the Study of Teaching and Policy, University of Washington, 2001), p. 19.

2. Estelle Fuchs, *Teachers Talk: Voices from Inside City Schools* (Garden City, NY: Doubleday, 1969), p. 21.

3. T. M. Wildman and J. A. Niles, "Reflective Teachers: Tensions Between Abstractions and Realities," *Journal of Teacher Education* 38, no. 10, 1987, pp. 25–31.

4. Gary Cornog, "To Care or Not to Care." In *Don't Smile Until Christmas: Accounts of the First Year of Teaching*, ed. Kevin Ryan (Chicago: University of Chicago Press, 1970), pp. 18–19. Copyright © 1970. Reprinted by permission of Kevin Ryan.

5. *What to Expect Your First Year of Teaching.* Available at: **http://www.ed.gov/pubs/FirstYear/ch6.html.**

6. Alliance for Excellent Education, *Issue Brief* (August 2005), p. 2. Available at: **http://www.all4ed.org/publications/TeacherAttrition.pdf.**

Chapter 15

1. Myron Lieberman, *Education as a Profession* (Englewood Cliffs, NJ: Prentice-Hall, 1956).

2. *U.S.A. Today.* Available at: **http://www.usatoday.com/news/education/2004-09-14-teachers-supplies_x.htm.**

3. Walter Boggs, quoted at 1963–64 convention of the National Commission on Teacher Education and Professional Standards; Myron Brenton, *What's Happened to Teachers?* (New York: Coward-McCann, 1970), p. 242.

4. Tanner, D., and Tanner, L. N. (1995). *Curriculum Development: Theory Into Practice*, 3d ed. (New York: Macmillian).

5. Ibid. Available at: **http://www.nbpts.org/nbct/index.cfm.**

6. NBPTS Five Core Propositions. Available at: **http://www.nbpts.org/about/coreprops.cfm#knowdo.**

7. Chester Finn and Danielle Wilcox, "Board Games: Failure of the National Board for Professional Teaching Standards to Accomplish Objective of Improving Quality of Teaching in the US; Business Backs a Losing Educational Strategy," *National Review* (August 9, 1999); and Frederick M. Hess, *Common Sense School Reform* (New York: Palgrave Macmillan, 2004).

8. National Education Association. Available at: **http://www.nea.org/aboutnea/index.html#mission.**

9. Ibid. Available at **http://www.nea.org/topics/index.html.**

10. Steven Chauffman, "The NEA Seizes Power: The Teachers' Coup," *The New Republic* (October 11, 1980), pp. 9–11.

11. Stanley Elam, "The National Education Association: Political Powerhouse or Paper Tiger," *Phi Delta Kappan* 63 (November 1981), pp. 169–174.

12. The Center for Responsive Politics: Public Sector Unions, PAC Contributions to Federal Candidates, 1997–1998, 1999–2000. Available at: **http://www.opensecrets.org/pacs/index/00003251.htm** and **http://www.opensecrets.org/pacs/index/00028860.htm.**
13. American Federation of Teachers. Available at: **http://www.aft.org.**
14. American Federation of Teachers. Available at: **http://www.aft.org/pubs-reports/american_teacher/oct03/organizing_side.html.**
15. National Education Association. Available at: **http://www.nea.org/aboutnea/index.html#neaft.**
16. National Education Association. Available at: **http://www.nea.org/student-program/about/index.html.**

Chapter 16

1. The Public Agenda, *A Sense of Calling: Who Teaches and Why* (New York: Public Agenda, 2000), p. 13.
2. Ibid.
3. Ibid., p. 36.
4. Ibid., p. 10.
5. Ibid.
6. Ibid., p. 12.
7. Ibid., p. 12.
8. Ibid., p. 10.
9. Ibid., p. 10.
10. Ibid., p. 12.
11. The Public Agenda, *Attitudes About Teaching* (New York: Public Agenda, 2003), p. 14.

Appendix

►Websites of U.S. State Teacher Licensure Offices

A teaching license is valid only in the state for which it is issued, and licensure and testing requirements are never static. If you are planning to move to another state, you should contact that state's licensure office, as listed below. Because the websites for these offices often change, if you experience difficulty reaching any one of them, you can link to any state agency by going to **http://www.ccsso.org** and clicking on the state education agencies bar.

When you contact the state licensure office, indicate the type of license you are receiving from your current state and which national tests you have taken, and ask for application materials and procedures for obtaining licensure in the new state. Another source of information about licensure requirements will be the actual districts to which you apply.

Alabama	www.alsde.edu/html/home.asp
Alaska	www.educ.state.ak.us/ teachercertification
Arizona	www.ade.state.az.us/certification
Arkansas	www.arkedu.state.ar.us/teachers/ teachers.html
California	www.ctc.ca.gov
Colorado	www.cde.state.co.us/ index_license.htm
Connecticut	www.state.ct.us/sde/
Delaware	www.doe.state.de.us
District of Columbia	www.k12.dc.us
Florida	www.fldoe.org/edcert
Georgia	www.gapsc.com/ TeacherCertification.asp
Hawaii	http://doe.k12.hi.us/teacher.htm
Idaho	www.sde.state.id.us/certification
Illinois	www.isbe.net/teachers.htm
Indiana	www.state.in.us/psb/
Iowa	www.state.ia.us/boee/
Kansas	www.ksbe.state.ks.us/cert/ cert.html
Kentucky	www.kyepsb.net/certification/ index.asp
Louisiana	www.doe.state.la.us/lde/tsac/ home.html
Maine	www.state.me.us/education/cert/ cert.htm
Maryland	https://certification.msde.state. md.us/
Massachusetts	www.doe.mass.edu/educators/ e_license.html
Michigan	www.michigan.gov/mde
Minnesota	http://education.state.mn.us/ html/intro_licen_first_time.htm
Mississippi	http://www.mde.k12.ms.us/ ed_licensure/index.html
Missouri	www.dese.state.mo.us/ divteachqual/teachcert/
Montana	www.opi.state.mt.us/cert/ index.html
Nebraska	www.nde.state.ne.us/tcert.html
Nevada	www.doe.nv.gov/licensure/
New Hampshire	www.ed.state.nh.us/education/ doe/organization/ programsupport/boc.htm
New Jersey	www.nj.gov/njded/educators/ license/
New Mexico	www.ped.state.nm.us/div/ais/ lic/index.html
New York	http://ohe33.nysed.gov/tcert/
North Carolina	www.dpi.state.nc.us/employment/
North Dakota	www.state.nd.us/espb/
Ohio	www.ode.state.oh.us/ teaching-profession/Teacher/ Certification_Licensure/ default.asp
Oklahoma	http://sde.state.ok.us/home/ defaultie.html
Oregon	www.ode.state.or.us/
Pennsylvania	www.teaching.state.pa.us/ teaching/site/default.asp
Puerto Rico	Phone: 787-754-0060

Rhode Island	www.ridoe.net/teacher_cert/Default.htm	**Vermont**	www.state.vt.us/educ/new/html/maincert.html#contact
South Carolina	www.scteachers.org/Cert/index.cfm	**Virginia**	www.pen.k12.va.us/VDOE/newvdoe/teached.html
South Dakota	www.state.sd.us/deca/OPA/index.htm	**Washington**	www.k12.wa.us/certification/
Tennessee	www.state.tn.us/education/lic/index.php	**West Virginia**	http://wvde.state.wv.us/certification/
Texas	www.sbec.state.tx.us	**Wisconsin**	http://dpi.wi.gov/tepdl/
Utah	www.usoe.k12.ut.us/cert/require/reqs.htm	**Wyoming**	www.k12.wy.us/ptsb/certification.htm
		U.S. Virgin Islands	www.usvi.org/education/

United States Department of Defense Dependent Schools   www.dodea.edu/pers/

Glossary

1890 institutions Colleges and universities created for African Americans as a result of the second Morrill Act passed by Congress in 1890.

academic engaged time The time a student spends on academically relevant activities or materials while experiencing a high rate of success.

academic freedom The freedom of teachers to teach about an issue or to use a source in teaching without fear of penalty, reprisal, or harassment.

academy A type of secondary school during the early national period that tried to combine the best of the Latin and English grammar schools. During the nineteenth century it took on a college preparation orientation.

acceleration A method of teaching gifted and talented students in which they do the same work as other students, but at a faster pace.

acceptable use policy A statement of rules governing student use of school computers, especially regarding access to the Internet.

active learning Learning in which the student takes control of or is positively involved in the process of his or her education; strongly associated with constructivism.

adequate yearly progress Students must show demonstrable improvement toward meeting state standards. Under NCLB, schools with students who do not make adequate yearly progress are subject to a variety of corrective measures.

aesthetics A branch of philosophy that examines the perception of beauty and distinguishes beauty from that which is moral or useful.

alternative licensure A procedure offered by many states to license teachers who have not graduated from a state-approved teacher education program.

American Federation of Teachers (AFT) The nation's second largest teachers' association or union. Founded in 1916, it is affiliated with the AFL-CIO, the nation's largest union.

assimilation The absorption of an individual or a group into the cultural tradition of a population or another group.

assistive technology The array of devices and services that help people with disabilities to perform better in their daily lives. Such devices include motorized chairs, remote control units that turn appliances on and off, computers, and speech synthesizers.

at-risk students *See* students at risk.

authentic (performance) assessment A recent trend in student evaluation that attempts to measure real student performance on significant tasks; the focus is on what we want the student to be able to do. Also called *performance assessment*.

axiology The philosophical study of values, especially how they are formed ethically, aesthetically, and religiously.

behaviorism A psychological theory asserting that all behavior is shaped by environmental events or conditions.

bilingual education A variety of approaches to educating students who speak a primary language other than English.

block grants Federal aid to education that comes with only minimal federal restrictions on how the funds should be spent. *Compare* categorical grants.

block scheduling An approach to class scheduling in which students take fewer classes each school day but spend more time in each class.

blog (Web log) A personal website that the user updates frequently, most are used like a journal or as a place to share personal opinions and information.

breach of contract A failure to fulfill the requirements of a legal agreement.

Brown v. Board of Education of Topeka U.S. Supreme Court ruling in 1954 holding that segregated schools are inherently unequal.

Buckley Amendment The shorthand name for the Family Educational Rights and Privacy Act, which outlines who may and may not have access to a student's records.

call to excellence An educational slogan pointing students to high standards.

career ladder A series of steps in an occupation. Usually the higher steps ("rungs" on the ladder) bring new tasks, more responsibility, increased status, and enhanced rewards.

categorical grants Federal aid to education that must be spent for purposes that are specified in the legislation and by the federal agency administering the funds. *Compare* block grants.

certification Recognition by a profession that one of its practitioners has met certain standards. Often used as a synonym for *licensure,* which is governmental approval to perform certain work, such as teaching.

character education Efforts by the home, the school, the religious community, and the individual student to help the student know the good, love the good, and do the good and, in the process, to forge good qualities such as courage, respect, and responsibility.

charter schools Public schools in which the educators, often joined by members of the local community, have made a special contract, or charter, with the chartering agency. Usually the charter allows the school a great deal of independence in its operation.

chief state school officer The executive officer of a state's board of education who is usually responsible for the administration of that state's public education. This person is also the head of that state's department of education. Also called *superintendent of education, commissioner of education,* and *superintendent of public instruction.*

choice theory A theory articulated by psychiatrist William Glasser holding that humans have fundamental needs such as survival, love, power, freedom, and fun, and that throughout our lives our actions are attempts to satisfy these needs.

civic learning (civic education) A part of social studies that emphasizes preparing students to be good citizens by becoming aware of our common heritage and engaging issues related to character and values. Students learn to apply principles of democracy to everyday concerns they will face as citizens.

classroom management The set of teacher behaviors that create and maintain conditions in the classroom permitting instruction to take place efficiently and effectively.

cognitive tools Computer applications that are used to engage and enhance thinking.

common schools Public elementary schools that are open to children of all classes. During the nineteenth century, the common school became the embodiment of universal education.

compensatory education Educational support to provide a more equal opportunity for disadvantaged students through such activities as remedial instruction and early learning.

constructivism A theory, based on research for cognitive psychology, that people learn by constructing their own knowledge through an active learning process rather than by simple absorbing knowledge directly from some other source.

content standards Statements of the subject-specific knowledge and skills that schools are expected to teach and students are expected to learn.

continuing contract An agreement between a school district and a teacher outlining the conditions and terms of work.

contract A binding agreement between parties.

cooperative learning An instructional approach in which students work together in groups to achieve learning goals. A variety of cooperative learning strategies exist.

core curriculum A common course of study for all students, often called for by essentialist reforms in the 1980s.

core knowledge *See* cultural literacy.

credential file A file established by college students—typically with the school's career planning and placement office—that contains materials important for securing a teaching job, for example, letters of recommendation, a transcript, and a résumé.

cultural literacy Being aware of the central ideas, stories, scientific knowledge, events, and personalities of a culture; also known as *core knowledge.*

culture shock The feeling of disorientation experienced by individuals when initially immersed in a society with different values, customs, and mores.

cultural pluralism An approach to diversity of individuals that calls for understanding and appreciating cultural differences.

culturally responsive teaching A method of embracing students' cultural backgrounds by modifying classroom conditions or activities to include elements that relate to the students' culture.

curriculum All the organized and intended experiences of the student for which the school accepts responsibility.

dame school A school run by a housewife during early colonial days.

database A software program that organizes and stores complex sets of information in the form of records that can be sorted according to different criteria.

deductive reasoning A type of reasoning from the general to the particular; reasoning in which the conclusion follows from the premise stated.

***de facto* school segregation** Segregation in the schools resulting primarily from residential patterns.

***de jure* school segregation** Segregation in the schools that occurs by law.

democratic reconstructionists Subscribers to an educational perspective that focuses on developing students who are prepared to make positive changes in a democracy.

differentiated instruction A variety of techniques used to adapt instruction to the individual ability levels and learning styles of each student in the classroom.

digital storytelling An instructional approach in which students use images, often digital photos, accompanied by their own written and recorded narrative to create a story that is stored digitally.

distance education The use of technology to link students and instructors who are separated in terms of location.

district school The type of school that succeeded the town school and moving school in New England. A township was divided into districts, each with its own school, its own schoolmaster, and funding from the town treasury.

drill-and-practice In educational technology, software programs that give students a series of tasks to reinforce a concept or to initially diagnose a student's level. These programs monitor progress, provide feedback, and present tasks accordingly.

due process The deliberative process that protects a person's constitutional right to receive fair and equal protection under the law.

economic reconstructionists Subscribers to an educational perspective or motivation that focuses on developing students who take a critical stance toward the dominant social and economic status quo.

education The process by which humans develop their minds, their skills, and their character. It is a lifelong process marked by continual development and change.

effective schools Schools that provide a significantly better education (usually measured by student test scores) for a much larger percentage of their students than do other schools serving similar student populations.

Elementary and Secondary Education Act (ESEA) The federal government's single largest investment in elementary and secondary education, including Title I. Originally passed in 1965 and periodically reauthorized by Congress, most recently in 2001 as the No Child Left Behind Act.

English grammar school A form of secondary education in the latter half of the colonial period that provided a practical alternative education for students who were not interested in college.

enrichment A method of teaching gifted and talented students in which they are allowed or assigned to do additional work to make regular class assignments more challenging or meaningful to them.

epistemology A branch of philosophy that examines the nature of knowledge, its origins, its foundations, its limits, and its validity.

equality of educational opportunity A concept that students from less advantageous backgrounds should have equal opportunities to experience success in school. Disagreement exists on whether this implies simply providing equal resources or ensuring equal success as more privileged students.

essentialism An educational philosophy that emphasizes a core body of knowledge and skills necessary for effective participation in society. Proponents believe that an educated person must have this core of knowledge and skills and that all children should be taught it.

ethics A branch of philosophy that examines the right and wrong of human conduct. The term can also refer to a particular moral code or system.

extrinsic rewards Rewards to an individual that are external to the activity itself, such as grades, gold stars, and prizes.

fair use A legal principle defining specific, limited ways in which copyrighted material can be used without permission from the author.

generational poverty Families living in poverty for two generations or longer.

grievance A formal complaint about working conditions. Procedures for filing grievances are often part of teachers' employment contracts.

Head Start A federally funded compensatory education program, in existence since the mid-1960s, that provides additional educational services to young children suffering the effects of poverty.

highly qualified teacher A teacher who has been licensed (via traditional or alternative routes) and has demonstrated a high level of competence in the subjects that he or she teaches.

inclusion The commitment to educate each child, to the maximum extent appropriate, in the regular school and classroom, rather than moving children with disabilities to separate classes or institutions.

individualized education program (IEP) A management tool required for every student covered by the provisions of the Individuals with Disabilities Education Act. It must indicate a student's current level of performance, short- and long-term instructional objectives, services to be provided, and criteria and schedules for evaluation of progress.

individualized family services plan (IFSP) Similar to an individualized education program for school-aged children, the IFSP specifies the services to be provided to developmentally delayed children from birth through age two. The IFSP is authorized by PL 99–457, the Education of the Handicapped Act Amendments.

inductive reasoning A type of reasoning, from the particular to the general, in which one can make a general conclusion based on a number of facts.

in loco parentis The responsibility of the teacher to function "in the place of the parent" when a student is in school.

integrated curriculum *See* interdisciplinary curriculum.

intellectual capital Another term for knowledge.

intelligent design theory A theory about the origins of life that suggests that the complexity of life is too great to be accounted for by standard evolutionary theories and that "an intelligence" either created or somehow guided its development.

interdisciplinary curriculum A curriculum that integrates the subject matter from two or more disciplines, such as English and history, often using themes such as inventions, discoveries, or health as overlays to the study of the different subjects. Also known as *integrated curriculum*.

intrinsic rewards Rewards to an individual that come from within, such as personal satisfaction or happiness.

junior high school A separate kind of school created typically for grades 7, 8, and 9. The first junior highs were founded in 1909–1910. In recent years, they have been gradually replaced by middle schools.

Kalamazoo **case** The 1874 U.S. Supreme Court decision (*Stuart and Others v. School District No. 1 of the Village of Kalamazoo and Others*) that upheld the right of states to tax citizens to create public high schools.

kindergarten A division of school for children below the first grade, usually for children between ages four and six; the concept, which means "garden of children" was imported into the United States from Germany during the nineteenth century.

Latin grammar school First type of secondary school in the American colonies, whose main purpose was to prepare students for college.

law The system of rules that governs the general conduct of a particular community's citizens.

LCD projector A projector that allows projection of the material seen on a computer screen to a larger screen for the whole class to see.

learning communities Organizations in which all members are engaged in continuous learning and improvement efforts.

learning style Characteristic way a student learns, including such factors as the way an individual processes information, preference for competition or cooperation, and preferred environmental conditions such as lighting or noise level.

least restrictive environment (LRE) A requirement of the Education for All Handicapped Children Act that students with disabilities should participate in regular education programs to the greatest extent appropriate.

liability A legal obligation.

licensure The approval given to an individual by a governmental agency, usually the state, to perform a particular work, such as teaching.

lifelong learners People who continue to learn new things after they leave school, throughout their lives.

limited English proficient (LEP) Term for students whose native language is not English and who have difficulty understanding and using English.

local school board The policymaking body of a school district, which represents the citizens of the district in setting up a school program, hiring school personnel, and generally determining local policy related to public education.

logic A branch of philosophy that involves the study of reasoning or of sound argument. In a more specific sense, logic is the study of deductive inference.

looping An educational practice of multiyear teaching in which the teacher follows students to the next grade level and stays with the group for several years.

magnet school An alternative school that provides instruction in specified areas such as the fine arts, for specific groups such as the gifted and talented, or for using specific teaching styles such as open classrooms. In many cases, magnet schools are established as a method of promoting voluntary desegregation in schools.

mainstreaming The practice of placing special education students in general education classes for at least part of the school day while also providing additional services, programs, or classes as needed.

McGuffey Readers A six-volume series of readers developed by William Holmes McGuffey that sold more than 100 million copies between 1836 and 1906. The readers served to create a common curriculum for many students.

mentor, mentoring A person who gives both personal and professional guidance to a novice.

metaphysics A branch of philosophy devoted to exploring the nature of existence of reality as a whole rather than to studying particular parts of reality as the natural sciences do. Metaphysicians try to answer questions about reality without referencing to religion or revelation.

middle school A school that bridges the grades between elementary school and high school, usually grades 6–8. It differs from a junior high school in that it is specifically designed for young adolescents, with a strong emphasis on personal growth and development, rather than mimicking the high school's emphasis on academics and sports, as junior high schools often did.

mind maps Graphical representations of a story or concept. *See also* webs.

Morrill Act Federal legislation passed in 1862 that granted each state federal land to establish colleges for the study of agriculture and mechanical arts. A second Morrill Act, passed in 1890, provided similar federal support to create "separate but equal" colleges for African Americans.

multicultural curriculum Several approaches to multicultural curriculum exist, but at its essence it promotes an understanding of and appreciation for cultural pluralism. It attempts to address issues of social injustice related to racism, sexism, and economic inequality by reducing prejudice and fostering tolerance through the formal curriculum.

multicultural education An approach to education that recognizes cultural diversity and fosters cultural enrichment of all children and youth.

multiple intelligences A theory of intelligence put forth by Howard Gardner that identifies at least eight dimensions of intellectual capacities that people use to approach problems and create products.

National Board for Professional Teaching Standards (NBPTS) A professional agency that is setting voluntary standards for what experienced teachers should know and be able to do in more than thirty different teaching areas.

national curricular standards Nationally dictated or recommended curriculum and levels of educational achievement.

National Education Association (NEA) The nation's largest teachers' association, founded in 1857 and having a membership of over 2.7 million educators.

National Education Goals (Goals 2000) Goals for U.S. education, established by the president and the fifty state governors and legislated by Congress, that were intended to be reached by the year 2000.

New England Primer The basic text used in schools during the eighteenth century. It was an illustrated book composed of religious texts and other readings.

news group A worldwide electronic network of users who share a common interest and post messages to one another.

No Child Left Behind Act (NCLB) The name of the 2001 reauthorization of the Elementary and Secondary Education Act. NCLB adds many new requirements for states and school districts.

Northwest Ordinances Passed by Congress in 1785 and 1787, these ordinances were concerned with the sale of public lands in the Northwest Territory (from present-day Ohio to Minnesota). Every township was divided into thirty-six sections, one of which was set aside for the maintenance of public schools. The 1787 ordinance reaffirmed that religion, morality, and knowledge were necessary to good government.

Old Deluder Satan Act A Massachusetts law passed in 1647 that strengthened an earlier law requiring parents to educate their children. It required every town of fifty or more families to pay a teacher to teach the children reading and writing so they could read the Bible and thwart Satan, who would assuredly try to keep people from understanding the scriptures.

parent-teacher organization (PTO) A local organization, usually centered around each school, that consists of both parents and teachers at that school. Its purpose is to serve as a communication mechanism between the school and the parents of the school's students.

participant observation In teacher education, the process of observing a class, recording one's observations, and comparing notes with other observers.

pedagogical content knowledge Teachers' knowledge that bridges content knowledge and pedagogy with an understanding of how particular topics can best be presented for instruction given the diverse interests and abilities of learners.

perennialism A particular view of philosophy that sees human nature as constant, with few changes over time. Perennialism in education promotes the advancement of the intellect as the central purpose of schools. The educational process stresses academic rigor and discipline.

performance pay (pay-for-performance) A financial reward given to teachers, based on the special quality of their work.

personal practical knowledge The set of understandings teachers have of the practical circumstances in which they work.

philosophy The love or search for wisdom; the quest for basic principles to understand the meaning of life. Western philosophy traditionally contains five branches of philosophy: metaphysics, ethics, aesthetics, epistemology, and logic.

phonics An approach to reading that teaches the reader to "decode" words by sounding out letters and combinations of letters.

Plessy v. Ferguson A Supreme Court decision in 1896 that upheld the constitutionality of separate but equal accommodations for African Americans. The ruling was quickly applied to schools.

portfolio A collection of a person's work. For students, portfolios are being used as a relatively new form of authentic assessment. They can contain a great range of work, from paper and pen work to sculpture.

private venture school A type of school in the middle states during colonial times, licensed by the civil government but not protected or financed by it.

privatization A movement to contract with private organizations, often for profit, to operate particular public schools whose students have been performing poorly on academic tests, or to provide specific educational services to public schools. The Edison Schools and Sylvan Learning Centers are examples of such providers.

problem solving The process of either presenting students with a problem or helping them to identify a problem and then observing and helping them become aware of the conditions, procedures, or steps needed to solve the problem.

profession An occupation or occupational group that fulfills certain criteria. Among other things, it must require training and knowledge, must perform a social service, must have a code of ethics, and must have a sense of autonomy and personal responsibility.

professional development The efforts by a school or school district to improve the professional skills and competencies of its professional staff. Also called "in-service" training in education. Also called *staff development*.

progressivism A form of educational philosophy that sees nature as ever changing. Because the world is always changing and new situations require new solutions to problems, learners must develop as problem solvers.

project approach An instructional method through which students engage in an in-depth investigation of a real world topic worthy of their attention and effort. The process often includes field trips or expert guests and a culminating event through which children present the results of their research.

project method A method of education in which students work in groups on a topic of interest to them. Developed by William Heard Kilpatrick, who believed that since students learn only what is of interest to them, they should be the ones to determine topics of study.

psychic reward Mental and spiritual benefits. Teaching has many.

public comprehensive high school The predominant form of secondary education in America in the twentieth century. It provides both preparation for college and a vocational education for students not going on to college.

real encounters Face-to-face experiences that are powerful sources of learning.

reduction in force (RIF) The elimination of teaching positions in a school system because of declining student population or funding.

reflection Conscious and analytical thought by an individual about what he or she is doing and how the action impacts others.

reflective teaching A teacher's habit of examining and evaluating his or her teaching on a regular basis.

resegregation Schools returning to a pattern of more racial segregation after a period of progress toward desegregation.

romanticism A child-centered philosophy of education that condemns the influences of society and suggests a child's natural curiosity and the natural world should be used to teach, instead.

scaffolding Providing assistance—some structure, clues, help with remembering certain steps or procedures, or encouragement to try—when a learner is on the verge of solving a problem but can't complete it independently.

school choice Allowing parents to select alternative educational programs for their children, either within a given school or among different schools.

school culture The prevailing mores, values, and rituals that permeate a school.

school vouchers (voucher plans) A type of educational choice plan that gives parents a receipt or written statement that they can exchange for the schooling they believe is most desirable for their child. The school, in turn, can cash in the received vouchers for the money to pay teachers and buy resources.

schooling Formal instruction typically conducted in an institution, adhering to standardized practices.

schools-within-schools In large schools, the establishment of "houses" of teachers and 100 to 400 students.

search engine A large database that has searched and indexed millions of web pages and helps users navigate the World Wide Web and pinpoint the information they need.

self-fulfilling prophecy Students' behavior that comes about as a result of teachers' expectations that the students will behave in a certain way. Teachers expect students to behave in a certain way; they communicate those expectations by both overt and subtle means; and students respond by behaving in the way expected.

sexual harassment Unwelcome sexual attention.

simulation A technique for learning or practicing skills that involves dealing with a realistic but artificial problem or situation. Typically, it provides an opportunity for safe practice with feedback on performance.

site-based decision making A school reform effort to decentralize, allowing decisions to be made and budgets to be established at the school-building level, where most of the changes need to occur. Usually teachers become involved in the decision-making process. Also known as *site-based management, school-based management,* or *school-based decision making.*

social bet The idea that the school curriculum represents a best guess or wager on what students will need to know to function in their society in the future.

social distance The psychological relationships between individuals, ranging from the formal to the familiar.

social reconstructionists Proponents of the theory of education that schools and teachers need to engage in the restructuring and reforming of society to eradicate its ills and shortcomings.

socialization The general process of social learning whereby children learn the many things they must know to become acceptable members of society.

socioeconomic status (SES) A system for measuring the economic conditions of people using the family's occupational status, income, and educational attainment as measures of status.

special education Educational programming provided by schools to meet the needs of students with disabilities.

spreadsheet An interactive software program allowing users to perform multiple calculations and view more than one answer at a time.

staff development The efforts by a school or school district to improve the professional skills and competencies of its professional staff. Also called "in-service" training in education.

state board of education The state's primary education policymaking body for elementary and secondary education.

state department of education The state bureaucracy, operating under the direction of the state board of education, whose responsibilities typically include administering and distributing state and federal funds, licensing teachers and other educational personnel, providing educational data and analyses, and approving college and university educational licensure programs.

students at risk Students judged to be in serious jeopardy of not completing school or not succeeding in school.

subject-matter curriculum A curriculum that focuses on bodies of content or subject matter, usually the traditional subject disciplines.

superintendent of schools Typically, a professional educator selected by the local school board to act as its executive officer and as the educational leader and chief administrator of the local school district.

teacher competency testing Examinations given to teachers to assess their professional knowledge and skills.

teaching journal A professional record of reflections, instructional ideas, and observations by a teacher or future teacher.

teaching portfolio Collection of such items as research papers, pupil evaluations, teaching units, and videocassettes of lessons to reflect the quality of a teacher's teaching. Portfolios can be used to illustrate to employers the teacher's quality or to obtain national board certification.

teaching to the test Instruction that is driven by the requirements or characteristics of a test, rather than the needs of students or the substance of a particular subject.

tenure A legal right that confers permanent employment on teachers, protecting them from dismissal without adequate cause.

Title I The section of the 1965 Elementary and Secondary Education Act that delivers federal funds to local school districts and schools for the education of students from low-income families and supplements the educational services provided to low-achieving students in those districts.

tools for learning Cognitive skills that make independent learning possible. They include advanced reading, remembering, recording, researching, test taking, analyzing, and creating.

town school A New England elementary school during the early colonial period, required in every town of fifty or more families.

tracking The homogeneous grouping of students for learning tasks on the basis of some measure(s) of their abilities.

tutorials A software application designed to provide initial instruction in a given topic, check for understanding throughout the process, and evaluate the learner's grasp of the topic once the program is completed.

ubiquitous computing Situations in which each student is provided access to some type of mobile computing device to use inside the classroom, out in the field, and at home.

universal education Schooling for everyone.

vicarious experiences Learnings gained not through direct experiences, but through observations or readings.

virtual fieldtrip Computer software that simulates the experience of an actual fieldtrip with the use of digital images and multimedia tools.

vocation A spiritual calling to do certain kinds of work. For many, teaching is more than a job; it's a vocation.

voucher plans (school vouchers) A type of educational choice plan that gives parents a receipt or written statement that they can exchange for the schooling they believe is most desirable for their child. The school, in turn, can cash in the received vouchers for the money to pay teachers and buy resources.

wait-time The time a teacher spends waiting for an answer after posing a question. Research indicates that good questioning practices involve giving students sufficient time to think about and respond to each question.

WebQuest An inquiry-based learning activity that directs learners in using information from the Web.

webs Graphical representations of a story or concept. *See also* mind maps.

whole language approach A teaching approach emphasizing the integration of language arts skills and knowledge across the curriculum. It stresses the provision of a literate environment and functional uses of language.

writing across the curriculum An instructional approach using writing as a tool for learning in all subject areas.

year-round education An educational reform, adopted in some states, where students go to school the same number of days as in traditional schools, but the school days are more evenly distributed throughout the school year.

zero-tolerance policies School policies calling for automatic suspension or expulsion of students who bring forbidden items, such as drugs or weapons, to school.

zone of proximal development A range of tasks that a person cannot yet do alone but can accomplish when assisted by a more skilled partner. This zone is the point at which instruction can succeed and real learning is possible.

Index

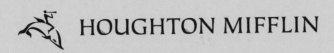

HOUGHTON MIFFLIN

GUIDES:

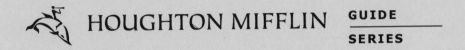

HOUGHTON MIFFLIN GUIDE SERIES

An Educator's Guide to
Teacher Reflection

Barbara Larrivee
California State University

James M. Cooper, Series Editor
University of Virginia

HOUGHTON MIFFLIN COMPANY   BOSTON   NEW YORK

CONTENTS

PREFACE

Houghton Mifflin Company publishes outstanding education textbooks in the areas of foundations of education, introduction to education, educational psychology special education, and early childhood education. These textbooks introduce students to many concepts, policies, and research that undergird educational practice. However, as is the case for virtually all introductory texts, many topics are introduced but not covered in great depth. The Houghton Mifflin Teacher Education Guide Series is designed to provide more in-depth coverage of selected educational topics studied in the teacher education curriculum.

At the present time, there are seven guides in the series:

- Classroom Management
- Field-based Classroom Observation
- Diversity in the Classroom
- Classroom Assessment
- Inclusion
- Technology Tools
- School-based Intervention Programs
- Student Motivation
- Teacher Reflection
- Differentiating Instruction

The topics for these guides were selected because they are addressed in virtually all teacher education programs, and contain vital information for beginning teachers if they are to be successful in the classroom. Instructors may use the guides either for required or enrichment reading.

Each of these guides provides pre-service teachers with greater in-depth knowledge, application suggestions, and additional resources on its particular topic. All the guides share a common format that includes an introduction to the topic, knowledge that the prospective teacher should possess about the topic, examples of and suggestions for how the knowledge can be applied, and resources for further exploration. Each guide also contains 10-15 questions designed to help the prospective teacher reflect on the concepts and ideas introduced in the guide, as well as a glossary of key terms.

Some teachers stagnate after a few years of teaching, falling into ruts and routines, while other teachers grow and continue to develop professionally over the course of their careers. A primary explanation for this phenomenon is the concept of teacher reflection. As Barbara Larrivee explains in this guide, teachers who develop the habit and skills of reflective practice are more effective in meeting student needs, in developing a more complex understanding of teaching issues, and in growing continuously as a professional teacher.

PART I: INTRODUCTION

WHY TEACHERS NEED TO BE REFLECTIVE PRACTITIONERS

There are many reasons for teachers to develop as reflective practitioners. Perhaps the most important is that teachers need to be reflective in order to deal with the inevitable uncertainties and tradeoffs involved in everyday decisions that affect the lives of students. Given all the complexities, ambiguities, and dilemmas that characterize today's classrooms, effective teachers will need to engage in both critical inquiry and thoughtful reflection, the hallmarks of reflective practitioners. Teaching is a complex and dilemma-ridden endeavor, necessitating ongoing learning as well as the capacity to be reflective. Many view the development of reflective practice as the foundation for the highest professional competence (Cole & Knowles, 2000; Jay, 2003; Larrivee, 2000; Osterman & Kottkamp, 2004; Steffy, Wolfe, Pasch, & Enz, 2000; Valli, 1997; York-Barr, Sommers, Ghere & Montie, 2001; Zeichner & Liston, 1996).

Because today's classroom represents increasing diversity among students, a teacher has to accommodate and adjust to this greater range of differences in ethnicity, socioeconomic status, developmental levels, motivation to learn, and achievement. Being responsive to this vast array of students' needs requires teachers who are reflective. Engaging in reflection helps teachers recognize behaviors and practices which impede their potential for tolerance and acceptance-the vital elements for meeting the needs of all students in a diverse society moving toward a global community.

Growing demands on teachers with recently imposed federal and state mandates often lead to a sense of alienation and isolation leaving teachers feeling like mere pawns in the system. However, teachers really can influence their practice much more than they may think by engaging in systematic reflection about their work. By taking control of their teaching lives they become empowered decision makers who can then begin to act on their world in a way that can change it. Reflective practitioners come to see themselves as change agents, capable of understanding not only what is, but also working to create what could be.

Another reason for developing as reflective practitioners is that it frees teachers from routine and impulsive acts, enabling them to act in a more deliberative and intentional manner. While following routine helps teachers manage the task of teaching, if teachers become slaves to routine they eventually come to feel powerless to influence their future careers. When teaching becomes so habitual that it is tantamount to a mechanical act it can be the path to burnout. Routine action is guided by circumstance, tradition and external authority (Zeichner & Liston, 1987). On the other hand, reflective practice entails voluntarily and willingly taking responsibility for considering personal actions.

A final reason is that emerging beliefs about quality teaching support teachers developing as reflective practitioners. What constitutes quality teaching is evolving. Major curricular changes that provide greater emphasis on curricular integration, teaching for meaning, interactive dialogue, socialization, and collaboration require fundamental changes in the way teachers view their role. These changing classroom demands redefine the teacher's role as social mediator, learning facilitator, and reflective practitioner (Larrivee, 2000). Being able to function in these roles begins with teacher self-awareness, self-inquiry and self-reflection. In fulfilling these roles, teachers in turn help students to learn to exercise self-direction, self-regulation and self-reflection – those qualities that are fundamental for democratic citizens.

This shift is characterized by a move from teacher-directed lessons to more participatory learning, from teacher solicitation of specific student responses to interactive dialogue, and from the teacher questioning students to students generating their own questions. Accordingly, the teacher role shifts from deliberately controlling learning to facilitating learning. The student role shifts from passive recipient of teacher-directed instruction to interactive participant, often functioning in a variety of collaborative modes with peers. This transformation is guided by the assumption that students construct their own meaning and take responsibility for their own learning.

REFLECTION IS A VITAL TOOL FOR NAVIGATING LIFE IN TODAY'S CLASSROOM

The explicit goal of reflective practice is to create deeper understanding and insight, forming the basis for not only considering alternatives, but also for taking action to continually improve practice throughout one's teaching career. Becoming a reflective practitioner means perpetually growing and expanding, opening up to a greater range of possible choices and responses to classroom situations. Building the habit of reflective practice allows teachers to remain fluid in the dynamic environment of the classroom.

Reflective practitioners operate in a perpetual learning spiral in which dilemmas surface, constantly initiating a new cycle of planning, acting, observing, reflecting, and adapting.

HISTORICAL PERSPECTIVE

John Dewey (1910/1933, 1938) is generally credited with the foundational influence on reflection in education. He made the distinction between action that is routine and action that is reflective, contrasting reflective thinking with habits of thought that are unsystematic, lack evidence, rely on mistaken beliefs or assumptions, or mindlessly conform to tradition and authority. Although Dewey first proposed his ideas nearly a century ago, the spirit of the concept remains essentially the same.

In the early 1980s, the notion of reflective practice in the United States was popularized primarily based on the work of Schön. Schön's (1983, 1987) work criticized the then reigning portrayal of teacher as technician. He challenged the belief system of teacher as technician, replacing it instead with teacher as committed and autonomous decision maker, or reflective practitioner. According to Schön, reflective practitioners continually learn from their experience, reconstructing experience through reflection.

The term reflection characterizes a way of thinking that accepts uncertainty and acknowledges dilemmas, (e.g., Dewey, 1933, 1938; Kelsey, 1993; King & Kitchener, 1994; Sparks-Langer & Colton, 1991; Osterman & Kottkamp, 2004). In his writings, Dewey asserted that the capacity to reflect is initiated only after recognition of a problem or dilemma *and* the acceptance of uncertainty. The dissonance created in understanding that a problem exists engages the reflective thinker to become an *active inquirer*, involved in both the critique of current conclusions and in the generation of new hypotheses. According to Dewey, reflective thinking requires continual evaluation of beliefs, assumptions and hypotheses against existing data and against other plausible interpretations of the data. Resulting decisions remain open to further scrutiny and reformulation.

Experiential learning theorists like Dewey and Jean Piaget maintain that learning is most effective when it begins with experience, in particular, experience that is problematic (Osterman & Kottkamp, 2004). Schön defined a problem as any "puzzling or troubling, or interesting phenomenon with which the individual is trying to deal" (Schön, 1983, p. 50). He suggested that such dilemmas practitioners face in the real world do not lend themselves to neat solutions. Instead, they require some improvising, inventing, and testing; that is, entering a reflective or inquiry cycle. A problem, defined as "a discrepancy between the present and the desired, or an intention and the actual impact", stimulates further inquiry, motivating a teacher to seek a deeper understanding of the situation at hand and to search for a better solution.

Regardless of the label, as uncertainty, dissonance, dilemma, problem, or conflict, some type of unsettling experience is a valuable stimulus to both cognitive growth as well as behavioral change. While experience is the starting point for learning, learning does not occur without reflection on experience. The old adage that experience is the greatest teacher tells only half the story. We actually learn only if we reflect on that experience.

PART II: KNOWLEDGE

DEFINING REFLECTIVE PRACTICE

Reflective teaching, reflective thinking, reflective inquiry, reflection and **reflective practice** are often used interchangeably, although there are slight distinctions (see Glossary). The term **reflective practice** is viewed here as the culmination of all other forms of reflection in that it is undertaken not solely to revisit the past but to guide future action.

Practice refers to one's repertoire of knowledge, attitudes, behaviors, and skills in specific areas of performance. For teachers, these areas include managing the classroom, designing instruction, establishing assessment strategies, and interacting with students, colleagues, and parents.

The following are some ways reflective practice has been described in the literature over the past two decades.

Reflective practice is:
- A dialogue of thinking and doing through which one becomes more skilled (Schön, 1987).
- A process that helps teachers think about what happened, why it happened, and what else could have been done to reach their goals (Cruickshank & Applegate, 1981).
- An inquiry approach that involves a personal commitment to continuous learning and improvement (York-Barr, Sommers, Ghere, & Montie, 2001).
- The practice of analyzing one's actions, decisions, or products by focusing on one's process for achieving them (Killion & Todnem, 1991).
- A critical, questioning orientation and a deep commitment to the discovery and analysis of information concerning the quality of a professional's designed action (Bright, 1996).
- A willingness to accept responsibility for one's professional practice (Ross, 1990).
- A systematic and comprehensive data-gathering process enriched by dialogue and collaborative effort (Osterman & Kottkamp, 2004).
- The use of higher-level thinking, such as critical inquiry and metacognition, which allow one to move beyond a focus on isolated facts or data to perceive a broader context.

for understanding behavior and events (Hatton & Smith, 1995).

- The capacity to think creatively, imaginatively and, eventually, self-critically about classroom practice (Lasley, 1992).
- An ongoing process of examining and refining practice, variously focused on the personal, pedagogical, curricular, intellectual, societal, and/or ethical contexts associated with professional work (Cole & Knowles, 2000).

As you can see from these definitions, reflection goes much deeper than thinking about how to keep students quiet and on task.

Reflective Teachers Vs. Non-Reflective Teachers

Teachers who operate at a non-reflective level react without conscious consideration of alternative responses. Settling too quickly on only one explanation of a behavior or situation leads to a narrow range of potential solutions.

Non-reflective teachers react to individual classroom situations without connecting them to other events. Their orientation is reactive, attributing ownership of problems to students or others. They view student and classroom circumstances as beyond their control, seeing themselves as victims of circumstances. They are willing to take things for granted without questioning, justifying teaching methods without exploring alternatives. They enforce predetermined standards of operation without adapting or restructuring based on students' responses.

Reflective teachers spend a lot of time thinking about classroom interactions and consider both the intended as well as the unintended consequences of their actions. They engage in the thoughtful reconsideration of everything that happens in their classroom with an eye toward improvement. Non-reflective teachers often fail to recognize dilemmas, have little impetus for improvement, and are consequently unlikely to achieve their professional potential.

While all teachers make mistakes, what differentiates non-reflective from reflective teachers is that reflective teachers recognize, learn from, and strive to correct their mistakes.

ATTRIBUTES AND ATTITUDES OF REFLECTIVE PRACTITIONERS

For teachers to become reflective practitioners they must possess certain qualities or attributes and sustaining attitudes that are distinctly different from non-reflective practitioners.

Reflective Practitioners Take an Inquiry Stance

A primary distinction between reflective and non-reflective teachers is taking an **inquiry stance**. An inquiry stance is an active search for understanding. In an inquiry stance you shift your internal orientation from certainty to curiosity, and from arguing your position to exploring other positions. Teaching practice is in constant formation and is always open to further investigation. A tightly wrapped argument with your own conclusions doesn't encourage further unfolding of ideas or solutions. An inquiry stance helps teachers construct their own meaning and become partners in helping others do the same.

A Closer Look

TEN ATTRIBUTES OF A REFLECTIVE PRACTITIONER

- Reflects on and learns from experience

- Engages in ongoing inquiry

- Solicits feedback

- Remains open to alternative perspectives

- Assumes responsibility for own learning

- Takes action to align with new knowledge and understandings

- Observes self in the process of thinking

- Is committed to continuous improvement in practice

- Strives to align behaviors with values and beliefs

- Seeks to discover what is true

KEY ELEMENTS OF REFLECTIVE PRACTICE

- A deliberate pause, a purposeful slowing down, to allow for higher-level thinking processes

- An open-minded stance, recognizing there are many ways to view a particular circumstance, situation, or event

- A receptiveness to changing viewpoint and letting go of needing to be right

- A mindful state, being conscious of both thought and action

- An acknowledgment that doubt, perplexity, and tentativeness are part of the process

Three Essential Attitudes of Reflective Practitioners

The three essential attitudes or habits of mind first described by Dewey are still considered the foundation of reflective practice. They are: open-mindedness, responsibility, and wholeheartedness.

Open-mindedness

Open-mindedness is a willingness to consider new evidence as it occurs and to admit the possibility of error. Open-mindedness means being open to other points of view, appreciating that there are many ways to view a particular situation or event, and staying open to changing your own viewpoint. Part of open-mindedness is also letting go of needing to be right or wanting to win.

It requires hearing different views as valid ways of thinking, not as threats. Zeichner and Liston (1996) have described open-mindedness as "an active desire to listen to more sides than one, to give full attention to alternative possibilities, and to recognize the possibility of error even in our most dear beliefs."

Being open-minded requires the capacity to criticize oneself. Teachers who are unable to acknowledge their errors tend to blame their students for any problems that arise. For example, if 90% of the class fails a test, teachers who are open-minded consider the possibility that the material, method or approach was lacking, rather than accuse students of not studying.

Open-minded teachers continually seek new information that might challenge their taken-for-granted assumptions about teaching, thus enabling them to envision a broad range of potential solutions and making it more likely that dilemmas will be resolved.

Responsibility

Responsibility is the careful consideration of the consequences of one's actions, especially as they affect students. For Dewey, reflective thinking leads to responsible action. Responsibility refers to a teacher's willingness to examine all decision making (e.g., decisions about curriculum, instruction, evaluation, organization, management) from a coherent philosophical framework of teaching and learning.

Responsibility is the willingness to acknowledge that whatever one chooses to do will impact the lives of students in both foreseen and unforeseen ways. Demonstrating responsibility means owning the many positive and negative ways your actions might influence others, regardless of how things turn out.

Wholeheartedness

Dewey believed that when people are thoroughly interested in a cause, they throw themselves into it with a whole heart. Teachers who are wholehearted approach all situations with the attitude that they can learn something new. The "need-to-know" is the driving force for their learning. Farrell (2004) characterized **wholeheartedness** as "a commitment to seek every opportunity to learn."

Three Essential Practices for Becoming a Reflective Practitioner

While it's not possible to prescribe a step-by-step procedure, there are actions and practices that are fundamental to developing as a reflective practitioner. The following three practices are essential: 1) Solitary reflection, 2) Ongoing inquiry, and 3) Perpetual problem-solving. The first creates an opening for the possibility of reflection while the others allow for a way of developing teaching practice that accepts uncertainty, recognizes contextual bounds and considers multiple plausible explanations for events and circumstances.

Solitary Reflection

Making time for thoughtful consideration of your actions and critical inquiry into the impact of your own behavior keeps you alert to the consequences of your actions on students. It's important to engage in systematic reflection by making it an integral part of your daily practice. Keeping a reflective journal is one vehicle for ensuring time is set aside for daily reflection.

Teachers also need reflective time to consider the inevitable tradeoffs involved in everyday decisions that affect students. Any effort to become a reflective practitioner involves negotiating feelings of frustration and insecurity. Taking solitary time helps teachers come to accept that such feelings are a natural part of teaching.

Ongoing Inquiry

This practice involves unending questioning of the status quo and conventional wisdom by seeking your own truth. Being a fearless truth-seeker means examining the assumptions that underlie both classroom and school practices.

Perpetual Problem-solving

Perpetual problem-solvers are never satisfied that they have all the answers and constantly seek new information. Problems present opportunities to find better solutions, build relationships, and to teach students new coping strategies. Your *modus operandus* is solving problems, not enforcing preset standards of operation. The classroom serves as a laboratory for purposeful experimentation. A practice or procedure is never permanent.

New insights, understandings and perspectives can bring previous
decisions up for reevaluation at any time.

WANTED
A Reflective Practitioner

A person who is inherently curious; someone who doesn't have all the answers and
isn't afraid to admit it; someone who is confident enough in his or her ability to
accept challenges in a non-defensive manner; someone who is secure enough to
make his or her thinking public and therefore subject to discussion; someone who
is a good listener; someone who likes other people and trusts them to make the
right decisions if given the opportunity; someone who is able to see things from
another's perspective and is sensitive to the needs and feelings of others; someone
who is able to relax and lean back and let others assume the responsibility of their
own learning. Some experience desirable but not as important as the ability to
learn from mistakes (Osterman & Kottkamp, 1993).

Activity Directions:

1. List all the qualities that are sought in this want ad.

2. Which ones do you possess?

3. Which one is your greatest strength?

4. Which one is your biggest challenge?

The following sections summarize various aspects that reflection entails so
you can develop a better understanding of its role in teaching as well as in
teacher development. Reflection is a complex and multifaceted term with
many different dimensions.

Developing the Capacity to be Reflective

The aim of reflective practice is to think critically about oneself, one's
assumptions, and one's teaching choices and actions (Cole & Knowles,
2000). Teachers who become reflective about their work come to know
what they are doing, why they are doing it, and what will happen as a
result of what they do. Whether focusing their reflection on subject matter,
students' understanding, or the larger social context, teachers who develop

as reflective practitioners understand and appreciate the complex realities of the classroom.

Focus and Goals of Reflective Practice

The focus of reflection can be at the level of examination of classroom practices and behaviors, goals and outcomes, or beliefs and values, manifested in expectations and assumptions. Teachers may reflect on the effects of a specific lesson or strategy, as well as on general practices, such as organizing the classroom, structuring the school day, establishing task structures and routines, interacting with students, and building relationships with both students and parents.

More in-depth reflection involves deliberations about one's aims and intentions, beliefs and values, as well as ethical dilemmas. Teachers may bring into question their goals, which encompass desired aims, outcomes, and intentions. They can be general such as creating the classroom as a learning community for students, or they can be more specific, such as assessing the impact of task structures like cooperative learning groups, buddy or peer groupings.

LEVELS OF REFLECTION

The term reflection is used to describe a vast array of practices. Just as with other popular terms, reflection can have a multitude of meanings as it is translated into professional teacher development. The literature describes numerous phases, levels, stages, types or dimensions of reflection. These descriptions range from mere thinking about a single aspect of a lesson to considering the ethical, social and political implications of teaching practice.

The various definitions evolving over several decades most commonly depict three levels of reflection (Day; 1993; Farrell, 2004; Handal & Lauvas, 1987; Jay & Johnson, 2002; Larrivee, 2004; Van Manen, 1977). In all of these descriptions of levels of reflection, critical reflection represents the zenith or ultimate aim.

The three levels are:

- An initial level focused on teaching functions, actions or skills, generally considering teaching episodes as isolated events.

- A more advanced level considering the theory and rationale for current practice.

- A higher order where teachers examine the ethical, social and political consequences of their teaching, grappling with the ultimate purposes of schooling.

Although there has been much discussion of the many different types and degrees of reflection, currently there is not any generally accepted terminology to define the various levels in the development of reflective practice. A point of deliberation is whether teachers should only reflect on behaviors and events within the confines of the classroom or whether they should also include the influence of the larger social and political contexts of the school community and the community at large.

The conceptual framework presented here represents a continuum of multiple levels adopting the terminology of surface reflection, pedagogical reflection, critical reflection and self-reflection.

Surface Reflection

At the first level, teachers' reflections focus on strategies and methods used to reach predetermined goals. They are concerned with what works in the classroom to keep students quiet and to maintain order, rather than with any consideration of the value of such goals as ends in themselves. At this level, the term technical has been most widely used (Van Manen, 1977). It has also been referred to as descriptive (Jay & Johnson, 2002). The term **surface reflection** is preferred by this author to depict a broader scope in this category, although still a low level of reflection.

Typical questions the teacher asks at the level of surface reflection are:

Did I spend too much time on groupwork today?

How can I keep students on-task?

Did I have enough (too many) activities?

How can I get students to pay better attention?

Pedagogical Reflection

At the next level, teachers reflect on educational goals, the theories underlying approaches, and the connections between theoretical principles and practice. This level has probably the least consensus in the literature as to its composition and label. It has been variously labeled practical, comparative, conceptual, contextual, theoretical, and deliberative. The term pedagogical is preferred by this author as a more inclusive term, merging all of the other concepts to connote a higher level of reflection based on application of teaching knowledge, theory and/or research.

Teachers engaging in **pedagogical reflection** strive to understand the theoretical basis for classroom practice and to foster consistency between espoused theory (what they say they do and believe) and theory-in-use (what they actually do in the classroom). Teachers reflecting at this level can determine when there is dissonance between what they practice and what they preach (e.g., seeing themselves as humanistic yet belittling students when they persist in disobeying rules).

Typical questions the teacher asks at the level of pedagogical reflection are:

How can I improve learning for all my students?

How can I build in better accountability for cooperative learning tasks?

Am I giving my students the opportunity to develop decision-making skills?

What else can I do to help students make connections to prior knowledge?

Is there a better way to accomplish this goal?

Teachers engaging in surface reflection, for example, may question how to limit the transition time between reading groups but may never question the larger issue of whether reading groups should exist (pedagogical reflection) or even if that structure limits the potential for some students with different cultural backgrounds (critical reflection).

Critical Reflection

At this next level, teachers reflect on the moral and ethical implications and consequences of classroom practices on students. They extend their considerations to issues beyond the classroom to include democratic ideals.

Acknowledging that classroom and school practices cannot be separated from the larger social and political realities, critically reflective teachers strive to become fully conscious of the range of consequences of their actions. Few teachers get through a day without facing ethical dilemmas. Even routine evaluative assessment of students' work is partly an ethical decision in that lack of opportunity to learn as well as impact on self-concept are ever-present considerations.

Although within the range of descriptions of reflective practice some incorporate a critical stance, many do not. Most typically, **critical reflection** is considered a higher-order level of reflection. Critical reflection adds the following dimensions:

- Questioning of underlying assumptions, biases, and values one brings to bear on their teaching.

- Conscious consideration of the ethical implications and consequences of practices on students and their learning.

- Examination of how instructional and other classroom practices contribute to social equity and to the establishment of a just society.

- Extended awareness beyond immediate instructional circumstances to include caring about democratic foundations and encouraging socially responsible actions.

The term critical reflection has the most consensus in the literature as a level of reflection examining the ethical, social and political consequences of one's teaching. Although even within this category there is considerable debate regarding the inclusion of self-reflection. Some definitions of critical reflection include the arena of self-reflection, also differentiated in the literature as *reflexive*, as distinguished from reflective. Some fail to acknowledge this category while others consider it to be imbedded in the category of critical reflection.

Typical questions the teacher asks at the level of critical reflection are:

Do all students in my class have daily opportunities to be successful?

Who is being included and who is being excluded in this classroom practice?

How might the ways I group students affect individual student's opportunity for success?

Does this classroom practice promote equity?

Do I have practices that differentially favor particular groups of students (e.g., males, females)?

Self-reflection

The conceptual models theorizing more than three levels generally single out the concept of **self-reflection** as a separate entity. Hatton and Smith (1995), Valli (1997), and York-Barr, Sommers, Ghere and Montie (2001) refer to this form of reflection as *dialogic, personalistic,* and *reflection-within,* respectively, highlighting the dimension of dialogue with oneself. However, the conceptualization of self-reflection presented here is a broader concept. Self-reflection focuses on examining how one's beliefs and values, expectations and assumptions, family imprinting, and cultural conditioning impact students and their learning (Larrivee, 2005). It is a process of search and discovery that uncovers the relationship of self to situation, of personal to professional. Based on the presumption that understanding oneself is a prerequisite condition to understanding others, self-reflection warrants distinction by itself.

The capacity for self-reflection is a distinguishing attribute of reflective practitioners. Self-reflection entails deep examination of **values** and **beliefs**, embodied in the assumptions teachers make and the expectations they have for students. Teacher behavior is driven by beliefs about students' capacity and willingness to learn, by assumptions about the behavior of students; especially those from different ethnic and social backgrounds, and by expectations formulated on the basis of the teacher's own value system.

Beliefs are convictions we hold dearly, having confidence in their truth, while acknowledging they are not susceptible to proof. They are enduring ideas about what is real.

Beliefs create the lens through which we view the world. Our beliefs shape our identity; hence shedding a dearly held belief shakes our very existence. For example, if a teacher tries to shed the belief that the teacher must be in total control to be effective, it means revealing uncertainty and vulnerability. A teacher's beliefs can be affirming or defeating, expansive or limiting.

Values are deeply held views about what we think is worthwhile. They steer how we behave on a daily basis and define the lines we will and will not cross. Values are our ideals; hence they are subjective and arouse an emotional response. In teaching, sets of values are often in conflict, challenging the teacher to weigh competing values against one another and play them off against the facts available. For example, a teacher may value being consistent while simultaneously valuing treating students justly. There are times when to be fair is to be inconsistent.

As teachers develop the capacity to be self-reflective, they become increasingly aware of how they are interactive participants in classroom encounters rather than innocent bystanders or victims. By developing the practice of self-reflection teachers learn to:

> (1) Slow down their thinking and reasoning process to become more aware of how they perceive and react to students

> (2) Bring to the surface some of their unconscious ways of responding to students.

Typical questions the teacher asks at the level of self-reflection are:

In what ways might I be modeling disrespect?

What is keeping me from trying to build a relationship with Pam?

Are there things I am doing that inhibit student self-management?

Why am I so intolerant of Adam's inappropriate behavior?

For teachers to continue to develop their professional work, they need to understand the formative as well as the continuing experiences and influences that have shaped and continue to shape their perspectives and practices.

Cole and Knowles (2000) distinguish between *reflective inquiry* and *reflexive inquiry*, describing the latter as tantamount to self-reflection as defined here. Underpinning reflective inquiry is the notion that assumptions behind all practice are subject to questioning. *Reflexive inquiry*, on the other hand, is reflective inquiry situated within the context of personal histories in order to make connections between personal lives and professional careers, and to understand personal (including early) influences on professional practice.

An example of progression from surface to self-reflection is depicted below.

A Closer Look | *Moving from Surface to Self-reflection*

Surface Reflection: *Are these good classroom rules for this group?*

Pedagogical Reflection: *Do my classroom rules represent reasonable expectations for my students?*

Critical Reflection: *Are the consequences for rule infractions just?*

Self-reflection: *Do I overreact when responding to Derrick's behavior because of my own biases?*

Teaching Practice Along the Reflective Continuum

Reflective practice is generally viewed as existing along a continuum. Although an individual teacher's progression is not necessarily linear, it is possible for teachers to reflect at different levels simultaneously or for various levels to be interwoven, depending on the topic of concern.

While each dimension of reflection can be useful in its own right as situations unfold, there is an implicit distinction in quality of reflection, with layers of quality moving from superficial to more significant to the potentially profound (Hatton & Smith, 1995; Hess, 1999; Jay & Johnson, 2002; Larrivee, 2004; McKenna, 1999; Smyth, 1989; Valli, 1997; Van Manen, 1977).

The increasing levels might also be characterized as falling along an "efficiency-value-worth continuum." At the first level the concern is mainly with means rather than ends. It entails selection and use of instructional methods primarily for their expediency. The second level adds questioning assumptions as well as consequences of particular strategies. Here teachers apply criteria to assess classroom practices to make individual and independent decisions about pedagogy. Teaching choices are based on a value commitment to a particular interpretive framework. The teacher analyzes and clarifies individual experiences, meanings, assumptions, and judgments for the purpose of making instructional decisions based on an interpretive understanding of what represents quality educational experiences. That is, decisions at the level of pedagogical reflection are based on a value judgment whereas decisions made at the level of critical reflection are based on a worth judgment. At the highest level of deliberation the worth of knowledge is in question. The teacher pursues worthwhile educational ends of self-determination based on the principles of justice, equality and freedom. This is what Van Manen (1977) referred to as the "classical politico-ethical meaning of social wisdom."

A Closer Look   *Vignette for Reflection*

While Ms. Dyer's class is working on story writing, she notices that Will is not working and is looking very frustrated. She asks him to brainstorm ideas for his story. He refuses, saying that he can't do it because he doesn't know how to spell.

Potential teacher's responses:
1. I would remind him that everyone is expected to be working. I would tell him to use the dictionary if he doesn't know how to spell the words. If he doesn't get started, I would tell him he can stay in for recess and do it then.

2. I would communicate that spelling is not important at this stage. What's important is to think of a story that the other students would enjoy reading. I would encourage him to use just the letters he hears for the words.

3. I would pair him with another student to work together.

4. I could allow him to dictate his ideas to me as I write them down.

5. Knowing that he has had little experience with the writing process, I would give further explanation of the brainstorming process as well as provide lots of modeling.

6. I could ask him to draw pictures to illustrate his thoughts and then dictate the story into a tape recorder.

7. I would remind myself not to merely respond to his refusal and to try to understand what the message is behind his refusal. Then I would respond to both the content and the emotion behind his words.

8. Because he has had some negative experiences with writing, making him apprehensive about putting his thoughts down on paper, I would try to build his confidence. I would make sure I provided a great deal of encouragement for every effort he makes.

Activity Directions:
For each of the identified options, note if you think it indicates reflective thinking. Then try to categorize the level of reflection evident in the teacher's response.

REFLECTION DIRECTION

While Schön (1983) initially made the distinction between *reflection-in-action* and *reflection-on-action*, Killion and Todnem (1991) added the concept of *reflection-for-action*, connoting a deliberate intent to change. York-Barr, Sommers, Ghere, and Montie (2001) used the terminology of reflection direction and added the concept of *reflection-within* depicting four different directions that can guide reflection. One can reflect in the present (in), reflect back (on), reflect forward (for action) or reflect within as described below.

Reflection-in-action is observing thinking and action as they are occurring for the purpose of making immediate adjustments as classroom events unfold. Here a reevaluation occurs on the spot. New data are linked to what is already known allowing the teacher to adapt in the moment. It is often difficult to reflect while events are occurring, but when it is possible, it is a very powerful type of reflection. Keen awareness of what is going on in the present allows the teacher to make adjustments while in the process of teaching or responding. It requires a high level of consciousness. With this type of reflection, for example, the teacher may notice that engagement is trailing off and will do something novel to regain students' attention. As Schön noted, this form of reflection is often tacit.

Reflection-on-action is looking back on and learning from experience or action in order to affect future action. Often reflection during, or simultaneous with, actions is difficult because of the multiple demands teachers have to juggle in the classroom. For instance, focusing attention on completing a lesson may distract from paying attention to the way in which the teacher interacts with students. Hence, reflection often requires a perspective of a meta-position, a looking back after the action has taken place. Van Manen (1991) referred to this as *recollective reflection* noting that it promotes deeper insight into past experiences. Reflecting after being removed from an event is probably the most frequently used form of reflection given that it may be too challenging to reflect while engaged in the teaching process with so many things vying for the teacher's simultaneous attention.

Reflection-for-action is analyzing behavior with the designated purpose of taking some action to change. What differentiates this type of reflection is that it is proactive in nature. Killion and Todnem contend that it is the desired outcome of both *reflection-in-action* and *reflection-on-action*. They make the case that reflection is not so much for the purpose of revisiting the past or becoming aware of our metacognitive processes, but to guide future action. Farrell (2004) noted that teachers can not only use this type of reflection to prepare for the future by using knowledge from what happened during class and what they reflected on after class, but also as a means of detecting inconsistencies between beliefs and practice.

Teachers use this type of reflection when they already recognize that they need to change something, such as a relationship with a student, or a task structure to enhance participation. Here the teacher entertains specific actions or interventions with students, the learning environment, or school community that are likely to produce more desirable results. The systematic investigation on classroom practices conducted via **action research** also falls into the category of reflection-for-action.

Teachers using reflection-for-action are able to move out of focusing on their dissatisfaction with what is happening now to concentrate on closing the discrepancy between the current situation and what they would like to see. By focusing on their vision for the preferred future they put their energy into closing the gap between what is and what might be.

Reflection-within is inquiring about personal purposes, intentions, and feelings. In this form of reflection, teachers might question what is preventing them from taking action or keeping their perspective limited. As such, this concept is very similar to self-reflection as defined earlier.

Here teachers may ask themselves questions like the following.

What were my intentions when I did that?

What triggered such an emotionally charged response?

Am I considering alternative explanations for what happened with Maria?

4-STEP PROCESS FOR GUIDING REFLECTION

The following process can guide reflection-on-action and reflection-for-action (York-Barr, Sommers, Ghere, & Montie, 2001). It moves through the sequence of asking what? why? so what? and now what?

A Closer Look	*Guided Reflection on a Significant Event*

Think about a significant event or interaction that occurred in your classroom that was unsettling or challenging. Consider the following questions to prompt your reflection about the experience.

1. What happened?
2. Why do I think things happened that way?
3. So what?
   Why was this significant to me?
   What have I learned?
   What questions remain?
4. Now what?
   What are the implications for action?

PART III: APPLICATIONS

THE CAPACITY TO REFRAME: A CRUCIAL ATTRIBUTE OF REFLECTIVE PRACTITIONERS

When faced with a problem, teachers basically have two choices--change the situation or change their reaction to the situation. Often teachers can't change the situation, but they can change how they respond by learning to **reframe** or reposition classroom situations and school circumstances. Reframing means putting the experience in a new frame, one that views the situation from a different angle or one that includes parts of the picture that weren't visible from the first vantage point.

The term **reposition** connotes the idea of changing your perception by moving out of your old position and creating a new position from which to view a situation (Larrivee, 1996). It involves developing the capacity to look at what's happening, withholding judgment, while simultaneously recognizing that the meaning you attribute to it is no more than your interpretation filtered through your cumulative experience.

Breaking through familiar cycles necessitates a shift in ways of thinking, perceiving and interpreting classroom events. When a student acts out, one teacher sees a personal attack while another sees a cry for help. It is the teacher's interpretation of the student's behavior, or the meaning attached to the behavior, that determines how the teacher will respond. It's a teacher's personal framing that shapes how he or she attributes meaning to classroom experiences.

Seeing new ways of interpreting a situation enables a teacher to move beyond a limited perspective and assign new meaning to the classroom situations encountered. By repositioning a seemingly negative event, the teacher seizes the opportunity to discover the potential in a situation.

A Closer Look   *Repositioning Events and Situations*

Some helpful ways of repositioning in the classroom include:
- Repositioning confrontation as energy to be rechanneled
- Repositioning an attack as a cry for help
- Repositioning conflict as opportunity for relationship building
- Repositioning defiance as a request for communication

> • Repositioning attention-seeking as a plea for recognition

Challenging Underlying Beliefs and Creating Dissonance

Teachers who develop as reflective practitioners continually challenge the underlying beliefs that drive their present behavior. However, the channel to changing beliefs is not direct; it is through critically examining assumptions, interpretations and expectations.

Questioning assumptions, naming issues, and confronting limiting beliefs is an emotional experience. Examining efficacy, value and worth of classroom practices necessarily creates tension. Promoting tension, uncertainty, and dissonance helps to unveil the multiple dimensions of dilemmas and consequently reveal a wider range of options. Reflecting on teaching practices can at times be discouraging and defeating, as well as empowering and exhilarating. Out of the conflict and discomfort can come invaluable learning and insight.

AVENUES TO DEVELOPING REFLECTIVE PRACTICE

To develop the habits of mind necessary to become reflective practitioners, preservice and novice teachers often need to be explicitly prompted to think, respond, and act in new ways. Reflection is enhanced when mentoring or coaching is provided that allows teachers as learners to tap into their own realm of experiences, reflect on those experiences, and construct personal meaning to inform their developing practice. Reflection, especially critical reflection and self-reflection, are complex constructs requiring strategically constructed mediation or facilitation.

Much of the literature grapples with moving beyond the surface level of reflection to engage in pedagogical reflection and critical reflection. According to the research conducted by Hatton and Smith (1995) with teachers in preservice training, teacher progression through various levels of reflection appears to be developmental in the sense that the technical level represents a useful starting point for addressing concerns. For example, they noted that teachers may need to reflect first on areas of technical skill before being able to compare different teaching strategies and weigh their relative merit.

Other researchers have identified processes that can help preservice and novice teachers move along the reflection continuum. The generally accepted position is that these teachers can be helped to reflect at higher levels with carefully constructed guidance (e.g., Putorak, 1993, 1996; Rudney & Guillaume, 1990; Wildman & Niles, 1987; Yost, Sentner, & Forlanza-Bailey, 2000). Collier (1999) noted that establishing self-monitoring and self-reflective activities early on can promote the kind of self-awareness that allows preservice teachers to hear and listen to their own voices. Focusing on what they already know and believe about teaching has proven to be a useful starting point (Wideen, Meyer-Smith, & Moon, 1998).

Some mediated structures and other vehicles that have been found to be useful in promoting reflection include journal writing, teacher narratives, autobiography, metaphor, critical incidents, support groups, critical friends, and action research. Merging these task structures in creative ways and utilizing them individually, collaboratively, and with facilitated coaching is likely to have the greatest potential for promoting higher-order reflection.

Journal Writing (open, reflective, interactive, and dialogue)

The act of maintaining and reviewing a journal over time can serve as a useful tool for reflection. Having a record of thoughts, feelings, issues and concerns can provide both a window of the past and a gateway to the future.

Practical Tips and Strategies	*Journal Writing for Reflection*

Journal writing can serve as a tool for:

- Looking more objectively at classroom behaviors

- Naming issues and posing questions

- Recording critical incidents

- Identifying cause and effect relationships

- Discovering habits of thought and behavior

- Working through internal conflicts

- Seeing patterns of unsuccessful strategies over time

- Tracing life themes

Journal writing as a systematic self-reflection process enables teachers to recognize their contribution to the experiences they encounter in the classroom. Making regular journal entries can help teachers become more aware of what is going on in both their inner and outer worlds. Journal writing also develops self-discipline.

Journal writing can be used in a number of ways to encourage reflection (Calderhead, 1991; Collier, 1999; Dobbins, 1996; Keating, 1993; Ross, 1990; Smyth, 1992; Surbeck, Han, & Moyer; Wiltz, 1999; Yost, 1997; Yost, Forlanza-Bailey, & Shaw, 1999). Reflection can be facilitated via guided prompts, structuring periodic rereading of previous entries to search for any emerging patterns, and posing questions in a nonjudgmental way as a means of creating ongoing dialogue.

One significant finding from Dobbins' (1996) research using journal writing with preservice teachers was that being specifically prompted to focus on their own learning produced reflections with a deeper focus in which they were able to confront broader educational issues in the process of clarifying their own beliefs. Similarly, there is evidence that when preservice teachers are engaged in journal writing over time they develop the habit of reflection (Yost, 1997, Yost, Forlanza-Bailey, & Shaw, 1999).

Dialogue journals, also referred to as interactive journals, are first individually written and then shared with another person who makes inquiries for the purpose of expanding thinking (Keating, 1993). That person might be an instructor, mentor, peer coach or critical friend.

Autobiographical journal writing coupled with deliberate questioning prompts can stimulate greater awareness of personal values and implicit theories of teaching (Ross, 1990). The regular feedback from a mentor serving in a coaching role can be a valuable tool to move teacher trainees along the reflection continuum.

Smyth (1991) found posing a series of four questions, respectively moving from description to meaning to confrontation to reconstruction, to be a powerful tool for prompting higher-order reflection. The questions are:

(1) What do I do?	*Description*
(2) What does it mean?	*Meaning*
(3) How did I come to be like this?	*Confrontation*
(4) How might I do things differently?	*Reconstruction*

Teacher Narratives (autobiography, metaphor, case story writing)

Narratives other than journal writing can render a rich understanding of what takes place in the minds of developing teachers as they construct their reality of teaching. **Teacher narratives** are stories written by and about teachers and can be used as the source of narrative inquiry (Cole & Knowles, 2000; Sparks-Langer & Colton, 1991; Zeichner, 1983). It is a more disciplined from of writing than journaling in that it has a structure and a focus, the intent to communicate a story. Either keen observers or teachers themselves write real stories about teaching that illuminate the realities, dilemmas and rewards of teaching. Reflecting on teacher narratives can yield insights about motivations for teacher actions, the complexities of teaching, and about teachers themselves (Sparks-Langer & Colton, 1991; Taggart & Wilson, 1998). Teacher narratives can also be specifically designed to be used as case studies with the explicit purpose of reflecting on a specific problem. Using a vehicle of case story writing based on student teaching experiences, Hunter and Hatton (1998) found that combined peer and instructor collaboration helped preservice teachers move toward critical reflection.

Autobiographical sketches, also called personal histories, are a specialized form of teacher narratives (Sparks-Langer & Colton, 1994). These stories of a more personal and in-depth nature offer insight into the past to uncover preconceived theories of practice. When teachers write about their own biographies and how they think these have shaped the construction of their values, then they are able to see more clearly how social and institutional forces beyond the classroom and school have had an influence.

Johnson (1994) and Lasley (1992) advocated the use of **metaphors** to help teachers become aware of their teaching identities and develop alternative ways to think about an issue. Marshall (1990) contends that the reflection that occurs in the examination of personal teaching metaphors involves reframing the lens through which a teacher perceives a problem. According to Schön, this is a critical attribute of reflective practitioners.

Metaphors bear the images teachers have of themselves as teachers, their professional identity (Bullough, Knowles, & Crow, 1992). The practical theories of teachers are often expressed as metaphors as opposed to the more logical forms of expression. They often appear in the natural language teachers use to talk about their teaching (Munby & Russell, 1990). The knowledge-in-action embedded in the practical theories of teachers often cannot be adequately depicted in their statements of knowledge; hence metaphor can be a way to bridge the known to the new.

Through metaphors teachers can elaborate and turn abstractions into real images, helping to give them firmer handles on slippery concepts such as teaching.

The following metaphors written by beginning teachers offer a glimpse of the images teachers have of themselves as teachers:

A teacher is like a song creating memories and bringing comfort when you hear it.

A teacher is like a caterpillar because you are continually stretching out then pulling back. It's pretty stressful if you try to be stretched out all the time, so you have to remember to pull back. But if you always pull back you go nowhere.

Critical Incident

Though generally conceived as a self-generated incident, a **critical incident** could also be a carefully chosen real-world example or case study of a teaching dilemma intended to serve as a springboard for reflection. Examining a critical incident can be a tool for deepening the level of reflection. Pultorak (1996) found that writing about critical incidents or dilemmas rather than typical daily events promoted critical reflection in novice teachers. Likewise, Griffin (2003) found that using critical incidents with explicit prompts and coaching increased the capacity of preservice teachers to engage in higher order reflection.

Descriptions of high and low moments in their practice, or details of significant incidents that stand out in their lives as teachers, provide the impetus to grapple with problems and dilemmas becoming the basis for critical investigation. By sharing critical incident responses, teachers come to realize that their individual stories have generic qualities and themes embedded within them. They discover that their personal struggles are not so different from those experienced by their colleagues. What they thought were idiosyncratic failings or inadequacies come to be seen as common experiences.

A Closer Look	*Critical Incident: Low Points of Practice*

Thinking back over the past few months, identify an incident that caused you the greatest distress in your teaching, one that may have kept you awake at night thinking about what you should have done. Write about where and when it happened, who was involved, and what it was about the incident that was so distressing to you.

Support Groups and Critical Friends

Teaching is a complex and personal expression of multiple and varied forms of knowledge and knowing. Much of what teachers do is implicit, hidden from the practitioner but observable by others. An individual teacher's thinking needs to be confirmed, modified, or stimulated to deeper levels of understanding by reflecting aloud.

A major purpose of reflective practice is to test for the presence of assumptions and biases in the information one accesses. The checks and balances of peers' and critical friends' perspectives can help beginning teachers recognize when they may be devaluing information or using self-confirming reasoning, weighing evidence with a predisposition to confirm a theory rather than consider alternative theories that are equally plausible.

Reflective practice involves teachers questioning the goals, values, and assumptions that guide their work, entailing critical questions about the means, ends, and contexts of teaching. Engaging in such questioning can best occur in a supportive learning community, such as that provided in **support groups** or **critical friends**.

Such support can help teachers keep from getting stuck in destructive habits to deal with the stress of teaching and provide a buffer against the inevitable low points enroute to becoming a reflective practitioner

(Brookfield, 1995). Ideally, a support group or critical friend provides a safe haven to be vulnerable, admit mistakes and ask for help.

Their function is not only to empathize with others' dilemmas but also to point out incongruencies in practice and fallacies in thinking. It often takes others to mirror back experiences and perceptions to open up a new way of seeing things.

It is important to build a support system to provide comfort and compassion as well as understanding, direction, and when necessary, redirection. Recurring problems can erode self-perceptions of ability to find adequate solutions to problems that plague teachers on a day-to-day basis, leading to a preoccupation with the negative aspects of teaching. Collaborative peer support is one vehicle for supplanting such negative attitudes and self-appraisals with encouragement.

Peer conversation helps to break down the isolation many teachers feel. Colleagues' perceptions help teachers realize the commonality of their individual experiences. There is often much more that unites them than they realize. Collaborative dialogue helps teachers become aware of how much they take for granted in their own teaching and how much of their practice is judgmental.

ACTION RESEARCH

One of the most widely recognized ways to reflect on and improve practice is action research (Carr & Kemmis, 1986; Cochran-Smith & Lyle, 1993; Cole & Knowles, 2000; Dana & Yendol-Silva, 2003; Glanz, 1998; McFee, 1993; Osterman & Kottkamp, 2004). It is a systematic inquiry process conducted by and for those taking the action. Teachers assume the role of researcher in their own classrooms as part of a professional reflective stance.

Action research is a form of disciplined inquiry ranging from simply raising a question about some educational practice and collecting information to answer the question, to doing statistical analyses to determine whether test results from an experimental group are statistically significant. The process is similar to other reflection frameworks with the primary distinguishing feature being the emphasis on formalizing research questions and then collecting and analyzing data to take informed action.

The purpose and intent of action research is not the development of universal principles to be applied to all teaching situations. Rather, each classroom is envisioned as a small culture created by teacher and students as they work together over a period of time. The ultimate intent of action research based on this view of teaching is to build and verify a coherent explanation of how a particular classroom works.

| A Closer Look | *Reflecting About a Teaching Practice* |

Mr. Bates was nearing the end of his first year of teaching fifth grade in an urban district. He wanted students to work together in his classroom and he believed that when students learned together they could all benefit. During the year, he had tried a variety of ways to gather his students into cooperative learning groups, but none got him the results he wanted. He needed to find more effective ways to organize for cooperative learning. He decided to conduct his own action research.

He learned from reading the research on collaborative learning that he needed to accomplish the following to be successful:

(1) Plan the groupwork to specifically align with the particular learning goals of the lesson.
(2) Provide a structure for the kind of social interaction he wanted to see among group members.
(3) Identify what kinds of group talk would serve as evidence that learning was being achieved during the group sessions.
(4) Exercise caution when entering the group setting not to disturb the dynamics already in place.

Mr. Bates realized that he had to be much more strategic in structuring the groups to accomplish the learning goals he had for his students. Adhering to these four guidelines, he changed the way he approached and structured group time with his class. He also made a plan to collect data to make sure these changes promoted the kind of collaborative climate he wanted.

Activity Directions:

1. Describe a situation you have had similar to Mr. Bates' where new information or research caused you to make a significant change in a teaching practice.

2. What information, knowledge, or research findings would you like to have about a teaching method you are currently using or would like to use?

3. What is an area of your teaching that you would like to see working better? What would you like to see that's not happening now?

PART IV: EXTENSIONS

BOOKS

Brookfield, S. D. (1995). *Becoming a critically reflective teacher.* San Francisco, CA: Jossey-Bass.

Farrell, T. S. (2004). *Reflective practice in action: 80 reflective breaks for busy teachers.* Thousand Oaks, CA: Corwin Press.

Jay, J. K. (2003). *Quality teaching: Reflection as the heart of practice.* Lanham, MD: Scarecrow Press.

Larrivee, B. (2005). *Authentic classroom management: Creating a learning community and building reflective practice.* Boston, MA: Allyn & Bacon.

Osterman, K. P., & Kottkamp, R. B. (2004). *Reflective practice for educators: Improving schooling through professional development.* Thousand Oaks, CA: Corwin Press.

York-Barr, J., Sommers, W. A., Ghere, G. S., & Montie, J. (2001). *Reflective practice to improve schools.* Thousand Oaks, CA: Corwin Press.

Zeichner, K. M., & Liston, D. P. (1996). *Reflective teaching: An introduction.* Mahwah, NJ: Lawrence Erlbaum.

FOR REFLECTION

1. Some might argue that teaching is too demanding to expect teachers to be reflective about their work. What do you think?

2. What things do you do automatically in the classroom without consciously thinking about them?

3. How have your past educational experiences influenced your understanding of yourself as a teacher?

4. What are some of the key experiences in your life that have had an impact on your current ideas about teaching and learning?

5. What is an example of an educational theory that you hold about teaching and learning that is based on your own experiences as a learner?

6. What ideas about how children learn are reflected in the organization of your school program?

7. What are the important values that underlie your approach to teaching?

8. What acts to constrain your view of what is possible in teaching?

9. What metaphor would you use to describe how you think about yourself as a teacher?

10. What student needs are not being addressed by your current teaching practices?

11. What avenues for reflection are best aligned with your learning style?

12. How might you create a "space" to reflect as a regular practice?

A Closer Look | *Reflective Practitioners Ask...*

What am I observing?
What would I like to see?
How might things be different?
What am I learning?
What possibilities are there for the future?

GLOSSARY

action research Any systematic inquiry conducted by teacher researchers or other stakeholders in the teaching/learning environment to gather information about how their particular schools operate, how they teach, and how well their students learn.

beliefs The conclusions we draw over time about our experiences that significantly influence our ways of thinking and behaving.

critical friends Both support and challenge each other to look critically at their classroom practices.

critical incident A vividly remembered event which is unanticipated and has significant implications related to your teaching.

critical reflection The conscious consideration of the moral and ethical implications and consequences of classroom practices on students.

inquiry stance A learning stance in which you actively search for understanding.

metaphor A way of illuminating features through comparison to understand and experience one kind of thing in terms of another.

open-mindedness Listening to other points of view, considering alternatives, and acknowledging our own potential for error.

pedagogical reflection At this level, reflection is guided by a conceptual framework and beliefs about teaching are grounded in theory or research.

reflective teaching Approaching teaching as a cyclical process in which teachers continually monitor, evaluate and revise their own practice.

reflective thinking   Involves developing the attitudes of open-mindedness, responsibility, and wholeheartedness.

reflection-for-action   Proactive thinking in order to guide future action.

reflection-in-action   Thinking about events in the classroom as they happen to make immediate adjustments.

reflection-on-action   Thinking back on what was done to gain deeper insight.

reflection-within   Inquiring about personal purposes, intentions, and feelings.

reflective inquiry   A systematic and disciplined approach to understanding problems, finding and implementing solutions, and assessing their results.

reflective practice   A questioning orientation toward one's actions, decisions, and outcomes and an acceptance of responsibility for one's professional practice.

reflective practitioners   Those who perpetually consider alternatives, taking action to continually improve practice throughout their professional career.

reframe   To put an experience in a new frame, one that views the situation from a different angle or includes parts of the picture that weren't visible from the first vantage point.

reposition   To change your perception by moving out of a limited perspective to see new ways of interpreting a situation.

responsibility   Taking ownership for the consequences of your actions and their impact on students.

self-reflection Examining how one's beliefs and values, expectations and assumptions, family imprinting, and cultural conditioning impact students and their learning.

support groups Can be either informal or formal groups of peers who meet on a regular basis to provide an opportunity for communication, reflection, and socialization.

surface reflection At this level of reflection, the teacher's examination of teaching methods is confined to tactical issues concerning how best to achieve predefined objectives and standards.

teacher narratives Stories written by and about teachers that can be used as the source of inquiry.

values Deeply-held views about what we think is worthwhile.

wholeheartedness Thoroughly committing yourself to seeking better solutions to perplexing concerns.

REFERENCES

Bright, B. (1996). Reflecting on "reflective practice." *Studies in the Education of Adults,* *28*(2), 162-184.

Brookfield, S. D. (1995). *Becoming a critically reflective teacher.* San Francisco, CA: Jossey-Bass.

Bullough, R., Knowles, J. G., & Crow, N. (1992). *Emerging as a teacher.* London: Routledge.

Calderhead, J. (1991). The nature and growth of knowledge in student teaching. *Teaching and Teacher Education, 8* (5/6), 531-535.

Carr, W., & Kemmis, S. (1986). *Becoming critical: Education, knowledge and action research.* London: Falmer.

Cochran-Smith, M., & Lytle, S. (1993). *Inside/Outside: Teacher research and knowledge.* New York: Teachers College Press.

Cole, A. L., & Knowles, J. G. (2000). *Researching teaching: Exploring teacher development through reflective inquiry.* Boston: Allyn and Bacon.

Collier, S. T. (1999). Characteristics of reflective thought during the student teaching experience. *Journal of Teacher Education, 50*(3), 173-181.

Cruickshank, D., & Applegate, J. (1981). Reflective teaching as a strategy for teacher growth: *Educational Leadership, 38*(7), 553-554.

Dana, N. F., & Yendol-Silva, D. (2003). *The reflective educator's guide to classroom research.* Thousand Oaks, CA: Corwin Press.

Day, C. (1993). Reflection: a necessary but not sufficient condition for professional development. *British Educational Research Journal, 19*, 83-93.

Dewey, J. (1910/1933). *How we think: A restatement of the relation of reflective thinking to the educative process.* Lexington, MA: Heath.

Dewey, J. (1938). *Logic: The theory of inquiry.* Troy, MO: Holt, Rinehart & Winston.

Dobbins, R., (1996). The challenge of developing a 'reflective practicum.' *Asia-Pacific Journal of Teacher Education, 24*(3), 269-280.

Farrell, T. S. (2004). *Reflective practice in action: 80 reflective breaks for busy teachers.* Thousand Oaks, CA: Corwin Press.

Glanz, J. (1998). *Action research: An educational leader's guide to school improvement* . Norwood, MA: Christopher-Gordon.

Griffin, M. L. (2003). Using critical incidents to promote and assess reflective thinking in preservice teachers. *Reflective Practice, 4(2),* 207-220.

Handal, G., & Lauvas, P. (1987). *Promoting reflective teaching.* Milton Keynes, UK: Open University Press.

Hatton, N., & Smith, D. (1995). Reflection in teacher education: Towards definition and implementation. *Teaching and Teacher Education, 11*(1), 22-49.

Hess, D. (1999). *Developing a typology for teaching preservice students to reflect: A case of curriculum deliberation.* Paper presented at the annual meeting of the American Educational Research Association, Montreal.

Hunter, J. & Hatton, N. (1998). Approaches to the writing of cases: Experience with preservice master of education students. *Asia-Pacific Journal of Teacher Education, 26,* 235-246.

Jay, J. K. (2003). *Quality teaching: Reflection as the heart of practice.* Lanham, MD: Scarecrow Press.

Jay, J. K., & Johnson, K. L. (2002). Capturing complexity: A typology of reflective practice for teacher education. *Teaching and Teacher Education, 18*, 73-85.

Johnston, M. (1994). Contrasts and similarities in case studies of teacher reflection and change. *Curriculum Inquiry, 24*(1), 9-26.

Keating, C. N. (1993). Promoting growth through dialogue journals. In G. Wells (Ed.), *Changing schools from within: Creating communities of inquiry* (pp. 217-236). Toronto, Canada: Ontario Institute for Studies in Education Press.

Kesley, J. G. (1993). Learning from teaching: Problems, problem-formulation and the enhancement of problem-solving capability. In P. Hallinger, K. A., Leithwood, & J. Murphy (Eds.), *A cognitive perspective on educational administration* (pp. 231-252). New York: Teachers College Press.

Killion, J., & Todnem, G. (1991). A process of personal theory building. *Educational   Leadership, 48*(6), 14-17.

King, P. M., & Kitchener, K. S. (1994). *Developing reflective judgment.* San Francisco, CA: Jossey-Bass.

Larrivee, B. (1996). *Moving into balance.* Santa Monica, CA: Shoreline.

Larrivee, B. (2000). Transforming teaching practice: Becoming the critically reflective teacher. *Reflective Practice, 1*(3), 293-307.

Larrivee, B. (2004). *Assessing teachers' level of reflective practice as a tool for change.* Paper presented at the Third International Conference on Reflective Practice, Gloucester, UK.

Larrivee, B. (2005). *Authentic classroom management: Creating a learning community and building reflective practice.* Boston, MA: Allyn & Bacon.

Lasley, T. J. (1992). Inquiry and reflection: Promoting teacher reflection. *Journal of Staff Development, 13*(1), 24-29.

Marshall, H. (1990). Metaphor as an instructional tool in encouraging student teacher reflection. *Theory into Practice, 29*(2), 128-132.

McFee, G. (1993). Reflections on the nature of action research. *Cambridge Journal of Education, 23*(2), 173-183.

McKenna, H. (1999). *A pedagogy of reflection: Pathfinding in times of change.* Paper presented at the annual conference of the American Association of Colleges of Teacher Education, Washington, D.C.

Munby, H., & Russell, T. (1990). Metaphor in the study of teachers' professional knowledge. *Theory into Practice, 29*(2), 116-121.

Osterman, K. P., & Kottkamp, R. B. (1993/2004). *Reflective practice for educators: Improving schooling through professional development.* Thousand Oaks, CA: Corwin Press.

Pultorak, E. G. (1993). Facilitating reflective thought in novice teachers. *Journal of Teacher Education, 44*, 288-295.

Pultorak, E. G. (1996). Following the developmental process of reflection in novice teacher: Three years of investigation. *Journal of Teacher Education, 47*, 283-291.

Ross, D. D. (1990). Programmatic structures for the preparation of reflective teachers. In R. T. Clift, W. R. Houston, & M. C. Pugach (Eds.), *Encouraging reflective practice in education: An analysis of issues and programs* (pp. 97-118). New York: Teachers College Press.

Rudney, G., & Guillaume, A. (1990). Reflective teaching for student teachers. *The Teacher Educator, 25*(3), 13-20.

Schön, D. A. (1983). *The reflective practitioner: How professionals think in action.* New York: Basic Books.

Schön, D. A. (1987). *Educating the reflective practitioner.* San Francisco: Jossey-Bass.

Smyth, J. (1989). Developing and sustaining critical reflection in teacher education. *Journal of Teacher Education, 40*(2), 2-9.

Smyth, J. (1991). *Teachers as collaborative learners.* Milton Keynes Open University Press.

Smyth, J. (1992). Teacher's work and the politics of reflection. *American Education Research Journal, 29*(2), 267-300.

Sparks-Langer, G., & Colton, A. (1991). Synthesis of research on teachers' reflective thinking. *Educational Leadership, 48(6)*, 37-44.

Sparks-Langer, G., & Colton, A. (1994). Reflective decision making: The cornerstone of school reform. *Journal of Staff Development, 15*(1), 2-7.

Surbeck, E., Han, E., & Moyer, J. (1991). Assessing reflective responses in journals. *Educational Leadership, 48*(6), 25-27.

Taggart, G., & Wilson, A. P. (1998). *Promoting reflective thinking in teachers.* Thousand Oaks, CA: Corwin Press. .

Valli, L. (1997). Listening to other voices: A description of teacher reflection in the United States. *Peabody Journal of Education, 72*(1), 67-88.

Van Manen, M. (1977). Linking ways of knowing with ways of being practical. *Curriculum Inquiry, 6*(3), 205-228.

Van Manen, M. (1991). Reflectivity and pedagogical moment: The normativity of pedagogical thinking and acting. *Journal of Curriculum Studies, 23*, 507-536.

Wideen, M., Mayer-Smith, J., & Moon, B. (1998). A critical analysis of the research on learning to teach: Making the case for an ecological perspective on inquiry. *Review of Educational Research, 68*(2), 130-178.

Wildman, T. M. & Niles, J. A. (1987). Reflective teachers: Tensions between abstractions and realities. *Journal of Teacher Education, 38*(4), 25-31.

York-Barr, J., Sommers, W. A., Ghere, G. S., & Montie, J. (2001). *Reflective practice to improve schools*. Thousand Oaks, CA: Corwin Press.

Yost, D. S., Sentner, S. M., & Forlenza-Bailey, A. (2000). An examination of the construct of critical reflection: Implications for teacher education programming in the 21st century. *Journal of Teacher Education, 51*(1), 39-48.

Yost, D. S. (1997). The moral dimensions of teaching and preservice teachers: Can moral dispositions be influenced? *Journal of Teacher Education, 48*, 281-292.

Yost, D. S., Forlenza-Bailey, A., & Shaw, S. F. (1999). The teachers who embrace diversity: The role of reflection, discourse, and field experience in education. *The Professional Educator, 21*(2), *1-14*.

Zeichner, K. M. (1983). Alternative paradigms of teacher education. *Journal of Teacher Education, 39*(3), 3-9.

Zeichner, K. M., & Liston, D. P. (1996). *Reflective teaching: An introduction*. Mahwah, NJ: Lawrence Erlbaum

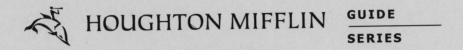

HOUGHTON MIFFLIN GUIDE SERIES

An Educator's Guide to
Technology Tools

Cheryl Mason Bolick
The University of North Carolina at Chapel Hill

James M. Cooper, Series Editor
University of Virginia

HOUGHTON MIFFLIN COMPANY   BOSTON   NEW YORK

CONTENTS

PREFACE

Houghton Mifflin Company publishes outstanding education textbooks in the areas of foundations of education, introduction to education, educational psychology, special education, and early childhood education. These textbooks introduce students to many concepts, policies, and research that undergird educational practice. However, as is the case for virtually all introductory texts, many topics are introduced but not covered in great depth. The Houghton Mifflin Teacher Education Guide Series is designed to provide more in-depth coverage of selected educational topics studied in the teacher education curriculum.

At the present time there are five guides in the series:

- Diversity in the Classroom
- Classroom Assessment
- Inclusion
- Technology Tools
- School-based Interventions

The topics for these guides were selected because they are addressed in virtually all teacher education programs, and contain vital information for beginning teachers if they are to be successful in the classroom. Instructors may use the guides either for required or enrichment reading.

Each of these guides provides pre-service teachers with greater in-depth knowledge, application suggestions, and additional resources on its particular topic. All the guides share a common format that includes an introduction to the topic, knowledge that the prospective teacher should possess about the topic, examples of and suggestions for how the knowledge can be applied, and both print and Web-based resources for further exploration. Each guide also contains 10–15 questions designed to help the prospective teacher reflect on the concepts and ideas introduced in the guide, as well as a glossary of key terms.

The use of computer technology in schools has increased dramatically in recent years and shows few signs of slowing down. Obtaining hardware and software is always a challenge for schools, but an even bigger challenge is helping teachers to use technology in ways that improve student learning. In this guide, Cheryl Mason Bolick explores different methods and tools teachers can use to develop an effective classroom learning environment for students of the digital generation. Moving from a teacher-centered environment to one in which students use technology to gather, analyze, and evaluate information, students learn to create new knowledge and to become critical thinkers by having greater control over their learning. Teachers can also use technology to increase their own productivity. Knowing how to use these technology tools effectively is a critical skill for teachers in the 21st century.

PART I: INTRODUCTION

TEACHING AND LEARNING WITH TODAY'S TECHNOLOGY TOOLS

The first morning bell rings and the students begin to file into Ms. Lane's seventh grade classroom. As the students settle in for the day they hang their coats in the classroom closet and pull their handheld computing devices out of their backpacks. Each cluster of desks has a computer with a device attached for synching information to and from the handheld. The students synch their **handhelds** and send their homework assignments and any notes from home to their teacher, while at the same time they download the handouts for the day's activities.

As the second bell rings, Ms. Lane asks the students to open the current events assignment on their handhelds. Ms. Lane has given the students web-based news sources from around the globe to read and summarize. Using their wireless handhelds, the students read their news clips and then join a class discussion about the day's current events and the media's interpretation of these events.

A Closer Look | Handheld Computing Devices

Most handhelds today are as long as an index card and as thick as a student's assignment pad. Prices range from $100 to $700. Software has been developed that permit handheld users to perform virtually every task that they could perform on their laptop or desktop computer.

Using their handhelds, students can create word-processed documents, enter data into spreadsheets, search databases, search the **Web** and send **e-mails**. Peripherals for handhelds extend the potential applications of the handheld. Peripherals include collapsible keyboards, global positioning systems, digital cameras, phones, audio recorders, and MP3 players.

After completing the current events activity, Ms. Lane asks the students to pull up their rainfall data from science class. The students quickly go to the interactive web site where they have been inputting environmental data and comparing it with student data from classrooms around the world.

Ms. Lane explains to the students that today they are going to continue their collaborative writing activity. In this activity, students synthesize the environmental data and collaboratively write five paragraph essays. In groups of three, students use the keyboard to collectively write the introductory paragraph on their handheld. The students spend the rest of the class period highly engaged in analyzing the different data sets and describing their findings in their essay.

Moments before the bell rings, Ms. Lane reminds the students to check their assignment sheets on their handhelds. There, she has prepared instructions for the students explaining that they will each write one paragraph of the essay for homework. Tomorrow in class they will beam their individual paragraphs to their group members and collaboratively write the concluding paragraph. The bell rings and the students quickly pack up their belongings and head to their next class.

Handheld devices and the **Internet** are just two technology tools that are transforming teaching and learning. From a small network of 23 computers in 1973 to the millions of networked computers today, technology is empowering teachers and students to revolutionize instruction. With the nearly ubiquitous access to the Internet in today's classrooms, the promise of technology to enhance learning is greater than ever; however, even though the majority of students use the Internet for school, this use occurs primarily outside of their classrooms and is outside the direction of their teachers (Levin & Arafeh, 2002). To best prepare students to be successful in our information-rich global society, teachers must understand the power and potential of technology tools.

Digital Classrooms

The printing press, camera, film projector, television, and VCR each have transformed education in unique ways. Likewise, revolutionary developments in today's field of technology are bringing drastic changes to the way we communicate with one another, the way we work, and the way we learn. Today's generation of students live in a society that surrounds them with audio, video, and interactive media. According to the Kaiser Family Foundation's study on children's use of computers (1999), nearly seven in ten kids have a computer at home and nearly half have Internet access from home. Many of today's students come to school expecting to use computers in their classrooms.

Classroom teachers must be prepared to provide their students with access to technology that enriches learning opportunities. Students need to develop skills that will allow them to be successful in today's technology-driven global economy. The most basic of these skills include manipulating data in a spreadsheet, developing multimedia presentations, or typing a word-processed document.

More than helping students develop basic computer literacy, however, today's teachers also should be prepared to help students gather, analyze, and evaluate information. Students must be able to use the information they find to become effective problem-solvers and critical thinkers. This Guide will explore different methods and tools teachers may use to develop an effective classroom learning environment for students of the digital generation.

The portrayal of Ms. Lane's classroom is a realistic scenario of technology tools being used to enhance classroom learning. Today, there are classrooms of varying grade levels using handhelds in similar lessons. It is essential to note that student learning is enhanced not just by the technology tools, but also by Ms. Lane's effective pedagogy. She planned her classroom carefully to be a student-centered classroom that promotes critical and higher-order thinking.

Technology tools such as the handheld computer are changing the face of today's classroom by offering teachers and students tools that can help teachers make the transition from traditional, teacher-centered environments to new learning environments. In order for students to learn with technology, however, teachers must understand how to create learning environments that promote meaningful and authentic learning. The International Society for Technology in Education (ISTE) has developed a series of standards to guide teachers as they learn not only how to use technology, but also how technology can be used to create new learning environments.

National Educational Technology Standards

Most states have technology competency requirements for both pre-service and in-service teachers. These standards follow closely the

ISTE's National Educational Technology Standards (NETS). ISTE has developed standards for both K–12 students and standards for teachers.

NETS are organized into six categories of performance indicators for classroom teachers: technology operations and concepts; planning and designing learning environments and experiences; teaching, learning and the curriculum; assessment and evaluation; productivity and professional practice; and social, ethical, legal and human issues. The NETS writing team has prepared a series of K–12 content-based lessons for each indicator. These lesson plans are available on the NETS web page (http://www.iste.org) or in the NETS printed publication.

A Closer Look   Sample NETS Lessons

- *Trigonometric Tables: Tangent:* Students enter data from rocket launches in Geometer's Sketchpad software to develop an understanding of the tangent table.
- *Who's in Control Here?* Simulation software and Internet resources provide students with information in which they must make decisions about sovereignty.
- *Electronic Book Discussion:* Students engage in an online threaded discussion after reading assigned books to further their understanding of the text and to promote equity among all students.
- *Cool Liquids:* Students record temperatures on their graphing calculators or a spreadsheet to develop an understanding of evaporation.

PART II: KNOWLEDGE

STUDENT LEARNING TOOLS

Schools are more high-tech today than they have ever been. Nationally, there are just over four students for every instructional school computer and the number of students per Internet-connected computer in schools dropped from 7.9 in 2000 to 6.8 in 2001 (Skinner, 2002). Beyond having access to computers, schools report that a majority of their teachers used the Internet for instruction. Given the increase in access to computers and reports of teacher usage, can one assume that technology is enhancing teaching and learning?

Unfortunately, we cannot. Many teachers are not using technology effectively. That is, many teachers use technology for technology's sake, rather than using technology to create meaningful learning environments. For example, drill and practice or playing math games are the most frequently reported uses of computers for math instruction (Skinner, 2002) rather than using technology tools to create student-centered learning environments.

ESTABLISHING NEW LEARNING ENVIRONMENTS
Incorporating New Strategies (NETS, 2002)

Traditional Learning Environments	New Learning Environments
Teacher-centered instruction	Student-centered learning
Single sense stimulation	Multisensory stimulation
Single path progression	Multipath progression
Single media	Multimedia
Isolated work	Collaborative work
Information delivery	Information exchange
Passive learning	Active/exploratory/inquiry-based learning
Factual, knowledge-based learning	Critical thinking and informed decision-making
Reactive response	Proactive/planned action
Isolated, artificial context	Authentic, real-world context

Teachers make decisions every day about how best to help their students learn. Before using technology tools in the classroom, teachers should ask themselves the following two questions (Harris, 1998):

1. Will technology allow me to do something with my students that I could not before technology?

2. Will technology allow me to do something with my students better than I'm doing it now?

Extending Classroom Learning Through the Internet

The Internet has opened classroom doors to resources that were not available to most classrooms. From paintings, books, and maps to movie clips, teachers and students can access thousands of resources that can be used to enhance classroom learning. These resources can either be online documents and data housed on the Internet or people who communicate through the Internet.

Online Research

In 1993, there were approximately 130 web sites; today there are hundreds of millions (Leiner, et al., 2000). These web sites provide teachers and students greater access to sources that otherwise would not be available for classroom learning. The table below highlights online resources available for various content areas that were not accessible by most teachers and students before the Internet.

A Closer Look	Online Content Area Resources
Content Area	**Sample Online Resources**

English / Language Arts	Mark Twain in His Times
	        http://etext.lib.virginia.edu/railton/
	Aesop's Fables
	        http://www.aesopfables.com/

Science	Science Junction
	        http://www.ncsu.edu/sciencejunction/
	Science Learning Network
	        http://www.sln.org/

A Closer Look	Online Content Area Resources
Content Area	**Sample Online Resources**

Mathematics	The Math Forum
	    http://mathforum.org/
	MicroWorlds Math Library
	    http://www.microworlds.com/library/math/

Health / Physical Education	PE Central
	    http://www.pecentral.org/
	Kids Health
	    http://www.kidshealth.org/

Social Studies	American Memory Project
	    http://memory.loc.gov/
	History Matters
	    http://historymatters.gmu.edu/

Art	Smithsonian American Art Museum
	    http://www.nmaa.si.edu/
	Art Safari
	    http://www.moma.org/onlineprojects/artsafari/
	    index.html

Music / Performing Arts	Instrument Encyclopedia
	    http://www.si.umich.edu/chico/instrument/
	The Drama Collection
	    http://eserver.org/drama/

The number of online resources available to enrich classroom learning today is phenomenal. Yet, the vast number of resources on the Internet can often seem unwieldy. Given that there are well over 500 billion documents on the Internet (Bergman, 2000), teachers must be prepared to teach their students effective research skills. Online research skills are important skills that students will use for a lifetime.

There are two types of search engines for identifying resources on the web: mechanical search engines and human-operated directories. Mechanical search engines use web robots to automatically search the web. Alta Vista (http://www.altavista.com) and Google (http://www.google.com) are examples of mechanical search engines. Human cataloguers, on the other hand, generate human-operated directories by using virtual libraries and categories of resources. Yahoo (http://www.yahoo.com) is an example of a human-operated directory.

When deciding which search engine to use, factors such as the size of the database, speed of the search process and frequency of updating should be considered. Frequency is an important factor because a search of the web is not a search of everything that is on the web at that given time, but rather, a search of the documents that were on the web the last time the database was uploaded.

There are a number of helpful guides and tutorials available online for teachers and students. Examples of these online guides are:

- KidsClick World of Searching
  http://www.worldsofsearching.org/

- UCBerkeley Search Strategies
  http://www.lib.berkeley.edu/TeachingLib/Guides/Internet/
  Strategies.html

Practical Tips and Strategies	**Search Strategies**

1. **Boolean search** operators (e.g., AND, NOT, OR, NEAR) narrow the search by limiting the number of documents that will be searched. For example, if searching for pages about William Shakespeare, you could search for either "WILLIAM AND SHAKESPEARE" or "WILLIAM NEAR SHAKESPEARE"
2. Most search engines have advanced sections that will allow you to search by "file format". This means you can search specifically for images, .pdf files, Word files, audio and video clips as well as PowerPoint presentations posted on the web.
3. Truncation and wildcards (e.g.,*) will help search for different variations of a word. For example, if looking for math lesson plans, enter "MATH*" so that the result would include all of the lesson plans with both math and mathematics in the descriptors.

Telecollaboration

In many ways, the best resource on the Internet is other people. **Telecollaboration** activities offer a variety of educational experiences for students in levels K12. Prior to the Internet, outside resources were limited to the traditional guest speaker, field trip, or pen pal. Now, there are voluminous ways to connect students with other people across the globe. Using e-mail, web-based discussions and video conferencing, teachers and students can connect in meaningful ways.

Harris' Virtual Architecture (1998) book and website are essential tools for teachers interested in implementing telecollaborative activities. Her work identifies three genres of telecollaborative activities:

- *Interpersonal Exchanges*: Students and teachers connect via the Internet with geographically disparate individuals.

- *Information Collection and Analysis:* Students gather authentic data and create projects to share and analyze with others.

- *Problem Solving:* Collaborative activities that engage students in critical thinking and problem-based learning.

Harris (1998) highlights how telecollaboration activities can benefit global education. It can expose students to "differing opinions, perspectives, beliefs, experiences, and thinking processes; allow students to compare, contrast, and/or combine similar information collected in dissimilar locations; and provide a platform where students can communicate with a real audience using text and imagery" (p. 55).

A Closer Look	Telecollaboration Activities
Activity Structures	**Curriculum Examples**
Keypals: students correspond with a partner via e-mail over a period of time	ePals.com is one of the largest Keypals services on the Interrnet. Teachers and students can register and connect with others across the globe to discuss a broad range of issues including: current events, Harry Potter, rainfall, or teacher professional development. http://www.epals.com/
Impersonations: Students engage in dialogue with historical figures	Ask Thomas Jefferson is an interactive web page that allows student to pose inquiries to "Thomas Jefferson". Students and teachers can also read through the collection of letters other students have sent to the

A Closer Look	Telecollaboration Activities
Activity Structures	**Curriculum Examples**
	site. http://www.monticello.org/education/asktj/instructions.html
Electronic Appearances: Students communicate with experts in a particular field.	Women of NASA Chat is a web page that facilitates discussion between the Women of NASA and teachers and students. Students can e-mail individual questions or engage in scheduled real-time chats or forums. Archives of all discussions are stored on the web page, along with helpful teaching resources. http://image.gsfc.nasa.gov/poetry/ask/askmag.html
Information Exchanges: Students collect local data and share it with others.	The GLOBE Program invites teachers and students to post and collect environmental data from their communities in the data archive. Students collaborate with other students and scientists from around the globe to learn more about local and global environments. http://www.globe.gov/
Electronic Publishing: Students create **hypertext** documents and share them with others.	MidLink is an online journal both for and by middle school students. Monthly themes are posted and students from around the world contribute poems, essays, art, and multimedia projects to be published. http://www.ncsu.edu/midlink/

Legal and Ethical Issues

Although the Internet is opening classrooms to the world in many positive and meaningful ways, the Internet also presents new challenges for teachers. Educators must be aware of legal and ethical issues surrounding technology. Two of the major concerns to address are Internet safety and copyright.

Teachers must be aware of risks and areas of concern associated with children's use of the Internet. The most prevalent risks include children communicating with **cyberpredators** on the Internet and children's access of inappropriate materials on the Internet. Unfortunately, there are cases each year that involve cyberpredators interacting with students on the Internet, which may lead to children being coerced into face-to-face meetings or to the children giving personal information such as passwords or credit card numbers to strangers. Teachers should work with colleagues and parents to establish an acceptable use policy (AUP) for Internet in their classrooms. AUPs will often include guidelines regarding publishing children's photographs on the web and student access of certain web sites. Students must be taught that the Internet is a public space and that there are guidelines to ensure safe use of the space.

Practical Tips and Strategies	Internet Safety Tips

1. The best way to ensure that young people are having positive online experiences is to supervise their activities. Monitor students' computer activities by placing the computer in an easily viewable area. Maintain open communication about information they have found, sites they have explored, and people with whom they have chatted.
2. Investigate the use of filtering software. Even with these controls, however, teachers still need to be involved. An excellent resource regarding filters can be found at http://www.cyberangels.org/parentsguide/filtering.html
3. Establish an acceptable use policy for the Internet. The National Center for Missing and Exploited Children (http://www.missingkids.com) has created a popular brochure that outlines suggested children's rules for online safety. (Berson, et al. 2001)

Copyright is another issue that must be addressed with students. Cutting and pasting are two **web browser** and word processing features that help make the software so user-friendly. Yet, these features also make it easy for students to cite their resources. Just as it is important to cite books and periodicals when doing research, it is important to cite online resources.

Teachers should ensure that students understand the importance of giving proper credit for resources they reference or quote. Once they understand this concept, they should be presented with proper guidelines for citing work. MidLink has a helpful web page that provides guides for citing electronic resources at http://www.ncsu.edu/midlink/citing.html. Forms to request permission to post graphics on your web page are also found on this web page.

Teachers should also help students develop strategies that will support their efforts of respecting copyright. One strategy is to use multiple windows when taking notes from a web page. That is, resize the web browser so that it vertically fits on the left half of the computer screen. Open a word processing document and resize it so that it fits vertically on the right half of the screen. When students use this strategy, they are more apt to paraphrase the information they are researching, rather than copy and paste verbatim.

Enhancing Classroom Learning with Software

In addition to the tremendous resources available on the Internet, educational software tools may also enhance classroom learning. Software programs are considered either instructional software (e.g., simulations and tutorials) or developmental software (e.g., spreadsheets or multimedia editing). The software industry is large and continues to grow. Two excellent resources that have extensive software evaluation databases are the California Learning Resource Network (http://www.clrn.org/home/) and the Children's Software Review (http://www2.childrenssoftware.com).

Simulations and Tutorials

Simulations are a genre of software that engages students in real-world problem-solving lessons that require critical thinking skills. Often, the software employs a degree of interactivity that requires the students to enter information throughout the simulation and respond to the consequences of their decisions. Multimedia features, such as sound and video, are engaging complements to the traditional text. Simulations have been developed for each content area and grade level.

"Prime Time Math: Fire" by Tom Snyder Productions is an example of a simulation. In this software, students assume the role of firefighters who must make mathematical decisions to combat a burning building, such as selecting the correct length and size of a hose and appropriate pressure. Audio and video clips, along with narratives lead the students through the scenario and call upon the students to apply mathematical concepts to the situation.

"Decisions, Decisions: The Environment" by Tom Snyder Productions is another example of simulation software. Students are assigned to play the role of different individuals (scientist, a campaign manager, an environmentalist, and an economist) who are impacted by the recent pollution of a town pond. Students are presented with a series of data and documentation from which they must make public policy decisions about how to address the pollution problem.

Tutorials are a second category of educational software designed to extend classroom learning. This type of software introduces students to new information, and then provides them with opportunities to apply the new information in a self-paced fashion. Musicianship Basics by New Horizons is an example of tutorial software in which students are introduced to fundamental music reading and listening skills. As students move through the program, they respond to a series of questions. A log tracks the student responses and suggests remediation activities based on the individual student.

World History: An Interactive Approach, by WorldView Software is another example of tutorial software. Students are presented with chronologically arranged world history modules. After reading through each module, students are presented with a series of objective questions to assess whether or not they have mastered this history content.

Development Software

Development software is specifically designed to allow teachers and students to enter and manipulate data for either individual learning or class presentation. Both categories can be used across content areas and grade levels, although there are some content-specific pieces of development software.

Spreadsheets, databases, and word processing software are generic software. That is, they are empty "shells" equipped to input numerical or textual data. Spreadsheets are designed specifically for the manipulation of numerical data. The basic function of most spreadsheets is the calculation of numerical formulas. Once data has been entered and calculated, students can choose to visually represent the data in charts or graphs. By giving students the opportunity to manipulate the data into different formats, they are able to explore the connection between numerical, algebraic and graphical representations of data.

Word processing software may be the most basic of the generic software, yet it has great potential in the classroom. Students across content areas and grade levels are using word processing software to prepare class assignments both in the classroom and at home. Teachers are maximizing the software by using the editing functions. The editing functions allow teachers and students to monitor revisions throughout the writing process. They also are useful functions when classroom activities are based around collaborative writing assignments.

In addition to tracking revisions, word processing software has the capability to insert hypertext links, digital images, spreadsheets, and graphs. The ability to add these extensions to an assignment holds great potential for students.

Imagine how dynamic a scientific lab report can be written using these features. For instance, beyond describing the steps taken and the results found in a lab activity that documents the growth of seeds, students can insert digital images of the seeds' growth throughout the germination period. The images would be displayed in chronological order along with the student narrative that describes the activity. The students could also insert the spreadsheet that was used to document the seeds' growth. Along with the numerical data, a line graph could be inserted to help illustrate the growth. Again, student narrative would accompany the data to describe the growth. Finally, if the students have done outside research on the growth of seeds on the Internet and found resources that enrich their understanding, they could insert **hyperlinks** to the web pages with this information.

A software program that allows the user to merge audio, text, images, animation and video is multimedia software. Typically, multimedia software is interactive; that is, the user has control over the program's actions. In addition to stimulating student interest and meeting the needs of different types of learners, multimedia software allows students to create and manipulate their own multimedia presentations.

Suppose a social studies class is researching their community's local history. Students can prepare multimedia presentations that incorporate audio and video clips taken from oral history interviews of local residents, images of buildings taken years ago and today, spreadsheet data of population growth over the years, and text that depicts that summarizes the local history. The Multimedia Ethnographic Research Lab at the University of British Columbia is home to a number of multimedia projects with children. Visit their homepage to view video from sample projects and to read descriptions of their work at http://www.merlin.ubc.ca/

Presentation software allows either the teacher or students to organize information and share it with the class as a presentation. Presentation software may be linear or non-linear. Linear presentations always follow the same sequence, while non-linear presentations do not follow any particular order.

"TimeLiner" by Tom Snyder Productions is an example of linear presentation software. Teachers or students can create a timeline by entering the span of dates along with events. Textual description, images, and video clips can be added along the timeline. A science teacher might use such software to help students understand the phases of the moon. For example, students could have their own timeline of thirty days. Each day students enter text that describes the moon and inserts a digital image of the moon they took the night before. At the end of the month, students will have a recorded collection of the moon's monthly cycle.

PowerPoint is another example of linear presentation software. Teachers or students can organize text, hyperlinks, audio, images, clipart, screen shots, or video on slides to create PowerPoint presentations. PowerPoint can be an excellent tool to assist teachers with the presentation of information. The key to effectively using PowerPoint is using it to enhance classroom learning beyond the traditional slide show.

Teachers can effectively structure class discussions by putting essential or key information on a slide. This could help students monitor their own note-taking skills in that the students would not merely copy notes word-for-word off of a screen, but rather they would rather understand the major concepts and record them in their notebook. Some teachers find that printing the slide handouts is an effective way to help teach students note-taking skills.

The ability to insert objects such as audio clips and images holds great potential to enhance classroom instruction. The slides below are taken from a lesson on the Treaty of Versailles. Note that the first slide has a link to an audio file of a speech by the Secretary of War. Below the link is a series of questions to help focus the students as they listen to the audio clip. The second slide is one that the teacher presented to guide the discussion on the impact of the Treaty of Versailles.

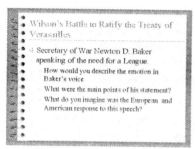
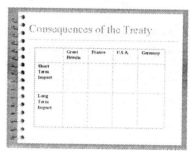

Inspiration is an example of non-linear presentation software. Inspiration is a tool that enables teachers and students to enter information and display it either as a concept map or as an outline. This is a useful piece of software to help students to map ideas and to organize their writing. Teachers may chose to prepare an Inspiration concept map to guide the class discussion or they may add to the concept map during the lesson. The example below is one that a teacher could create to guide student research on a famous person. The teacher would ask the students questions and guide their research so that they will be able to complete the concept map. After the class completes the concept map, the teacher may decide to view the information as an outline to allow the students to view the information in a linear format.

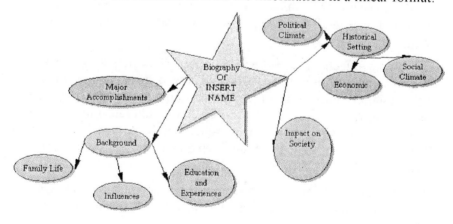

Inspiration comes with a library of clip art that may be inserted into the concept maps. There are also options that allow the user to change the display of the concept map, colors, and fonts. Kidspiration has been developed most specifically for young children. Visit http://www.inspiration.com for lesson ideas and examples.

Geometer's Sketchpad is another example of a non-linear piece of software. This software allows the user to create dynamic representations of mathematical concepts. Students are able to manipulate the representation to explore the meaning behind graphs and equations. The image below is a sample of the Pythagorean Theorem in which students manipulated the figures to arrive at an understanding of the mathematical concept. Visit http://www.keypress.com/sketchpad/ for more examples of how to use the sketchpad.

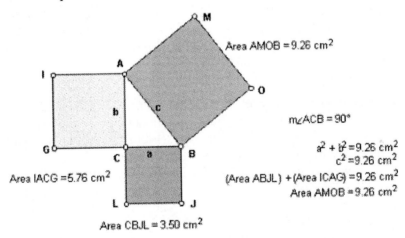

Area AMOB = 9.26 cm^2

m∠ACB = 90°

$a^2 + b^2 = 9.26$ cm^2
$c^2 = 9.26$ cm^2
(Area ABJL) + (Area ICAG) = 9.26 cm^2
Area AMOB = 9.26 cm^2

Area IACG = 5.76 cm^2

Area CBJL = 3.50 cm^2

TEACHER PRODUCTIVITY TOOLS

In addition to supporting classroom learning, technology tools can be used to enhance teacher productivity. Given the amount of time teachers dedicate to good teaching both inside and outside the classroom, productivity tools that help teachers maximize their time will also improve the quality of classroom instruction and student learning. Technology tools can help teachers communicate with parents, organize and manage information and engage in professional development opportunities.

Communication with Parents

Teachers and parents are discovering e-mail as a new and effective method to enhance communication. Teachers and parents alike find e-mail and web pages effective means to involve parents in daily classroom activities. E-mail messages can be used to send regular information to parents about what happens in the classroom during the day. Many of today's teachers have created **listservs** and send weekly informative e-mails to their students' parents. These e-mails may contain information such as the topics covered during the week, upcoming curriculum topics, daily schedules, homework assignments and due dates, school events, as well as extended activities to be completed at home. The extended activities could include suggested readings, links to resources on the Internet, or events in the community that connect to the classroom topics (e.g. a local museum exhibit).

It is essential for teachers to know their constituents and insure that they do not exclude students or parents by using e-mail. One way of doing this is to send home print copies of all informational e-mail messages to the parents who do not have e-mail access.

Informative e-mail messages are an effective way for parents to stay informed about what their children do in school each day. Teachers also find e-mail to be a helpful way to directly communicate with parents regarding students' progress. For example, sending a brief, daily e-mail to parents regarding their child's classroom behavior can be an effective and efficient way to follow up after a teacher-parent conference. It is also an efficient way for teachers to send individual student feedback to parents. The image below is one example of how a teacher could use e-mail to send "Great Day" messages to different students' parents throughout the school year.

A Closer Look | *Using E-mail with Parents*

Subject: Great Day!
Date: October 21, 2002
From: Ms. Lane
To: Students' Parents

Dear Mr. and Mrs. Caldwell,

This week in class the students finished their African Art projects. Jeremy's mural is a beautiful representation of his understanding of the ancient tribes! The pictures he brought in from home look fantastic in the print. I know you will enjoy seeing his final mural. You should be very proud of Jeremy's hard work! We've placed all of the projects on display in the cafeteria. Please feel free to come and look at all of the students' art.

Sincerely,
Ms. Lane

Class web pages are another technology tool that can be used to enhance parent communication. Much like the informative e-mails, class web pages can be a place to post information that help keep parents informed about what takes place in the classroom each day and suggestions for enhancing student learning. Student work and student contributions are another feature of class web pages to include. Some teachers ask a different student each week to post a summary of the week's events on the class web page for parents to read.

Organizational Tools

Generic software such as word processors and spreadsheets are the most commonly used organizational tools by teachers. Word processing software helps teachers generate and archive classroom materials. Lesson plans can be generated and archived according to standards taught, classroom objectives, or by unit. Teachers can revisit these lesson plans each year and easily update them and edit.

Spreadsheets or grading programs can be used to record and analyze student grades. Beyond averaging student grades at the end of the grading period, spreadsheets can help teachers analyze student grades by generating averages and distributions. Performing these calculations allows teachers to track student progress throughout the grading period.

Spreadsheets have been developed specifically to help teachers record and monitor student grades. Some schools have their own version of grade book software that allows teachers to automatically upload student grades at the end of the grading period. Other information may also be recorded in spreadsheets that can be used to help monitor student achievement, such as attendance.

Online grade books, such as GradePal (http://www.gradepal.com), have been developed for use by teachers. An added feature of using an online grade book is that parents and students may be given logins, which enable them to also monitor student progress.

A number of other software tools have been developed specifically for teachers, such as puzzle makers, rubric makers, test generators, and individualized education programs (IEPs). Again, the time a teacher saves by using one of these allows more time to be dedicated to good classroom instruction.

Practical Tips and Strategies	Teacher Tools
Puzzlemaker http://puzzlemaker.school.discovery.com/	
Barry's Clip Art http://www.barrysclipart.com/	
Worksheet Generator http://school.discovery.com/teachingtools/worksheetgenerator/	
Flash Card Exchange http://flashcardexchange.com/index.jsp	
Blank and Outline Maps http://geography.about.com/cs/blankoutlinemaps/	
Certificate Creator http://www.certificatecreator.com/	

Online Professional Development

Prior to the advent of the Internet, professional development for teachers was typically limited to local workshops that were scheduled after school hours or during the summer. The development of the Internet has ushered in numerous professional development opportunities for classroom teachers that are available any time, any place. In addition to providing teachers with professional development opportunities that are more convenient, online professional development provides teachers access to instruction not previously available and can lead to the development of online professional communities.

The number of online professional development opportunities for teachers is growing exponentially. School systems, universities, museums and other organizations are developing seminars and courses for teachers around the world. Some of these experiences are 100% online, while some use both face-to-face and online instruction. "Middle Educators Global Awareness" (MEGA) is an example of hybrid professional development. Hybrid professional development takes place both as face-to-face and online. Teachers participate in monthly workshops, but then also participate online throughout the year. For example, teachers may meet as a group to watch a demonstration on how to use GIS (geographic information systems) in the classroom. When they return to their own classrooms, they have a series of activities to complete and engage in online discussions with one another about the activities. They will meet again as a group on National GIS Day to demonstrate how they have incorporated GIS in their classroom.

Online instruction may be synchronous or asynchronous. Synchronous professional development opportunities are in real-time; for example, a videoconferencing session in which audio and video are transmitted over the Internet. The Annenberg/CPB Channel-sponsored workshop "Assessment in Math and Science: What's the Point?" is an example of synchronous professional development. In this workshop, teachers in geographically disparate locations viewed video clips about assessment strategies and then communicated directly with education experts who were in the studio for discussion about the video.

Professional development opportunities that are asynchronous are carried out over a period of time in which participants do not communicate with one another at the time. "Seminars on Science" is an example of online asynchronous professional development for teachers. This series of courses, sponsored by the National Museum of Natural Science, are taught by leading scientists to K-12 teachers across the country. The materials are web-based and provide teachers the opportunity to study with other professionals around the country and to learn about cutting-edge research. Visit "Online Professional Development: Suggestions for Success" at http://www.att.com/learningnetwork/virtualacademy/success.html to learn more about online learning and to learn more about your own learning styles.

Practical Tips and Strategies	Sample Online Professional Development Opportunities

Concord Consortium
http://www.concord.org

Riverdeep Professional Development for Teachers
http://www.riverdeep.net/pro_development/teachers_prof_dev.jhtml

ISTE Professional Development
http://www.iste.org/profdev/index.html

Library of Congress Professional Development
http://memory.loc.gov/ammem/ndlpedu/educators/index.html

iEARN Professional Development
http://www.iearn.org/professional/online.html

Lesley University Online Learning
http://www.lesley.edu/online_courses.html

PART III: APPLICATIONS

INQUIRY-BASED LEARNING

The previous section provided a description of a variety of technology tools. This section will look at specific applications of technology tools in the classroom. Each of the applications described is an inquiry-based lesson.

Inquiry-based learning is one of the most powerful teaching methods that technology can help facilitate. One of the essential elements of an inquiry lesson is the use of authentic data. Because the Internet provides teachers and students access to vast resources, technology promotes inquiry learning in a very powerful way. Additionally, technology tools such as spreadsheets and concept mapping software allow teachers and students to manipulate and interpret authentic data in a most effective way.

Different content areas have developed their own definitions of inquiry-based learning. However, a definition of "inquiry" developed by a team of cross-disciplinary researchers is as follows:

> Inquiry is an approach to learning that involves a process of exploring the natural or material world, that leads to asking questions and making discoveries in the search for new understandings (Exploratorium Institute for Inquiry, 1996).

Inquiry, in its purest form, requires students to play the leading role in answering questions that they themselves have asked. Molebash (2002) has outlined a "Spiral Path of Inquiry" that students should typically follow when completing an inquiry-oriented exercise.

- *Reflect* on previous or new material.
- *Ask questions* related to the topic.
- *Define procedures* for investigation.
- *Find and investigate data/information* that will help answer questions.
- *Manipulate the data/information* to answer questions.
- *Discuss* and defend results.

- *Reflect* on results...start the process over again if necessary.

As a teacher you can support student-centered inquiry. Here are some suggestions:

- Provide an interesting *hook* that students can reflect upon.

- Lead students to ask interesting *questions related to the topic.*

- When students define the procedures of their investigation, *ensure that the procedures are rigorous* enough to produce valid results.

- Assist students in *finding data resources* that will help answer their questions.

- *Provide students with access to data manipulation tools* (spreadsheet, database, or concept mapping software, etc.) as well as the prerequisite *skills* to use these tools.

Support students' efforts in presenting and defending results.

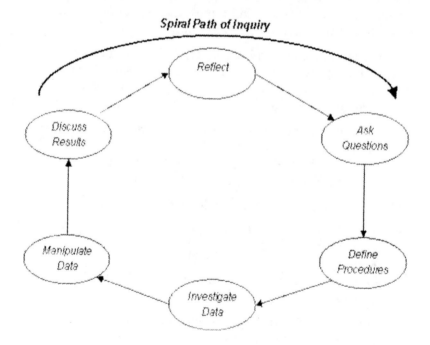

Spiral Path of Inquiry

Inquiry With Numerical Data

Technology tools provide students opportunities to gather and manipulate numerical data in very effective ways. Using the Internet, probes, or other technology tools, students are able to conduct research that provides them with authentic data. Using spreadsheets, databases, or other software, students are challenged to interpret and analyze the data. Inquiry-based lessons that involve students in the manipulation of authentic data engage students in higher-order thinking activities and promote the development of critical thinking skills.

Climate and Location

Students often do not understand the impact that latitude and longitude have on a city's climate. Using technology tools in this lesson, students will collect and analyze average temperatures from different cities and to deduce differences and similarities between their climates. This sample activity is one example of how technology tools can be used to support an inquiry-based science or math lesson.

Ask students to identify U.S. cities that are along similar lines of longitude and latitude. Sample cities are San Francisco, CA; Colorado Springs, CO; Dodge City, KS; and Norfolk, VA. Questions the teacher might ask students include: Which city is the warmest? Which city has the hottest summers? Which city is the coolest? Which city has the coolest winters? Which city gets the most snow? Which city has the lowest rainfall? While students should have conjectures for the questions posed, students may also begin to identify their own questions they would like to answer. The teacher should probe the students by asking them why they have these initial thoughts.

It is now time for students to begin researching on the Internet to start answering the questions. A suggested site to direct students to is the National Climatic Data Center (http://lwf.ncdc.noaa.gov/oa/ncdc.html). Once students locate the numerical data, they should enter it into a spreadsheet.

Working within the spreadsheet, students can calculate the mean and median monthly temperature as well as the range from the highest monthly temperature to the lowest monthly temperature. At this point the teacher should prompt the students by asking them if this is what they predicted? How do they think their calculations will appear on a line graph?

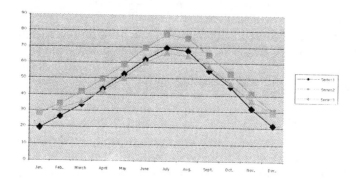

Using the graphing features of the spreadsheet software, students can create a line graph with the average monthly temperatures for each city. Once they have created the graph, ask the students to change the y-axis to highlight the extreme high and low temperatures. Students may be surprised to see how changing the y-axis can impact the data display.

From this activity, students could now conduct similar data collection and analysis of another set of cities along the same latitude or cities along similar longitudes. From their results, students should be able to hypothesize if there is a relationship between a city's location and their average temperature.

Practical Tips and Strategies	**Sample Online Sources of Numerical Data**
University of Virginia's GeoStat Interactive Data http://fisher.lib.virginia.edu/active_data/	
Weather.com's Average Temperature and Record Temperatures http://www.weather.com/common/home/climatology.html	
Historical and Current Oil Market Intelligence http://www.energyintel.com/DataHomePage.asp?publication_id=28	
National Forest Service Inventory and Analysis http://www.fia.fs.fed.us/	

Practical Tips and Strategies	Sample Online Sources of Numerical Data

Real Time Weather Data from the National Center for Atmospheric Research
http://www.rap.ucar.edu/weather/model/

Fleet Numerical Meteorology and Oceanography Center
http://www.fnoc.navy.mil/PUBLIC/

Inquiry With Online Primary Sources

Using online primary sources for instruction allows students to do the same work that scholarly historians do, that is: search, discover, and analyze primary sources to learn about people, trends, and events from the past. Online primary sources may in the form of hypertext documents, video, or audio. Because of technology, students not only have access to resources outside the classroom, but they are able to interact and manipulate these sources to make meaning of them. Essentially, using digital archives in the classroom allows students to actually "do history."

In addition to accessing resources available for the classroom, students also can manipulate authentic data in a rich and meaningful way. For example, students could download documents from existing online sources, use Inspiration to create concept maps from the information they discover, or use word processing tools to write historical fiction stories or newspaper accounts. Students could even create their own online community or personal histories!

Daily Life During the Civil War

Students are often required to memorize names, dates, and events when studying the American Civil War. Too seldom do they have the opportunity to do the work of historians and make meaning of the facts. This sample activity is one example of how technology can support an inquiry-based lesson.

The online primary sources used in this activity were digitized and archived by the University of Virginia's Virginia Center for Digital History (http://www.vcdh.virginia.edu). The Virginia Center for Digital

History is a collection of thousands of original documents related to America's history, as well as associated scholarly work placing these primary sources in an appropriate historical context.

The Valley of the Shadow Project is an online interactive archive of digitized primary sources that tells the stories of people in one southern and in one northern county before, during, and after the Civil War. Among the primary sources included in this digital history archive are letters, diaries, newspapers, census records, maps, photographs, church records, and military records. Each of these resources has either been scanned or transcribed and is accessible through the Internet.

Ask students what they know about what life was like during the Civil War, especially for someone their age. After the students generate a list of questions, direct them to the Valley of the Shadow website. Once here, students can read a series of letters written by families during this time period. These letters begin to tell the story of what life was like for everyday people during the Civil War.

The teacher should draw the students' attention to one letter, in particular. This letter is written by a young soldier to his sister at home:

From: Camp Gordonsville, Virginia

Aug 15th, 1862

Dear Sister,

I have wanted to write home but I have not had a chance I came up to Cousin John's for some bread and while they are cooking it I thought I would write a few lines home we have been on picket ever since Tuesday and just got of this morning. . . . I am carrying the colors for the Regiment it is not as much trouble as I thought it was at first they only trouble is I have is I cannot manage my horse very well.... I have seen Ash and Mike several times but have not seen Ned but once and then I passed while he was marching and I was caring a dispatch to Gen. Jackson so I could not have much talk with him he was looking very well, how is Sister Seal I hope she is not very sick give my love to her and tell her I will write to her soon give my love to Pa, Ma, Kate and Kelly and all others who ask for me you must excuse me for not writing sooner but I have written a good many times and when I have finished I would have to go some where and would put the letter in my

pocket until it was spoiled it is getting dark so I must stop I have to go
9 miles tonight so you must excuse me for not finishing this sheet.

Your Bro. Thos. M. Garber

Through class discussion, the students could make a list of what they .
learned about Thomas Garber from reading this letter. From reading the
letters, students will discover that Thomas is a soldier in the
Confederate Army in the American Civil War, he needs to ride a horse
to do his job, the leader of his company is C.J. O'Ferral, and he carries
the flags of his regiment.

Ask students what else they would like to know about Thomas Garber
and ask them for suggestions as to how they can learn more about him.
Explain to students that a valuable source for learning about Americans
who lived long ago is the population census. Explain to students that
the census is a list made of the entire United States population every
ten years. In addition to people's names, the census also records their
age, occupation, place of birth, and other information. Students can use
the online census tool at this website to locate census data on the
Garber family.

Once students have gathered information, they could begin to interpret the
primary sources and recreate the story of the Garber family. For example,
after students conduct a search of the census records, they will discover
Thomas was 14 in 1860, he did not own any property, he was white, and
he was born in Virginia. Students could deduce that Thomas was 16 or 17
when the letters were written in 1862-1863. You might ask students if they
know someone who is Thomas' age. Follow-up questions may include
asking students to imagine what it would feel like to be away from home
fighting in a war at this age; or asking them to hypothesize why someone
of this age would be fighting in a war.

To make meaning of this historical data, students need to place the
information in context and discover its relevance to their own lives. For
example, students could be asked to draw a picture or write a story
using the discovered information. Students are asked to write a letter
from Martha Garber to Thomas Garber. In order to do this, students
will need not only to show an understanding of nature of letters that

were sent from the homefront to soldiers during the Civil War, but also an understanding of family life during the Civil War. By studying the Garber family letters, students will discover not only how important letters from home were and the young age of many soldiers who fought in the war, but also that one family could have three sons fighting in the Civil War.

The activity described above is one in which students are going far beyond learning about history—rather, they are *doing* history!

Practical Tips and Strategies	Primary Sources and Hypertext Documents Online

Center for Electronic Texts in the Humanities
http://www.ceth.rutgers.edu/

Center for History and New Media
http://chnm.gmu.edu/

Documenting the American South
http://metalab.unc.edu/docsouth/

Electronic Text Center at the University of Virginia
http://etext.lib.virginia.edu/

The Geospatial and Statistical Data Center
http://fisher.lib.virginia.edu/

Library of Congress American Memory Project
http://memory.loc.gov/

Perseus Digital Library
http://www.perseus.tufts.edu/

Schoenberg Center for Electronic Text and Images
http://www.library.upenn.edu/etext/

World Languages Without Borders

Student and teacher foreign language resources have often been limited by school structures to textbooks, audiotapes, videotapes or the occasional school trip out of the country. Students who are at an entry level with their coursework often succeed in learning a world language in the classroom, but are not able to transfer the knowledge to an authentic environment. Technology tools are changing the traditional model of learning a foreign language and helping students to live within the discourse of another language.

Ask students what the current events of the day are in their community. Teachers may probe the students by asking what stories they heard on the radio or TV on the way to school or what news stories were in the morning newspaper. These could be categorized according to local, state, or national news. Questions to ask the students either through class votes or discussion include: Which news story was of most interest to you? Which story received the most press? Which stories do you want to know more about? Where could we look to learn more about these current events?

At this point, the teacher may display a web page with current news (e.g. http://www.cnn.com or http://www.nando.com). From this point, the teacher and students could learn more about the current events discussed earlier. The teacher should also ask the students to hypothesize how accessing current events from the Internet may be different that accessing them from the local radio, television, or newspaper. Students may discuss issues such as up-to-date news and different ways that the same news is portrayed.

The teacher at this juncture should guide the students towards wanting to know about current events around the world, in particular in areas where the language they are learning is spoken. Questions the teacher may ask include: What do you think are the top news stories in other areas? What differences do you think exist in how news is reported in other areas? Why do you think there might be these differences? What can we learn about other cultures by reading their news sources? How can we get access to news stories in other languages?

It is now time for students to begin researching these questions on the Internet. A suggested site to direct students to is MIT's online collection of foreign language newspapers (http://libraries.mit.edu/guides/types/flnews/). From this site, students could select one of many newspapers in a foreign language to read and interpret. Teachers may direct students to look for categories of news stories that are reported to compare the emphasis of different cultures and media sources. Teachers may also ask students to compare how world news is reported similarly or different. This could be an ongoing activity in which students record or track news stories over a period of time.

Having opportunities to practice reading a foreign language through activities such as these will help students enrich their understanding of a foreign culture and increase their vocabulary. It will also help them to understand the importance of media literacy skills and of foreign language skills in a global society.

Practical Tips and Strategies	Sample Online World Language News Sources

Latin American Network Information Center
http://lanic.utexas.edu/

Online Newspapers
http://www.onlinenewspapers.com/index.htm

Voice of America (audio world news)
http://www.voa.gov/

CNN.com: Europe (available in different languages)
http://europe.cnn.com/

Editorials, Columns, and Columnists
http://www.opinion-pages.org/

NewsLink
http://newslink.org/

PART IV: EXTENSIONS

TOMORROW'S CLASSROOMS

This guide has presented an overview of how technology tools are changing teaching and learning in today's classrooms. The technology applications explored are exemplars of how technology can be used to engage students in meaningful learning. These models should serve as springboards to guide continued exploration of the impact technology tools are having on teaching and learning.

Gordon Moore, the founder of Intel Corporation, observed that chip density doubles every eighteen months. This means that memory sizes, processor power, etc. all follow the same rate of growth. For example, today's Palm m100 has the same amount of memory as the computer that guided Apollo II to the moon in 1969. The rapid changes in technologies will continue to evolve and further change the way we teach and learn. Educators must respond to this exponential change by committing themselves to planning and implementing meaningful educational experiences for their students and engaging professional development for themselves. The resources listed below will help you continue your exploration into how technology tools can be used to enhance learning.

BOOKS

Barre, D., Hardy, J., & Harper, D. (2001). *Generation www.Y program and curriculum guide.* Eugene, OR: International Society for Technology in Education.

Bransford, J. D., Brown, A. L., & Cocking, R. R. (Eds.) (1999). *How people learn: Brain, mind, experience, and school.* Washington, DC: National Academy Press.

Collison, G., Elbaum, B., Haavind, S., & Tinker, R. (2000). *Facilitating online learning: Effective strategies for moderators.* Madison, WI: Atwood Publishing.

Cuban, L. (2001). *Oversold and Underused: Computers in the Classroom.* Cambridge, MA: Harvard University Press.

Forcier, R.D. (2002). *The computer as an educational tool: Productivity and problem solving.* Upper Saddle River, NJ: Prentice Hall.

Grabe, M. & Grabe, C. (2001). *Integrating technology for meaningful learning.* Boston: Houghton Mifflin.

Jonassen, D. H., Peck, K.L., & Wilson, B. G. (1999). *Learning with technology: A constructivist perspective.* Columbus, OH: Prentice Hall.

Kruger, L. (2001). *Computers in the delivery of special education and related services: Developing collaborative and individualized learning environments.* New York: Haworth Press.

Moersch, C. (2002). *Beyond hardware: Using existing technology to promote higher-level thinking.* Eugene, OR: International Society for Technology in Education.

Sharp, V., Levine, M. & Sharp, R. (2002). *The best websites for teachers.* Eugene, OR: International Society for Technology in Education.

Solomon, G. & Shrum, L. (2002). *Connect online: Web learning adventures.* Columbus, OH: Glencoe/McGraw-Hill.

Williams, R. & Tollett, J. (1998). *The non-designer's web book.* Berkeley, CA: Peachpit Press.

ARTICLES

Bull, G. L., Bull, G., Garofalo, J., & Harris, J. (2002). Grand challenges: Preparing for the technological tipping point. *Learning and Leading with Technology, 29*(8), 6–12.

Bush, G. (2001). Just sing: creativity and technology in the school library media center. *Knowledge Quest, 30* (2), 18–21.

Carroll, T. G. (2000). If we didn't have the schools we have today, would we create the schools we have today? *Contemporary Issues in Technology and Teacher Education, 1*(1). Available from http://www.citejournal.org/vol1/iss1/currentissues/general/article1.htm

Cooper, J., & Bull, G. (1997). Technology and teacher education: Past practice and recommended directions. *Action in Teacher Education, 19*(2), 97–106.

Dodge, B. (1997). Some thoughts about WebQuests. Available from http://edweb.sdsu.edu/courses/edtec596/about_webquests.html

Garofalo, J., & Pullano, F. (1997). Using graphing calculators to integrate mathematics and science. *Journal of Mathematics and Science: Collaborative Explorations, 1*(1), 53–64.

Hance, M. (2002). Playing catch-up with school technology. *Principal, (81)*5, 51–52.

Jester, R. (2002). If I had a hammer: Technology in the language arts classroom. *English Journal (91)*4, 85–88.

Means, B. (2000-2001). Technology use in tomorrow's schools. *Educational Leadership, 58*(4), 57–61.

Patterson, N. (2001). Computers and writing: feeling the power. *Voices from the Middle, 9*(1), 60–64.

Soloway, E. et al. (2001). Devices are ready-at-hand. Available from http://www.handheld.hice-dev.org/readyAtHand.htm

WEBSITES

International Society for Technology in Education's Teacher Resources
http://www.iste.org/resources
ISTE's large collection of educational resources offers listings of current Web sites, books, or periodicals that relate to educational technology.

Internet 101
http://www.internet101.org/
Created for beginners and advanced users of the Internet, this site explains the many different aspects of the Internet in a user-friendly format.

Bigchalk.com
http://www.bigchalk.com
Organized into sections for teachers, parents, and students, this site is a gateway to a comprehensive collection of educational resources.

The George Lucas Foundation: Edutopia Online
http://www.glef.org/
Edutopia is a collection of online videos and resources that explore effective teaching and learning in the digital age.

Concord Consortium
http://www.concord.org/
This non-profit agency's web site offers a variety of educational resources, including downloads and information on handheld computing, online learning, and modeling.

Global Schoolhouse
http://www.gsn.org/
The Global SchoolNet is a leader in telecollaborative projects. This site provides teachers and students opportunities to collaborate and communicate over the Internet.

U.S. Department of Education: Office of Education Technology
http://www.ed.gov/Technology/
The Office of Education Technology develops and implements national educational technology policy. This site houses many different reports and resources for educators.

Kathy Schrock's Guide for Educators
http://school.discovery.com/schrockguide/
One of the most extensive collections of educational resources, Kathy Schrock's Guide for Educators is a categorized list of lesson plans, professional development resources, reference materials, teacher tools, and student activities.

SOFTWARE

Decisions, Decisions

In this simulation program, students role-play a decision-maker faced with a critical situation drawn from historical events or contemporary issues. The online features allow classrooms to discuss and collaborate on the decision-making process across the Internet. Available from Tom Snyder Productions: http://www.teachtsp.com/

Learning to Speak Spanish

With lessons in vocabulary, grammar, and conversation, this software teaches students Spanish from the ground up. The digital teacher feature allows students to practice their conversation by talking into a computer microphone. Available from the Learning Company: http://www.learningcompanyschool.com/

LEGO MINDSTORMS: Robotics Invention System 2.0

This combination of toy LEGOs and the computer allows students to imagine and create a robot on the computer using RCX code. The infrared transmitter then lets the students test their inventions. Available from LEGO Mindstorms: http://mindstorms.lego.com/

Curriculum Pathways

This product is a web-based planning environment for teachers. It allows teachers to organize and access materials quickly, plan lessons efficiently, and spend more time with students. Available from SAS in Schools: http://www.sasinschool.com/

Geometer's Sketch Pad

Sketch Pad is a dynamic visualization tool that enables students to explore and understand mathematics through the process of discovery. Students can create an object and then explore its mathematical properties by clicking and dragging the mouse. Available from Key Curriculum Press: http://www.keypress.com/

Teacher's P.E.T.

This software for the handheld computer keeps track of student grades, attendance, and contact information. It is compatible with desktop spreadsheets and word processing software. Available from Palm: http://www.palm.com/

PROFESSIONAL ASSOCIATIONS

The Association for Educational Communications and Technology
1800 North Stonelake Drive, Suite 2
Bloomington, IN 47404
Phone: (812) 335-7675
Fax: (812) 335-7678
E-mail: aect@aect.org

International Society for Technology in Education (ISTE)
480 Charnelton Street
Eugene, OR 97401-2626
Phone: (800) 336-5191
Fax: (541) 302-3778
E-mail: iste@iste.org
Web: http://www.iste.org/

Society for Information Technology and Teacher Education (SITE)
P.O. Box 3728
Norfolk, VA 23514
Phone: (757) 623-7588
Fax: (703) 997-8760
E-mail: info@aace.org
Web: http://www.aace.org/site/default.htm

FOR REFLECTION

1. How has technology changed the K–12 classroom since you were a student?

2. Visit a school and record a specific list of technology tools available and how they are used. Did the list surprise or impress you?

3. How will you continue to learn about emerging technology tools for the classroom?

4. What can you do to ensure your students are safe while using the Internet?

4. How are students different today then they were ten years ago? How can teachers respond to these differences?

6. Review the NETS for your grade level and content area. What steps can you take to meet these standards?

7. List some effective Internet search strategies.

8. How can technology tools help students learn critical thinking skills?

9. Describe what you think a school will look like ten years from now.

10. How can you use technology for professional development activities?

GLOSSARY

boolean search   A method for searching that combines search terms with operators such as AND, OR, NOT. For example, "computers and art" searches for resources in which both "computers" and "art" appear.

cyberpredators   Individuals who seek to harm children through electronic communication.

e-mail A message sent over the Internet.

handheld   Portable computing device that can fit in your hand.

hyperlinks   Text or image that will take you to information stored at another location.

hypertext   Documents linked in a non-linear fashion with hyperlinks.

Internet   A global network of computers.

listserv An e-mail server with a list of e-mail addresses.

telecollaboration   Synchronous or asynchronous communication between two or more people via the Internet.

Web   A part of the Internet that hosts hypertext documents.

Web browser Software that enables users to access web pages.

REFERENCES

Bergman, M. (2000). The deep web: Surfacing hidden value. Retrieved August 20, 2002 from http://www.brightplanet.com/

Exploratorium Institute for Inquiry (1996). Inquiry Descriptions. Retrieved November 5, 2002 from http://www.exploratorium.edu/IFI/resources/inquirydesc.html

Harris, J (1998). *Virtual Architecture: Designing and directing curriculum-based telecomputing.* Eugene, OR: International Society for Technology in Education.

International Society for Technology in Education (2002). *National Education Technology Standards for Teachers: Preparing teachers to use technology.* Eugene, Oregon: Author, p. 5.

Kids & media @ the new millennium: A Kaiser Family Foundation report (n.d.). Retrieved August 20, 2002, from: http://www.kff.org/content/1999/1535/pressreleasefinal.doc.html

Leiner, B., Cerf, V., Clark, D., Kahn, R., Kleinrock, L. Lynch, D., Postel, J., Roberts, L., Wolff, S. (2000). A brief history of the Internet. Retrieved September 30, 2002 from http://www.isoc.org/internet/history/brief.shtml

Levin, D. & Arefeh, S. (2002). *The digital disconnect: The widening gap between Internet-savvy students and their schools.* Pew Internet & American Life. Retrieved August 30, 2002 from http://www.pewinternet.org/reports/pdfs/PIP_Schools_Internet_Report.pdf

Molebash, P., & Dodge, B. (2002). *WebQuests vs. inquiry: Whose question is it, anyway?* Paper presented at the Computer-Using Educators State Conference, Anaheim, CA.

Skinner, R. (2002). Tracking Tech Trends. *Technology Counts 2002: E-Defining Education, 21*(35), 53–56. Retrieved August 20, 2002 from http://www.edweek.org/sreports/tc02/article.cfm?slug=35tracking.h21

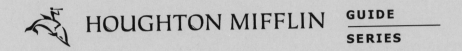

HOUGHTON MIFFLIN **GUIDE SERIES**

An Educator's Guide to
Diversity in the Classroom

Carl A. Grant
University of Wisconsin—Madison

James M. Cooper, Series Editor
University of Virginia

HOUGHTON MIFFLIN COMPANY   BOSTON   NEW YORK

CONTENTS

PREFACE

Houghton Mifflin Company publishes outstanding education textbooks in the areas of foundations of education, introduction to education, educational psychology, special education, and early childhood education. These textbooks introduce students to many concepts, policies, and research that undergird educational practice. However, as is the case for virtually all introductory texts, many topics are introduced but not covered in great depth. The Houghton Mifflin Teacher Education Guide Series is designed to provide more in-depth coverage of selected educational topics studied in the teacher education curriculum.

At the present time there are five guides in the series:

- Diversity in the Classroom
- Classroom Assessment
- Inclusion
- Technology Tools
- School-based Intervention Programs

The topics for these guides were selected because they are addressed in virtually all teacher education programs, and contain vital information for beginning teachers if they are to be successful in the classroom. Instructors may use the guides either for required or enrichment reading.

Each of these guides provides pre-service teachers with greater in-depth knowledge, application suggestions, and additional resources on its particular topic. All the guides share a common format that includes an introduction to the topic, knowledge that the prospective teacher should possess about the topic, examples of and suggestions for how the knowledge can be applied, and both print and Web-based resources for further exploration. Each guide also contains 10–15 questions designed

to help the prospective teacher reflect on the concepts and ideas introduced in the guide, as well as a glossary of key terms.
The makeup of children in America's schools is changing dramatically. Our culture is becoming much more diverse along a number of dimensions, including social class, ethnicity, race, and languages spoken. The overwhelming majority of teachers in the United States are middle-class white females. These teachers are being asked to "leave no child behind," including those whose backgrounds and culture are very different from their own. This is a challenging task for teachers, but one that must be taken very seriously.

In this guide, Carl Grant describes various kinds of diversity that students in American schools represent, and then offers suggestions to teachers on how to assist these students to meet challenging academic standards. In doing so, he examines the school curriculum, instructional practices, and ways that teachers and students communicate with each other.

PART I: INTRODUCTION

Nothing is distributed evenly across the United States. Not race, not religion, not age, not fertility and certainly not access to higher education. (Hodgkinson, 2000.)

The purpose of this guide is to discuss diversity—race, ethnicity, socioeconomic class, gender, sexuality, and language—in schools, paying particular attention to the classroom. To that end, the discussion will focus on teachers, curriculum, instruction, students, and a few other areas. To those who are moaning, "Here we go again—more diversity training," our hope is that your generation will get this "diversity thing" right, so that future generations of teacher candidates and beginning teachers will not echo a similar feeling. After September 11, 2001, you read about the importance of patriotism, and rightly so. In many cases, along with the reference to patriotism, you hear references to diversity as America's crown jewel, and rightly so. This crown jewel, however, unlike the image of patriotism with the very young drummer boy carrying the tattered and torn "red, white and blue" during the Revolutionary War, has a checkered history: enslaved people, resistance to voting rights and equal rights for women, reservations and the forfeiture of treaty rights for Native Americans, imprisonment of Japanese Americans during World War II, and immigration restrictions against Asian Americans and people from Southern Europe and Central and South America. Before dismissing these as your great grandfather's problems, there are numerous present-day diversity issues that are our problem. For example, race and gender discrimination are legally outlawed but commonly practiced, residential and school segregation are increasing, language and immigrant status are often combined with racial distinctions, and poor people are becoming poorer.

But let's not get ahead of ourselves in laying out this discussion. First, let's take a look at what is happening with diversity in society, and keep in mind that an often-overheard statement from any and all U.S. citizens is that schools are a microcosm of society. Schools reflect society's attitudes, beliefs, tensions, and struggles: the good, bad, and ugly. Since this statement has currency, let us first look at diversity in society.

WHO ARE THE NEW FACES AT THE MALL?

The United States is undergoing a major societal change. The population grew more between 1990 and 2000 than in any previously recorded decade—from 249 million to 281.4 million. During this same decade, the population of people of color increased by 35 percent, while the white population grew by 3.4 percent. Now, and especially during your children's lifetime, a reference to the "majority population" will not be a reference to white people, and this may lead to the term "majority" losing its status and popularity in the both the academic and popular press.

People of color are increasing, but how much money do they have in their pockets? The U.S. Census data estimates indicate a steady increase in the real median incomes for U.S. households. However, there is disparity between specific racial and ethnic populations. For example, although white, black and Hispanic groups earned the highest median income they have ever received, black and Hispanic groups continue to have the lowest median income at $27,900 and $30,700 respectively (U.S. Census Bureau, Current Population Report, 2001). U.S. Census Bureau estimates of 1999 suggest similar changes occurred with respect to national poverty rates. Though national poverty rates decreased to 11.8 percent—the lowest since 1979—24 percent of the U.S. black population lives in poverty. This is three times higher than the rate for white non-Hispanics (8 percent) (U.S. Census Bureau, Current Population Report, 2001, p.48, 51-52). What we're saying here is that in spite of increased wealth for whites as a group and people of color as a group, far more people of color are still affected by poverty.

Women are still in pursuit of gender equity and equality. Women constituted 51 percent of the U.S. population, and in 1999, men and women age 25 and older were equally likely to have completed high school, yet men were more likely than women to complete college—28 percent compared with 23 percent, respectively (U.S. Census Bureau, Current Population Report, 2001, p. 38). Also, according to the U.S.

Census Bureau's Current Population Report (2001), women earned about 72 cents for every dollar men made in 1999. This is two cents down from the all-time high of 74 cents earned in 1996 (p. 49).

The next time you see a handicap parking space, or see some mentally or physically disabled people in the mall remember that many among us, especially adults, have disabilities that we may not recognize. According to the U.S. Census Bureau's Current Population Report (2001), almost one in five adults had some type of disability and the likelihood of having a disability increased with age (p. 72). Also, the earning potential and power is lower for people with disabilities. The 1997 median earnings for people with no disability was $23,700, compared with $20,500 for those with a non-severe disability and $13,300 for those with a severe disability (U.S. Census Bureau, Current Population Report, 2001, p. 74).

Increasingly, you will hear different languages spoken. For example, at most major airports in the United States messages are given in three or four languages. Although, English will remain dominant, there are 176 living languages currently spoken in the U.S. (SIL, 2002, p. 1). For persons five years old and over, the most common language spoken in the U.S. is English, followed by Spanish and French, respectively (U.S. Census Bureau, Statistical Abstract, 2001a).

According to Vaid (1998), national public opinion research polls do not routinely incorporate demographic questions asking respondents about sexual orientation (Preface). Thus data about sexual orientation, as well as data on attitudes toward sexual orientation, are not widely available. However, in 1998, Yang, for the National Gay and Lesbian Task Force, collected and analyzed public opinion data covering a twenty-year period that addressed attitudes toward sexual orientation. Yang (1998) reports that empirical evidence strongly demonstrates that opposition to lesbian and gay equal rights is on the decline among most Americans. The author suggests that historically, public support for lesbian and gay rights have traditionally been on the issues of employment and housing equality. For example, from 1977 to 1996, Gallup Research indicates that support for equality in employment has increased from 56 percent to 84 percent (Yang, 1998). In addition, Yang (1998) points out that since the 1990s, the trend of stable disapproval of homosexual behavior began to dip, with nearly a 20 percent decrease in disapproval rates from the 1980s to the 1990s. However, Yang (1998) notes that although the disapproval rates have decreased in recent years, 56 percent of the respondents still disapprove of homosexual behavior. Discussions of sexuality and the knowledge that a person within the group is gay, although much improved in recent years, may still bring resentment and opposition toward that individual in many communities.

The religious face of the United States is changing. The changes are in numbers and in observable religious diversity. The next time you are at the mall or in the downtown area of a major city, pay attention to the people you can easily observe who are from different religious backgrounds. Eck (2001) claims that the United States has become the world's most religiously diverse nation. For example, there are more American Muslims than there are American Episcopalians, Jews or Presbyterians, and there are presently more than three hundred temples in Los Angeles, home to the greatest variety of Buddhists in the world.

Who raises the children you see dashing about the mall: mothers and fathers, single mothers, single fathers, grandparents, or others? According to the U.S. Census 2000, married couples with children make up 24 percent of all households, and single mother homes make up 7 percent of households. However, in 2.2 million households, single fathers raise the children. This is about one in 45, up 62 percent in 10 years (Armas, 2001). Also, children are increasingly being raised by an extended family, as more grandparents are taking on childcare duties of their children's children. Similarly, aunts and uncles are active in childcare. "It takes a village" to raise children today is an appropriate statement.

To listen to the media or read the press, especially the advertisements, it becomes easy to assume that *all* households have one or more computers. This is not so, according to the Current Population Survey: the U.S. Census Bureau estimates that in August 2000, only 51 percent of U.S. households had one or more computers. This number is up from 42 percent in December 1998 (U.S. Census Bureau, Current Population Reports, 2001, p. 1). Also, more than two in five households have Internet access. However, white children are more likely to have home computer access or use the Internet than are black or Hispanic children (U.S. Census Bureau, Current Population Reports, 2001, p. 2). In addition, this report suggests that girls are as likely as boys to use the Internet at home, and that high-income households (family households with incomes of $75,000 or more during the 12 months prior to the survey) were more likely to have computers or Internet access (U.S. Bureau, Current Population Reports, 2001, p. 2). In regards to school access, more school-age children have access to computer use at school than at home.

How many of your students have cell phones in their backpack? How many of these children are white and how many are children of color? With more and more functions being added to cell phones, including wireless Internet access, will cell phone ownership contribute to the already existing digital divide? While you will have to make that discovery yourself, based upon a survey mailed to all cellular, personal communications services, and enhanced special mobile radio systems, the 2001 Statistical Abstract of the United States reports that there are over 109 million cellular phone subscribers in the U.S. in 2000. This is up from the five million cell phone users reported in 1990 (U.S. Census Bureau, Public Information Office, 2002).

A Closer Look   *Diversity Facts and Figures*

Latinos and Asian Americans fueled the rapid growth of people of color. The Latino population increased by 58 percent and the Asian American population increased by 50 percent, while the African American population increased by 16 percent (American Council on Education, 2002). It is estimated that within the next two decades, 65 percent of the United States population will be people of color, particularly Latino and Asian immigrants (Hodgkinson, 2000).

Every fifth child faces hunger in the United States. As many as five and a half million children are hungry, and 13.4 million are growing up in conditions of poverty that make it difficult for them to develop their full potential (Bread For the World, 1992).

In all educational categories reported in U.S. Census Data, women earn less than their male counterparts who have comparable educational attainment (U.S. Census Bureau, Current Population Report, 2001, p. 49). This report also noted that female householder families with no husband present had the highest poverty rate at 28 percent. And though these families only made up 18 percent of all families, they accounted for 53 percent of poor families (U.S. Census Bureau, Current Population Report, 2001, p. 51).

The 1997 U.S. Census Data indicate that 53 million adults have disabilities, of which 24 million were men and 28 million were women. Among those with a severe disability, 15 million were men and 18 million were women (U.S. Census Bureau, Current Population Report, 2001, p. 72).

According to the U.S. Census from 1980-2000, U.S. residents indicate a preference for Protestant religious faiths (U.S. Census Bureau, Statistical Abstracts of the U.S, 2001b). In 2000, data taken from the Gallup Organization indicates that 56 percent of all respondents expressed a preference for Protestant faiths, followed by 27 percent who expressed a preference for the Catholic faith, and 2 percent who favored Jewish faith; 8 percent of the respondents expressed no interest in any religious faith (U.S. Census Bureau, Statistical Abstracts of the U.S. 2001b, p. 56).

For children ages 6 to 17 years old, computer use at school was more nearly equal across different income, race, or ethnic groups than computer access at home (U.S. Bureau, Current Population Reports, 2001, p. 5).

PART II: KNOWLEDGE

WHAT DO TEACHERS NEED TO KNOW ABOUT DIVERSITY?

According to the U. S. Census Bureau 2000, there are an estimated 51.5 million school-age children; children ages 5–13 are estimated at 35.8 million and children ages 14–17 are estimated at 15.7 million. Children in the United States continue to increase in racial and ethnic diversity. In 1999, 65 percent were white; 15 percent were black; and 16 percent were Latino; 4 percent were Asian/Pacific Islander; and 1 percent were American Indian/Alaska Native (America's Children: Key National Indicators of Well-Being, 2000). Given the dramatic social changes in society and schools, teachers are asking, "What do I need to know about diversity in order to be an effective and caring teacher?"

TEACHERS

Teachers who are active in attending to diversity in their classroom, and scholars and researchers who study diversity in the classroom, argue first and foremost that a teacher's knowledge of diversity must first start with her or himself. Teachers who advocate diversity recommend that teachers ask themselves the following questions in the "Who is the Person in the Mirror Survey?" Take the survey yourself and compare your answers to those of your classmates.

Who Is the Person in the Mirror?

1. What are my thoughts and behavior toward someone who is physically or mentally challenged?
    a. accepting
    b. tolerant
    c. I do not know
    d. I group them with others like themselves

2. How do I respond to students who are very intelligent, or students who are very much slower than other students?
    a. accepting
    b. tolerant
    c. I do not know
    d. I group them with others like themselves

3. How much do I know about the problems and issues facing gay, lesbian, and bisexual students?
    a. a great deal
    b. a fair amount
    c. a little bit
    d. next to nothing

4. How will I become prepared to provide gay, lesbian, and bisexual students with a caring classroom environment?
    a. read articles and books
    b. take university courses
    c. have discussions with people who are gay, lesbian, and bisexual
    d. I am not interested in any extra preparation to provide gay, lesbian, and bisexual students with a caring classroom

5. How much do I know about the problems and issues facing racial and ethnic groups other than my own?
    a. a great deal
    b. a fair amount
    c. a little bit
    d. next to nothing

6. If I am a teacher of color, do I believe that it is necessary for me to learn about diversity?
    a. yes
    b. no
    c. maybe
    d. not sure

7. Do I believe that single mothers with two or more children, who live at or below the poverty line, are living in these circumstances because they are lazy and want to get by on society?
   a. yes
   b. no
   c. maybe
   d. not sure

8. Will knowledge that the United States has become the world's most religiously diverse nation affect my teaching in any way?
   a. yes
   b. no
   c. maybe
   d. not sure

9. Do I believe that schools have a responsibility to provide instruction that will help English language learners to maintain their native language?
   a. yes
   b. no
   c. maybe
   d. not sure

9. Do I believe that all nine of Howard Gardner's multiple intelligences are equally important, or should be accommodated in the school setting?
   a. yes
   b. no
   c. maybe
   d. not sure

Perhaps you may wonder how your own responses compare to those of other teacher candidates or beginning teachers. Now is probably a good time to introduce you to two teacher education students, Sara and Elise, who will be with us throughout the guide. Let's give you some information about their backgrounds and then you can compare your own survey responses to their survey responses and their ideas on diversity.

Meet Sara and Elise

Sara Pedroni is bi-racial, Mexican and European American, and Elise Vanguard is European American. Sara and Elise will bear the burden of voicing some of the common expressions of interest and concern that we have heard in our travels both nationally and internationally.

Years ago, when Elise was very young, eight or nine years old, she said she wanted to be a teacher. Elise cannot remember exactly why she came to that conclusion. However, she has always enjoyed working with young people. Also, she contends her favorite Aunt, Mary Jo, may be influential, as she often hears Mary Jo talk about her students with such joy and excitement. In addition, Elise fondly remembers helping Mary Jo and some of the other teachers at her school get their classrooms ready for the start of the new school year. She did this from the time she was eight years of age until she was a sophomore in high school. She especially enjoyed being invited to sit with these teachers when they would eat lunch together. She felt like one of the "big girls." Also, being in the school when the other students were not there gave her a sense of privilege and being special.

Elise wrote on her admission essay to the teacher education program that she wanted to teach because she loves and wants to help children. Her discussion of "love and help" was characterized as narrow by three of the five reviewers/examiners. The reviewers noted that her discussion about her background lacked any discussion of culturally diverse knowledge or experiences and did not include any interaction with people of color. The community service projects she participated in during high school included working in the hospital in her community and serving food a couple of times in a homeless shelter. However, Elise's GPA and letters of recommendation were very strong. Also, she was the daughter of two very active alumni.

Elise attended both public and private schools for her K–12 education. When her mother and father were just getting their financial feet on the ground, Elise and her younger brother Mike Jr. attended public school. As the family began to prosper financially, which was around the time Elise began middle school, Elise and Mike Jr. were enrolled in an upscale private school. The school, The McArthur, was a short distance away from where the Vanguards purchased their home. The Vanguards have most of the adult "toys" they want (Mercedes, boat, and summer home), and give their children "toys" appropriate to their age and behavior. The family spends a good deal of time together, especially during holidays. Elise and Mike Jr. have visited most of the major cities in both the United States and Europe.

Elise was an excellent student throughout her K–12 education. Her GPA was 3.7. Her favorite subjects were mathematics and science, and she was well above average in the other subject areas. Elise was liked and admired by students and teachers. Some described her as humble, friendly, non-competitive and non-confrontational. Others describe her simply as "shy."

Elise was assigned to live in the same dorm, Lake Front, where her mother had lived when she was a college student. As the Vanguards were moving things (microwave, TV, computer, stereo, clothes) up to the room, they met Elise's roommate, Sara Pedroni.

Sara had already moved most of her stuff in. She greeted Elise with, "Hi, looks like you have cut your hair from the picture you sent me online. It's cute! This is my mother Amy and my uncle Ernest." Elise's response to Sara was, "Thanks. You are much taller than I imagined. You could be a model." Once the Pedronis and Vanguards greeted each other and helped the girls to arrange their stuff, they decided to go out and have dinner together.

Sara had come to State U on an academic scholarship, one designed to attract students of color to the University. Her high school guidance counselor, Ms. Kopper, had worked with Sara since her sophomore year. This was when she discovered that Sara had an excellent record of both standardized test scores and teachers' grades. Ms. Kopper called Sara's mother, Amy, at the end of her second year and suggested that they should discuss where Sara was going to go to college. Sara made the choice of State U after considering two other institutions. She was impressed with State U's reputation and that it was only a two-and-a-half-hour drive from her home. She wanted to be away from home, but not a long way away.

Sara declared education as her major only because she was tired of being bugged by her mother, relatives, and friends about what she was going to study in college. However, she took grief from many when she talked about becoming a teacher. Only her mother was very supportive and praised her. Sara did not dislike the thought of being a teacher, but the thought of teaching so many students who seem only to come to school because it was compulsory did not excite her. Her comfort in thinking about teaching was born out of several pieces of advice that Ms. Kopper gave to her. Ms. Kopper told her, "A teaching credential will allow you to get a job almost anywhere. Many women use teaching as a transition job to other professions; you have your summers off to pursue other career opportunities and to be with your children, should you choose to have some."

Sara was born in Texas, and lived with her mother and father in Houston until she was six. Shortly after her sixth birthday, her mother and father got a divorce, and she and her mother moved to Mexico. They moved to Mexico City to help her mother adjust to being a single parent and in order for her mother's family to give both of them emotional and financial support. They lived in Mexico City for five years. Sara became fluent in Spanish as her grandmother insisted that she both become fluent in Spanish and learn about her Mexican cultural heritage. Sara and her mother moved back to the U.S. when she was in middle school because the Mexican economy was going bad, her father was taking legal steps to see Sara more frequently, and Uncle Ernest got Amy a job working where he worked.

Sara's GPA is 3.98. She wrote on the admission essay that she is still deciding if she wants to teach; that she was only 70 percent sure. She wrote that if she decides to teach she wants to work in a Latino barrio. Also, she included numerous experiences she had during her high school years working as a volunteer translator in a community health center and at her high school, and tutoring middle school students. Also, as a high school student, Sara was in the school band and drama club and was very active in her church.

With that background of our two teacher candidates, let's move on to what teacher candidates and beginning teachers need to know about diversity—but first, let's get Sara and Elise's reactions to the "Person in the Mirror" Survey.

Elise: Wow! I had no idea that attending to diversity is so complex and involved. Most of the survey questions I have never considered seriously.

Sara: I agree. So much is dealing with teachers' attitude. For example, I haven't thought about how I feel about gays and lesbians, or how I am going to learn about providing a caring classroom for gay, lesbian, and bisexual students, or students whose religion is not Christian or Jewish.

Elise: Thanks for saying that, because I was starting to feeling awful, like I am a horrible person. I've never thought too much about non-English speaking students, or single mothers. Does this mean I have a bad attitude toward diversity?

Sara: No, I don't think the survey is intended to make us think that we are bad people or we will be bad teacher, because we didn't come across now as having a positive attitude about all of those different aspects of diversity. However, I think what we learn from the survey is that if we don't learn about the issues facing people who are culturally different and accept and appreciate those differences, then I think we become part of the problem in schools more so than part of the solution.

Elise: I wonder, other than knowing about ourselves, what else do we need to know about diversity?

You should tell Elise, after knowing about herself, that she needs to know about diversity in curriculum, instruction, students, language and several other areas.

Curriculum

Decades ago, the English philosopher Herbert Spencer asked a question that educators today still ask: "What knowledge is of most worth?" Spencer was criticizing classical education and asking for an inclusion of science. Since the civil rights movements for blacks, Native Americans, women, and gays and lesbians, some have extended Spencer's question to ask, "*Whose* knowledge is of most worth?" and "Who produces this knowledge?" These groups concerned with civil rights are asking where their voice is in the articulation and production of knowledge.

In schools, knowledge resides in the curriculum. Thus, one of the major focal points of diversity in school is the curriculum. However, many teacher candidates and beginning teachers are perplexed about what diversity needs to be included in the curriculum and how the curriculum needs to be changed. For some teachers this is troubling because they are being asked to change the curriculum they grew up on, a curriculum they know very well and achieved high grades from studying. Also, some of these teachers reason that textbooks have kept up with the times, so diversity needs have been taken care of by textbook publishers. They contend, for example, that they can recall that their K–12 textbooks included pictures and information on Martin Luther King, Jr., excerpts from Sojourner Truth's "Ain't I a Woman?" speech, Eleanor Roosevelt's contribution to World War II and race relations, and Betty Friedan's arguments about gender inequities. They read about the horrors of the Holocaust and the massacre at My Lai during the Vietnam War. In other words, they believe their textbooks took care of the diversity issues. But such is not the case.

In an analysis of 47 textbooks used in Grades 1–8, Sleeter and Grant discovered that much work still needs to be done. They examined social studies, reading and language arts, science, and mathematics textbooks. The highlights of what were found include the following:

> Whites consistently dominate textbooks, although their margin of dominance varies widely. Whites receive the most attention, are shown in the widest variety of roles and dominate the storyline and lists of accomplishments. Blacks are the next most included racial group. However, the books show Blacks in a more limited range of roles than whites and give only a sketchy account of Black history and little sense of contemporary Black life. Native Americans appear mainly as historical figures. . . . Males predominate in most books; but even in books in which females have a major presence, females of color are shown very little. One gains little sense of the history or culture of women, and learns very little about sexism or current issues involving gender. . . . Social class is not

treated in the book at all. . . . The image that books in all subject areas convey is that the United States is not stratified on the basis of social class, that almost everyone is middle-class, that there is no poverty and no great wealth. . . . Disability is ignored as well (Sleeter & Grant, 1991, pp. 97-98).

Sara: You know, now that I actually read about the treatment of people of color, women, and poor people in textbooks, I must admit that I don't recall seeing any major discussions of these groups in my K–12 texts. I rarely read about Latinos, and my people have been the fastest growing population. Also, I can't ever recall participating in a discussion on how cultural groups are represented in curriculum.

Elise: I am surprised that you didn't since many of the students at your high school were Latino and black. On the other hand, if the teachers want you guys to do well on the achievement tests, and test makers don't include this stuff on the test, would teachers be helping you if they spent time discussing it?

Sara: It's important, Elise! It's up to teachers and parents to point this out to the test makers. Do you know why more attention is given to blacks and women in the current textbooks? According to my Educational Policy professor, it's because in the 1960s and 1970s, parents and teachers demanded that publishers change their books. Black parents in urban areas, along with some of the teachers, communicated to textbook publishers that they were not going to allow the school to purchase the texts until there was better treatment of minorities in textbooks. Advocates for women's issues made a similar argument. Hearing the serious voices of African Americans and advocates for an anti-bias gender equity curriculum, textbook publishers responded—somewhat—to the pressure. Publishers did not want their bottom line affected.

In addition, my Ed Policy professor contends, quoting Belle & Ward (1994) ". . . that the school has played as major a role in dividing various ethnic and social class groups through the curriculum" (p. 99). Belle & Ward (1994) argue that student choices, for example, in "pursuing vocational and academic careers, is one major way in which divisions continue to be created. It is often the poor, minority student who is found in the vocational stream and the middle- or upper-class, and dominant group student who is in the academic stream. This tracking in the formal curriculum can be created and reinforced by the school using standardized test results for ability grouping, often beginning as early as kindergarten" (p. 99).

Elise: Do you believe all that you are hearing? I don't want to be disagreeable, but all that I keep hearing about is "diversity" or "multicultural education." It's been that way for the past four years. You've always gotten good grades, and have earned a scholarship to college. Don't you think all of this attention to "multiculturalism" will impede your progress? There is still very little multiculturalism on our exams, and not too much of it in schools.

Sara: No, I think we both need multiculturalism to teach, or to do any other job. Not only are the demographic population data changing, but a growing number of people are moving away from absolute answers to questions to viewing problems and issues from multiple perspectives.

What will probably surprise Elise and Sara, is that Grant & Sleeter's observations of classrooms (1996) indicates that there is more cultural diversity in the text materials teachers use than in the teachers' presentation (e.g., lectures, discussions). Whereas most teachers will use culturally diverse and non-sexist materials and will deal with a stereotypical statement about race made by a student head-on, most of these teachers do not refer very often to people of color, women, individuals with disabilities, and gay and lesbian people during their lectures and discussion. We saw many missed opportunities to point out the omissions of social justice and equity issues in textbooks and other curricular materials, and/or to clarify events in history or provide other points of view. Willis (2001) argues that attention to diversity needs to include how groups are represented in the curriculum in use; and what narratives of race and ethnic relations are constructed in schools and classrooms. Willis is interested in this question because he believes teachers should know if school knowledge prepares students for social critique and active citizenship in this increasingly diverse society.

Willis (2001) contends that what is missing from curriculum are meaningful representations of the actions and interactions of diverse groups as agents, actors, and subjects in U.S. history and society. He states, "Because diverse groups are missing in interaction in the social studies curriculum, school knowledge is a poor resource for enabling students to develop a discourse of contemporary race and ethnic relations that move beyond psychological understandings of racism to structural understandings of racism. As such, school knowledge provides an inadequate foundation for realizing a critical social studies education that will prepare students for active citizenship in our diverse society" (p. 44). Willis (2001) makes sense when he argues that "Meaning does not reside in texts, but in the interaction between the symbolic resources of texts and their readers in specific social, historical, and institutional settings. As such, the meaning of curricular content is a social accomplishment, and school knowledge is produced in the interaction between teachers, students, and curriculum" (p. 46).

Instruction

You may recall that your K–12 friends and maybe even you commented that a good deal of the K–12 classroom instruction was boring. This is not surprising, because it is argued that the teaching is not interesting for many students and even alienating for some students. Some observers of classrooms call the instructional environment emotionally flat (Goodlad, 1984). This is especially so for students of color, for students who are trying to keep their sexual orientation hidden in fear of the harassment they will face, and students who have physical and learning disabilities and are not included in the mainstream of the class (Grant & Sleeter, 1996). Contributing to the boredom is the overuse and misuse of worksheets. Everhart (1983) reminds teachers that the use of worksheets, especially ones that do not take into account students' experiential background, is a "no-no." Everhart describes an incident in a junior high classroom in which students were filling in a worksheet after reading about Switzerland in their textbooks. Not having been to Switzerland, and not having been provided experiences to develop visual, aural, or tactile imagery about Switzerland, the students discussed the weekend football game while completing an assignment that to them was merely verbal gymnastics.

Another instructional issue that affects diversity is the attention given to high-stakes testing and the pressure on teachers and students to be successful. This attention takes away from planning time needed for integrating multicultural issues into the curriculum (Johnson & Johnson, 2002).

During instruction time, students are alert to how their efforts are received by the teacher. This reception signals to all students, but especially those who are challenged by social justice issues, what teachers think about them. Grayson (1998) states, "As teachers, one of the measurable ways we manifest our perceived expectations for others is through our attention and to whom we give it. We are constantly reinforcing perceived high expectations for others by providing them with our undivided attention" (p. 19). Also of primary significance is the "quality" of attention. Grayson (1998) argues, "[W]hile frequency of distribution of our attention is extremely important, we must also look at the quality of attention" (p. 19). Attention, with quality, goes a long way in establishing a caring classroom. Noddings (1984) explains, "When a teacher asks a question in a class and a student responds, she received not just the 'response' but the student. What he says matters, whether it is right or wrong, and she probes gently for clarification, interpretation, and contribution. She is not seeking the answer but the involvement of the cared-for . . . The student is infinitely more important than subject matter" (p. 176).

Elise: For the most part my teachers made our work pretty interesting. They had many supplies and resources, and help for subjects if we needed it. You know, I hear a good deal of discussion about providing students of color and female students with instructional approaches that appeal to their learning needs. At my high school, this is the way it is. We would take field trips, see films, or read novels to learn about a concept. So, I don't know why a teacher would not be responsive to students' learning styles and needs.

Sara: Remember, your school was pretty well off. Many public schools, especially those in urban and rural areas, don't have those kinds of resources. Jonathan Kozol's book, Savage Inequalities, did an excellent job telling about the rich schools and the poor schools in this country and how money becomes the means of privilege and power and determines who receives a quality education and who does not.

Elise: Yeah, when I read that book, I found it hard to believe. I am not saying it isn't true, just hard to believe.

Sara: Elise, why do you think your mother and father transferred you and Mike Jr. to a private school? They know that money makes a difference in the quality of education kids receive.

Language

School policy may endorse language maintenance programs or transitional programs. Teachers nevertheless need to assess their attitude toward students whose first language is not English, and how they are going to work with them. Here, we're not discussing providing students with instruction in keeping with school policy, but the nature and quality of attention and interactions between teacher and student in regards to the student's first language. Language is a dimension of cultural heritage where some parents and students stand firm about the extent to which they will assimilate into the dominant culture and adhere to school policy. This is because language is a vital source of cultural and personal identity. Valenzuela (1999) helps teachers to understand this point when she argues that there are two types of caring found in schools: aesthetic and authentic. Valenzuela claims that aesthetic caring, which has to do more with the Americanization and assimilation of Latinos, is not good for Latino students' academic achievement and personal growth. This diminishes U.S.-Mexican students' culture and weakens their identities and prevents supportive and nurturing social ties from existing, eliminating resources critical to students' academic achievement. She goes on to explain that although aesthetic caring is intended to help students achieve, in reality this type of caring is subtractive, in that aesthetic caring reduces U.S.-Mexican students to ethnic minority students that are not identified with Mexico, nor are they equipped to operate competently with mainstream students. On the other hand, "authentic caring" expands on caring theory, which holds students' self-concept and background in high regard and gives pedagogical attention to questions of otherness, difference, and power that resides with the assimilation process itself (p. 25).

There are some within but mostly some outside of ethnic groups that believe the preservation of native language abilities by groups threaten the existence of the unifying elements in the overall culture of the United States. These individuals argue that U. S. society will not sustain its collective conscience if groups within it are permitted to reinforce a separateness based on language (La Belle and Ward, 1994, p. 108). Also, advocates of this position contend that schools should not base their approach to education on the primacy of ethnicity or other characteristics to the exclusion of the needs associated with citizenship in the larger society (Imoff, cited in La Belle and Ward, 1994).

There are committed advocates on both sides of the language debate. A position of neutrality will be a difficult position for a teacher to maintain. Therefore, beginning teachers must examine both sides of the "English Only" argument to determine where they will stand when they are called to stand; and for many teachers the time to take a stand is now.

Sara: You know in my house some of my relatives on my Mexican side are not proponents of their little children maintaining their Spanish. Some of them speak fewer words of Spanish than you do. It really makes my grandmother boil. We would really have hot family discussions over this issue!

Elise: If you have kids, what are you going to do? Will you push them to learn both English and Spanish?

Sara: No question, my grandmother would kill me if I don't teach them to speak Spanish. You know, when I lived in Mexico and she was teaching me Spanish and my cultural history, I resented it because it took playtime away, but now I am so happy that she did.

STUDENTS

Beside the teacher, students are the major challenge to successfully dealing with diversity in the classroom. Students come with their own "baggage," their likes and dislikes, their experiences and their absence of experiences. Wotorson (2001) argues that at as young an age as possible, children need opportunities to practice prosocial attitudes and behaviors, to learn about themselves and others, and to develop nonviolent responses to conflict. Wotorson (2001) contends that research studies report that young children begin to notice and evaluate differences very early in their development. He also reports research data that societal stereotyping and bias influence children's self-concepts and attitudes toward others.

Although these research data are available and are often taught in teacher education classes and staff development sessions, some pre-kindergarten teachers continue to ask, "Should I teach my students about diversity; and if so, what?" In response to this question, some reply that opportunities for children to engage in creative self-reflection and to explore the diversity around them in open, honest, and creative ways, while learning about the causes and effects of prejudice and bias, can help them begin a lifelong journey toward fairness, justice and nonviolence. Wotorson (2001) offers research data about other age groups of students to help teachers understand about diversity and kids:

- **Five-year-olds** begin to build a group ethnic identity, as well as an individual identity. They are able to explore the range of differences within and between racial and ethnic groups as well as the range of similarities between groups. Students at this age begin to understand scientific explanations for differences in skin color, hair texture, and eye shape. They are also beginning to understand the concept of family traditions and family history.

- **Six- to eight-year-olds** continue to recognize other group members and they are now beginning to understand that their ethnicity is not changeable. Their knowledge of history, local actions, and attitudes for and against cultural groups is budding. This new knowledge, which is influenced in part by the media, may foster personal prejudices that may become an integral part of a child's attitude and behavior. Students at this age are highly influenced by the way they see people interact and resolve conflicts. Many students in this age group learn about culture and race with greater cognitive depth and emotional connection than they did at earlier stages. They may begin to take pride in their own cultural identities and understand the experience of others. However the teacher plays a major role in the direction, depth and breadth of this learning.

- **Nine- to twelve-year-olds** may still be concrete thinkers primarily focused on their own experiences, but many are moving into more abstract thinking. They are gaining a greater understanding of the geographic and historical aspects of culture and becoming more aware of the attitudes and behaviors of persons in positions of authority within institutional settings, such as schools, places of worship, and youth agencies. Some are gaining an awareness and understanding of the various perspectives that are moored in ways of thinking that have a long racist, sexist, and social class history. Students at this age may understand personal and family struggles against bias and are often willing to discuss culture and race differences. Also, they are ready for more complex discussions of power and privilege and are ready to move from examples involving personal issues to examples in society. In addition, a more complex understanding of personal, family, and community identity based on cultural values may emerge, along with a more complex understanding of sexuality and religious intolerance. Students at this age are becoming increasingly aware of the valuing and devaluing of culture and race by their peers, the media, and the larger community. Many are ready for discussions of why this is taking place, which are located in historical and current ways of thinking that are continually reproduced. The advantages and disadvantages of some groups politically, educationally, and economically are becoming evident, and children may informally begin to discuss what they see as unfairness. Such informal discussions can be considered as invitations for the teacher to guide students to significant discoveries about life chances for people based upon their race, gender, sexuality, disability and social class. Or, such informal discussions may be left unguided and up to the personal explorations of only the students who raise them.

Most nine-to-twelve-year-olds can understand racial and cultural stereotypes; can speak from dominant and subordinate perspectives; can practice stating the strengths and positive aspects of various cultures; and can discuss how internalizing a negative view about self may affect someone's confidence. These students are ready for discussions of how race, class, gender and other characteristics intersect to shape how power and privilege are actualized in society.

Sara: Little kids and adolescents are pretty hip and smart. They have a great deal of learned knowledge and personal awareness. I wonder why teachers don't encourage a more substantive discussion of issues?

Elise: Yes, my brother Mike Jr. taught me this when he was about seven or eight. We were out shopping and I went from a large department store to a store for teens. I never expected that he would notice the differences in the store: the music, pictures, sale staff, and décor. He took in plenty and expressed it all at the dinner table that night. He mentioned how the teen store was more designed for girls like me and my friends, and they had pictures of good looking guys, looking cool all around, and there were a lot of pretty girls all around, but they were too old for him. However, the most revealing thing he said was that he didn't see any black kids in there, like we would see when watching videos on MTV.

Student-Student Interactions

How important do you think are student-to-student interactions across race and class lines? How much will you promote these kinds of interactions? In the elementary grades, teachers are often asked by parents, "Who are my kid's friends? I want to know because we are planning her birthday party. I want to contact the parents to invite them to the party." The teacher's response may not be race- and gender-inclusive if opportunities are not provided in the class for students to develop cross-race and -gender friendships.

Do you think such friendships are important enough to work to see that they take place? For some students, schools are the sites where they have their first sustained cross-racial experience. Orchestrating the cross-racial experience is often important to its success. There is increasing evidence that when students are able to interact with other students from varying racial, ethnic, and other backgrounds, it enhances their preparation for fuller participation in a diverse democratic society. The American Education Council (2002) reports that students who have experiences rich in diversity are more likely to contribute to community and volunteer efforts, to become active in politics, to demonstrate more cultural awareness and participate more often in activities that promote racial understanding, and are more likely to understand that awareness of racial and ethnic differences is crucial to ensuring that differences do not become divisive in our society (p.14). Also, when students from different racial and cultural backgrounds are in a classroom together, the learning environment is enhanced for both students and teacher. In addition, according to The American Council (2002), students who get to know people with a range of backgrounds and ideas are better critical thinkers, and also show greater social and interpersonal development than students with less exposure to diversity (p. 14).

In a classroom where there are more than two ethnic groups, especially blacks and whites, the possibility of an "us-versus-them" mentality, which often impedes students from forming friendships outside of their own ethnic group, can be reduced (Moody, 1997). In order to promote cross-racial friendships, Moody (1997) suggests that teachers encourage students of different races to join after-school clubs and participate in athletic activities. After-school programs help to reduce absenteeism, increase homework completion, and produce better school behavior and higher test scores (Center for Research on Out-of-School Time, 2001). In addition, Moody (1997) believes that teachers should take a different approach to assigning students to particular classes. For example, he contends that "instead of the 'dumb versus the smart' reading group, a teaching approach that can disproportionately assign minority students to less ambitious classes, you could mix the kids so they see each other as working together and see that these people are 'just like me'" (Huget 2002).

Sara: You know, you are the first Anglo that I have ever called a friend. We are friends, aren't we? I knew some white kids when I was in high school, but I mainly hung around with other Latinos. When I would go and visit my father, I would talk to a few white girls around where he now lives. We got along fairly well, doing small-talk kinds of stuff, but they never introduced me to any boys or invited me to go to a party with them. So after a while, I left them alone.

Elise: I bet you were much more popular than I was. It wasn't that I didn't know a lot of kids, and that they didn't like me, but I never really felt I could compete socially. I rarely had any dates, and I had a tough time getting a date for my senior prom. In fact, I believe my mother was behind it. There were very, very few kids of color at my school, maybe about a dozen, spread across the four grade levels. Now and again, I would talk to Ralph, this African American boy in my math class. But when I invited him over for a study session one Saturday, my folks were cool toward him. They did not say anything, but it did start me to think that we never had any people of color over to my house. My parents have never talked about any friends of color that they had when they attended State U. The only black and Latino items we have in the house are some CDs. My folks did watch the Cosby Show, and, oh yes, Mike Jr. does have a couple of posters of black ball players hanging on the wall in his room; but that's it.

Sara: Your parents treated me pretty well when I first met them. How do you explain that?

Elise: I don't know, but don't get the idea that they're monsters. I will tell you something, if you don't hold it against me. I never told my folks you were Latino and of course they couldn't tell from your last name before we arrived. Mother did ask me, when I walked them out to the car on the day we moved in, if I would be more comfortable with another roommate. Mike Jr. stood up for you. He said you are nice and your folks are nice, and besides you are pretty, and he is sorry that he is not older.

Sara: Wow Elise, am I seeing a new you? Maybe I have underestimated you. Yes, we do have a growing friendship. So, don't get angry at what I am about to say. Mike Jr. didn't stand up for me; he stood up for you and himself, and the elimination of racial prejudice.

Elise: Yeah, you're right.

Gay and Lesbian Students

How do you handle discussions of human sexuality? What is the attitude and behavior of your relatives and friends when people declare they are homosexual? How will you deal with homosexuality and heterosexuality in your classroom? The Gay, Lesbian and Straight Education Network (GLSEN) reports that schools are not doing enough to safeguard gay, lesbian, bisexual and transgendered students. GLSEN reports the results of a survey of 42 school districts across the country. The school districts were asked the following questions:

- Do the schools have policies protecting students and staff from discrimination or harassment based upon their sexual orientation?
- Does the staff receive training about dealing with gay and lesbian youth?
- Does the curriculum contain accurate information about gay people?
- Does the district support the formation of student clubs that seek to address prejudice at school?

GLSEN reports, "Sixteen of the districts got a grade of F, meaning that they answered yes to no more than one of the questions. . . . The average grade for the 42 school districts was a D, with three-quarters of the districts providing no training for teachers or staff on dealing with gay and lesbian students" (p. 1). GLSEN (1998) also reports that a survey by the state of Massachusetts found that 97 percent of suburban high school students had heard anti-gay slurs like "faggot" at school and a whopping 53 percent had heard such language from their teachers (p. 1). Also, increasingly in the research dealing with sexual orientation and youth suicide, there is evidence that existing data are sufficiently compelling in showing a connection. In addition, some studies are noting a stronger association between homosexuality and suicide in males more so than females (Remafedia, 1999).

Elise: Did you read about Derek Henkle who sued school officials in Reno, Nevada because he was constantly humiliated and beat up when he declared he was gay and intended to be open about it?

Sara: I saw it on television. He accepted a "$451,000 pre-trial settlement, the largest of its kind in history." (GLSEN, 2002). I know that sounds like a lot of money, but it is not nearly enough to pay for all of that emotional, physical and verbal abuse. I am going to let students know where I stand on this issue. What about you?

Elise: I will let students know that I will not tolerate any gay-bashing or name-calling, if one or two students has two moms and so forth. However, I think teachers also have to be careful and not purposely bring up issues that some parents may find objectionable.

Sara: Is that really enough? If you don't openly stand up for gay and lesbian students, especially when there are slurs called out so publicly in almost every school, then the gay and lesbian students will look at you as if you are condoning that behavior. Also, don't you think that the use of slurs is an indication of larger attitude problems that need to be dealt with?

Extracurricular Activities

Alongside the formal curricula in schools, there are also extracurricular activities. Eckhert (1989) contends that when students participate in extracurricular activities they are seeking to control their environment, define their age group, and set guidelines for interaction among themselves and adults. In middle schools and high schools, the establishment of these extracurricular organizations encourages the reinforcement of knowledge, skills and interests held by students. This often reflects particular socioeconomic and cultural backgrounds. As membership builds based upon socioeconomic class and culture, the sanctioned clubs and organizations reinforce separation on campus. For example, in some schools it is not uncommon to find academically oriented clubs (e.g., debate, chess, investment) and certain sports teams like polo, golf, and tennis dominated by white middle-class and upper-middle-class students, and other kinds of clubs (e.g., pop music, drama) and team sports like basketball and football dominated by African Americans from lower socioeconomic backgrounds. Thomas and Moran (1991) report that although some division along racial, ethnic, and class lines in the extracurricular activities can be seen as reflecting student choice, the school itself also reinforces and initiates such divisions. This occurs during new student orientation and when schools promote separate proms and graduation receptions.

It is argued that students of color demand these separate and equal events, and this is so. But the demand is located in students of color being denied equity and equality in school and classroom life and therefore emerges from a need for space where they and their culture will be respected.

Transiency

One form of diversity that many schools have to contend with is transiency. Hodgkinson (2002) tells us that "although about 3 million children are born each year, up to 40 million Americans move in that same period, making mobility far more important than births in explaining population changes. Many teachers have 22 students in the fall and 22 in the following spring, but 20 out of 22 are different students" (p. 3). Adding to students' transiency is teachers' transiency. Teachers' turnover at high-poverty schools—20 percent in comparison to 12.9 percent in low-poverty schools—can affect the diversity program in the school. Ingersoll (2002) reports that not only do teachers leave high-poverty schools, they often abandon the profession.

Sara: Do you still plan to get a teaching job in the suburbs?

Elise: Not really. I want to teach at a school like where I attended because I hear that the inner suburban ring will see a major increase in student diversity: more people of color, more immigrants, more students learning English as a second language (ESL), and more students of poverty. Teaching in an inner suburb will increasingly resemble teaching in an inner city (Hodgkinson, 2002).

Sara: I can't figure you out. For a while I thought you were becoming a proponent of diversity. But now I don't know, when I hear you say things like that.

Elise: Slowly, I am becoming a proponent of diversity. Let me be honest, old attitudes and habits die hard. I am working on my diversity hang-up, but it isn't easy. Sometimes, I am so torn and confused, and sometimes it's easier for me not to push myself in this area and to just do my work. Lord knows I have enough papers to write.

Sara: What about your students? Even if you are only teaching a class of all-white students, don't you think they need to know about diversity? Do you want them to think like you think about these issues? What will happen to your class of all-white students when they start communicating on the web with their peers in other regions of the U. S. or establishing pen pals with students who live in other countries? Our generation and their generation should eliminate the stereotype of the "ugly American."

PART III: APPLICATIONS

The struggles that Elise and Sara are having will be multiplied when they enter the classroom. Also, we must tell Elise that every school in the United States needs to have diversity included throughout teaching practices and policies. Here we are not only talking about developing tolerance for one another and eliminating hate words from our vocabulary, but implementing a concept of diversity that takes into account equity, power, and social justice while teaching. Willis (2001) helps to explain what is meant here. He studied elementary and middle school teachers teaching about the representation of segregation in *Young Martin's Promise* (1993) and the teacher's discussion of the book with her students. (Elise one day may use this book with her class.) What is significant to our discussion in Willis' (2001) analysis is the extent to which there are teaching silences or no discussions around white involvement and white agency in segregation. Willis explains it this way:

> For Janice and Susan [the teachers in the study] the story of Martin Luther King, Jr. is one of peaceful change, and the lesson is that conflicts can be resolved when people work together. . . . What is ironic in Susan's description of conflict resolution—'you listen to what each side has to say'—is that in the narrative of King's life, the white voice never gets to have its say, whether it is the pro-segregation white voice or the pro-desegregation white voice. It is the failure to explore the subjectivity of whites that leaves them missing in interaction in the narrative, and makes this an inadequate representation of race relations during this period. While the black opposition to segregation is audible and understandable, the white investment in segregation is silenced and inexplicable (p. 51).

Teaching the way Janice and Susan teach, notions of power and privilege are silent and diversity teaching is about superficially including one or two people from a different culture or background. Willis (2001) offers the following observation:

It is the possessive investment in whiteness, and the value of white identity in Southern society that is rendered invisible in the King narrative by ignoring white subjectivity and white agency in segregation. By focusing almost exclusively on the thoughts and feelings of young Martin as he experiences discrimination in a segregated society, the curriculum in use silences the perspectives of whites, fails to interrogate the meaning behind their actions, and obscures white agency in structuring and maintaining a system of privilege and power (p. 51).

Such analysis of diversity is often nonexistent in many classrooms. Developing the skills to do such analysis comes from commitment and motivation. Each teacher has to determine how committed they are to diversity teaching. Wotorson (2001) offers suggestions related to students, curriculum, instruction and parental involvement to help teachers with diversity in their classroom and school. He gives teachers six powerful suggestions for working with students.

Teaching Tips and Strategies	Discussing Diversity in the Classroom

- Studies have demonstrated a high correlation between teachers' respect for diversity and the learning potential of those students with whom schools have traditionally had the least success. It is critical that teachers have the proper preparation and materials to effectively teach respect for differences. By approaching diversity as an ongoing theme in the classroom, they encourage children to develop a lively interest in cultures, religions, ethnic traditions, and ways of being other than their own. This, in turn, will help young people mature into flexible, well-adjusted adults who are curious about their world rather than fearful of it. Teachers must also be encouraged to learn about their students' needs and cultures and to encourage their success.

- Teachers should investigate how much their students already know about various groups and the issues and concerns of these groups to determine a starting point for discussions on diversity issues.

Teaching Tips and Strategies	**Discussing Diversity in the Classroom (continued)**

- Schools greatly influence students' beliefs about the similarities and differences among people whether the subject of diversity is ever openly discussed or not. Students spend much of the day in school, and, for many, it is their main social milieu. They acquire attitudes from the absence as well as the presence of diversity in the student body and staff, in the curriculum, and in the physical environment. They learn by watching teachers who confront prejudice as it occurs and from those who choose to ignore it. Teachers are role models, and their actions say as much as their words, if not more.

- Sometimes when students are exposed to things or to situations that are outside the realm of their daily experiences, unfortunately, they may cope with their discomfort or feelings of inadequacy by making jokes or banding together to make fun of whatever it is they perceive as different. If that happens, they need to be told to stop and also told that what they are doing is hurtful. What's more important, however, is to think of ways that you can prevent that kind of behavior or use such experiences when they occur as "teachable moments."

- Children are naturally curious about the similarities and differences between themselves and other people, and their questions provide a wonderful opportunity to educate them about diversity and respect. During a discussion of family, the teacher might say, "There are all kinds of ways to make a family. Some families may have two moms or two dads. Some may have a mom and dad. Some may have one parent and sometimes families are made up of aunts and uncles raising their nieces and nephews or grandparents raising their grandchildren. What's most important about a family is that the people in it love each other." Whenever possible, try to help students recognize that there is more than one way to view an issue, more than one side to a story, more than one "right" cultural practice; and help them discern the standpoints from which other people's perspectives make sense.

- One way for students to learn about different kinds of family structures is to include books or other visual materials in your classroom that feature characters who are adopted, are living in single-parent homes, or who are being raised by two moms or dads, or by grandparents. The more diversity students are exposed to, the more accepting they will be of the differences that they encounter. If teachers have trouble answering questions about gay or lesbian families, for example, they may want to think about their own feelings about homosexuality. Since we live in a culture that is still rife with homophobia and heterosexism, it is important that teachers look closely at their own attitudes about it. To be truly effective in working with children on diversity issues, teachers must be willing to continue their own learning.

The curriculum is considered the lifeblood of the school. Wotorson (2001) offers the following comments about the significance of curriculum when attending to diversity.

- The curriculum materials teachers use should portray the contributions and perspectives of a variety of U.S. cultural groups: gays, lesbians, and bisexuals; people with disabilities; people of color; and both sexes. They should do so in a manner that does not reinforce and promote stereotypes or extol particular cultural groups. This material should also include discussions about who has power and privilege and whose interests are being served and at what cost.

- Teachers should examine the curriculum to determine whether it reflects multiple and divergent perspectives, engages all students in learning the different subject areas, and considers gender issues. Also, teachers should examine the curriculum to see how well it connects with the social context of their students' interests and experiential backgrounds, and with the types of information they would want to learn more about. In addition, the curriculum should be examined to see how it connects to the students' environment, including bulletin boards, books, videos, music, toys, and displays, to ensure that they are inclusive of all people and do not reinforce stereotypes.

- Teachers should tell students it is a reality of life that on virtually every issue there are multiple points of view. Yet, historically schools have tended to teach children to seek "the right answer."

Wotorson (2001) also tells teachers to examine the curriculum outside of their classroom. Pay attention to curriculum in the halls, in the school offices, and in the library and other resource rooms, He observes:

- What does your school look like? What do the halls look like? Whose pictures are displayed? Do they convey that power and privilege is represented across different ethnic groups, women as well as men? What do the visuals tell about the students? Do they clearly communicate that this is the school of all the students enrolled? Schools that appreciate and advocate diversity radiate life and diversity in visual displays. Posters depict people of different races, both sexes, and with disabilities, as well as extended and gay and lesbian families. Languages used by students and community members are used in the schools. Students' work is displayed. The school library houses a wide assortment of books featuring many different cultural groups. The school and classrooms are clean, warm, friendly, and inviting. Quotations and statements on posters encourage critical thinking about problems and issues students are facing.

Wotorson (2001) has a good number of good ideas to suggest to teachers about their teaching. He says:

- Teachers should allow time for the learning process to develop. Introduce less complex issues first, and create time to establish trust before moving on to more sensitive and complicated topics.

- Teachers must be prepared to respond to purposefully directed acts of bias. Students will carefully observe how you intervene when someone is the target of discriminatory or hate-based behavior. Silence in the face of injustice conveys the impression that the prejudiced behavior is condoned or not worthy of attention.

- Diversity teaching values small-group activities that allow students to get to know each other and to express their individuality. Thus, heterogeneous groups (in terms of race, gender, social class, and academic skill level), in which students work cooperatively, work well in many situations. Provide opportunities for students to work with students who are culturally different than they are; teachers should also monitor these groups to make certain that work on assignments is rotated, and student leadership depends on the task at hand.

- At the same time, homogenous groups are useful in some circumstances. In bilingual or multilingual classrooms, it is often helpful for students to work with others who speak the same language; talking over material in their first language helps them to learn. Sometimes girls work better in single-sex groups where they do not defer to the boys. Grouping practices should be flexible, and multiple groups should be used. Students need to learn to relate to their peers and not to categorize people on the basis of a permanent instructional group. At the same time, they also need the most optimal opportunity for learning.

- The concept of multilingualism should be presented in a positive manner, and the limitations of knowing one language should be discussed. Also, the languages students bring with them should be used as a teaching resource. In addition, language should be gender-inclusive, and free of gender bias.

- When teachers include diversity in their teaching they build a partnership among the home, school, and community. This partnership seeks to include parents in school activities and on decision-making and policy formation committees. The inclusion of diversity encourages communication in the parents' home language. It argues for meetings to be scheduled at convenient times and held in non-threatening locations.

- Teachers who include diversity in their teaching approach learning about the community both methodically and through various means. For example, they learn the community's history, become familiar with the housing patterns, introduce themselves to the community leaders, and visit organizations, associations, and religious institutions. They read the community newspapers and/or neighborhood bulletins. They communicate personally with parents, providing them with progress reports on their children, and they listen carefully to what parents say about their children and the school.

- Extracurricular activities are designed to avoid the perpetuation of stereotypes and categorization of students into stereotypic roles (e.g., boys as athletes and girls as onlookers cheering the boys). Students can join the activities of their choice, but they should be encouraged to cross boundaries and participate in activities that challenge the way they have previously thought about things (e.g., girls joining the mechanics club and boys joining the cooking club). The names and logos used to identify extracurricular activities (e.g., sports teams) should avoid using terms that may be offensive, such as a team using the name of a cultural group (e.g., the Mohawks).

Finally, Wotorson (2001) tells teachers to be active in their involvement of parents and other community members. He states:

- Involve parents, other family members, educators, youth service professionals, and other members of the community in the learning process. Acknowledge that the school, home, and community are interconnected and that all adults must work together to help children develop positive and healthy attitudes and behaviors.

Sara: What do you think about all of those suggestions for including diversity in your teaching? I think they are pretty good. I can use them.

Elise: Yes, they are pretty good, but what if you are teaching at a school where the other teachers are mostly ignoring diversity, and the principal is not promoting it? Don't you think it will be wiser not to rock the boat?

Sara: You are right that that could happen, but if you know better and do nothing, should you really teach? You are not helping to prepare kids for our changing society. In fact you are impeding social progress for many students who really need it, and this diversity thing continues to be a problem when there is no reason it should be a problem, especially in a democratic country like ours.

Elise: Okay, okay! I am going to come to your room and watch you teach. Maybe that will help to remove my resistance.

Sara and Elise are only two professional educators among many, who are sorting out what and how to deal with diversity. Hopefully, they will see that like their grandfather and grandmother, they too have challenges they must face and deal with in order for America's crown jewel to be appreciated, accepted and advocated by all.

PART IV: EXTENSIONS

There are many kinds of diversity present in American classrooms, and this guide has only touched the surface in addressing issues of diversity in the classroom. It has tried to help you to understand what some of these issues are and how they will affect you as a teacher. Further, it has tried to give you some ideas about how to treat diversity as an ongoing theme in your classroom, making it an environment that is accepting of the many differences that children bring to school. Look for ways to celebrate and incorporate these differences in your classroom, for by doing so, your students will learn good citizenship and their lives will be enriched.

This section provides you with more resources to explore issues of diversity in greater depth. Take advantage of them to help make yourself a more effective teacher for all the students you are likely to encounter.

BOOKS

Alas, R. (2001). Hispanic education in the United States. Lanham, MD: Rowman & Littlefield.

American Association of University Women. (1999). Gender gaps: Where our schools still fail our children. New York: Marlowe & Company.

Banks, J.A. (1997). Educating citizens in a multicultural society. New York: Teachers College Press.

Boyle-Baise, M. (2002). Multicultural service learning: Educating teachers in diverse communities. New York: Teachers College Press.

Bucher, R. D. (2000). Diversity consciousness: Opening our minds to people, cultures, and opportunities. Upper Saddle River, NJ: Prentice-Hall.

Cleary, L. M. & Peacock, T. D. (1998). Collected wisdom: American Indian education. Needham Heights, MA: Allyn & Bacon.

Crawford, J. (2000). At war with diversity: U.S. language policy in an age of anxiety. Cleveland: Multilingual Matters LTD.

Fine, M., Weis, L., Powell, L. C., & Wong, L. M. (1997). Off white: Readings on race, power, and society. New York: Routledge.

Grant, C. A. and Sleeter, C. E. (2003) Turning on learning: Five approaches for multicultural learning plans for race, class, gender and disabilities (3rd ed.). Hoboken, NJ: John Wiley & Sons.

Johnson, D. D. & Johnson, B. (2002). High stakes: Children, testing, and failure in American schools. Boulder, CO: Rowman & Littlefield.

Kohn, A. (1996). Beyond discipline: From compliance to community. Alexandria, VA: Association for Supervision and Curriculum Development.

Kozol, J. (1991). Savage inequalities: Children in America's schools. New York: Crown Publishers, Inc.

Ladson-Billings, G. (2001). Crossing over to Canaan: The journey of new teachers in diverse classrooms. San Francisco: Jossey-Bass.

Obidah, J. E. & Teel, K. M. (2001). Because of kids: Facing racial and cultural differences in the schools. New York: Teachers College Press.

Redman, G. L. (1999). A casebook for exploring diversity in K–12 classrooms. Upper Saddle River, NJ: Merrill.

Reyhner, J. (1992). Bilingual education. In Reyhner, J. (Ed.). Teaching American Indian students. Norman, OK: University of Oklahoma Press.

Rogers, L. J. & Swadener, B. B. (Eds.). (2001). Semiotics & dis/ability: Interrogating categories of differences. Albany, NY: State University of New York Press.

Rosenblum, K. E. & Travis, T-M. C. (1996). The meaning of difference: American constructions of race, sex and gender, social class, and sexual orientation. New York: McGraw-Hill.

Takaki, R. (1989). Strangers from a different shore: A history of Asian Americans. Boston: Little, Brown & Company.

Tatum, B. D. (1997). "Why are all the black kids sitting together in the cafeteria?: And other conversations about race." New York: Basic Books.

ARTICLES

Banks, J. A. (1993). The canon debate, knowledge construction, and multicultural education. *Educational Researcher, 22*(5), 4–14.

Cochran-Smith, M. (1995). Uncertain allies: Understanding the boundaries of race and teaching. *Harvard Educational Review*, *65*(4), 541–570.

Deschenes, S., Cuban, L., & Tyack, D. (August 2001). Mismatch: Historical perspectives on schools and students who don't fit them. *Teachers College Record*, *105*(4), 525–547.

Grant, C. A. (1994). Challenging the myths. *Multicultural Education*, 3-6.

Johnson, J. A. (1995). Life after death: Critical pedagogy in an urban classroom. *Harvard Review*, *65*(2), 213–230.

Kailin, J. (1999). How white teachers perceive the problem of racism in their schools: A case study in "liberal" lakeview. *Teachers College Record*, *100*(4), 724–750.

Ladson-Billings, G. (1995). Toward a theory of culturally relevant pedagogy. *American Educational Research Journal, 32*(3), 465–491.

Ladson-Billings, G. (1995). But that's just good teaching! The case for culturally relevant pedagogy. *Theory into practice, 34*(3), 159–165.

McIntosh, P. (1989). White privilege: Unpacking the invisible knapsack. *Peace and Freedom, July/August,* 10-12.

Tate, W.F. (1995). Returning to the root: A culturally relevant approach to mathematics pedagogy. *Theory Into Practice 34*(3), 166–173.

Tate, W. F. (2001). Science education as a civil right: Urban schools and opportunity to learn. *Journal for Research in Science Teaching, 38,* 1015–1028.

WEBSITES

Rethinking Schools
http://www.rethinkingschools.org
Rethinking Schools is an urban education journal dedicated to help teachers more successfully work with current educational problems and issues they are facing. of community life.

Digest of Education Statistics
http://nces.ed.gov/pubsearch/
The U.S. Department of Education's National Center for Education Statistics allows users of this site to search their publications using several criteria.

ASKASIA
http://www.askasia.org/
ASKASIA provides information on Asian culture, including articles on Asian philosophy and religion.

First Amendment Center
http://www.freedomforum.org/
The First Amendment Center provides materials for educators and others about the intersection of religion with teaching, character education, the Supreme Court, as well as other First Amendment issues.

National Association of State Boards of Education (NASBE)
http://www.nasbe.org/
NASBE's website provides varied publications for educators, parents, and community members on various educational issues including diversity, curriculum, family involvement, accountability, standards, and more.

PROFESSIONAL ASSOCIATIONS

National Coalition for Sex Equity in Education
P.O. Box 534
Annandale, NJ 08801-0534
Phone: (908) 735-5045
Fax: (908) 735-9674
Web: http://www.ncsee.org/

The American Association of University Women
1111 Sixteenth Street, NW
Washington, DC 20036
Phone: 1-800-326-AAUW
Web: http://www.aauw.org/

The Gay, Lesbian, and Straight Education Network
121 West 27th Street
Suite 804
New York, NY 10001-6207
Phone: (212) 727-0135
Fax: (212) 727-0254
Web: http://www.glsen.org/

The National Association for Multicultural Education (NAME)
733 Fifteenth Street, NW
Suite 430
Washington, DC 20005
Phone: (202) 628-6263
Fax: (202) 628-6264
E-mail: name@nameorg.org
Web: http://www.nameorg.org/

FOR REFLECTION

1. Which human characteristics and social factors do you include in your definition of diversity, and how do they interact?

2. Given the increasing changes in most social demographics, do you see your definition of diversity changing to remain current with the times?

3. To what extent did your high school embrace diversity as discussed in this Guide?

4. In what ways will you use the knowledge gained from learning the material in this Guide to influence the way you teach?

5. To what extent do you see a diversity connection between the formal curriculum and the extracurricular curriculum?

6. Which changes in demographic characteristics that occurred over the past decade are the most surprising to you and why?

7. What do you believe will happen to the students you teach if you ignore diversity in your teaching?

8. Have you known teachers like and Elise and Sara? Which one of these teachers would you like to have as the teacher of your son or daughter? Why?

9. Do you believe that students whose first language is not English should have programs available in the school to help them maintain their native language while they are learning English?

10. Which of your K–12 teachers was best at instruction? What did they do that you do and don't do?

11. Since six-to eight year olds are beginning to recognize diversity, and their actions and attitudes for and against cultural groups are growing, how will you teach students to accept and appreciate diversity if you classroom is racially homogenous?

12. The media plays a major role in shaping students' attitudes about diversity and other social issues—positively and negatively. To what extent will you teach your students to analyze what the media presents to them?

13. Given the growing religious diversity in the United States, how should teachers deal with the religion of students in their classroom?

14. What steps will you take to incorporate parents and community members into the educational process at your school and in your classroom?

15. Knowledge about diversity comes from inquiring about diversity in its many forms. How do you plan to continue your inquiry into this area?

REFERENCES

American Council of Education: Business-Higher Education Forum (2002). Investing in people: Developing. Washington, DC: American Council of Education.

Center for Research on Women, Wellesley College (2001). National Institute on Out-of-School Time fact sheet on school age children's out-of-school time. Available from http://www.niost.org/factsheet.pdf

Everhart, R. (1983). Reading, writing, and resistance. Boston: Routledge & Kegan Paul.

Federal Interagency Forum on Child and Family Statistics (2000). America's children: Key national indicators of well-being 2000. Retrieved August 25, 2002, from http://www.childstats.gov/ac2000

GLSEN (2002). Two landmark court settlements pave the way for a new era in school safety. Retrieved August 25, 2002, from http://www.glsen.org/templates/news/record.html?

Goodlad, J. I. (1984). A place called schools. New York: McGraw - Hill.

Grant, C. A. & Sleeter, C. E. (1996). After the school bell rings (2nd ed.). Barcombe, England: Falmer Press.

Grayson, D. A. (1998). Generating expectations for student achievement: An equitable approach to educational excellence. Canyon Lake, CA: Gray Mill.

Hodgkinson, H. (2001). Educational demographics: What teachers should know. *Educational Leadership 58*(4), 6–11.

Huget, J. (2002, June 11). Promoting cross-racial friendships in schools. *The Washington Post*, p. HE03. Available from http://www.washingtonpost.com/wp-dyn/articles/A27963-2002Jun10.html

Imhoff, G. (1990). The position of U.S. English on bilingual education. Cited in La Belle & Ward Ingersoll, R. M. La Belle, T.J. & Ward, C. R. (1994). Multiculturalism and education. Albany, NY: State University of New York Press.

Mirken, B. (1998). Public schools fail gay and lesbian kids. *The Progressive*. Retrieved August 25, 2002, from http://www.progressive.org/mpmirken998.htm

Nodding, N. (1984). Caring: A feminine approach to ethics & moral education. Berkeley, CA: University of California Press.

Remafedi, G. (1999). Sexual orientation and youth suicide. *msJAMA Review 282*(1291-1292). Retrieved August 28, 2002 from http://www.ama-assn.org/sci-pubs/msjama/articles/vol_282/no_13/jms90031.htm

SIL International (2002). Ethnologue: Languages of the world, 14th ed. Retrieved on August 25, 2002, from http://www.ethnologue.com/show_country.asp?name=USA

Sleeter, C. E. & Grant, C.A. (1991). Race, class, gender, and disability in current textbooks. In M. W. Apple & L. K. Christine-Smith (Eds.), The politics of the textbook (pp. 78–110). New York: Routledge.

Thomas, W. B. & Moran, K. J.(1991). The stratification of school knowledge through extra curricular activities in urban high schools. *Urban Education 26*(3), 285–300.

U.S. Census Bureau, Current Population Reports (2001). Home computers and internet use in the United States: August 2000. Retrieved on August 28, 2002, from http://www.census.gov/prod/2001pubs/p23-207.pdf

U. S. Census Bureau, Current Population Reports (2001). Population profile of the United States: 1999. Washington, DC: U.S.

Government Printing Office. Retrieved on August 28, 2002, from http://www.census.gov/prod/2001pubs/p23-205.pdf

U.S. Census Bureau, Public Information Office (2002). Cell phone courtesy. Retrieved on August 28, 2002, from http://www.census.gov/pubinfo/www/radio/pa0718.htm

U.S. Census Bureau, Statistical Abstract of the United States (2001a). Population. No. 47: Persons 5 years old and over speaking a language other than English at home by language: 1990. Retrieved on August 25, 2002, from http://www.census.gov/prod/2002pubs/01statab/pop.pdf

U.S. Census Bureau, Statistical Abstract of the United States (2001b). Population. No 66: Religious preference, church membership, and attendance: 1980-2000. Retrieved on August 25, 2002, from http://www.census.gov/prod/2002pubs/01statab/pop.pdf

U.S. Department of Commerce, Economics and Statistics Administration (1995). Bureau of the Census statistical brief: Women in the United States: A profile (SB/95-19RV). Retrieved on August 28, 2002 from http://www.census.gov/ftp/pub/apsd/www/statbrief/sb95_19.pdf

Vaid, U. (1998). Preface. In Yang, A. S. (1998). From wrongs to rights: Public opinion on gay and lesbian Americans moves toward equality. New York: The Policy Institute—National Gay and Lesbian Task Force.

Valenzuela, A. (1999). Substantive schooling: U. S.-Mexican youth and the politics of caring. Albany, NY: State University of New York Press.

Wotorson, M. (2001). Partners Against Hate: Program activity guide: Helping children resist bias and hate. Washington, DC: Anti-Defamation League.

Yang, A. S. (1998). From wrongs to rights: Public opinion on gay and lesbian Americans moves toward equality. New York: The Policy Institute—National Gay and Lesbian Task Force.

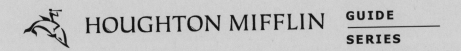

HOUGHTON MIFFLIN GUIDE SERIES

An Educator's Guide to
Field-based Classroom Observation

Gary D. Borich
The University of Texas at Austin

James M. Cooper, Series Editor
University of Virginia

HOUGHTON MIFFLIN COMPANY   BOSTON   NEW YORK

CONTENTS

PREFACE

Houghton Mifflin Company publishes outstanding education textbooks in the areas of foundations of education, introduction to education, educational psychology special education, and early childhood education. These textbooks introduce students to many concepts, policies, and research that undergird educational practice. However, as is the case for virtually all introductory texts, many topics are introduced but not covered in great depth. The Houghton Mifflin Teacher Education Guide Series is designed to provide more in-depth coverage of selected educational topics studied in the teacher education curriculum.

At the present time, there are seven guides in the series:

- Classroom Management
- Field-based Classroom Observation
- Diversity in the Classroom
- Classroom Assessment
- Inclusion
- Technology Tools
- School-based Intervention Programs

The topics for these guides were selected because they are addressed in virtually all teacher education programs, and contain vital information for beginning teachers if they are to be successful in the classroom. Instructors may use the guides either for required or enrichment reading.

Each of these guides provides pre-service teachers with greater in-depth knowledge, application suggestions, and additional resources on its particular topic. All the guides share a common format that includes an introduction to the topic, knowledge that the prospective teacher should possess about the topic, examples of and suggestions for how the knowledge can be applied, and resources for further exploration. Each guide also contains 10-15 questions designed to help the prospective teacher reflect on the concepts and ideas introduced in the guide, as well as a glossary of key terms.

Most teacher education programs now provide many opportunities for prospective teachers to observe in school classrooms and to partake in instructional activities. Integrating pedagogical training with experiences in schools allows teacher education students to merge theory with practice. In this guide, Gary Borich identifies key concepts and tools for helping teacher education students to focus their classroom observations so as to understand better the busy and complex interactions occurring in school classrooms. One researcher found that as many as 1000 interactions occur daily in elementary classrooms! Seeing and understanding what is happening in classrooms is not easy and requires considerable training and practice. Borich provides a number of different research-based lenses for viewing classroom behavior, and practice exercises to develop interpretative skill to make sense of the data collected. As prospective teachers take these tools into classrooms to collect and interpret information on classroom behavior, they will gain deeper understanding of the teaching and learning that occurs there.

PART I: INTRODUCTION[*]

Playing in the park, 3-year-old Jake looks up to see his mother approaching. He runs down the sidewalk to greet her. In his haste, he trips on an uneven stone and lands, unceremoniously, at his mother's feet.

For a moment, Jake looks stunned—about to cry. His mother wonders if he is hurt as he glances up at her face with a questioning look.

Laughing, Jake's mother scoops him into her arms. "Hi, honey!" she chuckles. "What fun to have you so excited to see me!"

The imminent clouds on Jake's face clear, and the toddler smiles.

How often have you observed a similar event—noting that split second when a child seems to decide how to respond to a given situation? Like Jake, each of us experiences many interactions with the world every day. As we try to make sense of these events, we create a personal framework or set of expectations about the nature of the world and our appropriate responses to events within it. This set of expectations influences what we see in a particular setting, as well as what we choose to ignore.

Many psychologists believe that professionals create frames for understanding within their chosen fields, just as individuals construct a frame for interpreting the events of daily life. Experts know what to look for and rapidly learn from what they see, and thereby rise to the top of their profession long before others who do not have a structure for sorting out the least relevant from the most relevant details. Sternberg (1995) believes that intelligent behavior may be marked more by the structure or frame one brings to a problem or task than by what one knows about the problem or task beforehand. Thus, developing a **professional frame** from which to evaluate and act objectively on events is a critical skill for becoming an expert.

---

[*] For further content on the field-based observation techniques in this booklet, see Borich, G. (2003). *Observation Skills for Effective Teaching*, (4th ed.). Upper Saddle River, NJ: Merrill/Prentice-Hall. The author thanks Debra Bayles Martin for contributions that appear in this booklet.

From observing the actions and interactions of professionals, less experienced individuals gain a sense of what is valued in a particular discipline and how professionals working in that field typically respond to events. But, while observation seems as simple and commonplace as dressing, eating, or driving a car, it is important to remember that, like Jake, each of us interprets the world and responds to it according to our personal frame. Without some outside direction, it is possible that our classroom observations may serve to validate much of what we already "expect" to see—allowing us to overemphasize some things and overlook others. As a result, observations need to be focused if they are to be helpful in our professional life.

The field-based observation techniques for the training of teachers come from more than twenty-five years of research on effective teaching and from national standards for the teaching profession representing how students and teachers best learn. For decades, teaching reflected a direct instruction model, where teachers were expected to present or "transmit" knowledge to students—who were expected to receive, store, and return information upon request. Many researchers and educators have challenged this view, suggesting that learners do not simply "receive" knowledge; rather, they actively construct knowledge through interacting with the social, cultural, and linguistic context in which an experience occurs (Richardson, 1997). Effective teachers function as able facilitators, coaches, and guides for students' knowledge-building processes.

Reflecting this more interactive view of teaching, the **National Board for Professional Teaching Standards (NBPTS)** was formed in 1987 with three major goals:

1. To establish high and rigorous standards for what accomplished teachers should know and be able to do;

2. To develop and operate a national, voluntary system to assess and certify teachers who meet these standards;

3. To advance related education reforms for the purpose of improving student learning in American schools.

During that same year, the **Interstate New Teacher Assessment and Support Consortium (INTASC)** was formed to create "board-compatible" standards that could be reviewed by professional organizations and state agencies as a basis for licensing beginning teachers. The INTASC standards (Miller, 1992) are written as 10 principles, which are then further explained in terms of teacher knowledge, dispositions, and performance. In other words, they describe what a beginning teacher should know and be able to do. Listed below are these 10 principles, which were intended in part to be acquired through field-based observation.

Principle 1:

The teacher understands the central concepts, tools of inquiry, and structures of the discipline(s) he or she teaches and can create learning experiences that make these aspects of subject matter meaningful for students.

Principle 2:

The teacher understands how children learn and develop, and can provide learning opportunities that support their intellectual, social and personal development.

Principle 3:

The teacher understands how students differ in their approaches to learning and creates instructional opportunities that are adapted to diverse learners.

Principle 4:

The teacher understands and uses a variety of instructional strategies to encourage students' development of critical thinking, problem solving, and performance skills.

Principle 5:

The teacher uses an understanding of individual and group motivation and behavior to create a learning environment that encourages positive social interaction, active engagement in learning, and self-motivation.

Principle 6:

The teacher uses knowledge of effective verbal, nonverbal, and media communication techniques to foster active inquiry, collaboration, and supportive interaction in the classroom.

Principle 7:

The teacher plans instruction based upon knowledge of subject matter, students, the community, and curriculum goals.

Principle 8:

The teacher understands and uses formal and informal assessment strategies to evaluate and ensure the continuous intellectual, social and physical development of the learner.

Principle 9:

The teacher is a reflective practitioner who continually evaluates the effects of his/her choices and actions on others (students, parents, and other professionals in the learning community) and who actively seeks out opportunities to grow professionally.

Principle 10:

The teacher fosters relationships with school colleagues, parents, and agencies in the larger community to support students' learning and well-being.

Much of classroom observation focuses on ways you can observe other teachers to learn about the teaching profession. The information you gain from these observations will help you expand your professional framework to include insights about teaching which follow the INTASC and NBPTS standards. But, classroom observation also addresses ways to apply observation techniques and insights to your own teaching. Thus, while you are observing others to learn about their approaches to teaching, you will also be learning to observe yourself—and to be observed by others. These observations can provide important insights about your growth and development as a teacher.

PART II: KNOWLEDGE

GOALS FOR FOCUSED OBSERVATIONS

The ability to consciously consider your personal growth is called *reflection*. There are many goals you will want to work toward in order to reflect on your own behavior. But some of the most important for focused observations are to achieve empathy, establish cooperative relationships, become realistic, establish direction, attain confidence, express enthusiasm, become flexible, and become self-reliant. As you observe professionals working to achieve each of these goals, you will want to reflect on your own development—and then set some goals for yourself. Because a cycle of observation, reflection, and goal setting is so important to becoming a productive and successful professional, let's consider these eight goals for focused observation in more detail.

Goal 1: To Achieve Empathy

Effective teachers exhibit *empathy*—a willingness to see events from different points of view and to appreciate others' interpretations or reasons for acting the way they do. An empathic approach can help you to understand student behavior from the student's point of view—which often provides insights for effective ways of dealing with problems or challenges. Your ability to empathize during classroom observations will serve you well both as an observer and as a teacher. For example, when you observe a teacher implementing an unusual classroom rule, you may be tempted to pass judgment on the teacher's effectiveness or on the rule's appropriateness—from your point of view. While your own experiences are an important source of information in evaluating what you observe, you will also benefit from trying to understand events from the teacher's vantage point. You may ask yourself, "Is what I am seeing working within the context of this classroom? Why or why not?" As you consider these questions, you may discover that a seemingly ineffective strategy in one context may be effective in another. As a result, your observations will extend beyond your personal and textbook knowledge of teaching to include an awareness of the variety of social and learning contexts that can influence a teacher's decisions. Enhancing your ability to empathize will help you approach your own teaching with more flexibility—and with the instructional alternatives you need to be an effective teacher.

Goal 2: To Establish Cooperative Relationships

Early on, effective teachers identify people who can help them in their teaching. They understand that, in the hectic and stressful environment of the classroom, people need other people to offer ideas, support, and collegiality. As you become involved in student teaching, and later in your beginning years of teaching, you will find a need to develop cooperative relationships with your colleagues. Experienced teachers have a wealth of information about students, curriculum, textbooks, and media with which you will be working. As you observe in different classrooms, you can and should take the opportunity to discover how professionals create and maintain cooperative relationships and how you can become an active participant in these relationships. These experienced teachers can answer many questions you will have now—and later.

Goal 3: To Become Realistic

Most beginning teachers understandably have an idealistic view of schools and teaching. While idealism motivates us to renew and extend our efforts, it also creates pitfalls when we are unreasonable in our expectations of students or ourselves. For example, beginning teachers who believe that schools *should be* a certain way may spend a great deal of time and effort trying to change a particular setting—failing to see and accept the strengths of the context they are working with. From your classroom observations, you will learn that schools and classrooms vary widely—and that each context offers both advantages and challenges. As you observe and reflect upon different classrooms, you will become more realistic in evaluating both what is desirable and what is possible in different classrooms.

Goal 4: To Establish Direction

Another purpose of classroom observation is to establish the professional goals toward which you will want to work during your student teaching and first years of teaching. By observing others, you will identify characteristics and practices you will want to emulate in your own teaching. Recording these characteristics and practices during observation can form the basis of short- and long-term goals of self-improvement. One of the advantages of focused observation is the opportunity to identify particular patterns and sequences of teacher behavior and to evaluate their effectiveness in a variety of settings. Over time, you should be able to identify teaching strategies specific to particular purposes and contexts that you value and to integrate them into your own teaching.

Goal 5: To Attain Confidence

Most of us in the course of learning to become teachers make judgments about what we believe is effective teaching. In the course of teaching, we then make decisions that follow from these judgments. Many of these decisions about what and how to teach represent gut feelings, the exact source of which may not be known to us. Some writers refer to this way of knowing as *tacit or practical knowledge* (Canning, 1991). Tacit knowledge represents what we know by experience, but rarely, if ever, articulate. Just as in the example with Jake, each of us compiles vast amounts of tacit knowledge through everyday experiences. This knowledge often guides our actions as effectively as does the knowledge we gain from formal instruction. Our tacit knowledge is put to use by acting, sometimes unconsciously, on thoughts and feelings acquired from day-to-day experiences. Tacitly acquired knowledge often helps us distinguish what is right from wrong, appropriate from inappropriate, and effective from ineffective. Through observation, beginning teachers learn to test their judgments and to trust their instincts.

Goal 6: To Express Enthusiasm

Effective teachers demonstrate an enthusiasm for the subject matter they teach, and for the teaching profession. The ability to express enthusiasm stems from a belief that what we do matters. Having an image of a future self who is growing provides us with the courage to work hard and attain the goals we select. You can enhance your personal enthusiasm and learn to calm your fears by seeing others attain goals, perform activities, and produce results that you would like to accomplish. As you observe successful teachers, you will find yourself saying, "I want to be like that." From this, you will set goals such as, "I want to *try* that." As you try various techniques, you then discover that you *can* accomplish particular goals, and your enthusiasm for teaching grows. Focused observation of successful and enthusiastic teachers can help you dare to express the enthusiasm within you.

Goal 7: To Become Flexible

A part of setting and achieving any goal is being willing to take risks. Effective teachers most often achieve their goals in the context of trial and error. This means that to develop as a professional, you must try new things and risk occasional failure. We seldom succeed in attaining a goal, performing an activity, or achieving the desired results the first time we try something. The key to our improvement is to persevere long enough for success to occur. Since some struggle is inevitable in becoming an effective teacher, it is important to develop a flexible attitude. For example, you may practice a behavior exactly as you observed it in a particular classroom—and not achieve the desired results. This is the time to consider various aspects of the behavior that could be adapted or altered in some way. The fact that you have observed teachers in many different settings will likely suggest variations you can try to improve your strategy. In other words, as you observe teachers implementing a strategy in different ways, you, too, can gain the ability to see and act more flexibly in your own teaching.

Goal 8: To Become Self-reliant

Perhaps the most important goal of focused classroom observation is becoming self-reliant. As you observe across many educational contexts, you will be building a professional frame from which to interpret events and make decisions. The greater the detail and scope of your observations, the greater your sense of personal confidence, enthusiasm, and flexibility will be in achieving your goals. Focused observation in classrooms will reveal that teaching is a complex profession for which no amount of formal training can provide all the preparation needed. It will also underscore the fact that effective teachers exist because of the challenges of teaching and that, with careful reflection and effort you can be one of them.

PROFESSIONAL GOALS FOR IMPROVEMENT

As you prepare to observe in classrooms, it is important to consider what sort of "lens" you will observe through. All of us develop our own views of the world or ways of looking at life. Our view is influenced throughout our lives by the experiences we have, the emotions we feel, and the way we choose to interpret them. What are the characteristics of your world view? How might they affect the way you "see" particular teachers or classrooms? Let's try a little experiment to find out. Read the sentences below (from a study by Sanford & Garrod, 1981, p. 114) and create a mental picture from the words.

John was on his way to school.

What picture formed in your mind as you read the sentence? How old is John? What does he look like? What time of day is it? What is the weather like? Remember what you pictured and read on.

He was terribly worried about the math lesson.

Now what is the picture you see? Has it changed? Does being worried about a math lesson "fit" the picture you have already developed in your mind about what John is like? Keep reading.

He thought he might not be able to control the class again today.

Has anything in your mental picture changed? What? Why? Now keep reading.

It was not a normal part of a janitor's duties.

What do you see now in your mental picture? How old is John? What does he look like? Were you surprised at the information in the last sentence? Why?

Just as you formed mental images and expectations while reading about John, you have probably formed a number of mental images and expectations about schools and classrooms. To explore a few of these images, take a minute and make a list with the following headings:

The perfect classroom	The perfect teacher	The perfect lesson
(how it looks, smells, feels, etc.)	(his or her classroom management, instructional methods and presentation style, etc.)	(subject, duration, type of activities, etc.)

Source: From Borich, G. (2003). *Observation Skills for Effective Teaching*, 4th edition. Upper Saddle River, NJ: Merrill/Prentice Hall. This and the following graphic reprinted with permission.

Now, take a minute to create a second list with these headings.

A terrible classroom	A terrible teacher	A terrible lesson
(how it looks, smells, feels, etc.)	(his or her classroom management, instructional methods and presentation style, etc.)	(subject, duration, type of activities, etc.)

What do you notice about the two lists you have created? Can you think of any specific experiences that may have influenced each of your lists?

WHAT REAL CLASSROOMS ARE LIKE

As you make formal and informal observations on your way to becoming a teacher, it is important to realize that you are about to enter a complex and demanding profession—a profession that requires not only intelligence, physical stamina, and motivation, but also an acute sense of sight and sound. Your ability to perceive what is happening in a classroom will be critical to your success as a teacher. Because the teaching profession is complex, it is important for you to consider how your preconceived ideas about teaching and students may influence what you see and hear—and how you interpret that information. No doubt you have already formed, from your years as a student, a set of beliefs about good and poor teaching, teachers, students, and lessons. While these opinions and beliefs comprise an important part of your view of education, they can also act as "blinders," and even limit your teaching goals for particular students or settings (Walqui, 2000). In order to look beyond personal experience to obtain a more complete view of classrooms, let's consider four characteristics of classrooms that will affect what you see: *rapidity, immediacy, interruption,* and *social dynamics.*

Rapidity

One of the first things you will notice from observing in classrooms is that events move rapidly. In fact, some authors have estimated that there are up to one thousand teacher-student interchanges in most classrooms in a single day. These interchanges include asking questions, soliciting information, clarifying answers, probing for details, reciting facts, and responding to student requests. In other words, events do not move slowly in classrooms; they are constantly changing at a rapid rate from teacher question to student response, and from student question back to teacher response—creating a momentum of classroom activity that puts the teacher on the front lines practically every minute of the day. The teacher's ability to move the class along at a brisk pace, keep transitions between major instructional events short and orderly, and establish milestones toward which all students work contributes momentum and a sense of accomplishment to the classroom. Being able to see how rapidly changing events in a classroom can be used to establish momentum is an important observation skill.

Immediacy

Closely related to the rapidity of life in classrooms is the immediacy of the interactions that occur within them. Immediacy pertains to the need to respond quickly to rapidly occurring events. For example, teachers often do not have time to think about how they will respond to a student question, but rather must have an answer—some answer—ready for almost any question or situation that may occur. To delay or ponder for very long over what to say may create an awkward void in the flow of classroom events that can, and often does, result in a loss of momentum and problems in classroom management (Emmer, Evertson, & Worsham, 2003). But even more important, the momentum of the classroom must be maintained with responses and interactions that satisfy student needs and instructional goals. Few reactions or responses of the teacher can be put off until tomorrow, until the end of the period, or even for a minute. Most of the queries, questions, and solicitations made by students need immediate responses if they are to be effective in satisfying student needs. This makes practically every exchange a test of the teacher's responsiveness. It also tests the teacher's skill at keeping the flow going in ways that respond to, rather than put off, student needs for information, clarification, or further discussion.

Interruption

Think back to some of your experiences as a student. How often were classroom routines interrupted by an unexpected announcement from the office or someone at the door? A third characteristic of classroom life that you will notice is the number of times the natural flow of the classroom is interrupted. A source of frustration for most teachers, such events can so alter the momentum within a classroom that both student achievement and classroom discipline can be affected by them. Perhaps in no other profession are individuals interrupted so frequently in the course of delivering or providing a message than in teaching. Even unsolicited salespeople generally are allowed to complete their message—and who ever heard of a surgeon being interrupted during an operation by a messenger at the door! Messengers, public address bulletins, students straggling in late for class, changing course schedules, getting parent signatures, and making announcements are only some of the many interruptions that invade the instructional routine of daily classroom life. As even your earliest classroom observations will reveal, teachers do a lot more than teach, and sometimes are interrupted more than they teach. Being able to see the many types of interruptions that occur in classrooms and how effective and ineffective teachers manage these interruptions is another important skill for observation—and for teaching.

Social Dynamics

The fourth characteristic of a classroom is its social dynamics. Let's not forget: teaching is a group process. Even in one-on-one encounters, students are aware of other members of the group, and so rarely perceive themselves as individuals in the classroom. As a result, teachers confront many important instructional and management decisions related to group dynamics (Borich, 2004, chapters 9 & 10).

In order to capitalize on the positive aspects of group membership and encourage a sense of inclusion, many teachers implement discussion sessions, student teams, small groups, and the sharing of instructional materials to create opportunities for positive social interaction among their students. But learning in groups can also create opportunities for social distraction—which may dampen the learning process. Friends and enemies are often found in the same class, and excitement and expectations that often start outside class are easily carried into the classroom. There is, in other words, ample opportunity for groups in school to behave as groups do outside of school, with all the same characteristics: jealousies, competition, playfulness, laughter, and argument. Although common outside the classroom, these characteristics can create social distraction and off-task behavior within the classroom. Few professions require their members to work in such a confined space with so many individuals for so long a time during the day as does teaching. Add to this scene the fact that some individuals do not want to be there, and you have the perfect social setting for learners to become distracted by one another. The teacher's ability to plan and carry out activities that promote cooperative interaction and discourage social distraction can make the difference between an effective and an ineffective classroom. Observing the social dynamics of classrooms will help you discover what types of activities minimize social distraction and maximize cooperative interaction among students. It will also help you understand how and why teachers can sometimes be unaware of how their own behavior contributes to or detracts from establishing a cooperative and cohesive learning environment that includes rather than distances learners.

BECOMING AWARE OF CLASSROOM BEHAVIOR: LENSES FOR SELF-IMPROVEMENT

Given the rapidity, immediacy, interruption, and social dynamics of classrooms, it is easy to see why teachers are busy people. Few occupations could boast of having a thousand or more interactions with clients or customers in a single day, yet teachers customarily do this not just for one day, but for practically every day of the school year. Add to this the fact that the teacher's job is to facilitate the learning of subject matter content and to determine that what is taught is learned, and we have a particularly demanding job. The effect of this ambitious undertaking is that most of a teacher's attention is focused on the subject matter and the students rather than on him or herself. Within the busy schedule of a school day, teachers do not have many opportunities to reflect on the relative merits of the strategies and methods they use. To pause for contemplation during instruction could disrupt the rapidity of classroom events, and almost surely would result in a loss of momentum; to pause after class or at the end of the school day would require the ability to accurately recall events that may have occurred hours earlier. As a result, teachers frequently can be observed performing behaviors that are unintentional and that they are unaware of, such as dominating discussions and allowing too little response time for students to think through an answer, staying with or encouraging answers from high-ability students more than low-ability students, calling on members of one sex more than the other, giving preferential treatment to high-achieving students and more frequently criticizing the wrong answers from low-achieving students, and responding to students from various cultures and linguistic backgrounds differently than to those from the teacher's own background. These behaviors have been observed even among experienced teachers, suggesting that at least some teachers may be so involved in conveying their subject matter content that they are unconscious of many of their own patterns of interaction.

A second reason teachers may be unaware of their teaching behavior is that they are not always given specific signs that define "good" teaching. Broad indexes of effectiveness, such as the number of students completing homework, high grades on classroom quizzes, accumulated points for work completed, and improvement from year to year on standardized tests, are often used to gauge progress within a classroom. Although these are convenient end products of individual student progress, their disadvantage for determining a teacher's effectiveness is that many factors other than the instruction being provided can contribute to them—student motivation, aptitude, past achievement, learning readiness, and home life, to name only a few. Also, since end products often result from many different instructional activities over an extended period of time, they rarely point explicitly to what should be changed to improve the quality of the outcome, and therefore provide little corrective value for changing teacher behavior.

Without clear signs of what to look for to evaluate their teaching, and without the time to consider and reflect on classroom events, many teachers fail to adequately consider their teaching behavior. Thus, focused observation activities and accompanying observation tools are needed to help you develop professional "lenses" for observing others, as well as for assessing your own development as a teacher. A detailed presentation of these professional lenses and tools for observation can be found in *Observation Skills for Effective Teaching,* 4th edition (Borich, 2003). Below we will present a brief introduction and synthesis of them.

As you learn to observe through these lenses, you will want to work toward four major goals: (1) to become aware of your own teaching behavior; (2) to discover alternative instructional practices and new solutions to instructional problems; (3) to learn your personal teaching strengths; and (4) to focus your reflections on important areas of teacher growth and effectiveness. Let's look at each of these goals for classroom observation.

To Become Aware of Your Own Behavior

Although teachers make many decisions each day about the instructional process (how to capture student attention, who they will call on, how they will structure the content, how to summarize the lesson, how misbehavior will be handled, what seatwork to assign, etc.), they sometimes make these decisions unconsciously in the course of meeting the demands of the classroom. They may become bound by routine, failing to recognize how easily decisions can be altered. Instead of being pulled along unconsciously by the stream of rapidly paced events in the classroom, teachers can and should be active decision makers who influence the quality and nature of events in the classroom. They should actively question their own assumptions, and seek input from parents and others on a regular basis (Compton-Lilly, 2000). As you observe in classrooms, you will become aware that the stream of events is not the same in every classroom, and that sometimes teachers make decisions simply out of habit. If your observations lead to questions such as "Should I be doing that?", "Could that work in my classroom?", or "Would I have done that?", your observations are beginning to make you more aware of your own teaching. That awareness can help you discover some of your own unconscious decisions and unchecked assumptions. Even after you complete your university preparation, taking the opportunity to observe others will help remind you of your own behaviors—and how they may appear to others.

To Discover Alternative Instructional Practices and New Solutions to Instructional Problems

Another goal for focused observation is to seek information and example behavior related to a specific area of interest. While each of us has experienced a number of instructional methods and practices as a student, there are many we did not experience—or that we experienced in a limited context. As you enter the teaching profession, it is natural to wonder about new instructional practices, methods, and strategies, and whether new and different educational ideas will help you become a more effective teacher. As you read textbooks, observe other teachers, and practice teach, you'll develop questions about the "how-to's" of teaching. Whether the basis of your curiosity stems from wondering about your own experiences as a student, from wanting to see some textbook procedure come alive in the classroom, or from having experienced a seemingly intractable problem in your own teaching, observation of other classrooms is often a practical solution for discovering and applying new ideas. For example, as you watch a teacher lead a class discussion, you may wonder how a teacher can successfully blend fact- and concept-type questions in the midst of the same discussion. Or you may encounter a problem with misbehavior in your own classroom and want to learn more about the variety of rules used by other teachers for keeping students from calling out without being acknowledged. Focused observations can be among the most rewarding, because they occur in response to an immediate need that has some sense of urgency for your thinking—and later, for your teaching.

To Determine Your Personal Teaching Strengths

Aside from helping you find solutions to instructional problems, focused observation helps put your personal teaching strengths in perspective. Teachers do not always see that a decision they have made, either consciously or unconsciously, could solve an instructional problem of another teacher. This may be due to the fact that many teachers rarely observe others and do not have sufficient opportunities to describe to others the positive achievements in their own classrooms. As you observe, you will discover areas where *your* knowledge and experience provide insights that can help other teachers address a particular challenge. Taking the opportunity to share insights about successes and challenges builds a healthy sense of competence and shared professionalism. This benefit alone is why so many career-ladder and professional development programs require peer observation.

To Focus Your Reflections on Important Areas of Teacher Effectiveness

Handbooks and reviews of classroom research, such as those by Banks and Banks (2001), Brophy (2002), and Richardson (2001) summarize the results of more than twenty-five years of research in classrooms. In these and related texts (Borich, 2004; 2003; Borich & Tombari, 2004, 1997; Cantrell, 1998/1999; Taylor, Pearson, Clark, & Walpole, 1999), the processes used by teachers to instruct students (for example, activity structures, questioning strategies, methods of organizing content) are related to student outcomes (such as engagement in the learning process and performance on classroom and standardized tests). This research has identified effective teaching behaviors related to: (a) the learning climate of a classroom; (b) classroom management; (c) lesson clarity; (d) instructional variety; (e) teacher's task orientation; (f) students' engagement in the learning process; (g) students' success; and (h) students' higher thought processes and performance outcomes.

PART III: APPLICATIONS

LENSES FOR VIEWING CLASSROOM BEHAVIOR

Because classrooms are busy and complex, observers often choose a particular professional frame-or lens-to gain insight regarding a particular aspect of classroom life. Over time, observations are completed using different lenses, resulting in a more comprehensive and detailed understanding of teaching and learning. While the lenses we will use are not the only ones that could guide observation in classrooms, each has been researched and has been found to influence the performance of learners. Other lenses for viewing classroom behavior are also available, and new lenses will undoubtedly emerge from classroom research in the future. For our purposes, the following lenses will serve as an introduction to acquiring classroom observation skills and beginning to teach effectively.

Area 1: Consider the Learning Climate

The **learning climate** of a classroom refers to its physical and emotional environment. Some observable features of the learning environment are (a) the warmth, concerns, and expectations conveyed to students by the teacher; (b) the organization of the physical aspects of the classroom, which promotes or precludes cohesion and interaction among students; and (c) the competitiveness, cooperation, or independence encouraged by the structure of activity within the classroom.

As you observe the learning climate of a classroom, you will want to note how students feel about themselves, about one another, and about their classroom, and the activities and materials that promote feelings most conducive to learning.

Area 2: Focus on Classroom Management

Classroom management involves how teachers organize the classroom and anticipate and respond to student behavior to provide an environment for efficient learning. Some observable features of classroom management are organizing the physical aspects of the classroom to match instructional goals; preestablishing and communicating classroom rules; developing and communicating instructional routines; establishing a system of incentives and consequences; and using techniques for low-profile classroom management. Because many beginning teachers find effective classroom management challenging, you'll want to pay close attention to how effective teachers orchestrate and facilitate learning with their classroom management skills.

Area 3: Look for Lesson Clarity

Lesson clarity refers to a teacher's ability to speak clearly and directly, and to organize and structure content at the students' current level of understanding. Some observable features of lesson clarity are informing learners of expected skills and understandings before a lesson; providing advance organizers that place the lesson content in the perspective of past and future learning; reviewing and summarizing; and using examples, illustrations, demonstrations and instructional media that can expand and clarify lesson content.

Area 4: Verify Variety

As you recall from your own experiences as a student, **instructional variety**, using different modes of learning (visual, oral, and tactile) maintains interest and attention. Effective teachers select an appropriate mix of instructional approaches to support particular learning objectives. Some observable features of instructional variety are the use of attention-gaining devices; variation in eye contact, voice, and gestures; use of alternate modes through which learning is to occur (seeing, listening, and doing); and using appropriate rewards and reinforcers to sustain student interest and engagement.

Area 5: Observe Task Orientation

Task orientation involves effective teaching practices that help the teacher maintain an instructional focus. It includes managing classroom activities efficiently; handling misbehavior with minimum disruption to the class; reducing instructional time devoted to clerical duties; and maximizing time devoted to content coverage. Some of the most observable features of task orientation are lesson plans that reflect the text and curriculum guide, use of rules and procedures that anticipate and thereby reduce misbehavior, and established milestones (for example, tests, reviews, and assignments) for maintaining instructional momentum.

Area 6: Examine Engagement

Students learn best when they become actively engaged in the learning process. Teachers promote **student engagement** by providing exercises, problem sets, and activities that allow students to think about, act on, and practice what they learn. Some observable features of teachers facilitating student engagement in the learning process are the provision of activities for guided practice; the use of feedback and correctives; the use of individualized and self-directed learning activities; the systematic use of meaningful verbal praise; and checking and monitoring of classroom assignments during seatwork.

Area 7: Measure Student Success

Students' learning is enhanced when they complete work at moderate to high levels of success. Some of the most observable features of teaching that promote **student success** are unit and lesson organization that reflects prior learning; immediate feedback and corrections; gradual transitions to new content; and a classroom pace and momentum that builds toward major milestones (for example, reviews, projects, practice exercises, and tests).

Area 8: Look for Higher Thought Processes and Performance Outcomes

Higher thought processes include decision-making, problem-solving, critical thinking, and valuing behaviors that alone cannot be measured by standardized tests of cognitive achievement. Some observable features of teaching for higher thought processes are using collaborative and group activities; demonstrating mental models and strategies for learning; arranging for student projects and demonstrations; engaging students in oral performance; providing opportunities for independent practice; and using performance assessments and student portfolios.

Although you will want to observe classrooms with specific questions or goals, your first few observations may be more general so that you can get a feel for particular grade levels or schools. These eight professional lenses can be used to help you consider the overall picture of a classroom. To see how all eight lenses can work together to inform your observation and suggest specific questions for further study, let's visit a fictional classroom taught by Ms. Koker. Before we begin, look over the eight professional lenses for focused observation below. Then, when you are finished reading about the events in Ms. Koker's classroom, complete the *General Observation Form* below to rate her classroom on each of our eight professional lenses.

General Observation Form

Instructions: On the blank for each lens place a check mark, closest to the word that best describes the classroom you are observing.

Learning Climate

Teacher Centered __ __ __ __ __ __ __ Student Centered

Classroom Management

Orderly __ __ __ __ __ __ __ Disorderly

Lesson Clarity

Clear __ __ __ __ __ __ __ Unclear

Instructional Variety

Varied __ __ __ __ __ __ __ Static

Teacher's Task Orientation

Focused __ __ __ __ __ __ __ Unfocused

Students' Engagement in the Learning Process

Students Involved __ __ __ __ __ __ __ Students Uninvolved

	Students' Success in Basic Academic Skills
	High __ __ __ __ __ __ __ Low
	Higher Thought Processes & Performance Outcomes
	Many __ __ __ __ __ __ __ Few

Source: From Borich, G. (2003). *Observation Skills for Effective Teaching*, 4th edition. Upper Saddle River, NJ: Merrill/Prentice Hall. Reprinted with permission.

A CLASSROOM DIALOGUE

The scene is a middle school social studies classroom. Ms. Koker is beginning a unit on forms of government. It is early in the school year, so the class is still new to her. The first several weeks of school were a bit rough for Ms. Koker because she was somewhat unprepared for the aggressive talking-out behavior of some of the students, and because of the new textbook, which devotes less time to some of her favorite topics. Things have calmed down somewhat now that Ms. Koker has established some classroom rules and has decided to organize her lessons more tightly with questions and recitation. Ms. Koker's goals for this lesson are to introduce three types of government, and then begin to develop the concept of democracy. Aside from a tendency to be loud and talkative, this class is composed of mostly average-performing students, with a few who are high-performing and a few who regularly challenge her authority.

Ms. Koker: Today we begin a unit on various forms of government. In the next few days, we will study the concepts of monarchy, oligarchy, and democracy, and how governments are formed using each of these three concepts. In fact, we will cover these three forms of government so thoroughly that at the end of the week, each of you will know how to create a government of your own using each—but, please, don't start any revolutions with what you learn! [Class laughs.] Let's start by defining what a monarchy is. Does anybody know? [At this point, some class members turn to their neighbors to ask if they know the answer.]

Ms. Koker: Please, no talking. Bobby, do you know what a monarchy is?

Bobby: No.

Ms. Koker: Christina, do you have any idea?

Christina: No, I'm afraid I don't, Ms. Koker.

Ms. Koker: Tim, you're not in your seat, so I'll have to ask you. Do you know what a monarchy is?

Tim: Yep, it's a butterfly. [Class bursts out in laughter.]

Ms. Koker: That's an extra assignment for you tonight. Okay, I'll tell you. A monarchy is a government that is ruled or governed by a single person. It's a form of government in which a single person, a king or queen for example, is the supreme head of a state for his or her entire lifetime. Now, what other names besides "King" or "Queen" do we have for individuals who serve as head of a country for a lifetime? Let's go from left to right across the first row.

Mary: I'm not sure what you mean, Ms. Koker.

Ms. Koker: Next. Felipe?

Felipe : You mean, what do we call someone who is just like a king, but called something else?

Ms. Koker: You're on the right track. Next. Anna?

Anna: Well, I would call a king an emperor.

Tim: [Talking out] Yeah, like in "The Emperor's New Clothes!" [Class laughs.]

Ms. Koke:r Okay, that's the second time you've spoken out of turn, Tim. You will answer two extra homework questions tonight if you don't want me to write up a detention slip. Now, go up and write your name on the board, so I won't forget to give you the assignment. [By now, talking has grown louder and a few students have left their seats waiting for Tim to return from the board.] Let's see now, where were we?

Student: [From somewhere in back of room] We were talking about emperors.

Ms. Koker: Yes, emperors, like kings, usually indicate a monarchy—or rule by a single person over a long time. Other names for heads of state that indicate a monarchy are *czar*, which was a title once used in Russia; *kaiser*, which was a term used in the early German empire; and *sultan*, which is a word still used today in the Middle East. These individuals, like kings and emperors throughout history, have often had absolute power over the people and lands they ruled. Traditionally, these rulers gained their power from the family they were born into, and not from any accomplishments of their own. In some cases today, a type of monarchy exists alongside some other form of government. Can anyone think of a country like our own that has a king or a queen? Let's go across the second row this time. Rashaun?

Rashaun: England. They have a queen and royal weddings and that kind of stuff that we don't have in this country.

Ms. Koker: Good, Rashaun. Some present-day monarchs, like the Queen of England, still exist. However, in England the queen possesses only minor authority and exists for mostly symbolic purposes, or as a way of showing the country's historical roots. Although kings and queens did at one time have absolute authority over England, today they serve mostly ceremonial functions. That was a good response, Rashaun. Now, before we move to another form of government, called an oligarchy, does everyone understand what a monarchy is? [No one responds.]

Ms. Koker: Okay, I guess we can go on. Let's see, where did we leave off in the second row? [Tricia meekly raises her hand.] Can you tell us what an oligarchy is, Tricia?

Tricia: I don't know.

Ms. Koker: Next. Raul?

Raul: Don't know.

Ms. Koker: Well, I guess I'll have to tell you—but it's in the chapter, which you should have read. An oligarchy is a form of government in which absolute power or authority is given to a few persons, instead of a single ruler as in a monarchy. These individuals usually come to power not through heredity or being born into the right families, but through some political struggle or compromise. Oligarchies, which were common in ancient times, are hard to find today, but some governments almost like an oligarchy still exist. Can anyone think of one? Jeff, Kathy, you're the last two in the second row. Any ideas?

Jeff : I'm not sure, but is it like a mother and father in a family?

Ms. Koker: What do you mean?

Jeff : Well, my parents have a kind of agreement—not written or anything like that—in which my mother is responsible for taking care of the house and my brothers and sisters, and my father is responsible for his job and doing repairs. That's a kind of sharing of responsibility, isn't it?

Ms. Koker: Yes, maybe. But it's not what we're talking about here. Kathy?

Kathy: I can't think of any examples.

Ms. Koker: Well, ancient Greece was ruled for a brief time by a group of persons called the Thirty Tyrants. This may have been the very first oligarchy. Also, we've been hearing a lot lately about a country called Yugoslavia. In that country power and authority used to be divided among individuals representing each of the states or regions. Now, let's compare the two forms of government we've been discussing—monarchy and oligarchy—with our own form of government. First, let's remind ourselves of what our form of government is called. Let's pick up with the first person in the third row. Quann?

Quann: I'm not ready.

Ms. Koker: Everyone should be ready when I call on them.

Quann: Well, I didn't get to read this yet. [Class begins to snicker at Quann getting in trouble.]

Ms. Koker: Okay, I'm going to make the rule that everyone must read the whole assignment before we begin a topic. That means that the reading for the entire week must be done by class on Monday. [Loud moans are heard.]

Tim: [Speaking without acknowledgment] But that means we'd have homework over the weekend, and no other teacher makes us do that.

Ms. Koker: [Ignoring Tim's comment] We still have one more form of government to discuss. Joan is next. [Class becomes noisy and restless at the thought of weekend homework.]

Joan: We live in a democracy.

Ms. Koker: What else can you tell us about a democracy?

Joan: Well . . . [Just as she is about to begin, the public address system clicks on.]

Principal: [On P.A.] I'm sorry to interrupt, but two lunchtime jobs are still available for any students who want to be paid for working in the cafeteria during the second half of their lunch. We need some workers for today, so, teachers, if anyone is interested, please write them a hall permit and send them to the office immediately. Thank you. [Roberto and Tim raise their hands, indicating their interest in the job. The teacher ignores Tim and writes a pass to the office for Roberto.]

Ms. Koker: Okay, we were discussing democracy. Time is short, so take out paper and pen and write down everything I say. Another rule we will start tomorrow, since you're not doing the reading, is to take notes on everything I say. The word *democracy* comes from the Greek word *demos*, which means "the people," and the Greek word *kratein*, spelled K-R-A-T-E-I-N, which means "to rule."

Brittany: [Calling out] How is that first word spelled?

Ms. Koker: [Responds by spelling the word.] D-E-M-O-S. So, who's next to be called on? [Rhonda raises her hand.] Okay. Rhonda, putting these two words together, what does the word *democracy* mean?

Rhonda: It means that the people rule.

Ms. Koker: Good. And who are the people in a democracy? Sam?

Sam I guess it's all of us—everyone that lives in a certain place.

Ms. Koker: Okay, a democracy differs from a monarchy and an oligarchy by who is given the authority to rule. As we have seen, in a monarchy, a single person, usually chosen through heredity, is given absolute authority, and in the case of an oligarchy, a small number of persons, representing only a fraction of all the people in the land, are given the authority to rule. In a democracy authority to rule rests in the hands of all the people. But how could such a system work when everyone has authority over everyone else? Next person. Diana?

Diana: We—or I should say all the people—elect persons to represent us. I guess that's what our senators and representatives do.

Ms. Koker: So when we say that all the people have the authority to rule in a democracy, we really mean . . . Next. That's you, Phil.

Phil: We elect persons—like Diana said—representatives and senators, and we give them the authority to rule.

Ms. Koker: Yes. So in a democracy like ours, the people have authority, but indirectly, through the election of individuals that represent their interests. In our form of democracy, called *representative democracy*, a legislature composed of senators and representatives is elected by the people. Does anyone know of any other kind of democracy? Mark, you're next.

Mark: Nope.

Ms. Koker: Did you take notes on the chapter?

Mark: I was going to do that tonight.

Ms. Koker: I will begin checking notes at the end of every class. Since some of you haven't read the assignment, we'll use the remaining time to read Chapter 7.

Reactions From Observing Ms. Koker's Classroom

Although this dialogue may not have been fair to Ms. Koker's everyday teaching, classroom exchanges such as this occur at almost all levels of schooling. They are, to be sure, uneven, rough, and sometimes even crude attempts to convey information in the midst of all sorts of competing forces—misbehaving and unprepared students, interruptions, quickly sketched lesson plans, and insufficient instructional time, to name only a few. The flow of events in a classroom, as shown in the dialogue, is not always a neatly packaged, smooth unit of instruction. Instead, teachers and students often struggle, sometimes with themselves and sometimes with each other, to complete the day's lesson. Although Ms. Koker's classroom may have had some problems, these problems are not uncommon for any teacher at one time or another.

Think back for a moment on the dialogue you have just read. In your opinion, was it an example of effective teaching or ineffective teaching, or did it contain some examples of each? What are your impressions of Ms. Koker as a person and as a teacher? What about her knowledge and use of instructional methods? Did she do the right things most of the time, even though not all the students conveniently cooperated, or did some of her decisions make it less likely that the goals of the lesson would be achieved? Do you believe the goals for this lesson, as stated before the dialogue, were met? If not, whose fault was it—Ms. Koker's, for not motivating the students; the students', for not reading the assignment; Tim's, for misbehaving; or the principal's, for creating a distraction at a crucial time?

Of course, all of these factors and others were instrumental in the way life in this classroom unfolded. But if we were to attempt to fully understand life in this classroom, each of the questions we asked ourselves would point us in equally narrow, and perhaps even biased, directions. A broader set of lenses than individual questions or idiosyncratic concerns that happen to gain our attention would be necessary to view classroom life. As you consider the interactions in Ms. Koker's classroom, look over the *General Observation Form* and complete your rating for each of our eight professional lenses for focused observation.

In what areas did you notice positive interactions? In what areas do you feel concern? Did seeing the observation form earlier help you "observe" Ms. Koker and her students more effectively?

The eight areas of effective teaching can help us achieve the breadth of vision we need to understand the events in Ms. Koker's classroom. Let's use each of these "professional frames" as a lens to achieve a more focused observation of life in Ms. Koker's classroom. After viewing the events through each of these lenses, we will bring all our data together to form some general impressions of the strengths and weaknesses of Ms. Koker's presentation. As you read the following discussion, add any notes to your *General Observation Form* that may help you remember key points about each of the eight lenses.

Consider the Learning Climate

Recall that the learning climate of a classroom involves the social and emotional environment in which learning takes place. Some of the most noticeable features of a learning climate are the warmth, concerns, and expectations conveyed to students by the teacher; the organization of the physical aspects of the classroom that promote or preclude cohesion and interaction among students; and the competitiveness, cooperation, or independence encouraged by the teacher's instructional routine. Using these aspects of the learning environment as our lens, let's look back at the dialogue to see how the learning climate may have influenced the achievement of Ms. Koker's goals for the lesson.

In many ways, the learning climate in Ms. Koker's classroom appears tense. On one hand, Ms. Koker seems genuinely committed to having students contribute their ideas to the development of the concepts she is teaching. But, on the other hand, few students seem to feel free or relaxed enough to share anything but the most obvious answers. As a result, very little genuine discussion takes place.

The manner in which Ms. Koker responds to students may also have increased the tension in the classroom. Rarely is an answer followed by another question to the same student. In the case of an inaccurate answer or no answer, the teacher quickly moves to the next student instead of staying with the student to correct a partially wrong answer, or drawing out a partially correct response that another student might build on. Even when opportunities present themselves to stay with a student and develop his or her response further, such as when Jeff equates the sharing of responsibilities among members of an oligarchy with the sharing of responsibilities between his mother and father, the teacher responds with a curt "But it's not what we're talking about here." These moves on the part of Ms. Koker enhance the competitive nature of this classroom by treating each individual student response as either all right or all wrong, thereby missing the opportunity to connect the discussion to the students' own experiences.

Another aspect of the tense learning climate results from Ms. Koker's desire to keep firm control of the events occurring in her classroom. Ms. Koker decided on a carefully controlled row-by-row recitation of answers instead of an open discussion. Perhaps in an effort to enhance classroom management, she restricts any interaction that is not a direct response to her questions. Consequently, she restricts the very type of response that her discussion-oriented agenda seems to call for. Without realizing it, Ms. Koker sets up a learning climate of opposing forces. The students resist being drawn into the discussion to avoid saying anything unacceptable; the teacher asks for student participation but responds with mostly unrewarding answers. Had the atmosphere of the classroom been less rigid, this class might have been more conducive to the cooperative interchanges being sought by the teacher. Now let's get a feel for some of the other lenses through which life in Ms. Koker's classroom can be observed.

Focus on Classroom Management

What did you notice about Ms. Koker's classroom management style? Did it appear to be more of a reaction to student behavior than a well-organized system of rules and procedures thought out in advance? At several points in the lesson, Ms. Koker seems to make up rules on the spot. Although sometimes necessary, this practice is risky. It can convey to students a sense of arbitrariness about the rule itself, making it seem less credible, and therefore less likely to be obeyed. Apparently, Ms. Koker failed to convey some basic rules earlier in the school year (for example, when to complete assigned reading and take notes). Without a well-organized system of rules and class procedures, Ms. Koker may continue to react defensively, at first tolerating a wide range of behavior, and later using valuable class time pulling back to respond to behaviors she didn't foresee.

Ms. Koker's classroom also exhibits problems with conduct. Talking out, for which presumably a rule was communicated earlier, seems to be a persistent problem. This comes as no surprise, because Ms. Koker's response to talking out, even in this short episode, was inconsistent. Notice that Ms. Koker is adamant at first about not speaking out. After reminding the class at the beginning of the lesson, "Please, no talking out," and reprimanding Tim for talking out, she accepts without reprimand a call out from an anonymous student. After which she switches unexpectedly to a nondirective style ("Let's see now, where were we?") more suited to an informal discussion session than the row-by-row recitation format she had pursued from the beginning of the lesson.

Did you also notice the amount of class time and resulting problems created by Ms. Koker's response to Tim's misbehavior? Although Tim's misbehavior might have been unpredictable, Ms. Koker's response to it may have created an even bigger problem. First, she responds by assigning extra homework, thereby equating homework with punishment. Second, during the time it took for Tim to leave his seat, go to the board to write his name, and return, the rest of the class waited without direction. The momentum, or pace, which previously kept the class moving forward and focused on the lesson, was lost. These momentary lapses, whether due to interruptions from misbehaving students, public address announcements, or visitors at the door, require special classroom management procedures to keep students engaged in the learning process. Ms. Koker's use of instructional time for discipline might have been avoided had she established and consistently reinforced an organized system of classroom rules and procedures from the start of the school year.

Looking for Lesson Clarity

Lesson clarity involves communicating clearly and directly, and presenting content at the students' current level of understanding. Clarity involves not only the visual and oral clarity of a teacher's delivery, but also the proper organization and structuring of the material to be taught. For example, to organize and structure the material to be taught, the teacher must know how much knowledge the students already have about the day's lesson. Notice that Ms. Koker begins the lesson by saying, "Let's start by defining what a monarchy is. Does anybody know?" The responses she receives, however, are not too encouraging. The first two students called on say no, after which Ms. Koker says, "I guess I'll have to tell you then" This beginning involves two aspects of clarity: checking for relevant prior knowledge, and summarizing or reviewing when it is discovered that the students do not have the knowledge necessary to understand the day's lesson. Had Ms. Koker not discovered early in the lesson that students had little or no knowledge of the day's topic, she might have gone on to more advanced concepts, never realizing her students did not have a basis for understanding the material she was presenting. As it was, most of the lesson seemed to cover the basics of what the students should have already learned from reading the text. Phrases such as "Okay, I'll tell you" and "It's in the chapter" are clues that not all of the class may have read the assignment, leading Ms. Koker to make explicit a rule that, in the future, all assigned reading be completed before a topic is discussed in class.

Some other aspects of clarity involve informing the students of the skills or understanding expected at the end of the lesson, and organizing the content for future lessons. Recall that, to some extent, Ms. Koker's opening remark reflects both these aspects of clarity. The students are informed of the three forms of government to be covered, and are told that they are expected to know how to form the three types of government at the end of the unit. Both of these ingredients of the day's lesson worked to make Ms. Koker's lesson more understandable.

Verifying Instructional Variety

Another lens through which to observe Ms. Koker's classroom is instructional variety. Instructional variety includes the varied use of rewards, reinforcements, and types of questions asked (for example, recall vs. application), as well as the teacher's use of instructional media to enhance student attention and engagement with the lesson. It also involves the flexibility of the teacher to change strategies or shift directions when needed. Variety can be enhanced by a teacher's animation (through variation in eye contact, voice, and gestures), as well as through the use of different instructional strategies and media within the same lesson. We did not see Ms. Koker teaching, but from what we read, there seems to have been little variety to her lesson. She persists with her questioning technique, even though she seems to have little success with it, until finally, out of necessity, she assumes a more direct lecture approach at the end of the lesson. Also, her questions call only for basic facts and definitions: "What is a monarchy?" and "Can you tell us what an oligarchy is?" instead of "What are its advantages and disadvantages?", "How is it formed?", or "What lessons can we learn from these three forms of government for governing ourselves?" Focusing only on factual recall may fail to engage some students in the learning process.

Instructional variety is also achieved by choosing specific activity structures to convey lesson content. The term **activity structure** refers both to how the students are organized for learning and how the lesson is organized. Both categories of structure appear in Ms. Koker's classroom. For example, we note that Ms. Koker chooses to organize her instruction around student recitation in an almost drill-and-practice format. We noted previously the possible mismatch between such a format and what appears to be the discussion-oriented goal of her lesson. At that time, we suspected that this structure was selected more as a way to manage classroom talk than as an effective vehicle for achieving the goals of the lesson. The choice of a recitation format led Ms. Koker to call on students one by one in a predesignated order, as might be done if students were giving their answers orally to questions from a workbook. The results were factual responses that avoided any risk on the part of the students, rather than the type of responses that could result in more complex or integrated learning.

Observing the Teacher's Task Orientation

Teacher's task orientation is the percentage of time allocated to a lesson in which the teacher is actually teaching material related to the topic. In the dialogue, attention to the misbehavior of individual students, time spent introducing new rules about conduct and academic work, and interruption from the school administrator all took their toll on the time that could have been devoted to instruction. As a result of these interruptions, the time Ms. Koker actually spent teaching the content was limited. When teachers inefficiently handle misbehavior or spend large amounts of class time doing clerical chores (for example, passing out papers, stapling and collating, reprimanding misbehaving students) which may be done more efficiently in other ways or at other times, instructional time may be only a small percentage of the total amount of time allocated to the lesson. Although we have no way of knowing the exact amount of time Ms. Koker's instruction was interrupted by noninstructional demands, a simple count of the total number of lines of dialogue minus the number of lines containing dialogue *unrelated* to the goals of the lesson reveals that about 34 percent of Ms. Koker's teaching was off-task. If this continued throughout the school day, more than 18 minutes of every hour would be devoted to noninstructional events.

Noninstructional events that compete for instructional time include formulating classroom rules, giving directives, administering reprimands, dealing with interruptions, creating orderly transitions between subjects or activities, and engaging in activities that structure the learning environment. The amount of time actually devoted to instruction often depends on how efficiently noninstructional activities are managed. Poor classroom management can detract from time spent on instructional tasks, decreasing students' engagement in the learning process and, predictably, interfering with success in completing assignments correctly. Although we saw only a brief view of Ms. Koker's classroom, she made some important decisions about classroom rules, the use of reinforcement, and the handling of misbehavior that affected the amount of time devoted to instruction during this lesson.

Examining Students' Engagement in the Learning Process

A sixth lens through which to observe a lesson is student engagement in the learning process. Like the task orientation of a teacher, this behavior is often measured as a percentage of time. Student engagement in the learning process pertains to the percentage of time the teacher presents instructionally relevant content (is task oriented) *and* the students are acting on, thinking about, or otherwise using the content being taught. In contrast to a teacher's task orientation, a student's engagement in the learning process may be much more difficult to determine. A student may look attentive or appear to be working through the workbook, but her thoughts may be miles away. In the example, part of the time Ms. Koker was teaching, at least some of her students were not engaged in the learning process.

By relying on individual recitation, Ms. Koker does little to involve students in the lesson. Aside from her questions and a few attempts to reward a correct answer with praise, Ms. Koker seems to encourage only a passive or mechanical involvement in the lesson. Absent from Ms. Koker's lesson is a broad range of questions that might excite the imagination of students and encourage them to keep trying after a wrong answer or no answer. Perhaps most relevant to the apparent disengagement of some of the students was Ms. Koker's drill-and-practice style, which requires students to respond in order across rows. This ordered-turns approach is often recommended for content in which many discrete pieces of knowledge with clearly defined right and wrong answers is being recalled. But Ms. Koker's content seems concept-oriented. After a time, students in the back half of the room could pretty much guarantee that they would not get called on during the class, providing even more opportunity for these students to disengage from the learning process. This, together with Ms. Koker's sometimes critical responses to a wrong answer or no answer, may have provided a reason for those who had already responded to turn their attention elsewhere. If more complicated and time-consuming responses were being sought, it may have been better for Ms. Koker to call on students who volunteered and who, therefore, may have provided answers around which she could have built lesson content. Ms. Koker could also have implemented any of a number of cooperative group activities to encourage greater student participation.

Measuring Student Success

What signs of student success did you see in Ms. Koker's classroom? Student success pertains to the percentage of correct responses given to classroom questions, class exercises, and workbook assignments. When an expository or didactic approach (which seems to fit Ms. Koker's recitation format) to learning is used, the percentage of student success after the first time through the material should be about 60 to 80 percent to encourage further response and engagement in the learning process. When the success rate is, on the average, less than 60 percent, it may indicate that the lesson content is too difficult or that the exercises are inappropriate for the material being taught. Ultimately, homework and further assignments should work toward creating an average success rate of 90 percent or higher.

Ms. Koker's students seemed reluctant to participate, avoiding, rather than engaging in, the lesson. Students found it safer to say "I don't know" than to risk a wrong or partially wrong response and be criticized for it. Ms. Koker seemed to accept only a narrow definition of correct responses. As a result, the success of her students in answering questions was not very high. Most students avoided answering altogether, and others failed to provide the correct answer. These two student behaviors tell us a lot about Ms. Koker's classroom. Failure to actively involve students in the lesson and present instruction that most students can respond to correctly are indications that the level of the lesson may not have been properly matched to the students' current level of understanding.

As was the case with student engagement, there are certain teacher activities that encourage a moderate to high success rate. These include providing correctives immediately following a wrong or partially right answer, dividing lesson content into small segments at the learner's current level of understanding, planning transitions to new content in small, easy-to-grasp steps, and continually relating the parts of the lesson to larger objectives and goals. Seatwork assigned prior to the day's lesson is one way to check student success rate. If a low success rate is confirmed, Ms. Koker could provide more practice opportunities or cooperative learning activities to actively engage students in the learning process before embarking on the next lesson.

Looking for Higher Thought Processes and Performance Outcomes

The final lens through which to observe Ms. Koker's classroom takes the previous lens, student success, to a higher level. For this lens our focus turns from the recitation of correct responses to higher thought processes, which arise out of teaching and learning activities that promote critical thinking, reasoning, and problem solving. These processes cannot be measured by tests of cognitive achievement alone. The higher thought processes required for analyzing, synthesizing, and decision making in adult contexts are stimulated by interacting with peers and adults and by increasing awareness of one's own learning.

By requiring oral responses, Ms. Koker encourages students to exhibit higher thought processes. But, Ms. Koker fails to follow up on her students' responses and lift them to a higher level. Recall that most of her responses were short and noncorrective, often moving to another student if the response was right, or failing to probe more deeply with another question if the response was incorrect. Ms. Koker saw each answer as either correct or incorrect—not as an opportunity to make a wrong answer right or a good answer better. This left her students responding at the lowest level of behavioral complexity, even though her lesson seemed, at times, aimed at acquiring concepts, patterns of thinking, and judgments.

In other words, Ms. Koker's presentation lacks a plan for helping her students meaningfully learn the content. For example, alerting her students at the start of the lesson to look for some of the features that could distinguish a monarchy from an oligarchy from a democracy might have encouraged her students to analyze the differences between various forms of government, their purposes in history, and advantages or disadvantages in today's world. Although not every lesson need achieve these types of higher thought processes, teachers can and should capitalize on potential opportunities whenever possible.

Also, while student collaboration was not a lesson objective, students collaborating with one another or building on the responses of others could have created classroom interaction that engaged more students and improved student understanding of the concepts being presented. Ms. Koker could have shaped responses in small steps or allowed the thoughts and judgments of individual students to inform the group, so that larger concepts, patterns of thinking, and judgments could have accumulated gradually and cooperatively. By using student responses and collaborative learning activities to encourage problem-solving and judgment skills, routine recitation at the beginning of the class might have turned into higher thought processes by the end of the class.

If you thought our description of Ms. Koker's classroom seemed a bit unfair, you're probably right. A lot happened to Ms. Koker in less time than it generally takes to teach a single lesson. Although our picture of Ms. Koker was compressed for illustrative purposes, teachers at all levels of experience and training are confronted with, and must manage, similar events. Real teachers in real classrooms are never immune from these and similar problems, despite the extent of their training or years of experience.

As we conclude our discussion of Ms. Koker's class, it is important to note the interrelationship among all eight lenses through which we viewed these classroom events. Seldom is the behavior observed under one lens independent of that being observed under others. This reflects the interactive nature of life in classrooms. In other words, if we were to observe Ms. Koker's classroom with only one or even a few of our lenses, an incomplete and possibly distorted observation would result. This is especially obvious when we consider how the learning climate established by Ms. Koker, her classroom management techniques, and the presentation of content all work to influence student behavior. Remember, too, that Ms. Koker's behavior, classroom management style, and presentation were influenced by her students' behavior during the lesson. Thus, it would be futile to separate these interactive aspects of a classroom in real life. Your final goal as an experienced observer is to understand the overall patterns and rhythms of classrooms using all of our lenses.

PART IV: EXTENSIONS

Because systematic observation involves observing and then recording behavioral signs in a form that can be retrieved and studied at a later time, it usually involves a record, or instrument. The instruments used for recording classroom behavior can range from relatively unstructured (taking notes), to highly structured (involving explicit procedures for when and how long to observe specific behaviors). In this section we briefly summarize some of the most frequently used tools to systematically observe and record classroom observations arranged from least structured to most structured. These and other recording formats and observation instruments are described in greater detail and illustrated in *Observation Skills for Effective Teaching*, 4th edition (Borich, 2003).

NARRATIVE REPORTS

Narrative reports represent the least structured method of recording classroom observations. Narrative reports do not specify the exact behavioral signs to be observed, but instead simply describe events, in written form, as they occur. Little guidance is given to the observer about what to include or exclude from the observation. Thus, narrative reports are sometimes referred to as *open-ended*, meaning that considerable flexibility about what events to record is given to the observer. You may find it helpful to think of narrative reports as note-taking activities. While there are many ways to take notes, four methods are particularly helpful for classroom observations: anecdotal reports, ethnographic records, thematic notes, and visual maps.

Anecdotal Reports

An **anecdotal report** describes a critical or unusual incident that occurs in the classroom which may be related to an event of larger consequence. It takes the form of a written paragraph that describes what, how, when, and to whom the critical incident happened. Because of the special significance of separating fact from interpretation, anecdotal reports are divided into two distinct parts: (a) facts (for example: "John began reading and the teacher asked him to read louder, saying, 'speak up, or you'll never be good at public speaking'") and (b) an interpretation of the facts (for example: "The teacher's comment to John in front of the class may have reduced his confidence and discouraged others from volunteering"). Anecdotal reports are most useful when they occur over time. For example, after an observer makes an initial interpretation, she returns to the classroom at a later date (perhaps several times) to clarify that interpretation. The focus of later observations is to expand on the interpretation's usefulness and validity.

Ethnographic Records

Ethnographic records report events sequentially, as they occur, without selecting a specific focus or incident. Ethnographic records differ from anecdotal reports in that the observer records a continuous stream of events on a laptop computer, usually for the duration of an entire class period and occasionally longer, and records all the behavior occurring, not just selected incidents. For example:

8:30 Children have just been let into the classroom. Several boys are in the corner fighting and some girls are sitting on the floor playing a puzzle. Teacher and teacher aide are in the back of the room talking.

8:35 Teacher says, "Blue group, get your folders and go up to the front. Green group, come here."

8:38 Noise level drops and children begin to follow directions, etc.

As with anecdotal reports, it is important that the observer record only what is observed, and avoid judgments or interpretations unless they are clearly divided from the factual portion of the record.

Thematic Notes

Thematic notes are facts recorded in traditional outline form, according to predesignated categories of observation. Much like the detective at the scene of a crime who jots down predetermined categories of facts, such as suspects, motives, times, and places, you can use thematic notes to jot down relevant data. Thematic notes can be recorded using Roman numerals (I, II, III, and so on), representing the major areas to be observed, and letters of the alphabet (A, B, C, and so on), representing the factual information observed under each of the more general areas. For example:

I.   Learning Climate

   A. Teacher's exchanges with kids are mostly businesslike.

   B. Atmosphere is competitive as workbooks are being checked.

   C. Teacher evaluates student workbooks orally by using phrases such as: "read over what you've written," "check your work," "follow directions."

To prepare thematic notes, first determine the precise themes or areas on which to focus the observation, and then jot down key facts corresponding to these areas as the action unfolds.

Visual Maps

Visual maps use pictures instead of words to serve much the same purpose as narratives. Visual maps portray the spatial relationships among physical objects—learning centers, reference libraries, groups at work—that may be important to fully understanding anecdotal reports, ethnographic records, or thematic notes. When you observe events that are clearly related to the spatial layout of a classroom, you'll want to construct a visual map to help you (and others) better understand your narrative record. Often, a visual map can help show how a particular instructional activity was implemented, or cooperative activities were organized (for example, how cooperative groups are spaced in the classroom to allow communication between the groups).

RATING SCALES

Narrative reports allow the observer a great deal of flexibility in choosing which behaviors will be observed. On the other hand, rating scales are more structured and offer you the opportunity to record not only what behaviors you observe, but also the degree of the behavior that you note. In order to use a rating scale, you identify, in advance, the behaviors you want to observe. Rating scales can be used individually or in conjunction with other observation tools such as narrative reports. Two common types of rating scale formats are checklists and summated rating scales.

Checklists

The simplest type of rating scale is **a checklist**. Checklists consist of a list of the behaviors to be observed alongside response boxes labeled yes/no or present/absent. Your job as an observer is simply to note the presence or absence of a particular behavior during an observation and mark it on the scale. (For example: Teacher asked higher order questions: Yes ☐ No ☐.) Simple checklists of this sort are most useful when you are observing behaviors that are difficult to evaluate in degree, but that can be identified as either occurring or not occurring.

Summated Rating Scales

Summated ratings differ from checklists in that more than two degrees of discrimination are possible. Summated rating scales help you focus more closely on the degree of behavior because they typically describe a behavior at its extremes and at selected intermediate points. As you observe a behavior, you compare what you observe with the scale and choose the degree or number that best matches your observation. When items represent a common underlying theme, scores across individual scales are summed and averaged, hence the name *summated ratings*. The most common summated rating scales offer five or seven degrees of discrimination. For example: This classroom is:

Teacher centered __ __ __ __ __ __ __ Student centered

You used a summated rating scale when you completed the *General Observation Form* to assess Ms. Koker's classroom.

CLASSROOM CODING SYSTEMS

Observation systems that help you record the *frequency* with which various teacher and student behaviors occur are called **classroom coding systems**. They are sometimes referred to as low-inference observation systems because they require fewer judgments or inferences on the part of the observer than summated ratings. Unlike the general concepts measured by rating scales, coding systems measure the frequency of specific and distinct units of behavior, such as "Teacher asks questions" or "Teacher used example," that can be tallied during relatively brief intervals of time. One of the most popular observation coding system is called a *counting* system. With a counting system, the observer counts the number of time intervals in which various teacher and/or student behaviors occur. A time interval (such as every five seconds), represents a frame for the observation that is established before the observation begins. Every time the interval or frame elapses, a tally is made to indicate which behavior on the instrument occurred during that interval.

FOR REFLECTION

1. Describe in your own words what a "professional frame" is and give several examples.

2. Of the eight goals for focused observation, what would be two toward which you would work the hardest?

3. Identify four characteristics of classrooms that make them unlike most other work environments.

4. Identify eight professional lenses for observing in classrooms. Describe the behavioral indices you would want to observe for two of them.

5. Using the *General Observation Form* used to observe Ms Koker, what were her strongest and weakest areas?

6. What is the purpose of a narrative report?

7. What are four methods for making a narrative report? Describe how you would record what you see for one of them.

8. How does a checklist differ from a summated rating scale?

9. How is a classroom coding system different from a checklist or summated rating scale?

10. With the help of *Observation Skills for Effective Teaching*, 4th edition, construct an example of a checklist, summated rating scale or classroom coding system for measuring one or more of the eight professional frames for focused observation.

GLOSSARY

activity structure This term refers both to how students are organized for learning and how the lessons are organized.

anecdotal report A form of narrative reporting that describes a critical or unusual incident that occurs in a classroom which may be related to an event of larger consequence.

checklists A list of the behaviors to be observed alongside a yes/no or present/absent response scale.

classroom coding systems Observation systems that record the frequency with which various teacher and student behaviors occur.

classroom management How teachers organize the classroom and anticipate and respond to student behavior to provide an environment for efficient learning.

ethnographic records A form of narrative reporting in which events are recorded sequentially, as they occur, without selecting a specific focus or incident.

higher thought processes Critical thinking, reasoning and problem solving behaviors that alone cannot be measured by formal tests of cognitive achievement.

instructional variety The teacher's use of different modes of learning (visual, oral, and tactile) to maintain interest and attention and promote learning.

Interstate New Teacher Assessment and Support Consortium (INTASC) NBPTS (see below) board compatible standards reviewed by professional organizations and state agencies as a basis for licensing beginning teachers.

learning climate The physical and emotional environment of the classroom indicating its degree of warmth, cohesion, interaction and cooperation.

lesson clarity The teacher's ability to speak clearly and directly to the class, and to organize and structure content at the students' current level of understanding.

National Board for Professional Teaching Standards (NBPTS)
A set of standards prepared mostly by and for teachers indicating what teachers should be able to do along with a voluntary system to certify teachers who meet these standards.

professional frame An objective viewpoint from which to evaluate and act on events critical to becoming an expert.

student engagement The teacher's ability to actively get students to think about, act on, and practice what they learn.

student success Student success pertains to the percentage of correct responses given to classroom questions, class exercises, and workbook assignments. When an expository or didactic approach to learning is used, the percentage of student success after the first time through the material should be about 60 to 80. Ultimately, homework and further assignments should work toward creating an average success rate of 90 percent or higher.

summated rating scales A type of scale in which the observer compares what is observed with what is on the scale and chooses the degree (number) that best matches the observation and then sums and takes the average of all the comparisons made, for example, as in five-point scales.

task orientation The teacher's use of practices that help maintain an instructional focus by managing classroom activities efficiently, handling misbehavior with a minimum disruption to the class and reducing instructional time devoted to clerical duties to provide students the maximum opportunity to learn.

thematic notes A form of narrative reporting in which facts are recorded in traditional outline form, according to predesignated categories of observation, much like a detective at the scene of a crime who jots down facts about suspects, motives, times and places.

visual maps A form of reporting in which pictures portray the spatial relationships among physical objects in a classroom, such as learning centers, reference libraries, groups at work.

REFERENCES

Borich, G. (2004). *Effective teaching methods,* (5th ed.). Upper Saddle River, NJ: Prentice-Hall/Merrill.

Borich, G. (2003). *Observation Skills for Effective Teaching,* (4th ed.), Upper Saddle River, NJ: Prentice-Hall/Merrill.

Borich, G. and Tombari, M. (2004). *Educational assessment for the elementary and middle school classroom,* (2nd ed.). Upper Saddle River, NJ: Prentice-Hall/Merrill.

Borich, G., & Tombari, M. (1997). *Educational psychology: A contemporary approach, 2nd edition.* New York: Addison-Wesley Longman.

Canning, C. (1991). What teachers say about reflection. *Educational Leadership, 48*(6), 69–87.

Cantrell, S. C. (1998/1999). Effective teaching and literacy learning: A look inside primary classrooms. *The Reading Teacher, 52*(4), 370–378.

Compton-Lilly, C. (2000). "Staying on Children": Challenging stereotypes about urban parents. *Language Arts, 77*(5), 420–427.

Emmer, E., Evertson, C., & Worsham, M. (2003). *Classroom management for secondary teachers* (3rd ed.). Englewood Cliffs, NJ: Prentice-Hall.

Interstate New Teacher Assessment and Support Consortium (INTASC) (1992). *Model standards for beginning teacher licensing and development: A resource for state dialogue.* Retrieved July 30, 2003 from http://www.ccsso.org/intascst.html

Richardson, V. (1997). Constructivist teaching and teacher education: Theory and practice. In V. Richardson (Ed.), *Constructivist teacher education: Building new understandings* (pp. 3–14). Washington, DC: Falmer Press.

Sanford, A. J., & Garrod, S. C. (1981). *Understanding written language.* New York: John Wiley & Sons.

Sternberg, R. (1995). *The nature of insight.* Cambridge, MA: MIT Press.

Taylor, B. M., Pearson, P. D., Clark, K. F., & Walpole, S. (1999). Effective schools/accomplished teachers. *The Reading Teacher, 53*(2), 156–159.

Walqui, A. (2000). Access and engagement: Program design and instructional approaches for immigrant students in secondary school [Monograph]. *Language in Education: Theory and Practice 94*(Topics in Immigrant Education 4). Washington, DC: Center for Applied Linguistics.

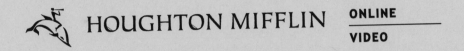

Video Cases Manual

HOUGHTON MIFFLIN COMPANY   BOSTON   NEW YORK

Table of Contents

The chapter titles below reference the chapters in *Those Who Can, Teach* Eleventh Edition.

The videos noted correlate with the corresponding chapter and include page references. Access the Video Cases online at

college.hmco.com/PIC/ryancooper11e

Select the student web site, and then click on HM Video Cases. You will be prompted to enter a passkey. Access is provided for free with the purchase of a new copy of Those Who Can Teach. If the passkey in your textbook has already been used, you can purchase a new passkey by visiting the Houghton Mifflin College Division Store at **college.hmco.com/students**.

Chapters from *Those Who Can Teach*	**Correlating Video Case**
Chapter 1: Why Teach? **VM - 5**	Video: Teaching as a Profession: Collaboration with Colleagues (page 9)
Chapter 2: What Is a School and What Is It For? **VM - 7**	Video: Parental Involvement in School Culture (page 48)
Chapter 3: Who Are Today's Students in a Diverse Society? **VM - 9**	Video: Culturally Responsive Teaching (page 56) Video: Inclusion: Classroom Implications for the General and Special Educator (page 66) Video: Motivating Adolescent Learners: Curriculum Based on Real Life (page 76) Video: Gender Equity in the Classroom: Girls and Science (page 78)

Chapters from *Those Who Can Teach*	Correlating Video Case
Chapter 4: What Social Problems Affect Today's Students? **VM** - 17	Video: Social and Emotional Development: The Influence of Peer Groups (page 101)
	Video: Social and Emotional Development: Understanding Adolescents (page 107)
Chapter 5: What Is Taught? **VM** - 21	Video: Elementary Reading Instruction: A Balanced Literacy Program (page 119)
	Video: Reading in the Content Areas (page 132)
	Video: Cooperative Learning at the Elementary Level: Jigsaw Model (page 134)
	Video: Cooperative Learning: High School History Lesson (page 136)
	Video: Academic Diversity: Differentiated Instruction (page 138)
Chapter 6: What Makes a Teacher Effective? **VM** - 31	Video: Writing Instruction: Process Writing (page 164
Chapter 7: What Should Teachers Know About Technology and Its Impact on Schools? **VM** - 33	Video: An Expanded Definition of Literacy: Meaningful Ways to Integrate Technology (page 185)
	Video: Multimedia Literacy: Integrating Technology into the Middle School Curriculum (page 190)
	Video: Using Technology to Promote Problem Solving (page 194)
	Video: Using Technology to Promote Discovery Learning (page 202)

Chapters from *Those Who Can Teach*	Correlating Video Case
Chapter 8: What Are the Ethical and Legal Issues Facing Teachers? **VM** - 41	Video: Legal and Ethical Dimension of Teaching: Reflections from Today's Educators (page 226)
Chapter 9: What Are the Philosophical Foundations of American Education? **VM** - 43	Video: Middle School Science Instruction: Integrating Technology (page 272) Video: Middle School Science Instruction: Inquiry Learning (page 279)
Chapter 10: What Is the History of American Education? **VM** - 47	Video: Bilingual Education: An Elementary Two-Way Immersion Program (page 321) Video: Diversity: Teaching in a Multiethnic Classroom (page 323)
Chapter 11: How Are Schools Governed, Influenced, and Financed? **VM** - 51	Video: Assessment in the Middle Grades: Measurement of Student Learning (page 342)
Chapter 12: How Should Education Be Reformed? **VM** - 53	Video: Assessment in the Elementary Grades: Formal and Informal Literacy Assessment (page 363) Video: Performance Assessment: Student Presentations in a High School English Class (page 364) Video: Portfolio Assessment: Elementary Classroom (page 365) Video: Elementary School Language Arts: Inquiry Learning (page 365)
Chapter 14: What Can the New Teacher Expect? **VM** - 61	Video: Elementary Classroom Management: Basic Strategies (page 430) Video: Secondary Classroom Management: Basic Strategies (page 432)

Chapters from *Those Who Can Teach*	Correlating Video Case
Chapter 15: What Does It Mean to Be a Professional? **VM** - 65	Video: Home-School Communication: Parent-Teacher Conference (page 471)

Chapter 1: Why Teach?

Video: Teaching as a Profession: Collaboration with Colleagues (page 9)

Collaborating with your colleagues takes time; it can also call into question your own strongly held beliefs about teaching. Yet collaboration can enrich your teaching across many dimensions, according to the teachers you will meet in this video. You'll see how elementary grade-level teachers work together to strengthen their math reporting system. You'll also see how they present their recommendations at a faculty meeting.

Video Questions

1. Teachers Ann Ruggiero and Jenerra Williams describe the benefits of professional collaboration. How will you transfer what you know about being a collaborator to your teaching career? Where will you begin?

2. What do you see as the greatest strength of the math work group that you observed? How might this group's work influence the way their fellow teachers view issues related to reporting student progress in math?

3. In the bonus video clip, "Challenges of Collaboration," Jenerra describes the challenges inherent in collaborating with other teachers, saying that it's time consuming and people have opinions you may not agree with. Suppose you were in charge of a math study group. How would you persuade other teachers to take a collaborative approach?

4. The Mission Hill School Student Report artifact includes two interesting categories: "Habits of Mind" and "Habits of Work." What might the rationale be for evaluating students in these areas along with more traditional academic areas?

5. In her interview, Ann Ruggiero stresses the importance of collaborating with other teachers. She advises you to find one person in your school to meet with on a regular basis -- a "collaboration partner." What do you think of Ann's recommendations?

Chapter 2: What Is a School and What Is It For?

Video: Parental Involvement in School Culture (page 48)

Making parents feel welcome in schools, and highlighting the fact that they're an important part of the school culture, is a surefire way to get parents involved. In this video, you'll see how literacy specialist Linda Schwertz engages parents in a book publishing project. You'll also hear from parents who explain why they are so eager to become involved in this and other school events.

Video Questions

1. Elementary school parent Patricia speaks to the advantages of being involved in her child's education. If you were to begin teaching tomorrow, how would you reach out to parents as allies in their child's progress?

2. Another parent, Monica, describes the sense of community she experiences when she gets to know teachers and other parents in her role of literacy volunteer. Can you think of any programs in schools you've visited that have fostered this sense of community?

3. According to Literacy Specialist Linda Schwertz, the Amigos School tries to entice parents to participate in a whole range of activities—some that are academic, and others, like a dance, purely social. Linda feels that it's the parents and students who create the culture of the school. Would you agree or disagree? Explain your thinking.

4. In the Bonus Video material, see the footage entitled "How Parents Become Involved." Linda discusses why she's flexible about the ways in which parents can help with the book publishing project. Given that time is of the essence for teachers and parents, what projects would you recommend that would result in a finished product that students can take pride in—all in a limited amount of time.

Chapter 3: Who Are Today's Students in a Diverse Society?

Video: Culturally Responsive Teaching (page 56)

We live in a multicultural society. Yet, classroom discussion of diverse societies often get short shrift in this age of high-stakes testing because many teachers worry about squeezing as much curriculum as possible into a school day. In this video, you'll see how Developmental Psychologist Dr. Francis Hurley weaves a lesson on multiculturalism into a traditional lesson on the five-paragraph essay.

Video Questions

1. Dr. Francis Hurley begins her lesson on multiculturalism by sharing her own story of coming to America from Canada. Do you think this is an effective strategy? If not, how would you introduce the topic of multiculturalism differently?

2. Thematic teaching allows students to study different topics through multiple lenses. In your experience, how does thematic teaching boost student learning?

3. If you were to begin teaching tomorrow and your goal was to teach using a multicultural perspective, how would you go about it? Explain your ideas.

4. Francis advises new teachers to become responsive multicultural educators by learning everything they can about countries around the world—one at a time. You have probably had the experience of studying particular countries. How has the experience broadened your world view?

5. Read Francis' lesson plan in the accompanying Classroom Artifacts section. What aspects of the actual lesson went far beyond the eight points you see here? How would you describe what actually took place?

Chapter 3: Who Are Today's Students in a Diverse Society?

Video: Inclusion: Classroom Implications for the General and Special Educator (page 66)

What does a third-grade inclusion classroom look like during a reading and language arts period? How does a skillful teacher work with specialists, such as an occupational and physical therapist to optimize learning for each student? In this video segment you will see how veteran teacher, Chris Colbath-Hess, collaborates with her colleagues to help every child succeed as a reader and writer.

Key Terms

Adaptive tools: Tools designed to accommodate the learning needs of children with individual needs.

Individualized Educational Program (IEP): A document that is mandatory for every child who is covered under the Individuals with Disabilities Act (IDEA) legislation. IEPs must include current performance levels, learning objectives, services to be provided and a plan for evaluating student learning.

Occupational therapist: A specialist who works with children to improve their sensory integration, coordination, and fine motor skills.

Video Questions

1. In reflecting on what she wishes she had known before becoming a teacher, Chris Colbath-Hess remarks that a) she hadn't anticipated teaching children with such a wide range of abilities; and b) that she could get the support of other staff members. Does Chris' realization that she doesn't have to know how to "do it all" reassure you about the teaching challenges you will face? Why or why not?

2. Many of Chris's students have an Individualized Education Program (IEP). What do you see as some of the most important advantages for students who have IEPs? What challenges do IEPs pose for teachers and specialists?

3. Peggy Tryon, the occupational therapist, offers several examples of low-tech adaptive tools that she has provided for students in Chris's classroom—everything from specialized paper to tennis balls that have been attached to chair legs to reduce noise. What do you see as the most important benefits of these tools? What would you do to avoid having students who use such tools be ostracized by their peers?

4. When Chris is unsure about what she should do next to help a child succeed, she sits back and watches. In your experience, what sorts of clues can students give you about their learning if you take the time to be a careful observer?

5. In the additional video segment, "An Inclusive Cooperative Learning Group in Action," Chris works with three students who revise their writing by adding "brighter words." How does Chris adapt her instruction for the three different learners in this group? (For example, Chris writes down the ideas of the boy sitting next to her).

Chapter 3: Who Are Today's Students in a Diverse Society?

Video: Motivating Adolescent Learners: Curriculum Based on Real Life (page 76)

In this segment you'll learn how sixth-grade teacher, Kelly Hammond-Franklin, breathes new life into her math curriculum by getting students involved in a real-world project—a student-operated school store. By taking turns working in the store, students gain first-hand experience in applying concepts, such as fractions and decimals, as part of selling notebooks, pens, and other school supplies. Through an interview, you'll hear Kelly reflect on students' increased enthusiasm for learning math once they understood its relevance to the world.

Video Questions

1. Kelly Franklin observed that before her students worked in the school store they just went through the motions of learning fractions, decimals, and percents. What aspect of the store do you see as the strongest motivator for her students in learning these math concepts?

2. One of the benefits of the store, according to Kelly, is that it increases students' sense of responsibility; essentially they are in charge of sales, keeping careful accounts, and handling the cash box. She trusts them to do so. In your experience, how can an increased sense of responsibility, combined with trust, foster academic success?

3. The students are not the only ones who have benefited from participating in the school store. In what ways do you think the story has helped Kelly become a better teacher?

4. The school store is just one example of math applied to a real-world setting. Can you recall examples of when your teachers helped you make similar connections? How would you approach real-life math learning in your own classroom?

5. In the bonus video material, you observed as Kelly led a math lesson. How and when did Kelly connect her instruction to the math involved in running the store? What visuals might you have added to the lesson (e.g., using the chalkboard or projecting a digital spreadsheet) to make the connections even more pronounced?

Chapter 3: Who Are Today's Students in a Diverse Society?

Video: Gender Equity in the Classroom: Girls and Science (page 78)

In this video segment you'll see how Robert Cho, a middle school teacher, promotes science learning for all his students: boys and girls. Rob describes how he keeps the girls in his classroom interested in science. He also reflects on the importance of role models and mentors who can help girls sustain their interest in science through adolescence and beyond, in his words: "a real-life human being who ten to twenty years ago was just like them."

Video Questions

1. What challenges does Rob face as a science teacher who is committed to having all his students succeed, regardless of gender? How does he approach this goal?

2. If you were to begin teaching science tomorrow, how would Rob's insights about girls and science influence your teaching?

3. What is the interplay between a regular science class and a Science Club for Girls? That is, how does one support the other? In your opinion, why is that important?

4. Rob encourages girls to pursue non-stereotypical roles in science, cautioning them against closing any doors. Can you think of other situations (such as sports or math) in which you could offer female students similar advice and encouragement? Conversely, can you suggest specific ways in which you could offer male students similar advice and encouragement in a different situation (such as drama or English)?

5. In the bonus video, you have seen how girls participated by leading the discussion of sandstone; laying out a plan for an experiment; examining rocks under a microscope; drawing conclusions; and examining rock components. What does the girls' behavior suggest to you about their level of confidence? What does it suggest about their enthusiasm for science? Can you recall examples of your teachers who boosted your confidence and interest in a similar way?

Chapter 4: What Social Problems Affect Today's Students?

Video: Social and Emotional Development: The Influence of Peer Groups (page 101)

Drama teacher, Voncille Ross, examines the issue of peer pressure head on with her sixth graders. In this video you'll see how Voncille draws her students out on their experiences with peer pressure (such as feeling the need to identify with a particular social group) through open discussion. Then you'll see how students use drama to gain perspective on the real-life situations they encounter, the different choices they can make, and the potential consequences.

Video Questions

1. "In drama, you can act out what you really wanted to do but it's not for real," observes Drama teacher Voncille Ross. Drama allows kids "to see all situations from all angles without actually experiencing [them] and getting into the real trouble," she continues. Can you think of any experience you've had with using drama to act out the dilemmas you've faced?

2. Voncille asks students why they don't seek out the advice of teachers when they're experiencing peer pressure. What do you think of the students' explanations and the way Voncille responds to them?

3. Adolescents deal with peer pressure every day. One reason for this, Voncille observes, is that students want to belong. Can you think of any ways that you could foster a sense of belonging among students to help lessen the pull of peer pressure?

4. Many of the students speak candidly about their experiences with peer pressure. One girl remarks that you never know when you will encounter peer pressure: it could sneak around the corner any time. What insights did you gain from listening to students discuss peer pressure? How will these insights influence your teaching?

5. Suppose you didn't have a teacher like Voncille in your school. How could you incorporate drama in your classroom to help students better understand issues such as peer pressure? Do the objectives outlined in the "Welcome to Theater Arts" blackboard (see artifacts) offer you food for thought?

6. In the bonus segment, "A Real Story about Bullying," Voncille describes two students in an advanced work class who are ridiculed for reading books during lunch. The students remark that while they're comfortable about being recognized for being smart, they want to fit in with everyone else; not stand out in any way. How can you help students realize that they can be strong academically and still fit in socially?

Chapter 4: What Social Problems Affect Today's Students?

Video: Social and Emotional Development: Understanding Adolescents (page 107)

How can we help adolescent boys deal with the anger they often feel in everyday life? And how can we help them devise solutions, drawn from their own experiences, which will deal with their emotions? In this video, you'll see a guidance counselor meet with a group of seventh grade boys to discuss their feelings and then generate a list of coping strategies. You'll also see Shaina share her insights about the psychology of adolescent boys with another teacher and how he responds.

Video Questions

1. Guidance counselor Shaina Martinez leads a small group discussion about effective strategies to help control anger in everyday life. What do you think of the way Shaina encourages students to devise strategies that will work for them?

2. Alan, a member of the group, appreciates being able to meet with Shaina and his friends to try to resolve issues related to anger. Do you think this type of discussion benefits other group members as well? What are some potential drawbacks to their free exchange of ideas?

3. How would you describe the way Shaina mediates a particular boy's concerns by discussing them with his teacher? How would you approach this type of discussion if you were in Shaina's position? What if you were in the classroom teacher's position?

4. Alan strongly advises teachers to really listen to seventh and eighth grade boys. Although sometimes they may sound angry and resentful, he points out, the boys want to make a connection with their teacher. Can you recall any of your own teachers who were especially good listeners? What effect did their ability to listen have on you and your peers?

Chapter 5: What Is Taught?

Video: Elementary Reading Instruction: A Balanced Literacy Program (page 119)

Through this glimpse of balanced literacy instruction in Sandra Jenoski's second-grade classroom, you'll come to understand the carefully laid foundation at the heart of her program. How does Sandra orchestrate various elements from a mini-lesson, to small group work, then guided instruction? How is it that young children work independently and purposefully on a range of literacy tasks—from building words with magnetic letters to reading with a buddy? Through an interview, Sandra describes the nuts and bolts of creating a balanced literacy program.

Video Questions

1. Sandra Jenoski remarked that it takes a good deal of time to establish a system for balanced literacy instruction—as long as six to eight weeks, beginning on day one. Does this amount of time surprise you? What do you see as the benefits of laying a foundation over a long period of time? What might the disadvantages be?

2. Sandra commented that it's important to begin her language arts block with a whole-class mini-lesson. What is her rationale for this? How did this lesson set the stage for the independent, partner, and small group work that followed?

3. Integral to Sandra's classroom are the various learning center options for students, such as word building, buddy reading, and writing. How would you characterize students' engagement with center activities? In what ways do the centers complement instruction?

4. In the bonus material, #3, "Word Building with Cards" you saw how a boy named Jeffrey built words with letters, and then created sentences with these words. What does this brief episode say about Jeffrey's ability to work independently with sustained, concentrated effort? Was this footage an eye opener for you?

5. In reviewing the artifacts from Sandra's classroom, what do you notice about the directions she offers students (as in "Read and sort the word cards into four columns.")? Why do you think it is essential to provide children with clear, concise directions even if they may not be ready to decode some of the key words?

Chapter 5: What Is Taught?

Video: Reading in the Content Areas (page 132)

How can teaching an interdisciplinary unit enrich students' understanding of both literature and history? In this video you'll see how high school teachers join forces to create a unit focused on the Roaring 20's. You'll learn how The Great Gatsby informs the study of this historic period and vice versa. You'll also hear students' reflections on how this interdisciplinary approach has increased their learning in both subject areas.

Video Questions

1. High school English teacher Tanya Earls-Milner recommends using multiple text genres––fiction, poems, and speeches—to breathe life into history. Can you recall examples of any of your teachers who used a similar approach? If so, describe your experience.

2. Tanya leads a discussion during which she adds information to a graphic organizer she's created to map out the socio-cultural forces of the 1920s. What are the benefits of graphic organizers, and for which types of learners? What are some other comprehension aids she might have used?

3. What do you think of the high school students' remarks about how studying literature and history together deepens their understanding of both topics? What could you do now to prepare for taking an interdisciplinary approach when you have your own classroom?

4. Laura Mosman also discusses several benefits of adopting an interdisciplinary approach from an English teacher's point of view. What might some of the challenges be in taking this approach, both in regard to content and coordination with a colleague?

5. After reading Eleanor's freewrite what would you say of her level of engagement with The Great Gatsby? If you were her English teacher, what type(s) of feedback would you provide given the interdisciplinary nature of this unit?

Chapter 5: What Is Taught?

Video: Cooperative Learning at the Elementary Level: Jigsaw Model (page 134)

The jigsaw model is one example of a cooperative learning strategy that can be particularly effective for students in the middle elementary grades. In this video you'll see how veteran fifth-grade teacher, Ilene Miller, dispatches students to small expert groups to study the ancient Olympics. Students then return to their "home group" to teach what they've learned to their classmates. Assessment is part of the process, with experts designing ways to measure what their classmates have learned. Throughout the video, Ilene reflects on how this strategy has increased student learning and made her a better teacher.

Video Questions

1. Teacher Ilene Miller describes the jigsaw model as a type of cooperative learning strategy in which children meet in their expert groups to learn about a particular subject. Then children meet with their home groups to teach and assess the information they've learned. What distinguishes the jigsaw model from other cooperative learning strategies you've observed or read about? What do you think of its effectiveness as a learning strategy?

2. When students teach a subject, Ilene remarks, they really learn it. Have you found this to be true in your experience both as a teacher and as a learner? Why or why not?

3. Students suggest several methods they might use in teaching peers about the ancient Olympics and then measuring what they've learned. What can you infer about the types of learning experiences students have had, based on their suggestions?

4. What do you think of Ilene's statement that she spends one to two hours planning her learning groups? In your experience, why is that important? How can the group dynamic, in general, affect learning?

5. What are some of the techniques Ilene uses for facilitating learning? Which of these techniques would you consider adding to your teaching repertoire?

6. In "Ms. Miller Introduces the Lesson," one of the bonus segments, we learn that children had been assigned homework in preparation for this activity. An oft-heard criticism of homework is that it's little more than rote busywork. What do you think of this assignment in preparation for the jigsaw activity? How might it have jump-started the class discussion?

Chapter 5: What Is Taught?

Video: Cooperative Learning: High School History Lesson (page 136)

In this high school classroom, you'll see how teacher Sarabinh Levy-Brightman assigns students to small groups to analyze texts and then respond to the question of what it means to be a human being. You'll also gain insights into how Sarabinh's sensitivity to group dynamics inform her teaching.

Key terms

Cooperative Learning: Approach in which the teacher orchestrates small heterogeneous groups in which students support each other in mastering specific skills.

Video Questions

1. High school history teacher Sarabinh Levy-Brightman asks students to meet in small groups to discuss what it means to be a human being. Sarabinh believes this method will help them develop their analytical reading and writing skills. In your experience, how can working cooperatively with peers be beneficial? Give one or two examples.

2. What do you think of Jake's description of the benefits of cooperative learning? Do his comments ring true to you? How might you apply his advice about creating well-matched groups to your next teaching assignment?

3. Sarabinh described her three goals for the lesson. How would you characterize her goals? What questions has this video raised about your own picture of how adolescents learn?

4. What advice about setting up ad hoc cooperative groups does Sarabinh offer in the bonus video entitled "The Benefits of Ad Hoc Cooperative Learning Groups"? How do you respond to her observation that some pairs of students work together far more effectively than she

would have imagined? What do you consider to be important criteria for setting up partners and groups?

5. In her interview, Sarabinh makes a provocative statement about cooperative learning. She remarks, ". . . some kids learn very well in cooperative environments and some don't. And, some can be super interactive and appear like they're learning and not really be learning. And some can be quiet but they get a lot out of it." Is Sarabinh's observation consistent with your experiences as learner and as a teacher? If so, give an example.

Chapter 5: What Is Taught?

Video: Academic Diversity: Differentiated Instruction (page 138)

One of the greatest challenges for teachers in teaching students in heterogeneous classrooms is to design instruction that meets the needs of different types of learners. In this video segment you'll see how third-grade teacher Chris Colbath-Hess uses "task analysis" to strategically plan a writer's workshop that brings out the best in all students as they learn to become writers.

Key Term

Differentiated instruction: A variety of techniques for adapting curriculum to meet the needs of a range of learners in regard to ability levels and learning styles.

Video Questions

1. Chris describes the way she plans three different focal points for her writing lessons. How is her description of three types of learners consistent with the students you've observed or taught? How might you adapt Chris's "prototypical kids" for a particular teaching situation you've encountered?

2. How does the storyboard technique help the struggling writer who works with the teaching intern? How does the boy respond to the visual and one-on-one support he receives? In your experience, have you seen or used similar types of graphic organizers? If so, what were the advantages (and perhaps disadvantages) of using these tools?

3. According to Karen Daniels, the Speech and Language Specialist, the portable keyboard can help struggling writers to formulate their ideas. If students had access to computers, what would you suggest as the next logical step?

4. Considering children's particular strengths when planning instruction is also essential, according to Chris. She looks for an area in which students are strong and "lets them sail there"

as a prelude to taking learning risks. Can you recall examples of teachers you had who built on your strengths? What was the result in regard to your own willingness to take academic risks?

5. On page 6 of Chris Colbath-Hess's interview transcript (toward the bottom of the page), she describes the range of issues her students have, from a child who has severe language processing challenges to a child whose cognitive functioning is a couple of years below grade level. Why is the differentiated instruction approach well suited to Chris' class? What do you think your biggest challenge will be in implementing differentiated instruction in your teaching in the future?

Chapter 6: What Makes a Teacher Effective?

Video: Writing Instruction: Process Writing (page 164)

How can a writer's workshop focused on historical fiction come alive for fourth graders? In this video you will see how a classroom teacher, in collaboration with the Literacy Coordinator, helps students at various stages of the writing process—from "planting seeds" to publishing their stories.

Key Terms

Rubrics: Guidelines for assessing student work, often generated by students themselves with teacher guidance. Rubrics may include examples, models, or charts.

Process writing approach: A learning-centered approach to writing in which students create their own pieces of writing based on their choice of topic, their awareness of audience, and their development of ideas from initial stages through revisions to final publication.

Video Questions

1. As part of a unit on the Middle Ages, a boy named Ryan shares a first person account he has written as if he were the son of Charlemagne. Why is it beneficial for Ryan to share his work with peers and receive their feedback? In what ways might the discussion of Ryan's story help others strengthen their compositions?

2. What is your response to the way teacher Kristen Nerich, in collaboration with Literacy Coordinator Patricia Donahue, has focused on nonfiction texts during writers' workshop? Do you agree or disagree with experts who advocate for greater emphasis on nonfiction texts in the primary grades? Explain your thinking.

3. Kristin conferences with a girl who has written a story from the point of view of Rosa Parks' granddaughter. What questions about conferencing does this segment raise in your mind?

4. "When [children] write a story that they want to get out it becomes such a fertile place to teach them how to write. . . they have this passion to make it wonderful," observes Patricia. To what extent do you think children should be encouraged to write about the subjects they are passionate about? Is there also a place for assigned writing topics? Why or why not?

Chapter 7: What Should Teachers Know About Technology and Its Impact on Schools?

Video: An Expanded Definition of Literacy: Meaningful Ways to Integrate Technology (page 185)

This video offers glimpses into the classrooms of several innovative, technology-using teachers. As you watch them teach, you'll gain insight into how they maximize the potential of new tools to help their students become strong readers, writers, and communicators.

Video Questions

1. In the first classroom you see, teacher Elizabeth Sweeney guides her high school students as they use primary source materials. What do you expect to be the most challenging problem you will encounter when you integrate new tools into your instruction?

2. In the second classroom, elementary grade teacher Sheryl Cebula discusses the importance of giving students guidelines when you assign an Internet-based research project. If you were to begin teaching tomorrow, what guidelines would you develop for your students to use when they are on the Internet?

3. In the third classroom, middle school teacher Gretchen Brion-Meisels comments that teaching with technology is about "giving kids the tools to represent themselves in a way that shows the best of who they are." Do you agree with Gretchen? Why, or why not?

4. Elizabeth Sweeney remarks that it's not enough to ask students to conduct research and write a report. Instead, they should "take it up a notch." Based on your own experience with technology, what does taking it up a notch mean to you? How will your beliefs influence the way you teach?

5. In the bonus video entitled "Josh Talks About the Forum Building Community," the teacher makes the case for how important it is to have students read in an environment in which "the text is alive." How does Josh use the online forum to realize his goal?

Chapter 7: What Should Teachers Know About Technology and Its Impact on Schools?

Video: Multimedia Literacy: Integrating Technology into the Middle School Curriculum (page 190)

How can new technologies be integrated into curricular topics in ways that matter? In this video you'll see how a seventh grade teacher assigns students to study groups that will research a particular topic, write an essay, and then communicate what they've learned via PowerPoint presentations. The subject is Costa Rica, a country several students in this class are familiar with. Best of all, students will visit Costa Rica after completing this unit.

Video Questions

1. Gretchen Brion-Meisels has her seventh graders work in small groups to study an aspect of Costa Rica, such as biodiversity, weather patterns, or natural disasters. Eventually, consistent with the jigsaw approach, students will teach others what they have learned. What do you see as the strength of the jigsaw model? What are some potential drawbacks?

2. Gretchen observes that this PowerPoint project contributes to students' overall literacy— "the ability to . . . read and write and communicate in the world." If you were to begin teaching tomorrow, would Gretchen's approach to combining technology with instruction impact your teaching? Why or why not?

3. During a lesson on how to create effective PowerPoint presentations, Gretchen asks students to critique several slides she's created, each of which contains a deliberate flaw. In your experience, how can the experience of critiquing someone else's work improve your project?

4. What has been added to the overall lesson by students' ability to conduct research on the Internet and create PowerPoint presentations? Would you integrate technology in a similar or different fashion if you were to teach a similar unit? Explain your thinking.

Chapter 7: What Should Teachers Know About Technology and Its Impact on Schools?

Video: Using Technology to Promote Problem Solving (page 194)

In today's schools, technology is often situated at the margins of a lesson, rather than embedded in a way that dramatically changes student learning. In this video, you'll see how high school biology teacher Ken Bateman maximizes student learning by using online tools that allow students to determine various genetic traits of dragons.

Video Questions

1. High school teacher Ken Bateman perceives several advantages for using technology to help students understand biology. Based on your own experiences, is the way he integrates technology an effective use of computers? Why or why not?

2. Many critics of new technologies maintain that computers turn students into "isolated nerds." Based on the student behavior and teacher interactions in this video, how would you respond to this assertion? What evidence would you use to agree or disagree?

3. In what ways do you see Ken acting as a facilitator of learning as opposed to a dispenser of knowledge? What are the learning implications of his approach for students in this class?

4. How do you plan to approach integrating new technologies into the curriculum when you have your own classroom? Has Ken influenced your thinking in any way? Explain your reasoning.

5. In reading the classroom artifact document entitled "Assignment", what do you notice about Ken's directions to students? In what ways are the directions traditional? In what ways do they make assumptions about students' sophistication in using new tools?

Chapter 7: What Should Teachers Know About Technology and Its Impact on Schools?

Video: Using Technology to Promote Discovery Learning (page 202)

In this high school geometry class, teacher Gary Simons uses a technological tool that allows students to investigate problems and create their own "conjectures." You'll see Gary in action—facilitating discussions, challenging ideas, and encouraging students to think through problems. Through his narration, you'll come to understand why Gary feels discovery learning is an important part of a teacher's repertoire and how technology can be integrated to help foster to student understanding.

Video Questions

1. High school geometry teacher Gary Simon maintains that technology is an essential teaching tool for a discovery learning approach. Is his statement consistent with your experience? Why or why not?

2. What do you think will be the most challenging aspect of using new tools to support discovery learning that you will encounter when you become a teacher? How will you approach this challenge?

3. You have probably encountered people who are skeptical about using new tools to support the discovery learning approach. They may think it's the teachers job to present ideas in "stand and deliver" fashion. Where do you stand on this issue? How do you support your point of view?

4. Can you think of any experiences you've had with discovery learning and technology? If so, describe how and what you learned.

5. In the bonus video entitled "Teacher Helps Guide Student Through Problem," what do you notice about Gary's teaching? How does the student respond? How would you characterize the give and take process?

Chapter 8: What Are the Ethical and Legal Issues Facing Teachers?

Video: Legal and Ethical Dimensions of Teaching: Reflections from Today's Educators (page 226)

What aspects of the law will be relevant to you as a teacher? In this video, you'll get to listen in on a conversation with a diverse group of teachers, an attorney who became a teacher (the moderator), and an elementary school administrator. The participants will discuss every-day issues they've encountered, including ethical dilemmas, concerns about child abuse, and how the law affects their course of action.

Video Questions

1. What is your response to teacher Kate Malinowski's discussion of how she strives to model ethical behavior for both her students and for her fellow teachers?

2. Can you think of any experiences you've had, or might have, with students in which you've needed to find out more about various laws to guide your decision? Describe such a scenario.

3. From a legal perspective, what questions has this video raised in your mind about what students can and can't say in school (e.g., making threats, cursing)?

4. What is your response to the advice that the panelists offer future teachers (i.e., contacting your local District Attorney or Union Representative for additional information)?

5. In the Bonus Video that accompanies this case, what is your response to the case that assistant principal Marlon Davis makes for examining both sides of an issue, such a student who behaves inappropriately? Are Marlon's views consistent with your own? Explain your thinking.

Chapter 9: What Are the Philosophical Foundations of American Education?

Video: Middle School Reading Instruction: Integrating Technology (page 272)

Meet Joshua Lawrence, a seventh-grade teacher who shows inner-city students how to make a personal connection to a Greek myth. You'll see the strategies Joshua uses to help students understand and respond to The Judgment of Paris. You'll also see how "every voice is heard daily" through an online discussion forum, a tool that offers students a novel way to express themselves in writing.

Video Questions

1. Teacher Joshua Lawrence helps students personally connect with a 3,000- year-old text, The Judgment of Paris, a Greek myth about the events that led up to the Trojan War. How does he do it? Can you recall examples of teachers who helped you relate to a classic text that seemed intimidating, or obsolete, at first? What can you learn from their technique?

2. Joshua states that teachers need to create a community in the classroom for a text to be meaningful and come alive. How do you interpret his statement? What can you do now to help foster a sense of community among the students with whom you have contact?

3. Joshua also uses an online forum to help students connect to the literature. How does this style of communication increase students' sense of community in spite of the fact that each student works independently at a computer? Do you think the online forum is an effective way to integrate digital technology? Elaborate.

4. Melissa, the girl in the interview, remarks that her teacher and classmates will read her online response in a nonjudgmental manner. Rather than looking for a right or wrong answer, her teacher and peers will be interested in how well she expressed what she thinks. What's your response to Melissa's statement?

5. "Learning to love reading and writing helps students become proficient readers and writers in any context; it's the most important thing we can do as teachers," according to Joshua. Would you agree? Why or why not?

Chapter 9: What Are the Philosophical Foundations of American Education?

Video: Middle School Science Instruction: Inquiry Learning (page 279)

In this video you'll see how a middle school science teacher uses inquiry learning in teaching a lesson on the geology of the Grand Canyon. As you watch students construct knowledge through experimentation, you'll also hear the teacher's views on the benefits of inquiry learning, as well as the challenges it presents, such as extra planning and general "messiness."

Key Term

Differentiated instruction: A variety of techniques for adapting curriculum to meet the needs of a range of learners in regard to ability levels and learning styles.

Video Questions

1. Middle school science teacher Robert Cho remarks that inquiry learning using hands-on tools is an effective way to help students understand a difficult subject such as geology. What value do you see in having students construct knowledge using physical tools as well as "what's inside their brains"?

2. Through hands-on experiments, student are "doing the science," not just reading about it or memorizing facts. It really hooks them on science, according to Robert. Do the students in Rob's class appear to be engaged with problem solving? Elaborate.

3. One of Robert's goals is to teach "habits of mind" that will help students think beyond science class. Do you agree that teaching students to become critical thinkers, to realize that they have the ability and tools to apply the discovery process, will serve them well in life? If so, what can you do now to help the students you work with develop strong habits of mind?

4. Robert remarks that a teacher's preparation for inquiry learning must be more intensive than for more traditional approaches. Based on your experiences in preparing lessons, do you agree with Robert? If so, would you agree that the payoff in student learning is worth the investment in time? Why or why not?

Chapter 10: What Is the History of American Education?

Video: Bilingual Education: An Elementary Two-Way Immersion Program (page 321)

Many students learn to become proficient in Spanish or English in school. What's especially interesting about this video is that you'll get to meet the two teachers and their students who are involved in a two-way bilingual program. That is, all students learn to read, write, and communicate in both English and Spanish in all subject areas.

Video Questions

1. The two teachers in this video segment, Sarah Bartels-Marrero and Sheila Donelan, work together closely to teach students in two different languages. What do you see as the strengths of the two-way bilingual method? What might some of the drawbacks be?

2. In your experience, how does this approach to bilingual education differ from many others that you've observed or read about?

3. The two teachers in this video made a concerted effort to not just repeat the lesson in both languages. Sheila set the stage by introducing the concept of estimation; Sarah showed children how to extend the lesson by creating bar graphs. In your opinion, how does this introduction, then extension strategy benefit students?

4. What do you think of the public debate over bilingual education? How does this video segment either challenge or support your views (or do a little of each)?

5. What do you notice about students' work samples in the Classroom Artifacts? Do you think the worksheet format has been successful in structuring the assignment? Why, or why not?

Chapter 10: What Is the History of American Education?

Video: Diversity: Teaching in a Multiethnic Classroom (page 292)

This video takes you inside a second grade classroom where students from diverse ethnic backgrounds collaborate on a special project— Japanese Kamishibai books. You'll come to understand why the teacher, in collaboration with the Japanese Language Teacher, decided to introduce an ancient art form as a window into Japanese culture.

Video Questions

1. Japanese Language Teacher, Akiko Kawai, mentions several of her goals for the Japanese students she works with. One is to create a welcoming school environment that will help her students feel at home. In what ways is the Kamishibai lesson consistent with Akiko's goals?

2. For the American-born students, the Kamishibai books offer an artistic approach to understanding one aspect of Japanese culture. Do you plan to draw upon the arts to foster multicultural understandings in your teaching? If so, how? Are there ways you can incorporate your own ethnic heritage?

3. Classroom teacher Jonathan Norwood believes that by having children present their original stories in the form of Kamishibai books they will learn to communicate in ways that will serve them well in life. Is Jonathan's belief consistent with your own experience? Elaborate.

4. Jonathan discusses the ethnic diversity of the students in his classroom and why it's important to help children understand other cultures. What would you say to people who claim that children should assimilate as soon as possible and focus on basic academic skills?

5. Jonathan remarks that he wished he had had more tools and techniques for teaching English Language Learners (ELLs) when he first began teaching. What have you learned about instructing ELLs that could be applied to a classroom such as his?

Chapter 11: How Are Schools Governed, Influenced, and Financed?

Video: Assessment in the Middle Grades: Measurement of Student Learning (page 342)

Marin Somers is a math teacher in an urban middle school. In this segment you'll see how he assesses his students' mastery of a particular unit. Perhaps more interestingly, you'll see how he prepares students for taking the assessment in two ways: By previewing the test as a whole-class activity and through small, peer-teaching groups. You'll learn how Martin uses assessments not just as a way to gauge student progress, but to also evaluate his own effectiveness as an instructor. Through an interview, you'll gain insight into how Karen, a student in Martin's class, uses assessment data to "know where she stands" as she prepares for high school and college.

Key Terms

Benchmark: A goal that one achieves on the way to mastery of a particular skill or subject area.

Standardized test: A test designed by experts in a particular field; its administration, scoring, and interpretation are standardized according to particular criteria.

Video Questions

1. The segment begins with a student named Karen remarking that early in the school year the math concepts she would be learning seemed "like high school." By the spring, when this video was filmed, Karen had learned many of the concepts that once intimidated her. What would you say to students who feel overwhelmed by new material at the beginning of the school year? How would you reassure them, while at the same time acknowledging that the material is indeed difficult?

2. Martin Somers advised new teachers to really get to know the students they're teaching— "the group that you have in front of you." What do you think of Martin's advice? What would you say to those who argue teachers are given a formal curriculum that they must teach regardless of their students' backgrounds and interests?

3. Martin encouraged students to prep each other on the math concepts they'd need to know prior to the test. What do you think of this practice? Do you think peer teaching gives students an unfair advantage, or do you think it allows them to answer test items in a way that more accurately reflects what they know? Does Martin's approach give you ideas for the types of review sessions you might institute in your classroom?

4. What did you notice about the way Martin helped students during the actual testing period itself? How would you describe the way he helped students think through problems just short of giving away the answer?

5. In the bonus video material you saw Martin working with a girl who was having difficulty with a test item. What types of questions did he ask her? What sort of reminders did he offer? Why is it significant that he gave her back her pencil and said, "You do it"? How might this exchange affect the girl's self esteem?

Chapter 12: How Should Education Be Reformed?

Video: Assessment in the Elementary Grades: Formal and Informal Literacy Assessment (page 363)

In this segment you will see how Chris Quinn, a second grade teacher, administers both a formal assessment (a standardized test on phonics) and an informal literacy assessment (a running record) to her students. You will also see students working on their assessment portfolios and reflecting on their growth as writers. Throughout, Chris explains why different types of assessments are important both for gauging students' learning and for planning instruction.

Key Terms

Formal assessment: A standardized approach to collecting test data under formal, controlled conditions.

Informal assessment: A non-standardized approach to collecting test data in which achievement is measured through observation.

Portfolio assessment: An approach to evaluating student progress that involves having students collect work that demonstrates their growth and achievement over time. Portfolios may include items such as reflective journals, artwork, completed projects, and so on.

Video Questions

1. What do you think of Chris Quinn's discussion of the insights she gains from using a variety of assessments? Would you approach the assessment of young readers and writers in a similar way, or do you hold different views?

2. Chris points out that assessment portfolios give students opportunities to reflect on their progress. What do you think is the value of having students critique their own work?

3. Chris believes it is important for children to be part of the assessment process, to be part of their education, and to share with others how far they've come. How do you see students benefiting from this philosophy? What might some of the challenges be for a teacher who shares this point of view?

4. The DRA Observation Guide for "Thin as a Stick," (Lesson 24, page 4) shows a record of a particular child's miscues. What do you notice about the miscues (such as clothes for close; writer for slither; show for shadow; and light for lightning)? Are these the sorts of miscues that impede comprehension? Why or why not? In what instances would a closer examination of context clues have helped the child decode an unfamiliar word? When was the context of the miscued word not helpful?

Chapter 12: How Should Education Be Reformed?

Video: Performance Assessment: Student Presentations in a High School English Class (page 364)

Working with partners, students in Laura Mossman's high school English class conducted research on 20th century writers – from Gertrude Stein to Langston Hughes. In this video, you'll gain a glimpse of their presentations. You'll also see how they evaluated each other's work using a set of criteria they helped to create.

Video Questions

1. High school English teacher Laura Mosman has assigned her students a research/discovery project on a famous author, such as Ezra Pound. What do you see as the benefits of such an assignment?

2. Laura has asked students to help create a scoring rubric for the literature project. In your experience, is seeking student input on grading an effective strategy? Why or why not?

3. Do you agree with Laura's statement that performance assessment gives students an opportunity to demonstrate their knowledge in ways that allow them to showcase what they've learned? Explain your reasoning.

4. During each performance, Laura's students critique each other's work. How would you respond to critics who maintain that only tests can measure student achievement; peers aren't capable of evaluating each other's work fairly or objectively?

5. Take a look at the student projects in the classroom artifacts that accompany this case. How would you characterize students' understanding of the authors they studied? Support your opinion with specific examples.

Chapter 12: How Should Education Be Reformed?

Video: Portfolio Assessment: Elementary Classroom (page 365)

What does portfolio assessment look like in the elementary classroom? In this video you'll see how teacher Fred Park helps students develop their writing for a piece that will become part of their portfolios. Through an interview with Fred, you'll gain insight into the strengths of portfolio assessment, as well as the classroom management challenges inherent in this approach.

Key terms

Portfolio Assessment: An assessment method that uses a collection of selected student work that is intended to demonstrate student effort and progress toward achieving particular learning objectives.

Video Questions

1. What is your response to the public debate about standardized assessment? How would you argue the position that portfolio assessment can help balance out a portrait of an individual learner?

2. Teacher Fred Park describes how he organizes the portfolio assessment process. He elaborates further on this in the bonus video titled "The Challenges of Portfolio Use in Today's Classrooms." What do you see as the most challenging aspect of his approach to portfolio assessment? How will you deal with these types of dilemmas when you have your own classroom?

3. Self-reflection is a hallmark of Fred's approach to portfolio assessment. How does he encourage students to reflect on their writing? What could you take from Fred's approach and apply to your own teaching?

4. Sara, one of Fred's students, has drafted a profile of her classmate Asa Benjerman. If you were conferencing with Sara about this profile, what strengths would you point out in her writing? What mini-lesson(s) would you provide to help Sara strengthen her composition?

5. When interviewed about Portfolio Assessment, Fred emphasizes how important it is for students to become self-reflective about their work. He explains how teachers can help by modeling their own reflections on daily events. What other techniques could you use to help students become self-reflective learners?

Chapter 12: How Should Education Be Reformed?

Video: Elementary School Language Arts: Inquiry Learning (page 365)

How can the inquiry learning approach be adapted for a lesson on writing poetry? In this video, you'll meet primary grade level teacher Jenerra Williams. You'll see how she structures a lesson in which children learn to write sensory poems by reaching inside paper bags to encounter strange and interesting objects which they will then write about. You'll also hear Jenerra's views on the pros and cons of combining the inquiry learning approach to poetry.

Video Questions

1. Inquiry learning, to teacher Jenerra Williams, means allowing children the opportunity to find the answers on their own; children are in charge of their own learning. What do you think of the way Jenerra applies this philosophy to a poetry-writing lesson?

2. How does Jenerra's view of herself as a writing coach influence the way she provides feedback on students' poems? What questions has this video raised about your own stance toward teaching writing?

3. Rather than telling students how to write a sensory poem, Jenerra sets the stage for them to figure out how to write one. Can you think of any other writing genres that lend themselves to the inquiry approach? If so, name a few.

4. In her interview, Jenerra points out that inquiry learning requires a lot of work. "To really make it work effectively," Jenerra maintains, "you have to put in the time and the energy to find those resources to have available for students." Can you recall examples of any of your teachers who used the inquiry learning approach? Would you say that it's well worth the effort in terms of learning? Why or why not?

5. Using a flipchart, Jenerra has written four sensory experiences and then added a statement below each one. In your experience, how can charts such as this one about sensory poetry help to anchor instruction?